PONTIFICAL INSTITUTE OF MEDIAEVAL STUDIES

STUDIES AND TEXTS

18

ROBERT OF FLAMBOROUGH

CANON-PENITENTIARY OF SAINT-VICTOR AT PARIS

LIBER POENITENTIALIS

A Critical Edition with Introduction and Notes

Edited by

J. J. FRANCIS FIRTH, C.S.B.

St. Joseph's College, Edmonton

TORONTO

PONTIFICAL INSTITUTE OF MEDIAEVAL STUDIES

1971

ISBN 0 - 88844 018-9

PRINTED AT UNIVERSA — WETTEREN (BELGIUM)

TABLE OF CONTENTS

BIBLIOGRAPHY

Some Useful Writings Related to Robert of Flamborough or to his Sources

I. — Ancient and Mediaeval Source Material

Abaelard, Abailard, Abelard — see below Peter Abelard.

ALAN OF LILLE (ALANUS DE INSULIS), *Liber poenitentialis* long tradition ed. Jean LONGÈRE, 2 vols. (Analecta mediaevalia Namurcensia 17-18; Louvain-Lille 1965); medium and short traditions ed. IDEM, *ArchivesHDLMA* 32 (1965) 169-242; short tradition ed. F. Charles DE VISCH, PL 210.279-304.

——, *De virtutibus et de vitiis et de donis Spiritus sancti* ed. Odon LOTTIN, *MedStud* 12 (1950) 20-56; more critically re-edited by the same in his *Psychologie et morale aux XIIe et XIIIe siècles*, VI (Louvain-Gembloux 1960) 27-92.

ALEXANDER III, Pope (Roland Bandinelli), *Epistolae et privilegia ordine chronologico digesta*, ed. J.-P. MIGNE (Paris 1855), PL 200.

——, *Stroma* (*Summa*), a commentary on Gratian, *Decretum,* ed. by Friedrich THANER along with some canonical *quaestiones* of uncertain authorship (Innsbruck 1874).

ANSELM OF LUCCA, Saint, *Collectio canonum*, ed. Friedrich THANER, *Anselmi episcopi Lucensis collectio canonum una cum collectione minore* I (Innsbruck 1906; reprinted Aalen 1965).

Apparatus: *Ecce vicit Leo*, anonymous commentary on Gratian, *Decretum*, St. Florian, Stiftsbibliothek MS XI.605, the entire MS.

Appendix concilii lateranensis, an important twelfth-century collection of decretal letters, ed. MANSI 22.248-454.

BARTHOLOMEW OF EXETER, *Liber poenitentialis* or *Poenitentiale*, ed. Adrian MOREY, *Bartholomew of Exeter, Bishop and Canonist* (Cambridge 1937) pp. 163-300.

BEDE, the Venerable (Beda venerabilis), *Historia ecclesiastica gentis Anglorum*, ed. along with his other historical works by Charles PLUMMER, 2 vols. (Oxford 1896).

BENEDICT THE LEVITE, *Capitularia*, ed. Georg Heinrich PERTZ, MonGerHist Leges (folio) II².17-158; PL 97.697-912.

BERENGAR FREDOLI, *Liber de excommunicatione*, ed. Eugène VERNAY, with introduction (Paris 1912).

BERNARD OF PAVIA (Bernardus papiensis), *Breviarium extravagantium*, afterwards called *Compilatio prima*, ed. Emil Albert FRIEDBERG, *Quinque Compilationes antiquae nec non Collectio canonum Lipsiensis* (Leipzig 1882) 1-65; cited 1 *Compil.*

——, *Summa decretalium*, ed. Ernst A. Th. LASPEYRES (Regensburg 1860; reprinted Graz 1956).

Breves dies hominis — see below *Summa: Breves dies hominis*.

BURCHARD OF WORMS, *Corrector*; this is Book 19 of his *Decretum* PL 140.919-1018.

——, *Decretum* PL 140.537-1058.

Die Bussordnungen der abendländischen Kirche nebst einer rechtsgeschichtlichen Einleitung, ed. F. W. H. WASSERSCHLEBEN (Halle 1851).

CAESARIUS OF HEISTERBACH, *Dialogus miraculorum*, ed. Joseph STRANGE, 2 vols. (Cologne-Bonn-Brussels 1851).

Canones apostolorum interprete Dionysio Exiguuo, ed. Cuthbert Hamilton TURNER, *Ecclesiae occidentalis monumenta iuris antiquissima* I[1] (Oxford 1899) 1-34.

Die Canonessammlung des Dionysius Exiguus in der ersten Redaktion, ed. Adolf STREWE (Arbeiten zur Kirchengeschichte herausgegeben von Emmanuel Hirsch und Hans Lietzmann 16; Berlin and Leipzig 1931).

Cantor — See Peter Cantor.

Capitula Theodori, Penitential canons of Frankish origin falsely attributed to St. Theodore of Canterbury, PL 99.935-952.

Chartularium Universitatis parisiensis, ed. Heinrich DENIFLE and Émile CHATELAIN, 4 vols. (Paris 1889-97).

Codex — see Justinian, *Codex*.

Codex canonum ecclesiae (*Collectio Dionysiana*) — see Dionysius Exiguus.

Collectio Seguntina, a twelfth-century collection of papal decretals, ed. with commentary by Walther HOLTZMANN," La 'Collectio seguntina' et les décrétales de Clément III et de Célestin III," *RevHistEccl* 50 (1955) 400-453. Full text is given only for decretals not available elsewhere.

Collectio Wigorniensis, a twelfth-century collection of papal decretals, ed. with introduction, notes and indices by Hans-Eberhard LOHMANN, "Die Collectio Wigorniensis (Collectio Londinensis Regia) Ein Beitrag zur Quellengeschichte des kanonischen Rechts im 12. Jahrhundert," *ZSavignyStRG* kan. Abt. 22 (1933) 36-187. Full text is not given for decretals available elsewhere.

Compilatio prima — see Bernard of Pavia, *Breviarium extravagantium*; also *Quinque compilationes antiquae*.

Corpus iuris canonici, ed. Emil Albert FRIEDBERG, 2 vols. (Leipzig 1879-81).

Corpus iuris civilis, ed. Theodor MOMMSEN, Paul KRÜGER, Rudolf SCHÖLL and Wilhelm KROLL, 3 vols. (Berlin 1877-94, later stereotyped editions also).

Courson, Courçon, Curzon, etc. — see Robert (of) Courson.

Decretales pseudo-isidorianae et capitula Angilramni, ed. Paul HINSCHIUS (Leipzig 1863).

De fructibus carnis et spiritus, anonymous, PL 176.997-1010.

De injungendis poenitentiis, a penitential contained within the *Summa: Breves dies hominis*, Bamberg, Staatsbibliothek MS Patr. 136, fols. 77rb-93vb.

Denifle, Heinrich, and Émile Chatelain — see *Chartularium*.

De poenitentia injungenda — see *Summa de poenitentia injugenda*; cf. above *De injungendis poenitentiis*.

De vera et falsa poenitentia, PL 40.1113-1130.

Digesta or *Pandecta* (in Roman Law), ed. Theodor MOMMSEN and Paul KRÜGER, *Corpus Iuris Civilis* I (Berlin 1922) part 2, pp. 1-994.

DIONYSIUS EXIGUUS (Denis the Short), *Codex canonum* or *Dionysiana*, a collection of canon law found in various redactions, several of which are edited PL 67.39-316; one by Adolf STREWE, *Die Canonessammlung des Dionysius Exiguus in der erste Redaktion* (Leipzig 1931); several scattered throughout the work of Cuthbert Hamilton TURNER, *Ecclesiae occidentalis monumenta iuris antiquissima*, 2 vols. in 9 parts (Oxford 1899-1939).

Durandus of Mende — see William Durand.

Ecce vicit Leo — see *Apparatus: Ecce vicit Leo*.

Ecclesiae occidentalis monumenta iuris antiquissima, Canonum et conciliorum graecorum interpretationes latinae, ed. Cuthbert Hamilton TURNER, 2 vols. in 9 parts (Oxford 1899-1939).

Epistolae Pontificum Romanorum ineditae, ed. Samuel LOEWENFELD (Leipzig 1885).

False Decretals — see *Decretales pseudo-isidorianae*.

Frédol — see Berengar Fredoli.

GALIENUS [?] *Summa juniorum*, Oxford, Bodleian Library, MS Bodley 655.

GANDULF OF BOLOGNA (Gandulphus Bononiensis), *Sententiarum libri quatuor*, ed. Johann VON WALTER (Vienna-Breslau 1924).

Garnerus, Garnier — see Warner.

GERHOCH OF REICHERSBERG, *Epistola ad Innocentium papam*, MonGerHist *Libelli de lite* 3.202-239; also published PL 194.1375-1426.

——, *Liber de duabus haeresibus*, PL 194.1161-84; portions also published Mon-GerHist *Libelli de lite* 3.284-288.

GILBERT OF POITIERS (Gilbertus Pictavensis, sometimes called Gilbert of la Porrée or Porretanus), *Epistola ad Matthaeum abbatem Sancti Florentii Salmuriensis*, PL 188.1255-58.

Glossa ordinaria (in Decretum Gratiani) chiefly by JOHN THE TEUTON (Joannes Teutonicus) edited in many early editions of the *Decretum*. Printed editions contain also many glosses by Bartholomew of Brescia, who wrote about thirty years after Joannes.

GRATIAN OF BOLOGNA (Magister Gratianus), *Decretum* or *Decreta*, originally entitled *Concordantia discordantium canonum*, ed. Emil Albert FRIEDBERG, *Corpus iuris canonici* I (Leipzig 1879).

GREGORY I, Pope (St. Gregory the Great), *Moralia*, an exposition of the Book of Job, PL 75.510-1162, 76.9-782.

——, *Registrum epistolarum*, PL 77.433-1352.

GREGORY IX, Pope, *Decretales*, ed. Emil Albert FRIEDBERG, *Corpus iuris canonici* II (Leipzig 1881) 1-928.

Gullielmus Durandus — see William Durand.

GUY OF ORCHELLES (Guido de Orchellis), *Tractatus de sacramentis*, ed. Damian and Odulph VAN DEN EYNDE (Franciscan Institute Publications, Text series 4; Louvain 1953).

GUY OF SOUTHWICK, *De virtute confessionis et utilitate et modo confitendi*, ed. André WILMART, "Un opuscule sur la confession composé par Guy de Southwick vers la fin du XIIᵉ siècle," *RechThAncMéd* 7 (1935) 337-352.

HINSCHIUS, Paul, *Decretales pseudo-isidorianae* — see *Decretales*.

Hispana (collectio), a collection of canon law attributed to St. Isidore of Seville, but formed at an earlier date than the "False-decretals"; PL 84.93-848.

HOLTZMANN, Walther, "Kanonistische Ergänzungen zur Italia pontificia," *Quellen und Untersuchen aus italienischen Archiven und Bibliotheken* 37 (1957) 55-102; 38 (1958) 67-175; also publ. separately (Tübingen 1959). Cited Holtzmann, *KanErgänz* followed by the number of the decretal.

——, see also above *Collectio Seguntina*.

HUGH OF ST-VICTOR, works sometimes attributed to him — see *Speculum de mysteriis ecclesiae; De fructibus carnis et spiritus*.

HUGUCCIO OF PISA, *Summa decretorum* or *Summa super Decretum*, a commentary on Gratian, *Decretum*, Paris, BN MS lat. 3891 and MS lat. 3892 (each consists of one copy). Folio numbers, unless otherwise indicated, refer to 3892. A small part of this work has been edited by J. ROMAN, "*Summa d'Huguccio* sur le décret de Gratien d'après le manuscrit 3891 de la Bibliothèque Nationale, Causa XXVII, Questio II," *RevHistDroitFE³* 27 (1903) 745-805. In spite of Roman's title, part of this edition is based, not on BN MS lat. 3891, but on BN MS lat. 3892.

INNOCENT III, Pope (Lothar of Segni), *De sacro altaris mysterio*, 6 books, PL 217. 773-916.

——, *Regesta sive epistolae*, ed. first by Étienne BALUZE, augmented by Louis G. O. F. DE BRÉQUIGNY and F. J. G. LA PORTE-DU THEIL and reprinted PL 214-216; supplement ed. J.-P. MIGNE, PL 217. All of this indicated by the abbreviation "Reg.".

Institutiones — see Justinian, *Institutiones*.

Isidore of Seville — see above *Hispana*.

Isidore (pseudo-), *Decretales* — see above *Decretales pseudo-isidorianae*.

IVO OF CHARTRES, *Decretum*, ed. Jean FRONTEAU (1647), PL 161.9-1036.

——, *Panormia*, PL 161.1037-1344.

JAFFÉ, Philippe, *Regesta pontificum romanorum, ab condita ecclesia ad annum post Christum natum MCXCVIII*, 2nd ed. revised by William WATTENBACH with the collaboration of Ferdinand KALTENBRUNNER, Paul EWALD and Samuel LOEWENFELD, 2 vols. (Leipzig 1885-88). Letters numbered 1-1065 are cited as JK, those numbered 1066-3386 as JE, those numbered 3387 ff. as JL.

Joannes Teutonicus — see *Glossa ordinaria*.

JOHN OF FAENZA (Joannes Faventinus), *Summa*, a commentary on the *Decretum* of Gratian, Paris, BN MS lat. 14606, fols. 1-166^v.

JUSTINIAN, *Codex*, ed. Paul KRÜGER, *Corpus iuris civilis* II (Berlin 1880).

——, *Digesta* — see *Digesta* (Roman law).

——, *Institutiones*, ed. Paul KRÜGER, *Corpus iuris civilis* I, part 1 (Berlin 1877, reprinted 1922) 1-56.

——, *Novellae*, ed. Rudolf SCHÖLL and Wilhelm KROLL, *Corpus iuris civilis* III (Berlin 1894).

Liber de vera et falsa poenitentia — see *De vera et falsa poenitentia*.

Liber poenitentialis exceptus de libris poenitentialibus M. Roberti confessoris et M. Petri et aliorum, Paris, BN MS lat. 14859 (Q in the present edition) fols. 304^r-311^r.

Loewenfeld — see above *Epistolae pontificum Romanorum*; also Jaffé.

Lohmann, Hans-Eberhard — see above *Collectio Wigorniensis*.

Lombard — see Peter Lombard.

Lothar of Segni — see Innocent III.

MARTÈNE, Edmond, *De antiquis Ecclesiae ritibus*, 2nd ed., 4 vols. (Antwerp 1736-38).

Novellae — see Justinian, *Novellae*.

Obituaire de la province de Sens (Recueil des historiens de la France, Obituaires 1-4) 4 vols. ed. Auguste MOLINIER and others (Paris 1902-23).

Ordo excommunicationis (anonymous), PL 138.1123-28.

PAUCAPALEA, *Summa*, a commentary on the *Decretum* of Gratian, ed. Johann F. VON SCHULTE (Giessen 1890).

PETER ABELARD, *Ethica*, also called *Scito teipsum*, PL 178.633-878.

PETER CANTOR, *Summa de sacramentis et animae consiliis*, ed. Jean-Albert DUGAUQUIER, 2 vols. as well as vol. 3, part 1, thus far (Louvain-Lille 1954-), also found in Troyes MS 276. References by volume and page (as I 90) refer to the above-mentioned edition; folio references refer to this MS.

——, *Verbum abbreviatum*, PL 205.21-370.

PETER LOMBARD, *Commentarium in psalmos davidicos*, PL 191.55-1296.

——, *Quatuor libri sententiarum*, 2nd ed. Collegio de S. Bonaventura, 2 vols. (Quaracchi 1916).

PETER OF ROISSY, *Speculum ecclesiae* or *Manuale de mysteriis ecclesiae* (longer redaction), Paris, BN Nouv. Acq. MS lat. 232.

Poenitentiale, published under the name of Theodore of Canterbury, ed. with commentary by Jacques PETIT, PL 99.901-1230.

Pontificale Romanum, various medieval texts published by Michel ANDRIEU, *Le Pontifical romain au Moyen-âge*, 4 vols. (Studi e testi 86-88, 99; Vatican City 1938-41).

POTTHAST, Augustus, *Regesta pontificum romanorum inde ab anno post Christum natum MCXCVIII ad annum MCCCIV*, 2 vols. (Berlin 1874-75). Cited Po. followed by the number of the decretal.

Quinque compilationes antiquae nec non Collectio canonum lipsiensis, ed. Emil Albert FRIEDBERG (Leipzig 1882).

ROBERT (of) COURSON (or Courçon, Curzon, etc.), *Summa*, Paris BN lat. 14524, fols. 1-186; folio references refer to this MS. A table of contents derived chiefly from this MS has been published by Vincent L. KENNEDY, "The Contents of Courson's *Summa*," *MedStud* 9 (1947) 81-107. Divisions 1-2, on penance, have been edited from Bruges 247 and Troyes 1175 by the same editor, "Robert Courson on Penance," *MedStud* 7 (1945) 291-336; "ed. Kennedy" refers to this edition in vol. 7. Divisions 11-12, on usury, have been edited from several Paris MSS by Georges LEFÈVRE, *Le traité "De usura" de Robert de Courçon* (Travaux et mémoires de l'Université de Lille, Tome 10, Mémoire no. 30; Lille 1902).

ROBERT OF FLAMBOROUGH, *Liber poenitentialis* partially edited by Johann F. VON SCHULTE, *Roberti Flamesburiensis Summa de matrimonio et de usuris* (Giessen 1868).

Roland Bandinelli — see Alexander III.

RUFINUS, *Summa decretorum* or *Summa in Decretum*, ed. H. SINGER (Paderborn 1902).

SENATUS OF WORCESTER, Two letters ed. Philippe DELHAYE, "Deux textes de Senatus de Worcester sur la pénitence," *RechThAncMéd* 19 (1952) 201-224.

SICARD OF CREMONA, *Mitrale* or *De officiis ecclesiasticis Summa*, PL 213.14-436.

SIMON OF BISIGNANO, *Summa decretorum*, a commentary on Gratian, *Decretum*; text of a projected edition by Terence P. MCLAUGHLIN, based chiefly on London, British Museum MS Royal 10.A.III. and on London, Lambeth Palace MS 411.

SIMON, Magister, *De sacramentis*, ed. Henri WEISWEILER, *Maître Simon et son groupe, De sacramentis* (Spicilegium sacrum Lovaniense, Études et Documents 17; Louvain 1937).

Speculum de mysteriis ecclesiae or *Speculum ecclesiae*, an anonymous work sometimes attributed to Hugh of St-Victor, PL 177.335-380.

STEPHEN OF TOURNAI (Stephanus Tornacensis), *Summa*, a commentary on Gratian, *Decretum*, ed. Johann F. VON SCHULTE (Giessen 1891).

Strewe, Adolf — see above *Die Canonessammlung* (under "C"); also Dionysius Exiguus.

Summa ad injungendam poenitentiam — see *Summa de poenitentia injungenda*.

Summa: Breves dies hominis, Bamberg, Staatsbibliothek, MS Patr. 136, fols. 1ra-98vb.

Summa de poenitentia injungenda or *Summa ad injungendam poenitentiam*, by one Ricardus, which has been sometimes attributed to Praepositinus of Cremona, Vienna, Nationalbibliothek MS 1413, fols. 129ra-132ra.

Summa: Ecce vicit Leo — see *Apparatus: Ecce vicit Leo*.

Summa juniorum — see Galienus.

Summa Parisiensis, an anonymous commentary on Gratian, *Decretum*, ed. Terence P. MCLAUGHLIN (Toronto 1952).

Synodicae constitutiones (decreed at Paris early in the early thirteenth century), PL
212.57-68; cf. *MedStud* 8.87.

Theodore of Canterbury, *Capitula* — see *Capitula Theodori.*

——, *Poenitentiale* — see *Poenitentiale* published under the name of ... .

THEODULF OF ORLÉANS, *Capitula ad presbyteros parochiae suae*, PL 105.191-208.

——, *Capitulare ad eosdem*, PL 105.207-224.

THOMAS DE CHOBHAM (or CHABHAM), *Summa confessorum*, ed. F. BROOMFIELD (Analecta
mediaevalia Namurcensia 25; Louvain-Paris 1968).

Turner, Cuthbert Hamilton — see above *Ecclesiae occidentalis monumenta iuris antiquissima.*

WARNER (Garnerus) OF ST-VICTOR, *Gregorianum*, 16 books, PL 193.23-462.

Wasserschleben — see above *Die Bussordnungen* (under "B").

WILLIAM DURAND OF MENDE, the elder, *Pontificalis ordinis liber*, ed. Michel AN-
DRIEU, *Le pontifical romain au moyen-âge* III (Studi e testi 88; Vatican City 1940).

II. — MORE RECENT STUDIES

ACHÉRY, Jean-Luc D', *Spicilegium* (re-ed. de la Barre, Paris 1723).

Acta Congressus iuridici internationalis - VII saeculo a Decretalibus Gregorii IX et
XIV a Codice Justiniano promulgatis, Romae habiti 12-17 nov. 1934 -
3 vols. (Rome 1935-36).

ADDLESHAW, George William Outram, *The Development of the Parochial System from
Charlemagne (764-814) to Urban II (1088-1099)* (Pamphlet, St. Anthony's
Guild: London 1954).

——, *Rectors, Vicars and Patrons in Twelfth and Early Thirteenth Century Canon Law*
(Pamphlet, St. Anthony's Guild: London-New York 1956).

ADELSON, Howard, and Robert BAKER, "The Oath of Purgation of Pope Leo III
in 800," *Traditio* 8 (1952) 35-80.

AMANN, Émile, A. MICHEL and Martin JUGIE, "Pénitence, "*DictThCath* 12¹.722-
1138; especially "2 Pénitence-sacrement" part I "La pénitence primitive,"
cols. 749-845 and part II "La pénitence privée: son organisation; premières
spéculations à son sujet," cols. 845-948, both by Émile Amann.

AMANN, Émile, "Petit, Jacques," *DictThCath* 12¹.1337-38.

ANDRIEU, Michel, *Le pontifical romain au moyen-âge*, 4 vols. (Studi e testi 86-88, 99;
Vatican City 1938-41).

ANCIAUX, Paul, *La théologie du Sacrement de pénitence au XIIᵉ siècle* (Universitas Catholica Lovaniensis: Dissertationes ad gradum magistri in Facultate Theologica
vel in Facultate Iuris Canonici consequendum conscriptae Series II - To-
mus 41; Louvain-Gembloux 1949).

BALDWIN, John W., "A Campaign to Reduce Clerical Celibacy at the Turn of the
Twelfth and Thirteenth Centuries," *Études d'histoire du droit canonique dédiées
à Gabriel Le Bras* (Paris 1965) II 1041-53.

——, "Critics of the legal Profession: Peter the Chanter and his Circle," *Proceedings
of the Second International Congress of Medieval Canon Law* (Vatican City 1965)
249-259.

BARON, Roger, "Hugues de Saint-Victor: Contribution à un nouvel examen de son
œuvre," *Traditio* 15 (1959) 223-297.

BAYART, P., "Autel," *DictDroitCan* 1.1456-68.

BLOCH, Marc Léopold Benjamin, "The Rise of Dependent Cultivation and

Seignorial Institutions," *The Cambridge Economic History of Europe* I (Cambridge 1941) 224-277.

——, *La société féodale: La formation des liens de dépendance* (L'évolution de l'humanité, synthèse collective dirigée par Henri Berr. 2ᵉ section, xxxiv¹; Paris 1939).

BLOOMFIELD, Morton W., "A Preliminary List of Incipits of Latin Works on the Virtues and Vices, mainly of the Thirteenth, Fourteenth and Fifteenth Centuries," *Traditio* 11 (1955) 259-379.

——, *The Seven Deadly Sins*, an introduction to the history of a religious concept, with special reference to medieval England (East Lansing, Michigan 1952).

BONNARD, Fourier, *Histoire de l'abbaye royale et de l'ordre des chanoines réguliers de Saint-Victor de Paris*, 2 vols. (Paris 1904-08).

BOURQUELOT, F., *Études sur les foires de Champagne* (Mémoires présentés par divers savants à l'Académie des Inscriptions et Belles-Lettres, 2ᵉ série, 5; Paris 1865).

BOYLE, Leonard E., "Three English Pastoral Summae and a 'Magister Galienus'," *Studia Gratiana* 11 (Collectanea Stephan Kuttner 1; Bologna 1967) 133-144.

BRÉHIER, Louis, *L'Église et l'Orient au Moyen-Age: Les Croisades*, 2nd ed. (Bibliothèque de l'enseignement de l'histoire ecclésiastique; Paris 1907).

BROWE, Peter, "Die Kinderkommunion im Mittelalter," *Scholastik* 5 (1930) 1-45.

BRYS, Joseph, *De dispensatione in iure canonico praesertim apud decretistas et decretalistas usque ad medium decimum quartum saeculum* (Universitas Catholica Lovaniensis, Dissertationes ad gradum doctoris in facultate Theologiae: Series 2, tome 14; Bruges-Wetteren 1925).

BULTOT, R., "L'auteur et la fonction littéraire du 'De fructibus carnis et spiritus'," *Rech ThAncMéd* 30 (1963) 148-154.

CABROL, Fernand, "Jeûnes," *DictArchChrLit* 7².2481-2501.

The Cambridge Economic History of Europe from the Decline of the Roman Empire, ed. J. H. CLAPHAM, Eileen POWER and others, vols. 1-3 (London 1941-63).

CHAMPEAUX, Ernest, "*Jus sanguinis*, trois façons de calculer la parenté au Moyen Age," *RevHistDroitFE*⁴ 12 (1933) 241-290.

CHENEY, Christopher Robert, "La date de composition du 'Liber Poenitentialis' attribué à Pierre de Poitiers," *Rech ThAncMéd* 9 (1937) 401-404.

——, *English Synodalia of the Thirteenth Century* (London 1941).

——, *Episcopal Visitation of Monasteries in the Thirteenth Century* (Manchester 1931).

——, *From Becket to Langton* (Ford Lectures 1955; Manchester 1956).

CHENEY, Mary, "The Compromise of Avranches of 1172 and the Spread of Canon Law in England," *The English Historical Review* 56 (1941) 177-197.

CHENU, Marie-Dominique, *La théologie au douzième siècle* (Études de philosophie médiévale 45; Paris 1957).

Congrès de droit canonique médiéval, Louvain et Bruxelles, 22-26 juillet 1958 (Bibliothèque de la Revue d'histoire ecclésiastique, Fasc. 33; Louvain 1959).

CONSTABLE, Giles, *Monastic Tithes from their Origins to the Twelfth Century* (Cambridge 1964).

——, "Resistance to Tithes in the Middle Ages," *The Journal of Ecclesiastic History* 13 (1962) 172-185.

CORIDEN, James A., *The Indissolubility added to Christian Marriage by Consummation*, An Historical Study of the Period from the End of the Patristic Age to the Death of Pope Innocent III (Univ. Greg. extract from a dissertation; Rome 1961).

D'Achéry — Achéry, Jean-Luc d'.

DAUVILLIER, Jean, *Le mariage dans le droit classique de l'Église depuis le Décret de Gratien (1140) jusqu'à la mort de Clément V (1314)* (Paris 1933).

DEANESLY, Margaret, *The Pre-Conquest Church in England* (An Ecclesiastical History of England 1; London 1961).

DEANESLY, Margaret, and Paul GROSJEAN, "The Canterbury Edition of the Answers of Pope Gregory I to St. Augustine," *Journal of Ecclesiastical History* 10 (1959) 1-49.

De Ghellinck — see Ghellinck, Joseph de.

DELHAYE, Philippe, "Deux textes de Senatus de Worcester sur la pénitence," *RechThAncMéd* 19 (1952) 203-224.

——, *Pierre Lombard, sa vie, ses œuvres et sa morale* (Conférence Albert le Grand 1960; Paris-Montréal 1961).

DEMAN, Thomas, "Probabilisme," *DictThCath* 13¹.417-619.

DESTREZ, Jean, *La Pecia dans les manuscrits universitaires du XIIIᵉ et du XIVᵉ siècle* (Paris 1935).

DICKSON, Marcel, and Christiane DICKSON, "Le cardinal Robert de Courson. Sa vie," *ArchivesHDLMA* 9 (1934) 53-142.

DIETTERLE, Johann, "Die 'Summae Confessorum' (sive de casibus conscientiae) von ihren Anfängen an bis zu Silvester Prieras (unter besonderer Berücksichtigung über den Ablass)," *ZKirchGesch* 24 (1903) 353-374, 520-548; 25 (1904) 248-272; 26 (1905) 59-81, 350-362; 27 (1906) 70-83, 166-188, 296-310, 431-442; 28 (1907) 401-431.

DOLLINGER, Philippe, *L'évolution des classes rurales en Bavière depuis la fin de l'époque carolingienne jusqu'au milieu du XIIIᵉ siècle* (Paris 1949).

DUGGAN, Charles, *Twelfth Century Decretal Collections and their Importance in English History* (University of London Historical Studies 12; London 1963).

ESMEIN, Adhémar, *Le mariage en droit canonique*, 2nd ed., 2 vols. (Paris 1929-35).

Études d'histoire du droit canonique dédiées à Gabriel Le Bras, 2 vols. (Paris 1965).

EUPEN, Th. VAN, "De praktijk van de boete in de middeleeuwen," *Tijdschrift voor Theologie* 2 (1962) 351-374; 3 (1963) 12-44.

EYNDE, Damien VAN DEN, "Les définitions des sacrements pendant la première période de la théologie scholastique," *Antonianum* 24 (1949) 183-228, 439-488; 25 (1950) 3-78; also published separately (Rome-Louvain 1950).

——, "The Theory of the Composition of the Sacraments in Early Scholasticism," *Franciscan Studies* 11¹ (1951)¹ 1-20, 117-144; 12 (1952) 1-26.

FIRTH, J. J. Francis, "The 'Poenitentiale' of Robert of Flamborough," *Traditio* 16 (1960) 541-556.

——, "More about Robert of Flamborough's Penitential," *Traditio* 17 (1961) 531-532.

——, « Report of a Thesis Defended at the Pontifical Institute of Mediaeval Studies : Robert of Flamborough, *Liber poenitentialis*, » *Med. Stud.* 30 (1968) 342-344.

——, *Thesis* — see below Appendix D at the end of this volume.

FISCHER, Eugen Heinrich, "Bussgewalt, Pfarrzwang und Beichtvater-Wahl nach dem Dekret Gratians," *Studia Gratiana* 4 (1956-57) 185-230.

——, the same article, *Theologische Quartalschrift* 134 (1954) 39-82.

FLICHE, Augustin, *La Réforme grégorienne et la Reconquête chrétienne (1057-1125)* (Histoire de l'Église 8; Paris 1944).

FLICHE, Augustin, Christine THOUZELLIER and Yvonne AZAIS, *La Chrétienté romaine (1198-1274)* (Histoire de l'Église 10; Paris 1950).

FLICHE, Augustin, Raymonde FOREVILLE and Jean ROUSSET DE PINA, *Du premier*

Concile du Latran à l'avènement d'Innocent III (1123-1198) (Histoire de l'Église 9, 2 parts; Paris 1946-53).

FOURNIER, Paul Eugène Louis, and Gabriel LE BRAS, *Histoire des collections canoniques en occident depuis les fausses décrétales jusqu'au Décret de Gratien*, 2 vols. (Paris 1931-32).

FRANKLIN, Alfred, *Histoire de la bibliothèque de l'abbaye de Saint-Victor à Paris d'après des documents inédits* (Paris 1865).

FREISEN, Joseph, *Geschichte des canonischen Eherechts* (Paderborn 1893).

GANSHOF, François Louis, *Qu'est-ce que la féodalité?*, 2nd ed. (Neuchâtel 1947).

GÉNESTAL, Robert, *Histoire de la légitimation des enfants naturels en droit canonique* (Bibliothèque de l'École des Hautes Études: Sciences religieuses 18; Paris 1905).

GHELLINCK, Joseph DE, "Un chapitre dans l'histoire de la définition des sacrements au XIIe siècle," *Mélanges Mandonnet* (Paris 1930) II 79-96.

——, *Le mouvement théologique du XIIe siècle* (2nd ed. Museum Lessianum, Section historique 10; Bruges-Brussels-Paris 1948).

——, "Pierre Lombard," *DictThCath* 12².1941-2019.

——, "Le traité de Pierre Lombard sur les sept ordres ecclésiastiques: ses sources, ses copistes," *RevHistEccl* 10 (1909) 290-302, 720-728; 11 (1910) 29-46.

GIBBS, Marion, and Jane LANG, *Bishops and Reform 1215-72 with Special Reference to the Lateran Council of 1215* (Oxford Historical Series; London 1934).

GILCHRIST, John, "'Simoniaca haeresis' and the Problem of Orders from Leo IX to Gratian," *Proceedings of the Second International Congress of Medieval Canon Law*, ed. S. Kuttner and J. Ryan (Vatican City 1965) 209-235.

GILLMANN, Franz, "Die Abfassungszeit der Dekretsumme Huguccios," *ArchivKKRecht* 94 (1914) 233-251.

——, "Der Ausdruck 'Sacramentum' bei Robert von Flamesbury," *Katholik*⁴ 8 (1911)² 450-457.

——, "Die Ehe ein Sakrament nach Sikard von Cremona," *Katholik*⁴ 6 (1910)² 479-481.

——, "Das ehemals zwischen der soboles ex secundis nuptiis und den Blutsverwandten des verstorbenen Eheteiles bestehende Ehehindernis," *ArchivKKRecht* 89 (1909) 447-470; also publ. separately (Mainz 1909).

——, "Das Ehehindernis der gegenseitigen geistlichen Verwandtschaft der Paten?" *ArchivKKRecht* 86 (1906) 688-714.

——, "Das Ehehindernis der gegenseitigen geistlichen Verwandtschaft der Paten bei Simon von Bisiano," *ArchivKKRecht* 88 (1908) 556.

——, "Das Ehehindernis der geistlichen Verwandtschaft aus der Busse," *ArchivKKRecht* 90 (1910) 236-261; also published separately (Mainz 1910).

——, "Huguccio über die Heiligung, über das Virginitätsgelübde und die Ehe des Gottesmutter," *Katholik*³ 29 (1904)¹ 304-308.

——, "Die Notwendigkeit der Intention auf seiten des Spenders und des Empfängers der Sakramente nach der Anschauung der Frühscholastik," *Katholik*⁴ 17 (1916)¹ 432-449; 18 (1916)² 40-55, 99-115, 163-179; also publ. separately (Mainz 1916).

——, "Die Resignation der Benefizien," *ArchivKKRecht* 80 (1900) 50-79, 346-378, 523-569, 665-708; 81 (1901) 222-242, 433-460.

——, "Die Siebenzahl der Sakramente bei den Glossatoren des Gratianischen Dekrets," *Katholik*⁴ 4 (1909)² 182-214; also published separately (Mainz 1909).

——, "Weibliche Kleriker nach dem Urteil der Frühscholastik," *ArchivKKRecht* 93 (1913) 239-253.

——, "Zur Ablasslehre der Frühscholastik," *Katholik*[4] 11 (1913)[1] 365-376.

——, "Zur Geschichte des Gebrauchs der Ausdrücke 'irregularis' und 'irregularitas'," *ArchivKKRecht* 91 (1911) 49-86, 557-560; also published separately (Mainz 1911).

——, "Zur kanonistischen Schuldlehre in der Zeit von Gratian bis zur den Dekreta'en Gregors IX," *ArchivKKRecht* 117 (1937) 329-362; also published separately (Mainz 1937).

GÖLLER, Emil, *Die päpstliche Pönitentiarie von ihrem Ursprung bis zu ihrer Umgestaltung unter Pius V*, 2 vols. each in 2 parts (Rome 1907-11).

GRABMANN, Martin, *Die Geschichte der scholastischen Methode*, 2 vols. (Freiburg im Br. 1909-11).

GROMMENGINGER, Alfons, "Bedeutet die Exkommunikation Verlust der Kirchengliedschaft?" *ZKathTh* 73 (1951) 1-71.

HANENBURG, Jacoba J. H. M., "Decretals and Decretal Collections in the Second Half of the XIIth Century," *Tijdschrift voor rechtsgeschiedenis* 34 (1966) 552-599.

HÄRING, Nikolaus M., "The Augustinian Axiom: *Nulli Sacramento Injuria Facienda est*," *MedStud* 16 (1954) 87-117.

——, "Berengar's Definitions of *Sacramentum* and their Influence on Mediaeval Sacramentology," *MedStud* 10 (1948) 109-146.

——, "Character, Signum und Signaculum," *Scholastik* 30 (1955) 481-512; 31 (1956) 41-69.

——, "Peter Cantor's View on Ecclesiastical Excommunication and its Consequences," *MedStud* 11 (1949) 100-112.

——, "Report of a Recent Thesis: One Baptism: An Historical Study of the Non-Repetition of Certain Sacraments," *MedStud* 10 (1948) 217-219.

——, "St. Augustine's Use of the Word *Character*," *MedStud* 14 (1952) 79-97.

——, "A Study in the Sacramental Theology of Alger of Liège," *MedStud* 20 (1958) 41-78.

HARTRIDGE, Reginald Alfred Rupert, *A History of Vicarages in the Middle Ages* (London thesis; Cambridge 1930).

HAURÉAU, Barthélemy, *Notices et extraits de quelques manuscrits latins de la Bibliothèque Nationale* 6 vols. (Paris 1890-93).

HEIMBUCHER, Max Joseph, *Die Orden und Kongregationen der katholischen Kirche*, 2 vols. (Paderborn 1933-34).

HEITMEYER, Heinrich, *Sakramentenspendung bei Häretikern und Simonisten nach Huguccio. Von den "Wirkungen" besonders der Taufe und Weihe in der ersten Causa seiner "Summa super Corpore Decretorum"* (Analecta Gregoriana fasc. 132. Series Facultatis Iuris Canonici: sect. B, no. 12; Rome 1964).

HEFELE, Karl Josef VON, *Conciliengeschichte* in Fr. tr. by Henri LECLERCQ, *Histoire des conciles*, 9 vols. (Paris 1907-31).

HERDE, Peter, "Römisches und kanonisches Recht bei Verfolgung des Fälschungsdelikts im Mittelalter," *Traditio* 21 (1965) 291-362.

HILL, Rosalind, "The Theory and Practice of Excommunication in Medieval England," *History* 42 (1957) 1-11.

HINSCHIUS, Paul, *System des katholischen Kirchenrechts mit besonderer Rücksicht auf Deutschland*, 6 vols. (Berlin 1869-97).

Histoire de l'Église depuis les origines jusqu'à nos jours, ed. Augustin FLICHE and Victor MARTIN, 20 vols. to date, some in two parts (Paris 1934 ff.).

Histoire de France depuis les origines jusqu'à la révolution, ed. Ernest LAVISSE, 9 vols. in 18 (Paris 1905-1911).

HÖDL, Ludwig, *Die Geschichte der scholastischen Literatur und der Theologie der Schüsselgewalt*, 1. Teil "Die scholastische Literatur und die Theologie der Schlüsselgewalt von ihren Anfängen an bis zur Summa Aurea des Wilhelm von Auxerre" (Beiträge 38.4, Münster 1960).

——, "Die *lex continentiae*, Eine problemgeschichtliche Studie über den Zölibat," *ZKathTh* 83 (1961) 325-344.

HOLTZMANN, Walther, *Kanonistische Ergängzungen zur Italia pontificia* — see above among ancient and medieval source materials.

——, "La 'Collectio seguntina' et les décrétales de Clément III et de Célestin III," *RevHistEccl* 50 (1955) 400-453.

——, "Zu den Dekretalen bei Simon von Bisignano", *Traditio* 18 (1962) 450-459.

HÖRMANN ZU HÖRBACH, Walther VON, *Die desponsatio impuberum*. Ein Beitrag zur Entwicklungsgeschichte des canonischen Eheschliessungsrechtes (Innsbruck 1891).

HUIZING, Peter, "The earliest development of excommunication latae sententiae by Gratian and earliest decretists," *Studia Gratiana* 3.277-320.

IMBERT, Jean, *Les hôpitaux en droit canonique* (Paris 1947).

JUNGMANN, Joseph A., *Die lateinischen Bussriten in ihrer geschichtlichen Entwicklung* (Innsbruck 1932).

——, "Kinderkommunion," *Lexikon ThKirche*[2] 6.154-155.

——, *Missarum sollemnia. Eine genetische Erklärung der römischen Messe*, 2 vols. (Vienna 1948); Eng. tr. *The Mass of the Roman Rite*, 2 vols. (New York 1951-55).

KANTOROWICZ, Hermann, *Einführung in die Textkritik, Systematische Darstellung der textkritischen Grundsätze für Philologen und Juristen* (Leipzig 1921).

KENNEDY, Vincent L., "The Date of the Parisian Decree on the Elevation of the Host," *MedStud* 8 (1946) 87-96.

——, "The Handbook of Master Peter, Chancellor of Chartres," *MedStud* 5 (1943) 1-38.

——, "The Moment of Consecration and the Elevation of the Host," *MedStud* 6 (1944) 121-150.

KIRSCH, Peter Anton, "Der sacerdos proprius in der abendländischen Kirche vor dem Jahre 1215," *ArchivKKRecht* 84 (1904) Heft 4, pp. 527-537.

KUTTNER, Stephan, "Bernardus Compostellanus Antiquus, A Study in the Glossators of the Canon Law," *Traditio* 1 (1943) 277-340.

——, "'Ecclesia de occultis non judicat' apud decretistas et decretalistas," *Acta Congressus juridici internationalis* - VII saeculo a Decretalibus Gregorii IX et XIV a Codice Justiniano promulgatis, Romae habiti 12-17 nov. 1934 - III (Rome 1936) 227-246.

——, the same article partially reproduced in *Jus pontificium* 17 (1937) 13-28.

——, "The Father of the Science of Canon Law," *Jurist* 1 (1941) 2-19.

——, *Harmony from Dissonance* (Wimmer Lecture 10 ; Latrobe, Pennsylvania 1960).

——, "An Interim Checklist of Manuscripts," *Traditio* 11 (1955) 439-448.

——, *Kanonistische Schuldlehre von Gratian bis auf die Dekretalen Gregors IX.* (Studi e testi 64; Vatican City 1935).

——, "Methodological Problems Concerning the History of Canon Law," *Speculum* 30 (1955) 539-549.

——, "Notes on the Roman Meeting, on Planning and Method," *Traditio* 11 (1955) 431-439.

——, "Pierre de Roissy and Robert of Flamborough," *Traditio* 2 (1944) 492-499.

——, *Repertorium der Kanonistik* (1140-1234), I "Prodromus corporis glossarum" (Studi e testi 71; Vatican City 1937). Since only one volume has been published, "Kuttner, *Repertorium*," refers always to this volume.

——, "The Scientific Investigation of Mediaeval Canon Law: the Need and the Opportunity," *Speculum* 24 (1949) 493-501.

KUTTNER, Stephan, and Eleanor RATHBONE, "Anglo-Norman Canonists of the Twelfth Century: An Introductory Study," *Traditio* 7 (1949-51) 279-358.

LACOMBE, Georges, *La vie et les œuvres de Prévostin* (Prepositini cancellarii parisiensis [1206-1210] *Opera omnia* I; Bibliothèque thomiste 11, section historique 10; Paris-Kain 1927).

LANDGRAF, Artur Michael, "Beiträge der Frühscholastik zur Terminologie der allgemeinen Sakramentenlehre," *DivThomFreib*[3] 29 (1951) 3-34.

——, "Cod. Bamberg Patr. 136. Cod. Paris Nat. lat. 3237 und der Magister Alanus," *Philosophisches Jahrbuch* 54 (1941) 476-490.

——, *Dogmengeschichte der Frühscholastik*, 4 vols. in 8 (Ratisbon 1952-56).

——, "Die frühscholastische Streitfrage vom Wiederaufleben der Sünden," *ZKathTh* 61 (1937) 509-594; reprinted in his *Dogmengeschichte der Frühscholastik* IV[1] 193-275.

——, "Grundlagen für ein Verständnis der Busslehre der Früh- und Hochscholastik," *ZKathTh* 51 (1927) 161-194.

——, "Die Lehre der Frühscholastik vom Episkopat als ordo," *Scholastik* 26 (1951) 496-519.

——, "Sünde und Trennung von der Kirche in der Frühscholastik," *Scholastik* 5 (1930) 210-247.

——, "Zur Konsekrationsgewalt des von der Kirche getrennten Priesters im 12. Jahrhundert," *Scholastik* 15 (1940) 204-227.

LA PORTE-DU THEIL, F. J. G., "Notice sur plusieurs lettres anecdotes du Pape Innocent III," *Notices et extraits des manuscrits de la Bibliothèque nationale et autres bibliothèques* 3 (1790) 617-650.

Lavisse, Ernest, Histoire de France — see Histoire de France.

LAVISSE, Ernest, and Alfred Nicolas RAMBAUT, *Histoire générale du IV*[e] *siècle à nos jours*, 12 vols. (Paris 1893-1904).

LE BRAS, Gabriel, "Le droit classique de l'Église au service de l'homme," *Congrès de Droit canonique médiéval* (Louvain 1959) 104-110.

——, *Institutions ecclésiastiques de la Chrétienté médiévale* (Histoire de l'Église 12) I, 2 parts (Paris 1959-64).

——, "Mariage: III La doctrine du mariage chez les théologiens et les canonistes depuis l'an mille," *DictThCath* 9[2].2123-2317.

——, "Les problèmes du temps dans l'histoire du droit canon," *RevHistDroitFE*[4] 30 (1952) 487-513.

——, *Prolégomènes* (Histoire du droit et des institutions de l'Église en Occident 1; Paris 1955).

LE BRAS, Gabriel, and Ch. LEFEBVRE and Jacqueline RAMBAUD, *L'âge classique, 1140-1378, Sources et théorie du droit* (Histoire du droit et des institutions de l'Église en Occident 7; Paris 1965).

Lefèvre, Georges, *Traité de Usura* — see Robert of Courson among the original source material.

LE GRAND, Léon, *Statuts d'Hôtels-Dieu et de léproseries* (Collections de textes pour servir à l'étude de l'Enseignement de l'histoire 32; Paris 1901).

LEONARDI, Corrado, "La vita e l'opera di Uguccione da Pisa Decretista," *Studia Gratiana* 4 (Bologna 1956-57) 37-120.

LESAGE, Germain, "Le 'Décret de Gratien' et la nature du droit canonique," *Revue de l'Université d'Ottawa*, Section spéciale 22 (1952) 207*-227*.

Loewenfeld, *Epistolae* — see above among catalogues and registers of papal letters: *Epistolae Pontificum Romanorum*.

LOHMANN, Hans-Eberhard, "Die Collectio Wigorniensis (Collectio Londinensis Regia)," *ZSavignyStRG* kan. Abt. 22 (1933) 36-187.

LOTTIN, Odon, *Psychologie et morale aux XIIe et XIIIe siècles*, 6 vols. (Louvain-Gembloux 1942-1960).

——, "Le tutiorisme du treizième siècle," *RechThAncMéd* 5 (1933) 292-301.

LUCHAIRE, Achille, *Les premiers Capétiens* (Ernest Lavisse, Histoire de France II, part 2, Paris 1901).

MACKINNON, Hugh, *The Life and Works of William de Montibus* (unpublished thesis).

McLAUGHLIN, Terence P., "The Teaching of the Canonists on Usury," *MedStud* 1 (1939) 81-147; 2 (1940) 1-22.

——, "The Extravagantes in the *Summa* of Simon of Bisignano", *MedStud* 20 (1958) 167-176.

MACHIELSEN, Lambert, "Les *spurii* de S. Grégoire le Grand en matière matrimoniale dans les collections canoniques jusqu'au Décret de Gratien," *Sacris erudiri* 14 (1963) 251-270.

MARTÈNE, Edmond, *De antiquis ecclesiae ritibus*, 4 vols. (Antwerp 1736).

MEERSSEMAN, Gilles G., *Dossier de l'ordre de la pénitence au XIIIe siècle* (Spicilegium Friburgense 7; Fribourg 1961).

MEERSSEMAN, Gilles G., and E. ADDA, "Pénitents ruraux communautaires en Italie au XIIe siècle," *RevHistEccl* 49 (1954) 343-390.

Mélanges Joseph de Ghellinck S.J., 2 vols (Museum Lessianum, Section historique 13, 14; Gembloux 1951).

Mélanges Mandonnet, Études d'histoire littéraire et doctrinale du moyen âge, 2 vols. (Paris 1930).

MEYER, Otto, "Überlieferung und Verbreitung des Dekrets des Bischofs Burchard von Worms," *ZSavignyStRG* kan. Abt. 24 (1935) 141-183.

MEYVAERT, Paul, "Les 'Responsiones' de S. Grégoire le Grand à S. Augustin de Cantorbéry," *RevHistEccl* 54 (1959) 879-894.

MICHAUD-QUANTIN, Pierre, "Un manuel de confession archaïque dans le ms. Avranches 136," *Sacris erudiri* 17 (1966) 5-54.

——, "A propos des premières *Summae confessorum*," *RechThAncMéd* 26 (1959) 264-306.

——, *Sommes de casuistique et manuels de confession au Moyen âge (XIIe-XVIe siècles)* (Analecta mediaevalia Namurcensia 13; Louvain-Lille-Montréal 1962).

Miscellanea Giovanni Mercati, 6 vols. (Studi e testi 121-126; Vatican City 1946).

MONTFAUCON, Bernard DE, *Bibliotheca bibliothecarum manuscriptorum nova*, 2 vols. (Paris 1739).

MOORMAN, John Richard Humpidge, *Church Life in England in the Thirteenth Century* (Cambridge 1945).

MOREY, Adrian, *Bartholomew of Exeter, Bishop and Canonist*, A Study of the Twelfth Century (Cambridge 1937). It contains an edition of Bart.'s penitential pp. 163-300.

MORIN, Jean (Joannes Morinus), *Commentarius historicus de disciplina in administratione sacramenti Poenitentiae in tredecim primis saeculis* (4th ed. Venice 1702).

Müller, Michael, *Ethik und Recht in der Lehre von der Verantwortlichkeit*, Ein Längsschnitt durch die Geschichte der katholischen Moraltheologie (Ratisbon 1932)

——, "Zur Frage nach der Echtheit und Abfassungszeit des Responsum b. Gregorii ad Augustum episcopum," *Theologische Quartalschrift* 113 (1932) 94-118.

Muzas, Joseph J., "The Concept of *Matrimonium ratum* in Gratian and the Early Decretists (1140-1215)," (Catholic Univ. of America Canon Law Studies 441; Washington 1964 ; an unpublished thesis ; photographic reproductions available from University Microfilms, Ann Arbor, Mich. ; cf. *Dissertation Abstracts* 26 [1965-66] 2229).

Newman, William Mendel, *Le domaine royal sous les premiers Capétiens* (Paris 1937).

Oakley, Thomas Pollock, "Alleviations of Penance in the Continental Penitentials," *Speculum* 12 (1937) 488-502.

——, "Commutations and Redemptions," *Catholic Historical Review* 18 (1932) 344-351.

——, *English Penitential Discipline and Anglo-Saxon Law in their Joint Influence* (New York 1923).

——, "The Penitentials as Sources for Mediaeval History," *Speculum* 15 (1940) 210-223.

Oesterle, G., "Dissolutio matrimonii rati et non consummati per subsequens matrimonium," *Studia Gratiana* 9 (1966) 27-43.

——, "Irrégularités," *DictDroitCan* 6.42-66.

Olsen, Glenn, "The Definition of the Ecclesiastical Benefice in the Twelfth Century: the Canonists' Discussion of Spiritualia," *Studia Gratiana* 11 (Collectanea Stephan Kuttner 1; Bologna 1967) 431-446.

Onclin, Willy, "L'âge requis pour le mariage dans la doctrine canonique médiévale," *Proceedings of the Second International Congress of Medieval Canon Law*, ed. S. Kuttner and J. Ryan (Vatican City 1965) 237-247.

Oudin, Casimir, *Commentarius de scriptoribus ecclesiae antiquis*, 3 vols. (Frankfurt-Leipzig 1722).

Paulus, Nikolaus, *Geschichte des Ablasses im Mittelalter*, 3 vols. (Paderborn 1922-23).

Perrin, Ch.-E., *Recherches sur la seigneurie rurale en Lorraine* (Paris 1935).

Petit-Radel, "Robert of Flamesbury, ou Flamesbourg," *HistLittFrance* 17 (1895) 402-404.

Porte-du Theil — see La Porte-du Theil.

Poschmann, Bernhard, *Die abendländische Kirchenbusse im frühen Mittelalter* (Breslau 1930).

——, *Busse und Letzte Ölung* (Handbuch der Dogmengeschichte 4³; Freiburg im Br. 1951). Eng. tr. *Penance and Anointing of the Sick* (Freiburg im Br. 1964).

Proceedings of the Second International Congress of Medieval Canon Law, Boston College, 12-16 August 1963, ed. Stephan Kuttner and J. Joseph Ryan (Monumenta iuris canonici; Series C: Subsidia 1; Vatican City 1965).

Prolégomènes — see Le Bras, Gabriel, *Prolégomènes*.

Prosdocimi, Luigi, "La 'Summa decretorum' di Uguccione da Pisa, Studi preliminari per una edizione critica," *Studia Gratiana* 3 (Bologna 1955) 349-374.

Rahner, Karl, "Bussdisziplin, altkirchliche," *Lexikon ThKirche*² 2.805-815.

Rambaud-Buhot, J., "Denys le Petit," *DictDroitCan* 4.1131-1153.

Russo, François, "Pénitence et excommunication. Étude historique sur les rapports entre la théologie et le droit canon dans le domaine pénitentiel du ixᵉ au xiiiᵉ siècle," *Recherches de science religieuse* 33 (1946) 257-279, 431-461.

Saltet, Louis, *Les réordinations* (Paris 1907).

SCHARNAGL, Anton, *Das feierliche Gelübde als Ehehindernis in seiner geschichtlichen Entwicklung* (Strassburger theologische Studien 9, Heft 2-3; Freiburg im Br. 1908; also re-ed. Amsterdam 1965).

SCHMOLL, Polykarp, *Die Busslehre der Frühscholastik* (Munich 1909).

SCHULTE, Johann Friedrich VON, *Die Geschichte der Quellen und Literatur des Canonischen Rechts von Gratian bis auf die Gegenwart*, 3 vols. (Stuttgart 1875-80).

SMITH, Albert Hugh, *The Place-Names of the East Riding of Yorkshire and York* (English Place-Name Society 14; Cambridge 1937).

STEPHENSON, Carl, *Mediaeval History* (New York 1935).

——, "The Origin and Nature of the Taille," *Revue belge de philologie et d'histoire* 5 (1926) 801-870.

Studia Gratiana post octava Decreti saecularia auctore Consilio Commemorationi Gratianae Instruendae edita directed by Giuseppe FORCHIELLI and Alphonsus M. STICKLER (Bologna 1953-).

TAYLOR, Henry Osborn, *The Medieval Mind. A History of the Development of Thought and Emotion in the Middle Ages*, 2 vols. (4th ed. London 1927).

TEETAERT, Amédée, *La confession aux laïques dans l' Église latine depuis le VIIIᵉ jusqu'au XIVᵉ siècle.* Étude de théologie positive (Universitas Lovaniensis: Dissertationes ad gradum magistri in facultate theologica, Series 2, no. 17; Bruges-Paris 1926).

——, "Le 'Liber Poenitentialis' de Pierre de Poitiers," *Aus der Geisteswelt des Mittelalters* (Beiträge Suppl. 3) I (Münster 1935) 310-331.

——, "Quelques 'Summae de paenitentia' anonymes dans la Bibliothèque Nationale de Paris," *Miscellanea Giovanni Mercati* II (Studi e testi 122; Vatican City 1946) 311-343.

——, "Raymond de Penyafort (Saint,)" *Dict ThCath* 13².1806-1823.

Thaner, Friedrich, *Die Summa Magistri Rolandi* — see Alexander III.

Theil — see La Porte-du Theil.

THOMAS, Paul, *Le droit de propriété des laïques sur les églises et le patronage laïque au Moyen âge* (Paris 1906).

THOMASSIN, Louis, *Ancienne et nouvelle discipline de l' Église touchant les bénéfices et les bénéficiers*, re-ed. and augmented by M. ANDRÉ as *Ancienne et nouvelle discipline de l' Église*, 7 vols. (Bar-le-Duc 1864-67).

THOMPSON, Alexander Hamilton, *Diocesan Organization in the Middle Ages: Archdeacons and Rural Deans* (Raleigh Lecture in History; offprint from the Proceedings of the British Academy; London 1943).

——, *The English Clergy and their Organization in the Later Middle Ages* (Ford Lectures 1933; Oxford 1947).

——, *The Historical Growth of the English Parish Church* (Cambridge 1913).

THOULOUSE, Jean DE, *Annales ecclesiae sancti Victoris Parisiensis*, Paris, BN lat. 14368-74 (7 vols. mostly autograph); another copy in BN lat. 14679-83 (5 vols. partly autograph).

TIERNEY, Brian, *Foundations of the Conciliar Theory*: the Contributions of the Medieval Canonists from Gratian to the Great Schism (Cambridge Studies in Medieval Life and Thought, New series 4; Cambridge 1955).

——, "Two Anglo-Norman Summae," *Traditio* 15 (1959) 483-491.

TORQUEBIAU, P., "Chapitres de chanoines," *DictDroitCan* 3.530-595.

ULLMANN, Walter, "Canonistics in England," *Studia Gratiana* 2 (Bologna 1954) 519-528.

VACCARI, Pietro, "La tradizione canonica del 'debitum' coniugale e la posizione di Graziano," *Studia Gratiana* 1 (1953) 535 547.

Van den Eynde — see Eynde, Damien van den.

VERBAARSCHOT, M., "De iuridica natura impedimenti consanguinitatis in theologia et in iure canonico a S. Petro Damiano usque ad Decretales Gregorii IX (ca. 1063-1234)" *Ephemerides theologicae Lovanienses* 30 (1954) 697-739.

VERLINDEN, O., "Markets and Fairs," *The Cambridge Economic History of Europe* III (Cambridge 1963) 119-153.

VERNAY, Eugène, Le *"Liber de excommunicatione" du Cardinal Bérenger Frédol précédé d'une introduction historique sur l'excommunication et l'interdit en droit canonique de Gratien à la fin du XIII*e *siècle* (Paris 1912).

VIARD, Paul, *Histoire de la dîme ecclésiastique principalement en France jusqu'au décret de Gratien* (Dijon 1909).

——, *Histoire de la dîme ecclésiastique dans le Royaume de France aux XII*e *et XIII*e *siècles* (Paris 1912).

WALLACH, Liutpold, "The Genuine and the Forged Oath of Pope Leo III," *Traditio* 11 (1955) 37-63.

——, "The Roman Synod of December 800 and the Alleged Trial of Leo III: A theory and the historical facts," *Harvard Theological Review* 49 (1956) 123-142.

WATKINS, Oscar Daniel, *A History of Penance*, Being a Study of the Authorities (a) for the Whole Church to A.D. 450, (b) for the Western Church from A.D. 450 to A.D. 1215, 2 vols. (London-New York 1920).

WEINZIERL, Karl, *Die Restitutionslehre der Frühscholastik* (Munich 1936).

——, "Das Zinsproblem im Dekret Gratians und in den Summen zum Dekret," *Studia Gratiana* 1 (1953) 551-576.

WEISWEILER, Heinrich, "Zur Einflusssphäre der 'Vorlesungen' Hugos von St. Viktor," *Mélanges Joseph de Ghellinck S.J.* II (Gembloux 1951) 527-581.

WENZEL, Siegfried, "The Seven Deadly Sins: Some Problems of Research," *Speculum* 43 (1968) 1-22.

ZIEGLER, Joseph Georg, *Die Ehelehre der Pönitentialsummen von 1200-1350* (Studien zur Geschichte der katholischen Moraltheologie herausgegeben von Michael Müller 4; Regensburg 1956).

TABLE OF ABBREVIATIONS

ambig.	— *ambiguus.*
ANCIAUX	— Paul ANCIAUX, *La théologie du sacrement de pénitence au XII*e *siècle.*
App ConcLat	— *Appendix concilii lateranensis* ed. Mansi 22.248-454.
Archives HDLMA	— *Archives d'histoire doctrinale et littéraire du Moyen-âge* (Paris 1926 ff.).
ArchivKKRecht	— *Archiv für katholisches Kirchenrecht* (Innsbruck and Mainz 1857 ff.).
BART.	— BARTHOLOMEW OF EXETER, *Liber poenitentialis* or *Poenitentiale* ed. Adrian MOREY (Cambridge 1937).
Beiträge	— Beiträge zur Geschichte der Philosophie und Theologie des Mittelalters (Münster 1891 ff.).
BN	— La Bibliothèque nationale at Paris.
BURCH.	— BURCHARD OF WORMS, *Decretum* PL 140.537-1058.
BURCHf	— BURCHARD OF WORMS, *Decretum* as cited in Friedberg's edition of GRATIAN, *Decretum.*
C.35 q.5 c.6	— GRATIAN OF BOLOGNA, *Decretum* Part 2, Causa 35, question 5, capitulum 6. References which begin with "C." refer to Part 2 of the *Decretum.*
1 *Compil.* 3.29.1-2	— *Compilatio prima* Book 3, title 29,' capitula 1-2; edited in *Quinque Compilationes antiquae* by Emil Albert FRIEDBERG (Leipzig 1882).
CorpusScrEccLat	— Corpus scriptorum ecclesiasticorum latinorum 80 vols. to date (Vienna 1866 ff.).
D.51 pr.	— GRATIAN OF BOLOGNA, *Decretum* Part 1, Distinction 51, prooemium (i.e. prologue to Distinction 51). References which begin with "D." refer to Part 1.
De consec. D.2 c.27	— GRATIAN OF BOLOGNA, *Decretum* Part 3 is designated as *De consecratione*; the reference is to Distinction 2, capitulum 7.
De poen. D.5 c.8 *decipi*	— GRATIAN OF BOLOGNA, *Decretum* Part 2, Causa 33, question 3 is designated as *De poenitentia* and subdivided into distinctions; this reference is to Distinction 5, capitulum 8, at the word *decipi.*
DictArchChrLit	— *Dictionnaire d'archéologie chrétienne et de liturgie* ed. Fernand CABROL and Henri LECLERCQ, 15 vols. in 30 (Paris 1924-53).
DictDroitCan	— *Dictionnaire de droit canonique* ed. R. NAZ and others, 7 vols. (Paris 1935-65).
Dict ThCath 7¹.347-369	— *Dictionnaire de théologie catholique* published under the direction of A. VACANT, E. MANGENOT and E. AMMAN, 15 vols. in 30 (Paris 1902-50); reference to volume 7, part 1, columns 347-369.
dictum p. c.5	— dictum post capitulum 5; in GRATIAN, *Decretum*, a passage

apparently by the author to comment on a preceding canon or group of canons.

Div ThomFreib — *Divus Thomas* (Freiburg, Switzerland) begun as *Jahrbuch für Philosophie und spekulative Theologie* (Paderborn-Münster 1887 ff.); 2nd series *Divus Thomas* (Vienna-Berlin 1914 ff.); 3rd series *Divus Thomas* (Freiburg, Switzerland 1923 ff.); 4th series *Freiburger Zeitschrift für Philosophie und Theologie* (Freiburg, Sw. 1954 ff.).

Du Cange — Charles du Fresne Du Cange, *Glossarium mediae et infimae latinitatis,* augmented and revised by Carpentier and Henschel, re-ed. by Léopold Favre, 10 vols. (Paris 1937-38).

Gratian — Gratian of Bologna, *Decretum,* ed. Emil Albert Friedberg, *Corpus iuris canonici* I (Leipzig 1879).

Grat — Gratian of Bologna, *Decretum* ed. Friedberg (in contradistinction to the Roman edition).

Grat* — Gratian of Bologna, *Decretum* Roman edition.

Hefele-Leclercq 5².1340 — Karl Joseph Hefele, *Conciliengeschichte,* revised in French transl. by Henri Leclercq, *Histoire des conciles,* 9 vols. in 18 (Paris 1907-31); reference to vol. 5, part 2, page 1340.

HistLittFrance — *Histoire littéraire de la France* begun by the Benedictines of Saint-Maur, 38 vols. (Paris 1865-49).

Hug. ad C.27 q.2 pr. *individuam* (fol. 287ʳᵇ; ed. Roman p. 748) — Huguccio of Pisa, *Summa decretorum* or *Summa in Decretum* etc.; reference to his commentary on Gratian, *Decretum* Causa 27, question 2, prooemium, comment on the word *individuam* (Paris, BN MS lat. 3892, fol. 287 recto side, col. 2; this text also ed. by Roman, *Nouvelle revue historique de droit français et étranger* 27[1903] 748).

Hugᵃ — Huguccio of Bologna, *Summa decretorum* according to Paris, BN lat. 3891.

Hugᵇ — Huguccio of Bologna, *Summa decretorum* according to Paris, BN lat. 3892 (in contradistinction to 3891).

Ivo 15.52 (PL 161.870) — Ivo of Chartres, *Decretum* Book 15, cap. 52 (Migne, *Patrologia latina* vol. 161, col. 870). If no work of Ivo is mentioned, the reference is understood to be to his *Decretum.*

Ivo *alia lectio* — Ivo of Chartres, *Decretum* according to a reading differing from the text of PL 161.9-1036.

Ivo *Decr* — Ivo of Chartres, *Decretum* PL 161 (in contradistinction to the *Panormia*).

Ivo *Pan* — Ivo of Chartres, *Panormia* PL 161.1037-1344.

JE 1843 — Ph. Jaffé, *Regesta pontificum Romanorum* 2nd ed. revised under the direction of William Wattenbach, 2 vols. (Leipzig 1885-1888). JE refers to the part revised by P. Ewald (namely A.D. 590-882); reference to letter no. 1843.

JK 768 (PL 62.80)— same work as the preceding. JK refers to the part revised by F. Kaltenbrunner, namely from the beginning of Christianity to A.D. 590; this reference is to letter no. 768, which is found in Migne, *Patrologia latina* volume 62, column 80.

JL 16580 (X 3.19.6) — same work as the two preceding items. JL refers to the part revised by S. Loewenfeld, namely A.D. 882-1198; this reference is to the letter numbered 16580; its text is found in the Decretals of GREGORY IX, Book 3, title 19, capit. 6.

KanErgänz — Walther HOLTZMANN, "Kanonistische Ergänzungen zur Italia pontificia," *Quellen und Untersuchungen aus italienischen Archiven und Bibliotheken* 37 (1957) 55-102; 38 (1958) 67-175; also published (Tübingen 1959). Cited by number of decretal.

Lexikon ThKirche² — *Lexikon für Theologie und Kirche*, new edition (Freiburg im Br. 1957 ff.).

MANSI — Giovanni Domenico MANSI, *Sacrorum conciliorum nova et amplissima collectio* (re-ed. Florence 1759-98) 31 vols.

MedStud — *Mediaeval Studies* (Toronto 1939 ff.).

MonGerHist — Monumenta Germaniae historica (Hanover 1835 ff.).

om. — *omittit.* The words of the text with which this variation deals are not found in the MS.

orig — The original (of a canon or patristic text).

PL (122.1128D) — *Patrologiae cursus completus*: Series latina, ed. J.-P. MIGNE (Paris 1844-64); (reference to vol. 122, column 1128, division D of this column).

Po. 2534 (PL 215.659) — Augustus POTTHAST, *Regesta pontificum Romanorum inde ab anno post Christum natum MCXCVIII ad annum MCCCIV*, 2 vols. (Berlin 1874-75). Reference is to letter no. 2534; this letter is published in PL, vol. 215, column 659).

pr. — prooemium (prologue); the introductory remarks of the author, usually in a division or subdivision of GRATIAN, *Decretum*.

praem. — *praemittit.* The words following this abbreviation are found in the MS immediately before the reading on which this variant is indicated.

Proleg. The Prolegomena of the present edition.

Rech ThAncMéd — *Recherches de Théologie ancienne et méviévale* (Louvain 1929 ff.).

Reg. 5.51 (PL 214.1018-19) — INNOCENT III, *Regestorum sive epistolarum libri* (PL 214-216 with suppl. PL 217); reference to Book 5 (containing the letters of the fifth year of his pontificate), letter no. 51 (PL volume 214, columns 1018-1019).

RevHistDroitFE³ — *Revue historique de droit français et étranger*, Series 3 (Paris 1877-1921); this series is also called *Nouvelle Revue historique de droit français et étranger*.

RevHistEccl — *Revue d'histoire ecclésiastique* (Louvain 1900 ff.).

RevScPh Th — *Revue des sciences philosophiques et théologiques* (Le Saulchoir, Kain, Belgium 1907-1912; Paris 1913 ff.).

RobertiFlSumma — ROBERT OF FLAMBOROUGH, *Liber Poenitentialis*, partial edition by Johann F. von SCHULTE, *Roberti Flamesburiensis Summa de matrimonio et de usuris* (Giessen 1868).

Sent. — PETER LOMBARD, *Quatuor libri sententiarum*, 2 vols. (Quaracchi 1916).

s.v. (s.vv.) — *sub verbo* (*sub verbis*) reference to the discussion in a dictionary or encyclopedia of the word(s) indicated.

THOMASSIN-ANDRÉ — Louis THOMASSIN, *Ancienne et nouvelle discipline de l'Église*, re-ed. and augmented by M. ANDRÉ, 7 vols. (Bar-le-Duc 1864-67).

X 3.31.12   — Gregory IX, Pope, *Decretales* ed. Emil Albert Friedberg, *Corpus iuris canonici* II (Leipzig 1881); reference to Book 3, title 31, capitulum 12.

ZKath Th   — *Zeitschrift für katholische Theologie* (Innsbruck 1877 ff.; Vienna 1947 ff.).

ZKirchGesch   — *Zeitschrift für Kirchengeschichte* (Gotha, Tübingen, etc. 1876 ff.).

ZSavignyStRG kan. Abt. — *Zeitschrift der Savigny-Stiftung für Rechtsgeschichte, Kanonistische Abteilung* (Weimar 1911 ff.).

Symbols:

( )   parentheses — used as punctuation. Words enclosed in parentheses belong to the text, but their meaning is parenthetical within the thought of the sentence.

[ ]   square brackets — enclose words which, in the editor's judgment, do not belong to the text. In the edition of the author's main text these signs enclose words which do not belong to the text of Form 3, but are found in several important MSS. Often they belong to Form 2; the *apparatus criticus* must be consulted for precise information. In the Prolegomena and in the notes these brackets enclose explanations of the editor judged necessary for a right understanding of the text. They are also used for parentheses within parentheses.

< >   pointed or diamond brackets — enclose words which, in the editor's opinion, should be included in the text, but are not found in the MS sources. Within the publication of the author's main text (Form 3) this occurs only in the case of rubrics. Rubrics are enclosed in these brackets if they are not found in the generality of MSS which contain the traditional rubrics even if one or other MS does contain them; in that case their presence in any MS is always indicated among the variants.

§   paragraph sign — used to indicate a paragraph or subdivision of an ancient or mediaeval text. For the method of citing Gratian, etc., see above in the table of abbreviations.

LIST OF SIGLA

Aa	= Ann Arbor, Univ. of Mich. 52		Ann Arbor, Univ. of Mich. 52		= Aa
Ab	= Paris, Arsenal 386		Avranches 230		= R
Ac	= Paris, Arsenal 526		Bamberg, Staatsb. Patr. 132		= Bm
Ad	= Paris, Arsenal 769		——, Staatsb. Theol. 207		= Bt
Bm	= Bamberg, Staatsb. Patr. 132		Basel, Universitätsb. B. VII. 30		= F
Bt	= Bamberg, Staatsb. Theol. 207		Berlin, Staatsb. Diez. B. Sant 16		= B
Cc	= Cambridge, Corpus Christi 441		——, see also Tübingen below		
Ci	= Cambridge, Univ. Libr. Ii. 6. 18		Cambridge, Corpus Christi 441		= Cc
Ck	= Cambridge, Univ. Libr. Kk. 6. 1		——, Univ. Libr. Ii. 6. 18		= Ci
Cp	= Cambridge, Pembroke Coll. 238		——, Univ. Libr. Kk. 6. 1		= Ck
D	= Berlin, Staatsb. Diez. B Sant. 16.		——, Pembroke Coll. 238		= Cp
E	= Erlangen, Universitätsb. 359		Erlangen, Universitätsb. 359		= E
F	= Basel, Universitätsb. B. VII. 30		Innsbruck, Universitätsb. 942		= I
G	= Leipzig, Universitätsb. 345		Leipzig, Universitätsb. 345		= G
H	= Paris, BN lat. 10691		London, Br. Mus. Royal 15. B. IV		= L
I	= Innsbruck, Universitätsb. 942		Paris, Arsenal 386		= Ab
J	= Vaticana Bibl. Regin. lat. 395		——, Arsenal 526		= Ac
K	= Vaticana Bibl. Regin. lat. 983		——, Arsenal 769		= Ad
L	= London, Br. Mus. Royal 15. B. IV		——, BN lat. 3529		= Z
M	= Paris, BN lat. 13454		——, BN lat. 10691		= H
N	= Paris, BN lat. 13455		——, BN lat. 13454		= M
O	= Paris, BN lat. 16418		——, BN lat. 13455		= N
P	= Prague, Univ. Libr. XXIII. E. 52		——, BN lat. 14859		= Q
Q	= Paris, BN lat. 14859, comprising :		fol. 306^r *Liber poen. exceptus*		= Pen
	Q^1 = fols. 328^r-331^v Form 1		fols. 328^r-331^v Form 1		= Q^1
	Q^{1*} = fols. 331^v-335^v Form 2		fols. 331^v-335^v Form 2		= Q^{1*}
	Q^2 = fols. 337^v-338^v Form 1		fol. 337^{r-v} from Form 2		= Q^{2*}
	Q^{2*} = fol. 337^{r-v} from Form 2		fols. 337^v-338^v Form 1		= Q^2
	Q^{2**} = fol. 338^v from Form 2		fol. 338^v from Form 2		= Q^{2**}
R	= Avranches 230		——, BN lat. 16418		= O
Sg	= Sigüenza, Cabildo 62		——, BN lat. 16506		= W
So	= Soissons 129		——, BN lat. 18082		= X
Ta	= Troyes 817		——, BN lat. 18201		= Y
Tb	= Troyes 1315		——, BN Nouv. Acq. lat. 232		
Tc	= Troyes 1339		Peter of Roissy, *Manuale*		= Pet
Tu	= Tübingen, Universitätsb., from		——, Bibl. de l'Univ. 1247		= U
	Berlin, Pr. Staatsb. lat. fol. 212		Prague, Univ. Libr. XXIII. E. 52		= P
U	= Paris, Bibl. de l'Univ. 1247		Sigüenza, Cabildo 62		= Sg
V	= Vendôme 150		Soissons 129		= So
W	= Paris, BN lat. 16506		Troyes 817		= Ta
X	= Paris, BN lat. 18082		Troyes 1315		= Tb
Y	= Paris, BN lat. 18201		Troyes 1339		= Tc
Z	= Paris, BN lat. 3529		Tübingen, Universitätsb., from		
			Berlin, Staatsb. lat. fol. 212		= Tu
Pen	= *Liber poenitentialis exceptus*, Paris,		Vatican City, Vat. Reg. lat. 395		= J
	BN lat. 14859 (Q) fol. 306^r		Vatican City, Vat. Reg. lat. 983		= K
Pet	= Peter of Roissy, *Manuale*, Paris,		Vendôme 150		= V
	BN Nouv. Acq. lat. 232				

PROLEGOMENA

FOREWARD

A critical edition of a manual of instruction for confessors is a useful instrument for research into the religious, moral and social climate of life in the Church. The *Liber poenitentialis* of Robert of Flamborough is particularly important in this regard. For it was through this work that the new, formal, "scientific" canon law, which had been developed during the eleventh and twelfth centuries, first became available to the ordinary confessor and so began to influence the consciences of individuals in a new, very effective way. The consequences of this will merit much study and investigation; it is hoped that the present edition will prove to be an aid for research of this kind.

This edition was prepared first as a doctoral thesis presented to the Pontifical Institute of Mediaeval Studies in Toronto, Ontario, Canada. The typewritten dissertation contains several discussions of considerable length for which there is no space here in the printed book. It will be available to those who wish to consult it.[1]

The editor wishes to express his gratitude to all who have helped him with this project, particularly to the staff of the Pontifical Institute of Mediaeval Studies. A special debt of gratitude is owed to Stephan Kuttner of the Institute of Research and Study in Medieval Canon Law at Yale University. Other indebtedness will be mentioned in connection with individual contributions.

THE AUTHOR

Various attempts have been made to identify our author's place of origin, which is indicated as *Flamesburc, Flamesburch, Flamesbore, Flamesbut,* etc. in the rubrics of the penitential in various MSS. Johann Dietterle reasoned that these forms must designate an English town named "Flamesbury," and many writers have followed him in calling our author "Robert of Flamesbury."[2] But there is no town of that name in England; nor has any such

---

[1] See below Appendix D; it is cited herein as FIRTH, *Thesis.*

[2] See DIETTERLE, "Die *Summae confessorum,*" *ZKirchGesch* 24 (1903) 365. This scholar re-

place been found mentioned in mediaeval charters. However the name
of a village now called "Flamborough" on the east coast of Yorkshire
was spelled in mediaeval documents as *Fleynesburg, Flamesburch, Flaynburgh,
Flaineburg,* also sometimes with endings in *-urch* or *urc*.[3] Hence George
P. Warner and Julius P. Gilson in their *Catalogue of Western Manuscripts
in the Old Royal and King's Collections*[4] named the author of our penitential
simply "Robert of Flamborough." This identification of the name has
been accepted by such authorities as Stephan Kuttner and Pierre Michaud-Quantin.[5] It is shown to be even more probable by the spelling
Flainesburc written with the *i* plainly stroked in the initial rubrics of two
of our MSS.[6] Thus the research conducted up to the present points to
the town of Flamborough in Yorkshire as the most likely place of origin
for the author of our penitential.[7]

mained dissatisfied with his own suggestion and later proposed the conjectural reading "Fl.
Amesbury," and the identification of our author with a certain Robert Pullen of Amesbury,
near Salisbury. See *ZKirchGesch* 26 (1905) 79; cf. Stephan KUTTNER, "Pierre de Roissy and
Robert of Flamborough," *Traditio* 2 (1944) 493 n. 5.

[3] See Albert Hugh SMITH, *The Place-Names of the East Riding of Yorkshire and York* (Cambridge
1937) p. 105; Eilert EKWALL, *The Concise Oxford Dictionary of English Place-Names* (4th ed. Oxford 1960) s.v. Flamborough.

[4] Vol. II (London 1921) 154, description of British Museum MS Royal 15.B.iv, item no. 23.

[5] See KUTTNER, *Traditio* 2.493; MICHAUD-QUANTIN, "A propos des premières *Summae confessorum*," *RecThAncMéd* 26 (1959) 268 n. 12.

[6] Namely MSS Ac and Z. Moreover the reading may be *Flainesburch* in CcF and *Flaines-
borc(h)* in CiO, but the spelling is less clear in these MSS. Cf. below p. 7, n. 35; KUTTNER,
Traditio 2.495 n. 21.

[7] Cf. FIRTH, *Thesis* I 11*-12* with notes. The possibility remains to be investigated that
Flensburg in Schleswig-Holstein, or perhaps some hitherto unnoticed place, might be referred
to. — The text of the penitential has very few indications which might point to the author's
nationality. His professed friendship with Richard Poore, Dean of Salisbury, to whom the work
is dedicated in the prologue (see below sect. 1 with notes), is no proof that Robert was English;
he might have met Poore as a student at the University of Paris, where the latter was educated.
He mentions two customs as prevailing *in Alemannia* (sects. 74, 114), both of which can be
traced with considerable probability to his sources. The mention of the custom in sect. 74 apparently depends on Huguccio, who (according to the copies of his *Summa* at my disposal) says
that it prevails *in Campania*; sect. 114 contains a reference to a decretal which speaks of the
practice *in terra teutonica* (see notes to these texts). On the other hand, our author's use of the
term *persona* would suggest an English or a French rather than a German background. For him
a *persona* is the rector of a parish, as in England or France, whereas in Germany a *persona* was
a dignitary in a chapter of canons (see below sect. 129 with notes; also Paul HINSCHIUS, *System
des katholischen Kirchenrechts* II 110-114). Further confusion is added to the problem of Robert's
origin by Jean de Thoulouse, seventeenth-century historian of the Abbey of Saint-Victor, who
describes him in his *Annales ecclesiae sancti Victoris parisiensis* as *natione scotus* (Paris BN lat. 14370,
fols. 2ᵛ, 329ʳ); cf. Fourier BONNARD, *Histoire de l'abbaye royale et de l'ordre des chanoines réguliers de
Saint-Victor de Paris* I 285.

It is not known where Robert of Flamborough obtained his education. His friendship with Richard Poore suggests that it may well have been at Paris; it is established that Richard studied there under Stephen Langton.[8]

At an unknown date, in any case before 1205, Robert became a canon regular at the Abbey of Saint-Victor in Paris.[9] This abbey, whose origins can be traced back to William of Champeaux near the beginning of the twelfth century, had already become famous as a centre of learning and as a model of religious observance.[10] It had undertaken the task of reforming other houses, and so the Order of Saint-Victor had come into being.[11]

Both in the rubrics of the penitential and in several contemporary papal letters our author is designated as *poenitentiarius*.[12] This word came into use about the beginning of the thirteenth century to designate a priest with special authority in regard to penance; indeed the papal letters just mentioned, dated 1205, 1206 and 1207, are the earliest known instances of the use of the term in precisely this sense.[13]

The fact that Robert was called *poenitentiarius* does not mean that he was the only priest of the abbey who heard confessions. There is good evidence that a number of priests at Saint-Victor, perhaps even all of them, were qualified and authorized to assign penances to the students of the University of Paris.[14] The word *poenitentiarius* normally meant one

---

[8] This friendship is expressed by Flamborough in his prologue (sect. 1). Regarding Richard Poore's studies see *Chronicon abbatiae de Evesham* (ed. William D. MACRAY, Rolls series 29; London 1863) p. 232; cf. Marion GIBBS and Jane LANG, *Bishops and Reform 1215-1272* (London 1934) pp. 26-27 with n. 8. Schulte's contention that Robert was a fellow student of Stephen of Tournai has been disproved by KUTTNER, *Traditio* 2 (1944) 495.

[9] He is designated as canon penitentiary of this abbey in the rubrics of many of our MSS and in a nearly contemporary work: *Liber poenitentialis exceptus* (see below pp. 6-7).

[10] See BONNARD, *Histoire de Saint-Victor* I 1-14; 85-141.

[11] See *op. cit.* I 141-189.

[12] Po. 2534 (PL 215.659; issued June 7, 1205) is addressed to three persons including *magistro R. poenitentiario S. Victoris Pari<si>ensis*. Po. 2750 (PL 215.866; issued April 16, 1206) and Po. 2751 (PL 215.861-862; issued two days later) refer to Robert as *poenitentiali* and *poenitenti* respectively, but these are obviously misprints or misreadings for *poenitentiario*. Finally in Po. 2995 (PL 215.1087; issued Feb. 1, 1207) he is mentioned thus: *R. Sancti Victoris poenitentiarum*, again an obvious mistake for *poenitentiarium*.

[13] See Emil GÖLLER, *Die päpstliche Pönitentiarie* I[1] (Rome 1907) 75-90; FIRTH, *Thesis* I 13*-14* with notes.

[14] Thus Robert Courson felt it necessary to remind his readers that the religious of Saint-Victor would not be competent to impose penances if they had not been authorized to do so by the Bishop of Paris; see his *Summa* 1.46 (ed. Vincent L. KENNEDY, *MedStud* 7 [1945] 326); cf. FIRTH, *Thesis* I 15* with notes.

who had special authority from the bishop, such as that granted a few years later by the Bishop of Amiens when he instituted such an office in his cathedral chapter:

> Poenitentiarius vero loco nostri confessiones audiet de quacumque parte dioecesis ad ipsum referantur, exceptis confessionibus curatorum nostrorum et magnatum et baronum, quas nobis reservamus. Ad illum etiam, tamquam illum quem post nos in hoc officio proximum esse volumus, dubitationes, si quae emergant in foro poenitentiali, jubemus reportari. Poenitentias injunctas ab aliis confessoribus relaxare poterit et mutare, prout secundum Deum viderit expedire. Provisionem etiam et curam domus hospitalariae ambianensis loco nostri habebit.[15]

The author of our penitential tells us, through the mouth of the priest in the dialogue, that he sought and obtained from two Bishops of Paris, one of whom succeeded the other in 1208, special authority to grant dispensations.[16]

The jurisdiction of the priest penitentiary of Saint-Victor, sometimes at least, went beyond what could be granted by the bishop of the city. In several instances popes or papal legates conferred on the abbot special authority to dispense or absolve.[17] A letter of January 23, 1212, reveals that authority to absolve students from excommunication for violence to clerics had been granted previously to the Abbot of Saint-Victor at the request of the students.[18] Ralph, the papal penitentiary, in another letter, written about 1218, implies that such authority granted to the abbot would often be exercised by the penitentiary of the abbey.[19]. It is very likely that Robert of Flamborough was granted some authority of this kind before the expiration of his office. He does not mention it in his penitential written for the average confessor, perhaps because it was so extraordinary that it would not likely be duplicated elsewhere. But he does mention the special authority to dispense which he had obtained from the bishop; the confessor who was to use his penitential might find it expedient to obtain similar authority in his own diocese.

In 1205, while he was penitentiary at Saint-Victor, Robert of Flam-

---

[15] Luc d'Achéry, Spicilegium (re-ed. de la Barre, Paris 1723) III 590; cf. Du Cange s.v. poenitentiarius. Regarding the duties of a penitentiary cf. Göller, Die päpstlicher Pönitentiarie I[1]. 75-85, 97-128.

[16] See below sect. 108 with notes.

[17] See Bonnard, Histoire ... de Saint-Victor I 195-197.

[18] See Po. 4371 (PL 216.510 no. 150; Chartularium Universitatis parisiensis ed. Heinrich Denifle and Émile Chatelain, I [Paris 1889] 74 no. 15).

[19] See Denifle-Chatelain, Chartularium I 85-86 no. 28; cf. F. Bonnard, Histoire de Saint-Victor I 196-197.

borough was delegated along with the archdeacon of Paris and Robert Courson to judge the case of Maheu or Matthew of Lorraine, Bishop of Toul, who had been accused of alienating church property.[20] When they went to try the case, the bishop demanded a delay; they continued in spite of his protests and declared him deposed.[21] Innocent III afterwards expressed surprise that these judges, who were *viri litterati providi et discreti*, should have proceeded with the case under the circumstances. The Pope quashed their sentence and granted the bishop a new trial. Eventually he was deposed from the see of Toul; this sentence was confirmed by Pope Innocent early in 1210.[22]

We do not know precisely when the author of our penitential became subprior of the abbey; it was certainly after John the Teuton had been elected abbot in 1203.[23] The most definite indication of the date is the statement of the historian, Jean de Thoulouse, that he was "new in this office" in 1213; in any case he was subprior by that year.[24]

The date of Robert's death is unknown. Jean Morin in his *Commentarius historicus* on the sacrament of penance says of him: *Obiisse dicitur anno 1224*.[25] Whatever be the value of this indication, it is certain that he had ceased to be subprior by 1234; for in that year Ralph, who had been subprior, became abbot.[26]

There are two entries in the obituary of Saint-Victor indicating the death of a subprior Robert, one on July 14, the other on September 19.[27] Jean de Thoulouse indicates July 14 as the day of Flamborough's death.[28]

---

[20] See Po. 2534 (PL 215.659; issued June 7, 1205); Po. 2750 (PL 215.866; issued April 16, 1206).

[21] See Po. 2751 (PL 215.861); Po. 2995 (PL 215.1087).

[22] See Po. 2995 (PL 215.1087); Po. 3875 (PL 216.169); Po. 5619 (Recueil des historiens des Gaules et de la France 19.638-639). Regarding the interesting story of Maheu (Maherus) or Matthew of Lorraine see F. J. G. LA PORTE-DU THEIL, "Notice sur plusieurs lettres anecdotes du Pape Innocent III," *Notices et extraits des manuscrits de la Bibliothèque nationale et autres bibliothèques* 3 (1790) 617-650; *Gallia Christiana* (Paris 1874) 1006-9.

[23] Abbot Joannes Teutonicus, not to be confused with the canonist of the same name, ruled 1203-1228 or 1229. When he was elected in 1203 Richard was subprior according to BONNARD, *Histoire de Saint-Victor* I 278.

[24] See JEAN DE THOULOUSE, *Annales* BN lat. 14370, fol. 2ᵛ; cf. BONNARD, *Histoire de Saint-Victor* I 285.

[25] JOANNES MORINUS, *Commentarius historicus de disciplina in administratione sacramenti poenitentiae* 7.22.7 (4th ed. Venice 1702, p. 340) cf. 10.25.2 (p. 538); PETIT-RADEL, *Histoire littéraire de la France* 17 (1895) 402.

[26] See BONNARD, *Histoire de Saint-Victor* I 307, cf. 344; *Gallia christiana* VII (Paris 1747) 676-7.

[27] See *Obituaires de la province de Sens* ed. by A. MOLINIER and A. LONGNON (Recueil des historiens de la France, Obituaires) I¹.569-570, 586-587.

[28] See his *Annales* BN lat. 14370, fol. 329ʳ; cf. BONNARD, *Histoire de Saint-Victor* I 303 n. 2.

There are good reasons, however, for preferring Sept. 19. On each date of this obituary the entries are generally arranged in chronological order. If this practice has been maintained in the entries on these dates, then the death of the subprior Robert on July 14 must have occurred in the twelfth century, while the entry on Sept. 19 refers to someone who died in the thirteenth, probably between 1219 and 1286.[29]

AUTHENTICITY OF THE PENITENTIAL

The *Poenitentiale* or *Liber poenitentialis* is the only known work of Robert of Flamborough.[30] It is expressly attributed to him in the rubric titles of twenty-seven of the thirty-seven MSS which contain the work; nine others are anonymous.[31] It is ascribed to him by Jean de Thoulouse, who quotes from it liberally.[32] Besides, there is a verbatim quotation from it in an anonymous work entitled: *Liber poenitentialis exceptus de libris poenitentialibus M. Roberti confessoris et M. Petri et aliorum.*[33] We have good reason to assign this anonymous work to the early thirteenth century, perhaps within the lifetime of Innocent III (1198-1216).[34] The first part of it is based on Flamborough's penitential and, according to the sole MS witness, cites it expressly thus:

---

[29] After the entry indicating the death of the subprior Robert on July 14 comes another: *It. Huldardis, abbatissa Edere* (p. 570). The editors indicate that she died about 1150. Then follows mention of Bishop Odo of Paris; this must be Odo of Sully who died in 1208. Hence this Robert is most probably not the author of our penitential; this work was completed only after the death of Odo. — The first entry for Sept. 19 (pp. 586-587) refers to King Louis VII, who died in 1180. After a number of commemorations of persons of uncertain date comes the anniversary of a certain Gervasius Anglicus, who donated certain books to the abbey. Alfred FRANKLIN, *Les anciennes bibliothèques de Paris* (Paris 1867) p. 140 n. 4, considers that this most probably refers to a certain Gervasius Melkeleius, and dates his gifts about 1219. Then follows mention of the subprior Robert. Next is commemorated Geoffrey, Cardinal of Saint Susanna; the editors indicate that he died after 1286. There is nothing then to prevent this indication on Sept. 19 from referring to Robert of Flamborough.

[30] The attribution of other works to our author by Fabricius and Hurter is based on some errors in a catalogue transcribed by Montfaucon; see FIRTH, *Thesis* I 19*-20* with notes. Cf. KUTTNER, *Traditio* 2.495-496.

[31] The anonymous MSS are AbBtCkILQTuUX. The remaining MS, namely D, contains an inscription, which seems to be a later addition, attributing the penitential to Peter Cantor. Since Cantor died in 1197, this attribution cannot be taken seriously.

[32] See his *Annales* BN lat. 14370 fols. 57r-60r, 97v.

[33] Paris, BN lat. 14859, fols. 304r-311r; cf. below p. 27.

[34] This is maintained by Amédée TEETAERT, "Quelques *Summae de paenitentia* anonymes dans la Bibliothèque nationale de Paris," *Miscellanea Giovanni Mercati* 2 (Vatican City 1946) 334-335 no. xii. The text of the work supports his contention. The author writes: *Idem quoque Innocentius*

Et magister Robertus sancti Victoris parisiensis canonicus et poenitentiarius ita dicit in poenitentiali suo: "Domine, non es ad praesens de foro meo; Deus enim ad libitum suum poenitentiam imponit [tibi *insert.*] quia infirmaris. Et ideo innuenda est tibi poenitentia et nulla injungenda, nisi haec tantum: ut studeas ad dolendum de universis peccatis tuis et de singulis et ad Deum diligendum, et firmiter proponas quod de cetero ab omni cavebis peccato, et quando convalueris ad me vel ad alium pro poenitentia revertaris."[35]

Dedication of the Work

The person who is addressed in the prologue as *decane salesburiensis* and near the end of Book 4 as *optime decane* can be none other than the prominent churchman Richard Poore, who was Dean of Salisbury 1198-1214.[36] Thereafter he became Bishop of Chichester, Salisbury and Durham successively, and played a leading role in the reform which followed in England upon the Fourth Lateran Council.[37]

Richard Poore lived and taught in Paris approximately 1208-1213.[38]

---

in nova decretali statuit ... (Paris, BN lat. 14859, fol. 309ʳ). The reference is probably to GRATIAN, *De poen.* D.5 c.8, which is actually a decree of Innocent II. But the fact that the author, thinking it to have come from Innocent III, calls it a new decree would indicate that he was writing during the lifetime of the latter or very soon afterwards. He refers to a council held in Paris under the presidency of the papal legate, Cardinal Guala, thus: *Sicut autem ab ipsius domini Gallonis ore accepimus* (fol. 311ʳ). Regarding the date of this council see Vincent L. KENNEDY, "The Date of the Parisian Decree on the Elevation of the Host," *MedStud* 8 (1946) 89 n. 16.

[35] Paris, BN lat. 14895, fol. 306ʳ. The quotation is from our penitential, below sect. 230. Robert of Flamborough is cited as *Robertus de Flaveny* of Saint-Victor at Paris in *Summa juniorum*, a book of instruction for confessors written about 1250 by a certain Magister Gal<ienus?>. The incipit *Res grandis* is mentioned there. See Leonard E. BOYLE, "Three English Pastoral Summae and a *Magister Galienus*," *Studia Gratiana* 11 (Collectanea Stephan Kuttner 1; Bologna 1967) 137 with n. 1.

[36] In the prologue (sect. 1) two English MSS have the reading *Ric. decane salesburiensis*; in Book 4 he is addressed in sect. 230. See Christopher R. CHENEY, *English Synodalia of the Thirteenth Century*, p. 54; Kuttner, *Traditio* 2 (1944) 495; cf. DIETTERLE, *ZKirchGesch* 24 (1903) 367 with n. 1. Dietterle's identification of Richard Poore with the canonist Ricardus Anglicus is now rejected; see Stephan KUTTNER and Eleanor RATHBONE, "Anglo-Norman Canonists of the Twelfth Century," *Traditio* 7 (1949-51) 329-332. Cf. Josiah Cox RUSSELL, *Dictionary of Writers of Thirteenth Century England* (London 1936) pp. 112-118.

[37] See RUSSELL, *Dictionary of Writers* pp. 118-119; CHENEY, *English Synodalia* pp. 51-57; GIBBS and LANG, *Bishops and Reform* (London 1934) pp. 25-27.

[38] Two papal letters were addressed to him there: one on Jan. 3, 1209, addressed to *Decano sarisberiensi Parisius commoranti* (Po. 3590; X 1.4.8; PL 215.1519), the other on April 9, 1213, addressed to him as *decano sereberiensi docenti Parisius sacram paginam* (Po. 4700; PL 216.801); cf. RUSSELL, *Dictionary of Writers* pp. 158-159. Some sermons he preached there have been found by Thomas KAEPPEL, "Un recueil de sermons prêchés à Paris et en Angleterre," *Archivum Fratrum praedicatorum* 26 (1956) 183 (no. 13), 184-185 (no. 28).

This was the period during which England was under interdict because
of the quarrel between King John and Innocent III over the elevation
of Stephen Langton to the See of Canterbury. Poore, a former pupil of
Langton, was out of favour with the King; it is not surprising that he
should have been at Paris.[39]

DATE OF THE PENITENTIAL

The penitential of Robert of Flamborough, as it is found in all of the
known MSS of it except QW, must have been composed not earlier than
the latter part of 1208. Johann Friedrich von Schulte discovered in it
a reference to a decretal of 1207;[40] it contains at least one reference to
a decretal of 1206.[41] Franz Gillmann found in it a mention of two bishops
of Paris, Odo of Sully and Peter of Nemours: *Ego autem ad istud vitandum
inconveniens a duobus parisiensibus episcopis Odone et Petro habui ut ubique eorum
auctoritate dispensarem ubi et ipsi dispensarent.*[42] Now Odo of Sully died in
July 1208 and Peter of Nemours succeeded him later in the same year.
These references are found in all the MSS used except BtDW. So the earliest
possible date of the penitential is 1208, verified in the case of Forms 2, 3
and 4. However Form 1, texts of which are found in MSS QW, may
have been composed as early as 1198 or 1199.[43]

The work must have been completed at least by 1215. This is evident,
as Schulte and Dietterle have pointed out, because it includes impediments to marriage which were abolished at the Fourth Lateran Council

---

[39] See Augustin FLICHE, Christine THOUZELLIER and Yvonne AZAIS, *La Chrétienté romaine*
(Histoire de l'Église 10; Paris 1950) pp. 94-96; Po. 2676 (Reg. 8.209 PL 215.792; issued Feb. 1,
1206); cf. RUSSELL, *Dictionary of Writers* p. 119.

[40] The decision of Innocent III mentioned below in sect. 55, is that contained in Po. 3168
(X 2.24.25; issued Sept. 1, 1207); cf. SCHULTE, *RobertiFlSumma* p. xxii n. 21.

[41] Po. 2749 (X 3.43.3; issued April 13, 1206) is cited in sect. 77. Probably also Po. 2836
(X 4.15.6; issued July 3, 1206) is cited in sect. 15; cf. SCHULTE, *RobertiFlSumma* p. xii n. 2.

[42] Below sect. 108; cf. Franz GILLMANN, "Das Ehehindernis der geistlichen Verwandtschaft
aus der Busse," *ArchivKKRecht* 90 (1910) 250 n. 3 (251).

[43] Regarding these Forms 1-4 see below pp. 34-51. Form 1 is found in W; moreover there
are two incomplete copies of it in Q designated as Q¹Q². None of these references is found in
these copies of Form 1, except for five words found in Q¹Q² which can hardly have belonged
to the text as originally composed, but almost certainly have been inserted at a later date;
see below pp. 38-39 with n. 99. But Q contains also fragments of Form 2; these are designated
Q *Q *Q **; see description of Q below. Q-* contains both the reference which indicates a
decretal of 1207 (fol. 333ʳᵃ) and the mention of Bishops Odo and Peter (fol. 334ᵛᵃ).

in 1215.[44] This is true of all forms of the work except Form 4, which is found only in MS X.[45]

There is some evidence for an even earlier date for the composition of our penitential. Much has been copied from it into the second redaction of Peter of Roissy's *Manuale de mysteriis ecclesiae*, which was most probably completed by 1213. Stephan Kuttner was the first to notice that many texts of Robert's penitential are also found in Peter's *Manuale*. He rightly concluded that it was Peter who copied from Robert.[46] Vincent L. Kennedy has shown that Peter of Roissy was chancellor of Chartres in 1208 and that he had ceased to be so in 1213.[47] He was not raised to a higher dignity; neither was he deposed from the chancellorship in disgrace; for he is remembered in his obituary as chancellor of the Church at Chartres, esteemed by his fellow canons.[48] So there is good reason to suppose that he died in 1213, if not earlier. It is reasonable then to conclude with considerable probability that the *Poenitentiale* of Robert of Flambourough was completed by 1213 at the latest.[49]

Thus on the basis of the information available at the present time we should date the work most probably 1208-1213, in any case within the period 1208-1215. This applies to the text as found in all the MSS except QW, which contain a form which may have been earlier, and X, which contains a later one.[50]

---

[44] The impediments expounded in Book 2 sects. 38-43 and 58 were greatly reduced at the Fourth Lateran Council and some of them were abolished; see c. 50 of this council (X 4.14.8). Cf. HEFELE-LECLERCQ 5².1372-1373; SCHULTE, *RobertiFlSumma* p. ix; DIETTERLE, "Die *Summae confessorum*," *ZKirchGesch* 24 (1903) 373.

[45] Regarding Form 4 see below p. 51.

[46] See "Pierre de Roissy and Robert of Flambourough," *Traditio* 2 (1944) 489-499, esp. 493, 498. Further evidence for the priority of Flamborough is presented in FIRTH, *Thesis* I 150*-152*.

[47] See "The Handbook of Master Peter, Chancellor of Chartres," *MedStud* 5 (1943) 1-5.

[48] See *ibid.* p. 2.

[49] This reasoning does not eliminate all other possibilities. For example Peter might have resigned his post with honour (as John the Teuton, Abbot of Saint-Victor, did in 1228 or 1229; see BONNARD, *Histoire* I 303) or the longer redaction of his *Manuale* might have been completed by his disciples. But in any case both Flamborough's penitential and this second redaction of Roissy's work must have been completed before the decrees of the Fourth Lateran Council became known; see KENNEDY, *MedStud* 5.4 n. 24; FIRTH, *Thesis* I 201* n. 12 (III 577*-578*).

[50] See above at nn. 44, 46. It will be shown that our penitential was probably brought to completion gradually from the primitive text represented in Form 1 in MSS QW to the final complete Form 3 through a series of revisions, chiefly additions, made by its author. Peter's *Manuale* contains several passages peculiar to Form 3, including part of the only one of them of any great length. Thus it bears witness to Form 3. However its readings show some affinity to those MSS which I call "intermediate MSS," which probably represent Form 3 in its earlier stages of development from Form 2; see below pp. 49-51. So it is possible that Robert might

The Character of the Penitential

The need for such a work.

By the early thirteenth century books of instruction for the confessor had evolved from mere tariffs of penances for various sins into manuals of pastoral instruction.[51] This process seems to have begun with Book 19 of Burchard's *Decretum* (composed within 1007-15); Book 19 was often copied separately as a penitential, called Burchard's *Corrector*.[52] The development continued through the penitential of Bartholomew of Exeter (approximately 1150-70), to issue in a varied assortment of small books, most of them still unpublished, which had begun to appear about the beginning of the thirteenth century.[53] Among these the penitential of Alan of Lille (1183-1203) was quite outstanding.[54] The character of such manuals had changed because of the growing conviction that confession and especially contrition were more important than the austerity of the penances.[55] Many of these new treatises included some ancient canons containing old traditional penances, but usually their main content was material based on current theology, sometimes also on mystical writings and on pastoral experience.[56]

have added a few short portions of text in the period 1214-1215. — Schulte concluded from the vague way in which Robert cited certain decretals that he did not have access to *Compilatio tertia*, which was issued in 1210; see *RobertiFlSumma* p. ix, p. xv n. 6. It was probably for this reason that he dated the work 1207-1210; see *Geschichte der Quellen und Literatur des canonischen Rechts* I 210. But Flamborough was not a teacher of canon law; he seems to have known decretals chiefly through the writings of canonists. So even after 1210 he might have referred to these decretals without using *Compilatio tertia*.

[51] Regarding these tariffs see Ludwig BIELER, "Penitentials," *New Catholic Encyclopedia* 11.86-87; regarding the development see KUTTNER, *Traditio* 2.493-494.

[52] Printed in PL 140.942-1014; see Pierre MICHAUD-QUANTIN, "A propos des premières 'Summae confessorum'," *RechThAncMéd* 26 (1959) 266. See also *Medieval Handbooks of Penance* ed. John McNEILL and Helena GAMER (Records of Civilization, Sources and Studies 19; New York 1938) pp. 321-345.

[53] Bartholomew's penitential is edited by Adrian MOREY in his monograph, *Bartholomew of Exeter, Bishop and Canonist* pp. 163-300. This development and a number of these manuals are the subject of an article by Amédée TEETAERT, "Quelques 'Summae de paenitentia' anonymes dans la Bibliothèque Nationale de Paris," *Miscellanea Giovanni Mercati* II 311-343.

[54] Edited by Jean LONGÈRE: Alain de Lille, *Liber poenitentialis*, 2 vols. (Louvain-Lille 1965); this is an edition of Alan's longer, final redaction. Two other forms of the text are edited by the same editor in *ArchivesHDLMA* 32 (1965) 169-242.

[55] Regarding these changes see Amédée TEETAERT, *La confession aux laïques dans l'Église latine depuis le VIIIe jusqu'au XIVe siècle*, esp. pp. 38-42; Artur LANDGRAF, "Grundlagen für ein Verständnis der Busslehre der Früh- und Hochscholastik," *ZKathTh* 51 (1927) 161-194.

[56] Alan of Lille's penitential contains many old canons along with a considerable amount of new material (see the analysis of this work by Jean LONGÈRE in his edition I 160-213), but some

However there was one important factor in the Church's contemporary life which had not begun to affect the practice of confession, namely the newly developed canon law. The great revival of church law, begun under the impulse of the Gregorian Reform of the eleventh century, had been given a fresh start with the publication of Gratian's *Decretum* about 1140, and had flourished in the schools under the influence of learned commentators on this great work as well as in the church courts by reason of the flow of decretal letters from Rome.[57]

In the early days of the Gregorian Reform canon law had been a powerful force for Christian living. Canonical texts and their commentaries had dealt, in addition to other matters, with the sacraments, with moral problems, with the general reformation of Christian life.[58] Practical manuals for confessors had used, and still continued to use, this old law quite freely.[59] But the fresh growth of canon law in the latter part of the twelfth century had been oriented chiefly towards the activity of the church courts. More and more frequently popes were appointing judges-delegate and in each instance would send a decretal letter to explain how and by what principles the case was to be judged. Or again, in answer to a bishop's query, the pope would explain in a decretal how he should judge a case in his court. The more noteworthy among these decretals had been preserved and were used as a kind of "case-law" for the church courts, but had rather little effect on the daily lives of Christians.[60] The teaching and writing of contemporary canonists too was oriented towards the application of law in court.[61]

On the other hand, zeal for reform of Christian living had been taken up by theologians such as Peter Cantor and his follower Robert Courson in the University of Paris. These men inculcated respect for the authority of the pope and of the bishops, and sometimes they cited canon law

---

of the treatises examined by TEETAERT, *Miscellanea Giovanni Mercati* II 311-343, contain only advice based on current theology and pastoral experience.

[57] See Stephan KUTTNER, "The Father of the Science of Canon Law," *Jurist* 1 (1941) 2-11; Gabriel LE BRAS, *Institutions ecclésiastiques de la Chrétienté médiévale* (Histoire de l'Église 12) I 1.45-63; FIRTH, *Thesis* II 443*-459*.

[58] For example, BURCHARD in his *Decretum* Book 4 (PL 140.727-750) deals with baptism and confirmation and in Book 10 (cols. 831-834) with the moral evil of superstition and discord; so also IVO, *Decretum*, Books 1 and 11 (PL 161.59-134, 745-780).

[59] See BIELER, "Penitentials," *New Catholic Encyclopedia* 11.86-87. Likewise Alan of Lille in his penitential makes considerable use of Burchard's penitential canons; see the edition by Jean LONGÈRE I 167-176, 255-257.

[60] See Charles DUGGAN, *Twelfth Century Decretal Collections and their importance in English History* pp. 12-25; FIRTH, *Thesis* II 449*-456*.

[61] See FIRTH, *Thesis* II 446*-448*.

in favour of the reforms they advocated.[62] But sometimes, too, they were critical of church law and called for changes in measures and policies which seemed to them inimical to proper Christian life.[63] Their attention was centred on the problems of the ordinary member of the Church, whether cleric or layman, on the Christian morality of his religious, social and personal life, and especially on the relation between diocesan authorities, pastors and people in the parishes. The lectures of Cantor and Courson were recorded and published; they had perhaps intended that their lectures and these books should be of service to the priest with care of souls. But their writings were long and tedious, and they often failed to come to any conclusion definite enough to be practical.[64] In much the same way as the ponderous tomes of canonists were inaccessible to the ordinary pastor, so also these records of rambling theological lectures were of little use to him.

There was need for a short, orderly, readable book if confessors were to learn how to proceed according to canon law. Meanwhile Robert of Flamborough had been hearing confessions at the Abbey of Saint-Victor, confessions chiefly of the students of the University of Paris, who were practically all clerics. It is evident from the words of the confessor in his penitential that, even before he wrote this work, Robert had been accustomed to insist that his penitent conform to the precepts of canon law.[65] After all, if a person's marriage were invalid, it seemed reasonable that such a one be obliged either to separate from his partner or to enter into a valid union with her. If he were debarred from orders by church law, it would be only right that he should refrain from receiving or exercising them unless dispensed by ecclesiastical authority. This policy, which he had already been following as confessor, he now presented for the instruction of other confessors by writing his *Poenitentiale.*

Outline of the work and its use of sources.

In all but two of the manuscripts the work is divided into books and chapters.[66] Flamborough himself explains in his prologue how he intends

---

[62] See Nikolaus HÄRING, "Peter Cantor's View on Ecclesiastical Excommunication and its Consequences," *MedStud* 11 (1949) 100-112.

[63] See John W. BALDWIN, "Critics of the Legal Profession: Peter the Chanter and his Circle," *Proceedings of the Second International Congress of Medieval Canon Law* pp. 249-259.

[64] Regarding the works of these theologians see ANCIAUX pp. 86-89; TEETAERT, *Confession aux laïques*, pp. 164-190. Regarding editions see above in the Bibliography.

[65] See e.g. below sect. 108.

[66] These two MSS (QW) contain portions of Form 1, which is probably an abbreviated and mutilated remnant of Flamborough's earliest redaction of his penitential; see below pp. 34-45.

to divide it; he states there also that it will proceed in the form of a dialogue between a priest and a penitent who comes to him for confession.[67] This dialogue does not represent a typical confession; such a priest and such a penitent never existed nor could exist. Rather the character presented in the role of penitent provides an opportunity for the author to instruct his reader, presumably a priest in need of instruction, with all the details which he thinks the latter should know. Matrimonial law of the time was very complicated; so the penitent is presented as having been involved in a series of marriages, each of such a kind as to illustrate some point of law. The confessor of the time would need to know much about holy orders and impediments to orders; so the penitent is presented as a priest who has never been ordained deacon, as illegitimate, but legitimated by a subsequent marriage, and so forth. He is not a real living person, but a conglomeration of cases in canon law. At other times he is a curious pupil, asking his confessor, now become his teacher, questions that will help clarify something for the benefit of the reader. In some places, in fact, the dialogue evolves into a short treatise on some point of theology or law.[68]

In Book 1 this dialogue begins; the confessor receives the penitent and explains to him with touching kindness and earnest zeal the basic requirements for a good confession. Some of the theology here seems to have been derived from the penitential of Bartholomew of Exeter, and some from that of Alan of Lille.[69] Here too the plan of the subsequent books is explained more fully. Robert insists that the penitent follow the order of the seven capital vices in his confession. This order was not new; it had already been suggested by earlier authors for the interrogation of the penitent.[70] Our author explains that it is necessary to follow such an order to avoid confusion in the minds of both penitent and confessor.[71] However he finds that it expedites the process if the two most difficult matters are dealt with separately beforehand: first marriage with its

---

[67] See below sects. 2-3.

[68] Thus the whole of Book 2 is a treatise on marriage; the questions of the penitent in sect. 58 thereof are evidently those of a pupil under instruction.

[69] See below sects. 3-8 with notes.

[70] See BURCHARD OF WORMS, *Decretum* (henceforth BURCH.) 19.6 (PL 140.976-977); IVO OF CHARTRES, *Decretum* (henceforth IVO) 15.52 (PL 161.870); BARTHOLOMEW OF EXETER, *Liber poenitentialis* (henceforth BART.) c.1 (ed. MOREY, *Bartholomew of Exeter* p. 175) and c.37 (p. 203); THEODULF OF ORLÉANS, *Capitulare*, PL 105.217, 219; below sect. 9.

[71] Following the theological doctrine of the time Robert conceives the principal function of the confessor as *injungere poenitentiam*. Now if the confessor is to estimate the penance properly he must have a clear notion of the sins which the penitent has committed; cf. below Appendix B sect. 383.

impediments, which will be treated in Book 2, then orders and impediments to orders, which will be the subject of Book 3.[72] Thereafter in Book 4 the interrogation on the vices can begin.

In Book 2 the dialogue continues according to plan and the confessor outlines for his penitent a short treatise on marriage, what is essential for it, the impediments which can invalidate it and others which merely forbid it. This teaching is derived chiefly from the *Summa decretorum* of the canonist Huguccio, along with material from the works of other canonists, from the teaching of Robert Courson, from papal decretals, including a few quite recent ones, and from sources still undiscovered.[73]

In Book 3 orders are treated in similar fashion: first what is essential, then impediments to orders. For the purpose of showing what is signified by each order, Robert copies from a long treatise dealing with the signification of sacred vestments, a treatise entitled *Speculum de mysteriis ecclesiae*, written by an unknown author belonging to the school of Hugh of Saint-Victor.[74] Here Flamborough shows an interest which is not canonical: the meaning of each order is presented in a way which will impress his reader, presumably a cleric, with the value and importance of the dignity to which he has been raised and with the need of bringing his life into conformity with the spirit and purpose of his calling. The sources of most of Book 3, however, are canonical. A long passage is taken almost word for word from the *Summa* of Huguccio;[75] in other places too this author and the others just mentioned as sources for Book 2 have been used.[76] Noteworthy among the impediments to orders are simony,

---

[72] See below sects. 2, 10.

[73] See below sects. 11-72 with notes. Sects. 14, 45-49, 51-54, 62-63, 65-70 have evidently close connections with HUGUCCIO; sect. 30 with *Apparatus: Ecce vicit Leo*; sect. 43 with both HUGUCCIO and RUFINUS; sect. 28 with the *Summa* of ROBERT COURSON. Sects. 39-41, while they show an analogy with Huguccio and some other canonists, most probably depend on another source yet unknown. Numerous decretals are cited throughout, some from the text of Huguccio; sect. 55 refers to a decretal of 1207 and sect. 15 contains a reference which is probably to a decretal of 1206.

[74] See below sects. 90-96. This treatise is published in the appendix to the dogmatic works of HUGH OF SAINT-VICTOR, PL 177.335-380; it was attributed to him in at least one mediaeval catalogue; see PL 175.cxlix-clii with nn. 203, 217. The author in the prologue calls it *Speculum ecclesiae* (col. 335). Regarding its authorship see Heinrich WEISWEILER, "Zur Einflusssphäre der 'Vorlesungen' Hugos von St. Viktor," *Mélanges Joseph de Ghellinck S.J.* II 534-570; cf. Damien VAN DEN EYNDE, "Deux sources de la Somme théologique de Simon de Tournai," *Antonianum* 24 (1949) 41.

[75] Namely below sects. 80-82.

[76] Sect. 103 and the first paragraph of sect. 107 are both related to the same passage in Huguccio; sects. 142-143, most of sects. 157-158 and sect. 172 are based on the same author. Sect. 176 is related to both Huguccio and Rufinus; the last paragraph of sect. 81 as well as sect.

which involves the most lengthy discussion of any topic in the penitential,[77] and homicide ; even accidental homicide is considered by Robert, in conformity with an old canonical tradition, as an impediment for which one must at least seek a dispensation.[78]

After the canonical discussion of these and other impediments, the dialogue turns to the confession at hand. The confessor interrogates his penitent first about his orders and possible impediments to orders, then about his matrimonial status.[79] Thus the pastoral interrogation of the penitent about marriage, which might logically have come in Book 2, actually comes at the end of Book 3.

In Book 4 comes the interrogation according to the seven capital vices outlined by Saint Gregory the Great.[80] First the penitent is asked about pride, the root of all vices, with its associated faults, then about vain glory, next envy, and so forth, each along with a list of associated faults. These lists of faults, begun by St. Gregory, had been enlarged by others; Robert adapted much of the content of his lists from an anonymous treatise *De fructibus carnis et spiritus* printed among the works of Hugh of Saint-Victor and from Alan of Lille, *De virtutibus et vitiis et de donis Spiritus sancti*.[81] Here again our author's teaching is theological and pastoral rather than canonical. But in his treatment of avarice and its associated vices he introduces discussion of the practical problems of restitution for theft or damage, of tithes and usury.[82] These are technical discussions such as are found in the two preceding books; they are based to a great extent on the *Summa* of Robert Courson and probably on the writings

84 contain a dictum of Praepositinus which Flamborough came to know most probably through Robert Courson's *Summa*. The sources of many passages are unknown. Many decretals are cited, a considerable number of them known through Huguccio; sect. 77 refers to a decretal of 1206.

[77] Sects. 110-140.

[78] See sects. 103-109 with notes; cf. Stephan Kuttner, *Kanonistische Schuldlehre von Gratian bis auf die Dekretalen Gregors IX* esp. pp. 185-247; Michael Müller, *Ethik und Recht in der Lehre von der Verantwortlichkeit* esp. pp. 71-101; Firth, *Thesis* II 483*-485* with notes.

[79] The interrogation about orders is in sects. 178-187; it involves a number of canonical points not previously mentioned. The interrogation about marriage is in sects. 188-196; there is presented a long marriage case involving four real or putative marriages. The confessor is concerned with two problems: the matrimonial status of his penitent, and possible irregularity which he may have incurred.

[80] Sects. 197-229; cf. St. Gregory, *Moralia in librum Job* 31.45.88 (PL 76.621).

[81] Robert uses *De fructibus carnis et spiritus* cc. 3-11 (PL 176.999-1002); regarding this work see R. Bultot, "L'auteur et la fonction littéraire du 'De fructibus carnis et spiritus'," *RechThAncMéd* 30 (1963) 148-156. He uses Alan, *De virtutibus* cap. 2 art. 1 (ed. Odon Lottin, *Psychologie et morale* VI 68-75; ed. Idem, *MedStud* 12 [1950] 40-45).

[82] Sects. 204-220.

of Peter Cantor as well, also to some extent on Huguccio and on papal decretals.[83]

At the end of the interrogation our author avoids any precise computation of penance for the penitent's numerous sins by presenting him as a sick person, on whom no penance should be imposed as long as the sickness endures.[84] By this device he also instructs his reader how to deal with such a contingency. Thus the confession is completed and the dialogue comes to an end. Book 4 is terminated with a short treatment of the kinds of penance which may be imposed and some general advice about dealing with penitents.[85]

In his prologue Robert of Flamborough announced a fifth book in which he would set forth the penances proper to various sins.[86] The long series of penitential canons, which makes up approximately the last third of the whole work, fulfils this purpose of the author. After a short introduction explaining how these canons are to be used,[87] Book 5 is subdivided into five parts, each beginning with its own list of titles.[88] Each of these five parts consists of a series of old canons; each canon outlines, often in considerable detail, the penance to be performed for some particular sin. Many of these canons are copied from the penitential of Bartholomew of Exeter, who in turn had obtained many of them from the *Decretum* of Ivo of Chartres.[89] Robert himself took many more canons from Ivo; a few others he seems to have found in Book 19 of the *Decretum* of Burchard, and perhaps some of them even elsewhere in the latter's *Decretum*.[90]

Flamborough is, of course, only the compiler, not the author, of these canons. It is probable that he was aided in his work of compilation by others, perhaps by some of his fellow religious at the Abbey of Saint-

---

[83] See notes to our text; sect. 208 and the central part of sect. 213 correspond quite remarkably with Courson.

[84] See sect. 230.

[85] See sects. 231-233; cf. sect. 2.

[86] See sect. 2.

[87] Sects. 234-241. This passage has been taken as belonging to the beginning of Book 5 because of the opening words of sect. 234 which indicate the intention of the author to turn at this point to consideration of penances for different kinds of sins; cf. FIRTH, *Thesis* II 342*-351*.

[88] Sects. 242, 271, 298, 308 and 323. The list of titles in sect. 336 does not introduce a new part of Book 5, but a short subdivision (sects. 336-339) of the last part.

[89] Regarding Bartholomew's use of Ivo see Adrian MOREY, *Bartholomew of Exeter* pp. 170, 173-174, 308-311; regarding Flamborough's use of Bartholomew see FIRTH, *Thesis* II 417*-418*; cf. *Traditio* 16.551; below in the table of citations.

[90] Our penitential contains many canons found in Ivo, *Decretum*, but not in Bartholomew's penitential, for example the first three canons of sect. 243. The second paragraph of sect. 316 and the second one of sect. 351 are found also in Book 19 of BURCHARD, *Decretum*. Regarding Robert's possible use of other parts of his *Decretum* see FIRTH, *Thesis* II 420*-421*.

Victor.[91] But we have every reason to believe that Robert of Flamborough planned the whole work and saw to the editing of it as his penitential.

In one or two places in Book 5, where no source for a paragraph has been found, it is not clear whether our author copied it from a source or composed it himself.[92] But there can be little doubt that the long paragraph at the end of the whole work is his composition. For it is a final exhortation to the confessor, in which Robert explains in a very personal way, as he has done before, his policy of assigning penances in conformity with the ancient canons.[93]

The general plan of our penitential resembles the arrangement of Book 19 in the *Decretum* of Burchard of Worms. It too consists of a confession in dialogue form followed by a long list of penances.[94] A somewhat similar plan had already been adopted in other works as well.[95]

Importance and influence of the work.

Flamborough's penitential differs from previous manuals for confessors in one important respect: the author has included in it the new canon law of the decretists and of the decretals, that law which had been developed in the schools and rendered effective by papal initiative throughout the Church. Alan of Lille had quoted some of the new decretals in his penitential, but only those which involved matters of public order, such as ecclesiastical burial.[96] It seems that he and others hesitated to bring to

---

[91] This can be surmised from the fact that several canons are repeated. For example the second paragraph of sect. 244 is repeated in slightly different form in the first paragraph of sect. 250. The scribes of several MSS avoided copying some of the repeated canons over again by writing instead *ut supra*.

[92] This is the case in regard to sect. 299, with the last paragraph of sect. 307 and with sect. 341. Moreover no source has been found for sect. 249, which is a comment on the preceding section of canons, and likewise none for a few shorter comments.

[93] Sects. 355-356; cf. sects. 234-235, 241.

[94] BURCH. 19.4-7 (PL 140.950-978) consists of a confession in dialogue form; thereafter chapters 8-72 (cols. 978-1000) deal with the principles and practice of penance and then cc. 73-159 (cols. 1000-14) consist chiefly of traditional penances for particular kinds of sin.

[95] Bartholomew of Exeter's penitential does not contain a dialogue, but in cc. 1-40 (ed. MOREY pp. 175-210) the author explains how the penitent is to be received and inculcates some general principles about penance. Then in cc. 41-135 (pp. 210-300) he copies some old traditional penances for particular sins.

[96] Of the 24 texts listed in Jean Longère's edition of Alan's penitential (II 204) as being found also in *Compilationes* 1-3, the majority are either old penitential canons or moral dicta from the fathers of the Church. The rest deal with ecclesiastical burial. Two other public matters appear in these texts, namely the excommunication and deposition decreed for a cleric who receives a church from a layman (ALAN 3.33) and the prohibition of tournaments (ALAN 3.18), but these

bear upon the conscience of a penitent the rigid formalities of this new law as it was expounded by canonists in their commentaries. Insofar as can be determined at the present state of research, Flamborough was the first to make available to confessors in a short, readable, comprehensive work the new law of the decretists and of the decretals, organized in a practical way for solving cases of conscience.[97] For the first time this juridical offshoot of the Gregorian Reform extended its influence beyond synods and church courts and was put at the service of the ordinary confessor, through whose ministry reform measures could now present a more insistent appeal to the individual conscience.[98]

Flamborough's manual was soon followed by others in which similar use was made of the new law: the penitentials of Paul of Hungary, of Saint Raymond of Peñafort and of many others.[99] But for a long time Robert's work continued in use. The considerable number of its manuscripts which have survived is witness to its widespread influence. From Spain eastward to Czechoslovakia, from England southward to the Austrian Tyrol, they are scattered throughout Western Europe. Many of them have belonged to monasteries or convents of various religious orders, at least three to cathedral libraries, one to a secular canon, another to an *officialis* of a diocesan curia, and another to the rector of a parish.[100] The copies of our penitential found in the majority of these manuscripts

too seem to have been included because of their connection with burial. Moreover Alan simply copies the whole text of a decretal in the style of the ancient canonists; he does not seek from it precise solutions for cases. The three texts he has taken from BERNARD OF PAVIA, *Summa decretalium* (see ed. LONGÈRE II 202) are theological rather than canonical in character.

[97] I have investigated all the pastoral books of instruction for confessors of any considerable length known to have been composed in the period 1200-1215. Some, such as the works of William de Montibus (made known to me through the kindness of Hugh McKinnon), do make a little use of the new canon law, but without the technical, juridical details expounded by Flamborough. Others, such as the *Notabilia de excommunicatione et poenitentia* mentioned by KUTTNER in his *Repertorium* pp. 240-241 (cf. ANCIAUX p. 123), do treat of canon law in a juridical way, but they are quite limited in scope; they do not treat in a general way of the knowledge the confessor should have. See FIRTH, *Thesis* II 459*-466* with notes.

[98] Reform synods were becoming common in the early thirteenth century; see Augustin FLICHE, Christine THOUZELLIER and Yvonne AZAIS, *La Chrétienté romaine (1198-1274)* (Histoire de l'Église 10) pp. 146-176.

[99] See KUTTNER, *Traditio* 2.493-495.

[100] See below pp. 20-31. MS O was donated by a canon of Beauvais to the Sorbonne; Tu belonged originally to an *officialis* of the Brandenburg curia; Cp to a rector of Teversham. It is probable that still more of them belonged formerly to individuals of the secular clergy; these would be inclined to make donations to religious houses or to cathedral libraries, rather than vice versa. Moreover the numerous copies in the libraries of mendicant orders, or of canons such as the Premonstratensians, who engaged in pastoral work, probably had a considerable influence on the practice of confession.

were transcribed during the thirteenth century, but at least five of them were copied in the fourteenth.[1] Thus the work continued to be used for over a century. The provenance of three other manuscripts is unknown; many more copies have probably been lost.[2] All of this indicates an influence on confessors, and hence on the consciences and lives of men, that must have been considerable.

One important feature of the new law that had been developed since the *Decretum* of Gratian was its sharper precision, its insistence on conformity with the letter of the statutes and on their interpretation according to fixed canonical principles. This type of precision had been unknown in the time which preceded the Gregorian Reform and even during the Reform itself in the eleventh and earlier part of the twelfth century.[3] It had been developed with a view to the application of law in the ecclesiastical courts; so far as can be determined at present, up to the time of Flamborough's publication it had never been included in a comprehensive manual of pastoral instruction for the confessor. But in his work a zeal for this new juridical precision, an insistence on observance of the law in its canonical details, is quite evident.[4]

In fact our author manifests an earnest zeal for observance of all law, both old and new. His reverence for the old canons prescribing penances "handed down from the holy fathers" was severely criticized by his confrere at Saint-Victor, the canon Peter of Poitiers.[5] Robert himself admits that most people will no longer accept such penances;[6] yet a similar respect for the old canons is evident in a number of other works of about the same time, and some signs of reverence for them can be observed for several centuries afterwards.[7] On the other hand, his intro-

---

[1] BtCiCkTaTuZ are indicated in the descriptions of MSS below as belonging to the fourteenth century; however the script of Z could also have been copied in the late thirteenth. On the other hand, V could belong to the fourteenth. There are also annotations in a fourteenth century hand in Bm which indicate an interest in the text for pastoral use.

[2] A list of lost copies which have come to my attention is given below p. 32. It is reasonable to surmise that many more have been lost. A practical book for pastoral use that had been out of date for more than a century is not the type of book that a scholar in past times would have been easily motivated to keep.

[3] See Stephan KUTTNER, "The Father of the Science of Canon Law," *Jurist* 1 (1941) 2-19; Gabriel LE BRAS, *Prolégomènes* (Histoire du droit et des institutions de l'Église en Occident 1) pp. 154-162.

[4] See below e.g. sects. 18-54, 103-109, 143-157.

[5] Robert's reverence is seen below sects. 234-235, 356; Peter's criticism is transcribed by A. TEETAERT, "Le 'Liber Poenitentialis' de Pierre de Poitiers," *Aus der Geisteswelt des Mittelalters* (Beiträge Suppl. 3) I (Münster 1935) 325; recopied by FIRTH, *Traditio* 16.552.

[6] See below sects. 234, 241.

[7] This respect is evident in the penitential of Alan of Lille. This author admits more readily

duction of the new law with its spirit and its methods, its technicalities
and its precision, into a penitential was the beginning of a kind of re-
volution.[8] The full implications of such a momentous change merit
further study and research. If we open any manual of moral theology
published in the last few centuries, we find a mass of technical details,
a rigorous insistence on observance of precepts and statutes, an effort
to establish precise boundary-lines between what may be tolerated in
a penitent and what must be condemned. All of this is the result of a
gradual development over a long period of time. It would be too much
to say that Robert of Flamborough was responsible for this tradition,
but it does seem safe to say that his work represents one of its historical
roots.

MANUSCRIPTS

The manuscripts of Flamborough's text are treated in alphabetical
order of their sigla, followed by an account of the manuscript of Peter
of Roissy, *Speculum*, which contains numerous quotations from Flamborough.[9] Then some lost MSS will be indicated.

Aa = Ann Arbor, Michigan, Univ. of Mich. Libr. 52, fols. 2r-41v.[10]
— 13th century; from France, probably from the Abbey of Saint-Denis
near Paris.[11]

Initial rubric: *Incipit liber poenitentialis magistri Roberti canonici sancti Victoris parisiensis poenitentiarii.*[12]

---

than Flamborough the propriety of mitigation in his own time (2.5-14 [ed. LONGÈRE II 45-57]
4.21-22 [II 174-177]); yet he copies many such canons with evident respect (2.15-152 [II 57-123]).
Great reverence for these ancient canons is evident also in some notations made on Bm in a
fourteenth century hand indicating alternative lengths of penances; also in a manual for the
confessor edited in the appendix of a very early printed edition of GRATIAN, *Decretum* (publisher
Johann PREVEL 1526).

[8] See FIRTH, *Thesis* II 443*-500*.

[9] Limited space available permits only a very brief account of each MS here; more complete
descriptions are found in FIRTH, *Thesis* I 32*-138*. Please note that some of the sigla used by
FIRTH, *Traditio* 16.541-556, have been changed as indicated in *Traditio* 17.531.

[10] Folios in this MS are not numbered. I am following the system of numbering indicated
by Seymour DE RICCI and W. J. WILSON, *Census of Medieval and Renaissance Manuscripts in the
United States and Canada* II 1112; according to this a loose flyleaf is fol. 1, two loose gatherings
are numbered fols. 2-17 and the continuous book fols. 18-76. Stephan KUTTNER, *Traditio* 2.497
n. 30, outlines the contents of this MS according to another system of numbering, also used by
the present editor in *Traditio* 16.541-544; see FIRTH, *Thesis* I 34*-37*.

[11] See SEYMOUR and RICCI, *Census* II 1112; KUTTNER, *loc. cit.*

[12] Not all rubrics of the MSS are indicated here or in the *apparatus criticus* to the text, but only
those of AdC iZ, as well as those of other MSS which are judged to be of special interest to the
reader.

An incomplete text intermediate between Forms 2 and 3. The first part is on two loose gatherings (fols. 2-17); it is broken off near the end of sect. 115 with the words *teneor non benefacere* followed by the catchword *spiritualiter*. Then a gathering is missing. Book 4 (sect. 197) begins on fol. 18ʳ. Thereafter the work is complete, but sects. 312-315 are out of place; they come after *ad perfectionis gratiam pervenire* of sect. 327.

Ab = Paris, Bibl. de l'Arsenal 386, fols. 183ʳ-225ʳ.
— 13th century; from the Abbey of Saint-Victor at Paris.[13]

A complete text of Form 2.

Ac = Paris, Bibl. de l'Arsenal 526, fols. 1ʳ-39ᵛ.
— 13th century; from the Abbey of Saint-Victor at Paris.[14]

Initial rubric: as in the present edition, at the beginning of sect. 1 below.
A complete text of Form 3 followed on fols. 39ᵛ-40ʳ by the anonymous appendix printed below as Appendix A. This is followed on fols. 41ʳ-42ʳ by diagrams of affinity and of consanguinity.[15]

Ad = Paris, Bibl. de l'Arsenal 769, fols. 84ᵛ-109ᵛ.
— 13th century; early or middle part; from the Abbey of Saint-Victor at Paris.[16]

Initial rubric: *Incipit prologus in librum poenitentialem magistri R. canonici S. Vict. Par.*
Form 3. AdZ lack the list of titles *De ebrietate et gula* in sect. 336. Along with CcCi, which are very similar, Ad is probably the best witness to Form 3.

Bm = Bamberg, Staatsbibl. Patr. 132, fols. 1ᵛ-64ᵛ.
— 13th century; formerly at the cathedral library of Bamberg.[17]

Final rubric : *Explicit poenitentialis magistri roberti viri authentici et illustrissimi confessoris.*
Form 3. The prologue is lacking. The text of Bm has some affinities with that of MSS intermediate between Forms 2 and 3.

---

[13] See Henry MARTIN, *Catalogue des manuscrits de la Bibliothèque de l'Arsenal* I (Catalogue général des manuscrits des bibliothèques publiques de France; Paris 1885) 247-248; cf. Vincent L. KENNEDY, "The Date of the Parisian Decree on the Elevation of the Host," *MedStud* 8 (1946) 89.

[14] See H. MARTIN, *Catalogue ... Arsenal* I 377-380.

[15] These diagrams are quite similar to those found in the appendices of many printed editions of Gratian, except that the degrees of both affinity and consanguinty are extended here to the seventh degree, according to the canon law before the Fourth Lateran Council. These may well be the diagrams mentioned by Flamborough below sect. 42.

[16] See H. MARTIN, *Catalogue ... Arsenal* II (Catalogue général; Paris 1886) 89-92; cf. Stephan KUTTNER, *Repertorium der Kanonistik* p. 435; IDEM, "Bernardus Compostellanus Antiquus," *Traditio* 1 (1943) 331 n. 40; KENNEDY, *MedStud* 8 (1946) 89-90.

[17] See Friedrich LEITSCHUH and Hans FISCHER, *Katalog der Handschriften der königlichen Bibliothek zu Bamberg* I (Bamberg 1895-1906) 1.519-520.

Bt = Bamberg, Staatsbibl. Theol. 207, fols. 68ʳ-76ᵛ,
— 14th century; formerly at the Dominican convent in Bamberg.[18]

Final rubric: *Expliciunt canones poenitentiales.*
An incomplete text of Form 3, consisting only of sects. 288-356.

Cc = Cambridge, Corpus Christi Coll. Libr. 441, pp. 37-134.
— 13th century; formerly at Christ Church, Canterbury; originally in the peculium of Richard of Weynchepe, who became prior of Dover in 1268.[19]

Initial rubric: *Incipit liber poenitentialis magistri R. de Flainesburch* [vel *Flamesburch*] *kan*** s. v*** par. et p****.
A complete text of Form 3; AdCcCi are the best witnesses to this form.

Ci = Cambridge, Univ. Libr. Ii. 6. 18, fols. 3ʳ-129ᵛ.[20]
— 14th century; apparently from the library of Norwic. More.[21]

Initial rubric: *Incipit liber poenitentialis magistri R. de flainesborch* [vel *flamesborch*] *canonici sancti victoris parisius poenitentiarii.*
A complete text of Form 3; AdCcCi are the best witnesses to this.

Ck = Cambridge, Univ. Libr. Kk. 6. 1, fols. 1ʳ-97ᵛ (the whole MS).
— 14th century; provenance unknown.[22]

Intermediate between Forms 2 and 3. Fol. 91 is missing, omitting most o sects. 250-251 *bibat cunctis diebus — ipse et sui.* The text breaks off at the end of fol. 97ᵛ with the words *et aqua poeniteat et septem se-*; the rest is lacking.

Cp = Cambridge, Pembroke Coll. Libr. 238, fols. 153ʳ-179ᵛ.
— 13th century; legacy of Walter de Stratton, rector of Teversham (1337-49).[23]

---

[18] See Leitschuh and Fischer, *Katalog* I 1.778-779.

[19] See Montague Rhodes James, *A Descriptive Catalogue of Manuscripts in the Library of Corpus Christi College Cambridge* II (Cambridge 1912) 349-355.

[20] The numbers by which I am designating the folios here are those marked in the MS itself. Because fol. 3 is the first on which there is any writing, the catalogue designates this as fol. 1, the following as fol. 2 etc. See *A Catalogue of Manuscripts Preserved in the Library of the University of Cambridge* III (Cambridge 1858) 516-517, no. 1897.

[21] Cf. Thomas Tanner, *Bibliotheca Britannico-Hibernica* (London 1748; reprinted Tucson, Arizona, 1963) p. 286. Tanner refers to our author as *Richardus de Flamesborg*; the only two MSS that he has seen (CcCi) in their initial rubrics have abbreviated *Robertus* to *R.*

[22] See *Catalogue ... University of Cambridge* III 708 no. 2081.

[23] See Montague R. James, *A Descriptive Catalogue of the Manuscripts in the Library of Pembroke College Cambridge* (Cambridge 1905) pp. 214-215. The notice of this legacy (quoted by James on p. 214) leaves it uncertain whether at that time Robert's penitential (which is now the last complete work in the volume) was part of the book donated. Regarding Walter de Stratton see Alfred Br. Emden, *A Bibliographical Register of the University of Cambridge to 1500* (Cambridge 1963) p. 563.

Rubric title: *Incipit prologus in libro poenitentiali magistri Roberti sancti Victoris.*
A composite text intermediate between Forms 2 and 3. It breaks off near the
end of sect. 334 with the words *Si quis praecantaverit ad fascinum vel quascumque,* probably because of loss of the last folio.

D = Berlin, Deutsche Staatsbibl. Diez. B Sant. 16, fols. 121ᵛ-140ᵛ.

— 13th century; from the Benedictine Abbey of St-Jacques at Liège;
it was also at one time at the church in Tongres. It belonged afterwards to
the library of Laurens van Santen, whence it passed in 1800 into the possession of Friedrich Heinrich von Diez.[23a]

Form 3, with some affinity to the MSS intermediate between Forms 2 and 3. The
text is very incomplete. A portion *dicente propheta — Sed, quantum-* (sects. 25-62) is
missing between fols. 128 and 129, perhaps by reason of the loss of a gathering of
eight folios. The text is broken off an end of fol. 140ᵛ with the words *Haec est
Huguccionis* of sect. 107; apparently this folio has been separated from those which
originally followed it. The rest of the penitential is now lacking in D.

E = Erlangen, Universitätsbibl. 359, fols. 8ᵛ-22ᵛ.

— 13-14th centuries; formerly at the Cistercian Abbey of Heilsbronn
near Ansbach.[24]

Initial rubric: *Incipit poenitentiale magistri Ruberti poenitentiarii sancti victoris parisius
authenticatum in concilio lateranensi.*
An incomplete copy of Form 3; the text breaks off near the beginning of sect. 230
with the words *ad dolendum de universis,* probably because fols. 23-33 have been
lost.

F = Basel, Universitätsbibl. B. vii. 30, fols. 1ʳ-30ᵛ.

— 13th century; formerly at the Dominican convent in Basel.[25]

[23a] See Valentin Rose, *Verzeichniss der lateinischen Handschriften der königlichen Bibliotheken zu
Berlin* II (Die Handschriften-Verzeichnisse der königlichen Bibliothek zu Berlin 13) 1 (Berlin 1901)
326 note. Rose designates it as a MS of the 14th century, but the script of these folios belongs evidently to the 13th. The information he gives has been supplemented by further data kindly
supplied by the staff of the Deutsche Staatsbibliothek. I am grateful also to Louis Bataillon of
the Leonine Commission at Le Saulchoir for information which led to my locating this MS.
There is no rubric title properly so called for our penitential, but someone has written at the top
of fol. 121ᵛ in coloured ink: *Liber factus ad decanum salabriensem De poenitentia*; and someone else
has written below this in black ink, also in a mediaeval hand: *Summa magistri Petri Cantoris de
poenitentia, sed non est completa.*

[24] See *Katalog der Handschriften der Universitätsbibliothek Erlangen* I "Die lateinischen Pergament-
handschriften," by Hans Fischer (Erlangen 1928) 423-425. Fischer dates this MS in the early
thirteenth century, Dietterle, *ZKirchGesch* 24 (1903) 365-366, assigns it to the fourteenth.
The script seems to belong to the end of the thirteenth century or to the fourteenth.

[25] See *Die mittelalterlichen Handschriften der Universitätsbibliothek Basel,* Abt. B *Theologische Per-
gamenthandschriften* ed. Gustav Meyer and Max Burckhardt I (Basel 1960) 796. There is an
inscription on fol. 1ʳ: *Nota subtractum hunc librum reddi debere henr.' sacerdoti capellano sancti Joannis
in hofsteten dioc.*

Initial rubric: *Incipit liber poenitentionalis magistri Rob. de flamesburch* [vel *flaines-burch*] *canonici sancti Victoris parisiensis poenitentiarii*

Final rubric: *Explicit liber poenitentialis magistri Roberti viri authentici illustrissimi confessoris beati Victoris parisien.*

A complete text of Form 3.

G = Leipzig, Universitätsbibl. 345, fols. 38ʳ-69ᵛ.

— 13th century; from the Benedictine Abbey of Pegau near Merseburg, Saxony.[26]

Initial rubric: *Poenitentiarius magistri Roberti canonici sancti Vitoris parisiensis.*
Final rubric: *Explicit speculum christianae religionis.*
Form 3. The text has some affinities to the peculiarities of KP; several lists of titles have been enlarged.[27] Several penitential canons have been omitted or shortened when they repeat what was contained in an earlier canon.

H = Paris, BN lat. 10691, fols. 1ʳ-96ʳ (the whole MS).

— 13th century;[28] inscription inside the front cover: *Bibliothèque de Rosny.*

Initial rubric: *Incipit liber poenitentialis roberti canonici sancti victoris parisiensis poenitentiarii.*

Intermediate between Forms 2 and 3.

I = Innsbruck, Universitätsbibl. 942, fols. 1ʳ-47ᵛ.

— Early 13th century; it belonged in the 13th century to the canons of Brixen; afterwards it was found at the Carthusian Monastery of Schnals.[29]

A complete text of Form 3, which shows some affinity to those MSS intermediate between Forms 2 and 3.

J = Vatican City, Bibl. Vaticana, Regin. lat. 395 (Montfaucon 106), fols. 37ʳ-58ᵛ.

---

[26] See *Katalog der Handschriften der Universitäts-Bibliothek zu Leipzig* IV, "Die lateinischen und deutschen Handschriften," 1 "Die theologischen Handschriften" by Rudolf HELSSIG (Leipzig 1926-35) 502-503; *op. cit.*, 3 "Die juristischen Handschriften" by the same author (Leipzig 1905) 329.

[27] Cf. F. FIRTH, "The 'Poenitentiale' of Robert of Flamborough," *Traditio* 16 (1960) 547 n. 35; IDEM, "More about Robert of Flamborough's Penitential," *Traditio* 17 (1961) 531.

[28] Cf. Léopold DELISLE, "Inventaire des manuscrits conservés à la Bibliothèque impériale sous les nos. 8823-11503 du fonds latin," *BiblEcChartes* 24 (1863) 197; IDEM, *Inventaire des manuscrits latins conservés à la Bibliothèque Nationale sous les numéros 8823-18613* (Paris 1863-71) I 88.

[29] The handwriting is rather early because the scribe still uses "e" with cedilla for classical "ae" and "oe"; the provenance is indicated in a handwritten catalogue preserved in the library, of which the librarian, Herr Direktor Wieser, has kindly supplied me with a photographic copy. On fol. 1ʳ is written *Carthúsiae Snalia*; the evidence for the canons of Brixen is found on fols. 49ᵛ-50ᵛ. I am grateful to Pierre Michaud-Quantin of Paris for bringing this manuscript to my attention.

— 13th century; originally from the Abbey of Saint-Denis near Paris; afterwards in the library of Alexandre Petau.[30]

Initial rubric: *Incipit liber Poenitentialis Magistri R. Canonici Sancti Victoris pari-<si>ensis.*

Intermediate between Forms 2 and 3. It lacks the first canon of sect. 294. In two places, after sect. 16, and again in place of the word SACERDOS in the middle of sect. 117, extraneous canons have been interpolated into the text. These seem to have nothing to do with the penitential of Robert of Flamborough.[31]

K = Vatican City, Bibl. Vaticana, Regin. lat. 983 (Montfaucon 1244), fols. 1ᵛ-69ᵛ.

— 13th century; formerly at the Abbey of Saint-Denis near Paris, afterwards in the library of Alexandre Petau.[32]

Initial rubric: *Incipit prologus poenitentialis magistri Ruberci canonici sancti Victoris Parisiensis.*

Final rubric similar with *Ruperti* corr. ad *Roperti.*

Form 3 with some peculiarities found only in KP; Book 5 has been subdivided into six books, making ten books in all.[33] It lacks only a few penitential canons, namely sect. 255 (along with GPX), the canon *Episcopis — cesset* of sect. 298 (with P), and the first short canon of sect. 313. After our penitential there follows on fols. 69ᵛ-71ᵛ the anonymous passage published below in Appendix A.

L = London, Br. Museum, Royal 15. B. iv, fols. 146ʳ-153ᵛ.

— 13th century; provenance unknown.

An incomplete copy of Form 3; the text breaks off in the middle of sect. 175 with the words *vel per te vel per alium hoc*, apparently because of separation from the gathering which originally followed.[34]

M = Paris, BN lat. 13454, fols. 1ʳ-47ᵛ.

— Late 13th century; formerly at the Abbey of Saint-Germain-des-Prés in Paris.[35]

---

[30] See Andrew WILMART, *Codices Reginenses Latini* II (Vatican City 1945) 445-451.

[31] See FIRTH, *Thesis* I 68*-71*.

[32] See A. RAES, *Les manuscrits de la reine de Suède au Vatican*, Studi e Testi 238 (Vatican City 1964) 68 and Emil GÖLLER, *Die päpstliche Pönitentiarie* I 1.58 n. 4, 59 n. 1. A table of contents on fol. 1ʳ corresponds to that given by Bernard DE MONTFAUCON, *Bibliotheca bibliothecarum manuscriptorum nova* I 40 for MS 1244 of the library of the Queen of Sweden. The spelling *pagiement* for the vernacular word in sect. 217 and *aligenus* for *alienus* in many places indicates a text from Italy or southern France.

[33] See FIRTH, *Traditio* 16.547 with notes.

[34] This volume is a collection of many gatherings of various origins; our text covers one gathering; see G. F. WARNER and J. P. GILSON, *Catalogue of Western Manuscripts in the Old Royal and King's Collections* II 153-155.

[35] See Léopold DELISLE, "Inventaire des manuscrits latins de Saint-Germain-des-Prés," *BiblEcChartes* 29 (1868) 232; or IDEM, *Inventaire des manuscrits latins conservés à la Bibliothèque Na-*

Initial rubric: *Incipit liber poenitentialis Magistri Roberti de Flamesbore cano<ni>ci sancti Victoris Parisiun. et poenitentiarII.*

Final rubric: *Explicit liber poenitentialis Magistri Roberti de Flamesbore, canonici sancti Victoris periti et authentici, cujus anima requiescat in pace. Amen.*

A complete copy of Form 3.

N = Paris, BN lat. 13455, fols. 25^r-100^v.

— 17th century; completed by 1677; made at the Abbey of Saint-Victor at Paris, afterwards found at the Abbey of Saint-Germain-des-Prés.[36]

Initial rubric: *Incipit liber poenitentialis M. Roberti de flammesbure canonici S. Victoris paris. et poenitentiarii.*

Final rubric similar, except for *Magistri Roberti flammesburc.*

A complete text of Form 3.

O = Paris, BN lat. 16418, fols. 2^r-60^v (the whole MS).

— Early 13th century; donated in 1790 to the Sorbonne library by l'Abbé Dans, a canon of the cathedral of Beauvais. Another inscription reads: *S. Tiersonnier 1708.*[37]

Initial rubric: *Incipit liber poenitentialis magistri R. de flamesborc* [vel *flainesborc*] *canonici sancti Victoris parisius et poenitentiarii.*

A text of Form 2 that is almost complete. The original scribe stopped copying at the end of sect. 353 near the top of fol. 60^v. Another scribe of the fairly early thirteenth century began to copy two paragraphs higher up, thus repeating the last two paragraphs of sect. 353. The writing of this second scribe is designated as O^2; it conforms generally to Form 3. It continues until cut off at the end of the same fol. 60^v, probably by reason of separation from the folio which originally followed it, ending with the words *quam aliqua in hac vita* somewhat below the middle of sect. 356. This is the end of the MS. The second scribe is probably the same as the one who corrected the MS in a number of places, inserting portions of Form 3 missing from Form 2. The writing of the first scribe in this MS is the best witness to Form 2 which has been preserved. It has some peculiar texts and arrangements in Book 5 which may perhaps pertain to the original Form 2.[38]

P = Prague, Universitni knihovna XXIII. E. 52 (formerly Lobkowitz Libr. 432), fols. 1^r-67^v.

---

tionale sous les numéros 8823-18613 (Paris 1863-71) II 104; also RICHARD OF SAINT-VICTOR, *Liber exceptionum* ed. Jean CHATILLON (Paris 1958) p. 42 no. 124.

[36] See FIRTH, *Thesis* I 79*-81*; cf. DELISLE, *locc. citt.*; TEETAERT, "Le 'Liber Poenitentialis' de Pierre de Poitiers," *Aus der Geisteswelt des Mittelalters* (Beiträge, Supp. 3) I (Münster 1935) 313-314.

[37] These inscriptions are on the inside front cover; see FIRTH, *Thesis* I 82*-84*; IDEM, *Traditio* 16.542-546.

[38] The chief peculiarities of Form 2 are indicated below in Appendix C. The last 8 items (portions 20-27) are these peculiarities of MS O in Book 5.

— 13th century, probably completed by 1233; from the Premonstratensian Monastery of Weissenau near Ravensburg.[39]

Initial rubric: *Incipit prologus poenitentialis magistri Roberti canonici sancti Victoris Parisiensis.*

Final rubric: *Explicit poenit. magistri Ruberti.*

Form 3 with some peculiarities found only in KP; Book 5 has been subdivided into six books, making ten books in all.[40] It lacks only two penitential canons as indicated above in the description of K. After our penitential there follows on fols. 67ᵛ-68ᵛ the anonymous passage published below in Appendix A.

Q = Paris, BN lat. 14859, fols. 328ʳ-335ᵛ and 337ʳ-338ᵛ.

— 13th century; most probably from the Abbey of Saint-Victor at Paris.[41]

Towards the end of the thirteenth century the main parts of this volume consisted of two distinct books, each belonging to the Abbey of Saint-Victor, but by the fifteenth century these had been united along with other material to form a single volume of 341 folios, for which is a table of contents on fol. Aᵛ.[42] This included on fols. 304ʳ-311ʳ the work *Liber poenitentialis exceptus de libris poenitentialibus M. Roberti confessoris et M. Petri et aliorum*, based on the penitentials of Robert of Flamborough and Peter of Poitiers, both canons of Saint-Victor.[43] Afterwards, at the latest by 1897, the material which formerly occupied fols. 328-341 was replaced by two gatherings differing noticeably from each other, fols. 328-335 and 336-339 of the present volume.[44] The first is filled completely with texts from Flamborough; the second contains a varied assortment of texts relating to penance, a number of which have been taken from our author's work. These are arranged and designated as follows:

Q¹ = fols. 328ʳ-331ᵛ, containing the greater part of Form 1, from immediately after sect. 365 (corresponding to sect. 11) as far as the end

---

[39] The handwriting belongs to fairly early in the 13th century; on the last folio of the whole MS is a receipt dated 1232, according to Johann F. SCHULTE, *RobertiFlSumma* pp. vii-viii, or rather 1233, according to DIETTERLE, *ZKirchGesch* 24.365 no. 1. The provenance is shown by an inscription *Biblioth. Weissenav.* on fol. 1ʳ; see also Paul LEHMANN, *Mittelalterliche Bibliothekskataloge Deutschlands und der Schweiz* I (Munich 1918) 409, 412.

[40] See FIRTH, *Traditio* 16.547-548.

[41] The main parts of this MS certainly come from Saint-Victor; this includes the *Liber poenitentialis exceptus* fols. 304ʳ-311ʳ. There is good reason to surmise that the gatherings containing our texts, which have apparently been added to the MS within the period 14th-19th centuries (see following paragraph), belonged to Saint-Victor also. I am indebted to Stephan Kuttner for drawing my attention to this MS.

[42] See FIRTH, *Thesis* I 88*-91*.

[43] Cf. above pp. 6-7.

[44] These gatherings differ from each other in parchment and script; in both cases however the handwriting belongs to the 13th century. An inscription on the paper flyleaf of the present bound volume *Volume de 339 feuillettes plus la feuillette A préliminaire 22 juin 1897* shows that these gatherings had been incorporated by that time.

of the first paragraph of sect. 395 (*Matrimonium est legitima — quantamlibet alleviationem*).[45]

Q¹* = fols. 331ᵛ-335ᵛ, containing portions chosen from Form 2, from within sects. 18-156.[46]

Q²* = fol. 337ʳ⁻ᵛ, containing a portion of Form 2 from near the end of sect. 100 to near the end of sect. 108 with a few short omissions (*Sunt quaedam quae — incestuosos et graviores*).

Q² = fols. 337ᵛ-338ᵛ, containing a considerable part of Form 1 from immediately after sect. 365 as far as immediately before sect. 368 (*Matrimonium est legitima — sine dispensatione papae*).[47]

Q²** = fol. 338ᵛ, containing fragments from Form 2 sects. 141-145 with many omissions (*excommunicatio impedit promotionem — tandem subjuncta absolutione*).

The scribe who chose the first series of texts (Q¹ and Q¹*) from Flamborough's work copied from Form 1 more than is now found in Q¹; the first part has been lost, probably because of separation of fols. 328-335 from what originally preceded them.[48] It seems that the same scribe afterwards looked through Form 2 seeking parts not already copied from Form 1.[49] The scribe who chose the second series (Q², Q²* and Q²**) copied shorter portions from each form of our work; however he seems to have followed a somewhat similar policy.

R = Avranches 230, fols. 174ʳ-186ᵛ.

— 13th century; almost certainly from the Abbey of Mont-Saint-Michel.[50]

Somewhat intermediate between Forms 2 and 3. It lacks the last canon of sect. 313.

Sg = Sigüenza, Bibl. del Cabildo catedral 62, fols. 61ʳ-101ᵛ.

— 13th century; provenance unknown.

Initial rubric: *Incipit poenit * * * magistri roberti canonici sancti victoris.*[51]

---

[45] See below Appendix B pp. 286-302.

[46] See FIRTH, *Thesis* I 92*-98*, where these portions are indicated in detail.

[47] See below Appendix B pp. 286-290.

[48] See FIRTH, *Thesis* I 93*-94*.

[49] See *loc. cit.*

[50] Most of the MSS of Avranches come from Mont-Saint-Michel; see *Catalogue général des manuscrits des bibliothèques publiques de France, Départements* X (by H. OMONT; Paris 1889) 1-3. Moreover the presence on fol. 186ᵛ of fragments attributed to a penitential of Fulbert of Chartres corresponds to what is said by MONTFAUCON, *Bibliotheca* II 1360 no. 197, about a MS then at Mont-Saint-Michel. MS R is described by OMONT, *Catalogue général, Départements* X 109-110.

[51] The title is not visible on the microfilm at my disposal; the reading was supplied by Gérard Fransen of Louvain. I am deeply indebted to him; he first informed me of the existence of this MS on the basis of J. Rius SERRA, "Inventario de los manuscritos de la catedral de Sigüenza," *Hispania sacra* 3 (1950) 458, and afterwards obtained a microfilm copy for me.

A complete text intermediate between Forms 2 and 3. There follows on fols. 101ᵛ-102ᵛ the passage published below in Appendix A.

So = Soissons 129, fols. 108ʳ-128ʳ.
— Late 13th century; from the Abbey of Prémontré.[52]

Final rubric: *Explicit poenitentiarius magistri Roberti viri authentici et illustrissimi, Confessoris beati Victoris.*
Form 3. It lacks only the prologue and a short penitential canon at the end of sect. 267.

Ta = Troyes 817, fols. 160ʳ-207ᵛ.
— 14th century (at least for the pertinent folios); provenance unknown.[53]

Initial rubric: *Incipit prologus in librum poenitentialem magistri Roberti de sancto Victore.*
Form 2. Along with BtGRX it lacks the last canon of sect. 313.

Tb = Troyes 1315, fols. 1ʳ-44ʳ (the whole MS).
— 13th century; from the library of Montiéramey (Montier-Ramey) near Troyes.[54]

Initial rubric: * * * *poenit* * * * *Roberti* * * * *sancti* * * *.
An incomplete copy of Form 3 with an affinity to MSS intermediate between Forms 2 and 3. Sect. 58 is lacking, probably because its contents were soon rendered obsolete by the Fourth Lateran Council.[55] Four folios have been lost involving loss of text as follows: between fols. 17 and 18, one folio missing, involving omission of *Praeterea contra conscientiam — vel fidejussorem si causa* (sects. 139-145); between fols. 18 and 19 two folios missing, involving omission of *sed poenitentiam petet a papa — sub hoc sensu: Si aliquis in sacro ordine* (end of sect. 154 to sect. 170); between fols. 19 and 20 one folio missing, involving omission of *ab episcopo coronam suscipere —* SACERDOS. *Violenta fuit coactio* (sects. 178-189).

Tc = Troyes 1339, fols. 129ʳ-170ᵛ.
— 13th century; from the Abbey of Clairvaux.[56]

Initial rubric: *Incipit liber primus magistri Roberti de flammesbuc* [vel *flainesbuc*] *canonici sancti Victoris parisien. et poenitentiarii.*
A complete text of Form 3, which shows some affinity to MSS intermediate between Forms 2 and 3.

Tu = Tübingen, Universitätsbibl., deposit from the Deutsche Staatsbibl. of Berlin, lat. fol. 212, fols. 56ʳ-65ʳ.

---

[52] See *Catalogue général, Départements* III (Paris 1885) 109-110; description by A. MOLINIER.
[53] See *Catalogue général des manuscrits des bibliothèques publiques des départements* (quarto series) II (Paris 1855) 340.
[54] See *op. cit.* II 541.
[55] See above pp. 8-9 with n. 44.
[56] See *Catalogue ... départements* (quarto) II 557.

— 14th century, written about 1376, at any rate completed by 1380; originally a notebook of Nicholas Bernardi, *officialis* of the Brandenburg curia, afterwards in the Dombibliothek at Brandenburg.[57]

It contains an incomplete text intermediate between Forms 2 and 3. Near the top of col. 2 on fol. 65[r] the writing comes to an end with the words SACERDOS. *Scivit hoc ordinator tuus?* POENITENS. *Non.* SACERDOS. *Si* close to the beginning of sect. 179.

U = Paris, Bibl. de l'Université 1247, fols. 10[r]-33[r].

— 13th century; formerly at the Collège Maître Gervais, where it was designated: Louis-le-Grand, 189, 2, 30. - MS t. IV. 30.[58]

A complete text intermediate between Forms 2 and 3.

V = Vendôme 150, fols. 17[r]-50[v].

— 13th-14th centuries.[59]

Initial rubric: *Incipit primus liber p * * * flamesbut can * * *.*
Form 3 with a few characteristics of MSS intermediate between Forms 2 and 3. It lacks the prologue and a part of the first canon of sect. 250.

W = Paris, BN lat. 16506, fols. 19[r]-25[r].

— 13th century, probably about 1235-1250; formerly at the Sorbonne. Delisle describes the script of this MS as Italian.[60]

---

[57] See Valentin ROSE, *Verzeichniss der lateinischen Handschriften der königlichen Bibliothek zu Berlin* II (Die Handschriftenverzeichnisse der königlichen Bibliothek zu Berlin 13) 2. Abteil. (Berlin 1903) 896-898 no. 823. Nicholas Bernardi identifies himself on fol. 174[r] and says that he began to exercice the office of *officialis* in 1376 and mentions various incidents involved in this activity year by year up to 1380. Since he was *officialis* in the curia, he probably found in our penitential a convenient summary of the main points of canon law with which he had to deal, rather than a manual for hearing confessions. This would explain why the scribe stopped copying where he did; it was perhaps realized that nothing more in the work would serve the purpose for which this copy was intended.

[58] See *Catalogue général des manuscripts des bibliothèques publiques de France, Université de Paris et Universités des Départements* (Paris 1918) pp. 287-288, description by Ch. BEAULIEUX. I am indebted to Mlle d'Alverny and to *l'Institut de recherche et d'histoire des textes* of Paris for their research by which this MS was discovered.

[59] This MS is described in *Catalogue ... France, Départements* III 442; regarding possible provenance see introduction by H. OMONT pp. 393-395.

[60] See L. DELISLE, "Inventaire des manuscrits latins de la Sorbonne conservés à la Bibliothèque Impériale sous les nos. 15176-16718 du fonds latin,"*BiblEcChartes* 31 (1870) 147; or IDEM, *Inventaire* IV 63. The script of fols. 4[r]-31[r] is the same, a Gothic of the early or middle part of the 13th century. A *terminus a quo* for its dating is provided by the penitential of Odo of Cheriton, which is found on fols. 7[r]-19[r]. A. FRIEND, "Master Odo of Cheriton," *Speculum* 23 (1948) 653-658, has concluded that this must have been composed not earlier than 1235 because it uses the *Summa casuum* of St. Raymond of Peñafort. For more detailed discussion of this MS see FIRTH, *Thesis* I 120*-123*. Cf. TEETAERT, *Miscellanea Giovanni Mercati* II 341-343.

Final rubric: *Explicit poenitentiale magistri Roberti sancti Victoris.*
The best and most complete copy still extant of Form 1. The penitential canons
at the end are lacking. The author states that he is about to transcribe some
penances for special kinds of sins, and then the work abruptly ends. There is
evidence of inversion and abbreviation in other places as well. It is not clear
whether this is peculiar to MS W or belongs to Form 1 as such.[61]

X = Paris, BN lat. 18082, fols. 236v-283v.
— Latter part of the 13th century; formerly at the Dominican convent
on rue Saint-Honoré in Paris.[62]

The only surviving copy of Form 4, which is a modification of our penitential
by someone other than its author.[63] Besides lacking a number of portions which
are missing also in Form 2, this MS lacks five of the penitential canons.

Y = Paris, BN lat. 18201, fols. 127r-157r.
— Latter part of the 13th century; formerly at the Priory of Saint-
Martin-des-Champs at Paris.[64]

Initial rubric: *Incipit liber poenitentialis magistri Roberti de Flammesbuc canonici sancti
Victoris parisiensis et poenitentiarii.*
A complete text of Form 3.

Z = Paris, BN lat. 3529, fols. 1r-87v (the whole MS).
— 14th century; it formerly belonged to a Duke of Noailles, Marshal
of France.[65]

Initial rubric: as in the text of the present edition (at the beginning of sect. 1).
Form 3. The text is almost complete; it lacks the short list of titles in sect. 336,
and is cut off at the bottom of fol. 87v, ending with the words *secundum poenitentias
canonicas et authenticas* near the end of sect. 356. Evidently the last folio of our MS
has been separated from other folios which originally followed it.

One manuscript containing the longer redaction of the *Manuale de
mysteriis ecclesiae* of Peter of Roissy:
Pet = Paris, BN Nouv. Acq. lat. 232, fols. 4r-163r.

---

[61] See below pp. 34-37.

[62] See DELISLE, "Inventaire des manuscrits latins de Notre-Dame et de divers petits fonds
conservés à la Bibliothèque Nationale sous les nos. 16719-18613 du fonds latin," *BiblEcChartes*
31 (1870) 539; or IDEM, *Inventaire* V 79; cf. Barthélemy HAURÉAU, *Notices et extraits de quelques
manuscrits latins de la Bibliothèque Nationale* VI 12-18.

[63] See below p. 51.

[64] See DELISLE, *BiblEcChartes* 31 (1870) 545; or IDEM, *Inventaire* V 85; cf. HAURÉAU, *Notices* VI
78-89.

[65] See *Catalogus codicum manuscriptorum Bibliothecae Regiae* III (Paris 1744) 429; cf. Louis SAL-
TET, *Les réordinations* (Paris 1907) p. 351 nn. 2-3. The Duke in question was probably either Anne-
Jules (marshal 1693, died 1708) or his son Adrien-Maurice (marshal 1734, died 1766).

— Early 13th century; provenance unknown.[66]

Numerous, lengthy quotations from Flamborough are incorporated into Peter's *Manuale* on fols. 120ʳ-162ᵛ.[67] These are from Form '3; for they include several passages found in Form 3, but not in Form 2.[68] However, the quotations show an affinity to MSS which are intermediate between Forms 2 and 3.[69]

MANUSCRIPTS NOW LOST

At least ten other MSS containing Flamborough's penitential are reported to have existed, but have now perished or cannot be located:[70]

In England

Two MSS at Peterborough Abbey.
One at Saint Augustine's Abbey, Canterbury.

In France

Chartres 254 (formerly 300).[71]
One MS at the Abbey of Longpont, Soissons.[72]
Two MSS at the Grande-Chartreuse.

In Germany

At least one at Münster.[74]

In Italy

Two MSS at the Convent of San Domenico in Perugia.[75]

---

[66] See Marie-Thérèse D'ALVERNY, "Les mystères de l'église, d'après Pierre de Roissy," *Mélanges offerts à René Crozet* II (Poitiers 1966) 1093; cf. Vincent L. KENNEDY, "The Handbook of Master Peter Chancellor of Chartres," *MedStud* 5 (1943) 5-38.

[67] For a detailed list of quotations see FIRTH, *Thesis* I 131*-138*; cf. 247*-248*.

[68] See FIRTH, *Thesis* I 198*-201*. The most noteworthy instance is Peter's copying of sects. 138-139 of our penitential almost completely, along with the beginning of sect. 140. V. KENNEDY has quoted part of this passage from Peter in *MedStud* 5.11 with n. 74.

[69] See FIRTH, *Thesis* I 223*-226* with notes; cf. 230*-231*.

[70] Information about the first eight of these MSS was obtained from KUTTNER, *Traditio* 2.496 n. 24. I am indebted to Leonard Boyle, who informed me about the two from Italy. No doubt a search in mediaeval catalogues would reveal indications of several additional ones.

[71] This MS perished in the Second World War.

[72] MS D. 6; see A. MOREY, *Bartholomew of Exeter* p. 166. This MS is probably not the same as our MS So; for the latter came to Soissons from the Abbey of Prémontré.

[74] DIETTERLE, *ZKirchGesch* 24 (1903) 365 note, mentions a MS of our penitential in Münster: *Bibliothek d. Akad. 316 fol. (Bd. XIV)*. A recent communication from Ruth Steffen, Bibliotheks-Assessorin in Münster, cites Joseph STÄNDER, *Chirographorum in Regia Bibliotheca Paulina Monasteriensi catalogus* (Breslau 1889) as mentioning MS 195 (279) containing *Roberti canonici Parisiensis et poenitentiarii Liber poenitentialis*. This MS perished in the Second World War.

[75] See Tommaso KAEPPELI, *Inventari di libri di San Domenico di Perugia (1430-80)* (Sussidi eruditi 15; Rome 1962) pp. 75 (A 310) 109 (B 251) 147 (C 268) 226 (D 94).

Manuscripts of the Different Forms

Form 1 (formerly Form W). An abbreviated, mutilated rendering of what was quite probably Flamborough's earliest redaction of his work, composed apparently within 1198-1208:
W = Paris, BN lat. 16506 — the best, most complete copy.
Q = Paris, BN lat. 14859 — containing two incomplete copies:
Q^1 = fols. 328^r-331^v. Q^2 = fols. 337^v-338^v.

Form 2 (formerly Form O). Prior to Form 3, completed within 1208-1213:
O = Paris, BN lat. 16418 — best copy of this form.
Ab = Paris, Arsenal 386.   Ta = Troyes 817.
Q (see above under Form 1) contains several collections of fragments of Form 2:
Q^{1*} = fols. 331^v-335^v. Q^{2*} = fol. 337^{r-v}.
                                             Q^{2**} = fol. 338^v.

Intermediate MSS: between Forms 2 and 3. In three groups:
Tu = Tübingen, Universitätsbibl.   Aa = Ann Arbor, Univ. 52.
    deposit from Berlin, Staatsbibl.   Cp = Cambridge, Pembr. 238.
    lat. fol. 212. Closest of the   J = Vat. Reg. lat. 395.
    intermediate MSS to Form 2.   R = Avranches 230.
                                        Sg = Sigüenza, Cabildo 62.
                                        U = Paris, Université 1247.
Ck = Cambridge, Univ. Libr. Kk. 6. 1.   V = Vendôme 150.
H = Paris, BN lat. 10691.   Pet = Peter of Roissy, *Manuale de mysteriis eccl.* in Paris, BN Nouv. Acq. 232.

Form 3 (formerly Form A). Flamborough's final, complete form. MSS classified in four groups:
Ad = Paris, Arsenal 769.   Ac = Paris, Arsenal 526.
Cc = Cambr. Corpus Chr. 441.   E = Erlangen, Univ. 359.
Ci = Cambr. Univ. Libr. Ii. 6. 18.   M = Paris, BN lat. 13454.
    These are the best witnesses to Form N = Paris, BN lat. 13455.
    3; associated with them: Tb = Troyes 1315.
Z = Paris, BN lat. 3529.   Y = Paris, BN lat. 18201.

The third group containing a slight revision:
K = Vat. Reg. lat. 983   P = Prague, Univ. XXIII. E. 52.
Associated with these: G = Leipzig, Univ. 345.

The fourth group, other composite MSS:
Bm = Bamberg, Staatsb. Patr. 132.   Bt. = Bamberg, Staatsb. Theol. 207.
D = Berlin, Staatsb. Diez. B Sant. 16.
F = Basel, Univ. B. VII. 30.   I = Innsbruck, Univ. 942.
L = London, Br. Museum, Royal 15. B. IV.
So = Soissons 129.   Tc = Troyes 1339.

Form 4 (formerly Form X) in only one MS: X = Paris, BN lat. 18082.

Textual Criticism

Form 1 (formerly called Form W)

The form of our penitential which is most different from the others is found in W; there are also two incomplete copies of the same form in Q; these are designated as Q^1Q^2. This form is called Form 1; it is edited in Appendix B of the present edition.

Form 1 is much shorter than the other forms and is very different from them all. The prologue is similar, but it lacks the part describing the division of the work into books and chapters.[76] As as matter of fact, Form 1 is not divided into books or chapters; it has neither lists of titles nor rubrics. In a number of places its text corresponds quite closely to Forms 2 and 3; in others it differs considerably, not only in wording, but even in the maintenance of different positions on some canonical or moral questions.[77] The main feature of Form 1 is the dialogue between the confessor and the penitent, which is the penitent's confession of sins. This form shows less tendency than the others to evolve into a formal treatise on some point of theology or canon law. At the end of the confession the author tells what sort of penance he might impose on such a penitent and adds a few more comments, as in the other forms, about his policy in assigning penances.[78] Then he says that he is about to copy out some penances for particular sins, and the work abruptly comes to an end.[79] Quite probably in its original state Form 1 continued here with some penitential canons such as occupy the greater part of Book 5 in the other forms, but these canons have not been preserved in any known MS of Form 1.

Since no evidence for the relation of Form 1 to the other forms is available outside of the MSS themselves, the best that can be established regarding this complicated question is the most plausible hypothesis. This will be attempted in four steps:

1. Form 1 is evidently a rearrangement or abbreviation.
2. It is not simply a rearrangement or abbreviation of any other existing form of the work, but rather of something else.

---

[76] Namely sect. 2 is lacking in W.

[77] Two of these differences are discussed below pp. 41-43; regarding others see Firth, *Thesis* I 161*-163*, 178*-180*.

[78] See below sects. 395-396; cf. sects. 230-233.

[79] See below sect. 397.

3. This "something else" is not derived from Form 3, and seems to have been composed at a date even earlier than Form 2.

4. It is most reasonable to suppose that Robert of Flamborough was the author of that earlier form of the work, i.e. that this was the first redaction of his penitential.

1. *Form 1 is evidently a rearrangement or abbreviation.*

It has just been pointed out that the original text of Form 1 probably continued farther than it does now so as to include some penances for particular kinds of sins. Apparently it has afterwards been abbreviated so as to omit them.

Moreover within the text of Form 1 the word SACERDOS, which introduces the words of the confessor in the dialogue, occurs in several places where the context does not require it.[80] Perhaps something has been omitted before the unnecessary word, or SACERDOS with the words which follow it has been moved to its present position from elsewhere. This is especially significant when it occurs immediately after a statement about plurality of benefices introduced by the word *Postremo*.[81] This statement corresponds to a discussion in Form 2, which is the last one in a long series of discussions under the title *De simonia*.[82] At the end of this statee ment in Form 1 it is the confessor who has been speaking. Yet the passag which follows it in Form 1, which also pertains to the topic of simony, begins with the word SACERDOS.[83] It is quite probable that the statement about plurality was originally at the end of the part dealing with simony in Form 1 also, and that the words which follow it in Q¹W have been moved there from elsewhere.[84] Something similar is suggested by the absence of the word POENITENS or SACERDOS at one or two places in Form 1 where the context seems to require it.[85]

Some of these instances may be the result of scribal error. But the following situation in the early part of Form 1 as found in W is an especially evident example of both rearrangement and abbreviation. The beginning of the dialogue-confession, which in Forms 2 and 3 is found

---

[80] See below nn. 83, 88-89.

[81] At the beginning of sect. 380 below in Appendix B.

[82] This is sect. 128; sects. 129-140 are lacking in Form 2.

[83] SACERDOS. Decimas umquam non tuas habuisti? and ff. (sects. 380-381).

[84] Sects. 127 and 126 contain the texts of Forms 2 and 3 which correspond to most of sects. 380-381 of Form 1.

[85] For example, in the middle of sect. 380 the word SACERDOS after *recepi* is missing in W, although found in Q¹; a more evident example of a lack of each of these words is found in the text next to be quoted in these prolegomena.

in sects. 3-6 of the present edition, occurs in Form 1 without many notable differences. In particular the dialogue of sect. 4 about the penitent's parochial status and his permission to come to an alien priest occurs in W with practically the same words. But the mention of a possible vow by the penitent, which in our text comes at the end of sect. 6, becomes in Form 1 an occasion for the confessor to digress on the subject of vows. Thus the discussion of vows, which in the other forms occurs in the tract on marriage, comes in Form 1 a little earlier, as part of the preliminary dialogue concerning the requirements for a good confession.[86] Soon after this discussion of vows in W the same question of sect. 4 is asked again. The text in W, which is our only witness to Form 1 here, proceeds as follows:

> SACERDOS. De ovili nostro es?
> Sed de licentia abbatis mei ad vos venio. Monachus enim sum et prior.
> Alioquin adultera esset confessio, immo nec confessio.[87]

Thus the same text, which has already occurred integrally in W, is repeated here in abbreviated and mutilated form.

2. *Form 1 is not simply an abbreviation of Form 2 or Form 3, but rather of something else.*

One piece of evidence just presented to show that Form 1 must be rearrangement or abbreviation is the presence of the word SACERDOS at several places in the text where the context does not require it. It seems likely that in each of these cases the sentence must have formerly been found in a context where the word did belong. Apparently someone has altered the order of the text without eliminating the word SACERDOS, even though it was no longer necessary. Now, as a matter of fact, in only one of the four instances cited above is the same sentence found in Forms 2 and 3 introduced by the word SACERDOS.[88] In another of those instances practically the same sentence is found in the regular

---

[86] This part of Form 1 is not found in Q^1 or Q^2. However a remark in the text of Q^{1*} shows that whoever chose the portions of Form 2 to be quoted there had been copying from a text of Form 1 in which the discussion of vows came very near the beginning; see FIRTH, *Thesis* I 93*-94*.

[87] Sect. 365 *circa finem* (below p. 286); cf. sect. 4 with varr. for it in W (below p. 284).

[88] W (but not Q^1Q^2) has a text to correspond to sect. 6 of the present edition. W lacks line 3 of p. 59; yet begins line 4 SACERDOS. *Singillatim ...* as in our text. Here the omission in W is almost certainly the result of homoeoteleuton on *ista quatuor observare*. This may be a peculiarity of the one MS.

text, but without this introductory word. In the other three instances the corresponding sentence in the regular penitential is phrased somewhat differently, in one case introduced by the word SACERDOS, in the other two not.[89] So, if the presence of this word in these places in Form 1 is evidence of rearrangement or abbreviation, it seems that some text other than Form 2 or Form 3 has been rearranged or abbreviated.

Form 1 does not depend on Hugucc o as a source nearly so much as Forms 2 and 3. His name is not mentioned in our copies of Form 1. However there are some passages in this form which are based on Huguccio's *Summa*. They occur with little difference in the other forms also.[90] One of them deserves special consideration here. What follows is a quotation from Form 1 (words in square brackets found only in Q¹Q², not in W; other variants omitted):

> Maleficium etiam perpetuum et impedit et dirimit matrimonium; non perpetuum nec hoc nec illud facit. Numquam passus es tentiginem [vel erecta sunt virilia]; praesumitur de frigiditate tua; alias maleficiatus es.[91]

This passage is evidently based on a portion of Huguccio's text of which these are the most pertinent sentences:

> Sed qualiter potest cognosci inter frigidum et maleficiatum? Dico: si numquam passus est nocturnam pollutionem, si numquam virga ejus est erecta, si numquam passus est tentiginem et non potest coire, praesumitur esse frigidus; sed si talia ei quandoque contingunt vel continent<er> et non potest coire, praesumitur esse maleficiatus.[92]

The words *Numquam passus es tentiginem*, found only in Form 1, are valuable evidence that the author of Form 1 had access to Huguccio's text independently of those other forms of the penitential. This is a strong

---

[89] (1) A sentence which corresponds rather closely to the opening sentence of sect. 374 in Form 1 is found at the beginning of sect. 182, but without any introductory word to correspond to SACERDOS at the beginning of sect. 374. (2) The question SACERDOS. *Decimas umquam non tuas habuisti?* of sect. 380 corresponds to the question *Decimas habuisti nisi nomine ecclesiae tuae?* which has no introductory word, in sect. 127 (cf. above n. 75). (3) The question *Cum masculo peccasti?* at the beginning of sect. 388 corresponds to the question *Umquam cum masculo?* of sect. 223; in this case both questions are introduced by the word SACERDOS.

[90] Besides sects. 14-15, which will be discussed here immediately, sects. 32, 34 and 36, which are apparently based on Huguccio, are found also in Form 1. Moreover the paragraph *Umquam officium — detulisti* near the end of sect. 393 corresponds to the second paragraph of sect. 105, and is apparently based on the same text of Huguccio.

[91] See variants to sect. 14 below in Appendix B, p. 286.

[92] HUGUCCIO, *Summa decretorum* ad C.33 q.1 dictum p. c.4; text based on Paris BN lat. 3892 (fol. 320ᵣᵃ) and BN lat. 3891 (fol. 264ᵛᵇ); quoted at greater length in FIRTH, *Thesis* I 173*-174*.

indication that Form 1 is not simply an abbreviation or rearrangement of one of the other forms, but of something else.

3. *This "something else" is not derived from Form 3, and seems to have been composed at a date even earlier than Form 2.*

The date of a work such as this is indicated chiefly by its use of sources. It has been shown that Forms 2 and 3 must have been completed within the period 1208-1215. They cannot be earlier than 1208 because they contain a mention of two bishops of Paris one of whom succeeded the other in 1208; they also contain citations of a decretal of 1207 and of at least one decretal issued in 1206. They cannot be later than the Fourth Lateran Council held in 1215 because they teach matrimonial impediments abolished at that council.[93]

Form 1 cannot be later than the council of 1215 because it expounds the same matrimonial impediments as the other forms. But it may be earlier than 1208. No mention of the two bishops is found in it and, apart from a few words in $Q^1 Q^2$ which seem to be a gloss that has crept into the text,[94] no mention of the decretals of 1206 and 1207. The latest decretals used in Form 1 are decretals of Innocent III issued in 1198, also perhaps one issued in 1199 and possibly even one or two issued in 1201.[95]

The difference of Form 1 from Forms 2 and 3 in one of these places deserves special consideration here. Part of this passage in Form 1 has just been quoted to show that this form depends on Huguccio independently of the other forms. Form 1 continues thereafter, in agreement with the other forms, as follows:

> Usque ad triennium praesumitur maleficium temporale esse, deinde perpetuum. Tamen in favorem matrimonii semper praesumendum est maleficium fuisse post contractum matrimonium, et vix est aliquis ita maleficiatus quin aliquando possit resolvi.[96]

This depends on the following sentences found a little farther along in the text of Huguccio:

> Item qualiter discernetur an maleficium sit perpetuum an sit temporale? Usque ad triennium semper praesumitur temporale, exinde semper perpe-

---

[93] See above pp. 8-9.

[94] See below pp. 38-40.

[95] See Firth, *Traditio* 16.542-543 with notes, 550 with n. 59; Firth, *Thesis* I 171*-172* with notes. It is sect. 24 and the latter part of sect. 114 which also occur in Form 1 and contain references to recent decretals, possibly also sects. 377 and 393.

[96] Sect. 14.

tuum nisi aliud appareat. ... Item qualiter discernitur an maleficium praecedat an sequatur? Dico quod semper praesumitur secutum post matrimonium nisi aliud appareat, et hoc favore matrimonii, et quia maleficia
semper ex magna parte solent sequi matrimonium, et quia vix est aliquis
ita maleficiatus quin possit solvi, praesertim per actorem maleficii ....[97]

Immediately after the text just quoted from our penitential there follows in Form 2 and in Form 3 a paragraph in which a judgment of
Innocent III is explicitly cited; the reference is probably to a decretal
issued in 1206.[98] There is no trace of this paragraph in W, but in Q^1Q^2
it is indicated by these words in the text: *De virga ingrossata per morbum.*[99]
Then comes the following paragraph in all the forms:

> Ideo tutius dicit ecclesia Romana, et de frigido et de maleficiato, quod
> si non potest habere suam ut uxorem, habeat ut sororem.[100]

This is based on a decretal of Alexander III,[1] but is also closely related
to the following words of Huguccio which occur a little farther along in
the passage of his work which has just been quoted:

> Et propter istas difficultates et dubitationes quae vertuntur circa maleficium
> si dicatur impedire matrimonium, dicunt quod nullum maleficium in aliquo
> casu impedit vel dirimit matrimonium, et Romana ecclesia sic tenet, scilicet
> quod numquam propter maleficium debeant aliqui separari, in extra. *Super
> illo,*[2] ubi generaliter videtur dici quod nec propter maleficium nec propter
> frigiditatem debeat quis separari ab uxore sua; si enim non potest eam
> habere pro uxore, habeat eam pro sorore, sicut ibidem dicitur et supra eadem
> *Requisisti.*[3]

The judgment of Innocent III cited in Forms 2 and 3 appears then as
an interruption in a discussion of *maleficium* based on a text of Huguccio.
This interruption is not found in W. So it seems probable that the original
form of this text is that of Form 1 as found in W, into which the paragraph citing Innocent III has been inserted by a later addition. This
reasoning is not invalidated by the presence of the words *De virga ingrossata
per morbum* found at this point in Q^1Q^2, the two other copies of Form 1.

---

[97] HUG. *loc. cit.* (above n. 92).

[98] The first paragraph of sect. 15, probably citing Po. 2836 (X 4.15.6).

[99] These words are in the texts of Q^1Q^2 immediately after the word *resolvi* at the end of the
last passage from Form 1 cited in these prolegomena. They are followed immediately by the
paragraph next to be cited below.

[100] Below sect. 15.

[1] JL 14075 (1 *Compil.* 4.16.2).

[2] *Loc. cit.* Paris, BN lat. 3891 may perhaps read *Super eo*; cf. variant in FRIEDBERG, *Quinque
compilationes antiquae* p. 51.

[3] HUGUCCIO, *loc. cit.* (above n. 92); final reference is to C.33 q.1 c.2. Cf. FIRTH, *Thesis* I 175*
n. 55 (III 558*-559*).

It is difficult to see how an abbreviator could have written these words into his text with the expectation that they would make some sense to his reader.[4] Form 1 elsewhere does not contain such phrases unconnected with the surrounding text. It is much more likely that these words were written into the margin of an earlier MS of Form 1 and afterwards copied into the text of Q^1Q^2; it can be shown that these MSS have been affected elsewhere by contamination from Form 2.[5] So it is still quite probable that W contains the text of Form 1 for this passage as it was originally written, based on the commentary of Huguccio. The paragraph about the judgment of Innocent III seems to have been incorporated into it when the penitential was revised to make Form 2.

This hypothesis is strengthened by the word *Ideo* which begins the third of the three paragraphs just cited from the penitential. This word does make some sense in the context in which it is found in the regular forms of the work. But it makes much better sense in W, where it follows immediately after the last sentence of the first paragraph cited above:

> Tamen in favorem matrimonii semper praesumendum est maleficium fuisse post contractum matrimonium, et vix est aliquis ita maleficiatus quin aliquando possit resolvi.[6]

Then follows immediately in W:

> Ideo tutius dicit ecclesia Romana, et de frigido et de maleficiato, quod si non potest habere suam ut uxorem, habeat ut sororem.[7]

Together with this indication, suggesting that the reference to Innocent's decretal is an insertion, must go the evidence gathered a little earlier in these prologemena, that this same part of Form 1 depends on Huguccio's *Summa* independently of the other forms.[8] The ensemble of evidence found in this passage gives us good reason to conclude that Form 1 is most probably an abbreviation of an earlier text of this work, and that this text was probably the source of Forms 2 and 3.

There are other indications as well. In several instances in which the teaching found in Form 1 differs from that found in the other forms, the doctrine of Form 1 seems to be derived from authors who went out of date at the end of the twelfth century, while the doctrine of the other forms agrees rather with works whose influence still flourished in the thirteenth.

---

[4] See above n. 99.
[5] See Firth, *Thesis* I 192* with nn. 16-17 (III 570*-572*).
[6] Below sect. 14.
[7] Below sect. 15.
[8] See above pp. 37-38.

The most notable difference in moral doctrine occurs in connection with vows as impediments to marriage. This is the text of W, our only text of Form 1 for this part of the penitential:

> Si ergo post votum simplex cum aliqua contraxisti publice vel privatim, et exigere potes et reddere secundum primam opinionem; secundum alteram, quae tutior videtur, numquam exigas vel reddas. Immo ante permittas te excommunicari secundum quosdam, quibus in hoc non consentio, quia majus peccatum est scandalum facere excommunicationem sustinendo quam debitum reddere uxori putativae; sic enim quilibet propria ab ecclesia posset recedere excommunicationem sustinendo.[9]

The author of this form is quite convinced that even a private vow will invalidate a subsequent marriage. However, he maintains that ecclesiastical authorities are to be obeyed if they insist under penalty of excommunication on matrimonial life for the couple. This policy, by which obedience to church authority is preferred to one's private conviction about validity, is in conformity with the teaching of some anonymous twelfth-century canonical writings published by Friedrich Thaner,[10] and even to some extent with a decretal of Celestine III, issued apparently in 1191.[11]

In Forms 2 and 3 this text begins with practically the same words as the first sentence quoted above, but in the following sentence the author agrees with those who would have one suffer excommunication rather than live in an invalid marriage. This opinion is in conformity with the teaching of Huguccio (1188-90)[12] and of Robert Courson (1204-08)[13] and with a decretal of Innocent III issued in 1209.[14]

---

[9] Below sect. 28 with variations of Form 1 in Appendix B p. 285.

[10] See F. THANER, *Die Summa magistri Rolandi* (Innsbruck 1874) pp. 272-274, 288-291. These sources did not necessarily influence the respective texts of our penitential, but they are examples of the thinking current in the different periods.

[11] See JL 16611 (2 *Compil.* 4.13.2). Walther HOLTZMANN has shown that there is good reason to ascribe this decretal to Celestine III; see "La 'Collectio Seguntina' et les décrétales de Clément III et de Célestin III," *RevHistEccl* 50 (1955) 431-432 no. 44. Cf. also JL 13907 (2 *Compil.* 4.7.1).

[12] See his *Summa* ad C.30 q.5 c.1 *non dubitantur* (fol. 303va). This work was much used in Flamborough's time.

[13] "Si autem econtra ecclesia excommunicando cogit eam ad reddendum debitum ubi prius vovit Deo suam virginitatem, non ideo faciet ea primam fidem irritam, immo prius permittet se excommunicari et manebit in tali sententia." Robert COURSON, *Summa* 21.10 (Paris BN lat. 14524, fol. 81v); cf. FIRTH, *Thesis* II 407*-409*, where Courson is quoted more extensively.

[14] See Po. 3668 (X 5.39.44; issued apparently in Feb. 1209); cf. FIRTH, *Thesis* II 405*. The fact that the reading of Form 1 regarding this matter reappears also in Form 4 (found in X) suggests that the change of this text from Form 1 to Form 2 may have taken place at a relatively late date, late enough to have been influenced by this decretal. The evolution from Form 1

According to Form 1 only the pope can dispense one who has been *furtive ordinatus*.[15] This is in conformity with a decretal found in the collection called *Appendix concilii lateranensis*;[16] this decretal, so far as can be determined from printed sources, did not find its way into later collections. In the other forms of the penitential one's own bishop has power to dispense such a one unless the order was conferred or received by an excommunicated person.[17] This is based on another decretal also found in *Appendix concilii lateranensis*, but this decretal was included also in *Compilatio prima* and so passed into more general use.[18]

In other places it is not so much a difference between earlier and later sources which supports the priority of Form 1, but rather the fact that Forms 2 and 3 give evidence of a more thorough acquaintance on the part of their author with sources and doctrines current in the late twelfth and early thirteenth centuries.[19] Mention has already been made of the much more extensive use made of Huguccio's *Summa* in Forms 2 and 3.[20] This is especially evident when the author is dealing with the man who has committed incest with a relative of his wife. In Form 1 this problem is settled in accord with a decretal of Alexander III.[21] The author has heard of another opinion, but does not favour it. The treatment of the same subject in Forms 2 and 3 is based on Huguccio, who declares that Alexander's position must be modified.[22] Before the composition of these forms, Innocent III had applied the teaching of Huguccio on this point in at least three decretals, thus reversing the stand of his predecessor.[23] Since Flamborough shows considerable acquaintance with other decretals of Innocent, he may well have been influenced by these.[24] In the same

---

to Form 2 was probably a gradual process. Cf. FIRTH, *Traditio* 16.543 n. 6, 548-549 with n. 49; FIRTH, *Thesis* I 215*-217*; II 250*-251*; below Appendix C n. 7.

[15] See below in Appendix B sect. 374.

[16] See JL 14197 (*Appendix conc. lat.* 26 c.26; MANSI 22.372-373). Concerning this collection see Charles DUGGAN, *Twelfth Century Decretal Collections* pp. 53-54, 56, 135-139; IDEM, "English Canonists and the 'Appendix Concilii Lateranensis', with an Analysis of St. John's College, Cambridge, MS 148," *Traditio* 18 (1962) 459-468.

[17] See below sect. 182.

[18] See JL 13988 (*Appendix conc. lat.* 26 c.9; 1 *Compil.* 5.25.un.; X 5.30.1).

[19] Cf. FIRTH, *Thesis* I 161*-163*; 171*-180*, esp. 178*-179*.

[20] See above pp. 14 and 37.

[21] See below Appendix B sect. 387; JL 13163 (1 *Compil.* 4.13.2). Cf. FIRTH, *Thesis* II 479*-481*.

[22] See below sects. 65-66 with notes; cf. FIRTH, *Thesis* II 368*-371*, where Hug. is quoted.

[23] See Po. 1182 (X 4.13.6; issued probably Nov.-Dec., 1200); Po. 1836 (Reg.6.2 PL 215.10-11; issued Feb. 24, 1203); Po. 2656 (X 4.13.10; issued probably Jan., 1206). Innocent declared that the blameless wife was to be urged to observe continence, but that, if she would not and there was fear of a *lapsus* on her part, *vir ejus poterit et debebit tamen cum timore Domini debitum ipsi solvere conjugale*. Cf. FIRTH, *Thesis* I 216*; II 404*-405*, 479*-481*.

[24] See FIRTH, *Thesis* II 383*-385*, 393*-402*, 404*-405*; cf. IDEM, *Traditio* 16.550-551.

passage of Forms 2 and 3 the language of Huguccio himself is modified by use of the method of computing degrees of consanguinty derived from Roman law.[25] Here then in Forms 2 and 3 is manifested the influence of a complicated combination of sources not used in this context by the author of Form 1.

So it would be difficult to conceive how Form 1 could be an abbreviation of Form 2 or of Form 3 of the penitential. To maintain that, one would have to find an explanation why someone so diligently and so efficiently extirpated from Robert's text much of the influence of later sources, leaving a primitive, simpler doctrine derived chiefly from earlier writings.[26] This is unlikely. It is much more probable that an earlier text with less developed doctrines has been abbreviated and mutilated to give us the form of the penitential now found in Q^1Q^2W.

This hypothesis receives further confirmation from a comparison of the individual readings of the different MSS. Generally the reading of Q^1Q^2W seems to be the source of the readings found in the other MSS.[27]

4. *It is more reasonable to assume that Robert of Flamborough was the author of this earlier text of the work, i.e. that it was the earliest redaction of his penitential.*

If we suppose then, as seems most reasonable, that Form 1, at least in its original state, was composed before either Form 2 or Form 3, the question of the author of Form 1 remains to be determined. It has been shown that Forms 2 and 3 must be the work of Robert of Flamborough.[28] The texts of Form 1 in Q are anonymous. W has nothing to indicate authorship at the beginning of the penitential, but at the end the scribe

---

[25] According to this method brother and sister are related in the second degree, uncle and niece in the third, and first cousins in the fourth; see FIRTH, *Thesis* II 365*-372*. Cf. GRATIAN C.33 q.5 c.2; Joseph FREISEN, *Geschichte des canonischen Eherechts* pp. 406-411; Ernest CHAMPEAUX, "*Jus sanguinis,* trois façons de calculer la parenté au Moyen âge," *RevHistDroitFE*[4] 12 (1933) 241-290.

[26] Moreover, if this happened, it would necessarily have been within the period 1208-1215, since Form 2 comes within this period and Form 1 is necessarily prior to 1216; see above pp. 8-9, 38. If some less knowledgeable person had undertaken to revise Flamborough's work thus within his lifetime, it is difficult to understand how two copies of such a corruption of his esteemed penitential could have come to be inserted into Q, a MS of Saint-Victor; cf. above pp. 27-28 with notes.

[27] MS W has a considerable number of scribal blunders peculiar to itself. But rarely, if ever, do Q^1Q^2W, or (where Q^1Q^2 are lacking) W and other MSS agree on any significant reading which cannot have been the source of the readings found in the other forms.

[28] See above pp. 6-7. The quotation found in the *Liber poenitentialis exceptus* is from Form 3; Form 2 is very similar at that point. The quotation has no relation to Form 1.

has written: *Explicit poenitentiale magistri Roberti sancti Victoris*. In view of the close conformity of many parts of Form 1 with the text of other forms, it is most unlikely that anyone but Robert of Flamborough is meant by this inscription. Further considerations, far from contradicting this attribution, show his authorship to be all the more reasonable.

All the forms of the work are dedicated to someone who is addressed in the prologue with the same words of respect and affection. In MS W he is addressed as *decane*; in the other forms he is called expressly *decane salesburiensis*.[29] Now the Dean of Salisbury from 1198 until 1214 was Richard Poore, who was addressed in contemporary papal letters as *decane salisburiensis*.[30] If we suppose that Robert was the author of Forms 1, 2 and 3, the words of address in the prologue are easily explained: he apparently dedicated his work to Richard Poore when he first composed Form 1 about the beginning of the thirteenth century and then maintained this dedication when he revised it to make Forms 2 and 3, both probably within the period 1208-1213.

There is moreover a uniformity between Forms 1, 2 and 3 in general outlook and manner of expression which suggests that they have the same author.[31] The differences can be explained by a slight development in the author's style and especially in his knowledge of canonical sources after he had completed Form 1. In this interval he seems to have become much better acquainted especially with Huguccio and with the teaching of Robert Courson, and to have come to know a number of more recent decretal letters.[32] For example, in Forms 2 and 3 Flamborough does not hold, as he seems to have maintained in Form 1, that one should obey ecclesiastical authorities when commanded under pain of excommunication to remain in a marriage which one knows to be invalid. That opinion has apparently been overthrown by the influence of Huguccio and of Robert Courson, and perhaps also by a decretal of Innocent III.[33] But still our author will not counsel a cleric to refuse to obey his bishop who commands him to receive orders, not even a cleric who knows that he is irregular by reason of a *crimen maximum occultum* for which a dispensation from the pope is strictly necessary. The reason given for this in Forms 2 and 3 is precisely the same as that given in Form 1 in regard to marriage: if disobedience in this case were to be approved, anyone might be justified in rebelling against authority.[34]

[29] Below sect. 1; also Appendix B sect. 395.
[30] See above p. 7 n. 38.
[31] See FIRTH, *Thesis* I 182*-186*.
[32] See above pp. 37-43. Cf. FIRTH, *Thesis* I 172*-179*; II 353*-417*.
[33] See above p. 41 with notes.
[34] See below sect. 101.

Publication of Form 1.

In view of the evidence just presented that Form 1 is most probably our author's first redaction of his penitential preserved in a somewhat abbreviated and mutilated state, the readings found in MSS of Form 1 can be of considerable help in reconstructing the probable origin of some readings found in other forms. In Form 1 we have what is most likely the source from which some of the other readings have been derived; readings of the source of a text can be of great help in understanding the text itself.

Moreover our penitential is important chiefly because it is the first comprehensive manual for the confessor in which is incorporated the new canon law. Form 1 is most probably this first canonical book of instruction in the earliest stage of its development. In it we can study with considerable probability the development of the author's mind concerning penance and his attitude regarding law. According to the most plausible hypothesis, this is the beginning of a beginning.

For these reasons Form 1 is made available in Appendix B of the present edition. Where it corresponds fairly closely to Forms 2 and 3, only the variations of its MSS from the main text are indicated; where it differs considerably, the text of Form 1 is printed and the apparatus beneath indicates all significant variations of its MSS.

The best and most nearly complete copy of Form 1 is in W; Q^1Q^2 are less complete and have been influenced by contamination from readings of other forms. Hence the edition of Form 1 is based chiefly on W; Q^1Q^2 are helpful for correction of W's fairly numerous scribal blunders. Where there is not text in Q^1 or Q^2, these are corrected by conjectural emendation.

FORM 2 (formerly called Form O)

The other forms of the penitential are much more like one another. Form 3 is the author's final complete redaction published in the text of the present edition. Form 2 differs from it chiefly by the lack of certain portions of text found in Form 3. The peculiarities of Form 2 are enumerated below in Appendix C. First are listed nine portions, numbered 1-9, which are lacking in the text of O and in the text of at least one of $AbQ^{1*}Q^{2*}Q^{2**}Ta$. Then follow nine other portions, namely 10-18, which are missing or out of place in at least two of these and a few other MSS as well. Portions 1-9 will be considered here; portions 10-18 will be considered in the following part of these prolegomena, the part dealing with the intermediate MSS.

Concerning portions 1-9 it will be shown that:

1. There is good reason to believe that the author of these portions is Robert of Flamborough.
2. It is very probable that the penitential was written first without these portions and that they have been added to it afterwards.

1. *There is good reason to believe that the author of these portions is Robert of Flamborough.*

These portions of text are found in the great majority of manuscripts as part of the penitential; most of these MSS have rubrics in which the work is ascribed to Robert of Flamborough.[35] To reject these passages would involve rejecting the testimony of the great majority of the MSS.

There is, moreover, nothing in these passages out of harmony with the mind or the style of the author as found in the rest of his work. This is most evident in the only one of them which is of considerable length, namely portion 5; in this passage one case after another is treated in a way which is quite characteristic of Robert of Flamborough.

In this passage, too, there is a defence of Robert's policy in regard to orders and to the exercise of orders. He declares that these impediments, which we call irregularities, remain even after penance has been done for the sin, and that only the pope can dispense from them except where the bishop has been granted power to do so.[36] This policy is expressed elsewhere and applied quite consistently to the solution of many cases.[37] The manner in which this is defended in portion 5 resembles Flamborough's defence of some of his policies elsewhere.[38]

There is then very good reason to accept the testimony of the MSS that Robert is the author of this passage. Since portions 1-9 are found for the most part in the same MSS, it is likely that they all have the same origin as portion 5.

Further evidence in favour of Flamborough's authorship of these portions of text is found in the two contemporary works which contain quotations from his penitential. The second, longer redaction of Peter of Roissy's *Manuale de mysteriis ecclesiae*, a work composed before 1215 and quite probably at the latest by 1213, which includes texts borrowed from

---

[35] Cf. FIRTH, *Thesis* I 196*.

[36] This is in sects. 138-139 below; here our author opposes the teaching expounded in the anonymous appendix published below in Appendix A.

[37] This teaching is expressed below in sects. 101, 103, 107-108; it is applied to cases in sects. 104-106, 109.

[38] Compare the passage under discussion with sects. 27-29, 230-235, 241, 356.

many authors, contains numerous passages from the *Poenitentiale* of Robert of Flamborough.[39] Now in every case in which Peter makes use of a passage in which Form 3 differs from Form 2, it is Form 3 which he uses. This includes an abbreviation of portion 1, a quotation of considerable length from portion 5, and a garbled adaptation of portion 6.[40]

Moreover the anonymous *Liber poenitentialis exceptus de libris poenitentialibus M. Roberti confessoris et M. Petri et aliorum*, a work composed in the very early thirteenth century, quotes from Flamborough, naming him explicitly. Two words of the passage quoted, namely *quia infirmaris*, are missing from Ta and are insertions into the texts of AbO; apparently these words do not belong to Form 2, but only to Form 3. Yet they are included in the quotation in this almost contemporary work.[41]

Now it is hardly likely that interpolations inserted into the work of an author by someone else should have become current as the author's own words so soon after the composition of the work. These features were part of his penitential about 1215, and so must have been Robert's own handiwork.

2. *It is more probable that the penitential was composed first without these portions and that they have been added to it afterwards.*

Portions 5 and 9 are most evidently additions to the text. Portion 5 begins in the midst of a series of questions addressed to the penitent about simony. The question preceding portion 5 is introduced by the word *Postremo*; one would expect it to be the last question.[42] It is the last question regarding simony in AbOTaX; this was, no doubt, the original form of the text. In the MSS of Form 3 portion 5 follows here with further questions pertaining to simony; this portion is evidently an addition to the text in its original state.[43]

Portion 9 consists of a few words in the midst of a penitential canon; these words are not found in the source of the canon. The absence of the same words in some of our MSS is most easily explained if we suppose that Robert first based his text on the source alone, then afterwards in-

---

[39] See above pp. 9, 31-32 with notes.

[40] See FIRTH, *Thesis* I 198*-201*; cf. above p. 32 with n. 68.

[41] See above pp. 6-7 with notes; below sect. 230 with variants. It is quite probable that Flamborough wrote the words of the confessor here in Form 2 as they would be addressed to a sick penitent; he would not need to be told he was sick. Then, realizing that his would not be clear to his reader, he seems to have added the extra words in Form 3.

[42] See below sect. 128.

[43] Portion 5 consists of sects. 129-140; see below Appendix C. Cf. FIRTH, *Thesis* I 203*-204*; IDEM, *Traditio* 16.544.

serted these extra words. They constitute a kind of gloss explaining the word *carcerem* found in the canon.[44]

It is evident then that portions 5 and 9 have been added to the text after it was first composed. Since portions 1-9 are missing, for the most part, in the same MSS, it is reasonable to conjecture that all of them have had this same history. This is the more understandable because in each case the penitential makes good sense without the passage. Yet each adds something to the meaning: a further explanation or precision, a cautious qualification or a short discussion of a related topic. All of this is easily explained if we suppose that Robert wrote his penitential without these extra portions and afterwards added them to clarify his meaning or to elaborate something that had occurred later to his mind. Reasons why these portions should have been omitted from the text in some MSS would not be so easy to find.[45]

This conclusion is not invalidated by the lack of a passage in AbTa which has evidently been dropped from the text after it was first composed, namely the portion of text *Item oportet — dicitur unius uxoris virum* in the middle of sect. 168.[46] This portion is found in O, which is the best witness to Form 2. Lack of this portion is not a feature of Form 2, but rather an evident error common to MSS AbTa, which are both of composite text.[47]

Thus Form 2 represents a redaction of the penitential by the author himself which he later enlarged somewhat and perfected into his final complete redaction which is Form 3. If Form 1 be understood to be his first redaction, which has been shown to very likely, then Form 2 will be his second. That Form 2 is a source of Form 3 is further confirmed by the fact that, in a majority of cases in which priority of readings is evident, the readings of AbOTa, and especially of O, is seen to be the source of the readings found in the other MSS of Forms 2 and 3.[48]

---

[44] Portion 9 below in Appendix G comes in sect. 245; cf. FIRTH, *Thesis* I 203*; IDEM, *Traditio* 16.545-546.

[45] Cf. FIRTH, *Thesis* I 204*-205*.

[46] This portion must have belonged to the text originally because it ends with a quotation from Scripture, while the following words, which are in all the MSS, are a gloss on these words of Scripture. Actually the situations in Ab and Ta are not exactly parallel; in Ta the preceding words *quod impedit promotionem — in duo non divisisti* are lacking also, but this is quite probably the result of homoeoteleuton on the word *divisisti*.

[47] See FIRTH, *Thesis* I 205*-207*.

[48] One very evident instance can be seen by comparing the readings for *vel aliud* after *deest* in sect. 87. The reading of O is most likely the original, that of AbQ¹*Ta quite evidently formed from it by homoeoteleuton on the word *deest*, the reading of Form 3 is almost certainly an attempt to make more sense out of the resulting mutilated text. See FIRTH, *Thesis* I 207*-209*.

The most important variations of Form 2 from Form 3 are indicated below in Appendix C. Portions 1-9 as well as portions 10-18 are lacking in Form 2, but found in the fully developed Form 3. Portion 19 seems to have belonged to Form 2, but not to Form 3, although it has found its way into composite MSS of the latter form. Portions 20-27 are special features in Book 5 of O, which is throughout the best witness to Form 2. It is quite probable that portions 20-27 reflect features of the original Form 2, but this is less certain.[49]

Significant readings of MSS of Form 2 are also included in the *apparatus criticus* of our main text, according to the general policy for indicating variants to be explained at the end of these prolegomena. MS O is the best witness to Form 2, Ab the next best. However, both of these have probably been affected to some extent by infiltration from Form 3. $Q^1*Q^2*Q^2**Ta$ have composite texts, combining even more features of Form 3 with a text of Form 2.[50]

THE INTERMEDIATE MANUSCRIPTS

Besides the nine portions of text numbered 1-9 below in Appendix C, which are lacking only in two or more of AbOTa and also sometimes in the fragments of Q, there are nine other portions, namely 10-18, which are missing or out of place in several of these same MSS and in some others as well, namely AaAcCkCpHJRSgTbTuUV. No one of these portions is missing in all or nearly all of these MSS; each of them lacks one or two or three of these portions, which are also missing in Form 2. Among these MSS, AcTb manifest affinity with this group to a lesser extent than the others; AcTb will be treated among MSS of Form 3. The rest of them, namely AaCkCpHJRSgTuUV, are called herein "the intermediate MSS," because they are intermediate between Forms 2 and 3. They belong for the most part to Form 3, but differ in each case by the lack of a very few of portions 10-18; some of them moreover have one or several of these portions out of place.[51] Closely allied with these MSS in some of their readings are the texts copied by Peter of Roissy; these are indicated in the apparatus by the siglum: Pet.[52]

---

[49] Cf. FIRTH, *Thesis* I 210*-212*. In Appendix C of this thesis portion 10 of the present edition is not found; hence portions (10)-(17) of the thesis are equivalent to portions of 11-18 of the present edition, and so forth.

[50] Cf. FIRTH, *Thesis* I 210*-221*.

[51] Cf. FIRTH, *Thesis* I 222*, 232*.

[52] See FIRTH, *Thesis* I 224*-226*, 230*-231*, 237*-238*; cf. above pp. 31-32 with notes.

Portions 10-18 are missing also in Form 2, which is the source of Form 3; moreover portion 11, which consists of two lines of poetry ascribed to Stephen Langton, is missing in the *Speculum ecclesiae*, the source from which Flamborough derived the text surrounding them in Forms 2 and 3. It is more probable then that the text was first composed without these portions and that they are additions to it.[53]

Now there is fairly good reason to suppose that it was Robert of Flamborough himself who added them to his work, as he added also portions 1-9. The anonymous *Liber poenitentialis exceptus*, an almost contemporary work which in one place quotes from our penitential expressly and in several other places uses its text as a source, seems to have used a copy which included portion 15.[54] It is reasonable to accept as genuine a text current so soon. And it is logical to surmise that portions 10-18 have most probably the same history, i.e. that they are part of Flamborough's work.

Each of the intermediate MSS has a composite text. In the marginal or inserted corrections apparent on some of them, the general tendency is to correct from Form 2 or from something intermediate in the direction of the finally complete Form 3. This has apparently happened also in many of the MSS from which the intermediate MSS are derived. An indication of this is the fact that many of the latter have one or more of portions 10-18 in the wrong place. A portion of text being inserted into a MS can easily come to be inserted into a wrong place.[55]

However, it is unlikely that every one of portions 1-18 found in these MSS has obtained entry in this way. It is much more likely that most or even all of these MSS represent some intermediate stage or stages in the development of the penitential from Form 2 into Form 3, conceivably a stage in which portions 1-9 had already been incorporated, but not portions 10-18.[56]

The intermediate MSS fall into three groups. Tu stands somewhat alone, closest of all to Form 2. CkH form another group and AaCpJRSgU a third. The texts of Cp and Sg are more evidently composite than these

---

[53] See FIRTH, *Thesis* I 223*-226*; cf. IDEM, *Traditio* 16.543-544.

[54] See FIRTH, *Thesis* I 226*-231*; cf. above pp. 6-7. A question in the *Liber poenitentialis exceptus*: *Ad menstruatum, judaeam vel gentilem?* reveals the presence of mention of intercourse with a Jewish or pagan woman in sect. 225 of the text at the author's disposal, i.e. the presence of portion 15.

[55] See FIRTH, *Thesis* I 230*-233*. For example in the margins and between the lines of MS Aa there are corrections in at least four different hands; most of these are corrections to the reading of Form 3.

[56] See FIRTH, *Thesis* I 233*-239*.

others. Likewise V has a very composite text. V has not been included
in the groups just mentioned; it seems to belong rather with BmBt, MSS
of Form 3 which have an affinity with the intermediate MSS.[57]

FORM 4 (formerly called Form X)

Form 4 is found only in X. It is a revision of the penitential by someone other than the original author; many lists of titles and rubrics have
been revised and a large number of changes have been introduced into
the text. In several places mention is made of the Fourth Lateran
Council which was held in 1215; it is called in this MS "Second Lateran
Council."[58] The text which was revised seems to have manifested some
characteristics of all three preceding forms of the work, nc uding even
the peculiar doctrinal position expressed in Form 1 concerning marriage
after a private vow.[59] Probably the text used for the revision was a composite one containing some remnants of a very early stage in the development of Flamborough's penitential.[60]

MANUSCRIPTS OF FORM 3 (formerly called Form A)

The text of Form 3 is pub'ished in the present edition; it is Robert of
Flamborough's final, complete redaction of his work. An outline of it
has been given above.[61]

Among the MSS of Form 3, the two most closely allied are KP; they
agree on almost every reading. These contain evidence of slight revision;
their titles and rubrics have been altered, especially by subdividing Book 5
into six books, to make ten for the whole work. Now the text on which
this revision was based seems to have been an early text of Form 3. For
this reason the readings of these two MSS, when they agree with the
readings of other MSS of Form 3, are of considerable value as witnesses
to the original. P is a little more valuable than K in this regard. MS G,
and probably also Bt, have some affinity to KP.[62]

---

[57] See FIRTH, *Thesis* I 240*-249*.

[58] Regarding the numbering of this council see Christopher R. CHENEY, "La date de composition du 'Liber Poenitentialis' attribué à Pierre de Poitiers," *Rech ThAncMéd* 9 (1937) 401-3.

[59] This doctrinal position is quoted above p. 41. Regarding Form 4 see FIRTH, *Thesis* II
250*-265* with notes; IDEM, *Traditio* 16.548-549.

[60] Cf. FIRTH, *Thesis* I 214*-217*.

[61] Pp. 12-17.

[62] See FIRTH, *Thesis* II 293*-302*; IDEM, *Traditio* 16.547-548. The text of our penitential
in Bt is so short that its affiliations are not easy to determine.

Ad CcCi form another group, which generally has the readings which are the source of the other readings of MSS of Form 3. AdCcCi also have some slight evidence of "tidying up" or rectification of the text. Of these three, Ad, a MS from Saint-Victor, seems slightly superior, Ci next; CcCi are often in agreement with each other. Z and, to some extent, Tc are allied with this group. Tc is also related to the intermediate MSS.[63]

AcEMNTbY form a third group. Of these Ac, another MS from Saint-Victor, is by far the best and most faithful to the original. Its readings are less often the source of the other readings of Form 3 than is the case with AdCcCi; however, Ac seems to have escaped the "tidying up" process undergone by the text of AdCcCi. For example, Ac and KP, along with some others, have the canon *De hospitalibus* only at the end of the penitential in sect. 357, where it was most probably placed originally. On the other hand, AdCcCi have it after sect. 322, a more logical place for it, to which it was probably moved.[64]

The other MSS, namely BmBtDFILSoVY, are composite MSS of little value. I seems to have a little more authority than the rest of these on account of its early date, but it too has a composite text.[65]

THE PRESENT EDITION

The purpose of the present edition is to present the original text of the author in Form 3 as faithfully as possible. Sometimes the character of the readings themselves or their relation to the sources used by Flamborough makes clear which reading was most likely the original reading of Form 3.[66] When these indications are wanting, the relative authority of the MSS must be decisive. There are three principal witnesses to the text of Form 3: the group AdCcCi, Ac and P; K is normally omitted because it is almost always in agreement with P. Of great importance also is the reading of the source; now Form 2, which is found at its best in O, and also in AbQ¹*Q²*Q²**Ta, is the proximate source of Form 3. AdCcCi together are of such great authority that when they are in agreement with any one of the other authorities, that is with Ac or with P or

---

[63] Regarding AdCcCi and connected MSS see FIRTH, *Thesis* II 302*-326*.

[64] Regarding AcEMNTbY see *loc. cit.*; the canon *De hospitalibus* is discussed pp. 311*-316*, relative value of AcEMNTbY on p. 327*.

[65] See FIRTH, *Thesis* II 327*-329*. MSS DISg are not included in the textual criticism of the thesis.

[66] See FIRTH, *Thesis* II 259*-293*; Hermann KANTOROWICZ, *Einführung in die Textkritik* (Leipzig 1921) esp. pp. 9-12, 29-35.

with Form 2, this authority of AdCcCi should prevail. But when the group AdCcCi is alone against all of these, which happens very rarely, then its reading is considered an instance of "tidying up," not as evidence for the original Form 3.[67]

In the *apparatus criticus* of the main text all significant variants, i.e. all except slips of the pen and variations in word order and spelling, will be indicated from AbAcAdCcCiO. The same will be done in the case of AaCkHJPQ¹*RTaTcTuUZ, except that here the variant will be omitted when only one of these, and no other among those mentioned thus far, varies significantly from our text on the word or phrase in question.[68] Variants from the other MSS, namely BmBtCpDEFGIKLMNQ²*Q²**Sg-SoTbVXY, will be indicated only in special cases, and then in parentheses.[69]

In the apparatus for Appendix A all significant variants from AcP will be indicated, and in Appendix B with its apparatus all significant variants of Q¹Q²W.

---

[67] See FIRTH, *Thesis* II 330*-336*; cf. 259*-329*.

[68] This is the policy also in regard to Pen (readings from the *Liber poenitentialis exceptus*) and to Pet (readings from the *Manuale* of Peter of Roissy).

[69] Regarding this and the following paragraph cf. FIRTH, *Thesis* II 336*-341*. This method of indicating variants is based to a considerable extent on the policy suggested by Stephan KUTTNER, "Notes on the Presentation of Texts and the Apparatus in Editing Works of Decretists and Decretalists," *Traditio* 15 (1959) 458-461.

INCIPIT LIBER POENITENTIALIS MAGISTRI ROBERTI DE FLAINESBURC CANONICI SANCTI VICTORIS PARISIENSIS ET POENITENTIARII

INCIPIT PROLOGUS

1 Res grandis immo permaxima, cujuslibet nedum meis impar viribus, 5
contra quemlibet ad excusationem mihi satisfecisset ut eam declinarem,
si non tantus institisset amicus ut cui meipsum totum dedi, nihil dandum
retinui.[1] Nemo igitur arrogantiae nota me maculet; amicitia est enim
quae res impossibiles ad possibilem facultatem, immo ad facilem reducit
possibilitatem.[2] Hilaris igitur, laetus et securus aggredi tentabo quod 10
petitis, decane salesburiensis,[3] hilaris et laetus quod, ad quidlibet me
vocat vestra voluntas, securus de erratorum meorum (quippe qui sciens
et prudens manum mitto in flammam) venia et emendatione, a benigni-
tate vestra veniam, a discretione et litteris emendationem exspectans.
Imperfectum enim *meum viderunt oculi* vestri et noverunt.[4] Non igitur in 15
hac re perfectionem exspectetis; *inscrutabile est* enim *cor* hominis et *quis
cognoscet illud*?[5] Si viam viri adolescentis penitus ignoravit sapientissi-
mus,[6] quot capitum tot sententiarum vias quis investigabit?[7] Accipite

---

1-4 *Pro varr. hujus tituli vide descr. MSS supra in Proleg ad pp. 20-31.* (*Sectionibus 1-3 carent*
BmSoV). 5 Res] Quaestio O. cuilibet Cc cujuslicet Tc *corr. ab* cujus Ck.
nedum] nondum Ck ne de O *corr. ad* ne non Ab. 9 facultatem] facilitatem Ad. 10
impossibilitatem J *corr. ab* impossibilitatem Aa. igitur *add.* et PTu. 11 petis AaJ-
OU(CpMX) petistis AcPRZ(KNY petisti FTb Petrus L petitis W). Ric. decane CcCi.
salesberiensis R salesbiriensis H(Sg salebiriensis I) saledinensis *corr. ad* saleburienis Tc sa-
leburgensis PTa(K) saluburiensis Ab (saleburiensis CpTb salesburiensium M salesburnensis
E *corrupio pro* salemburgensis F saliberiensis G saluberiensis L salubriensis DX) saresberiensis
AdJ(N) saresbergensis Z sarum Ck. (decane salesburiensis *om.* W). quod] quo
AbRTa. quodlibet Tc quilibet CcTu. 12 de *om.* Ck *add.* venia PTu. 13 veniam et emendationem AdCkP. 15 enim *corr. ab* hoc Tc *om.* AbORTaTu (*om.* W).
16 exspectans CcCi. 17-18 sapiens Ad. 18 quis *add.* cognoscit aut Ta *add.* cognoscit
aut *insert. alia manu* P.

---

[1] Cf. *Tractatus de conscientia ad religiosum quemdam ordinis cisterciensis* pr. (PL 184.551-553).
[2] There is a marginal note on these words in Ad: "Sumptum est ex libro pla. ubi dicitur quod
sola virtus est quae res impossibiles ad possibilem facilitatem ducit."
[3] This is Richard Poore; see above Proleg. p. 7.
[4] See *Ps* 138.16.
[5] See *Jer* 17.9; cf. *Tractatus de conscientia* c.1 (PL 184.553B).
[6] Cf. *Prov* 30.18-19.
[7] Cf. TERENCE, *Phormio* 2.454; HORACE, *Sermones* 2.1.27-28.

ergo, dilectissime, quamcumque exilem pauperculae venae stillulam, et affectum effectui commensurare nolite, sed ex altero perpendite al- 20 terum.

2 Quia ergo distincta melius servantur et compendiosius inveniuntur, opusculum istud in quinque partes sum partitus sive libros, et unumquemque librum per capitula sua. In primo libro ostenditur quomodo suscipiendus sit poenitens, et hoc in primo capitulo; in secundo, quae 25 exiguntur a poenitente; in tertio, quomodo confiteri debeat poenitens, scilicet gradatim et ordinate de omnibus septem vitiis capitalibus, primo de primo, secundo de secundo, et sic de singulis propter compendium. [Tamen] In quarto capitulo ostenditur quod separatim et in primis agendum sit de matrimonio et simonia et aliis quae circa clericos atten- 30 duntur, ut ordinibus et ordinum impedimentis; de illo in secundo tractabitur libro, de istis in tertio. In quarto gradatim et ordinate singula percurram vitia et singulorum species; in fine aliqua apponam huic negotio necessaria. In quinto proponere proponimus poenitentias peccatis competentes.[8]   35

Verumtamen, quia ad propositum, ut puto, plus facit et in eo quem quaeritis modo plus consonat, dialogum si placet in medium producamus, videlicet ut vicissim uterlibet, poenitens scilicet et sacerdos confessor, prout res postulaverit, tum interrogans tum introducatur respondens.

EXPLICIT PROLOGUS   40

20 affectum] effectum OR (ad effectum W).   effectui] affectui CkZ(IMSg) affectui *insert*. Cc *corrupt*. Ac.   22 et] vel O.   23 sive] sicut Ck *om*. Aa. 24 librum *om*. CkTa. 26-27 poenitens scilicet] peccatum suum R peccata sua Tu.   27 scilicet] sacerdoti Z *corr*. *ad* sacerdos Aa.   28-29 propter compendium Tamen *om*. Tu.   29 Tamen AaAcCkH-JORTcUZ(CpEFGMNTbXY) tum *delet*. Ab (tum Sg) *om*. AdCcCiPTa(DIKL).   30 et de aliis AaJTuZ.   31 ut] scilicet de HJUZ *add*. de AaP *add*. in Tc.   illo] illis PTu. 32 ordinate] ordine Cc.   33 singulorum *add*. vitiorum CcCiTc.   aliqua] autem O autem alia Tu autem *add*. aliqua *insert*. Aa.   33-34 in fine — necessaria *insert*. Ad.   34 proponere proponimus] proponemus TaTu.   proponimus] proposuimus CcCkH.   34-35 In quinto — competentes *om*. O (*cf. infra var. ad lineam 38*) *add*. Dividitur quintus liber in sex partibus CcCi.   36 Verumtamen] Verum AbORTa.   ut puto *om*. OTu.   37 producamus] proponamus R procuramus sive producamus U.   38 utrumlibet O uterque RTa utraelibet *corr*. *ad* uterlibet Aa.   poenitens *add*. est. In quinto proponere proponimus poenitentias peccatis competentes O (*cf. supra var. ad lineas 34-35*).   confessor *om*. CkR *corr*. *ab* confessos J.   39 tum[1] *corr*. *ab* cum O inde R.   tum[2]] cum *corr*. *ad* tu O inde R.

[8] Regarding the general structure of this penitential see above Proleg. pp. 12-17; regarding further details and problems concerning divisions of it see FIRTH, *Thesis* II 342*-351*.

3 i. Quomodo suscipiendus sit poenitens.

ii. Quae exigantur a poenitente.

iii. Quod poenitens debeat confiteri gradatim et ordinate et de omnibus septem vitiis capitalibus et eorum speciebus.   45

iv. Quod in primis et seorsum agendum sit de matrimonio et simonia.

<INCIPIT LIBER PRIMUS>

< Cap. > i. QUOMODO SUSCIPIENDUS SIT POENITENS

POENITENS. Suscipe me, domine, miserum peccatorem.

SACERDOS. Suscipiat te, fili, misericordia illa cujus non est numerus. 50
Suscipiat te ille qui in omnium amplexus brachia sua expandit in cruce,
qui ipsum cor suum lancea perforatum etiam persecutoribus suis, pro
quibus et oravit, aperuit. Ante omnia, fili, de illius spera misericordia qui,
cum inimici ejus essemus, ut nos sibi reconciliaret, ut quod nos debebamus,
scilicet pessimum et aeternum genus tormentorum, ipse pro nobis sol- 55
veret, sputa, clavos et lanceam, opprobria et derisiones, fel et acetum
et arundinem, tandem mortem abjectissimam gratis sustinuit, quantacumque sint, quantula sunt peccata tua respectu illius misericordiae quae
totius mundi, immo infinitorum mundorum, suffecit absorbere peccata.

De me quoque, fili, licet indigno ejus et misero ministro, tamquam de 60
teipso confidas, cui nemini carissimo tuo revelanda confiteri proponis.
Aeque enim mea agitur causa ut tua; quia si caecus caecum ducit *ambo*

---

41 LIBER *om.* Ad.   *Variationes rubricarum plerumque non indicantur in hoc apparatu; cf. supra*
in Proleg. ad p. 20 n. 12.   42-46 *Hic et alibi numeros titulorum om. plures MSS.*   42 sit *om.*
Ab.   43 exiguntur AaCkHJTcUZ.   44 debet OP.   et ordinate et *om.* R.   et²
om. Ta.   50 fili *add.* mi AaJTuU *add.* carissime *insert.* AcAd.   52 cor] corpus PTa-
TuZ.   etiam] et RTc *add.* pro PR.   52-53 pro — oravit *om.*] Ck.   53 et *om.* AaJ-
TaUZ.   et oravit aperuit] aperuit oravit H.   aperuit] apparuit Ck *om.* Tu.   54
ejus *om.* Ta.   ut² *om.* JTaUZ *insert.* Aa.   debeamus CcCiCk *corr. ab* deleamus Tc
(debeamus omne W).   56 sputa] imputa CcCi *om.* J *insert.* Aa *delet.* H.   et² *om.* Ci-
Ck.   et³ *om.* CkU.   acetum *add.* sputa H.   57 et *om.* OU.   57-58 quanta-
cumque] quantulacumque Ck.   58 quantula] quanta U.   quantula sunt *om.* Ta.
sunt] sint AaCkJOTu.   quae] qui AaTu quam Ta.   59 sufficit CcH.   60 De]
confide tamen de O.   licet] mi CcH *om.* TuU.   61 carissimo tuo *om.* Ta.   62
ducat R duxerit Tc.

in foveam cadunt,[1] et utriusque anima de manu ducentis requiretur.[2] Ambo igitur diligentes et attenti simus coadjutores Christi ad animas nostras salvandas, tu nude et aperte proponendo quae memoriter tenes, ego 65 sollicite et quasi proterve et improbe quae aperta sunt rimando vulnera, et si quae latent cicatrices aperiendo.

4 Sed antequam ulterius procedamus, dic mihi: De ovili nostro es an non ?

POENITENS. Non sum, sed de licentia abbatis mei ad vos venio. 70

SACERDOS. Alioquin adultera esset confessio tua, immo nec confessio.[3] Nullus enim te ad poenitentiam recipere potest sine ejus licentia qui tui curam habet, nisi forte in necessitate, ut si forte pastorem tuum habere non potes, vel si forte ita contumax es quod ei nullo modo confiteri velis. Tunc quidem te admittam ad poenitentiam, ne forte vel inconfessus mo- 75 riaris vel sine consilio a me recedas; ad consilium enim quemlibet admittam.[4]

---

63 requiritur HTa require J.   66 et[2] *corr. ad* id est *a scriptore originali in textu* O. improbe *add.* et O.   68 Sed *om.* Ci. an] aut CcCiOP(K vel So) (an W).   70 mei] nostri O.   73 in *om.* AaAbHJTuU(BmCpISgSoVX) (*om.* W).   74 forte *om.* OTu.

---

[1] See *Matt* 15.14; cf. *Luc* 6.39.

[2] Cf. *Ezech* 3.17-21, 33.2-9.

[3] Cf. GRATIAN, *Decretum* C.16 q.1 c.9 & dictum post c.19; *De poen.* D.6 c.3; BERNARD OF PAVIA, *Summa decretalium* 5.33.5 (ed. LASPEYRES pp. 270-271); Peter Anton KIRSCH, " Der sacerdos proprius in der abendländischen Kirche vor dem Jahre 1215", *ArchivKKRecht* 84.4 (1904) 527-537; Philippe DELHAYE, "Deux textes de Senatus de Worcester sur la pénitence", *RechThAncMéd* 19 (1952) 221-222.

[4] Cf. ALAN OF LILLE, *Liber poenitentialis* 4.18 (ed. LONGÈRE II 172-173). Gratian, on the basis of a text from the pseudo-Augustinian work *De vera et falsa poenitentia,* allows one to confess to another priest if one's own is ignorant. (see *De poen.* D.6 c.1, dictum post c.2 & c.3; cf. Eugen Heinrich FISCHER, "Bussgewalt, Pfarrzwang und Beichtvater-Wahl nach dem Dekret Gratians", *Studia Gratiana* 4 [1956-57] 185-230). Canonists generally follow him, admitting this exception to the general rule (see e.g. HUGUCCIO, *Summa super decretum* ad *De poen.* D.6 c.3 *ignorantia,* fol. 341[ra]). Theologians often oppose this exception. Robert Courson distinguishes between *consulere, poenitentiam indicere* and *poenitentiam injungere.* Another priest, if he is well-informed and prudent, can advise the penitent and evaluate a suitable penance; but he cannot enjoin or impose penance except by permission of one's *proprius sacerdos* or of a higher prelate. See COURSON, *Summa* 1.46 (ed. KENNEDY p. 326); cf. FIRTH, *Thesis* II 429*-431*; *Summa: Breves dies hominis* quoted by ANCIAUX p. 601. Flamborough is treating here of a slightly different matter, but he may have been influenced by these opinions.

\<Cap.\> ii. QUAE EXIGANTUR A POENITENTE

5   A poenitente duo exiguntur: ut christianus sit et poenitens. Ad chris-
tianitatem quatuor exiguntur: fides, spes, caritas et operatio. Fides tibi 80
illuminabit, spes animabit, caritas producet, operatio consummabit.

Fidem tenes rectam et firmam, an instruendus es ?[5]

POENITENS. Teneo per gratiam Dei, semperque tenebo.

SACERDOS. Bene speras de Dei misericordia, an admonendus es ?

POENITENS. Spero, domine; *etiam si me occiderit, sperabo in* eum.[6]   85

SACERDOS. Deum diligis ante omnia et times, et postea proximum ?[7]

POENITENS. Diligo, domine, et timeo.

SACERDOS. De quarto, id est operatione, quid est ? Quae et qualia sunt
opera tua, directa an prava et distorta ?

POENITENS. Vae mihi; directa quam paucissima, prava et distorta quam 90
plurima et maxima. Vae mihi.

SACERDOS. Age igitur quod restat: quidquid *potest manus tua instanter
operare*; quia ecce nox instat in qua non licet operari.[8] Fac *dignos fructus
poenitentiae*,[9] et per opera poenitentiae redime mala quae fecisti ut ad innocentiam reducaris; postea de merito cogita, et sint *sicut mercenarii* dies 95
tui.[10]

6   Dixi quod duo exiguntur a poenitente: christianitas et poenitentia.[11]
Diximus de christianitate; consequenter de poenitentia agamus.

Ad poenitentiam quatuor exiguntur: dolor de praeteritis, cautela de 99
futuris, integra et nuda confessio et obedientia. Vis ista quatuor observare ?

---

79 poenitens *add.* sit O.   80 exiguntur *add.* scilicet O.   et *om.* CkHJ.   tibi] te
CcHTaTuUZ(BmEFGLMNSgSoV Christi X) (tibi W).   (80-81 tibi illuminabit] Christi
illuminabit tibi Tb).   84 Dei *om.* J *insert.* Aa.   87 domine] Dominum Z *om.* CkO.
88 id est] scilicet CcCiP *add.* de AaCkJPRTaTcUZ(BmCpGKLMNSgSoX) (*add.* de W).
Quae *om.* O.   et *om.* Cc.   89 tua *add.* operari AaCkHJTcUZ(CpMNSgY) *add.*
operari *insert.* Ac (*add.* operari hoc E).   instanter *add.* operari Tb).   97 Dixi *add.* quidem O.   a] de O.   scilicet christianitas P *add.* scilicet CkHJUZ.

[5] Cf. BARTHOLOMEW OF EXETER, *Liber poenitentialis* cc.1-5 (ed. MOREY pp. 175-177); *Summa:
Breves dies hominis* quoted by ANCIAUX p. 129 n. 4.

[6] See *Job* 13.15.

[7] Cf. *Matt* 22.37-39; *Marc* 12.30-31; *Luc* 10.27; FIRTH, *Thesis* II 431*-435*; GRATIAN *De
poen.* D.4 c.49.

[8] See *Qoheleth* (*Eccles*) 9.10; *Joan* 9.4.

[9] See *Luc* 3.8.

[10] See *Job* 7.1.

[11] See above sect. 5.

POENITENS. Non plane intelligo quid sit ista quatuor observare.

SACERDOS. Singillatim ista tibi exponam. De universis peccatis tuis doles tu et de singulis? 5

POENITENS. Doleo.

SACERDOS. Vis tu ab omni peccato abstinere mortali?[12]

POENITENS. Non possum.

SACERDOS. Hoc videris dicere quod talem te creavit Deus ut non peccare non possis. Fili, absit ab omni fideli hoc credere de Deo, qui etiam 10 ultra quam possumus tentari nos non permittit.[13] Si tamen ad hoc induci non potes ut omni velis renuntiare peccato, aliquo retento de aliis ad poenitentiam te recipiam.

POENITENS. Numquid valebit mihi poenitentia talis?

SACERDOS. Non est bonum quod non valeat. Valebit igitur tibi quoad 15 quid, scilicet ut ad gratiam Dei recipiendam habilior sis; sed fructuosa tibi non erit, id est nec ad meritum nec ad peccatorum remissionem.[14]

Sed attende tibi, fili. Hinc est tibi Deus a dextris, qui tot tibi bona temporalia, tam spritualia quam corporalia, contulit, qui tot et tanta aeterna promittit, qui de tua continue sollicitus est salute. Illinc a sinistris est 20 tibi diabolus, qui de tua continue sollicitus est perditione. Vis ergo pro delectatiuncula instantanea et turpissima Deum derelinquere et diabolo adhaerere in aeternum moriturus?[15]

POENITENS. Absit hoc a me, domine.

---

4 ista] illa U *om.* CcCiP *add.* quatuor TaR.   9 non *om.* Cc.   10 non *om.* CkJ. qui] quia Ad.   11 possimus AaAdCcCiCkRUZ(FM) (possumus W).   12 ut ab omni O.   abrenuntiare Ta renuntiari CkTu.   aliquo retento *om.* J *insert.* Aa.   14 valet Tu.   15 valet O *corr. ab* valet Cc.   tibi *om.* AbTaU.   16 recipiendam *om.* Cc.   17 nec¹] non RTc *om.* Ta.   18 tibi¹ *om.* Tu.   fili *add.* mi O.   tibi² *om.* Ta.   tibi³ *om.* CkO.   19 tam] quam JTu.   21 tibi *om.* CkTaU.   continue *corr. ab* continere Ci *om.* RTu *insert. alia manu* Cc.   ergo] igitur OP.   22 delectantiuncula J delectamento R delectatione prava O delectanti vincula Tu *corr. ab* delectati vincula Ci.   relinquere AaJZ delinquere Cc.

---

[12] Cf. *Synodicae constitutiones* cap. 6 no. 8 (PL 212.61). This is a decree of a council held at Paris under Bishop Odo of Sully (A.D. 1196-1208); cf. Vincent L. KENNEDY, "The Date of the Parisian Decree", *MedStud* 8 (1946) 87.

[13] Cf. 1 *Cor* 10.13.

[14] Cf. FIRTH, *Thesis* II 431*-439*, esp. p. 439* n. 58 (quoting HUG. ad *De poen.* D.5 c.8 *decipi* fol. 340rb) and n. 59 (quoting *Liber poenitentialis exceptus* fol. 309^r, and citing JL 13772 [X 5. 38.5]).

[15] Cf. ALAN OF LILLE, *Liber poenitentialis* 2.2-3 (ed. LONGÈRE II 46-47; cf. *ArchivesHDLMA* 32.198-199; PL 210.289-290).

SACERDOS. Vis igitur, ut dixi, ab omni abstinere mortali?   25
POENITENS. Volo.

SACERDOS. Alioquin, uno peccato mortali retento omnia retinentur.
Vis ergo omnia peccata tua retinere?

POENITENS. Immo omnibus renuntio.

SACERDOS. Deo gratias.   30

POENITENS. Voto vel sacramento obligare me non audeo.

SACERDOS. Nec votum nec sacramentum a te exigo.[16] Sed tu videris:
si aliquod tibi assumpsisti, redde, sive simplex sit sive sollemne.

7   Vis integre et nude confiteri omnia ac si numquam confessus fuisses?

POENITENS. Numquid et illa confitebor quae alii confessus sum?   35

SACERDOS. Sic est, ex quo tu mutas confessorem.[17] Non enim truncare
debes confessionem, ut quaedam mihi, alii alia, confitearis.[18]

POENITENS. Igitur nude et integre omnia confitebor.

SACERDOS. Vis tu obedire et facere quod tibi injungetur?

POENITENS. Volo.   40

SACERDOS. Frequenter et libenter confiteris?

POENITENS. Non.

SACERDOS. Frequenter confitere et statim quando opus est; quia, quanto
plus et plus differs confiteri, tanto pejor et pejor efficieris. Licet non nisi
in uno solo mortali fueris peccato, libenter confitere et in hac vita punia- 45

---

25 abstinere] cavere Tc *add.* peccato CcCiP.   28 tua *om.* CkTu.   29 POENITENS *om.*
J.   immo *add.* etiam AaJU.   33 aliquid HTaU aliquot Ac.   redde *om.* JZ *insert.*
Aa.   sit *om.* CkU.   sit sive sollemne] sive sollemne fuerit Tu.   34 ac] at J aut
H.   35 et alii AaJ et aliis Tu.   36 est *om.* OTa.   37 alii] aliis JTuZ.   alia]
quaedam AaCkTa.   39 quod *insert.* Ck quae Tu.   injungitur CkTa injunguntur Tu.
43 Frequentur *add.* et libenter Ad.   quanto] quando Cc.   44 et plus *om.* OTu.
confiteri *om.* PTa.   efficeris AaTaZ efficaris R.   45 in[1] *om.* J.   in uno *corr. ad*
minimo Aa.   uno] minimo Tu.   peccato fueris *add.* alioquin Tu.   confitere *add.*
alioquin AaAdCkJTcUZ(GSg *add.* alioquin *insert.* Bm).   et] ut H(M) *om.* AaJZ(KSgVY)
et nisi *insert. alia manu* P *add.* nisi Ta.

---

[16] Cf. ROBERT COURSON, *Summa* 1.44 (ed. KENNEDY, *MedStud* 7.324-325).

[17] Cf. COURSON, *Summa* 1.27-30 (ed. KENNEDY pp. 308-310); PETER CANTOR, *Summa de sacramentis et animae consiliis* Part 2 Appendix 2 from Paris MS c. 4 *ad finem* (ed. DUGAUQUIER II
p. 433 lines 153-155); see also. Artur Michael LANDGRAF, *Dogmengeschichte der Frühscholastik*
IV.1.193-275 (cf. *ZKathTh* 61 [1937] 509-594).

[18] See *De vera et falsa poenitentia* c. 15 no. 31 (PL 40.1125-26) quoted in GRATIAN, *Decretum,
De poen.* D.5 c.1 §7. Cf. ALAN OF LILLE, *Liber poenitentialis* 2.8, 4.31 (ed. LONGÈRE II 51, 183;
cf. *ArchivesHDLMA* 32.201, 233; PL 210.292B, 303-304). Alan bases this repetition of confession on the notion that the guilt of past sins returns when new ones are committed. He is
not sure it is necessary, but declares that it is safer and that the confessor should insist on it.

ris; alioquin in futuro vel in perpetuum damnaberis vel per purgatorium transibis, cujus acerbitas in hac vita excogitari non potest.[19]

8 Frequenter doles de peccatis tuis?

POENITENS. Aliquando.

SACERDOS. Immo semper studeas ad dolendum; quia summa poeni- 50 tentia est dolor et contritio.[20] In tantum enim dolere poteris quod ulterius non punieris.[21]

POENITENS. Quantus dolor sufficit ad hoc?

SACERDOS. De quovis minimo mortali plus debes dolere quam si omnia amisisses quae citra Deum amitti possunt. Et probo: Nonne quovis minimo 55 mortali amisisti Deum, et Deus omnibus aliis praestantior est? Ergo plus debes dolere de Dei amissione quam aliorum omnium.

Frequenter meditaris?

POENITENS. Raro.

SACERDOS. Frequenter cogita de vitae brevitate et fragilitate, de poe- 60 narum inferni acerbitate et aeternitate; et ita timorem tibi incuties, licet servilem, tamen multum expedientem. Cogita de Deo, quanta sollicitudine, quanta caritate, quanto desiderio tuae semper egit et agit curam salutis, et vitae aeternae gloria et ineffabilitate. Numquam sine medita-

---

45-46 punieris AaAdCkJUZ(Sg *corr. attentat. ad* punieris Bm *om.* Y ne puniaris SoV *add.* pro peccatis 1).   46 alioquin] aliter CcCi vel R et Ck(Bm) ne Tu *om.* AbAdTaTc(SoV sin autem X sin autem vel DISg).   (in] vel Cp).   alioquin in futuro *om.* AaJUZ(G *add.* puniaris Y).   vel[1]] et Tu(N et *corr. attentat.* Bm) *om.* Ta(DIX).   49 Aliquando *add.* SACERDOS. (*om.* Aa) De universis peccatis tuis doles? POENITENS. Doleo. SACERDOS. Doles tu et de singulis? POENITENS. Doleo. H *add. idem insert.* Aa *cf. supra in sect.* 6 *ad lineas* 4-5. 51 dolere poteris] potes dolere Tu poteris (*insert. in rasuram vel lacunam*) dolere Ck.   54 quovis] quolibet JUZ *corr. ab* quolibet *add.* peccato Aa peccato mortali CcCiPTa *add.* peccato JU. 55 Et *om.* Ad *add.* hoc TcTu.   quovis] quolibet JUZ *corr. ab* quolibet Aa.   minimo *om.* P.   55-56 mortali minimo *add.* peccato Aa.   56 mortali] melior Ta *om.* Ck. et *om.* O.   58 SACERDOS. Frequenter HU.   60 et de fragilitate O *add.* et CkO.   61 timorem *insert.* Ci timores J *add.* Dei CkJTcUZ.   tibi *om.* CkTu.   incutias Tu incuties AbAc induces Ck injicies U.   62 tamen *add.* saltem O.   quanta sollicitudine *om.* Ta. 64 salutis *add.* et ita amorem Dei in te semper accendes O *cf. infra var. ad lineam 66.*   et[1] *add.* de O.   aeternae] aeternitate AaJZ.   gloriam Tu *add.* et fervorem O *cf. infra var. ad lineam 66.*   Numquam *add.* sis O.

---

[19] Cf. *De vera et falsa poen.* 18.34 (PL 40.1128) quoted by GRATIAN *De poen.* D.7 c.6 §2; ALAN, *Liber poenitentialis* 4.26-30 (ed. LONGÈRE II 179-183; cf. *ArchivesHDLMA* 32.230-233; PL 210. 302-303).

[20] Cf. *De vera et falsa poen.* 19.35 (PL 40.1128-29) quoted by GRATIAN *De poen.* D.3 c.4.

[21] Cf. LOMBARD, *Sent.* 4.20.2-3; ALAN, *Liber poenitentialis* 2.5 (ed. LONGÈRE II 47-48; cf. *ArchivesHDLMA* 32.199; PL 210.290-291).

tione, timida, frequens et fervida erit oratio, ad opus bonum eris promp- 65
tus et hilaris; et ita amorem Dei in te semper accendes et fervorem.

<Cap.> iii. QUALITER CONFITERI DEBEAT POENITENS

9 Fere omnes inordinate confitentur; quia omisso ordine vitiorum ordinem aetatis, locorum et temporum observant, dicentes: "In illa aetate
feci illam fornicationem, illud adulterium, illud furtum, illud perjurium, 70
illud homicidium. Item in illa aetate feci illum incestum, illam monialem
procatus sum, illud sortilegium feci." Et ita et se et sacerdotis memoriam
confundunt.

Mihi placet ut incipiens a superbia, quae est radix omnium malorum,
singula cum suis speciebus confitearis gradatim vitia prout unum ab alio 75
nascitur et procedit: scilicet prius vanam gloriam, secundo invidiam,
tertio iram, quarto accidiam, quinto avaritiam, sexto gulam, septimo
luxuriam.[22]

<Cap.> iv. QUOD IN PRIMIS ET SEORSUM AGENDUM SIT
DE MATRIMONIO ET SIMONIA   80

10 Ego in primis de difficilioribus me expedire consuevi, de matrimonio
scilicet cum laicis, de simonia et aliis quae circa clericos attenduntur cum
clericis. Sed quia de matrimonio etiam cum clericis non numquam est
disputandum, in sequenti secundo libro de matrimonio tractabimus; et
primo videbimus quid sit matrimonium, secundo quae exigantur ad ma- 85
trimonium et sint de substantia matrimonii,[23] tertio quae impediant et
dirimant matrimonium, quarto quae impediant tantum matrimonium.

---

65 timidi Ta timenda Ck.   fervens CkHJU fecunda P.   oratio *add.* et JO *add.* nec
Ta *add.* nec non Tu *add.* nec *insert.* P.   66 et ita— fervorem *om.* O *vide supra varr. ad lineam* 64.
accendens Ta attendens Aa accende Cc.   68 Fere] Vere J Ecce P.   70 illud²] illum
corr. ad istud Aa.   illud³] istud *hic et* ʃ *usque ad linaem 72* Ci.   71 illum] illud CkJTc.
72 precatus JRZ.   et² *om.* PTa.   et se *insert.* H.   et³ *om.* Tu *insert.* Aa.   74 in-
cipiatis Tu incipietis Ck.   76 prius] primo O *om.* RTa.   et secundo P postea Ck.
79 ET SEORSUM *om.* Ad.   81 Ego *add.* cum *delet.* O.   82 scilicet *om.* JPTaZ *insert.*
Aa.   84 sequenti *add.* in O.   secundo *om.* Ta *delet.* Tc.   85 primum OTc.
exiguntur CkHORTuU.   86 et¹ *add.* quae CkHOTcUZ(BmCpELMSoTbV).   sint]
sunt H *sic* Cc.   impediunt AdCkHJRTuUZ(BmCpDEIMSgSoV) *corr. ab* impediunt Aa.
86-87 et dirimant *om.* Ck *insert. alia manu* P *cf. infra var. ad* tantum.   87 dirimunt AaHJ-
RTuUZ(CpDEIMSgSoV disjungunt Bm).   impediant CcOP(FKLN) impediunt *cett.*
quarto — matrimonium *om.* Tu (*homoeotel.*).   tantum] et dirimunt Ck *cf. supra var. ad lineas*
86-87.

[22] Cf. Alan, *Liber poenitentialis* 1.4 (ed. Longère II 27); Siegfried Wenzel, "The Seven Deadly Sins: Some Problems of Research", *Speculum* 43 (1968) 1-22, esp. 4-5; above Proleg. p. 13
with n. 71.

[23] Regarding this use of the word *substantia* cf. below sects. 74 and 76 with nn. 6 and 9.

INCIPIUNT CAPITULA SECUNDI LIBRI

11   i. Quid sit matrimonium.
   ii. Quae sint de substantia matrimonii.[1]
   iii. Quae impediant et dirimant matrimonium.
   iv. Quae impediant tantum.   5

INCIPIT SECUNDUS LIBER

<Cap.> i. QUID SIT MATRIMONIUM

Matrimonium est legitima viri et mulieris conjunctio, individuam vitae
retinens consuetudinem.[2] *Legitima* dicitur contra naturalem conjunctio-
nem; quia inter patrem et filiam, matrem et filium et alias consanguineas 10
personas est conjunctio naturalis, non legitima, id est non secundum leges
introducta. *Individuam* dicitur propter easdem personas quae ab invicem
[non] separantur.[3] Unde Dominus in evangelio: *Propter ·hoc*, id est propter
matrimonium, relinquet *homo patrem et matrem et adhaerebit uxori suae.*[4]

2-5 Quid —tantum *om.* RTaTu Pet.   4 impediunt... dirimunt CkHUZ *corr. ab* impediunt
...dirimunt Aa.   5 impediunt AaHU.   tantum *add.* matrimonium HTc.   6-7
INCIPIT — MATRIMONIUM *om.* Ci.   8 Matrimonium *ss. incipit* Pet *usque ad finem*
sect. 72 in variis partibus foliorum 142ᵛ-159ᵛ.   9 contra] circa Tc *corr. ad* circa Ci propter Tu.
10 filiam] filium AbAcCkTc *corr. ab* filium R *add. et* ORTu.   12 individua HOTaTcTu
Pet(BmCpDFGIKLMNSoTbX *om.* E).   13 non JOTu (*insert.* Y) *om. cett.*(*cett.*) *Vide adnota-*
tionem ad hunc textum.   Propter *om.* PTa.   14 patrem — suae] etc. U.   et² —
suae] etc. CkTu *add.* et erunt duo etc. H *add.* et erunt duo in carne una JTc.

[1] Cf. below sects. 74 and 76 with nn. 6 and 9.

[2] Cf. "Matrimonium igitur conjunctio maris et feminae legitima, individuam vitae consuetudinem retinens." HUG. ad C.27 pr. (fol. 281ᵛᵇ); "Matrimonium est viri et mulieris legitima
conjunctio individuam vitae consuetudinem retinens." BERNARD OF PAVIA, *Summa decretalium*
4.1.4 (ed. LASPEYRES p. 131). Regarding the development and interpretation of this definition
see JUSTINIAN, *Institutiones* 1.9; cf. ALEXANDER III (Roland Bandinelli) *Stroma* ad C.27 pr. (ed.
THANER p. 114); PAUCAPALEA, *Summa* ad C.27 pr. (ed. Johann F. VON SCHULTE p. 111); J. FREISEN,
Geschichte des canonischen Eherechts pp. 22-24; Joseph Georg ZIEGLER, *Die Ehelehre der Pönitentialsummen von 1200-1350* p. 34.

[3] See variants. There is good reason to believe that Robert first wrote *non* in his text, there-
by adopting the traditional interpretation of canonists for this word *individuam*, namely "un-
divided". It is probable that the other meaning of *individuus*, namely "individual" or "distinct", was in the mind of the scribes who omitted *non*. According to the evidence of the MSS
this change took place before the completion of Form 3 and was allowed to stand, no doubt
inadvertently, by the author himself. The quotation from Scripture which follows immediately
in the text shows that the word is understood by the author to mean that common life in marriage is indivisible and that married persons are not to be separated from one another.

[4] See *Matt* 19.5; cf. *Gen* 2.24, *Eph* 5.31.

12 Tria exiguntur ad matrimonium: consensus animorum, consensus corporum, id est consensus in carnalem copulam, et personarum regularitas ad contrahendum.[5] Unde et beata Virgo in carnalem consensit copulam; conditionaliter enim vovit virginitatem.[6]

Ubi ergo deest aliquod istorum trium, non est matrimonium. Unde 20 pueri ante septennium, quia non sentiunt nec consentiunt, ideo nec contrahunt, nec etiam sponsalia.[7] Cum aliqua infra septennium contraxisti; propter hoc non impedieris ea dimissa quamlibet ejus consanguineam ducere; cum alias, si esset septennis vel major, nullam ejus consanguineam ducere posses, licet plus non esset actum quam quod per verba de 25 futuro cum ea contraxisses.[8] Eadem ratione qua puer, et furiosus non contraheret, nisi in tempore quietis si forte interpolatus sit furor.[9]

13 Similiter impossibilitas coeundi impedit matrimonium; ut semel castratus de cetero non contrahat, et si contraxerit non erit matrimonium. Si post contractum matrimonium sectus fuerit, non ideo dirimitur matri- 30

16-27 Tria — furor *abbrev.* Pet *fol. 144*ra-b.   16 consensus[2]] et habilitas Tc.   consensus corporum] habilitas corporum *insert. in lacunam* O.   18 et] etiam O *om.* AcTc.   20 trium *om.* Tc Pet.   est *om.* Cc *insert.* P.   21 septennium] septimum annum HJUZ septem annos Ck.   non] nec Ac neque Ck.   sentiunt nec *om.* R.   sentiunt nec consentiunt] consentiunt neque dissentiunt O.   nec[1]] neque AaCkHJUZ.   nec[2]] non JPTaU Pet. 22 nec] Si Tc *delet.* O *add.* habent Tu.   etiam *add.* si OR *add.* si *insert.* Ab.   aliqua] autem AaTu *om.* Cc.   aliqua infra] ante *corr. ad* aliqua Ci.   23 dimissa] divisa O. 24 cum] tum Ci tamen illa Ck.   esses HP essent J.   25 quam] nisi R.   quod *om.* PTaTc.   27 contrahet AcCkP contrahat Tu.   28 Similiter] Simpliciter O Si Tc.   28-31 *Textus alienus substitutus* Pet.   28 semel] senilis Cc *corr. ab* senilis Ci. 29 contrahet CcOTa.   erit] est Ck esse Tu.   30-31 Si post — dirimitur matrimonium *om.* J *insert.* Aa (*homoeotel.?* *om.* W).   30 matrimonii O.   sectus] castratus O. dirimetur H dimittitur Tc *corr. ab* dimittetur Aa.

---

[5] Cf. ALEXANDER III (Roland Bandinelli) *Stroma* ad C.27 pr. (p. 114).

[6] Cf. HUG. ad C.27 q.2 c.3 *Nisi Deus aliter* (fol. 287vb, ed. ROMAN pp. 752-753); Damian and Odulph VAN DEN EYNDE in their edition of GUY OF ORCHELLES, *Tractatus de sacramentis* (Louvain 1953) Prolegomena pp. XXXI-XXXII; Franz GILLMANN, "Huguccio über die Heiligung, über das Virginitätsgelübde und die Ehe der Gottesmutter", Katholik[3] 29 (1904)[1] 304-308 (quoting Huguccio).

[7] Cf. GRATIAN C.30 q.2 pr., c.un.; Po. 535 (X 4.2.13; issued probably Sept.-Dec., 1198).

[8] Cf. Po. 876 (Reg. 2.233; PL 214.791-792; issued Nov. 24, 1199); 1 *Compil.* 4.2.5, 6, 8 (X 4.2.4, 5, 6; JL 13947, 13887, 14032). Cf. also below sect. 51 with n. 11.

[9] Cf. HUG. ad C.32 q.7 c.26 (fols. 318vb-319ra).

monium.[10] Idem dico de frigido naturaliter; quia ejus membra dicuntur paralytica ut non possint erigi. Talem si te dixeris et relicta tua accesseris ad aliam et cognoveris, probaberis non esse frigidus et cogeris redire ad primam.[11] Si tu et uxor tua confitemini frigiditatem tuam, commanebitis tamen per biennium, et post jurabitis ambo quod ita est, et sic fiet divor- 35 tium.[12] Si non ambo confitemini et mulier probabiliores rationes inducit, ei credetur; alioquin viro credetur, quia caput est mulieris.[13] Si vir vel non velit vel non possit probare, probet mulier per aspectum corporis et publicam famam et juramentum testium, quorum numerus sit in arbitrio judicis. 40

14 Maleficium etiam perpetuum et impedit et dirimit matrimonium; non perpetuum nec hoc nec illud facit. Numquam erecta tibi sunt virilia; praesumitur de frigiditate tua; alias maleficiatus es. Usque ad triennium praesumitur maleficium esse temporale, deinde perpetuum. Tamen in favorem matrimonii semper praesumendum est maleficium fuisse post 45 contractum matrimonium; et vix est aliquis ita maleficiatus quin aliquando possit resolvi.[14]

15 Aliquis aliquo morbo virgam habuit ingrossatam, quod virginem non potuit deflorare, sed corruptas cognoscere. Contraxit cum virgine, quam

33 et eam cognoveris AaHJTaUZ.　　probaris PTa probaveris J.　　34 tua *om.* Aa Pet. confiteamini ORTa.　　35 tamen] tantum O.　　36 inducat U *corr. ad* inducat Aa induxerit Pet.　　37 vel *delet.* O.　　38 probabit O.　　mulier *add.* vel AaJZ.　　et] vel AaJUZ *add.* per AaCkHJTcUZ Pet.　　41 etiam] enim AaJZ *om.* R.　　et[1] *om.* ORTaTu Pet autem H.　　impendit CcCi.　　42 non] nec O.　　nec[1]] non O.　　erepta O. 43 fragilitate O.　　43-44 de frigiditate — praesumitur *om.* J (*homoeotel.*).　　44 esse] fuisse Ad *om.* Z Pet *insert.* Tc.　　in perpetuum AaTu.　　Tamen *om.* Cc *corr. ad* non Tc. 46 ita *om.* Cc.　　47 resolvi] redimi O.　　48 aliquo] alio AaTu.　　grossatam CkJUZ tam grossam *corr. ad* grossatam H.　　49-50 quam cum] quamcumque Tu (quantum L).

[10] Cf. Hug. ad C.27 q.2 dictum p. c.28 §2 *Item Nicholaus* (fol. 290vb ed. Roman p. 782); Gratian C.27 q.2 dictum p. c.29.

[11] Cf. Gratian C.33 q.1 c.2; 1 *Compil.* 4.16.1 (X 4.15.1; F. W. H. Wasserschleben, *Die Bussordnungen der abendländischen Kirche* p. 652).

[12] This period of two years is in conformity with Justinian, *Codex* 5.17.10; most twelfth-century decretists preferred to follow the three years indicated in the *Novellae* 22.6; see e.g. Hug. ad C.33 q.1 c.2 *propinquorum* (fol. 319[ra-b]); Rufinus, *Summa* ad C.33 q.1 pr. (ed. Singer p. 497). Robert may have been influenced by Bernard of Pavia, *Summa decretalium* 4.16.4 (ed. Laspeyres p. 177).

[13] Cf. Gratian C.33 q.1 c.3; Hug. ad C.27 q.2 c.29 *probare* (fols. 290[vb]-291[ra]); JL 16081 (X 2.19.4).

[14] See Hug. ad C.33 q.1 dictum p. c.4 (quoted above Proleg. pp. 37-39 and more fully in Firth, *Thesis* I 173*-174*; cf. *ibid.* I 172*-177*).

cum ipse cognoscere non potuit, facto divortio alii nupsit, et ab eo est 50 deflorata et cognita. Quod cum comperisset prior, eum repellit et judicio Innocentii papae obtinuit.[15]

Ideo tutius dicit ecclesia romana et de frigido et de maleficiato quod, si non potest habere suam ut uxorem, habeat ut sororem.[16]

Idem videtur esse dicendum de stricta quae nec arte nec natura potest 55 fieri habilis, vel si per infirmitatem fiat inhabilis irrecuperabiliter, quod de frigido et maleficiato dictum est.[17]

Itaque consensus animorum et habilitas corporum ad carnalem copulam exiguntur ad matrimonium, et eorum defectus impedit matrimonium.

<Cap.> iii.   DE HIS QUAE IMPEDIUNT ET DIRIMUNT MATRIMONIUM 60

16   Impediunt etiam matrimonium votum, ordo, habitus, dispar cultus, error personae, cognatio, agnatio sive affinitas, publicae honestatis justitia, delicti enormitas, coactio, raptus. [tempus feriarum, interdictum ecclesiae.][18]

---

50 cum *om.* Z(ETb).   (Quod — repetiit *om.* Cp Qui cum eam [*add.* prior So] reperisset, repetiit SoV).   reperisset AbOTaTu(FMSoVX) pepercisset Tc (comperuisset DSgTb *corr. ab* reperisset Bm).   eum] eam AbAdCcCiCkHJTuU(BmEFLMNSgX) *corr. ad* eam Aa *corr. ab* eam Tc.   petiit Cc *corr. ab* petiit Ci.   52 papae] tertii AaCkH *add.* tertium Z *add.* tertio Pet.   53 tutius *om.* Tc.   de² *om.* AaU.   quod] quia JZ.   54 ut¹ *om.* CkU. ut² *om.* Ck.   55 esse *om.* AaCcCiOP.   56 irrecuperabiliter] metu probabiliter Cc *corr. ab* metu probabiliter Ci.   quod] quid Ad.   57 et de maleficiato AcJTaZ.   58 Itaque — habilitas] Itaque legitimos personarum, consensus animorum et habilitas *insert. in lacunam* O.   corporis O.   59 impedit matrimonium *invers. add. aliam materiam* Pet *fol. 144ᵛ-148ʳ*.   61 impedit HJUZ *corr. ab* impedit Aa (impedit W).   etiam] autem Ac *om.* Pet.   62 cognatio *add.* sive RTa.   agnitio O (agnitio W) *om.* Tu.   63 tempus feriarum *insert. alia manu* O *add. et* Z.   63-64 (raptus — ecclesiae] interdictum ecclesiae tempus feriarum raptus Tb tempus feriarum raptus interdictum X).   tempus — ecclesiae *om.* AcCcCi(DEFIN) *insert.* Ad.   interdictum ecclesiae] ecclesiae interdictum Z (*om.* Cp). (64 ecclesiae *om.* Y).

[15] Cf. Po. 2836 (X 4.15.6; issued July 3, 1206); above Proleg. pp. 38-40; FIRTH, *Thesis* II 262*-263*, 319* n. 11 (III 623*-626*), 397*-399*.
[16] See HUG. *loc. cit.* (quoted above Proleg. p. 39); cf. above Proleg. pp. 38-40 and GRATIAN C.33 q.1 c.2.
[17] Cf. JL 14179 (X 4.15.3).
[18] Cf. RUFINUS, *Summa ad* C.27 pr. (ed. SINGER p. 433).

De voto 65

17 Votum est conceptio melioris boni, animi deliberatione firmata.[19] Licet alias aliter distinguatur votum, ad propositum sic sufficit distinguere votum: votum aliud simplex, aliud sollemne. Simplex est quod nullo extrinseco fulcitur adminiculo.[20]

De simplici voto 70

18 Vovere potest quaelibet persona quae sui juris est, et statim, ut puto, quando doli capax est. Persona quae alii subjecta est sine ejus consensu vovere non potest; ut monachus vovere non potest sine consensu sui abbatis, nec mulier sine consensu viri sui, nec filia quamdiu est in potestate sui patris sine ejus consensu; et fortasse servus sine consensu domini sui 75 non potest aliquid vovere in praejudicium domini sui.[21] Tamen quaelibet talis persona aliquod modicum habet proprium quod sine aliorum consensu potest vovere; ut mulier potest vovere quod non exiget a viro suo debitum.

Si aliqua dictarum personarum vel similium de consensu sui superioris 80 aliquid voverit, ille superior ratione inspecta potest illud revocare; ut si de consensu viri vovit aliquid mulier, vir potest ratione inspecta illud votum revocare et illa tenetur obedire. Idem est in monacho et abbate

66-67 Votum — distinguere votum *om.* Pet.   66 firmata *add.* Deo oblata Tc *add.* Deo oblata *insert.* O.   votum² *om.* TaTu.   68 votum *incipit* Q¹*.   68-69 intrinseco Tu exteriori Ta.   72 est² *om.* Cc.   73 vovere non potest² *om.* CkJZ *insert.* Aa. 74 sui *om.* Q¹*Tu.   quamdiu] quando H Pet.   74-75 quamdiu-consensu] nec consensu Cc sine consensu patris quamdiu est in potestate sua Q¹*.   75 sui¹ *om.* R *insert.* Aa.   fortasse] forte JQ¹*U *corr. ab* forte Aa.   sui²] Si enim *corr. ad* Servus enim O. 76 Tamen *add.* et O.   77 aliquid AaCkHJTaTcUZ Pet(CpLSoV) ad O(I).   modicum *om.* Q¹*Ta *insert.* Aa.   78 ut — vovere *om.* Tu *insert.* Ad (*homoeotel.*).   quod] ut OTu. exigat PTu.   80 Si *add.* autem O.   consimilium AaHJTcZ *add.* personarum Ab. de] sine U *corr. ad* sine Aa.   sui *om.* Tu Pet.   81 illud] istud Ci *add.* votum Aa. revocare *add.* votum CkJ.   81-83 ut si — revocare *om.* CkJ(D) *insert.* AaTc (*homoeotel.*). 82 de] sine TaU(GMSgSoX) *corr. ad* sine OP(Bm) *om.* AbAd.   voverit PZ Pet *corr. ab* vovet J.   ratione inspecta *om.* Tc Pet.   83 votum *om.* Cc.   in] de OTuU. et² *add.* in JR.

[19] Cf. Rufinus, *Summa* ad C.27 q.1 pr. (p. 435).
[20] Cf. *ibid.*; also Hug. ad C.27 q.1 pr. (fol. 282ʳᵃ).
[21] Cf. Alexander III (Roland Bandinelli) *Stroma* ad C.27 q.1 (ed. Thaner pp. 115-117).

suo;[22] de aliis non ita constat. Item vir potest revocare votum mulieris quod ipsa ante conjugium emisit. Ad hujus similitudinem dicunt aliqui 85 quod abbas potest revocare votum abstinentiae quod monachus emisit ante conversionem.[23]

19 Ita secundum aliquos votum uxoris revocat maritus, sive ante matrimonium emissum fuerit, ut Causa xxxiii. quaest. v. *Noluit*,[24] sive post matrimonium, ut Causa xxxiii. quaest. v. *Manifestum*,[25] etiam si de con- 90 sensu viri emissum fuerit, et etiam si votum fuerit continentiae.[26] Utique vir peccat si sine causa rationabili revocat uxoris votum; illa autem sine culpa est propter obedientiam.[27] Semper tamen captare debet opportunitatem ut votum servet, et hoc secundum quosdam; secundum alios non oportet; sed primum tutius est.[28] Si autem sollemniter vovisset vir 95 continentiam vel quod numquam debitum exigeret, fortasse non posset uxoris votum continentiae revocare.[29]

Alii aliter judicant de voto continentiae quia illud nulla ratione potest revocare vir si ejus consensu vovit uxor; quia consentiendo videtur et 99 ipse vovisse continentiam, vel perpetuam si sic vovit mulier, vel tempora-

---

84 ita est constat Cc *add.* est   *delet.* Ci.   85 commisit CkTu.   86 continentiae
Tc *corr. ab* contienentiae *forte manu originali* Aa.   88 Ita] Item PQ¹*Tu.   aliquos]
alios AaCcTu *corr. ab* alios Ci.   89 Noluit] Voluit CiRTu *corr. ab* voluit Ad Voluerit O
Voluntas Ta *om.* U.   90 Manifestam Ta *corr. ab* Maritum O *om.* U *add.* est JTc.
92 sine *insert.* Aa *rasura* Cc absque HU.   94 quosdam] alios AaCkHU.   alios] quosdam AaCkHU.   97 uxor J *corr. ab* uxor Aa.   98 quia] quod CkJPTu.   99 uxor]
mulier CkJU mulier *corr. attentat.* Aa.   et] etiam O.   99-1 quia — mulier *insert.* AaJ
(*homoeotel.*).   1 continentiam] continere Ad.

---

[22] Cf. GRATIAN C.20 q.4 c.2; HUG. ad C.33 q.5 c.16 *vovere* (fol. 344ᵛᵃ).

[23] Cf. HUG. ad C.20 q.4 c.2 *frangendum* (fol. 255ʳᵃ); *Apparatus: Ecce vicit Leo* ad C.33 q.5 c.16 *non persolvat* (St. Florian, Stiftsbibliothek MS XI. 605, fol. 114ᵛᵃ).

[24] This is a reference to GRATIAN, *Decretum* C.33 q.5 c.16. When such references are given in the text, the footnote will henceforth indicate only what is lacking or erroneous there. Thus this reference would be *Cap.* 16.

[25] Cap. 11.

[26] GRATIAN C.33 q.5 dictum p. c.20 and HUGUCCIO ad C.33 q.5 c.11 *nisi auctor* (fol. 344ʳᵃ) restrict this to *votum abstinentiae*, that is to a vow which does not involve deprivation of the act of intercourse. However a decretal of Alexander III (1 *Compil.* 3.28.1; JL 13946; X 3.32.1; cited by Flamborough below in sect. 22) and another of Celestine III (JL 16794; X 3.32.11; *Collectio seguntina* no. 95 *RevHistEccl* 50.445) might seem to imply that the same was true of *votum continentiae*.

[27] Cf. GRATIAN C.33 q.5 c.11; HUG. *loc. cit.*; these are speaking about *votum abstinentiae*.

[28] Sources not found.

[29] Cf. BERNARD OF PAVIA, *Summa decretalium* 3.28.2 (ed. LASPEYRES p. 112); also decretals cited above in n. 26.

lem si sic vovit. Si etiam votum peregrinationis concessit vir mulieri, si
moritur illa in peregrinatione, ex voto continere tenetur vir usque ad
tempus quod suffecisset mulieris peregrinationi.[30]

20 Sed dico: Quando petit mulier ut vir voto ejus consentiat, quod- 5
cumque illud sit, et vir consentit: aut vir simul se obligat cum muliere
eodem voto, et tunc non potest uxoris votum rcvocare, quodcumque
illud sit; aut sibi reservans jus suum servat se liberum a voto (ac si dicat
uxori: "Aliter non consentio ut voveas, nisi ut jus meum in te quando
voluero habeam et te ad libitum meum utar"), et tunc sine peccato illud 10
votum revocare potest et illa obedire tenetur; aut quasi brute et indis-
crete clausis oculis nescio quomodo consentit; tunc, ut credo, simul vovisse judicandus est, et tunc non potest revocare. Sic videtur mihi in
quolibet voto distinguendum.[31]

21 Revocatur etiam votum sollemne; ut, si vir vel mulier reliquo vel 15
invito vel ignorante claustrum intrat, a reliquo revocabitur; sed si super-
vixerit tenetur ad religionem.[32]

Similiter, si propter fornicationem alterius alter religionem intrat non
prius per judicium ecclesiae celebrato divortio, qui religionem intravit
a reliquo revocabitur, nisi ille qui intravit in continenti alterius adulterium 20
probare voluerit; tunc enim, ut credo, revocandus non est.[33]

---

3 moriatur O.   ex voto continere *om.* Tu.   continere] continentiae J *forte corr. ab*
continentiae Ad *om.* Q1*.   tenetur *insert.* Aa videtur O.   4 sufficeret Ck fecisset O.
mulieri J mulier Pet *corr. ad* mulier O.   mulieris peregrinationi] ad mulieris peregrinationem Ck.   peregrinationi *corr. ad* peregrinationem O *add.* continere Tu.   6 aut] ante
O.   7 uxoris] vir ejus AaCkHJUZ.   10 utar] uti possim O.   12 et *om.* U *insert.*
Ck.   12 oculis *add.* et Ad.   13 est *om.* CcCi.   15 vel2 *om.* AaCkTaTc.   17 religionem *add.* redire P *add.* convolare Ck *add.* revocatus scilicet *insert.* Ad.   20 a reliquo] ab
altero Ta.

---

[30] Cf. Hug. ad C.33 q.5 c.10 *sed similiter convertatur* (fol. 343vb).

[31] Cf. the following remark in a commentary on Gratian: ". . . extra. *De conversione conjugatorum* c.1 contra (1 *Compil.* 3.28.1 [?]) ubi dicitur quod potest revocari vir quamvis licentiam
uxor dederit. Sed in tali casu intelligitur quando uxor consensit ita: Volo quod sis monachus,
sed non continebo." *Apparatus: Ecce vicit Leo* ad C.33 q.5 c.3 *Mulier si sine licentia* (fol. 114va).
Cf. also JL 16794 (X 3.32.11; *Collectio seguntina* no. 95 *RevHistEccl* 50.445).

[32] Cf. Gratian C.27 q.2 cc.20, 21; Hug. ad C.27 q.2 c.21 *conjugii* (fol. 290ra-b, ed. Roman
pp. 775-776).

[33] Cf. Bernard of Pavia, *Summa decretalium* 3.28.1-2 (ed. Laspeyres p. 112); Hug. ad C.
27 q.2 c.21 *nec quondam* (fols. 289vb-290ra, ed. Roman pp. 772-773).

Item qui juravit se numquam debitum exacturum vel sollemniter continentiam vovit ñon potest allum revocare.[34]

22 Item, etsi de licentia uxoris intrans religionem monachis et sacerdote praesentibus vir in manus se dedit abbatis, sed episcopo ignorante, si mulier 25 nec perpetuam vovit continentiam nec cum viro religionem intravit, potest eum revocare episcopus, ut in decretali *Praeterea* in titulo *De conversione conjugatorum*.[35] Quod sic intelligo, quod episcopus potest et debet virum ad mulieris petitionem revocare si illa in ingressu viri protestata est se nolle continere.[36] Quod enim dicitur, quod votum sollemnizatur quando 30 aliquis se in manus dat abbatis, de solutis intelligitur personis, non de conjugatis; quia nec vir nec mulier sine episcopi auctoritate religionem intrare potest.[37] Unde iste conjugatus, qui sine auctoritate episcopi in manus se dedit abbatis, nihil fecit.

De sollemni voto   35

23 Votum tribus modis sollemnizatur: ordine, habitu et professione;[38] *ordine*, ut quando aliquis suscipit sacrum ordinem, ut subdiaconatum vel majorem; *habitu*, ut quando aliquis suscipit religionis habitum; *professione*, ut cum in praesentia episcopi praesente clero vovet aliqua continentiam

---

22 jurat Ac juraverat Aa juraverit JTuU.   23 voverit U.   24 etsi] si Tu *om*. Cc.
25 dederit HO Pet.   si mulier] similiter CcCiCkQ^{1}*Z *corr. ab* similiter HO similiter si mulier P.   26 nec^{1}] non RTa.   27 in^{1}] habetur in Ck *om*. O *add*. tali Tu.   decretali *add*. hac O.   29 in] ante Z *om*. Tu.   ingressum CiZ *corr. ab* ingressum O.
31 dat] dederit H *om*. CkTu.   solutis] subditis AaCkHJTu subditis *corr. ad* absolutis O.
32 conjugatis] subditis sive conjugatis Ac subditis sive de conjugatis R.   33 poterit
CkHJZ.   35 *tit*. De sollemnitate voti Ad.   voto *om*. AbO.   36 Votum *ss. desinit*
Q^{1}* *usque ad sect. 30*   et *om*. OPTa.   38 habitum O.   39 cum] quando Tu quae
Pet *add*. aliqua Z *corr. ad* qui Aa.   ut cum *corr. ab* qui O.   voverit O vovit HJTuZ.
aliquam AaCcCkJTcZ(BmDEGLMSgSoTbVY) *corr. ab* aliquam AbAcO(Cp) *corr. ad* aliquam
Ci aliam Tu *om*. Pet (aliqua *add*. mulier N).

---

[34] Cf. Bernard of Pavia, *loc. cit.*

[35] See 1 *Compil.* 3.28.1 (JL 13946; X 3.32.1); cf. above sect. 19 with notes.

[36] Cf. Hug. *loc. cit.* (in n. 33); *Apparatus: Ecce vicit Leo* ad D.32 c.14 *in vita* (fol. 15ra); ad C. 27 q.2 c.21 *ne forte ejus voluntate* (fol. 101rb).

[37] Cf. Gratian C.27 q.2 c.23; Bernard of Pavia, *Summa decretalium* 3.28.3 (p.113); below sect. 195 with n. 31.

[38] Cf. Bernard of Pavia, *Summa decretalium* 4.6.1-2 (pp. 149-150); Hug. ad D.27 pr. (fols. 31vb-32ra); *Glossa ordinaria in decretum* ad D.27 c.2 *post votum*; ad C.27 q.1 c.1 *sub testimonio*; Ludwig Hödl, "Die *lex continentiae*, Eine problemgeschichtliche Studie über den Zölibat", *ZKathTh* 83 (1961) 338-343; below sect. 195.

manens in saeculo, cujus vir intrat religionem. De cetero enim sic vovens, 40
licet manens in saeculo, propter voti sollemnitatem nubere non potest;
et hoc dico si perpetuam vovit continentiam. Si autem usque ad mortem
viri vovit, post mortem viri nubere potest.[39]

24 Similiter in praesentia abbatis et aliquot fratrum dat se aliquis religioni per verba de praescnti; licet habitum non mutet, illius abbatis jam 45
factus est monachus vel canonicus ac si in capitulo factum esset.[40] Plus
etiam dicitur in decretali quadam: Si ad infirmum aliquem vel alium
quemcumque mittitur unus aliquis monachus vel canonicus auctoritate
abbatis ut eum in monachum vel canonicum suscipiat, si eum recepit
per verba per quae solent recipi intrantes religionem, jam monachus ef- 50
fectus est.[41] In tantum sollemnizat votum auctoritas praelati, ut episcopi
vel abbatis vel prioris domus in qua non est abbas.

POENITENS. Numquid ita est in aliis praelatis?

SACERDOS. Non legi.

Ubi ergo nulla istarum intervenit sollemnitatum, votum est simplex.   55

25 Quidquid igitur vovisti, vel simpliciter vel sollemniter, redde; ut si
in facie ecclesiae cum aliqua contraxisti, licet ficte, vel habitum religionis
suscepisti, vel crucem per te privatim vel in populo publice portasti, ad
solutionem teneris; quia in talibus propter sollemnitatem plus est quod

---

44 Similiter *add.* si Z Pet. si dat Ta.   dat se aliquis] si aliquis se dat Ck.   44-45 ad
religionem OTu.   46 factum] fratrum AbAcCkTaTu(ELNTbY) *corr. attentat.* ad factus O
(factus CpV).   47 dicitur *insert.* O.   48 unus *om.* CkHJRTaUZ(BmCpEFGLMNSgSo-
TbV) *add.* scilicet Pet.   unus aliquis *insert.* (unus *delet.*) Aa.   unus aliquis monachus]
monachus aliquis muntius Tu.   aliquis *om.* JPUZ(CpKLSgV *om.* W) *add.* alius Tc.
49 suscipiat] recipiat AaTc (Sg) suscipiet Tu.   recepit] recipit AbCkHJOPRTaTcTuUZ
Pet(BmDEFILMNSoXY) receperit Ci(Tb reciperit Sg recipiat K suscipit V suscipiat Cp recipit W).   50 per[2] *om.* CkTa.   in religionem AaJOZ.   50-51 factus AaOPTaTu
Pet(KSgV).   51 votum *insert.* O.   ut] aut Ta vel J et Tu.   56 igitur] ergo
CcCiHJOPRTu(BmIKLSoV *om.* EG).

---

[39] Cf. 1 *Compil.* 3.28.8 (JL 13972; X 3.32.8); HUG. ad C.33 q.5 c.10 *sed similiter convertatur*
(fol. 343[vb]). Huguccio teaches that such a person must be requird to enter a monastery if he
or she is young, or at least to profess perpetual continence if more advanced in age. But if this
person, contrary to the law, should have professed continence only until the death of the marriage partner, then he or she may marry after that partner's death. Cf. below sect. 195.

[40] Cf. Po. 572 (X 3.31.13; issued January 11, 1199); cf. also decretals cited in the following
note.

[41] See Po. 502 (X 3.31.17; issued Dec. 23, 1198); cf. Po. 434 (X 3.31.16; issued Nov. 23,
1198); also decretal cited in the preceding note and FIRTH, *Thesis* II 394*-396*.

est in opinione quam quod est in rei veritate. Alioquin quilibet posset 60
deludere ecclesiam dicendo se hoc vel illud ficte fecisse.[42]

POENITENS. Unde habet hanc votum virtutem?

SACERDOS. Quia de jure est naturali, lege scilicet vel evangelio, dicente propheta: *Vovete et reddite*.[43] Contra legem autem vel evangelium
nemo dispensare potest; lex enim et evangelium ab ore Dei edita sunt. 65
Quis autem verba Dei irritare praesumet?[44]

26   Simplex tamen votum quod tibi est importabile potest tibi commutare episcopus tuus, et etiam quaedam sollemnia, ut peregrinationis. De
aliis sollemnibus consule papam ipsum. Jus etiam ipsum in quibusdam
dispensat; ut si intrasti religionem tibi importabilem, de licentia abbatis 70
tui et conventus intra leviorem.[45]

27   POENITENS. Si teneor adimplere simplex votum, quid dicit Augustinus quod votum simplex impedit matrimonium contrahendum et non
dirimit contractum?[46] Esto quod post votum simplex matrimonium cum
aliqua privatim solus cum sola contraxi; cui adhaerebo, voto an matri- 75
monio?

---

61 ficte *om.* J *insert.* CcCk *om.* jocando *insert.* Aa.   63 naturali] de natura *corr. ad* de naturali
O a naturali Z.   lege scilicet] et lege P lege Ta vel lege scilicet Tu.   (*post* evangelium
desinit D *usque ad lineam 49 in sect. 62 octo foliis perditis*).   64 reddite *add.* Domino AaU.
Contra] circa CcCi.   vel] et CkHJUZ Pet.   65 enim] autem OTu.   66 autem]
enim Tc Pet ergo R.   praesumeret O praesumat CkTaTuU praesumit *corr. ad* praesumet
Pet.   69 sollemnitatibus AbCkO Pet.   ipsum[2] *om.* AaJ.   72 quid] quod CkRTa.
73 quod] quid J *om.* Tu.   et] sed TuU *om.* J.   74 post votum *invers.* CcCi.
75 contraxerim Ck contraxerit Tu.

[42] Cf. HUG. ad D.27 c.6 (fols. 32vb-33ra); *Glossa ordinaria in Decretum* ad D.27 c.6 *et finxit*;
FIRTH, *Thesis* II 474*-493*. Cf. also James A. BRUNDAGE, "Cruce Signari": The Rite for Taking
the Cross in England," *Traditio* 22 (1966) 289-310 (esp. 289).

[43] *Ps* 75.12; cf. *Qoheleth* (*Eccles*) 5.3-4; *Deut* 23.21-23. Regarding this view of "Natural law"
cf. GRATIAN D.1 pr.; HUG. ad D.27 pr. (fol. 32va); Gabriel LE BRAS, Ch. LEFEBVRE and J. RAM-
BAUD, *L'âge classique 1140-1378, Sources et théorie du droit* (Histoire de droit et des institutions de
l'Eglise en Occident 7) pp. 367-379, 564-565; Ricarda WINTERSWYL, "Das neue Recht, Untersuchungen zur frühmittelalterlichen Rechtsphilosophie", *Historisches Jahrbuch* 81 (1962) 58-79.

[44] Cf. GRATIAN D.9 dictum p. c.11; D.13 pr.; Joseph BRYS, *De dispensatione in jure canonico* pp. 126-131, 209-213.

[45] Cf. 1 *Compil.* 3.27.1 (JL 13972) *ibid.* c.2 (JL 13849; X 3.31.7).

[46] Cf. GRATIAN D.27 c.2, dictum p. c.8; C.27 q.1 c.41; Anton SCHARNAGL, *Das feierliche Gelübde* pp. 52, 106-164; AUGUSTINE, *De bono viduitatis* cc. 9-10 (nos. 12-13; CorpusScrEccLat 41.
317-320; Pl. 40, 437-438).

SACERDOS. Fere omnes dicunt quod matrimonio, tum propter auctoritatem Augustini, tum quadam subtilitate juris. Verbi gratia, unam et eandem rem duobus promisi, sed uni tantum eorum eam tradidi; ejus erit res. A simili, promisi me Deo et mulieri, sed mulieri tradidi me; 80 ideo ejus ero.

28 Non nulli aliter dicunt, quorum opinio mihi placet, quia subtilitas illa juris quae contra nos inducitur pro nobis facere videtur; quia, statim cum voveo Deo continentiam, obligo me et trado Deo; ergo ejus ero potius quam mulieris cum qua postea contraho. Augustinus ergo, ut dicimus, 85 voluit ut simplex votum impediret matrimonium quodcumque contrahendum et non dirimeret contractum, supple "solemniter"; quod verum est, quia sola sollemnitas voti hoc facere potest. Vel forte votum simplex vocavit Augustinus sponsionem de futuro, quae utique nullum matrimonium dirimit.[47] 90

Si ergo post votum simplex cum aliqua contraxisti vel publice vel privatim, et exigere potes et reddere secundum primam opinionem; secundum secundam, quae tutior videtur, numquam exigas nec reddas; immo ante permittas te excommunicari secundum quosdam, quibus in hoc consentio.[48] Ego in tali casu consulerem ut, si obtinere posses a muliere 95 licentiam, religionem intrares vel aliter eam pie deluderes; quia non est matrimonium inter te et eam.

---

77 tum] tamen Cc *om.* R.   78 tum] tamen R *om.* Cc.   quadam subtilitate] propter quandam subtilitatem P propter (*delet.*) quadam subtilitate Tc propter quandam subtilitate Tu quadam sollemnitate Pet.   juris *om.* Cc.   79 eam *om.* R insert. Aa.   ejus *add.* ergo Ck *add. et* Aa.   80 erit *corr. ad* eadem Aa *add.* eadem Tu.   81 ideo] ergo U nonne Aa.   82 aliter] autem P Pet.   85 diximus CkHJPTcZ Pet(BmCpFGIKLMNSgSoTbVX) *corr. ab* diximus Ci *corr. ad* diximus U dicens *vel* Dominus Cc (dicimus W). ut dicimus *om.* Tu *cum additione inserta* ut dicens *vel ut* Dominus Aa.   89 vocat CkHJU-(CpIVX) *corr. ab* vocat Aa (vocat W).   utique *add.* sponsio AaHJUZ.   91 Si] Sic Ta. aliqua] qua OTaTu.   contraxi RTa.   vel[1] *om.* AaHJU.   92 et[1] *om.* AcP. potest Ta potero R.   93 nec] neque Z numquam Pet.   94 ante] etiam AaCkHU *add. ante insert.* Aa autem Ci.   te *om.* OTu *insert.* Aa.   quibus] quibusdam Tu. in hoc] non Ck.   (in hoc non consentio... X *vide supra in Proleg. ad p. 51 una cum n. 59*). 95 Ego *add.* itaque Ac.   consulem CkJ *insert.* Aa.   possis CkHJ *corr. ab* possis Aa. 96 licentiam] bonam O *om.* Ta *delet.* Ab.   96 intres CkH.

---

[47] Cf. HUG. ad C.27 q.1 pr. (fol. 282[ra-b]); ad C.27 q.1 c.41 *Nuptiarum* (fol. 285[va]); ad C.17 q.2 c.2 *Nos novimus* (fol. 244[va]). Huguccio interprets *votum simplex* as *votum de futuro*. See also following note.

[48] See Robert COURSON, *Summa* 21.10 (Paris, BN lat. 14524, fols. 81[ra]-82[ra]); cf. above Proleg. p. 41 with nn. 13-14; also FIRTH, *Thesis* I 161*-162*, 177*-178*, 215*-217*, II 250*-251*, 405*-409*, 462*-463*, 487*-488*.

29 POENITENS. Nonne frequenter cum subdiacono dispensat papa ut matrimonium contrahat ?[49] Ergo vel dispensat contra votum sollemne, oo quod videtur contra rationem, vel ad minus vera est illa opinio quae dicit quod votum simplex nullum dirimit matrimonium.

SACERDOS. Utique aliquis illorum qui hoc dicunt, legens Parisius in decretis, concessit mihi quod etiam cum sacerdote posset papa dispensare ut contraheret matrimonium, eadem ratione cum abbate cisterciensi; 5 et hac ratione quia votum, inquantum est votum, non dirimit matrimonium, sed hoc habet ex sui sollemnitate,[50] et hoc contulit sollemnitati institutio ecclesiae. Sed, quod instituit ecclesia, hoc potest destruere; ergo hoc potest papa, cui contulit ecclesia plenitudinem potestatis,[51] scilicet hoc auferre sollemnitati voti, vel generaliter si vellet, vel personaliter, 10 ut fit in subdiacono qui matrimonium contrahit.[52] Sed, salva sit papae reverentia, quod dixi tutius videtur.

30 POENITENS. Si bene memini, dixisti quod episcopus potest commutare votum aliquod, et papa similiter, sed non dispensare contra aliquod, id est ex toto irritum facere.[53] Dic quaeso quod votum est commutabile, 15 quod non.

SACERDOS. Dicunt quod illud votum est commutabile quo aliquid melius, vel cui aliquid par vel aequale, inveniri potest; ubi vero neutrum

98-22 Sects. 29-30 abbrev. Pet.   99 contrahatur Tu.   vel] ibi Tu om. Aa.   1 videtur add. fieri CkHJPUZ add. vel O.   illa] mea O.   est illa] ipsa Tu.   2 nullum] non AaCkHJTuUZ.   3 illorum] eorum OPTc.   Parisius] parum AaCcCiJPTcU. 4 possit CkHJ corr. ab possit Aa.   5 contrahet Ck contraret Ci.   eadem ratione] vel O.   6 quia] quod JR.   est om. AaRTc.   8 potest] poterit Ta corr. ab possunt O.   9 potest om. AaHJZ.   9-10 scilicet] sed Ta om. Ck.   10 hoc om. O. personaliter] specialiter personaliter Ck corr. ab specialiter Tc.   11 fit] sit AdOR. sit] sic P om. TcTu.   13 POENITENS reincipit Q1*.   memini add. quod HR.   14 et om. Cc.   15 facere add. POENITENS AbPTaZ add. POENITENS insert. Aa.   18 cui om. O corr. ab in Aa.   aliquid] aliquod TcTuZ(CpFMXY) aliud AaH(BmSg) a^d AdQ1*TaU aliud vel Ck alicui O aut CcCi (om. L).   vel2] et P om. Cc.   invenire AbJ.

[49] See 1 Compil. 4.6.3, 4, 5 (JL 13904, 13983, 14101); ROBERT COURSON, Summa 23.3 (quoted by John W. BALDWIN, "A Campaign to Reduce Clerical Celibacy at the Turn of the Twelfth and Thirteenth Centuries", Études d'histoire du droit canonique dédiées à Gabriel Le Bras II 1051-52; cf. ibid. II 1045-47, 1050-53).

[50] Regarding this theory see SIMON OF BISIGNANO, Summa decretorum ad C.27 q.1 pr.

[51] Regarding this plenitude of power cf. HUG. ad D.4 dictum p. c.3 (fol. 5ra; partly quoted by Brian TIERNEY, Foundations of the Conciliar Theory p. 145 n. 2); cf. TIERNEY, op. cit. pp. 141-148. The plenitude is sometimes mentioned in papal letters, e.g. Po. 83 (Reg. 1.89 PL 214.77; issued April 17, 1198).

[52] This discussion corresponds rather closely with one found in HUG. ad C.27 q.1 c.2 velatae (fol. 282va-b); cf. FIRTH, Thesis II 462*-463*.

[53] See above sects. 25-26.

invenitur, est incommutabile. Verbi gratia, voto peregrinationis et abstinentiae aliquid melius inveniri potest; unde commutabilia sunt. Voto 20
continentiae et religionis nihil aequale vel majus invenitur; unde commutari non possunt.[54]

31 Ita de voto dictum sit; sequitur ut de ordine dicamus et habitu.

De ordine et habitu

Ordo et habitus impediunt matrimonium et dirimunt; quia, si ordi- 25
nem sacrum vel habitum religionis assumpsisti tibi publice, licet ficte,
praejudicabitur tibi ne possis contrahere, et si contraxeris dirimetur matrimonium; alioquin posset illudi ecclesiae.[55]

32 Tamen, si tantum ad probandum intrasti religionem, scilicet non
praemisso voto religionis cum proposito manendi in ea, toto tempore 30
probationis potes redire ad saeculum; quia, licet publice habitum religionis suscepisti, tamen publice protestatus es quod non voto monachandi,
sed tantum proposito probationis, illum suscepisti. Si autem votum religionis emisisti postquam fueris ingressus religionem, non exibis.[56]

---

19 est om. J insert. Aa.   commutabile RTu.   et] vel AdQ¹* om RTc.   21 ma-
jus] magis AaCk melius O.   23 Ita ss. desinit Q¹* usque ad lineam 48 in sect. 44, interpo-
latis aliis sectionibus ut suis locis notabitur.   Ita add. demum CkHJUZ(CpIKVX add. deinde
Sg Cum ita L) add. demum corr. ad dictum est Aa.   de — sit] demum (dictum insert.) sit
P dictum de voto sit AdCc (dictum est de voto quid sit F demum de voto sit I).   sit] est
TcTu(GTb om. So).   dictum sit] sit dicendum H sic dictum U sic dictum est J(V) sit dictum
delet. et iterum insert. Aa add. demum R(N) add. demum vel deinde insert. Ac (add. deinde ESgTbY
add. demum vel deinde M).   ut add. deinde Ck.   Ita — habitu om. Pet.   sequitur
— habitu om. (unum vel duo vocabula illegibilia insert.) O.   et habitu] et de habitu U om. AbHJP
insert. Aa.   26 vel] et PR.   tibi] ubi H om. Pet.   tibi — ficte] licet ficte et publice
JU licet ficte tamen publice Z licet ficte publice tibi Ck corr. ab licet tibi ficte et publice Aa.
27 tibi om. H insert. Ci.   (possent Sg).   illudere Cc deludi Tu illud J corr. ab illud Ci.
28 ecclesia JRTcTuUZ(BmCpFGILMNSoV ecclesia assidue W) ecclesiam Cc.

---

[54] Cf. Apparatus: Ecce vicit Leo ad C.27 q.1 c.21 Proposito meliore (fol. 99ᵛᵇ quoted in FIRTH,
Thesis II 378*); also JL 13848 (X 3.34.4).

[55] Cf. above sects. 16, 23 and 25 with notes; HUG. ad D.27 c.6 se sub (fols. 32ᵛᵇ-33ʳᵃ).

[56] Cf. HUG. ad C.20 q.1 pr. (fol. 253ʳᵃ); 1 Compil. 3.27.9 (JL 13946; X 3.31.9); Po. 2209
(X 3.31.20, issued May 15, 1204); Po. 3265 (Reg. 10.186 PL 215.1281C; issued Jan. 9,
1208).

33 Item propria voluntate intrasti monasterium in minori aetate; cum 35
veneris ad annum quintum decimum, stabitur arbitrio tuo ut maneas
vel recedas.[57]

Si in minori aetate, sed doli capax, quod fit in anno septimo, traditus
fuisti a parentibus monasterio et consensisti, numquam exibis; si non consensisti, in anno quinto decimo stabitur arbitrio tuo ut maneas vel non. 40
Hoc est verum de masculo; quia mulier in anno duodecimo ad arbitrium
suum vel manebit vel recedet.[58] Secundum Caelestinum et secundum
alios, si in minori aetate traditus es a parentibus monasterio, capax doli
vel non, consentiens vel non, sed habitum et tonsuram suscepisti, numquam exibis; quia monachum facit vel propria devotio vel paterna tra- 45
ditio.[59]

34 Si subito et sine probatione factus es monachus, secundum Alexan-
drum, ut dicunt, potes infra triduum redire ad saeculum;[60] non tamen
est tutum, nec post instans, ut credo.[61]

De cultu dispari   50

35 Dispar cultus impedit et dirimit matrimonium; ut si fidelis contrahat

---

38 Si] sed AaJ.   sed] vel Pet *om.* Ta.   40 quindecimo OR.   arbitrio] judicio
O in judicio Tc Pet.   ut] vel O.   42 vel[1] *om.* HTa.   secundum[2] *insert.* O.
43 in *om.* CcCi.   44 non[1] *om.* PTu delet. HO.   consentiens vel non *om.* Z *insert.* H.
sed *om.* Cc corr. *ab* se Ci.   accepisti Aa.   45 vel[1] *om.* AaCkHJ.   45-46 traditio
add. quia jam consensisse videris P *add. idem insert.* Ac.   48 infra] in Cc corr. *ab* in Ci.
49 post *corr. ab* potest Aa.   post instans] potest stare Tu.

---

[57] Cf. GRATIAN C.20 q.1 c.10; HUG. *loc. cit.* (fol. 253[ra-b]; cf. Paris BN lat. 3891, fol. 218[va]);
1 *Compil.* 3.27.11 (JL 10604; X 3.31.11).

[58] Cf. BERNARD OF PAVIA, *Summa decretalium* 3.27.8 (pp. 109-110); ALEXANDER III (Roland
Bandinelli) *Stroma* ad C.20 q.1 (p. 71); SIMON OF BISIGNANO, *Summa* ad C.20 q.1 pr.

[59] Regarding Celestine III see JL 16637 (X 3.31.12). Good evidence that this is a decretal of
Celestine is presented by Walther HOLTZMANN, "La 'Collectio seguntina' et les décrétales de
Clément III et de Célestin III", *RevHistEccl* 50 (1955) 400-421 (esp. 417) 436 no. 59. Celestine quotes *Monachum facit . . . paterna traditio* as partial basis for his solution of the case, implying
however that personal consent of the religious is also necessary (cf. FIRTH, *Thesis* II 387*-393*).
These nuances seem to have escaped Robert; he apparently takes the decretal for a rigid application of the old maxim. In fact this is the position which he himself prefers; see below sect.
54. Regarding *alios* see GRATIAN C.20 q.1 c.3 dictum p. c.8; 1 *Compil.* 3.27.11 (JL 10604; X
3.31.11).

[60] See 1 *Compil.* 3.27.8 (JL 13854; X 3.31.8).

[61] See ". . . quod tamen ego non credo etiam post unam horam." HUG. ad C.17 q.1 c.1 (fol.
244[rb-va]).

cum infideli, non est matrimonium, ut dicunt.[62] Unde Esdras separavit
filios Israel a babyloniis cum quibus contraxerant; quod non fecisset si
fuisset ibi matrimonium.[63]

36 Inter infideles autem est matrimonium, sed non ratum.[64] Unde, 55
si tu conversus es et illa non vult converti, sed tantum commanere, non
potes ea sic vivente aliam ducere. Si autem discedit in odium christia-
nitatis, ducas aliam si vis; et ideo non est ratum matrimonium infide-
lium.[65] Hoc autem intelligendum est de illis qui contraxerunt in infide-
litate; quia si fideles contraxerunt et alter apostatat, et tamen non vult 60
manere nisi blasphemans, vel forte discedere vult, non potest remanens
fidelis cum alia contrahere vivente prima, quia ratum fuit matrimonium.[66]

In solis judaeis aliter est; quia, quidquid sit, neuter reliquum potest
retinere nisi ambo convertantur.[67] Solutum est ergo matrimonium; licet
quidam dicant quod non, et male, ut videtur, quia sic cogeretur quis invi- 65
tus continere.[68]

De errore personae

37 Error personae impedit et dirimit matrimonium; ut voluisti contrahere cum Berta et supposita est tibi Teberga; non est matrimonium,
nisi postea consenseris in Tebergam.[69]   70

---

53 contraxerunt Aa ipsi contraxerunt Tu.   56 tantum] tamen PRTaTcTu.   tantum
commanere] tamen tecum manere Pet.   57 discedat AdTc Pet discessit Tu cedit P om.
Ta.   59 intelligendum est] intelligi debet O intellige Tu.   63 sit] fit AaCkZ.
reliquum] neutrum O relictum Tu alterum Pet.   64 obtinere HJUZ corr. ab obtinere Aa
remanere corr. ad obtinere Ck.   est insert. O.   Solutum est] solvitur Tu solveret Cc.
65-66 invite RZ maritus O.   69 Teberta HTc.   70 consentias Aa consentis Tc.
Thebertam Tc Tebertam H.

[62] Cf. GRATIAN C.28 q.1 dictum p. c.14.
[63] See Ezra (1 Esdras) 10.11; GRATIAN C.28 q.1 pr.
[64] Cf. GRATIAN C.28 q.1 dictum p. c.17; Po. 684 (X 4.19.7; issued May 1, 1199); Joseph
J. MUZAS, "The Concept of Matrimonium ratum in Gratian and the Early Decretists", (unpublished thesis; Washington 1964); Dissertation Abstracts 26 (1965-66) 2229.
[65] Cf. GRATIAN C.28 q.2 dictum p. c.2; JL 16595 (2 Compil. 3.20.1; Collectio seguntina no.
25 RevHistEccl 50.427; Clement III); Po. 684 (X 4.19.7); Franz GILLMANN, "Zur Geschichte
der kanonischen Ehescheidung", Katholik[3] 29 (1904)[1] 191-212, esp. 205 n. 1.
[66] Cf. GRATIAN ibid.; Po. 684 (ibid.).
[67] Cf. GRATIAN C.28 q.1 c.10.
[68] See HUG. ad C.28 q.1 dictum p. c.10 perditionem (fol. 295[vb]; quoted in FIRTH, Thesis I
172* n. 45 [III 556*-557*]); he cites Cardinalis as holding that the marriage is not dissolved.
Cf. JL 16595 (2 Compil. 3.20.1; cf. above in n. 65).
[69] Cf. GRATIAN C.29 q.1 §2, §3.

Item error conditionis impedit et dirimit matrimonium; ut voluisti contrahere cum libera et comperta est esse ancilla, non est matrimonium, nisi postquam hoc scivisti accessisti ad eam.[70]

Alius error, ut virginitatis, paupertatis, pulchritudinis, non nocet matrimonio.[71]   75

De cognatione

38 Cognatio impedit et dirimit matrimonium, sed in linea ascendente vel descendente, quae eadem est, in infinitum; quia, si hodie viveret Adam, cum nulla posset contrahere.[72] In linea transversa etiam in septimo gradu dirimitur matrimonium; dispensari tamen potest, sed a solo papa, et 80 tantum ultra tertium gradum;[73] quia in lege inhibetur contractus in primo et secundo et tertio gradu;[74] papa autem contra legem vel evangelium, ut superius dictum est, dispensare non potest.[75]

De agnatione

39 Agnatio, immo potius affinitas, impedit et dirimit matrimonium.   85
Sunt autem tria genera affinitatis. Primum genus hoc modo dinoscitur:

---

71 ut *add. si* RTa Pet.   72 est¹ *insert.* O.   esse] tibi Ck *op.* Aa.   73 accesti Ci *corr. ab* accesti Tc.   74 ut *om.* Cc.   74-75 matrimonio *om.* Tu.   77 sed] si TaTc quia Tu *corr. ab* sit Ab *add.* non AaJZ.   78 vel descendente *om.* Tu Pet *insert.* Tc.   hodie *om.* O. 79 linea *add.* vero O.   etiam] et AaR Pet *om.* O.   80 dirimit Cc.   82 et tertio] in tertio Cc et in tertio U tertioque AaHJZ vel tertio R.   vel] et PTuU.   85-24 Agnatio — affinitate *una cum alia materia substituta et interpolata* Pet *fol. 161ʳ⁻ᵛ*.   84 agnatione *add.* et affinitate Cc.   85 Cognatio JTu.   potius] etiam PTu.   85-87 *alibi derivatum* Pet.   86 autem *om.* AcCk.

---

[70] Cf. GRATIAN C.29 q.2 dictum p. c.3, c.4; HUG. ad C.29 q.2 c.5 *sciens* (fol. 298ᵛᵃ⁻ᵇ); 1 *Compil.* 4.9.2 (JL 14021; X 4.9.2); Jean GAUDEMET, "Droit canonique et droit romain: A propos de l'erreur sur la personne en matière de mariage (C.XXIX, qu.1)", *Studia Gratiana* 9.45-64.

[71] Cf. GRATIAN C.29 q.1 §5; GAUDEMET *loc. cit.*

[72] Cf. HUG. ad C.35 qq.2-3 pr. (fol. 347ʳᵃ).

[73] Cf. HUG. ad C.35 q.8 pr. (fol. 354ʳᵇ). In this, as in several other texts of his penitential, Robert seems to be indicating the number of degrees according to the method of computation used in Roman law; see above Proleg. p. 43 with n. 25; cf. FIRTH, *Thesis* II 365*-373*. Regarding consanguinity and affinity as impediments at this time cf. M. VERBAARSCHOT, "De natura iuridica impedimenti consanguinitatis", *Ephemerides theologicae Lovanienses* 30 (1954) 697-739; John W. BALDWIN, "Critics of the Legal Profession: Peter the Chanter and his Circle," *Proceedings of the Second International Congress of Medieval Canon Law* pp. 249-259.

[74] Cf. *Lev* 18.6-18; 20.17, 19; also preceding note.

[75] See above sect. 25.

omnes consanguineae uxoris tuae tibi sunt affines in primo genere. Et
habet septem gradus sicut consanguinitas, quos hoc modo dinosces: in
quoto gradu consanguinitatis est aliqua uxori tuae, in toto gradu primi
generis affinitatis est ipsa tibi; ut soror uxoris tuae est tibi in primo gradu 90
primi generis affinitatis. Quantum ad matrimonium contrahendum et
dirimendum et dispensandum, in eis aequis passibus currunt consanguinitas et primum genus affinitatis,[76] sed non quantum ad poenitentiam; plus
enim puniam illum qui accessit ad sororem suam, quam illum qui ad
duas sorores accessit. 95

40 Secundum genus affinitatis nascitur ex primo hoc modo: si affini tuo
in primo genere jungatur persona per carnis copulam, erit tibi affinis in
secundo genere, ut uxor fratris uxoris tuae. Et durat istud genus usque
ad quintum gradum eodem modo judicandum ut primum; "usque" dico 99
exclusive. Gradus dinoscuntur hoc modo per primum genus: in quoto
gradu est aliquis tibi affinis in primo genere, in toto gradu secundi generis est tibi affinis persona illi juncta per carnis copulam; ut frater uxoris
tuae est tibi in primo primi; ergo ejus uxor est tibi in primo secundi.[77]

Tertium genus nascitur ex secundo hoc modo: aliquis est tibi affinis 5
in secundo genere; ergo persona illi juncta per carnis copulam est tibi affinis
in tertio genere. De isto genere judicandum est per omnia sicut et de
aliis usque ad secundum gradum; "usque" dico inclusive. Gradus istius
sic dinoscuntur: in quoto gradu est tibi aliquis in secundo genere, in toto
tertii est tibi persona illi personae juncta per carnis copulam.[78] 10

87 consanguineae *corr. ad* consanguines J *corr ab* consanguines Aa. 88 dinoscetur O.
89 quoto] quarto CcCkPTa *corr. ab* quarto Aa quo J. consanguinitas Aa *om.* RTa.
uxoris J *corr. ab* uxoris O. tuae *add.* consanguinea CkH. 91 contrahendum et *om.*
Ta. et *om.* Z. 92 in is *om.* OPTu. 98 genus *add.* exclusive Z. 99 pri-
mum] prius AaJ. 1 dinoscitur AaJRTaTuUZ dinoscatur Ck. primum *sic omnes MSS*
(*omnes*) *vide* FIRTH, *Thesis II 263*-264**. quoto] quarto CkPTaTu quotu Ci quarto
corr. ad quanto vel quoto J quinto Tc. 2 in primo genere *delet.* Ci. in²] vel
Cc *corr. ab* vel Ci. 3 illi] illa Cc. 4 tibi¹ *add.* affinis PTu. primo¹ *add.* gradu
PRTaU. primi *add.* generis JRU. 6 ergo *om.* OTu. 7 est *om.* RTa.
et *om.* AdCcCkHJRTuUZ(EFGISgTbXY) *insert. post* de Aa. 9 dinoscitur J Pet di-
noscantur Ta. quoto] quarto CkTa quarto *corr. ad* quanto vel quoto J. tibi *om.* O.
10 personae *om.* RU *insert.* Ad.

[76] Cf. Hug. ad C.35 qq.2-3 pr. (fols. 346ᵛᵇ-347ʳᵇ); RUFINUS, *Summa, ad eundum locum* (pp.
512-513); STEPHEN OF TOURNAI, *Summa, ad eundum locum* (ed. Johann F. VON SCHULTE pp. 250-
251); GRATIAN C.35 qq.2-3 dictum p. c.21.
[77] Cf. Hug. *ibid.* (fol. 347ʳᵃ); RUFINUS *ibid.* (pp. 513-515); STEPHEN *ibid.* (p. 251); below
sect. 225 with nn. 52-53.
[78] Cf. Hug. *loc. cit.*; RUFINUS *loc. cit.*; STEPHEN *ibid.* (p. 250).

41   Ista genera docet haec regula: Persona apposita personae per carnis copulam mutat genus, non gradum; ut fratri uxoris tuae appone per sonam per carnis copulam et da ei uxorem, quae erit tibi in secundo genere; cui si apposueris personam per carnis copulam, erit tibi in tertio genere.[79] Et vide quod ex parte appositionis attenditur omnis affinitas; 15 verbi gratia, ex parte uxoris tuae judicavimus omnem affinitatem tuam. Tuus enim filius potest contrahere cum filia uxoris tuae.[80]

Item gradus in quolibet genere docet haec regula: Persona apposita personae per carnis propagationem mutat gradum et non genus; ut uxori fratris uxoris tuae appone personam per carnis propagationem ut sit ejus 20 filia, et erit tibi in secundo gradu secundi generis. Ista duo genera affinitatis vix servat ecclesia.[81]

42   Propter multam intricationem quae hic invenitur in consanguinitate et affinitate, necessarium est hic arborem consanguinitatis et affinitatis prae oculis ac manibus habere; cujus arboris picturam in fine libri ap- 25 ponemus.[82]

De cognatione spirituali

43   Cognatio etiam spiritualis impedit et dirimit matrimonium. Septem igitur sacramentalia, non dico sacramenta, sunt in baptismo.[83] Primum est pabulum salis. Secundum est aurium et narium sputo linitio. 30 Tertium est in ecclesiam introductio secundum quosdam,[84] vel melius in fronte et pectore crucis signatio. Quartum est olei sacri perunctio. Quin-

---

12 genus *add.* et CkR *add.* et *insert.* Ad.   16 judicamus TaTcTu ut judicamus O.
18 apposita] addita RTc.   21 tibi *om.* O.   24 hic *om.* CiJUZ.   24-26 necessarium
— apponemus *om.* Pet.   29 igitur *om.* Ta *eras.* Aa.   30 salis] salutis CkTu.   est²
om. AaCkRTuUZ.   32 et in pectore HJ.

[79] Cf. Hug. *ibid.* (fol. 346vb); Rufinus *ibid.* (p. 515); Stephen *ibid.* (p. 250).

[80] Cf. Hug. *ibid.* (fol. 347ra-b); Huguccio comes to the same conclusion from the opposite formula: *Gradus affinitatis computatur ex parte consanguinitatis et non ex parte appositionis.* Cf. also Po. 919 (X 4.14.5; issued Dec. 31, 1199).

[81] Cf. Hug. *ibid.* (fol. 347ra); Rufinus *ibid.* (p. 515); Stephen *ibid.* (pp. 250-251); Baldwin *loc. cit.* (above in n. 73).

[82] Two tables or diagrams, one of consanguinity and one of affinity, are found in Ac after this penitential and its appendix; see above Proleg. p. 21.

[83] Cf. Hug. ad C.30 q.1 c.1 *septem dona baptismi* (fol. 299va-b); Rufinus *ad eundem locum* (p. 461); Firth, *Thesis* II 377* n. 83 (III 660*).

[84] Cf. Gratian C.30 q.1 c.1; Alexander III (Roland Bandinelli) *ad eundem locum* (p. 145).

tum est aquae ablutio. Sextum est chrismatis in vertice perunctio. Septimum est ejusdem facta in fronte consummatio. Quae omnia et singula creant spiritualem cognationem et impediunt et dirimunt matrimonium;[85] 35 quia potius in singulis diversi debent ministrare patrini quam aliqui in omnibus.[86]

44 Unam solam filiam meam suscepisti de sacro fonte; illam nullus filius tuus potest habere; sed quamlibet aliam filiam meam potest quilibet filius tuus habere.[87] Dicunt tamen quidam quod filiolam meam potest 40 filius meus ante compaternitatem natus habere in uxorem, sed errant.[88] Idem dico de illa quam tenuisti ad confirmationem.[89]

Uxor tua suscepit filium Petri de sacro fonte; mediante uxore tua factus es compater Petri. Si mortua uxore tua Petrus contrahat cum alia, illius non eris compater; quia compaternitas non transit in tertiam 45 personam. Sed mortuo Petro non potes ejus uxorem ducere, quia tua commater est.[90]

Aliqui dicunt commatres esse illas quae filium alicujus simul de sacro fonte suscipiunt; quod non credo, quia unam post aliam potest quis ducere.[91] 50

33 est² *om.* AbP Pet.   34 est *om.* Tu.   consummatio] confirmatio AdOP(BmK Q¹Q² GRATIAN HUG.) consignatio Pet.   36 aliquis O.   38 illam] eam OTcTu Pet.   39 quilibet *om.* JRZ.   41 meus] tuus AbTu *corr. ab* tuus O.   41-42 errant Idem] erratum quidem Tu.   42 Idem *add.* enim O.   42 de illa] de ea *insert.* O.   44 es] est O *corr. ab* est Ci.   Petri *add.* quia tu et uxor tua effecti estis una caro sed Tc *add.* sed si postea tu et uxor tua facti estis una caro *insert.* O.   mortua *add.* Petrus J.   tua] Petri RTu sua H Pet.
48 Item aliqui O.   Aliqui *usque ad finem sectionis 55* Q¹* *in variis partibus foliorum 332ʳ-33ʳ.*

[85] Cf. RUFINUS, *Summa, ad eundem locum* (p. 461); HUG. *loc. cit.*; FIRTH, *Thesis* II 377* n. 83 (III 660*).

[86] Cf. GRATIAN, *De consec.* D.4 c.100.

[87] Perhaps Flamborough has misunderstood the opinion usually cited in this context. According to it, brothers and sisters of the baptized person born before the baptism might marry the natural children of the god-parent, but not those born afterwards. That distinction is rejected by most authors; they declare that all of the brothers and sisters of the baptized person may enter such a marriage, but not the baptized person himself. See e.g. HUG. ad C.30 q.3 c.5 (fol. 302ʳᵃ); RUFINUS, *Summa* ad C.30 q.3 c.4 (pp. 463-464).

[88] Cf. RUFINUS, *loc. cit.*; GANDULF OF BOLOGNA, *Sententiarum libri quatuor* 4.294 (ed. WALTER pp. 564-565). Like Flamborough, these authors mention this opinion without accepting it.

[89] Cf. RUFINUS, *Summa* ad C.30 q.3 pr. (p. 463).

[90] Cf. RUFINUS, *Summa* ad C.30 q.4 pr. (pp. 464-465).

[91] Cf. STEPHEN OF TOURNAI, *Summa* ad C.30 q.4 pr. (p. 243); Franz GILLMANN, "Das Ehehindernis der gegenseitigen geistlichen Verwandtschaft der Paten?" *ArchivKKRecht* 86 (1906) 688-714 (also publ. separately); IDEM, "Das Ehehindernis der gegenseitigen geistlichen Verwandtschaft der Paten bei Simon von Bisiniano," *ArchivKKRecht* 88 (1908) 556.

45 Item uxor mea Mathilda facta est commater Bertae, cujus filium de baptismo suscepit. Si post illam compaternitatem factus sum una caro cum uxore mea, non possum ducere Bertam mortuis ejus viro et uxore mea; alioquin potero Bertam ducere illis mortuis. Sic sentit Gratianus.[92] Huguccio sic: Si compaternitas praecedit carnalem copulam, licite potest 55 habere duas commatres, unam post aliam; aliter si sequitur. Verbi gratia, Martinus et ejus uxor Maria suscipiunt filium Bertae, vel illa illorum filium; Martinus numquam poterit ducere Bertam. Sed si Berta suscepit filium Mariae non de Martino genitum, Berta potest Martino copulari post Mariam vel ante.[93] Nihil enim refert an antequam cognoverim uxo- 60 rem meam, an post, ipsa facta sit commater alicujus mulieris, dummodo ante commaternitatem illam contraxerim cum uxore mea et eam cognoverim.[94]

46 Non exspectes ut sacerdos extrahat infantem de sacro fonte et postea tibi tradat. Si tamen statim extractum et elevatum suscipis de manu 65 presbyteri, non minus es compater; quia ea quae in continenti fiunt inesse intelliguntur. Extrahe ergo de fonte simul cum sacerdote. Si enim aliquantulam moram interponis, aliquid faciendo quod ad propositum non pertinet, non credo quod compater fias si postea suscipias, neque si prius uni porrigatur, postea tibi, postea alii.[95]   70

Sponsa mea etiam de praesenti, quam nondum cognovi, commater est

---

51 Matella P Matildis R Matilla Tc Balda Pet.   52 baptismo] sacro fonte RTu.   sum *om.* RTu.   53 mea *om.* AaJ.   mortuo JPRTa mortua Tu *corr. ab* mortuus [?] Ab mortuus Pet *add.* enim O *add.* enim *insert.* Aa.   53-54 mortuis — ducere *om.* Ck (*homoeotel.*). 54 possum JTaZ potest Tu.   54-58 illis — Bertam *om.* J (*homoeotel.*).   54 sensit OZ. 55 Hugo CkHPTaUZ Huguico O Huguntio Ci unctio Tc.   praecedat Ta. 56 si] sic Aa non PTu.   57 illorum] eorum AaHTuUZ.   58 suscipit OR susceperit Tc *om.* Pet.   60 an *om.* Tu *insert.* OTc.   61 dummodo] de modo J *corr. ab* de modo O.   62 eam] illam AaCkHZ ante illam Tu.   65 tamen] tu Ta *corr. ab* non Tc. statim *add.* extra Q^{1*}.   contractum O.   suscipis *corr. ab* sucepit O.   65-66 de manu presbyteri *om.* U.   66 presbyteri] sacerdotis Q^{1*}Tu.   es] est Aa.   simul inesse CcCi *om.* P.   67 simul *om.* Q^{1*}Tc.   69 non²] nec O.   fiat O. 70 postea tibi *om.* Ci.   postea²] praeterea O *insert.* Cc.   71 Item sponsa O. mea etiam] etiam mea JO Pet etiam Non Tu.   est] sit *insert.* O fit Pet.

---

[92] See C.30 q.4 dictum p. c.5. Our author has obtained this citation from the text of Huguccio (see following note). Cf. FIRTH, *Thesis* II 363*, 379*-380* with notes; also below sect. 225 with nn. 52-53.

[93] See HUG. ad C.30 q.4 pr. (fol. 302ʳᵇ; quoted in FIRTH, *Thesis* II 266*-268*).

[94] This sentence seems to represent an illogical abbreviation of Huguccio's text; see FIRTH, *Thesis* II 264*-272*; also below sect. 225 with nn. 52-53.

[95] See HUG. ad C.30 q.4 c.3 *suscepit de sacro fonte* (fol. 302ʳᵇ⁻ᵛᵃ); cf. IDEM ad C.30 q.4 c.6 *minime praesumant* (fol. 303ʳᵇ; GILLMANN, *ArchivKKRecht* 86.703).

alicujus mulieris; ideo sponsa mea mortua possum ducere illam mulierem. Non enim viro acquiritur per ejus uxorem compaternitas nisi post carnalem commixtionem, sicut nec affinitas viro adveniens mediante uxore.[96]

47 Si aliqui sunt compatres, unus est pater vel mater carnalis, alius spi- 75 ritualis.[97] Est hic pater spiritualis et mater et filius et filia et frater et soror, sed non nepos vel neptis; nec ultra procedendum est.[98]

Judaeus baptizavit aliquam. Ante conversionem suam contraxit cum ea. Propter hoc non separabitur ab ea post conversionem, et fortasse post conversionem potest cum ea contrahere, quia ecclesiasticis consti- 80 tutionibus non constringitur judaeus.[99]

Credo quod fratrem et nepotem tuum potes baptizare et de baptismo suscipere, cum non sit prohibitum.[100]

Monachis interdicitur compaternitas suscipiendo, non baptizando; quia major solet ibi esse familiaritas quam hic, osculando, donando.[1]   85

Filius baptizantis frater est baptizatae; ideo non potest cum ea contrahere, et sic de aliis sacramentis.[2]

---

75 Item si O.   sunt] sint JOTc.   est *om*. OTc.   pater] compater AaJ.   mater] commater AaJ.   76 pater] compater J.   et[1]] vel CkHJZ.   mater] commater HJ. 79 fortasse] forte Q[1]* *om*. Ta.   80-81 institutionibus OTc Pet consuetudinibus JU. 81 astringitur Ck astrictus est R.   82 fratrem *add*. tuum AaCkTcU.   tuum *om*. AaCk. 82-85 Credo — donando *om*. Q[1]*.   82 et[2] *om*. HJU *insert*. Aa.   85 quam hic *om*. R *add*. esse AaCkHJZ.   osculando *add*. et P *add*. et *insert*. Ci.   86-87 Filius — sacramentis *om*. Pet.

---

[96] See Hug. ad C.30 q.4 c.3 *effecti una caro* (fol. 302[va]).

[97] Cf. Hug. ad C.30 q.4 c.6 *sed ut puritas* etc... *infamia* (fol. 303[ra-b]; Gillmann, *ArchivKKRecht* 86.702-703).

[98] Cf. Hug. ad C.30 q.3 pr. (fol. 301[rb]).

[99] Cf. Hug. ad C.30 q.1 c.1 *septem dona baptismi* (fols. 299[vb]-300[ra]). In the first case considered by Robert the impediment of disparity of cult would invalidate the marriage. Huguccio more logically considers the case of a Jew acting as sponsor to someone in the ceremonies preparatory to baptism and then marrying that person before the baptism of either. He also considers the case of a Jew who has baptized someone and married that person's unbaptized mother before his own baptism.

[100] See Hug. ad C.30 q.1 c.7 *nec debe<re> separari* quod esset *contra prae<fatas> auctoritates* (fol. 300[rb]). This and the following six paragraphs seem to be based on the same part of Huguccio's *Summa*.

[1] See Hug. ad C.30 q.1 c.8 *quia scriptum est* (fol. 300[rb]).

[2] See Hug. *ibid*. (fol. 300[rb-va]).

48   Sacerdotis filius non est frater spiritualis illius quam sacerdos ad-
mittit ad poenitentiam; ideo potest cum ea contrahere. Joannes dicit
quod hoc ideo fit quia plura sacramenta sunt in baptismo quam in poeni- 90
tentia, utpote resurrectionis et aliorum.[3] Sed privata poenitentia nullum
est sacramentum; et ideo per eam non generatur compaternitas vel fra-
ternitas spiritualis.[4]

   Item non est prohibitus contractus cum poenitentiali patris, et ita
intelligitur concessus; et haec regula in omnibus talibus sufficit.[5]   95

   Item sacerdos non potest baptizare filium suum. Numquid potest ei
poenitentiam dare, vel uxori suae? Potest; tamen tutius alius dabit.[6]

   Esto quod sacerdos possit contrahere; numquid cum sua poenitentiali?
Potest; quia non est ibi tanta compaternitas quae impediat matrimonium 99
si contractum fuerit.[7]

49   Item pater spiritualis potest accipere sororem filii spiritualis et
neptem et quamlibet de ejus cognatione, quia ad tales personas non extenditur talis cognatio.[8]

---

88 sacerdos] presbyter AaCk.   92 compaternitas] paternitas R *corr. ad* paternitas Cc.   94 poenitentiali] spirituali TcTuZ.   ita] ideo OR.   95 concessus]
consensus HJZ *corr. ab* consensus Aa.   96 ei] et O.   97 suae *add.* et O.   98-1
Esto — fuerit *om.* Q¹*.   98 sua] sola Ck filia R filia sua Ci.   poenitentiali] spirituali
Pet.   98-99 sua — Potest] filia sua potest contrahere spirituali O.   99 compaternitas
om. J *insert.* Aa.   tanta compaternitas] causa U.   impedit AaAcCkJTuU *corr. ab* impedit
O.   3 et *om.* AaTu.

   [3] I have not found this doctrine in John of Faenza's commentary on the *Decretum* at this place.
But Hug. *loc. cit.* assigns it to *Magister Joannes*. Regarding the impediment thought to arise
from the administration of penance see Franz Gillmann, "Das Ehehindernis der geistlichen
Verwandtschaft aus der Busse," *ArchivKKRecht* 90 (1910) 236-261 (also publ. separately). This
author quotes from many mediaeval canonists. Cf. Idem, "Zum Ehehindernis der geistlichen
Verwandtschaft aus der Busse," *ArchivKKRecht* 91 (1911) 178-179.
   [4] See Hug. *loc. cit.* (cf. Paris BN lat. 3891, fol. 247ᵛᵃ). It is commonly maintained by canonists of this time that only public penance is a sacrament. Cf. Rufinus, *Summa* ad C.1 q.1 c.74
(p. 216); *Glossa ordinaria in Decr.* ad C.1 q.1 c.74 *impositio*; Anciaux pp. 365-370; Magister
Simon, *Tractatus de sacramentis* ed. Weisweiler pp. 22-23.
   [5] See Hug. *ibid.* (fol. 300ᵛᵃ; cf. Paris BN 3891, fol. 247ᵛᵃ; quoted by Gillmann, *Archiv-
KKRecht* 90.248 n. 3).
   [6] See Hug. *loc. cit.*
   [7] See Hug. *loc. cit.* Gillmann, "Das Ehehindernis," *ArchivKKRecht* 90.250-251, expresses
the opinion that Robert, in speaking here of this impediment as merely impedient rather than
invalidating, is differing from Huguccio. I cannot find any such difference. Flamborough's
words are based upon a passage in Huguccio quoted by Gillmann himself p. 248 n. 3; cf. *ibid.*
pp. 246-249.
   [8] See Hug. ad C.30 q.3 c.7 *filiam* (fol. 302ʳᵃ).

Item pater potest accipere filii sui filiam spiritualem, quia non ascendit 5
vel descendit talis cognatio.[9]

50 Collige ex praemissis quod est cognatio carnalis et est spiritualis,
de quibus dictum est. Est et legalis, quae fit per adoptionem, quando
aliquis adoptat alium in fratrem vel filium vel nepotem, et sic usque ad
septimum gradum. Secundum aliquos ista etiam cognatio impedit ma- 10
trimonium,[10] sed hodie non tenetur.

De justitia publicae honestatis

51 Justitia publicae honestatis impedit matrimonium; ut per verba de
futuro contraxisti sponsalia cum septenni vel majori; licet ulterius non
est processum, nullam ejus consanguineam habere poteris.[11]   15

Igitur matrimonium rite contrahitur inter puberes. Pubertas autem in
masculis attenditur a quarto decimo anno et deinceps, in femina a duodecimo et deinceps.[12]

Sponsalia vero a septennio et deinceps contrahuntur, quia tunc in-
cipimus esse doli capaces. Si ante septennium contracta fuerint sponsa- 20
lia, non tenent nisi inter doli capaces; quia consentire non possunt nisi
sentiant; non sentiunt autem furiosi et alii adulti doli non capaces. "Non
sentiunt," id est non sapiunt vel intelligunt.[13]

5-6 Item — cognatio *om.* Ck *infra post* est[1] *ad lineam 8* Tc.   7 quod] quid U quae Pet *add.*
non Tu.   quod est] talis O.   (est[1] *om.* I).   carnalis] spiritualis TaR.   et
om. AbAc(ENY).   et est *invers.* CcCiCkHZ(FLV est etiam I).   est[2]] quae Pet *om.*
JOQ[1]*TcU(CpMSoTb etiam X).   spiritualis] carnalis RTa cognatio spiritualis CcCiP.
8 Est et *invers.* P Est etiam Tc.   9 aliquis] quis TcTu Pet.   alium] filium *delet.* J *om.*
Tu filium alterius Pet.   10 aliquos] alios AbTaR.   13-16 Justitia — Igitur *om.* Q[1]*.
15 est] sit R.   sis processus Pet.   potes O potest Tu.   16-60 matrimonium —
recedere *intperpolat. post sect.* 63 Q[1]* *fol.* 332[r].   17 a[2] *om.* AaO.   17-18 in femina —
deinceps *om.* CkR (*homoeotel.*).   duocecimo *add.* anno CiJOTa.   22 sentiant] con-
sentiant Pet.   23 sentiunt] consentiunt Cc Pet *corr. ab* consentiunt Ci.   vel] neque
Ck nec U *add.* non *insert.* Aa.

[9] See *loc. cit.*
[10] Cf. Hug. ad C.30 q.3 pr. (fol. 301[rb]); Rufinus, *Summa, ad eundem locum* (p. 463); 1 *Compil.*
4.12.un. (JE 2812; X 4.12.un.; Nicholas I).
[11] Cf. Hug. ad C.27 q.2 c.11 (fol. 288[va]; ed. Roman pp. 760-761); also above sect. 12 with
n. 8.
[12] See Hug. ad C.30 q.2 pr. (fol. 300[vb]; cf. Paris BN lat. 3891, fol. 247[vb]).
[13] See *loc. cit.*

52 In matrimonio contrahendo duo sunt necessaria: ut possint consentire et commisceri. Unde minores duodecim annis et castrati et frigidi et non possunt contrahere matrimonium. Furiosi et adulti non capaces doli possunt commisceri, sed non consentire; unde non possunt contrahere matrimonium.[14]

In sponsalibus contrahendis unum solum est necessarium, scilicet mutuus consensus, quorum terminus, ut diximus, est septennium; quia ante 30 non contrahuntur sponsalia nisi inter doli capaces; ut in extra. *Accessit* septennium dicitur tempus discretionis sive doli capacitatis.[15] Secundum alios a quarto decimo anno incipit discretio aut doli capacitas;[16] ex tunc enim possunt jurare, ut Causa xxii. quaest. v. c. *Parvuli*,[17] item votum facere, ut Causa xx. quaest. ii. c. *Puella*,[18] item matrimonium contrahere. 35

53 Ante pubertatem contraxerunt aliqui sponsalia; numquid adveniente pubertate possunt ab invicem discedere et se de juramento absolvere? Secundum quosdam possunt, cum ita sit in aliis contractibus.[19] Dico quod non possunt; quia sponsalia sunt praeparatoria matrimonii et ideo censentur ejusdem juris cum illo, quod non potest dirimi sola voluntate con- 40 jugatorum. Compellendi sunt igitur impuberes ut servent sponsalia, et sese invicem debent exspectare, sive ambo sint impuberes, sive alter tantum.[20] Alii dicunt quod admonendi sunt sed non compellendi, quia libera debent esse matrimonia.[21] Sed hoc de primo consensu dicitur, quia postquam consenserint compellendi sunt.[22]   45

---

26 Furiosi et adulti] et adulti et furiosi O.   31 extra.] decretali extra. H ecclesia J Causa x. P.   33 alios] aliquos OTu.   quinto decimo H duodecimo Ta.   34 c.] titulo J *om.* Ta Pet *insert.* Cc.   35 Causa *om.* CkTa Pet.   xx.] xxii. PTu *corr. ab* xxii. Tc. ii.] v. CkQ¹*Ta secundo O.   c.] titulo J *om.* Ta Pet.   36 contrahunt RTa.   37 possent JU.   ab] ad O.   39 possunt *om.* ORTa.   40 quod] quia Tc propter quod Ta.   non *om.* J *insert.* Ac.   possunt Ta   dirimi] demi O.   41 igitur] ergo CkJ.   42 impuberes] puberes Cc *corr. ab* puberes Ci.   45 consenserunt CkO Pet conserunt Ci.

[14] See *loc. cit.*

[15] See *loc. cit.*; Huguccio cites this decretal: 1 *Compil.* 4.2.6 (JL 13887; X 4.2.5).

[16] Cf. JOHN OF FAENZA, *Summa* ad C.30 q.2 c.un. *tempus discretionis* (Paris BN lat. 14606, fol. 140vb; quoted by Walther VON HÖRMANN, *Die desponsatio impuberum* p. 92); HUG. ad C.30 q.2 c.un. *ad tempus discretionis* (fol. 301ra); RUFINUS, *Summa* ad C.30 q.2 pr. (p. 462).

[17] Cap. 14, cf. capp. 15-16.

[18] Cap. 2.

[19] Cf. 1 *Compil.* 4.1.11 (JL 13903; X 4.1.2); *Glossa ordinaria in Decr.* ad C.30 q.2 *Nihil.*

[20] See HUG. ad C.30 q.2 c.un. *consensus utriusque* (bis) (fol. 301$^{ra\_b}$).

[21] See 1 *Compil.* 4.1.12 (JL 15165; X 4.1.17; *KanErgänz* no. 207, LUCIUS III), cited by Huguccio.

[22] See HUG. *loc. cit.*; cf. IDEM ad C.27 q.2 c.33 *non negetur* (fol. 291vb, ed. ROMAN p. 792); Walther VON HÖRMANN, *Die desponsatio impuberum* pp. 202-205.

Ambo adulti contraxerunt sponsalia. Ante carnalem copulam possunt se ab invicem absolvere, sed non auctoritate sua, sed praelati sui, id est episcopi ad minus.[23] Ut videtur, eodem modo possunt se absolvere impupuberes.

54   Ecce parentes ante septennium compromittunt et jurant sponsalia; 50 filii in septennio nolunt consentire. Non debent cogi parentes, quia non tenent sponsalia. Si enim filii admoniti, prout debent, nolunt consentire, nihil est quod parentibus debeat imputari, nec poena forte interposita; nec juramenti sunt rei vel perjurii; quia sub conditione intelliguntur jurasse, scilicet si filii in septennio consentirent. Si vero hanc conditionem 55 omiserunt, de temeritate sunt arguendi.[24]

Diximus superius: Si aliquis in minori aetate traditur a parentibus religioni, quidquid contingat non potest recedere, quia monachum facit paterna traditio.[25] A simili parentibus qui juraverunt sponsalia tenentur obedire impuberes ut numquam possint ab invicem recedere.   60

Quae dirimant sponsalia

55   Item secundum dominum Innocentium dirimuntur sponsalia inter adultos si post sponsalia contracta inventa est sponsa ante carnalem copulam vel matrimonium contractum fornicata fuisse, vel leprosa, vel

---

47 ab] ab RTa.   id est] scilicet AaHJUZ.   50 septimum annum AaJU.   51 filii *add.* sui AaHJUZ.   parentes *add.* ejus J *add.* ejus *delet.* Aa.   53 nihil] non O nec J nil Tu.   a parentibus O *add.* suis Tc Pet.   debent J debet P.   debeat imputari] imputari possit Ck.   nec — interposita *om.* OZ nec poenitentia imponi P.   poena *om.* JU.   poena forte *insert.* Aa.   interpositii JU interponenda Tc imposita Ta.   54 nec *om.* JU.   56 omiserint JTaTu comiserint Ck omiserint *cum* vel -runt *suprascr.* H omittere voluerint *cum* omiserunt *suprascr.* O.   57-60 Diximus — recedere *om.* Pet.   57 aliquis] quis OTc.   traditus sit JZ sit traditus AaCkHU.   58 quidquid] quicumque O quid Tu. 59 juraverant OU juraverint AaTu.   sponsalia *om.* AaTa.   60 obedire] observare AaCkJUZ.   recedere] discedere Tc separari AaJU *add.* usque ad pubertatem P *add.* usque ad pubertatem *insert.* Ac.   61 *In* HPTa(CpEFIKLM) *titulus vel spatium pro titulo sequitur paragraphum hic sequentem.*   62 Item *om.* O.   62-66 Item — paralytica *infra post finem paragraphi sequentis* Q[1]*.   62 domnum AcTu.   Innocentium *add.* tertium AaHJUZ.

---

[23] Cf. 1 *Compil.* 4.1.11 (JL 13903; X 4.1.2); 1 *Compil.* 4.4.5(7) (JL 12293).

[24] See Hug. ad C.30 q.2 c.un. *consensus utriusque* (bis) (fol. 301ra); Hörmann, *Die desponsatio impuberum* pp. 187-201.

[25] See above sect. 33 with n. 59; cf. Firth, *Thesis* II 478*-493*.

mutilata unde deformis fieret, vel oculum amisisse vel nasum, vel si tur- 65
pius aliquid ei evenerit, vel paralytica.[26]

Dirimuntur sponsalia sicut et matrimonium; quia impuberes qui contraxerunt sponsalia debent sese invicem exspectare usque ad pubertatem,
uterque usque ad alterius pubertatem: puer usque ad puellae annum duo-
decimum, puella puerum usque ad annum quartum decimum. Tunc uter- 70
que in principio suae pubertatis potest sola sua voluntate commanere vel
recedere, quia tunc primo possunt consentire in matrimonium.[27] Consensus autem est de substantia matrimonii, et sine consensu non est matrimonium, ut superius dictum est.[28]

56   Ex favore religionis dirimuntur sponsalia; quia, si alter in principio 75
pubertatis suae ante carnalem copulam intraverit religionem, remanens
in saeculo nubat in Domino cui voluerit.[29]

In adultis etiam post contractum matrimonium ante carnalem copulam,
maxime infra duos menses, potest uterque reliquo invito intrare religionem; et imponunt Alexandro quod manens in saeculo statim potest 80
nubere;[30] quod ego non audeo consulere.[31]

---

65 fierit] fuerit CkP.   amisisse *om.* Ta.   66 aliquid *corr. ab* ad O *om.* R.   ei]
eidem Z *om.* JP.   advenerit OTcTu evenisset Pet *om.* R.   paralytica *add.* minuitur [?]
matrimonium O.   67 Dirimuntur] minuuntur O.   67-68 qui — sponsalia] contraxerunt sponsalia qui R.   contraxerint J contraxerant U.   68 sese] se JTaTuUZ *om.*
Ck *add.* ad Ta Pet.   73 autem *om.* Q1*R.   est *om.* Cc.   74 ut — est *om.* Q1*
Pet.   est *om.* Cc.   75 Ex *ss. desiniunt lectiones usque ad lineam 16 in sect. 59* Q1*.
76 intravit CkOPTa.   79 reliquo] altero AaJU.   80 et] ut P *add.* etiam Ta.   81 ego
lacuna O.

[26] See Po. 3168 (X 2.24.25; issued Sept. 1, 1207).

[27] Cf. 1 *Compil.* 4.2.9, 10, 11 (JL 13767 X 4.2.7; JL 13765 X 4.2.8; JL 14126).

[28] See sect. 12.

[29] Cf. GRATIAN C.27 q.2 dictum p. c.26, cc.27-28; 1 *Compil.* 3.28.9 (JL 11865).

[30] See 1 *Compil.* 3.28.7 (JL 13787; X 3.32.7); 1 *Compil.* 3.28.2 (JL 14091; X 3.32.2). Probably Robert derived his knowledge of these decretals from the following passage in Huguccio:
"Frangitur ergo matrimonium dum est in probatione? Dico quod non, quia non transivit ad
religionem, sed ad probationem religionis. Non ergo frangitur antequam fiat monachus vel
canonicus regularis vel ibi conversus. ... Sed postquam transit ad religionem et eam sumit,
statim dissolvitur matrimonium. Sed numquid sponsus relicta poterit statim contrahere cum
alio? Dico quod sic, scilicet statim et postea." HUG. ad C.27 q.2 c.27 *eligere matrimonium* (text
established from BN lat. 3892, fol. 290va, and 3891, fol. 238rb). Huguccio then cites both
decretals of Alexander III just mentioned; see *ibid.* (fol. 290va-b, ed. ROMAN pp. 779-780).
Cf. HUG. ad C.27 q.2 dictum p. c.26 (fol. 290va, ed. ROMAN pp. 778-779); also below sect. 195;
also James A. CORIDEN, *The Indissolubility added to Christian Marriage by Consummation.*

[31] It is possible that Flamborough here rejects the notion, which Huguccio also rejects, that
the partner remaining in the world may marry as soon as the other has first entered the mo-

Item etiam in adultis dirimuntur sponsalia; quia, si post sponsalia ante carnis copulam alter alterum reliquerit et cum alio matrimonium contraxerit, stabit matrimonium, et relictus nubat in Domino cui voluerit. Ideo dixi "ante carnalem copulam," quia si sponsalia secuta est carnalis 85 copula, consummatum est matrimonium, nec umquam dirimetur. Et hoc dico si maritali affectu convenerunt; alioquin puto non est matrimonium. Sed tamen semper praejudicabitur illis et stabitur pro matrimonio.[32]

57   Item etiam in adultis dirimuntur sponsalia; quia, si clericus contraxit 90 cum aliqua sponsalia et ante carnis copulam intellexit eam esse corruptam, non tenetur tenere sponsalia. Alioquin praejudicabitur illi quod non poterit promoveri quia contraxerit cum corrupta; ipse autem intelligitur jurasse sponsalia "omni jure suo salvo."[33]

---

82 si *om*. OR.   83 carnis] carnalem   AaAbOPRTu(BmCpFGIKMSgSoX) car. Z(L). copulam *add*. si *insert*. O.   86 dirimitur CkJ.   87 convenerint AaAdPR conveniunt J convenirent Tu.   ut puto O puta Ta.   est] esse Tc Pet.   88 stabit CkTu *add*. matrimonium Tu.   90 etiam] et CcO *om*. CkHR.   contraxerit AaAbCcCkOPRTcTu-(CpFGIKMSgSoTb contrahit LX).   91 carnis] carnalem HOPTu.   intellexerit HO-PRTu(KLMSoX intelligit BmSg).   93 contraxit AaCkHJOPRTaTuUZ(CpEFGKNTbVX contraxerunt Bm contrahit Sg).   94 sponsalia *om*. TaU.   omni] cum Ta quasi R.

---

nastery to begin his or her period of probation. However, it seems much more likely that he disagrees with Huguccio, who has said that *statim*, i.e. just as soon as the other partner has made his or her vows, and so become definitely a monk or nun, the one remaining in the world may marry someone else (see preceding note). If such be the case, then Robert denies freedom to marry to the one remaining in the world. This will then be another instance in which Robert sees nothing unreasonable in disabilities being imposed on human beings without their consent; see FIRTH, *Thesis* II 478*-493*. Elsewhere too he has shown reluctance to accept decisions of ecclesiastical authority that seem to him opposed to God's law; see above sects. 29 and 34. In other texts he follows Huguccio; here he differs from him. But throughout he is following the principle enunciated by Huguccio that "from the Law or the Gospel no one can dispense" (above sects. 25 and 38); cf. below sects. 65-66.

[32] Cf. HUG. ad C.27 q.2 dictum p. c.45 *Sed concedatur* (fol. 292vb, ed. ROMAN p. 799-801); ad C.27 q.2 c.51 *vel etiam pro consensu* (fol. 293ra, ed. ROMAN p. 804); ad C.29 q.2 c.5 (fol. 298va); 1 *Compil.* 4.4.6(8) (JL 14234); JL 13902 (X 4.1.15); J. FREISEN, *Geschichte des canonischen Eherechts* pp. 190-210; below sects. 171, 192, 195; Appendix B sect. 392. See John T. NOONAN Jr., "Marital Affection in the Canonists," *Studia Gratiana* 12 (Collectanea Stephan Kuttner 2; Bologna 1967) 479-509; Gerard OESTERLE, "Dissolutio matrimonii rati et non consummati per subsequens matrimonium," *Studia Gratiana* 9.27-43; Joseph J. MUZAS, "The Concept of *Matrimonium ratum* in Gratian and the Early Decretists (1140-1215)," (Catholic Univ. of America Canon Law Studies 441; cf. *Dissertation Abstracts* 26 [1965-66] 2229); Terence P. McLAUGHLIN, "The Formation of the Marriage Bond according to *Summa Parisiensis*," *MedStud* 15 (1953) 208-212.

[33] Cf. HUG. ad C.27 q.2 c.33 *non negetur* (fols. 291vb-292ra, ed. ROMAN p. 792).

58   Item de secunda duarum uxorum patris tui natus es; nullam con-95
sanguineam prioris habere poteris usque ad quartum gradum; usque
dico inclusive.[34] Ita tenet ecclesia; alii dicunt usque ad septimum,
sed non tenet ecclesia.[35] Quidam dicunt quod hoc est quartum genus
affinitatis; sed nihil est.[36]
                                                                      99
POENITENS. Numquid ita est in contrario; scilicet, si natus sum de
priore duarum uxorum patris mei, non possum habere aliquam consanguineam secundae uxoris patris mei usque ad quartum gradum?
   SACERDOS. Non legi.
   POENITENS. Quae est hic ratio?   5
   SACERDOS. Institutio ecclesiae; aliam non legi.[37] Talem tamen possumus assignare: Pater meus factus est una caro cum prima uxore sua;
ergo mediante patre meo factus sum quasi consanguineus priori uxori
patris mei; sed hoc non esset si natus essem de prima uxore patris mei.[38]

De delicti enormitate   10

59   Delicti enormitas impedit matrimonium, ut in uxoricida, non ta-

---

(95-9 Item — mei *om.* Tb).   97-98 alii — ecclesia *om.* JTaZ Pet *insert.* Aa *vide infra*
var. ad lineam 99.   97 septem AdCc *corr. ab* septem Aa.   98 hoc *om.* J *insert.* Aa sed
add. hoc OTc.   99 est *add.* alii dicunt usque ad septem sed non tenet ecclesia Z *vide supra*
var. ad lineas 97-98.   1 scilicet] sed Aa *om.* Ta.   sum *om.* JTc.   sum de] sive
Ta.   2 priori AaAbCkJORTaUZ(BmFI MSgSoVX).   mei *om.* Aa.   non] numquid non Aa numquam O.   2-3 non — mei *om.* JTu (*homoeotel.*).   5 hic] haec Ck Pet
om. Tu.   7 sua *om.* PTu.   8 quasi] sicut J tamquam P *om.* O.   prioris Ta Pet
pariter O.   uxoris Ta *om.* Pet.

---

[34] Cf. 1 *Compil.* 4.15.1 (JL 14022); GRATIAN C.35 q.10 c.4; Franz GILLMANN, "Das ehemals
zwischen der *soboles ex secundis nuptiis* und der Blutsverwandten des versterbenen Eheteiles bestehende Ehehindernis," *ArchivKKRecht* 89 (1909) 447-470.

[35] Cf. LOMBARD, *Sent.* 4.41.2 (II 983-985).

[36] Cf. HUG. ad C.35 q.10 pr. (fol. 355va-b; GILLMANN, *ArchivKKRecht* 89.454 n.4 [pp. 454-
455]). Huguccio cites Gan<dulphus?> as holding this opinion. However WALTER, the
editor of GANDULF, *Sententiae*, has found therein nothing indicative of this position; see his edition, Prolegomena p. xxxvii.

[37] Cf. Huguccio: "Quid ergo prohibet tales copulari inter se? Dico quod sola honestas
publica sive publicae honestatis justitia; et fuit hoc statutum propter commixtionem sanguinis.
Unde, si uxor mea habet filiam ex alio viro antequam mihi misceatur, illa filia bene potest
copulari cuilibet meo consanguineo; sed si habet illam postquam commixta est mihi, tunc non
potest copulari meis consanguineis quibusdam, impediente non consanguinitate vel affinitate
(quia nulla est ibi) sed sola publica honestate propter jam factam commixtionem sanguinis inter
me et uxorem meam." HUG. ad C.35 q.10 pr. (text established from BN lat. 3892, fol. 355vb
and 3891, fol. 279vb).

[38] Cf. LOMBARD, *Sent.* 4.41.2 (II 983-985).

men in matricida, licet majus sit peccatum; quia in quo deliquit quis
puniendus est.[39]

Item cognovisti consanguineam uxoris tuae in primo vel [in] secundo
vel tertio gradu; sine spe conjugii manebis.[40]   15

Ista duo, scilicet uxoricidium et incestus cum consanguinea uxoris
tuae in primo vel secundo vel tertio gradu, impediunt, ut puto, contrahendum, sed non dirimunt, ut puto, contractum.[41] Omnia praedicta
impedimenta et impediunt contrahendum et dirimunt contractum.

60   Quaecumque delicti enormitas impediat contrahendum, nullum 20
tamen dirimit contractum, nisi forte in duobus casibus (ubi tamen ecclesiastica constitutio magis dirimit quam criminis enormitas):[42] scilicet
si adulter adulterae fidem dedit vivente ejus marito quod eo mortuo
eam duceret, vel si adulter vel adultera ejus viri machinatus sit in mortem; et hoc cum effectu.[43] Non enim sufficit machinari nisi et occidat; nec 25
etiam ei imputabitur ad matrimonium contrahendum vel dirimendum si
ab altero illorum occidatur vir casu vel certa scientia vel alio quolibet modo,
nisi tantum ideo interficiatur ut post ejus mortem adultera ab adultero
ducatur.[44]

Item, si publice vivente viro suo tenuisti uxorem ejus, illo mortuo non 30

---

12 delinquit JTaUZ.   quis *om.* Aa *add.* in eo Ta *add.* in hoc Z.   14 in[2] CcCiCkJOTa
Pet(CpV) *om. cett.(cett.).*   15 vel] et Ac *add.* in CkO.   manebit CcTc maneas Tu.
16 Ista duo *usque ad finem sectionis 63*] *interpolatio post finem sectionis 30 supra* Q[1]*.   17-18.
matrimonium contrahendum Tc *add.* matrimonium JP.   18 sed — contractum *om.* J
(*homoeotel.* ?).   ut puto *om.* TaZ *insert.* Aa.   18-19 Omnia — contractum *om.* Z *insert.*
Aa (*homoeotel.* ?).   19 et[1] *om.* AaTa.   et — contractum *om.* U.   20 Quaecumque
corr. ab Quandoque O.   impedit CkTu *corr. ad* impedit O.   nulla PTa non Q[1]*.
21 duobus *corr. a* duabus AbTc.   in duobus casibus] duabus causis P.   22 institutio
TaTcTu Pet consuetudo CkHJUZ.   criminis] delicti OTu.   23 dederit OTu.   24
machinata Ta machinata machinatus Aa machinata vel machinatus J machinatus vel machinata
U machinati P.   sint P est Ta.   in *om.* OTu.   25 hoc *add.* est AaAcHJQ[1]*UZ-
(CpELMNXY).   et[2] *om.* P.   nisi et] ubi et si non O.   26 ei *om.* OTu.   27 il-
lorum] eorum Tc *om.* R.   occiditur TaTc.   vir] vel AaJZ.(CpFNX in Tb) *corr. ab*
vel Ac *corr. ab* in O.   alio quolibet] aliquo alio O.   28 tantum] tamen O.   interfi-
ciatur] occidatur R instituatur Ck.   30 suo *om.* Q[1]*TaTu *delet* Ac.

---

[39] Cf. Hug. ad C.33 q.2 c.8 *venialiter* (fol. 321[rb]); ad C.33 q.2 dictum p. c.11 (fol. 321[vb]).
[40] Cf. below sects. 65-66; above sect. 38 with n. 73.
[41] Cf. Hug. ad C.33 q.2 dictum p. c.11 (fol. 321[vb]).
[42] Cf. Hug. ad C.31 pr. (fol. 304[vb]).
[43] Cf. Hug. ad C.31 q.1 pr. (fol. 304[vb]).
[44] Cf. Hug. ad C.31 q.1 c.5 *occidisse* (fol. 305[rb-va]).

potes illam ducere, et si duxeris dirimetur matrimonium; et hoc secundum quosdam.[45]

61   Ista tria, si impediunt generaliter matrimonium contrahendum, non tamen generaliter dirimunt, sed tantum inter illas personas de quibus dictum est. Verbi gratia, si fidem dedisti alicui vivente marito suo quod [35] eam duceres, si mortuo viro ejus contraxeris cum ea, dirimetur matrimonium. Item, si aliquem interfecisti ut ejus uxorem duceres, si eo interfecto duxeris eam, dirimetur matrimonium. Item, si mortuo viro cujus uxorem publice tenuisti eo vivente contraxeris cum ea, dirimetur matrimonium.[46] Cum aliis quam [cum] istis tribus si contraxeris, non diri- [40] metur matrimonium.

De coactione

62   Coactio absoluta et violenta, quae scilicet cadit in virum constantem, et impedit contrahendum et dirimit contractum, ut minae mortis, verbera, captio corporalis; et licet proferat haec verba et nolit consentire, [45] scilicet "Accipio te in meam," non tamen consentit nec vult consentire. Sed, quantumcumque aliqua coacta fuerit, si postea moram fecerit cum viro et cum potuit non recessit, videtur consensisse.[47]

Item, quantacumque fuerit coactio, si post illam facta est aliqua

---

31 illam] eam CkHQ[1]*RTcUZ Pet(CpEGIMSgVXY) eam *delet.* Aa *om.* Tu (*corr. ab* aliam So).   hoc *om.* Tc.   et hoc *om.* R.   33-41 Ista — matrimonium *om.* R.   33 si] etsi CkTa scilicet O *om.* J *delet.* Tc *insert. post* generaliter Aa.   matrimonium *om.* HUZ Pet.   34 generaliter *om.* O *insert.* Aa.   35 marito] viro Q[1]* Pet.   36 ejus *om.* Ta. viro ejus] marito suo AdTu.   37 Item *add.* videtur Aa *add.* ut H.   38 eam] uxorem ejus JUZ ejus uxorem CkH uxorem suam Aa.   viro] ejus viro Ck *add.* ejus HJTaTc. cujus *om.* TaTu.   39 si contraxeris Tu *corr. ad* si contraxeris Tc.   40 cum[2] JHOTaTuU *delet.* Aa *om. cett.*   si *om.* AbO.   43 in] inter Tu.   44 et[1] *om.* PTu.   impedit *add.* matrimonium AaCkTaU.   contrahendum *add.* matrimonium Pet.   45 corporaliter O corporea Aa. noluit J nolet Tu.   46 non] nec Tc Pet.   consenserit O.   nec] non O.   47 (-cumque aliqua coacta *reincipit* D).   fecit Tc Pet.   49 quantumcumque JOR *corr. ab* quamcumque Ci.   fuit Tc Pet.   est] es Tu fuit R.   facta est *corr. ab* fuerit Tc.   aliquam CiTc aliam Cc alia Tu *om.* R *add.* ita J.

---

[45] Cf. Hug. ad C.31 q.1 c.4 *anathematizamus* (fol. 305rb, cf. BN lat. 3891, fol. 251rb).

[46] Cf. JL 16602 (X 4.7.4; *KanErgänz* no. 206; *Collectio seguntina* no. 112 *RevHistEccl* 50.449, Celestine III).

[47] This and the following paragraph are apparently based on Hug. ad C.31 pr. (fol. 304vb); cf. Firth, *Thesis* II 489*-492*.

volens, non impeditur matrimonium; licet quidam dicant quod con- 50
sensus coactus non facit matrimonium, quia semper ab initio debet
esse spontaneus. Talis enim exceptio in aliis contractibus locum habet,
in matrimonio nequaquam; sed nec in aliis quantum ad Deum; quia,
si coactus juras aliquid quod non est peccatum, fac illud.[48]

De raptu 55

63 Raptus etiam impedit matrimonium; quia si innubilem rapuisti
ad matrimonium vel nubilem ad stuprum, reddes eam. Tamen qua-
liscumque fuerit raptus, si rapta et raptor libere et liberaliter in matrimonium consenserint, stabit matrimonium.[49]

Tibi desponsatam rapuisti; non cades a jure tuo, tum favore matri- 60
monii, tum quia uxor alligata est legi viri.[50]

Clericus qui innubilem rapuit sibi non desponsatam, vel nubilem
ad stuprum, deponatur si corrigi noluerit, vel fortasse etiam si poeniteat et satisfaciat. Laicus, si hoc fecerit, excommunicetur, ut Dist.
lxxxvi. Tanta.[51] 65

64 Ex praedictis collige quod quandoque separantur conjugati ita
quod matrimonium dirimitur, ut in supra dictis; et tunc post divortium
uterque nubet cui voluerit; quandoque separantur quantum ad cohabi-
tationem ita quod non dirimitur matrimonium. Verbi gratia, convi-
cisti uxorem tuam in jure de fornicatione, vel in jure confessa est. Potes 70

50 impedietur H impedit O.   51 ab initio] consensus O ab invicem Ck.   52 exceptio]
acceptio Tu *corr. ab* exspectatio O *add.* et AcTa *add.* et *insert.* Tc.   56 etiam *om.* AaJO (*om.*
Pet *sed forsitan ex revisione*).   58 fuit Tu Pet.   libere] libera OTu.   59 consenserunt
CkOTu consentiunt RTa consenserat Ad.   60 Tibi] Si *add.* tibi *insert.* O.   tum] tamen
CcQ¹*RZ *corr. ab* tamen O cum CkH *add.* de OR.   61 tum] tamen Cc *om.* R.   62
nubilem Ci.   non *om.* CkTu.   63 voluerit TaTc.   etiam si] si etiam PR non Tu.
64 ut] ubi Cc *om.* O *add.* ff. [?] U *add.* ff. *delet.* Aa.   65 lxxv. TcTu Pet *add.* vel Tc *add.*
c. *insert.* Aa.   66-76 Ex — relinquere *om.* Q¹*.   67 ut in] velut O.   in *om.* Ck.
68 nubat CkTu *add.* in Christo Ck.

[48] See Hug. *loc. cit.* (quoted in Firth, *Thesis* II 490*-491*).
[49] Cf. Hug. ad C.36 q.1 dictum p. c.3 (fol. 356rb); Po. 1066 (X 5.17.7; issued probably
May-June 1200).
[50] Cf. Hug. ad C.36 q.2 c.5 (fol. 356va).
[51] Cap. 24. This paragraph is evidently based on Hug. ad C.36 q.2 c.1 (fol. 356va). Huguccio cites this canon, which has nothing to do with *raptus*, as evidence that one may be deposed or even excommunicated, i.e. excluded from the sacraments, for a time as a penalty for
crime even after repentance.

eam judicio ecclesiae dimittere et ea invita religionem intrare; sed
neuter reliquo vivente potest nubere. Hoc dico si immunis es a fornicatione et occasionem non dederis ei fornicandi nec post fornicationem
eam cognoveris; si aliquod istorum fuerit, non potes eam relinquere.[52]

65   Item cognovisti duas sorores quarum neutra tua fuit uxor nec tu 75
uxoratus; acta poenitentia potes nubere.   Alexander sic distinguit:
Cognovisti consanguineam uxoris tuae ignoranter; in quocumque gradu
attineat, non separaberis ab uxore tua; tamen ad cautelam imponetur
tibi poenitentia. Si scienter et manifestum est, si illa attinet uxori tuae
in primo vel secundo vel tertio gradu, ut mater, soror, filia vel neptis, 80
perpetuo separaberis ab uxore tua quantum ad carnalem copulam.
Si vero eandem cognovisti sed occultum est, reddes, sed non exiges.
Si vero attinet uxori tuae in quarto vel ulteriori gradu, sive sit occultum
sive manifestum, accepta poenitentia et reddes uxori et exiges, ut in
extra. *Ad aures.*[53]   85

66   Sed nonne haec est iniquitas ? Uxor non vult dimittere; quare ergo
privatur jure suo ex quo non peccavit ? Item apostolus dat optionem
dimittendi ut reconcilietur viro vel maneat innupta; similiter de viro

---

71 judicio] de jure O.   72 es *corr. ab* est Aa.   73 dederis Aa *corr. ab* dederis Ck.
75 Item *reincipit* Q[1]* *fol. 333*.   Item si cognovisti AaCkHPTuU Item si cognoveris J.
sorores] uxores CkR *corr. ab* uxores AaAd Pet.   fuerit CcCiO sit H.   75-76 nec tu
uxoratus *om.* Z.   tu uxoratus] uxoratus es O tu uxoratus es Tu.   77 Si cognovisti AaCkJU.   78 tua *om.* CcTu.   imponatur OTu Pet praeponatur Tc.
79 manifestum] matrimonium O.   attineat AbTu.   80 vel in secundo CiO.   vel
in tertio O *om.* Z.   gradu *om.* J *insert.* Aa.   82 sed[1]] et Q[1]* quod Tu.   sed[2]] et
JQ[1]*U.   83-84 Si vero — exiges *om.* Q[1]*.   83 in] tertio vel TuZ(EY) vel in tertio
vel Aa quinto vel Ck *add.* tertio vel JR(MV) *add.* tertio vel in H(Cp *add.* primo vel secundo
vel tertio vel ISg *om.* Tb).   84 sive *add.* sit JOTc.   et[1] *om.* AaJU.   uxori *om.*
R *add.* tuae CkHTc.   in *om.* CkR.   86-92 Sed — exigere *om.* Q[1]*.   86 haec]
hoc AaCkHJOPRTaU Pet(DEGIKMSgSoTbY *om.* X).   quare] quae O.   87 peccaverit O.   apostolicus AaU papa Z.   optionem] adoptionem Pet *corr. ab* adoptionem
Aa occasionem J *corrupt.* U.   88 dimittenti AbAcAd(Hug.) *corr. ad* dimittenti U dimittendae
PTu(K) *om.* R.   concilietur Ab.   viro *add.* suo CkHJTu.

---

[52] Cf. Bernard of Pavia, *Summa decretalium* 4.20.2-5(pp. 187-189); Gratian C. 32 qq.6-7.
[53] See 1 *Compil.* 4.13.2 (JL 13163). This and the following paragraph are apparently based
on Hug. ad C.27 q.2 dictum p. c.30 *licet ei vel adulterae* (fol. 291[rb-va], ed. Roman pp. 787-788,
quoted in Firth, *Thesis* II 368*-371*). Cf. above Proleg. pp. 42-43; also below sect. 225 with
nn. 52-53.

si ipsa ei debet reconciliari.[54] Item Dominus: "Non dimittas uxorem nisi propter fornicationem,"[55] ejus scilicet. Dico ego quod in tali casu, 90 si velit uxor retinere maritum, non est ab eo separanda; et ille debet reddere debitum, sed non potest exigere. Idem dico usque ad tertium gradum, sive sit occultum sive manifestum. In quarto vero et ulteriori et exiges et reddes, sive sit occultum sive manifestum, ut in extra. *Si quis parochianorum.*[56]   95

67 Sponsa de futuro etiam vivente sponso alii nubet quando propter fornicationem ab eo recedit.

Illam quam polluisti adulterio non ducas etiam mortuo marito suo. Tamen Gratianus ita distinguit: Si vivente viro ejus polluisti eam, num- 99 quam duces eam; si mortuo viro ejus cognovisti eam, poteris eam ducere.[57] Cardinalis ita dicit: Si occultum est adulterium tuum, potes eam ducere; si publicum, non potes.[58] Ego credo quod, sive publicum sive occultum sit, non potes eam ducere; si tamen post adulterium occultum contraxeris cum ea, non dirimetur matrimonium; si post pu- 5 blicum, dirimetur.

89 si] sed AcCcCiOPRU(CpDFIKLMNSoXY).   ei debet] debet et O.   deberet P dat J. Dominus *om.* Pet *insert.* Tc.   dimittes Ck dimmittas Tu.   uxorem *add.* tuam AaCkJTuU. 90 scilicet] sed OTcTuZ(BmEFGILNSoTbX) similiter P(KV) Sacerdos JU.   quod] si JU *add.* si HOR si *corr. ad* quod si Aa quia *add.* si *cum signis ad ponendum post* casu Tc.   91 si *om.* AaHJORTcU.   92 potes Aa debet Ta *om.* PU.   Idem] Item AaCkJTu *om.* R.   93 sive² *add.* sit AbAcTaZ Pet.   quarto] quinto O.   vero *om.* O *add.* gradu Ck.   93-94 In quarto — manifestum *om.* CcTuU (*homoeotel.*) *infra in linea 95 post* parochianorum Ck.   94 et¹ *om.* AcCk.   occultum sive *om.* J *add.* sit AbAcAdTcZ.   95 parochiarum O parochianum Pet.   96-6 Sponsa — dirimetur *om.* Pet.   96 de futuro etiam] etiam de futuro CkP.   sponso *add.* si *corr. ad* suo O.   98 Illam *ss. desinit usque ad sect. 71* Q¹*.   99 ita] sic AaCkJ ista Tu.   1 ducas JU.   potes Ta.   2 dicit *om.* RTa.   est *om.* Cc.   poteris JTaU.   3 poeteris Ta *om.* O.   quod *om.* TuU.   4 poteris Ta.

[54] See 1 *Cor* 7.11.

[55] See *Matt* 5.32.

[56] See 1 *Compil.* 4.20.6 (JL 13162); citation derived from Hug., *loc. cit.*

[57] Robert seems to have misinterpreted Huguccio's reference to Gratian C.31 q.1 dictum p. c.2; Huguccio refers to this in his commentary on the prooemium of this question. See Firth, *Thesis* II 363* with n. 40 (III 649*-650*).

[58] Reference apparently derived from Hug. ad C.31 q.1 pr. (fol. 304ᵛᵇ; quoted in Firth, *Thesis* II 447*).

68 Sponsalia et matrimonium etiam inter absentes contrahi possunt per nutus et signa, litteras et nuntium. Sed ecce ante quam nuntius veniat ad illam, iste revocat consensum; illa tamen consentit nuntio. Non est matrimonium. Alioquin est matrimonium, etiam si iste dormit 10 quando illa consentit, quia consensus intelligitur inhaerere et durare adhuc; et ita praesens consensus istius et praeteritus jam illius, qui tamen intelliguntur adhuc durare, faciunt matrimonium. In nullo mandato fit aliquid nisi consensus mandantis inhaereat ipsi facto, id est perduret usque ad illud. Fiet tamen ei praejudicium nisi poterit pro- 15 bare quod revocaverit mandatum.[59]

69 Cum sollemnitate debent fieri matrimonia; filii enim clandestini sunt legitimi quantum ad successionem et testimonium et accusationem in saecularibus causis, sed sunt illegitimi quantum ad promotionem, testimonium et accusationem in ecclesiasticis causis.[60]   20

In clandestinis matrimoniis non est interpretandum in melius, ut scilicet praedicentur legitima, ne sub tali praetextu adulterium et fornicatio committantur. Sunt tamen matrimonia vera. Si ergo est publica fama quod matrimonium est inter eos, vel si publice uterque se gessit pro conjuge erga alterum, cessat, ut credo, omnis talis canonis 25 mala suspicio, et ut de certo matrimonio judicabit ecclesia, non praesumet de incerto.[61]

8 et[1]] etiam Ac per CkTu.   signa add. et CkPRTa add. et per Aa add. per HJU. nuntius om. HJ insert. Aa.   9 illam] eam O illum Tc istam corr. ad illam Ck.   iste] ille Ta ista Tc.   illa] iste Tc.   10 est[2]] esset AaJU.   11 adhaerere OP.   12 jam om. O.   13 intelligitur CcCkJTuU corr. ab intelligitur Aa.   facit Tc.   14 nisi] nec J corr. ab nec Aa.   mandatis CkU.   id est] et CkJ.   15 duret HJU. possit PTa.   16 revocasset Ta.   18 testimonium] testamentum AaCkHJTcU Pet(FGX) testium CcCiTu(LMSo) contract. ambig. AbAcAdTa(V testimonii Cp).   accusationem] actionem Ta.   18-19 et[2] — causis] in saecularibus causis et ad accusationem H.   19 sed] et AcR.   promotionem add. et Tc add. et insert. O.   19-20 sed — causis om. Ck Pet(V) (homoeotel.).   20 testimonium] testium AbORTcTu(KLMNSo) contract. ambig. AcP testimonii Aa(ISg testamenti F) om. Ta.   et om. TcTu delet. O.   accusationem] actionem AaAbAcAdHTuUZ(EGN) contract. ambig. CcCiTaTc(M).   22 et] vel JU.   23 committatur Ck commutantur Cc admittantur Tu.   est om. CcTc insert. Ci.   24 est] sit AaCkHJTaU.   25 alterum] alium Tc Pet adulterum R.   erga alterum] ergo P.   cessit O crescat J.   cessat — omnis] cessat omnis credo Cc.   26 de certo] decetero Cc corr. ab decetero Aa.   non] nec Ab Pet.

[59] See Hug. ad C.30 q.5 c.8 duceretur uxor (fol. 304[rb]); cf. ad C.30 q.2 c.un. consensus utriusque (fol. 301[ra]).
[60] This and the following section are apparently based on Hug. ad C.30 q.5 c.1 non dubitantur (fol. 303[va], cf. Paris BN lat. 3891, fol. 250[ra]).
[61] See loc. cit.; cf. 1 Compil. 4.1.14 (JL 13969; X 2.23.11).

70 Simplici verbo volunt in facie ecclesiae asserere quod contraxerunt; credetur eis? Non, nisi publica fama hoc habeat. Si non est fama, contrahant publice, quia hoc tutius est. Item, si volunt jurare se 30 contraxisse, audiantur; nec postea audiantur in contrarium; quia nonne crederetur eis si jurarent se in praesenti contrahere? Quidam dicunt quod in quolibet casu debent contrahere publice coram ecclesia; secundum alios sufficit si coram judice in jure confiteantur se esse conjuges.[62] 35

Item clandestine contraxisti cum aliqua, postea publice cum alia; tandem poenitens vis redire ad primam. Excommunicat te ecclesia. Quid fiet? Respondeo: Excommunicet te potius quam adultereris cum secunda.[63]

71 Sunt et alia quae matrimonii impediunt effectum, id est carnis 40 copulam: locus sacer, tempus sacrum. Credo tamen quod, ubicumque et quandocumque exactus fueris, reddere tenearis, nisi cum omni pace evadere possis.[64]

De fornicariis aliter judico quod, si aliquis in vigilia paschae fornicatus est simplici fornicatione vel graviori, propter recens facinus in die 45 paschae a sacra eum arcebo communione. Idem facerem de conjugato libidinose exigente, sed non de exacto. Quid si causa incontinentiae

28 Si simplici PRTa Pet Si *insert.* simplici O *add.* vero OTu.   quod] quam Cc.
contraxerint PTa.   29-45 credetur — die *insert.* Ck.   eis *corr. ab* eisdem Ab.
Non[1] *rasura* Ab.   31 nec] ne J non Tc.   postea] post O.   nonne] non CkOP
corr. ad non Aa vere Tu.   32 jurarunt J jurent Ta praesentarent O.   Quidam
add. autem O.   36 cum alia] confiteatur *script. in lacuna vel rasura* Cc.   37
tandem] tamen PR.   38 adulteraris Cc adulteris J.   40 Sunt *ss. reincipit* Q[1]* *fol.*
333[r].   et *om.* Q[1]* *insert.* Aa autem Pet.   Sunt et] Inter U.   alia] plura Q[1]*
om. Pet.   quae] autem U et quae sunt Tu.   matrimonium AbJTc.   impediant
Ad *add.* non J.   effectum *add.* scilicet Ab.   41 copula PTu.   ubicumque et *insert.*
Aa.   42 et *om.* Pet.   et quandocumque *insert.* H.   quandocumque] quocumque
R *corr. ab* quantumcumque Tc quamcumque Tu.   omni *om.* O.   44 fornicatoriis O.
44-45 fornicatus est *om.* Q[1]*.   45 est] fuerit CkjTa.   die *add.* sacro AaJTaU *add.*
sancto H.   46 sacra] sacro Cc.   a sacra eum arcebo] arcebo eum a Q[1]*.
eum — communione] cum acerbo dolore communione abstinebit Ta.   arcebo] acerbo
R.   communicatione U conventione J.   47 de *om.* JTuU *insert.* Aa.

[62] See Hug. *loc. cit.*
[63] See *loc. cit.*; cf. Firth, *Thesis* II 462* n. 54 (III 742*).
[64] Cf. Hug. ad C.33 q.4 pr. (fol. 341[rb-va]).

exigit? Si contritus est, conscientiae suae eum relinquam,[65] ut si esurierit manducet, alioquin credat tantum et manducavit.[66]

<Cap.> iv. QUAE IMPEDIUNT MATRIMONIUM TANTUM   50

72 Tempus feriarum et interdictum ecclesiae impediunt matrimonium; quia in adventu, in quadragesima et interdicto ecclesiae non contrahuntur matrimonia, id est non debent contrahi. Quandocumque tamen contracta fuerint, stabunt.[67]

---

48 exigerit CkHJU exegit P exigitis Tu.   Si *om.* Tu.   Si contritus est *om.* Cc. contrictus O constrictus Tc.   relinquant J relinquo Tu.   49 credat] recedat Ck eradat Tu.   tantum] eum O.   manducaverit AaCkJQ¹*U.   50 IMPEDIANT AbAd.   *tit. om.* JOTaTc.   51 Tempus *desinit* Q¹* *usque ad sect. 74.*   et *om.* J *insert.* HTu.   52 quia *om.* Tu.   in quadragesima] quadragesima scilicet Tu. in quadragesima et interdicto *om.* J.   et *add.* in AdHPU *add. ex Pet.*   interdictio Tu *corr. ab* interdictio Aa.   52-53 et interdicto — matrimonia] non contrahuntur matrimonia nec in interdicto ecclesiae R.   53 Quandocumque] Quaecumque Tu *corr. ad* Quaecumque Tc.   tamen *om.* J *insert.* Tc.

---

[65] Cf. Hug. ad C.33 q.4 c.7 *suo judicio* (fol. 342ra-b); Courson, *Summa* 1.11 (ed. Kennedy, p. 299); Michael Müller, *Ethik und Recht* pp. 48-64, 77-89. Regarding Robert's attitude towards marital intercourse cf. Rudolf Weigand, "Die Lehre der Kanonisten des 12. und 13. Jahrhunderts von den Ehezwecken," *Studia Gratiana* 12 (Collectanea S. Kuttner 2; Bologna 1967) 443-478, esp. 468-473. The case which Robert considers here is complicated by the fact that marital intercourse was forbidden during lent in the ancient canons (see below sect. 296); the first paragraph of this sect. 71 indicates that Robert has this circumstance in mind.

[66] See Augustine, *Tractatus in Joannis evangelium* 25.12 (*ad Joan* 6.29; PL 35.1602) quoted in Gratian *De consec.* D.2 c.47 and in Lombard, *Sent.* 4.9.1 (II 793); cf. Courson, *Summa* 1.14 (ed. Kennedy p. 301; in this edition it comes before c.13).

[67] Cf. Hug. ad C.33 q.4 dictum p. c.1 (fol. 342rb); ad C.33 q.4 c.10 *separentur* (fol. 342va); 1 *Compil.* Book 4, tit. 17 (X book 4, tit. 16); Bernard of Pavia, *Summa decretalium* 4.17.1 (ed. Laspeyres pp. 180-182). By the impediment *interdictum ecclesiae* was understood at this time a prohibition proceeding from ecclesiastical authority forbidding certain persons to marry, usually until their freedom to marry should be established in the church courts.

INCIPIUNT CAPITULA TERTII LIBRI

73   i. Quid sit ordo et qui.

    ii. Quae exigantur ad ordinem et sint de substantia ordinis.[1]

   iii. Quae impediant ordinem et ordinis exsecutionem.

   iv. Quae impediant exsecutionem tantum.   5

INCIPIT LIBER TERTIUS

Pertransitis pro modulo nostro quae ad propositum de matrimonio pertinent, secundum ordinem praelibatum ad ea quae in clericis attenduntur progrediamur, ad ordines scilicet, dignitates, simoniam, etc.[2] Sed quia ordo clericum facit et sine ordine laicus est quilibet, licet litte- 10 ratus sit,[3] ab ordine incipiamus.

<Cap.> i. QUID SIT ORDO

74 Ordo est potestas officiandi ecclesiam, alicui a pontifice vel sacerdote collata per verba ab ecclesia ad hoc instituta.[4] Officiat ecclesiam qui ministrat in ecclesia. Ministrat autem non quilibet in officio quo- 15 libet, sed in illo ad quod institutus est. Unde et ab officiis diversis diversa sortiti sunt nomina ministri, ut alius dicatur lector, alius ostiarius, et sic de aliis.

---

1 LIBRI *om.* Ci.   TERTII LIBRI *om.* Cc.   INCIPIT LIBER TERTIUS; CAPITULA III. LIBRI *insert.* Ad.   2-11 *sect.* 73 *om.* Pet.   2 (Quid — qui *om.* DI).   et qui *om.* AaCkHJORUZ(CpGLNVX).   qui *om.* PTaTu(BmKMSoTb *ita conjunguntur duo tituli*) add. conferant Ad.   3 exiguntur AaCkHJOTcU(CpDEGISgTbVX).   sunt JTc.   4 impediunt AaHRTuZ(BmCpDEGISgTbXY).   5 Quae — tantum *om.* U *aliter* P (*aliter* X). impediunt AaCkHJTu(CpDEGISgTbXY).   8 praelibatis AaOTaTu *om.* J.   9 aggrediamur O.   ad *om.* OTu.   simoniae O *om.* J.   11 sit *om.* O.   13 Ordo reincipit Q1* *fol.* 333ra.   Ordo *usque ad finem sect.* 141 (*aliquibus omissis et aliis mutatis*) Pet *fols.* 134v-139v.   15 quilibet *add.* in ecclesia JU.   17 sortita O *corr. ab* sortita Tc. sortiti sunt] sortiuntur AaCkHJU.

---

[1] Regarding this use of the word *substantia* see below sect. 74 with n. 6 and sect. 76 with n. 9.

[2] See above Book 1 sect. 10.

[3] Cf. JL 12701 (LOEWENFELD, *Epistolae Pontificum Romanorum ineditae* no. 262, pp. 148-149).

[4] I have not found the source of this definition; regarding the institution of the words by the Church cf. below n. 6.

Instituitur autem minister ecclesiasticus non a quolibet, sed ab epis- copo suo vel sacerdote; ut ordo psalmistae, sive ille qui dicitur corona 20 apud nos, a lombardis clerica, olim a simplici conferebatur sacerdote et adhuc hodie in Alemannia confertur.[5] Confirmabant etiam olim simplices sacerdotes. Alii ordines ab episcopo conferuntur.

Instituitur autem minister ecclesiasticus non sine consecratione. Consecratur autem per verba ab ecclesia ad hoc instituta; unde et 25 verba illa, ut puto, de substantia ordinis sunt.[6]

75   Octo sunt ordines. Psalmistae ordo sive prima tonsura sive cle- rica sive corona, quocumque istorum modorum dicatur, idem puto est ordo.[7] Secundus ordo est ostiarii, tertius lectoris, quartus exorcistae, quintus acolythi, sextus subdiaconi, septimus diaconi, octavus sacer- 30 dotum.[8]

19-23 Instituitur — conferuntur *om.* Q[1]*.   19 Instituuntur Ac *corr. ab* Instituuntur J. ministri ecclesiae Ac.   19-20 a suo episcopo AaJU Pet.   20 vel a sacerdote CkJTuU Pet.   21 lumbardis AaAdHU Pet(BmGSg lumbardeis D) lumbrandis O longobardis P (lanbardis F).   22 Alemonnia Cc Almania Ci Alemania U Alemaninnia Ab.   in Alemannia] manet quia O.   etiam] autem O Pet.   24 sacratione O.   25 con- secratur] consecrator CcTu.   Consecratur — instituta *om.* Q[1]*.   verba *add. ante* O. ab ecclesia *om.* R Pet.   institutam Ck consituta O.   26 ut puto] utpote Ck *om.* Ta. 27 sive[2] *om.* RTa.   28 corona *add.* sive O.   puto *om.* AaCkHU.   idem puto] ut puto idem Tu.   30-31 sacerdotis AaAdRTa sacerdos Ck.

---

[5] *Alemannia,* which in the early Middle Ages designated the district now called "Swabia," by the thirteenth century had come to be used for the whole territory of the German Empire; cf. e.g. Po. 29 (Reg. 1.19; PL 214.19); also below sect. 114 with n. 9. Regarding the conferring of tonsure by a simple priest see HUG. ad D.23 c.20 *absque scientia episcopi sola jussione presbyteri* (fol. 26[vb]). According to the text of his *Summa* at my disposal, Huguccio says it is the custom *in Campania.*

[6] Cf. Huguccio: "Nihilominus tamen hodie unctio sacerdotalis est de substantia consecratio- nis; quia non est mirum sub alia forma consecrationem modo fieri et sub alia olim. Nam ecclesia circa talia satis potuit immutare ecclesiasticam formam sacramenti, sicut patet in multis exem- plis. Nam ex permissione Gregorii simplices sacerdotes chrismabant in fronte, ut Dist. xcv. *Pervenit* (cap. 1), et erat verum sacramentum." HUG. ad D.23 c.12 *neutris agitur* (text established from Paris BN lat. 3892, fol. 26[rb] and 3891, fol. 26[ra]); cf. also ad D.23 c.14 (fol. 26[rb]). The word *substantia* seems to have been used to designate what is essential to a sacrament first by Peter Lombard; see his *Sententiae* 4.3.1 (II 755) and 4.28.2 (II 926); cf. Damian VAN DEN EYNDE, "The Theory of the Composition of the Sacraments in Early Scholasticism," *Franciscan Studies* 11[1] (1951)[1] 3-4. Cf. below n. 9.

[7] Cf. HUG. ad D.21 c.1 *psalmista* (fol. 20[rb-va]); FIRTH, *Thesis* II 364*-365* with notes 53-54 (III 654*-655*) where Huguccio is quoted.

[8] Although Robert follows Huguccio in considering first tonsure as an order, he does not follow the latter's position that the episcopacy too is an order (see e.g. HUG. ad D.21 c.1 *epis-*

\<Cap.\> ii. QUAE EXIGANTUR AD ORDINEM ET SINT DE SUBSTANTIA ORDINIS

76   De substantia ordinis sunt sexus, baptismus, prima tonsura cete-
rorum ordinum, potestas ordinantis et ejus intentio, et forte intentio 35
ordinati et verba.[9]

De sexu

Sexus est de substantia ordinis ; quia mulieres benedicuntur, non ordinantur ; licet inveniatur quod aliquando fuerunt diaconissae. Sed
in alio sensu dicebantur diaconissae quam hodie diaconus; numquam 40
enim habuit femina illud officium quod modo habet diaconus. Nec
hermaphroditus, etiam si in eo praevaleat sexus virilis.[10]

De baptismo

77   Baptismus est etiam de substantia ordinis; quia baptismus est
janua et fundamentum non solum ordinum, sed etiam omnium sacra- 45

---

35 ordinatis Tu ordinandi HJTa.   36 ordinanti *add.* ejus Tu.   et *add.* ejus AaHJ.
39 fuerint AaHOPQ¹*RTaU(FGIKMNSoTbVX).   41 illud] idem Ac vel Ta.   habuit—diaconus] officium habuit femina quam modo diaconus Tu.   42 praevalet Tu prae-
valeret Ck praevaluit H.   44 est¹ *om.* R.   etiam *om.* OQ¹*TuZ(DEILSgSoTbXY).
etiam est AdCkTa Pet(G) est etiam est Aa.   est — ordinis] etiam de substantia ordinis
est HJU(CpV).   est² *om.* R *add.* etiam Tc.   45 ordinis JO.   etiam] et AdTu *om.*
AaJRU.

---

copus). In regard to this Flamborough follows rather the tradition of the theologians, notably
Lombard, that the episcopacy is a "dignity," but not an order distinct from the priesthood.
This is followed by Rufinus, Stephen of Tournai and many others (see e.g. the anonymous *Speculum ecclesiae* PL 177.349-352). See Robert P. STENGER, "The Episcopacy as an Ordo according to the Medieval Canonists," *MedStud* 29 (1967) 67-112; Gabriel LE BRAS, *Institutions ecclésiastiques de la Chrétienté médiévale* (Histoire de l'Église 12) I¹ (Paris 1959) 151-152; Artur LAND-
GRAF, "Die Lehre der Frühscholastik vom Episkopat als ordo," *Scholastik* 26 (1951) 496-519,
esp. 506-508, where Huguccio is treated.

   [9] Cf. Peter CANTOR, *Summa de sacramentis et animae consiliis* Part 3, c.34, § 286 (fol. 128ᵛᵇ;
cf. ed. DUGAUQUIER III¹ 127-128); the author is dealing here with baptism, but his treatment
of it shows some similarities with our text. Cf. also COURSON: "Ad esse baptismi ista tria re-
quiruntur, scilicet debita forma verborum et elementum ad hoc deputatum et intentio ipsius
baptizantis, scilicet ut intendat baptizare in forma ecclesiae." ROBERT COURSON, *Summa* 38.1
(fol. 120ʳᵃ). Cf. above n. 6.

   [10] Cf. HUG. ad C.27 q.1 c.23 *ordinari* (fol. 284ʳᵇ); Franz GILLMANN, "Weibliche Kleriker nach
dem Urteil der Frühscholastik," *ArchivKKRecht* 93 (1913) 239-253 (quoting Huguccio pp. 246-249)

mentorum. Unde baptismo non habito nullus ordo, nullum sacramentum suscipitur.[11]

Dicit tamen dominus Innocentius quod, si quis habet fidem, licet nec aqua baptizatus fuerit nec sanguine proprio, ut fit in martyrio, ordinem suscipit; baptizatur enim quis in spiritu, et ex quo habet fidem, 50 habet et Christum; et ita in Christo baptizatus est, qui est omnium bonorum fundamentum. Sacerdotem tamen non baptizatum fecit baptizari et reordinari quia sic senserunt praedecessores ejus; et hoc tutius est.[12]

De prima tonsura

78 Sicut baptismus est fundamentum omnium sacramentorum, ita et 55 secundum quosdam prima tonsura est fundamentum omnium ordinum, et illa non habita nullus ordo suscipitur.[13] Unde si aliquis non habita prima tonsura accedit ad acolythatum, postea ad subdiaconatum, deinde ad sacerdotium, nullum ordinem habet; immo, si vult in aliquo ordine ministrare, oportet quod suscipiat primam tonsuram et deinde 60 acolythatum, postea subdiaconatum, et sic deinceps.

Alii dicunt quod hoc totum falsum est et quod non praehabita prima tonsura quilibet ordo haberi potest.[14] Qui ergo non praehabita prima

---

48 dominus] papa Z *om.* Aa.   dominus Innocentius] Innocentius papa Pet.   quod *om.* JU.   habuerit AaJU.   49 nec[1]] non AaQ[1]*Tc Pet(EGKLSgXY) *add.* in U Pet(Cp).   aqua *add.* non Ck.   fuerit] sit P Pet.   50 sucepit PRTu *add.* quis Tu.   baptizatus Tu Pet.   enim] autem AaHJTaU.   in] etiam AbQ[1]*Tc *om.* OTu.   et] etiam OTu *om.* AbPQ[1]*RTa.   51 et[1] *om.* ORTaU.   52 non baptizatum] inbaptizatum OTu.   53 ordinari JU recoronari Z.   ejus] sui P nostri Z *om.* OQ[1]*Tu.   55 et] etiam JP *om.* HRTa.   56 est fundamentum *om.* AaJ.   58 accedat R accidit Cc.   acolythum TcU acolatum O.   subdiaconum Tc *add.* et sic deinceps P *add.* postea ad diaconatum U Pet *add.* deinde ad diaconatum Tu.   58-59 postea — sacerdotium] et sic ad alios Tu.   59 ad *add.* diaconatum et Ad *add.* diaconatum et sic ad H.   sacerdotem O.   habet] suscipit O.   aliquo] alio CiO.   60 accipiat HJU.   et *om.* AaHJOQ[1]*U.   60-61 deinde ad acolythum Tc deinde ad acolythatum Pet deinde [ad *insert.*] acolythatum Aa.   61 postea ad subdiaconum Tc postea ad subdiaconatum Pet *om.* Ta.   62 falsum] factum CcCk.   habita R habita prius O.

---

[11] Cf. Hug. ad D.52 c.un. *redire ad officia majora* (fol. 65[ra-b]); probably this paragraph and certainly the following one are based on the decretal cited in the following note.

[12] See Po. 2749 (X 3.43.3; issued April 13, 1206).

[13] Cf. Hug. ad D.52 c.un. *redire ad officia majora* (fol. 65[ra-b]). Huguccio maintains that tonsure or some other minor order is necessary as a foundation for valid reception of any major order.

[14] Source not found.

tonsura ulteriorem ordinem suscepit, accipiat primam tonsuram, et
tamdiu ab omni cesset administratione quamdiu caruit corona vel 65
prima tonsura, ut fit in aliis ordinibus transitis.[15]

Ego omnes sine prima tonsura ordinatos ad dominum papam transmitto et ab omni administratione suspendo. Idem facio de illis qui
prima tonsura a simplici sacerdote suscepta ulteriores susceperunt
ordines, nisi sint in partibus illis in quibus adhuc de antiqua consue- 70
tudine primam tonsuram simplices benedicunt sacerdotes.[16]

De potestate ordinantis

79   Potestas ordinantis est de substantia ordinis. Sed nota quod quandoque potestas ordinandi in aliquo omnino non est, ut in non sacerdote
quantum ad coronam conferendam, et non episcopo quantum ad 75
ordines ulteriores. Episcopo catholico et catholice viventi inest potestas ordinandi soluta et libera in suo episcopatu; in alieno est ligata.
Nullus enim alienum clericum nec in episcopatu alieno sine licentia
ordinare debet.[17]

Ligatur etiam ista potestas in suspenso, schismatico, excommunicato 80
et haeretico; ligatur, inquam, in istis ordinandi potestas, quia ea uti
non possunt, id est non debent ordinare. Utrum tamen ordines conferant quaestio est, et maxime de haeretico, de quo diversae sunt opi-
niones.

64 susceperit R habebit J habebit *corr. ad* suscipit Aa.   65 ab omni *insert.* Aa.
ab omni cesset] cesset ab P.   ministratione O Pet.   corona vel *om.* Tc.
65-66 vel prima tonsura *om.* R.   66 ut] et Tu.   ut fit] sed *corr. ad* ut fit sed O.
aliis *om.* J *insert.* Aa.   67-68 mitto AaU.   69 sucipiunt Ta suceperint AaJ acceperunt
Tc.   69-70 ulteriorem... ordinem Tc.   70 ordines *om.* U *insert.* O.   sint] sicut
vel sunt O.   antiqua] prima Ta *om.* Ck.   de antiqua *om.* R.   71 primam *om.* P.-
primam tonsuram *insert.* Cc.   73 nota] notandum O.   nota quod *om.* Ta.   74 im
nino *om.* JR.   non[2] *op.* CkTcTu.   in non] non in Pet.   75 non] in non Ta in
CkTu.   76 et *om.* HP.   vivente OQ[1]*.   76-77 ulteriores — ordinandi *om.* Tu.
77 episcopio AbOQ[1]*Ta episcopatu vel episcopio Tc.   77-78 in alieno — alieno *om.* R
(*homoeotel. post inversionem*).   78 nec] non Tu *add.* suum in O *om.* Ta.   79 ordinare
add. se Tu.   ordinare debet] ordinandi R.   80 etiam] enim AaJ in istis Tc *vide
infra var. ad lineam 81.*   ista] illa H Pet ordinandi Tc.   81 et *om.* Q[1]*R.   in istis
om. Tc *vide supra var. ad lineam 80*   ea uti] eum O vitari autem Tu.   83 quaestio] quod
OTu.

[15] Cf. below sect. 183.
[16] Cf. above sect. 74 with n. 5.
[17] Cf. GRATIAN Dist. 71.

80   Dicunt aliqui: Si accepit quis ultimam manus impositionem, id 85
est ordinem episcopalem (qui sic dicitur quia post illum nullus ordo
confertur), si ergo illam accepit in ecclesia, id est in unitate ecclesiae,
ordinem confert; si extra, non, et qui ab illo accipit nihil accipit.[18]
De corpore Christi dicunt quod a nullo tali, id est extra ecclesiae uni-
tatem constituto, confici potest,[19] argum. xxiv. quaest. i. *Schisma*.[20]   90

Huguccio dicit quod quilibet episcopus, sive excommunicatus sive
non, sive catholicus sive haereticus, sive ultimam manus impositionem
accepit in ecclesia sive extra, ordinem confert, similiter et ordinatus ab
illo, et sic in infinitum,[21] argum. i. quaest. i. *Dominus*.[22]

81   Hoc autem dico, si forma conferendi sacramenta servetur; alio- 95

85 accipit Cc Pet accipiat O suscepit Aa.   87 acceperit OTa Pet.   88 illo] eo
J alio Tu.   accipit[1]] accepit CkJTcTu Pet.   accipit[2]] accepit CkTcTu.
90 constitutio Cc.   constituto confici potest] confici potest constitutor O.   argumento
Ad argumento *insert.* O ab Tc quia Ck Resp. J *om.* Tu.   xxiii. J xiii. *corr. ad* xxiv. Aa.
91 Hugo AaCkHJOTc Pet.   93 accepit *add.* si J *add.* si *corr. ad* sive Aa.   ecclesia]
ecclesiastico *corr. ad* ecclesia sive extra Aa.   sive extra] suscepit AaJ.   et *om.* AaHJU
insert. Ck.   93-94 ab illo *om.* Ta.   94 argum. *add.* c. AaU.   i.[1]c. J *om.* Tc.
95 sacramentum Ta.

[18] This is the theory of the school of Bologna. See ALEXANDER III (Roland Bandinelli) *Stroma*
ad C.1 q.7 (p. 15); note that, according to Huguccio and Robert (see next sect. 81), the same
Alexander III acted as Pope according to a doctrinal position different from that which he had
maintained as canonist. Cf. also RUFINUS, *Summa* ad C.1 q.1 c.17 (p. 206); ad C.9 q.1 pr. (p.
298); GRATIAN C.1 q.1 dictum p. c.97 § 4; Louis SALTET, *Les réordinations* pp. 291-316; Nikolaus
HÄRING, "The Augustinian Axiom: *Nulli sacramento injuria facienda est*," *MedStud* 16 (1954) 87-
117, esp. p. 111.
[19] This is maintained by GERHOCH OF REICHERSBERG, *Epistola ad Innocentium papam* Mon-
GerHist *Libelli de lite* 3.225-227; IDEM, *Liber de duabus haeresibus* MonGerHist *Libelli de lite* 3.287-
288; cf. Nikolaus HÄRING, "A Study in the Sacramental Theology of Alger of Liège," *MedStud*
20 (1958) 68-69, 75-76. This is also maintained by SIMON OF BISIGNANO, *Summa* ad C.1 q.1 c.16
inexpiabilis, c.30 *sed non contaminabitur donum* Dei *per illum*, c.72 *perfidiam dignis increpationibus re-*
pulit. Rufinus vacillates; see his *Summa* ad C.1 q.1 c.30 (p. 211) c.87 (p. 218). See also Artur
LANDGRAF, "Zur Konsekrationsgewalt des von der Kirche getrennten Priesters im 12. Jahrhundert," *Scholastik* 15 (1940) 204-227.
[20] Reference to GRATIAN C.24 q.1 c.34; in such references the initial *Causa* is often omitted,
as here, in mediaeval works; henceforth only missing data as *Cap. 34* will be indicated. —
Sects. 80-82 of this Penitential are paraphrases of HUG. ad C.9 q.1 pr. (fol. 176[rb-va]).
[21] See HUG. *ibid.* (quoted FIRTH, *Thesis* II 354*); cf. IDEM ad C.1 q.1 c.17 *Qui perfectionem*
(fol. 109rb); c.30 *Si fuerit justus* (fol. 111ra). Cf. also Heinrich HEITMEYER, *Sakramentenspendung*
bei Häretikern und Simonisten nach Huguccio (Analecta Greg. 132; Rome 1964).
[22] Cap. 87.

quin nihil agitur, ut i. quaest. i. *Si qui confugerint*[23] et quaest. vii. *Dai-bertum*.[24] Unde, si cum talibus dispensetur, oportet eos reordinari, ut habetur in praedictis capitulis; alii non debent ordinari, argum. i. quaest. i. *Quod quidam*.[25] Quod bene ordinavit Alexander in schismate 99 Octoviani. Lucius tamen papa, ut dicunt, fecit reordinari ordinatos ab illis qui ultimam manus impositionem acceperant extra ecclesiam, et mirum fuit quod cardinales consenserunt. Forte sequebantur primam pravam opinionem, vel hoc fecerunt in odium schismatis.[26]

Sic ergo a quocumque episcopo datur ordinatio, dummodo fiat in 5 forma ecclesiae et intendatur fieri quod facit ecclesia, ordinatur;[27] sed exsecutionem ordinis nullus potest dare nisi in ecclesia, ut i. quaest. i. *Qui perfectionem*, Verum etiam, *Arrianos*.[28]

96 nihil *om.* O.   ut *add.* c. JU *add.* in Tu *add.* capitulo *corr. ad* in prima quaestione Aa.   vii.] viii. OQ¹*RTaTc nona Tu.   96-97 Diabertus O Diabertum Pet Diabolo Tu Dabertum Ta Dalbertum H Sabbatum AaJU.   97 eos *om.* PTc(CpDFIKN) *delet.* Ac(Bm) *add.* ordinatos ab illis *insert.* O.   reordinari] recoronari Z *add.* ordinatos ab illis AcPTc(BmCpFGKMNSgSoY) *add. et* ordinatos ab illis R (*add.* scilicet ordinatos ab illis F).   98 non debent ordinari] dicunt non ordinari Tu.   reordinari Z(Hug.). argum.] ab Tc articulo Tu *add.* c. AaJU.   98-8 argum. — Arrianos *om.* Q¹*.   99 ordinantur O *om.* Tu.   Alexander *add.* papa AaHJU.   1 Octaviani AaCiPTc-(BmIKNSgXY) Octani Tu (*corrupt.* Octa- LSo) Octoviani *cett.*(*cett.* Hug.).   Lucius] Innocentius OTu.   feci Tu facit eos O.   4 hoc *om.* CcTa.   5 episcopo *om.* TaTu.   6 ordinatur *add.* quidem Ad.   7 exsecutionem — dare] exsecutio nullius ordinis potest dari JU.   ordinis *om.* P *insert.* Tc.   ut] si Ci *om.* Ck *add.* c. AaJ. i.² *om.* Cc.   8 etiam] et Pet *om.* P.   Arrianus RTaU(GETb) Arcianus Tu Arianos *corr. ad* Arianus Aa Anianus J (Arrianos *corr. ad* Arrianus Bm).

[23] Cap. 52 The incipit of this canon in our editions of Gratian is *Si quis confugerit*, and Rufinus comments on it under this incipit, *Summa* (ed. SINGER p. 213). Huguccio, according to the MSS at my disposal, comments on it as *Si qui confugerint* in his *Summa* (fol. 112ᵛᵃ), and cites it in the same way in the passage on which this is based (see FIRTH, *Thesis* II 355*) as well as ad C.1 q.1 c.30 (fol. 111ʳᵃ).

[24] Cap. 24; cf. Huguccio's commentary on this canon (fol. 126ᵛᵃ).

[25] Cap. 97.

[26] See Hug. ad C.9 q.1 pr. (quoted in FIRTH, *Thesis* II 354*). Regarding these historical events cf. SALTET, *Les réordinations* pp. 326-330; our knowledge of them seems to have come to us only through Huguccio.

[27] The phrase *et intendatur fieri quod facit ecclesia* is not found in Huguccio's text on which this passage is otherwise based (see above n. 20); cf. HEITMEYER, *Sakramentenspendung* pp. 52-68. There is reason to believe that Flamborough obtained it from Praepositinus by way of Robert Courson. Regarding Praepositinus see Franz GILLMANN, "Die Notwendigkeit der Intention. . .," *Katholik*⁴ 18 (1916)² 111-113; cf. Artur M. LANDGRAF, "Beiträge der Frühscholastik. . .," *DivThomFreib*³ 29 (1951) 9-34; FIRTH, *Thesis* II 363* with n. 44. Regarding Courson see his *Summa* 38.10 (fol. 121ᵛᵃ⁻ᵇ); cf. FIRTH, *Thesis* II 411* with n. 77.

[28] Reference to C.1 q.1 cc.17, 18, 73 is apparently intended. However the incipit of c.18, *Ventum est*, has been incorrectly reproduced both by Huguccio and by Robert of Flamborough; see FIRTH, *Thesis* II 363* n. 43 (III 651*), where Huguccio is quoted.

82   Scienter ordinatus ab illo qui ultimam manus impositionem accepit
extra ecclesiam non accipiat dispensationem; ignoranter, per dispen- 10
sationem toleratur in illo ordine, sed ad majorem non promovetur,
ut infra eadem, quaest. i. *Ordinationes*.²⁹

Ordinati ab illis qui ultimam manus impositionem acceperunt in
ecclesia, sed postea excommunicatis et ab ecclesia separatis, dispensative tolerantur in suis ordinibus etiam scienter a talibus susceptis, ut ix. 1
quaest. i. Qui *ab excommunicatis*,³⁰ sed ad majores non promoventur, ut i.
quaest. i. *Si quis haereticae*,³¹ nisi maxima utilitas vel necessitas exigat,
ut ix. quaest. i. *Ab excommunicatis*.³² Dispensative, inquam, tales tolerantur in suis ordinibus, nisi in quinque casibus: si sint iterata unctione
maculati, id est in eisdem ordinibus ordinati, ut i. quaest. vii. *Saluber*- 20
rimum,³³ vel si simoniace vel a simoniaco ordinati, ut ix. *Ab excommuni-*
catis,³⁴ vel si fecerint jacturam unici lavacri, scilicet rebaptizati, ut *De*
consec. Dist. iv. *Eos quos*,³⁵ et si ad subversionem fidei adhaeserint haereticis, et si elegerint ordinari ab haereticis cum aliter possint.   In his

9 ordinatos O *corr. ab* ordinatos *manu originali* Ci.   illo] eo OTc.   accipit OTu in-
cepit Ci.   10 accipit O.   11 ad *om.* Tu.   ad majorem] amplius U.   promoveretur O promovebitur P *add.* ad majorem U.   12 infra eadem] prima Causa Cc c. i.
JU Causa *add.* v. *vel* i. *suprascr.* Aa in exemplari Tu.   eadem *om.* CkPTa.   i. *om.* Ci.
14 post AbP.   et *om.* O insert. P.   14-15 dispensatione Cc dispensationem Pet dispensantem Ta *corr. ab* dispensantem Ac.   15 inceptis O ceptis Tu *om.* Ck.   ix.] in ix.
Z viii. Ta x. Cc *corr. ab* ii. Aa.   16 Qui] quia Tu *om.* Ck.   ab *om.* CcCiR.
16-17 Qui — quaest. i. *om.* U.   16 non *om.* Ck insert. Tu.   18 quaest. i.] Si Ad *om.*
AbOQ¹*Ta.   excommunicetis O.   dispensatione Tu Pet dispensationem *corr. ad* per
dispensationem Ac dispensatem Ci.   inquam] non R *om.* Tu insert. Aa.   inquam ta-
les] tamen quidam J.   19 sit JU.   iterata] in iterata R tanta JTu cathafrisi O.
21 si *om.* AcJP insert. Aa.   ix.] Causa ix. AaJU extra. Z *om.* Ta *add.* quaest. i. CkHJRU
add. quaest. ii. Pet.   Ab] Qui ab J Pet.   21-22 excommunicetis O.   22 reprobapti-
zati Ci baptizati Ta *add. versum* Z.   23 Dist.] autem Tu *om.* J.   Dist. iv. insert. O.
iv.] iii. Ta.   adhaeserunt AdCkJOPTu(BmI affuerunt G).   24 elegerunt PTu.
possunt JTc Pet.

²⁹ This reference is taken from the same commentary of Huguccio, on C.9 q.1 pr. (fol. 176ᵛᵃ),
on which sects. 80-82 of this penitential are based; there it refers to cap. 5 of the same question
in Gratian (C.9 q.1).
³⁰ Cap. 4. The incipit of this canon is *Ab excommunicatis*, as it is cited twice below in the same
paragraph of this penitential. Here Robert has probably mistaken *q.* (underlined) in his MS
of Huguccio for *Qui.*
³¹ Cap. 42.
³² Cap. 4.
³³ Cap. 21.
³⁴ C.9 q.1 c.4.
³⁵ Cap. 118; cf. in Part I of the *Decretum* D.50 c.65; D.51 c.5, and in Part II C.1 q.7 c.10.

quinque casibus non dispensatur cum talibus in suis ordinibus; papa 25
autem dispensare potest cum talibus si vult.[36]

83 Quod dictum est de ordinibus intelligendum est de omnibus sacramentis, consecrationibus et benedictionibus. Ego autem omnes
tales, tam ordinantes quam ordinatos, si ordinaverint vel ordinati fuerint in suspensione, schismate, excommunicatione, haeresi, ad dominum 30
papam transmitterem.

Ecce qui sciens et prudens ad aliquem ordinem suscipiendum se bis
benedici permittit vel baptizari irregularis est, nec potest in ordine suscepto ministrare nec ulterius promoveri sine papae dispensatione.[37]
Nonne idem judicium est de illo qui sciens et prudens aliquem ad eun- 35
dem ordinem bis benedicit vel bis baptizat? Credo. Nonne multo
fortius idem judicium est de illo qui sciens et prudens in eadem hostia
eucharistiae benedictionem vel consecrationem vel confectionem rei-
terat? Credo.[38]

De intentione ordinantis 40

84 Intentio ordinantis est de substantia ordinis, ut scilicet intendat
facere id quod ecclesia intendit facere in cujuslibet ordinis collatione.
Idem dico in omnibus sacramentis, consecrationibus et benedictionibus [39]

24-26 In his — autem] solus papa Q[1]*. 27-28 sacramentis *add.* et U *add.* in J. 30
schismate *add.* vel ORU *add.* vel *insert.* Aa. 31 transmitto Ck transeunt *add.* Tam (*pro
tamen?*) unctio olei in manibus sacerdotum non est de substantia ordinis secundum meum magistrum; tamen si praetermittatur addenda est. Tu (*hic finitur sectio in* Tu). 32-39 Ecce —
Credo *insert.* AbO *abbrev.* Pet *supra ad finem sectionis 82* Tu; *cf. infra in* Append. C *no.* 1. 33
nec *corr. ab* sine Aa *om.* Tu. 34 administrare U imministrare Ci imministrares O.
nec] vel P Pet. 35 et prudens *om.* Ab. 36 vel] et CiJPQ[1]*Tu. 38 eucharistia
R *om.* AbO. 39 Credo *add.* Unctio olei in manibus sacerdotis non est de substantia ordinis
secundum meum magistrum. Si tamen praetermittatur, addenda non est. P (*similis additio*
GK; *cf. variationem supra in linea 31*). 41 ut] in Tu *om.* Ta. scilicet *insert. ante* ut O.
42 id *om.* CcR *insert.* Tu. ecclesia — facere] facere in ecclesia tendit Ta. intendit
facere] ut O facit JQ[1]* (*auctor videtur scripsisse* facit *in Forma 2*). 43 et *om.* TaTc.

[36] This is the end of the passage based on Huguccio; see above n. 20. Regarding these five
"exceptions" cf. Hug. ad C.1 q.1 c.42 *maneat* (fol. 112ra); Idem ad C.1 q.7 c.21 *iterata unctione*
(fol. 126va).
[37] Regarding this use of the word *irregularis* see Franz Gillmann, "Zur Geschichte des Gebrauchs der Ausdrücke 'irregularis' und 'irregularitas'", *ArchivKKRecht* 91 (1911) 49-86, 557-
560; cf. Firth, *Thesis* II 453*-454* with n. 30 (III 731*). Regarding mediaeval abhorrence
of iteration of sacraments, see N. Häring, "The Augustinian Axiom", *MedStud* 16 (1954) 87-
117. Regarding thes eirregularities see] Gratian C.1 q.7 cc.10, 21; *De consec.* D.4 cc.117-118;
cf. above sect. 82.
[38] Cf. *Summa parisiensis* ad C.1 q.1 c.74 (p. 85; cf. *MedStud* 16.111); cf. below sect. 202.
[39] Cf. above sect. 81 with n. 27. Hug. ad *De consec.* D.4 c.31 *mimice* (fol. 387[vb]) declares the

85   Sed, licet intentionem rectam habeat, multotiens tamen multa omittit. Diligenter igitur considerandum est an omissum sit de sub- 45 stantia conferendi sive ordinis sive sacramenti sive consecrationis sive benedictionis, quia sine hoc nihil actum est. Verbi gratia, in baptismo sunt aqua et verba haec: "Ego baptizo te in nomine Patris et Filii et Spiritus sancti. Amen." Si ergo aliquis immergat in quocumque alio liquore quam in aqua, non baptizat.[40]   50

Item, si mutet verba et dicat "Ego immergo te," vel "intingo", non baptizat.[41]

Item, si truncat verba dicendo "Ego baptizo te in nomine Patris," nisi plus addat, non baptizat.

Item, si interrumpat verba, ut si postquam dixerit "Ego baptizo te 55 in nomine Patris," transeat ad actum contrarium, ut ad ostium clau- dendum vel ad cereum incendendum, non baptizat.[42] Contrarius actus intelligitur qui non pertinet ad propositum; tussis vero et suspirium et emunctio non sunt actus contrarii, quia non intelliguntur disrumpere formam verborum.[43]   60

Item, si corrupte proferat verba sponte et ex certa scientia, cum sciat et possit recte proferre, vel si sic proferat ut errorem introducat, non baptizat.[44] Oportet igitur ut forma verborum sit integra, perfecta et ordinata. Idem dico in aliis sacramentis.

---

44 habeat] quis habeat P *add.* quis *insert.* Ac.   45 igitur] ergo HOTcU ergo *insert.* Tu tamen J sibi R *om.* Cc.   47-64 Verbi — sacramentis *abbrev.* Pet.   47 baptismo *add.* tamen J.   48 sunt *add.* haec CkHJU.   haec *om.* Ck.   49 immergo Ab emergat Tc intingat Tu.   51 mutat TaTu immutat AaJ immutet CkHU.   mergo TaTu inungo J. te *om.* Ta-Tu.   intingo *add.* te PTa.   51-52 Item — baptizet *om.* Q¹*R *post sequentem paragraphum* AaHJU.   54 addat] dicat TaTu dixerit AaHJU.   nisi plus addat *insert.* Ad.   55 si¹ — ut *om.* Q¹*.   ut *corr. ab* et O.   dixit Ta.   56 ut] vel J *corr. ab* vel Aa.   ad² *om.* Tc *delet.* O.   57 incedendum O accendendum HJU.   58 tus- sis] risus O.   vero] ergo Cc.   59 munctio Ac *add.* narium Ta.   et emunctio *om.* CcHO.   contrarii *add.* et emunctio H.   dirumpere AaCiJ.   62 recte *om.* AbOQ¹*TaTu *add.* formare et U.   si *om.* CkJR.   introducat] inducat Tu *corr. ab* inducat AaU.   64 et *om.* CkP.   Idem] Item CkTa.   in *add.* omnibus RTa.

---

necessity of intention on the part of the one conferring a sacrament, but without explicitly saying that one must intend to do what the Church does or what the Church intends to do.

[40] Cf. Hug. ad *De consec.* D.4 c.1 (fol. 384va-b); Peter Cantor, *Summa* 1.33 (I 94-95).

[41] Cf. Hug. *De consec.* D.4 c.82 (fol. 392rb) partly quoted in Firth, *Thesis* II 361* n. 32 (III 644*-645*); Cantor, *Summa* 1.26-32 (I 84-94); Courson, *Summa* 39.3-6 (fol. 122va-b).

[42] Cf. Hug. *ibid.* (fol. 392va); Cantor and Courson, *locc. citt.*

[43] Cf. above sect. 46 with n. 95.

[44] Cf. Gratian *De Consec.* D.4 c.86; Cantor, *Summa* 1.29 (I 90-91); Courson, *Summa* 39. 5-6 (fol. 122vb).

86 Si vero omittitur aliquid quod non est de substantia rei, postea 65 supplendum est. Unde graviter offendunt simplices sacerdotes qui, cum parvulus aliquis in necessitate baptizatur aliquo sacramentali vel aliquibus omissis, non supplent, ut pabulum salis, narium linitio et in ecclesia introductio; omnia enim praeter substantiam baptismi quae omissa sunt supplenda sunt. Baptismus autem jam collatus est, et ideo 70 non est iterandus.[45] Idem dico de aliis.

87 Item in altari non numquam accidit quod super panem canone prolato in calice nihil reperitur. Consulunt ergo quod vinum cum aqua in calicem infundatur, et priori pane retento incipiat sacerdos *Te igitur* et ordinate usque in finem prosequatur. Hoc ideo dicunt quia 75 sacramenti altaris duplex est forma: *vocalis* scilicet, id est verba ipsa sic prolata ut debent, *forma realis*, panis et vinum;[46] et ubicumque aliquod istorum trium deest, vel aliud quod est de substantia sacramenti vel ordinis vel consecrationis vel benedictionis, nihil actum est. Mihi videtur tutius quod novus panis apponatur sicut novum vinum, et 80

65 Si *ss. desinit* Pet *usque ad lineam 86 in sect. 88.* — omittatur Tc dimittatur J. — non *om.* Ck *insert.* O. — 67 necesse Ck ecclesia Ta. — 68 sal] salutis Tu *corr. ab* salutis Aa. — 68-69 et — introductio *om.* J *insert.* Aa. — 69 ecclesiam CkHPTaU. — enim *om.* AaJ. — 70 omissa sunt] omittuntur O. — sunt[1] *om.* Ck. — sunt[2] *om.* Tu. — autem *om.* JU *insert.* Aa. — est *om.* Q[1]*R. — 70-71 et — iterandus *insert.* Ad. — 72 super] praeter R *corr. ab* praeter O. — 73 consulerem O consulo R consultum est P consultum Tc. — 74 in calice *insert.* O. — calice CcQ[1]*RTu. — infundantur HJ. — 75 dico CkO. — quia] quod CkOTu. — 76 sacramenti *corr. ab* sacramentum OR. — scilicet *om.* AaO(Y). — id est *om.* AcJOTaTuU(BmCpDEGLMNSoTbXY). — ipsa] illa O *om.* CkTu. — 77 et *om.* AbORTaTu. — aliquid CiTaTu. — 78 vel aliud] non consecratur; est enim generale: ubicumque aliquid deest O *om.* AbQ[1]*Ta (*cf. supra in Proleg. ad p. 48 n. 48*). — aliud] aliquod CiJ(Cp) aliquid AaTu(DLSoVX). — est *om.* Ab.

[45] Cf. CANTOR, *Summa* 1.35 (I 99-100); Po. 2138 (X 1.15.un.; issued Feb. 25, 1204); Po. 2350 (X 1.16.1; issued Dec. 19, 1204). In these decretals Innocent III is speaking about ordination and confirmation, not about baptism, but his decisions are parallel to the policy here enunciated by Flamborough.

[46] The term *forma* was used in the twelfth century to indicate the sensible sign of a sacrament. In this usage it designated both the matter and the form of later terminology. See Sicard of Cremona as quoted by Franz GILLMANN, "Taufe 'im Namen Jesu' oder 'im Namen Christi'", *Katholik*[4] 10 (1912)[2] 365 n. 4 (p. 366); cf. IDEM, "Die Ehe ein Sakrament nach Sikard von Cremona", *Katholik*[4] 6 (1910)[2] 479-481. Cf. HUG. ad *De consec.* D.2 c.1 *In sacramentorum* (fol. 367va); RUFINUS ad *De consec.* D.2 c.1 (p. 551); ad *De consec.* D.4 c.31 (p. 564); ANCIAUX p. 145 n. 5. See also Damian VAN DEN EYNDE, "The Theory of the Composition of the Sacraments in Early Scholasticism", *Franciscan Studies* 11[1] (1951)[1] 15-20, 126-136; Artur LANDGRAF, "Beiträge der Frühscholastik zur allgemeinen Sakramentenlehre", *Div ThomFreib*[3] 29 (1951) 4-6.

missa ordinate completa panis prior extra altare per totam missam cum reverentia conservatus ab aliqua persona cum reverentia sumatur.[47]

88   Diligenter igitur attendendum ad quid institutus sit ordo vel sacramentum vel consecratio; quia illud est de substantia ordinis vel consecrationis vel sacramenti, et illo omisso nihil agitur, immo reite- 85 randum est. Ad quid autem sit institutus ordo vel consecratio vel sacramentum, vel quid pertineat ad illa, ex verbis pontificis consecrantis perpendi potest, cum dicitur: "Accipe potestatem" vel "Esto" vel "Sis" vel simile aliquid. [Nos tamen in proximo capitulo breviter ostendemus.]   90

Quid ad quemlibet ordinem pertineat

89   Ad ostiarium ecclesiae claves pertinent, ut claudat et aperiat templum Dei et omnia quae intus sunt et extra custodiat, fideles recipiat, excommunicatos et infideles excipiat.[48]

Ad psalmistam pertinet quidquid pertinet ad cantandi peritiam: 95 benedictiones, laudes, sacrificium et responsoria.

Ad lectorem pertinet lectiones pronuntiare et prophetias populis praedicare.

Ad exorcistam pertinet exorcismos memoriter retinere, manusque 99 super energumenos et catechumenos in exorcizando imponere.

Ad acolythum pertinet praeparatio luminarium; ipse cereum portat; ipse suggesta pro eucharistia calicis praeparat.

---

81 completa] celebrata AaHJU. — reverentia *om.* U (*homoeotel.*). attendendum *add.* est OPTu. R.   86 Ad *reincipit* Pet. sic U sis *insert.* Aa *om.* J. Hoc O (Quod nos L). *cett.*(*cett.*) Cf. *infra in Append.* C *no. 19.* cludat Ta.   95 pertinet[1] *add.* omne O. U *om.* Cc (*homoeotel.*). pertinent JTu *om.* Ta. vel praeparat Ta.

82 observatus AaHJTu servatus Tc.   conservatus   83 Diligenter *ss. desinit* Q[1]* *usque ad lineam 42 in sect. 100.* 84 quia illud] quod Ck quod idem Tu.   est *add.* quod 87 illa] ipsa Pet *corr. ab* illam O.   88-89 vel "Sis"] 89 Nos *ss. desinit usque ad sect. 97* Pet.   Nos] Non *corr. ad* 89-90 Nos — ostendemus AbORTaTu(BmLMSo) *insert.* Aa *om.* 92 includat O.   94 excipiat] rejiciat P excludat Ta.   quidquid pertinet] quaecumque pertinent quidquid — peritiam] quod cantandi peritiam habeat Ta.   97 2 pertinet *om.* Ta.   3 praeparet Cc *corr. ab* praeparet Aa portat

---

[47] Regarding this problem as it was discussed at the time see Vincent L. KENNEDY, "The Moment of Consecration and the Elevation of the Host", *MedStud* 6 (1944) 121-150; IDEM, "The Date of the Parisian Decree on the Elevation of the Host", *MedStud* 8 (1946) 87-96. Regarding this solution cf. INNOCENT III (Lothar of Segni) *De sacro altaris mysterio* 4.22, 24 (PL 217.872-873). Cf. also below sect. 202.

[48] This section shows some affinity to GRATIAN D.25 c.1, but shows in some ways closer affinities to Ivo, *Decretum* 6.20 (PL 161.448-449) and *Panormia* 3.41 (PL 161.1137-1139), and still closer affinity to BURCHARD, *Decretum* 3.50 (PL 140.681-682).

Ad subdiaconum pertinet calicem et patenam ad altare Christi deferre et levitis tradere eisque ministrare, urceolum quoque et aqua- 5
manile, manutergium tenere episcopo et presbytero et levitis pro la-
vandis manibus, ante altare aquam praebere.

Ad diaconum pertinet semper assistere sacerdotibus et ministrare
in omnibus quae aguntur in sacramentis Christi, in baptismo scilicet,
in chrismate, in patena et calice, oblationes quoque offerre et disponere 10
in altari, componere etiam mensam Domini atque vestire, et crucem
ferre, et praedicare evangelium et apostolum. Nam sicut lectoribus
vetus testamentum, ita diaconibus novum praedicare praeceptum est.
Ad ipsum quoque pertinet officium precum et recitatio nominum.
Ipse praemonet aures ad Dominum; ipse hortatur orare; ipse clamat 15
et pacem ipse annuntiat.

Ad presbyterum pertinet sacramentum corporis et sanguinis Domini
in altari Domini conficere, orationes dicere et benedicere dona Dei.

Ad episcopum pertinet basilicarum consecratio, unctio altaris et
confectio chrismatis. Ipse praedicta officia et ordines ecclesiasticos 20
distribuit, ipse sacras virgines benedicit.[49]

De sacris vestibus

90 In vestibus etiam sacris per earum significationes intelligitur quid
de earum sit substantia benedictionum. Alba, id est tunica illa quae
graece poderis, id est talaris, dicitur, significat munditiam in anima; 25
zona castitatem in corpore, quod ad temperantiam pertinet; superhumerale, quod hebraice dicitur ephod, justitiam; rationale, quod graece
dicitur *logios*, sapientiam. Superhumerale portabant in veteri testamento in humeris, rationale in pectore. Utriusque typum hodie tenet

---

5-6 aqua manile Ci(CpMN) aquam anile Z aquam et ancule Tu aquam manile CcCkJOPTc-
(FKNSo aquammanile X aquam malini L aquam mantile DIV aquam Tb aquam *cum lacuna*
Bm) *om.* U *add.* id est AaHJTcTu(CpG) *add.* et *corr.* ad id est O *add.* et Cc(SgVX) *add.*
scilicet R.   6 manutergium *add.* scilicet AcAdCcTcZ(EFGILMNSoTbY *add.* debet L).
8 ministrare *add.* semper O.   9 in²] cum Ad *om.* AaH.   10 et¹] in H scilicet in Aa.
calice *add.* et O.   11 etiam *om.* Ab.   atque] et Ta.   12 et apostolum] ad populum
CkTu ad populum *corr.* ad ad apostolum et populum O.   16 et *om.* JR.   18 Domini
om. JTc.   23 etiam] autem Ck enim P.   significationes] signa Ck.   24 substantia
add. signis JU *add.* signis *corr.* ad signif. Aa.   benedictionem J *corr. ab* benedictionem Tc.
26 castitatem *add.* significat RTa.   quod] quae JU.   28 logion AdJTa(BmDGIX
orig).   28-29 testamento] lege Ac.

---

[49] Cf. *locc. citt.*

amictus; unde et humeros protegit et pectus. Stola, quae alio nomine 30
dicitur orarium, per sinistrum humerum transiens ad dextrum, in
prosperis et adversis fortitudinem significat; longitudo stolae perse-
verantiam. Idem facit alba in hoc quod talaris est. Stola cum zona
colligatur quia virtutes sibi invicem conjunguntur. Casula, quae planeta vel infula dicitur, caritatem exprimit, quae loco prudentiae po- 35
nitur; quia *plenitudo legis est dilectio.*[50] Mappula quae in sinistra ponitur
ad tergendum oculos significat vigilantiam pro accidia, quae saepe
mentibus accidit et post supra dictas virtutes subrepit, saepe remo-
venda et abstergenda ab oculis rationis sive animae.[51]

91   Dalmatica etiam qua utuntur levitae latitudine sui idem signi- 40
ficat quod casula, id est caritatem. Per duas lineas coccineas quibus
ipsa ante et retro a summo usque deorsum decoratur utriusque testamenti praedicatio, Dei et proximi dilectio figuratur. Duodecim fim-
briae linearum utrimque duodecim ramos caritatis exprimunt, quos
apostolus enumerat dicens, *Caritas patiens est, benigna est,* etc.[52] Tertia 45
linea, quae inter duas est, tribus fimbriis ante et retro insignitur, caritatem fide sanctae Trinitatis condecoratam demonstrat. Per fimbrias
in sinistro latere sollicitudo activae vitae circa plurima intelligitur;
per dextrum latus, quod caret fimbriis, contemplatio caelestium sine
multitudine perturbationum significatur.[53]   50

---

30 quae *add.* in JO *add.* et U.   31 dicitur *om.* JU.   32 et in adversis AaJPRTaU-
(CpKSgSoTb).   34 invicem] mutuo O.   36 mapula AcAdH(CpDFGINV) manipula JPRTaTuU(EKMSgTbXY *orig*) mappula *corr. ad* manippula Z mapula *corr. ad* manipula Tc mapula *corr. attentat. ad* manipula O manipula *corr. ad* mapula Ab (*om.* So).
sinistro JTu *add.* parte O.   in sinistra] a sinistris H.   37 pro accidia] per accidiam Z
corr. ab qua (*insert.*) prava cogitatio peracordia O.   38 saepe *om.* Aa *add.* sit O.
39 sive] et H *corr. ab* suae R.   sive animae] et scientiae Ck.   40 etiam] et Tu *om.* P.
42 decoratur] ornatur *insert.* O.   43 duodecim] duos Cc.   46 est] cum Ck *om.* JPTaU.
47 condecoratum Ck decoratam PTa(BmDGIKLSoV) et decoratam Tu(F) insignitam OZ(X).
49 caelestis AaJ.

---

[50] See *Rom* 13.10.
[51] Sects. 90-96 of our penitential are derived, almost by copying literally, from an anonymous work which has in some way been influenced by Hugh of St-Victor and has sometimes
been attributed to him: *Speculum ecclesiae* or *Speculum de mysteriis ecclesiae.* These sections are based
on chapter 6 (PL 177.352-355); cf. Heinrich WEISWEILER, "Zur Einflusssphäre der 'Vorlesungen'
Hugos von St. Viktor", *Mélanges Joseph de Ghellinck S. J.* II 534-570; FIRTH, *Thesis* II 413*-
415*.
[52] 1 *Cor* 13.4.
[53] See *Speculum de mysteriis ecclesiae* c. 6 (PL 177.353).

92 Quod autem pontifices utuntur duabus tunicis, praeter poderis
qua ceteri communiter utuntur, monstrat quod proprium est eorum
scientiam habere duorum testamentorum, ut sciant *de thesauro suo*
proferre *nova et vetera*.[54] Praeter haec et unaquaeque ex tribus tunicis
typum gerit proprium. Poderis enim, in eo quod byssina vel linea, 55
munditiam significat; quia, sicut in bysso vel linea candor qui non
est per naturam contingit per exercitium abluendi, ita munditiam quam
natura non administrat sancti per industriam juvante gratia acquirunt,
dum per exercitium bonorum operum corpus macerant et mundi-
ficant. Secunda autem tunica serica, quae originem traducit a ver- 60
mibus, qui sine coitu creantur et parvuli sunt, castitatem demonstrat
et humilitatem. Tertia vero tunica, sicut olim erat, jacintina est,
concolor lapidi jacinto, qui aetheris serenitatem imitatur; sanctos
significat cogitantes et imitantes caelestia. Et merito haec tunica
jacintini est coloris; quia, sicut ille lapis imitatur colorem cum aere, 65
in sereno aere serenus est et in obscuro aere pallidus, sic specialiter et
proprie decet episcopum *gaudere cum gaudentibus* et *flere cum flentibus*.[55]

93 Mitra pontificis corniculata duo praetendit testamenta, quibus
ipse debet expugnare hostes ecclesiae.[56] Sandalia quibus utuntur

---

51 poderim PTa(BmDFGIKSoV) poderem H(*orig* poderum LX ponderis Sg) poderes J *add.*
vel quam poderem O.   52 qua] quia OTu.   monstratur Ck *corr. ad* monstratur Ab.
54 haec] hoc Tc hoc *corr. attentat.* O *om.* Z.   haec et] et *corr. ad* haec Aa.   56 linea]
lino AaHJOPRU(GIKSgTbVXY *orig*) *corr. attentat. ad* lino Ad (lineae Bm).   56-57 non
est per] est praeter JU.   57 per[1] *corr. ab* praeter Aa.   contigit O.   ita munditiam]
sic munditia O.   58 natura *delet.* O.   61 demonstrant RTaZ *corr. ab* demonstrant
HO *corr. ad* demonstrant Tc.   62-63 jacintina — aetheris] jacintinarum jacintus qui
colorem habet aethereum Ta.   63 concolor] color Ck cum color CcCi.   concolor
lapidi jacinto *corr. ab* candor lapidis jacinti O.   jacinto] jacinti Ta jacintino JR jacintae
corr. ad jacintino Aa.   65 jacintina JTu.   est *om.* Aa.   imitatur] mutat OTu(So *orig*)
immutat R imitatur *sive* mutatur Ac(TbX mutatur V) *Secundum testimonium MSSorum auctor
scripsit in Forma 3 imitatur sed forsitan intellexit sub sensu* mutat, *sicut* Du Cange *s. v.* immutatio
asserit nomen imitatio *aliquando habere sensum* immutatio.   colorem cum aere] aerem in
colore Ta.   66 in sereno *insert.* Tc.   in sereno aere *om.* Cc (*homoeotel.*).   aere[1]]
cum aere *corr. ad* enim aere O cum aer AaAbHJTaU(SgVX) tamen aer Ck (aer M *om.* Y).
et[1] *om.* PR.   aere[2] *om.* R(G *orig*).   pallidus *add.* est Ck-Ta.   sic] sicut CkR *corr.*
ab sicut O.   specialiter] spiritualiter HJRTu(DINSoXY *orig*).   68 pontificalis CkOP-
Tu.   69 expurgare AbJ *corrupt.* Ta.

---

54 Cf. *Matt* 13.52.
55 See *Rom* 12.15; *Speculum* 6 (PL 177.353-354)
56 See *Speculum* 6 (PL 177.354).

episcopi et cardinales integra sunt inferius, quia non debent inhiare 70
terrenis; desuper sunt perforata, quia oculos mentis debent aperire ad
ea quae sursum sunt. Quod enim in quibusdam locis sunt aperta, in
quibusdam sunt integra, monstrat aperte quod caelestia sacramenta
quibusdam sunt revelanda et quibusdam sunt tegenda. Unde Dominus
in evangelio: *Vobis datum est nosse mysterium* etc.[57] Horum calceamen- 75
torum mysteria consideravit qui ait: *Quam speciosi pedes* annuntiantis
pacem.[58] Caligae pontificales significant praeparare iter et festinare
ad praedicandum.[59]

94   Anulus enim episcopi fidei signaculum; quia, sicut antiquitus in
sigillo anuli nomen et imago regis exprimebatur, ita et in fide catholica 80
nomen Regis caelestis et imago declaratur; verbi gratia, nomen ejusdem
cum dicitur, *Dominus Pater, Dominus Filius, Dominus Spiritus sanctus,*
quia *Dominus nomen est illi.*[60] Imago autem ejus ostenditur, hoc est qualis ipse sit, cum dicitur "Deus omnipotens" et "aeternus" et his similia,
licet secundum proprietatem loquendi nulla qualitas vel diversitas 85
in eo reperiatur. Gerit itaque episcopus anulum pro ecclesia, quam
ornare debet fide et caelesti sponso castam exhibere sponsam, juxta
illud *Despondi enim vos uni viro* etc.,[61] et ut sponsa cantare possit *Anulo
suo subarrhavit me Dominus Jesus Christus.*[62] Quod anulum in manu gerit
episcopus docet quod fidem in opere monstrare debet.[63]   90

73 sunt *om.* CkHJU.   74 et *om.* AaCkHJPTaU(BmCpDIKLMSoVX).   (sunt[1] —
sunt[2] *om.* Sg).   sunt[2] *om.* AaCkHJRTaTuU(CpLVX *orig*).   (sunt tegenda] non DI).
75 etc.] et bene O regni caelorum R regni Dei etc. H regni Dei, ceteris autem in parabolis Z.
76 mysteria] ministeria AbJ.   annuntiantis] evangelizantium RTa.   79 enim] autem
Tu(BmDILTbVX *orig*) *om.* RTa(G).   signaculum *add.* exprimit P *add.* significat *insert.* O.
80 exprimitur Aa exprimebantur U.   80-81 exprimebatur — Regis *om.* Tu (*homoeotel.*).
81 ejusdem] est ejusdem Tu ejus ostenditur P.   nomen ejusdem] ut Ta *om.* AaCkHJU.
82 Dominus[1]] Deus *insert.* Ad (Deus IV).   Dominus[2]] Deus AbAcAdCcCi(IVY).
Dominus[3]] Deus AbAcAdCi(IVY) *om.* Cc.   83 (Dominus] Deus V).   ejus] eis Ck
insert. Aa *om.* R.   est[2] *om.* O.   hoc est] id est R.   83-84 hoc — sit *om.* Ta.   84
dicitur *add.* ipse O.   Deus] Dominus CcCkO(So) *corr. ab* Dominus Ac (*om.* GN *orig*).
85 et licet Ta *om.* J.   87 ornare] ordinare AaCkHJ ornate Cc.   88 enim *om.* JP.
uni viro *om.* CkOTc.   etc.] virginem castam Tu virginem castam etc. P virginem castam
exhibere Christo Z.   89 Dominus *add.* meus HPTu.   Dominus Jesus Christus] etc. TaZ.

[57] See *Marc* 4.11; *Luc* 8.10.
[58] See *Rom* 10.15; *Is* 52.7.
[59] See *Speculum, loc. cit.*
[60] See *Symbolum "Quicumque" pseudo-Athanasianum; Ps* 67.5.
[61] 2 *Cor* 11.2.
[62] See *Pontificale Romanum* "De benedictione et consecratione virginum" (Michel ANDRIEU,
Le Pontifical Romain au Moyen-âge I 165).
[63] See *Speculum, loc. cit.*

Per chirothecas in manibus exempla sanctorum, quae in operibus habenda sunt, intelliguntur, et quod opera ab omni inquinamento mundanda sunt ne *modicum* fermenti *totam massam* corrumpat.[64]

95   Baculus pastoris rectitudinem sive rectum regimen significat. Quod autem una pars curva et altera acuta monstrat   95

Parcere subjectis et debellare superbos.[65]

Unde dictum est:

Curva trahit mites; pars pungit acuta rebelles.

Et iterum: 99

Curva trahit quos virga regit; pars ultima pungit.

Item:

Attrahe per curvum, medio rege, punge per imum.[66]

[Et iterum secundum magistrum Stephanum de Langetonne:]

Collige, sustenta, stimula vaga, morbida, lenta;   5
Hoc est pastoris; hoc virga figurat honoris.[67]

92 habenda sunt *om.* AaCkHJU.   94 pastoralis CkHPU.   sive rectum regimen] regiminis Ta.   regimen *insert.* O regnum Cc.   95 et] est et P *om.* AaJ.   altera] alia AaTc.   96 subjectis] mitibus Ta *corr. ab* subditis Ck.   superbos *praem* rebelles Cc. 98 rebelles] superbos CkH.   99 Iterum] verum J item Tc *Vide var, infra ad lineas 4-6* R. (99-1 Et — pungit *om.* So).   1 (Curva — pungit *infra post* lenta *in linea 5 ubi praem.* Et iterum L).   quos] quod O.   2 Item *om.* Ck (Et iterum LN Etiam item X) *Vide var. infra ad lineas 5-6* Ck.   3 curvum] primum AaCkJ(CpLSoV) summum Ta(Tb).   4 (Et iterum] Item BmSoTb).   Et iterum — Langetonne] Item AdH Demum Z *om.* CcCiCk-P(KL).   Langetone Tc (Langetona Bm Langedun So Languetonne F Langi. I Long. Cp Longetudine G).   de Langetonne *om.* R (Delongaton M).   4-6 Et iterum — honoris *om.* AaAbJTaTuU(SgVX) *insert.* O *supra post* rebelles *in linea 98* R *Cf. infra in Append.* C *no.* 11. 5-6 Collige — honoris *supra post* pungit *in linea 1* Ck.   5 morbida] languida Ck.   6 Hoc[1]] haec P.   Hoc[1] — honoris *om.* H   hoc[2]] haec P.   honores Ck honorem P(K).

[64] See 1 *Cor* 5.6; *Gal* 5.9.

[65] VIRGIL, *Aeneid* 6.853. The *Speculum de mysteriis ecclesiae*, at least in the text found in Migne's *Patrologia latina* (177.354), does not quote Virgil verbatim. But Robert of Flamborough has the original text of this poetry as quoted by SICARD OF CREMONA, *Mitrale* 2.5 (PL 213.80).

[66] I have not found the original source of these Leonine hexameter lines; they are quoted in *Speculum de mysteriis ecclesiae, loc. cit.*; and by SICARD OF CREMONA, *loc. cit.*

[67] These two lines are not quoted in the sources just cited. The *Speculum* (PL 177.354) has another short quotation at this place, but this was probably lacking in the MS at Robert's disposal. The first of these lines is quoted by INNOCENT III, *De sacro altaris mysterio* 1.62 (PL 217.796) and a similar line is combined with one of our preceding lines by PETER CANTOR, *Verbum abbreviatum* 56 (PL 205.176). See variants to this text; cf. FIRTH, *Thesis* I 223*-224*, 236*, II 414*-415*.

Pallium quod superapponitur archiepiscopis torquem et bravium significat quod legitime certantes accepturi sunt, et disciplinam exprimit qua se superinduere et constringere ad exemplum subditorum debent.[68]   10

96 Coccinea vero planeta, qua induitur apostolicus quocumque proficiscitur praedicando, martyrium declarat. Crucem praecedere hunc significat magis ei convenire illud *Mihi absit gloriari* etc.[69]

Tonsura capillorum in clericis docet omnia superflua esse resecanda ut libere possint audire et videre legem Dei. Corona monstrat cle- 15 ricos spiritualiter esse regnum Dei.[70]

Quod manus sacerdotis inunguntur oleo significat eos habere per Spiritum sanctum virtutem consecrandi, et quod manus ejus debent esse porrigibiles et non aridae et curvae ad retinendum.[71]

De intentione ordinati   20

97 Intentio ordinati est de substantia ordinis; quia, nisi intendat quis suscipere ordinem, forte non ordinatur. Asserunt tamen aliqui quod dormiens et invitus ordinantur; et hoc ideo quia non reordina-

---

7 superponitur RTa supra ponitur Cc.   torqueri J torquet Tu.   9 induere] inducere CkJ. exemplar AaJU exempla P.   11 vero *add.* et O.   13 Mihi *add*, autem CkJRTuU. etc.] nisi in cruce Domini etc. Ck nisi in cruce Domini nostri etc. Z Domini nostri Jesu Christi Ta *om.* P.   14 esse *om.* O.   15 possunt Cc possit Z.   16 regnum] reginem AbCc-CiJTcTuZ(DEISgGTbY) sub regmine R (regendos BmLSo).   17 inungitur AaJRTu. 21 Intentio *reincipit* Pet.   23 invitus] mutus AaJORTaTc(CpEFLSgSoY) in vitiis Tu (inviti G invitur I).   ordinatur CkHOPRTaTuU(CpFIKLMNVX *corr. ab* ordinatur Bm).   23-24 reordinantur P(EGKV ordinabuntur So recte ordinabuntur Sg) reordinabitur Ta(IX) recordabuntur CkTu.

---

[68] See *Speculum, loc. cit.*; cf. 1 *Cor* 9.24-27; *Eph.* 6.14-17.

[69] See *Gal* 6.14; *Speculum de mysteriis ecclesiae* 6 (PL 177.354-355). Regarding the title *apostolicus* see Michael J. WILKS, "The *Apostolicus* and the Bishop of Rome", *The Journal of Theological Studies*[2] 13 (1962) 290-317; 14 (1963) 311-354 (esp. 14.318).

[70] See *Speculum* 6 (PL 177.355).

[71] See *Speculum, loc. cit.*; cf. *Sirach* (*Ecclus*) 4.36.

[72] This is the position of SIMON OF BISIGNANO, *Summa ad* D.74 c.7 *quae in episcopum*, of HUGUCCIO ad D.74 c.7 *in episcopum* (fol. 84rb) and of ROBERT COURSON, *Summa* 24.6 (fol. 86vb); see Franz GILLMANN, "Die Notwendigkeit der Intention," *Katholik*[4] 18 (1916)[2] 43-45 (regarding Simon) 100-101 (regarding Huguccio) and 115 (regarding Courson); cf. *ibid.* pp. 169-170; cf. Artur LANDGRAF, "Beiträge der Frühscholastik zur Terminologie der allgemeinen Sakramentenlehre", *DivThomFreib*[3] 29 (1951) 9-29; Yves M.-J. CONGAR, "Ordinations *invitus, coactus*, de l'Eglise antique au canon 214", *Rev. des sciences phil. et théol.* 50 (1966) 169-197 esp. 183.

buntur.[72] Idem in baptismo.[73] Sed quia' serio et cum deliberatione
talia fieri debent in ecclesia, hujusmodi ordinationibus supersedemus.[74] 25

98 Ecclesia consecratur ut in ea cetera fiant sacramenta; coemeterium,
ut in eo fideles sepeliantur et a malignis spiritibus non vexentur; altare,
calix et corporalia, ut in eis corpus Christi consecretur; patena, ut
in ea corpus Christi fidelibus ministretur; baptisterium, ad baptizandum.

De verbis 30

99 Verba quoque de substantia sunt ordinis, sicut et sacramentorum,
ut patet in baptismo et in altaris sacramento.[75]

<Cap.> iii. QUAE IMPEDIUNT ORDINEM ET ORDINIS
EXSECUTIONEM

100 Quae dicta sunt de substantia ordinis ita ordini adhaerent quod 35
a nullo, nec etiam a domino papa, aliquis ordo confertur si illorum
aliquod omittatur. Quae autem sequuntur ordinum sunt impedimenta,
sed fortasse non ut omino ordo non conferatur, sed ut conferri non
debeat. Unde, si vult, cum homicida dispensare potest papa, sicut
fecit Alexander tertius;[76] et homicida, si ad ordinem accesserit, etsi 40

---

25 hujus CkO.   26-29 Ecclesia — baptizandum *om.* Pet.   30 *tit. om.* Z *et perplurimi*
alii.   31 sunt *insert.* Cc.   sicut *om.* Cc.   33 Impediant Z.   35 adhaerent]
accidunt *script. in lacuna* O.   37 aliquod] aliquid HTaTu.   38 omnino] canonice
O ideo P.   ordo *om.* CcOR.   conferantur O.   39 debeant O.   homicidio
Cc.   dominus papa JU.   40 homicidia Cc.

[73] Simon is less definite in regard to baptism, but Huguccio maintains the same in this regard; see ad D.45 c.5 *associatos, vinctos, corporis Domini* (fol. 52[rb]); so also ROBERT COURSON, *loc.*
cit. (cf. fols. 121[va], 123[va]). Cf. GILLMANN and LANDGRAF, *locc. citt.*

[74] The opinion which required for validity some intention on the part of the one receiving
a sacrament was suggested by RUFINUS, *Summa* ad D.45 dictum p. c.4 (p. 106) mentioned by
STEPHEN OF TOURNAI, *Summa* ad C.1 q.1 dictum p. c.58 (p. 133) and expressed with some degree of clarity by NICHOLAS OF AMIENS, *Ars catholicae fidei* 4.9 (PL 210.616; cf. GILLMANN, *Ka-*
tholik[4] 18.110). It was maintained by RADULF ARDENS, *Speculum universale* (quoted by LAND-
GRAF, *Div ThomFreib*[3] 29.15) and definitively taught by INNOCENT III, Po. 1479 (X 3.42.3; issued
probably Sept.-Oct. 1201). Thereafter it generally prevailed; cf. *Glossa ordinaria in Decr.* ad
D.45 c.5 *coacti sunt.* See GILLMANN, "Die Notwendigkeit" *Katholik*[4] 18 (1916)[2] 170-171; LAND-
GRAF, *loc. cit.* (above in n. 72).

[75] Cf. above sects. 74, 85 and 87 with notes; also FIRTH, *Thesis* II 426* n. 12 (III 700*-701*).

[76] This seems to refer to JL 13912 (*AppConcLat* 26.13; MANSI 22.369-370) which is probably one decretal with JL 13917; see Stephan KUTTNER and Eleanor RATHBONE, "Anglo-Norman Canonists in the Twelfth Century", *Traditio* 7 (1949-51) 310 with n. 44 and p. 356 tit. 9
q.3.

non debeat ordinari, ordinatur tamen, sed ordinis exsecutionem sine
papae auctoritate non habebit. Sunt autem quae de ordinis substantia
non sunt, et ordinem eo modo quo diximus, id est ne conferri debeat,
impediunt et ordinis exsecutionem: crimen, conditio, casus. Et primo
de crimine dicamus.   45

De crimine

101 Criminum aliud est maximum, aliud medium, aliud minimum:
maximum ut incestus, simonia, haeresis, apostasia, homicidium, etc.;
medium ut adulterium, perjurium, etc.; *minimum* ut fornicatio simplex
et similia.[77]   50

Post media etiam publicata potest quis promoveri per dispensationem episcopi et ad pristinum gradum reparari; multo fortius si occulta
fuerint, peracta tamen poenitentia vel bene inchoata; multo fortius
etiam post minima.[78]

Post maxima et publicata non datur dispensatio ad promovendum 55
nec ut ad pristinum gradum restituatur; papa tamen, si vult, potest
dispensare cum talibus.[79]

Si occultum est crimen tuum maximum, tutius non promoveberis,
et tutius ad pristinum gradum non reverteris si post ordinem lapsus
fueris; quia si cogat te praelatus tuus, ut episcopus vel abbas, non 60
audeo consulere quod resistas; alioquin posset quilibet non obedire

---

42 habebit *add. aliam materiam* Pet.   Sunt *reincipit* Q¹* (*incipit* Q²*)   43 eo] eodem
CcTu.   ne] nec O non P.   44 conditio *add.* et O.   47 criminis Ab crimen Ck.
est *om.* AaCkJTcTuU.   aliud² *add.* est PR Pet.   aliud³ *add.* est R Pet.   48 ut
om. O.   homicidium *om.* O.   49 adulterium *add.* et AaTu.   50 similia] hujusmodi H cetera similia Z.   51 media etiam *invers.* Ab.   etiam] autem H et *insert. ante*
media O.   promoveri *add.* etiam AaJU.   53 tamen *om.* Q¹*Tc Pet.   54 post
minima *om.* Tc Pet.   55 et] ut Tu etiam P *om.* J Pet.   publica AaJTu.   promo-
vendum] proponendum *add.* vel ad promovendum *delet.* O.   56 ut] non Z *om.* Pet *insert.*
O.   ad] in *insert.* Ab.   si vult *om.* O.   60 ut] vel O id est Q¹* *om.* Ta.
61 consulere] dicere Q¹*.   quod] ut JOTu *corr. ab* ut Aa.   potest O *post haec corr.*
ad sed Aa.

---

[77] Canonists do not usually mention the *crimen minimum*, but the distinction between *maximum* or *enorme* and *mediocre* is common enough; cf. Hug. ad D.50 pr. (fol. 56ᵛᵇ); Rufinus, *Summa*
ad D.50 pr. (pp. 115-116). See also Stephan Kuttner, "Ecclesia de occultis non judicat", *Jus
pontificium* 17 (1937) 17-18 with nn. 8-10; Idem, *Kanonistische Schuldlehre* esp. pp. 6-22.
[78] Cf. Hug. *loc. cit.*; ad D.50 c.22 *multotiens* (fol. 59ʳᵇ); ad D.81 dictum p. c.1 (fol. 88ᵛᵇ);
ad C.1 q.7 dictum p. c.5 (fol. 125ᵛᵇ); Rufinus, *Summa* ad D.81 pr. (p. 171); JL 14206 (X 3.3.4).
[79] Cf. Hug. ad D.50 pr. (fol. 56ᵛᵇ) quoted in Firth, *Thesis* II 471* n. 85 (III 750*-751*).

et rebellis esse.[80] Nonne hodie multi incestuosi et sodomitae promoventur et post lapsum ministrant? De consilio tamen meo, numquam sine dispensatione papae promovebitur, nec post lapsum pristinum recuperabit gradum, homicida, simoniacus, haereticus, apostata qui a 65 fide recessit.[81]

102 Igitur crimen impedit promovendum et dejicit promotum, ut homicidium, simonia, excommunicatio, sortilegium, sollemnis poenitentia, infamia, rebaptizatus, reordinatus, adhaerens haeretico, ab haeretico ordinatus, qui differt baptismum usque ad mortem vel infirmi- 70 tatem. De homicidio primo dicamus.

De homicidio

103 Homicidium tum fit facto, tum lingua; *facto*: tum ipso facto, tum auxilio; *lingua*: tum praecepto vel auctoritate, tum consilio. Sive interficiatur christianus, sive judaeus, sive gentilis, sive haereticus, sive 75 alius quicumque, indifferens est quantum ad promotionis impedimentum.[82]

Si igitur occidisti, vel mutilasti, vel in causa sanguinis signasti, vel auctoritatem vel consilium vel auxilium vel aliquod adminiculum ad hoc praestitisti, non ordinaberis. Si in conflictu fuisti in quo ex adversa 80 parte aliquis interfectus fuerit, non promoveberis.[83] Si alicubi ad hoc interfuisti ut caperetur vel judicaretur vel signaretur aliquis mutilandus,

---

62 Nonne] sicut OQ1*TaTu. 65 qui] quia Cc. 67 ut *om.* O. 71 De — dicamus *om.* Ta(KQ2*TbX) *script. sicut rubrica* O. 73 tum fit] fit tum R fit tam Ta fit cum Pet *add.* in Tc. tum2] tam Ta cum Pet *add.* fit Ck *add.* fit in Tc. facto2 *om.* AcTc. tum3] ut Ck cum HJ Pet. 74 lingua *om.* Ta. tum2] cum Pet *om.* Ac. vel] tum AaCkOTu *corr. ab* tum Tc *om.* Ac. tum3] cum Pet *om.* AcTu. Sive *corr. ad* Si quis O *insert.* Tc. 75 interficitur *add.* sive O. 78 vel1] sive Tc Pet. in *om.* AaZ. in causa sanginis *om.* AbQ1*TaTu(Q2*Tb) *insert.* AdO. 79 aliquod *om.* O. 81 aliquis *om.* O. fuit CkJ est P. alicubi] alicui AaJTu alic1 AbTcQ1* *corr. ab* alicui O *add.* alicui CkUZ. hoc] haec O. ad hoc] alicui H *om.* Aa. 82 vel1] et AaJ. vel judicaretur *om.* Ck.

---

[80] Cf. Hug. ad D.25 c.6 *peccati* (fol. 31ra) quoted *ibid.* (III 749*-750*); also above Proleg. p. 44.

[81] Cf. below sects. 108, 138-139; Firth, *Thesis* II 463*-466*, 471*, 494*-497*.

[82] Cf. Hug. ad D.50 dictum p. c.36 (fol. 61ra-b).

[83] Cf. below sects. 245-246, 251, 256; also Gratian C.23 q.8 c.34; 1 *Compil.* 5.21.3 (JL 14006; X 5.25.3); JL 17676 (X 5.25.4; *Collectio seguntina* no. 20 *RevHistEccl* 50 [1955] 426; Clement III); Po. 390 (X 5.37.5; issued Oct. 10, 1198). Regarding Flamborough's rigour concerning homicide see above Proleg. p. 15 with n. 78.

vel auctoritatem vel consilium vel auxilium ad hoc praestitisti, non
ordinaberis. Si litteras legisti vel scripsisti vel dictasti vel sigillasti ad
aliquem mutilandum vel interficiendum vel signandum, vel si ad tales 85
litteras incaustum praestitisti vel cultellum vel pennam vel pluteum
(dico cum effectu), de consilio meo sine papae dispensatione non ordinaberis. Rideat qui velit.

104   Si abortivum fecit mulier quia vim vel metum ei fecisti, vel ex
veneno tuo vel potione, non ordinaberis; et hoc dico si animatus fuerit 90
embryo, id est foetus; alioquin forte non impedieris ordinari.[84] Si auctoritate tua vel consilio vel auxilio projectus est parvulus aliquis, qui
ex inedia vel casualiter mortuus est vel non inventus, consilio meo
non ordinaberis.

     Ad iram commovisti aliquem unde in acutam vel tertianam vel dys- 95
enteriam incidit et mortuus est; numquid non causam mortis ei dedisti?
De consilio meo antequam ordineris papae pete dispensationem.

105   Si fuisti vel advocatus vel testis, maxime contra reum cujus sanguis
effusus est, non ordinaberis, vel si etiam pro reo simili modo stetisti 99
contra actorem ad talionem.[85] Quid si aliquod istorum fecisti et non est
secuta sanguinis effusio?

---

84 vel scripsisti *om.* PU.   85 aliquem] quem O.   86 praestitisti *om.* AaJU.   plu-
teum] plumbum OPTaTu(CpFKTbVX *corr. ad* pumicem M) *add.* dederis U.   vel pluteum
om. R.   87 cum] tamen Ck tamen cum PTu.   cum effectu] eum J.   papae dispen-
satione] dispensatione papae *add.* hoc *insert.* O.   87-88 ordinaberis] promoveberis Ta promoveberis nec ordinaberis Pet.   89 fecerit OR.   90 tuo *om.* AaJR.   vel *add.* ex
AaJRU.   potatione CcRTu *add.* tua Tu.   91 impediaris Tc impediaris *corr. ad* impediris
Cc.   92 vel auxilio *om.* JTc.   93 ex *om.* O.   casualiter] casu CcH casu aliquo Z.   est *add.* aliter Cc.   95 Si ad O.   aliquem *om.* J *insert.* Tc.   tertiam
O terciariam Cc.   96 causa AcTu.   97 De] igitur AaAbJQ^1*TaTuU(BmCpFSgSo)
Igitur de OTc(M) Ergo de G *om.* P(K).   (De consilio meo *om.* Q^2*).   De — or-
dineris] Igitur antequam ordineris de consilio meo R Ergo antequam ordineris de consilio
meo Pet.   antequam] numquam Ck Ta.   ordineris] promoveberis Ta.   98 vel^1
om. AaCcCkHTa(DFIMQ^2*SgX).   sanguinis JOU *corr. ab* sanguinis Tc.   99 etiam
pro reo] pro eo etiam Ta.   reo simili] consimili Ck reo sine *vel* sive Tu.   simili modo *om.* Q^1*.   stetisti] fecisti AaCiCkHJOPQ^1*RTcU Pet(BmCpDGIKLMNSgSoVX).
(99-4 vel — ordinaberis *om.* Tb *homoeotel.*).   1 auctorem *add.* teneris Ta.   Quid] quod
AcOPRTaTcTuU(BmEFGKLMNQ^2*SoVY quia X).   aliquid CcH Pet *corr. ab* adeo Ci.

---

84 Cf. GRATIAN C.32 q.2 cc.8-10; Po. 4312 (X 5.12.20). This last-mentioned decretal, issued
Oct. 4, 1211, is probably later than the composition of our text.
85 Cf. HUG. ad D.51 c.1 *in forensi exercitatione versati sunt* (fol. 64^{rb-va}); also following note.

Si semel officium scribatus suscepisti, licet non exercueris, non ordinaberis. Officium scribatus est saeva praecepta regis exercere et forisfacta sanguinis scribere et regi deferre; secundum aliquos si hoc officium 5
semel suscepisti, licet eo numquam usus fueris, non ordinaberis.[86]

Si furem vel alium mutilandum proclamasti, vel insecutus es cum
aliis, vel fugam ejus quominus evaderet impedivisti, vel ubi lateret
prodidisti, et captus mutilatus est vel signatus, non ordinaberis.[87]

106 Clericus relinquens clericatum et arma ferens non promovebitur.[88] 10
Aliis praeeuntibus clericus aliquis cum gladio insecutus est aliquem
ad interficiendum, qui antequam adveniret clericus interfectus est; a
viro litterato et discreto consultum est eidem clercico ne ad ordines
sine dispensatione papae accederet. In tantum districte considerandum est ne causae sanguinis aliquod adhibeatur adminiculum. 15
Haec de homicidio voluntario dicta sunt.

107 Si casualiter interfecisti hominem, si omnem quam debuisti adhibuisti diligentiam et rei licitae institisti, licite promoveberis; si autem
debitam non adhibuisti diligentiam, licet rei licitae institeris, non
promoveberis. Si rei illicitae institisti et aliquem interfecisti, quam- 20

---

3 exerceris Ta exercens P.   4 regis] legis CkH Pet.   4-5 forefacta Ta(SoXY) fo-
rifacta Ad (forisfactum Tb) forsitan CkTc(E) *corr. ab* forma O.   forisfacta sanguinis] foris
factam sanguinis effusionem H.   5 differre Cc referre U.   6 suscepisti] sumpsisti O.
7 secutus Cc.   8 qua minus Ck cum minus Tu.   inevaderet O fugeret Tu.
impedisti AaJOU.   9 prodisti Tu *corr. ab* prodisti P indicasti AaJU dicasti H.   ordinaberis *add.* Credo quod si rem meam portet et aliter non possum eam rehabere, tunc possum
reclamare et insequi Z.   11-16 Aliis — sunt *om.* Q1*.   11 praeeuntibus] praecedentibus OQ1*TaTc Pet praecentibus *corr. ad* praecedentibus Ab poenitentibus Tu.   est *om.*
JRTu.   12 veniret Q1* *corr. ab* ve Ck adveniat J.   clericus *om.* Q1*.   13 discreto *om.* O.   eidem] ipsi AaU ei J illi P.   clerico] domino *obscur.* O.   14 domini
papae Ta domini *cum* papae *insert.* H.   districte] discrete OTa.   districte consideran-
dum] cavendum R.   15 causae] in causa Pet *corr. ad* causa Tc.   17 casualiter] causa
litis J *corr. ab* causa litis Aa.   18 et] ad Tu *om.* Ta.   instituisti Cc *corr. ab* instituisti
Ck.   17-20 Si — promoveberis *om.* Q1*(Q2*).   19 debitam *om.* O.   20 licitae
CkO *corr. ab* licitae AaTc *add.* non *incert.* J.   institeris HU.   interfecisti] occidisti
CkHJU.

---

[86] Cf. Hug. ad D.51 c.4 *gravia* (fols. 64vb-65ra; cf. Paris BN lat. 3891, fol. 61va-b); Huguccio
mentions the last opinion presented by Robert in this paragraph, but does not accept it. Cf.
also Christopher Reginald Cheney, *From Becket to Langton* pp. 16-18, 21-24; also below sect.
172 with the passage from Huguccio which is source of that section (see n. 86). Cf. also below sects. 247-250.

[87] Cf. Peter Cantor, *Summa de sacr.* fol. 139va-b.

[88] Cf. Gratian C.23 q.8 cc.5-6.

cumque adhibuisti diligentiam, non promoveberis. Haec est Huguccionis distinctio.[89]

Secundum alios, quod tutius videtur, quocumque modo post baptismum occideris, non ordinaberis;[90] nec mirum, quia dicitur quod
generaliter pro quolibet crimine post baptismum commisso repellitur 25
quis a promotione, ut Dist. xxv. c. i.,[91] etiam si occultum sit.

108 Unde tutius pro quolibet crimine, etiam occulto, antequam ordineris petenda est dispensatio, vel a papa si minor non potest dispensare,
vel ab episcopo si dispensare potest. Graviter igitur, ut mihi videtur,
offendunt simplices sacerdotes confessores qui sine dispensatione et sola 30
sua auctoritate ordinari permittunt perjuros, fures, fornicatores, adul-
teros, incestuosos et graviores.[92] Ego autem ad istud vitandum inconveniens a duobus parisiensibus episcopis Odone et Petro habui ut
ubique eorum auctoritate dispensarem, ubi et ipsi dispensarent.[93]

109 Pueris biennibus ludentibus alter alterum in ignem intrusit, qui 35
et mortuus est; superstitem ut ordinaretur ad papam transmisi.

20-21 quantamcumque TcTu Pet quanticumque Aa.   21 adhibueris RTa.   21-22 Hu-
gonis AaCkHPTuZ.   (22 distinctio *ss. cessat* D).   23 quod] quos R *insert. alia manu*
Aa.   24 mirum *add.* est O.   26 xxv.] xxx. Ta xl. O.   27-28 ordinetur AaJU.
ordineris petenda est] petenda est ordinis Tu.   29 Graviter *om.* Q[1]*.   ut *om.* HQ[1]*.
31 sua *om.* JO.   perjures CcTu.   32 et *om.* Cc.   (*post* graviores *terminatur* Q[2]*).
evitandum JU.   33 parisiensis CkH pariter O.   episcopis *add.* scilicet J.   Odone
ad. scilicet Q[1]*.   34 ubicumque RTa Pet(CpEFLMNTb ubicumque *corr.* attentat. Bm) *add.*
ex Tc.   eorum *om.* J.   eorum auctoritate] ego R.   ubi] ibi Pet(FTb nisi So)
nobis Ta.

---

[89] See HUG. ad D.50 dictum p. c.36 (fol. 61rb; partly quoted by MÜLLER, *Ethik und Recht*
p. 76 nn.); cf. IDEM. ad D.50 c.37 (fol. 61rb); FIRTH, *Thesis* II 483*-486* with nn. 19-32 (III
759*-765*).
[90] Cf. STEPHEN OF TOURNAI, *Summa* ad D.50 c.8 (pp. 69-70); *Apparatus: Ecce vicit Leo* ad D.
50 c.6 (fol. 20ra); *Summa parisiensis* ad D.50 pr. (p. 44): *Summa Bambergensis* quoted by KUTTNER,
Kanonistische Schuldlehre p. 370 n. 2. This opinion is mentioned, but not accepted, by HUG.
ad D.50 dictum p. c.36 (fol. 61[rb]). BERNARD OF PAVIA, *Summa decretalium* 5.10.5 (pp. 222-223)
recognizes Huguccio's distinction regarding the guilt of homicide, but says that clerics are deposed for homicide unless dispensed. Regarding the treatment of accidental homicide by canonists of this period see above Proleg. p. 15 with n.78; also KUTTNER, "Ecclesia de occultis non
judicat", *Jus pontificium* 17 (1937) 13-28, esp. p. 23.
[91] Perhaps an error for D.24 C.7.
[92] Cf. below sects. 138-139 and Appendix A; FIRTH, *Thesis* II 453*-455*, 461*-466*, 471*.
[93] Cf. above Proleg. pp. 8 and 38.

Quinquennis quidam coaequaevum suum ludendo in brachio junco
acuto vulneravit, quo in tumorem converso mortuus est vulneratus;
superstitem ut ordinaretur ad papam transmisi.

Duobus presbyteris simul ludentibus alter, ut socium suum non 40
tangeret, sed jocose terreret, lapidem projecit, qui non ex ictu directo
in eundem socium pervenit, sed in parietem, et ex reverberatione modicum vulnus ei in capite inflixit; qui sui curam minus caute agens post
aliquot dies defunctus est. Superstitem, ut ordinis recuperaret exsecutionem, ad papam transmisi, quam vix tandem cum magna difficultate 45
obtinuit.[94]

De simonia

110 Consequenter de simonia dicamus. Simonia est studiosa voluntas
vendendi vel emendi aliquod spirituale vel adnexum spirituali. "Cum
effectu" debet intelligi; quia, si voluisti et non fecisti, non est simonia.[95] 50

Triplex est munus: *a manu*, ut pecunia; *a lingua*, ut promissum, adu-
lationes et similia; *ab obsequio*, ut obsequium indebite exhibitum, ut si
clericus fiat armiger vel notarius foeneratoris.[96] Quocumque istorum
interveniente obtinuisti ordinem vel beneficium vel dignitatem, simonia
est.   55

Item, si aliquod istorum secutum est quia obtinuisti aliquod istorum,

---

37 quidam] quidem J *om.* Aa.   quinquennis quidam] qui quamvis Tu quoniam quamvis Pet.   coaevum PQ¹*TuU coaequum O.   suum *add.* qui Aa.   brachio *add.*
suo RTc Pet.   juncto CcJ unco P cutello O.   38 vulneraverit Aa *om.* J. tumorem]
timorem Tc timorem *corr. ad* timore J tremorem Q¹*.   40 Duobus *ss. desinit* Q¹* *usque ad
sect. 118.*   presbyteris] pueris AaJTu.   41 joco (*corr. ab* jocose?) Ab.   ex *om.*
O.   42 et] sed H *om.* AaTcTu.   43 infixit CcCiZ(BmGLMSo) inflexit Ck(V) influxit
AaJ *corr. ab* influxit Tc.   45 vix *om.* RTa.   quam vix] quamvis JZ quamvis vix Pet.
tandem] tamen JR *om.* Ta.   49 aliquid Pet *om.* Ta *add.* beneficium O.   51 Triplex
ss. desinit Pet *usque ad sect. 138.*   munus] hoc *corr. ad* munus scilicet J *add.* ut Tc.   ut¹]
ex Tc et Tu.   51-52 adulationis JU *corr. ab* adulationis Aa.   52 indebito J indebitum
RU.   53 notorius TcTu.   56 Iterum O.   secutus es O.   quia] quod J
et P.   56-57 Item — est *om.* Aa (*homoeotel.*).

---

[94] Cf. Hug. ad D.50 c.39 *ipse et sui* (fol. 61va). A similar decision was made by a pope in
JL 16609 (2 *Compil.* 5.6.5; *Collectio seguntina* no. 1 *RevHistEccl* 50.422; Clement III); see Firth,
Thesis II 483*-484* with nn. 19 and 21 (III 759*-761*); 494*-497*.

[95] Cf. Hug. ad C.1 pr. (fols. 106vb-107ra); Rufinus, *Summa* ad C.1 pr. (pp. 197-198).

[96] Cf. Gratian C.1 q.1 c.114; Hug. *ibid.* (fol. 107ra); Rufinus, *ibid.* (pp. 198-199); Le Bras,
Institutions ecclésiastiques I 273-275; below sect. 207.

simonia est. Specialiter tamen dicitur giezia. Simon autem ante
obtulit; Giezi post exegit.[97]

111   Simonia quandoque est in promovendo et non in promotione,
quandoque e contrario, quandoque in utroque. Primum est quando 60
aliquis laborat pro se ut ordinetur, nec ordinatur. Secundum est
quando te nesciente aliquis laborat pro te, et tu ordinaris.[98]

    Dicamus itaque breviter. Quandoque aliquis scienter obtinet ali-
quid simoniace, quandoque ignoranter; si scienter, statim renuntiet
obtento, quidquid illud sit, quia eo retento non potest poenitere;[99] 65
et praeterea de jure stricto sciat se ad omne tale esse irregularem, nec
aliquod tale de cetero potest habere sine ipsius papae speciali dispensatione; vel ad minus et sine dubio illud quod male habuisti de cetero
non habebis sine dispensatione papae. Unde frequenter quidam et
seducti sunt et alios seducunt. Renuntiat enim aliquis ecclesiae vel 70
praebendae quam emit et reddit eam episcopo in manum et sic recedit
vacuus, et post tres dies vel quatuor revocat eum episcopus et reddit
ei praebendam; dico quod solus papa hoc facere potest.[100]

112   Quod dixi de dignitate, dico de beneficio, hoc addito quod, si
ecclesiam emisti, secundum quosdam deponeris in perpetuum ab omni 75

---

57 specialitate R spiritualiter Ck *corr. ab* spiritualiter Ac spiritualis Tu.   tamen] autem
Ta *om.* Tu.   dicitur *om.* JRTa.   giezia] gloria J iezia P.   autem] enim Ta.
autem ante] autem *corr. ad* ante O.   ante] prius AaJU.   58 Giezi] iezi P *corr. ab* et
O gesy et Tu.   59 Simonia *add.* est J *add.* autem P.   est *om.* HOTu.   et] est O
om. H.   61 nec ordinatur *om.* CkR.   62 et] ut ORTa.   tu *om.* Ta.   ordineris OTa.   63 itaque] ergo RTu.   quando R.   66 stricto] scripto P *insert.* O.
67 aliquid CcPRTu aliud Z.   speciali] spirituali CkJTu.   68 et *om.* JTu.   quod
add. de *corr. ad* tu O.   70 enim *delet.* Cc.   aliquis] quis AaJU.   71 episcopo in
manum] in manu episcopi CkTaU in manum episcopi HJ in manus episcopi Aa.   manus
Cc manu Ta *corr. ad* manu O.   72 reddet AcCkCi.   praedictam praebendam Cc.

---

[97] Usually canonists distinguished between *simonia* as buying and *giezia* as selling spiritual
goods; cf. Hug. ad C.1 pr. (fol. 107[ra]); Rufinus, *Summa* ad C.1 pr. (p. 198). A similar distinction to that made here is made by Rufinus, *ibid.* (p. 199) and by Peter Cantor, *Summa de
sacr.* fol. 165[rb]. Cf. *Act* 8.18-19; *2 Reg* (*4 Reg*) 5.20-24.

[98] Cf. Rufinus *loc. cit.*; Hug. *loc. cit.* quoted by Heitmeyer, *Sakramentenspendung* p. 164, n.
138.

[99] Cf. Hug. ad C.1 q.5 pr. (fol. 124[rb]); Idem ad C.1 q.5 c.1 *pro magna misericordia* (fol. 124[va]).

[100] Cf. Hug. ad C.1 q.5 c.3 *ex concessione episcopi* (fol. 124[vb]) quoted in Heitmeyer, *Sakramentenspendung* p. 164 n. 140. Cf. also below sects. 138-139; Appendix A sect. 363; Firth, *Thesis*
II 471* n. 85 (III 749*-751*).

ordine, quia fecisti te indignum ad omnem ecclesiam officiandam.[1] Et ita simoniacus amisit ordinis exsecutionem, etiam si ante simoniam commissam ordinatus sit, et maxime si post simoniam quocumque modo ordinatus sit et ad cujuscumque beneficii titulum.[2]

Eodem modo, si ordinem emisti, ab omni ordine de rigore debes 80 deponi.[3] Immo generaliter secundum quosdam quocumque modo factus es simoniacus vendendo vel emendo, numquam promoveberis, numquam in suscepto ordine ministrabis sine speciali papae dispensatione.[4]

113 Si te nesciente, sed alio pro te laborante, aliquid habes simoniace, 85 nisi statim cum adverteris simoniam renunties male acquisito, idem est ac si ipse laborasses ad simoniam.[5] Dicunt tamen aliqui quod, si aliquid alio mediante obtinuisti simoniace, non solum statim quando simoniam adverteris, sed etiam multo tempore post, potest tecum dispensare episcopus tuus;[6] quod non credo. Haec de ementibus. 90

Si vendendo aliquid es simoniacus, jus conferendi quodlibet tale perdidisti, quod solus papa tibi restituere potest. Unde dico: Si abbas aliquis semel aliquem novitium simoniace suscepit, de cetero numquam erit abbas sine dispensatione papae.[7]

---

76 officiendum Cc afficiendam Tu.   77 amittet OTc amittit P.   77-79 Et — titulum *om.* AbTa *insert.* O *cf. infra in Append. C no. 2.*   78 sit] est P sum Ck.   80 rigore *add.* juris CkZ.   81-84 Immo — dispensatione *om.* AbTa *insert.* O *cf. infra in Append. C no. 3.*   82 es] est AcCi *corr. ab* est Ad.   83 in *om.* OTc.   ministrabit Tud ebes ministrare Aa.   speciali] spirituali J spiritali Tu.   85 sed] vel TcTu. alio] aliquo OTa.   86 averteris JOR advertis P.   87 ipse] ille Tu *om.* HR.   88 alio] aliquo AaCkHJPRTaUZ(CpEIKLMNSgTbY) a° AbAcAdCi(G) vel Cc (illo V). 89 advertis P.   etiam] in J *om.* R.   90 tuus *om.* JZ.   quod] ut O.   Hoc OTu.   91 aliquis O.   es] est OTu factus es P.   quilibet J quaelibet Ck quod licet Cc.   93 novitium] monachum O.   recepit R.   94 domini papae HTc.

---

[1] Source not found. Cf. 1 *Compil.* 5.2.12 (JL 13843; X 5.3.13); also texts cited in the preceding note. Cf. also Glenn OLSEN, "The Definition of the Ecclesiastical Benefice in the Twelfth Century: The Canonists' Discussion," *Studia Gratiana* 11 (Collectanea Stephan Kuttner 1; Bologna 1967) 431-446.

[2] Cf. HUG. ad C.1 q.5 c.1 *Quicumque* (fol. 124rb).

[3] Cf. HUG. ad C.1 q.5 c.3 *Praesentium* (fol. 124va); *Glossa ordinaria in Decr.* ad C.1 q.5 c.3 *Praesentium.*

[4] Source not found. Cf. 1 *Compil.* 5.2.10 (JL 14110; X 5.3.11); 1 *Compil.* 5.2.12 (JL 13843; X 5.3.13).

[5] Cf. STEPHEN OF TOURNAI, *Summa* ad C.1 q.4 c.1 *Nullius crimen* (p. 149).

[6] Source not found; cf. below Appendix A sect. 360 also *ibid.*

[7] Cf. below sect. 126 with n. 34.

114   His intellectis, es ab omni simonia immunis ? Numquid aliquid 95
dedisti vel promisisti, vel sacramentum fecisti vel promisisti te post
facturum, vel indebitum obsequium exhibuisti pro te vel pro alio, vel
aliquis alius tale aliquid pro te fecit, vel pro ordine vel beneficio vel
alio spirituali ?   99

Aliquod beneficium habuisti ?

POENITENS. Immo diversa; quia patronus fui cujusdam ecclesiae,
ad quam meipsum episcopo praesentavi, qui me instituit.

SACERDOS. Salva sit episcopi gratia, non licuit, quanticumque meriti
fuisses.[8]   5

POENITENS. In alia ecclesia praebendam dedit mihi pater meus, quia
ejus erat canonicos eligere, ut sunt praepositi in Alemannia.

SACERDOS. Et hoc prohibitum est in decretali quadam.[9]

95-99 Numquid — spirituali *interpolat. infra post sect. 120* Q[1]* *fol. 334*[vb].   96 te post *om.*
Aa.   post *om.* CcCk.   97 vel[1] *om.* Tu.   exhibuisti *add.* vel AaJTuU.   alio]
aliquo CkTaTc *add.* vel aliquo alio Aa.   98 alius *om.* Ta.   aliquid] quid Ta(V) *om.*
AaAbAdJOQ[1]*(BmCpFSo).   tale aliquid *om.* Tu(F).   pro te *om.* AaCcCiCkHJPUZ-
(GINSgV tale K).   vel[1] *om.* AaJU.   vel[2] *add.* pro Tc(GIKTbY) *add.* alio HO *add.*
pro alio AbCkQ[1]*RU(BmFMX) *add.* pro aliquo TaTu(So).   vel[3] *add.* pro Tu.   99
alio] aliquo H(BmCpEINSoTbY *om.* X).   99-1 alio spirituali Aliquod] aliquod spirituale
J(G).   1 Aliquod] aliquot Ta *om.* J *add.* enim AbOR.   2 POENITENS] peccator O.
cujusdam] ejusdem CkOP.   4 non licuit] non potuit vel licuit Ad.

---

[8] Cf. Po. 275 (X 3.38.26; issued June 11, 1198).— This position of "patron", called *patronatus*,
in English "patronage" or "advowson", was a survival of the former ownership of churches by
laymen. In the earlier part of the Middle Ages the feudal lord considered that he owned the
church on his estate. Afterwards the Gregorian reformers insisted that church property belonged to God and that its revenues should support the clergy and the poor. But they left the
former lay owner with the privilege of naming the rector and the other clergy who should serve
and administer the church. The patron would choose some cleric to be rector and present him
to the bishop, who would then install him. This right of naming the holder of an ecclesiastical office came to be called "patronage" or "advowson". Advowsons were often acquired by
clerics or by monasteries. See 1 *Compil.* 3.33 (X 3.38); Paul THOMAS, *Le droit de propriété des
laïques sur les églises et le patronage laïque au Moyen âge* (Paris 1906) esp. pp. 105-159; THOMASSIN-
ANDRÉ, *Ancienne et nouvelle discipline* III 415-444, 544-556; John R. MOORMAN, *Church Life in
England in the Thirteenth Century* (Cambridge 1945) pp. 2-8; G. W. O. ADDLESHAW, *The Development of the Parochial System from Charlemagne (764-814) to Urban II (1088-1099)* (London
1954); IDEM, *Rectors, Vicars and Patrons in Twelfth and Early Thirteenth Century Canon Law* (London-New York 1956); also below sects. 129 and 131.

[9] The reference is apparently to JL 17606 (2 *Compil.* 3.4.3; *Collectio seguntina* no. 115 *Rev-
HistEccl* 50.449; CELESTINE III). These *praepositi* were ecclesiastics, regularly in major orders;
cf. P. HINSCHIUS, *System des katholischen Kirchenrechts* II 88-92, 95. The decretal forbade *praepositi* to promote their own sons whom they had begotten in sacred orders. It would not seem
to have necessarily excluded legitimate sons, begotten perhaps in marriage before ordination.
Flamborough's presentation of the decretal does not make this clear. However other decre-

115 Poenitens. Ad preces patris mei, qui foenerator fuit, obtinui
ecclesiam quandam a potente quodam, cui frequenter servierat pater 10
meus, ut fit frequenter, in munusculis, in obsequiis diversis, in accommo-
datione pecuniae et similibus.

Sacerdos. Si motus fuit princeps ad talia obsequia et pater tuus
tali intentione principaliter ea porrexit, simonia est.[10] Idem dico si
unicum vel minimum fuerit obsequium a patre tuo exhibitum unde 15
pater tuus vel princeps ille moveri potuit.[11] Sed si per hujusmodi obsequia comperta liberalitate patris tui voluit et princeps liberalis patri
tuo esse, non credo quod sit simonia, quia simonia est studiosa voluntas emendi vel vendendi aliquod spirituale. Numquid si aliquis benefacit
mihi non spiritualiter, teneor non benefacere ei spiritualiter? *Durus* 20
est sermo iste.[12]

Poenitens. Intentionem eorum non novi.

Sacerdos. De eo de quo tu nihil scis quomodo te judicabo? Si re-
murmurat conscientia tua, consule papam ut tecum dispenset.

116 Poenitens. De tertia ecclesia contendebamus ego et alius; quis 25
potior fuerit in jure nescio. Aliquid dedi, aliquid promisi, ut ipse de-
sisteret a lite, et ita obtinui ecclesiam.

---

11 ut fit frequenter] ut solet fieri Ta *om.* AaJ.   in[1] *om.* JR.   in[2] *om.* R.   diversis
add. et AaU.   11-12 commodatione R.   13 fuerit AaAcJOU(CpFLNSgSoTbY) fue-
rat H.   14 ea]ei O *om.* Tu.   porrexerit O.   15 fuit CkPTu.   16 potuerit O
poterat Tc.   hujusmodi] hujus TcTu.   17 comperta] comparata Cc.   liberalitate]
libertate AaCcCiCkHJORTcTuZ(BmCpEILMSgSoTbVY) *corr. ab* libertate Ab.   et] etiam
et P *om.* Ta.   19 emendi — spirituale] etc. Ta *add.* vel spirituali adnexum R.   bene-
faciat AbCiPZ.   20 *post* benefacere *textus desinit usque ad finem libri 3, octo foliis perditis, sed add.*
spiritualiter *tamquam vox reclamans* Aa.   20-21 Durus — iste *om.* H.   21 iste] hic CkPTaTc.
23 de[2] *om.* OTu.   de quo] quod H.   te *om.* CkRTc.   24 remurmuret JU.
conscientia] cogitatio O.   papa [?] AdJ.   25 tertia] tali OTu.   26 fuerit] esset
Ta foret U fieret J.   ut] et ut Cc.

---

tals, e.g. Po. 2599 (Reg. 8.147; PL 215.724; issued Oct. 27, 1205), forbade sons to succeed
fathers in the same benefice, without making any distinction between the legitimate and the
illegitimate.

[10] Cf. Hug. ad C.1 q.1 c.116 (fol. 119[rb]); ad C.1 q.1 c.21 *in aliquo tempore sive ante* etc. *acci-*
pere enim est quandocumque (fols. 109[vb]-110[ra]). Both Cantor and Courson speak at length about
those who perform some service for someone and obtain a benefice from him. Both declare
that much depends on the intention of the one who serves and of the one who confers the benefice; see Courson, *Summa* fols. 40[ra] and 52[vb]; Cantor *Summa de sacr.* fol. 165[rb]. Cf. below
sects. 135-136.

[11] Cf. Hug. ad C.1 q.1 c.23 *quinque tantum obolorum sint contenti, quod utinam non pretium villa-*
rum sed tantum quinque obolos acciperent (fol. 110[rb]).

[12] See *Joan* 6.61; cf. Cantor and Courson *locc. citt.*

SACERDOS. Intrinseca fuit transactio et ideo secundum quosdam non
est simonia, quia tu credebaris aliquid juris habere et ille; sed si tertius, de quo constaret quod nihil juris in ea haberet, tibi vel illi aliquid 30
dedisset vel promisisset, et ita ecclesiam obtinuisset, simonia fuisset
utrimque et extrinseca.[13] Sed quia rei veritas est quod alter vestrum
nihil juris in ea habuit, licet nesciatur uter, alter vestrum vel vendidit
uni quod habuit, et ita simonia fuit, vel cum nihil juris habuerit, pro
nihilo pecuniam accepit et ita rapuit. Rectius videntur dicere alii 35
qui non admittunt transactionem in spiritualibus nisi quando aliquis
scienter liberat vel redimit quod suum est.[14]

117 POENITENS. Cujusdam vicini mei ecclesiam concupivi, quia ditior
mea fuit et praeter spiritualia habuit etiam agrum; mea autem tota
fuit spiritualis. Refudi ergo ei decem libras.   40

SACERDOS. Si utraque tota esset spiritualis, manifesta esset simonia;
si altera tantum vel neutra, refusio fieri potest, ut videtur velle Alexander.[15] Ita, inquam, refusio fieri potest, ut pro temporali tantum detur
temporale tantum, et non permisceantur spiritualia et temporalia, ut

---

28 SACERDOS] Scilicet J *add.* si Tc.   ideo] ita O.   29 est] fuit JR.   juris *om.* J
add. in ea P *add.* te R.   30 quod] quia O.   ea] eo O eam Tu.   32 uterque (?)
corr. ad utrobique O *add.* intrinseca PTu.   et *om.* HR.   alterum Tc aliter P.
33 nihil — vestrum *om.* O (*homoeotel.*).   habuisset AbCkJTaTcTuU(IMSgSo) haberet R
(habuerit X).   uter] verum Tu utrum CcZ(MSoTbV ut Cp quis X) *om.* J.   (uter
alter] alteruter I).   vestrum *om.* P *insert.* H.   vel vendidit] vel vendit Ta vel emit vel
vendidit H vendidit vel R.   34 uni] vel *add. lacunam in qua scriptum est* emit O *om.* Tu (jus
VX).   fuerit Cc *om.* Ta.   habuerit] habuit CkHPTuUZ(EGKMNSg) haberet Ta(So).
39 etiam] et O.   autem] enim *insert.* O *om.* Ta.   41 SACERDOS] *interpolatio (vide su-*
pra in Proleg. ad p. 25) J.   esset¹] fuit J fuisset Tu *om.* P.   esset²] fuisset PTu.
43-49 Ita — conferendo *om.* AbOTaTu *post* fieret *ad lineam 49 infra* H; *cf. infra in Append. C*
no. 12.   43-44 detur temporale tantum *insert.* Tc.   44 tantum *om.* J.

---

[13] Alexander III and his immediate successors forbade transactions for an ecclesiastical office as having the appearance of simony; in matters such as the tithe they admitted them.
Perhaps someone concluded that because this practice was simply said to have *species mali* it
could be licit. In JL 14103 (1 *Compil.* 1.27.4; X 1.36.4) Alexander distinguishes between *spe-*
cies mali and *malum*; hence in this decretal he understands *species mali* as "the appearance of evil".
See also 1 *Compil.* 1.27.5-6 (X 1.36.5-6); 2 *Compil.* 1.16.1, 3-5 (X 1.36.7-10) also 2 *Compil.* 1.16.2;
these are JL 13832, 13159, 14177, 14102, 15186, 17675 (i.e. 17055; see *Collectio seguntina* no. 108
RevHistEccl 50.448), 14195.

[14] Cf. HUG. ad C.16 q.7 c.7 (fol. 240rb); CANTOR, *Summa de sacr.* fol. 93ra; COURSON, *Summa*
9.6 (fol. 44va).

[15] Reference apparently to JL 16580 (X 3.19.6; *Collectio seguntina* no. 15 *RevHistEccl* 50.424;
CLEMENT III).

dicatur quod "Pro ecclesia ista et agro isto habebis ecclesiam illam 45
et pecuniam illam" vel aliud temporale; sed prius commutetur temporale tantum pro temporali tantum nulla facta mentione de spiritualibus,
postea de spiritualibus disponat episcopus, quod voluerit cui voluerit
conferendo.[16] Forte tutius non fieret.

118 POENITENS. Praebendam aliquam dedit mihi episcopus in aliqua 50
ecclesia, sed investire me noluit antequam jurassem indemnitatem ecclesiae.

SACERDOS. Simonia fuit; quia tale sacramentum ante donationem vel
institutionem fieri non debet; sed postquam integre et plenarie receptus
fueras, licite potuisses fecisse.[17]   55

POENITENS. Ideo mihi cavi in alterius praebendae susceptione; nolui
enim antequam canonicus fierem jurare, sed promisi quod postea
jurarem.

SACERDOS. Et istud quoque simonia fuit, quia quodlibet spirituale
pure et sine omni conditione conferri debet. Tu autem per hoc quod 60
promisisti te postea juraturum praebendam obtinuisti.[18]

POENITENS. Quid est ergo quod in multis ecclesiis consuetudo est

---

45 habebit JRU.   illam] istam RU *om.* P.   46 illam] istam R.   aliud]
illud R aliquod P.   48 voluerint[1] R.   cui voluerit] aliquid J *om.* P.   49 non
om. JZ.   50 POENITENS *reincipit* Q[1]*.   55 fueris Tu fuisses P.   59 istud] illud
PTa.   quodlibet] quolibet Ci quod hoc *script. in lacuna* Ck.   62 est] sit U fit J.

---

[16] See *ibid.*; cf. below Appendix C no. 12; cf. also below sects. 136-137.
[17] This opinion, based on GRATIAN C.8 q.3 pr., seems to have been current in the latter part
of the twelfth century; cf. CANTOR, *Summa de sacr.* fols. 97[rb-va], 136[vb]. Huguccio distinguishes
more reasonably thus: "Sed distingue: tale juramentum aut praestatur ante electionem aut
post; item aut praestatur subditis, aut praelato. Si praestatur subditis ante electionem, simoniacum est, quia videtur praestari ut eligatur, ut infra c.i. <Idem> [Item MS] credo si
non praestetur, sed promittatur ante electionem praestari post electionem, ut infra eadem *Ar-
taldus* (c.2). . . . Si vero tale juramentum praestetur praelato, sive ante electionem sive postea,
sive ante confirmationem sive postea, sive ante consecrationem sive postea, licitum est et
licite potest exigi a superiori." HUG. ad C.8 q.3 pr. (fol. 175[va]). More reasonably still Courson
says: "Nos in his credimus esse distinguendum: quia aut exigitur juramentum de eo quod licitum est et ad quod quilibet tenetur, aut est juramentum de illicitis aut de indifferentibus quae
cooperari videntur ad impetrandum facilius beneficium. In primo casu et ante et post in-
vestituram licitum est juramentum, ut si jurem quod nec nocebo ecclesiae, nec dedi aliquid
pro beneficio." COURSON, *Summa* 9.6 (fol. 44[rb-va]). Flamborough's presentation seems to be
based on a literal interpretation of Gratian.
[18] Cf. GRATIAN, *loc. cit.*; HUG. *loc. cit.*; *Apparatus: Ecce vicit Leo* ad C.1 q.2 c.2 *omnis pactio* (fol.
37[ra]).

quod, in die in qua canonizatur quis, fratres reficit; et in monasteriis, quando aliquis monachatur, fratres reficit vel ex condicione vestes secum defert.   65

SACERDOS. Pessima est consuetudo.[19]

119 POENITENS. Vicinum habui canonicum vetulum. Rogavi episcopum meum ut post mortem ejus praebendam suam mihi conferret; quod et factum est.

SACERDOS. De re non vacante non fit promissio, salva sit episcopi 70 gratia. Unde si non fuerit simonia, pessima fuit intrusio, nec potuisti praebendam retinere. Prohibitum est enim ne aliquo vivente ejus beneficium alicui personae promittatur, ne mors possidentis desideretur vel procuretur.[20] Sed de collegio vel loco religioso talis non debet haberi suspicio; unde collegio et locis religiosis talis potest fieri pro- 75 missio.[21]

120 POENITENS. Consuetudo est in partibus nostris ut persona aliqua habens ecclesiam aliquam alii personae det pensionem ut ei succedat.[22] Ego alicui habenti ecclesiam dedi decem marcas ut mihi talem daret pensionem; quod et fecit; et sic eo mortuo obtinui ecclesiam.   80

SACERDOS. Simonia fuit et venatio pessima.

POENITENS. Abbas patronus cujusdam ecclesiae exegit a me censum antequam mihi illam daret; et sic illam obtinui.

SACERDOS. Simonia fuit; et non sunt creandi novi census sine episcopi auctoritate.[23]   85

---

63 die *add.* illa P.   in[2] *om.* O *insert.* H.   canonizatus Tu canonicatur U. reficiat Tu restitit J.   64 conditione] ordine AbQ[1]*TaTu *corr. ab* ordine O.   vestes *om.* O.   65 deferat Tu portat JU desunt Ci.   66 est] haec est H *add.* haec JTa.   68 meum *om.* JR.   69 et *om.* CkJPTuUZ.   70 sit *om.* AbORTaTu.   71 fuerit] fuit JPRTaTuU(CpEIKSgTb) sit H.   fuit] fuerit AbAcCcCiO(*et nulli alii*) tamen fuit H est Q[1]*.   72 aliquo] alio JUZ.   73 ne] nec CkTc.   75 haberi] fieri Tu fieri vel haberi Ta.   81 venatio] conventio J *om.* U.   84 et] quia Ac.   84-87 SACERDOS — obtinui *om.* Cc (*homoeotel.*).

[19] Cf. GRATIAN C.1 q.2 cc.2-3; COURSON, *Summa* fol. 38[rb-va]; cf. below sect. 126.

[20] Cf. 1 *Compil.* 3.8.2 (X 3.8.2; this is 3 Conc. Lat. c.8 quoted HEFELE-LECLERCQ 5[2].1094; MANSI 22.222).

[21] Promise to a religious house seems to be implicitly approved by INNOCENT III Po. 3077 (Reg. 10.45 PL 215.1138; issued April 6, 1207).

[22] Cf. JL 13933 (X 2.13.9); below sect. 130 with notes.

[23] Cf. Po. 751 (Reg. 2.115 PL 214.672; issued June 26, 1199); 1 *Compil.* 3.34.8 (JL 13162: X 3.39.8); 1 *Compil.* 1.26.6 (JL 13816; X 3.39.11).

POENITENS. In alia ecclesia sua recepit pensionem aliquam; qua a me augmentata ecclesiam illam obtinui.

SACERDOS. Simonia fuit; quia veteres census non sunt augmentandi sine episcopi auctoritate.[24]

121 POENITENS. Pauper eram et archidiaconi cujusdam optabam fa- 90 miliaritatem.[25] Praestiti ei mutuo viginti libras, et sic me ad se recepit; et post aliquantulum tempus ecclesiam mihi contulit, et tacuimus ambo de mutuo meo.

SACERDOS. Pessima fuit venatio, et simonia, et fortasse usura,[26] et fortasse si mutuum tuum repetivisses vel tibi solutum fuisset, ex quo 95 tali intentione et calliditate ad eum intrasti.

122 Umquam annuale vel tricennale[27] vendidisti, vel sepulturam, vel extremam unctionem, vel baptismum, vel aliud aliquod tale sacramentum ? 99

POENITENS. Non vendidi, sed sponte oblatum recepi.

SACERDOS. Non judico simoniam; sed si extorsisses simonia fuisset.[28]

---

86 alia] aliqua JPQ¹*U.   accepit OTc.   aliquam] aliam Tu *om.* U.   qua] quae Tu quam J.   87 illam] suam P aliam O *om.* Ta.   89 auctoritate *add.* Numquid — spirituali *ex lineis 95-99 supra in sect. 114* Q¹*.   90 captabam HJU captivi Ck. 91 Praestiti *corr. ab* praestitistis O *add.* enim Q¹*TcTu.   viginti] decem JHUZ.   92 aliquantum P aliquod Q¹*Ta.   94 fortasse] forte CcCkR.   94-95 et fortasse] etiam P.   95 fortasse] forte Tu.   repetisses J repetiisses U recepisses Ta.   vel] non JU sic P *insert.* Ad.   97 Numquam CkJO Umquamne Z SACERDOS. Umquam P. triennale CkJ.   98 vel per baptismum O.   aliud *om.* CkRTaTu.   aliud aliquod tale] aliquid tale H aliquid tale vel aliud J aliquid tale vel aliquod U.   1 oblatum *corr. ab* ablatum O ablatam Tu.   2 esset JTuU.

---

[24] Cf. Po. 751 (see preceeding note); 1 *Compil.* 5.2.17 (JL 13816); JL 16600 (X 3.39.15; *Collectio seguntina* no. 8 *RevHistEccl* 50.423; CLEMENT III).

[25] Regarding the office of archdeacon at this time, see Alexander Hamilton THOMPSON, *The English Clergy and their Organization in the Later Middle Ages* pp. 57-63, 70-71.

[26] Cf. CANTOR, *Summa de sacr.* fol. 97ra-b; COURSON, *Summa* 11.3, 5 (fol. 52rb-vb; ed. LEFÈVRE pp. 1ī, 19); *Apparatus; Ecce vicit Leo* ad C.1 q.1 c.114 *ab obsequio* (fol. 36rb).

[27] *Annuale* and *tricennale* in this context regularly signify a series of masses to be celebrated for a year and for thirty days respectively; see DU CANGE s.vv. Cf. CANTOR, *Summa de sacr.* fol. 82rb; COURSON, *Summa* 8.7-8 (fols. 36vb, 37ra); 49 (fol. 181va); THOMASSIN-ANDRÉ, *Ancienne et nouvelle discipline de l'Église* VI 475, 478. Courson's opposition to payment for celebration of masses can be seen from his *Summa* 2.11 (ed. KENNEDY p. 333).

[28] Cf. GRATIAN C.1 q.2 c.4; C.13 q.2 c.12; C.1 q.1 c.103; 1 *Compil.* 5.2.7-8 (X 5.3.8-9; these are Council of Tours (A.D. 1163) c.6 and 3 Conc. Lat. c.7 respectively; see HEFELE-LECLERCQ 5².972, 1093).

123   Umquam sacerdos vel diaconus vel subdiaconus mercenarius fuisti?

POENITENS. Fui; tum enim per annum sexaginta recepi solidos, tum
quadraginta solidos et medietatem altaris, tum altare tantum.[29]   5

SACERDOS. Primum simonia fuit pura, quia officium tuum, quod est
spirituale, vendidisti; secundum simonia fuit, sed non ita pura, eadem
ratione; tertium omnino non est simonia.

POENITENS. Mirum est valde quod dicis: ubi recepi sexaginta solidos
puros, judicas puram simoniam; ubi recepi altare purum, judicas omnino 10
non esse simoniam. Esto quod non valuerit altare nisi sexaginta solidos;
ergo indifferens videtur sive unum sive aliud recipiam.

SACERDOS. Licet paria sint, tamen altare recipitur nomine ecclesiae;
quod licitum est, quia qui servit altari de altari vivat.[30] Denarii recipiuntur
nomine bursae, maxime ex quo taxati sunt in numero.   15

124   Umquam recepisti ab aliquo vel donum vel obsequium indebitum
vel promissionem, ut pro eo intercederes ut ordinem ab aliquo reciperet,
vel beneficium ecclesiasticum, vel licentiam in aliquo ordine ministrandi,
vel aliud spirituale? Si fecisti, simonia est.

Umquam archidiaconatum tuum vel aliam dignitatem alii locasti, 20
vel simile quid ab alio conduxisti? Si fecisti, simonia est.[31]

     3-15 *sect. 123 om.* Q[1]*.   3 Numquam Ck Numquid Tc SACERDOS. Umquam P.
fuisti *add.* p. lx. l. v. sol. O.   4 tum[1] *om.* O.   sexaginta] quadraginta TcTu.
4-5 tum quadraginta solidos *om.* CcO.   5 quadraginta] sexaginta CkTc.   solidos
om. PTa.   et] tum JU.   tum] tertio (*forte corr. ad* tertio) O.   8 est] fuit
PTu.   9 sexaginta] quadraginta TcTu.   puram *add.* esse TaZ.   judicas puram]
puram judicas esse P.   11 non[1] *om.* Cc.   valuerat Cc valuit P.   sexaginta] quadraginta JTu.   solidos *add.* vel quadraginta U.   12 alium AbAcAdCiOZ(FN) alterum JU (reliquum Cp).   13 sunt AbCk.   14 qui *om.* Cc.   altari[1]] altare O.
altari[2]] altario PU.   15 sunt *om.* TaTu.   16 SACERDOS. Umquam PU.   vel[2] *om.*
O.   17 aliquo] alio CcTu.   reciperes TcTu.   18-19 vel licentiam — spirituale *om.* AbOQ[1]*Ta *cf. infra var. ad lineam* 21 *et in Append. C no. 4.*   19 aliud] aliquid
AcRTcTuZ(CpEFNTbXY) aliquod U(MSo alterum Sg aliquod tale Bm).   20 SACER-
DOS. Umquam P Numquam CkO.   20-21 Umquam — simonia est *om.* R.   20 alii]
alicui Ad tu alii U.   21 quid] aliquid Tu aliquod Tc.   alio] illo J aliquo Tc.
conduxisti *add.* vel licentiam in aliquo ordine ministrandi vel aliquid (?) spirituale *insert.*
O *vide supra var. ad lineas 18-19.*

     [29] The word *altare* in this context signifies an ecclesiastical revenue. Cf. GRATIAN C.1 q.3
cc.4, 14; Paul THOMAS, *Le droit de propriété des laïques sur les églises et le patronage laïque au Moyen
âge* pp. 76-79; P. BAYART, « Autel: V. L'autel comme bénéfice,» *Dict Droit Can* 1.1467-68. Cf.
also Reginald Alfred Rupert HARTRIDGE, *A History of Vicarages in the Middle Ages* pp. 36-37.
     [30] See 1 *Cor* 9.13-14. Cf. below sects. 129-130 with n. 41.
     [31] Cf. below sect. 132 with n. 48. Cf. also THOMASSIN-ANDRÉ, *Ancienne et nouvelle discipline
de l'Eglise* VI 501.

125 Archidiaconus parochiae sive archidiaconatus sui ecclesias visitat, a quibus procurationem recipit. Occurrit ei sacerdos dicens: "Domine, non visites ecclesiam meam: dabo tibi viginti solidos; vel ad minus non visites in propria persona, sed per clericum tuum, et dabo tibi decem 25 solidos." Simonia est; quia vendita et empta est visitatio, quae spiritualis est. Sed quia visitationi adnexa est et debita procuratio, postquam archidiaconus visitaverit ecclesiam, potest pro procuratione sua aliquid accipere et sacerdos dare.[32]

126 Umquam judicium vendidisti, vel subtraxisti ubi fieri debuit vel 30 accelerasti vel tardasti pro pecunia? Si fecisti, simonia est.[33]

Monachus gratis factus es?

Poenitens. Immo simoniace, et etiam prior; et ut idem aliis fieret saepius cooperator fui.

Sacerdos. Renuntia prioratui et numquam praelatus sis, numquam 35 ad novitium recipiendum intersis sine speciali dispensatione papae; et postea religionem quam intrasti simoniace exi, et artiorem intra; vel si gravior importabilis est tibi, quasi novitius intra eandem, tamen de speciali licentia papae.[34]

127 Decimas habuisti nisi nomine ecclesiae tuae? 40

Poenitens. Quasdam emi ab ecclesia, quasdam a persona laica.

22 Poenitens. Archidiaconus P *add.* sui U. sive] suae AbJ suae sive Tu *corr. ad* suae O vel Tc. parochiae sive *om.* RTa. sui] sine *vel* sive Ab *corr. ad* qui O. visitans CkZ. 23 a quibus — recipit *om.* Ta. recepit CcHO. et occurrit ei Z cui occurrit Ta. 26 solidos *om.* aliquid *illegibile insert.* Ad Sacerdos P *add.* Sacerdos TcU. 27 visitatio Tu visitationibus JU. et *om.* CkHPR. 28-29 recipere CcCkHPTc. 29 dare *add. interpolat.* Q[1]* *vide* Firth, *Thesis I 97*; *hic desinit* Q[1]* *usque ad sect. 141.* 30 Numquam Ck Sacerdos. Umquam P. 32 Sacerdos. Monachus P. 36 speciali] spirituali JTu *corr. ab* spirituali O *om.* P *insert.* Ad. 38 est] sit Tc *om.* Cc. de *om.* CkR. 38-39 speciali] spirituali JOTu. 40 Sacerdos. Decimas PU. habuisti] emisti JU. nisi] sine Tu non Ad *om.* JZ.

[32] This *procuratio* was originally the support of the visitor and his retinue during the visitation; later a payment of money was often substituted. Cf. 1 *Compil.* 3.34.6 (X 3.39.6; 3 Conc. Lat. c.4 Hefele-Leclercq 5[2].1091); JL 15342 (X 3.39.14); Thomassin-André, *Ancienne et nouvelle discipline* VII 41-45; Thompson, *The English Clergy* pp. 60-62; Christopher Robert Cheney, *Episcopal Visitation of Monasteries in the Thirteenth Century* pp. 104-118.

[33] Cf. Peter Cantor, *Verbum abbreviatum* c. 23 (PL 205.85-86); 1 *Compil.* 5.2.13 (X 5.3.14); JL 15192 (X 5.3.24).

[34] Cf. JL 14149 (X 5.3.19); JL 16562 (X 5.3.25; *Collectio seguntina* no. 6 *RevHistEccl* 50.323; Clement III); Po. 1403 (X 5.3.30; probably issued May-June 1201); Hug. ad C.1 q.3 c.8 *monachum* (fol. 122[va]); Rufinus, *Summa* ad C.1 q.3 c.8 (pp. 229-230); Courson, *Summa* 8.13 (fol. 38[va]). Cf. also above sect. 113.

SACERDOS. Nullius licentia potuisti decimas emere vel redimere ab ecclesia, quia hoc est simonia.[35] A persona laica non potes decimas emere vel redimere, nisi illas quae de jure tuae sunt ecclesiae, sine auctoritate episcopi loci in quo sunt decimae vel ecclesiae cujus sunt de jure.[36] Si ergo 45 tales emisti vel redemisti, satisfacies episcopo vel ecclesiae cujus sunt decimae de jure. Si in vadio tales decimas recipisti, scilicet non tuas, sine episcopi loci auctoritate vel ecclesiae cujus sunt de jure, redde decimas et quidquid ultra sortem percepisti, quia usura est.[37]

128 Postremo diversas ecclesias singulas tibi sufficientes sine speciali 50 licentia papae habuisti. Male fecisti; quia qua ratione hoc fecisti?

POENITENS. Ut consanguineos meos sufficienter sustentarem in torneamentis et in aliis saecularibus.[38]

SACERDOS. Mortaliter peccasti. Immo, etiam si pro fine honesto et justa causa, scilicet ut clericis profusior esses et ecclesiis diversis consilio et pro- 55 videntia provideres, sine culpa esse non posses. Ego tamen hoc damnare non auderem, maxime ubi pauca est beneficiorum pluralitas, vel multa cum papae dispensatione.[39]

42-44 ab ecclesia — redimere *om.* Ck *insert.* Tc (*homoeotel.*). 45 loci *add.* illius HTa. 46 satisfacias CcP. 47 scilicet] id est Ta solet Cc. 48 loci *om.* JU. 49 recipisti CcJHRTaUZ(BmCpLTbVX) cepisti Tu. 50 Postremo *add.* si Tc *add.* si *insert.* O. speciali] spirituali JOTu. 51 quia *om.* TaTc. 52 sufficienter *om.* JU. 53 in *om.* CkJPRTa. 54 SACERDOS] personis O. 55 clericus Ta cleris H ceteris JU eleemosynis Z. et in ecclesiis OP. 56 posses *add. notam scriptam alia manu tredecimi saeculi:* Tamen quinque casus excipiuntur H. tamen] autem CkP.

---

[35] Cf. HUG. ad C.16 q.7 c.7 (fol. 240rb).
[36] Cf. GRATIAN, C.16 q.7 c.39; 1 *Compil.* 3.33.21 (JL 14203; X 3.38.17); 1 *Compil.* 5.28.3 (X 5.33.3; 3 Conc. Lat. c.9 HEFELE-LECLERCQ 5[2].1095-96; MANSI 22.222-224); Po. 322 (X 3. 10.7; issued July 7, 1198); Paul VIARD, *Histoire de la dîme ecclésiastique dans le royaume de France aux XIIe et XIIIe siècles* pp. 139-144; HARTRIDGE, *History of Vicarages* esp. pp. 4-10; Giles CONSTABLE, *Monastic Tithes from their Origin to the Twelfth Century* pp. 83-197.
[37] Cf. *Apparatus: Ecce vicit Leo* ad C.1 q.3 c.14 *decimas* (fol. 37vb); also texts cited in preceding note. Regarding tithes see below sects. 213-215; regarding usury sects. 216-219.
[38] At this time tournaments were forbidden by canon law, although this was not always enforced in practice. See 1 *Compil.* 5.11.1 (X 5.13.1; 3 Conc. Lat. c.20 HEFELE-LECLERCQ 5[2].1102); 1 *Compil.* 5.11.2 (EUGENE II in council of Rheims; HEFELE-LECLERCQ 5[1].825); Po. 2927 (Reg. 9.197 PL 215.1035-36; issued Dec. 10, 1206); Po. 3127 (Reg. 10.74 PL 215.1174-75; issued June 25, 1207).
[39] Plurality of benefices was forbidden many times; see 1 *Compil.* 3.4.3 (X 3.4.3; 3 Conc. Lat. c.13 HEFELE-LECLERCQ 5[2].1098); 1 *Compil.* 3.5.6 (X 3.5.5; 3 Conc. Lat. c.14 HEFELE-LECLERCQ 5[2].1098-99); 1 *Compil.* 5.27.1 (JL 14192; X 5.31.1). The same laws testify to widespread abuses in this regard; cf. JL 13966 (X 3.5.15); Po. 420 (3 *Compil.* 3.5.4; issued Nov. 13, 1198). Ca.

129 POENITENS. Patronus prasentavit me ad ecclesiam quandam episcopo. Episcopus dixit: "Clerico meo R. dabo personatum, et te perpe- 60
tuum recipio vicarium ut annuatim decem percipias marcas."[40]

SACERDOS. Simonia est; quia tantum nomine bursae decem percipies
marcas, et ita mercenarius es; et illae decem marcae non sunt signum
alicujus futuri beneficii quod tu exspectes, sed jam suscepti officii mercedis quantitas taxata.[41]   65

---

59 *Sectionibus 129-140 carent* AbOTa(X); *cf. infra in Append. C no. 5.*   POENITENS *om.*
CcTuZ.   61 percipias] recipias CiJPTuU participes Cc.   62 percipias CkPTc participes CcJ recipias Tu.   63 sint AcAdCiZ(Tb).   64 tu *om.* HP.   64-65 mercedem CcHTcZ mercedes Tu *add.* scilicet Tc.

---

nonists recognized that it could be licit under certain conditions; see HUG. ad D.89 c.1 *singula
officia* (fol. 96rb); ad C.21 q.1 pr. (fol. 255rb); RUFINUS, *Summa* ad D.89 (p. 180); *Glossa ordinaria in Decr.* ad C.21 q.1 pr. & c.1. Popes also granted dispensations and recognized exceptions; see THOMASSIN-ANDRÉ, *Ancienne et nouvelle discipline* IV 622-624. Peter Cantor had harsh
things to say about those who held several benefices; see THOMASSIN-ANDRÉ, *op. cit.* IV 634-
635. Yet he himself by papal dispensation held two, according to ROBERT COURSON, *Summa*
17.3 (fol. 73va). Courson thought that there had been good reasons for this exception to the
law, but considered that it gave bad example, and so ought not be done in the future even
for such good reasons; see his *Summa* fols. 72ra-74rb. Regarding this practice of pluralism see
also Alexander Hamilton THOMPSON, *The Historical Growth of the English Parish Church* pp. 10-
23; John Richard Humpidge MOORMAN, *Church Life in England in the Thirteenth Century* pp. 24-33.

[40] *Personatus* is the office of parson or *persona*, who held the principal title as rector of a church.
He was often represented in the parish by a vicar who ordinarily exercised care of souls in his
absence; however sometimes even the vicar failed to reside and provided a substitute. See 1
Compil. 1.20.2-5 (X 1.28.1-4); Po. 2597 (Reg. 8.145 PL 215.723; issued Oct. 27, 1205). See
also THOMASSIN-ANDRÉ, *Ancienne et nouvelle discipline* I 488-494; VII 25-28; THOMPSON, *The
English Clergy* pp. 102-106, 116-122; CHENEY, *Becket to Langton* pp. 122-126, 129-136; HART-
RIDGE, *History of Vicarages* pp. 11-35, 48; G. W. O. ADDLESHAW, *Rectors, Vicars and Patrons in
Twelfth and Early Thirteenth Century Canon Law.* The aforementioned literature deals with the
Church in England and to some extent in France. In Germany a different meaning was attached
to the term *persona*; see above Proleg. p. 2, n. 7.

[41] Cf. GRATIAN C.21 q.2 c.5, which is the last sentence of c.10 of 2 Conc. Lat. (HEFELE-LE-
CLERCQ 5[1].728); it forbids churches to be entrusted to "hired priests." HUG. ad eundem locum (fol.
256ra-b) maintains that this forbids a vicar to be hired for an annual price to rule the church
and have care of souls, but he says one may be so engaged to carry out certain duties for the
parson if he is impeded. This prohibition is repeated in c.5 of the Council of Tours under
Alexander III (1 *Compil.* 5.3.3; X 5.4.3; see HEFELE-LECLERCQ 5[2].728; A.D. 1163). This canon
forbids the *regimen* or headship of a church to be committed to a priest for an annual price.
Flamborough maintains throughout that a priest may never be hired for a stated sum to exercise care of souls or any spiritual ministry. But it may be stipulated that such a one is to receive
the revenue of a church, or a certain portion of it, e.g. one third, or all of it except a fixed sum.
Regarding this see the following sect. 130; cf. above sect. 123. Regarding the pension as sign
of one's expectation of a future benefice cf. above sect. 120 and see again the following sect. 130
with notes.

130 POENITENS. In alia ecclesia receptus sum persona ut annuatim duos aureos perciperem vel marcam argenti, et residuum ecclesiae vicarius perpetuus.[42]

SACERDOS. Hic non judico simoniam; quia nomine ecclesiae recipit vica- 70 rius quod recipit, et nihil nomine bursae taxatum,s ed nomine ecclesiae; ut si diceretur "Habeat vicarius tertiam partem ecclesiae" vel "totam praeter marcam" vel aliquid aliud; quod licitum est.[43] Quod autem tibi taxatur marca non est mercedis tuae quantitas, ut videtur, sed signum quod futurum exspectes beneficium, scilicet residuum ecclesiae. Sed alia ratione judico illud vitiosum, quia statim cum institueris promittitur 75 tibi beneficium vicarii non vacans, quod est illicitum; immo tibi datur jus obtinendi illud beneficium statim post mortem vicarii, quod majus puto peccatum.[44] Idem dico si et vicarii et personae portio taxata sit, sed tantum nomine ecclesiae, non nomine bursae; ut si personae assignata sit tertia pars ecclesiae et vicario residuum.   80

131 POENITENS. Dum eram abbas, ecclesiarum multarum patronus eram. Dedi ergo episcopo loci ecclesiarum multarum jus patronatus, ut in ec- clesia majori canonicum me faceret, id est ut monasterium meum perpe- tuam in ea haberet praebendam, et ut alias ecclesias, in quibus tantum jus patronatus habebam, in usus suos proprios idem monasterium meum 85 converteret.[45]

67-68 vicariis perpetuis AcRTc vicarius praepositus P.   69 Hic] hoc JPU.   judico] video AcRTcTu(BmEFGMNSoTbY) dico P(K indico *vel* iudico Sg).   recipit] recepit JP *corr. ab* recepit CcTc.   70 recipit] recepit JP.   72 aliquid *om.* H *insert.* Ad. aliquid aliud] aliud tale P aliud aliquid tale U *add.* tale J.   autem] ante Ci *om.* AcRTc. 77 majus] magis AcJRTcU(BmCpFGMNSgTb).   78 et[1] *om.* AcPRTc(BmCpEFGKLMNSg- SoTb etiam V).   83 monasterium meum] ecclesia mea JU.   84 alias] aliquas JU. 85 suos *om.* JTcU.   idem] id est Z *om.* R.

---

[42] See above n. 40 and below n. 44.

[43] See above n. 40. Similar arrangements seem to have been implicitly approved byAl exander III; see 1 *Compil.* 5.3.4 (JL 13910; X 5.4.4); JL 13844 (*AppConcLat* 8.14; MANSI 22, 308).

[44] See above sect. 119 with n. 20. Cf. Po. 510 (Reg. 1.50 PL 214.461-462; issued Dec. 30, 1189); Po. 2334 (Reg. Suppl. 87 PL 217.125; issued Dec. 1, 1204); Po. 2600 (Reg. 8.148 PL 215.724; issued Oct. 27, 1205); Po. 4176 (Reg. 13.205 PL 216.372-373; issued Jan. 31, 1211); Po. 4218 (Reg. 14.26 PL 216.404; April 12, 1211).

[45] See the decretal: "Significarunt nobis prior et conventus — harum tenore tacito impetra- tae." *Collectio Wigorniensis* 7.77 (ed. LOHMANN, *ZSavignyStRG* kan. Abt. 22.146-147); cf. *ibid.* 7.78 (p. 147); FIRTH, *Thesis* II 4034. Regarding patronage see above sect. 114 n. 8; regarding pa- tronage and ownership of churches by monasteries see HARTRIDGE, *History of Vicarages* pp. 4- 33; THOMPSON, *The Historical Growth of the English Parish Church* pp. 10-23. Regarding monks and monasteries holding prebends, i.e. places of dignity in chapters, see THOMASSIN-ANDRÉ, *Ancienne et nouvelle discipline* VI 607-615.

Sᴀᴄᴇʀᴅᴏs. Simonia est; quia praebendam et ecclesias recepisti, quae sunt pure spirituales, et jus patronatus dedisti, quod non est pure spirituale; quod patet quia vendi potest et praescribi, saltem cum universitate.[46]

Pᴏᴇɴɪᴛᴇɴs. A milite jus patronatus cujusdam ecclesiae emi pro vi- 90 ginti marcis.

Sᴀᴄᴇʀᴅᴏs. Simonia fuit; quia dedisti argentum, quod est temporale purum, et jus patronatus recepisti, quod non est purum temporale; quod patet quia per se emi non potest.[47]

132 Pᴏᴇɴɪᴛᴇɴs. Sunt in partibus meis decani rurales qui pro decanatu 95 annuum solvunt censum; et hoc ex antiquo pro causis et judiciis quae exercent.

Sᴀᴄᴇʀᴅᴏs. Pessimam hoc judico simoniam, et causam in subditos sae-viendi et occasionem.[48]
99

133 Pᴏᴇɴɪᴛᴇɴs. Peritus eram in jure; et associavit me sibi episcopus ut coadjutor ejus fierem in causis decidendis et consiliis et aliis spiritualibus, et sub conditione annuatim viginti percipiendi marcas.

Sᴀᴄᴇʀᴅᴏs. Credo quod simonia est, quia pro spirituali officio tuo nu-meratam percepisti sub conditione pecuniam.
5

Pᴏᴇɴɪᴛᴇɴs. Quid ergo in tali faciendum est casu?

Sᴀᴄᴇʀᴅᴏs. Credo quod licite dicere potest clericus episcopo: "Domine, non sufficio mihi ut propriis meis vobis militem stipendiis,[49] sed honorifice mihi ministrate necessaria et vobis devotus serviam."[50] Sed non credo

---

87 praebendas AcHJTcTu(CpFMNSgSoTbY).   ecclesiam AcHJPRTcU(CpFGKNSg-SoTbY ecclesiae L).   89 vendi vel P *add.* non *partim erasum* Ac.   90-91 viginti] decem CkJ.   91 marcas JTu.   92 fuit] est Tu est vel fuit Ck.   95 meis] nostris HJ. 96 annuunt J annuatim Tu annuatim *corr. attentat.* Cc.   1 quidam episcopus JU. 9 ministrare CkJTu.

---

[46] Cf. 1 *Compil.* 3.33.9 (JL 13953; X 3.38.7); Hᴜɢ. ad C.16 q.1 c.56 (fol. 231vb); ad C.16 q.7 c.26 (fols. 241vb-242ra); *Apparatus: Ecce vicit Leo* ad C.16 q.7 c.40 *vel quocumque commercio vendere* (fol. 76rb); Cᴀɴᴛᴏʀ, *Summa de sacr.* fol. 94^{ra-vb}; Cᴏᴜʀsᴏɴ, *Summa* 8.20 (fol. 40ra).

[47] Cf. 1 *Compil.* 3.33.19 (JL 14158); 3.33.20 (JL 13798; X 3.38.16); also texts cited in preceding note.

[48] Cf. 1 *Compil.* 5.3.1 (X 5.4.1; 3 Conc. Lat. c.15 Hᴇғᴇʟᴇ-Lᴇᴄʟᴇʀᴄǫ 5^2.1099); 1 *Compil.* 5. 3.2 (X 5.4.2; Council of Tours [A.D. 1163] c.7 Hᴇғᴇʟᴇ-Lᴇᴄʟᴇʀᴄǫ 5^2.972 Mᴀɴsɪ 21.1178-1179); Po. 2116 (Reg. 6.225 PL 215.255-256; Feb. 6, 1204). Cf. above sect. 124. Both Cantor and Courson inveighed at length against the rapacity of rural deans, who, they maintained, used to "fleece" their flocks by bribery and extortion.

[49] Cf. 1 *Cor* 9.7.

[50] Cf. Hᴜɢ. ad C.21 q.2 c.5 (fol. 256^{ra-b}); Cᴏᴜʀsᴏɴ, *Summa* fol. 45^{ra-b}.

quod liceat ei vel victum taxare vel vestitum, ut dicat "Tot et talia volo 10
habere sircula, et tot vestes et tales"; sed neque in generali necessaria, ut
dicat "Pro necessariis meis annuatim dabitis mihi decem libras"; ne, si
modicum taxaverit, cogatur clericus vel mendicare vel turpiter negotiari,
si nimium, de quaestu infametur; sed secundum apostolum habens victum
et vestitum his contentus sit.[51]   15

POENITENS. Numquid idem liceret clerico diviti?

SACERDOS. Non auderem consulere.[52]

POENITENS. Propriis igitur militabit stipendiis?[53]

SACERDOS. Non tenetur.

POENITENS. Quid si pauper clericus non invenitur?   20

SACERDOS. Quid si caelum caderet? Nonne *pauperes semper habetis vobiscum*?[54] Idem videtur dicendum de sacerdote quem sibi advocat dives
aliquis ut sibi celebret divina.

POENITENS. Numquid potest clericus tantum spiritualiter serviturus
episcopo cum eo de praebenda pacisci?   25

SACERDOS. Qui admittunt commutationem spiritualium dicant in quo
hic sit simonia.[55] Ego nihil definio.

134 POENITENS. Postquam per aliquot annos pro viginti marcis annuatim servieram episcopo, tandem sufficienter beneficiavit me in praebenda et dixit mihi: "Frater, jam sufficis tibi; propriis tuis mihi servias 30
expensis sicut consuevisti." Quid facere debui?

SACERDOS. Si sic te beneficiavit parisiensis episcopus in parisiensi ecclesia, forte rationabiliter videtur alicui quod, in his quae ad parisiensem pertinent ecclesiam et ad commune bonum, ei servire debeas, sed non in propriis episcopi negotiis. Item, si ad preces episcopi parisiensis in carnotensi 35
beneficiatus es ecclesia, forte nec episcopo parisiensi nec ecclesiae, nisi
ex liberalitate, teneris servire.

---

13 taxatur J taxetur U.   vel[1] *om.* PTu.   vel mendicare *om.* R.   15 contemptus JR.
16 licet JP.   20 invenietur TcTu.   21 habebitis AcHPR.   24 spiritualiter] specialiter PZ.   27 hic] haec J ibi U.   sit] fit Tu fieret Cc.   28 aliquos CcJTu.
30 sufficit Tc *corr. ab* sufficit Cc conficis Tu.   33 alicui *om.* CkH.   37 libertate CcRTu.

---

[51] See 1 *Tim* 6.8.
[52] Cf. GRATIAN C.1 q.2 cc.6-9.
[53] See 1 *Cor* 9.7.
[54] See *Joan* 12.8.
[55] Cf. below sects. 136-137 with nn. 60-61; sect. 140 with n. 77.

135 Poenitens. Ad firmam ecclesias habui.[56]

Sacerdos. Si ad officiandum ecclesiam non te obligasti, non audeo hoc damnare nisi inhonesta cupiditas suffuerit.[57] Si autem ad officiandum ecclesiam principaliter te obligasti solum Deum ante oculos habens, et quia ultra necessaria tibi suffecit ecclesia aliquid ex condictu personae refudisti, non credo quod sit simonia.[58] Si autem ad lucrum tantum oculum direxisti, et propter pinguius lucrum ad officiandum ecclesiam te obligasti, credo quod simonia est; quia officium tuum, quod est tantum spirituale, et denarios tuos dedisti pro fructibus ecclesiae, qui sunt tantum non spirituales; et, licet hic et ibi idem emergat emolumentum, alia tamen est hic forma contractus quam ibi, et fortasse alius contractus, et intentio alia; et intentio tua operi tuo nomen imponit.[59]

136 Poenitens. Ecclesiam totam spiritualem commutavi pro alia tota spirituali, de qua commutatione prius tractaveramus ego et socius meus.

Sacerdos. Dicunt aliqui quod simonia est; quia aliquid dedisti, scilicet

---

38 ecclesiam AcJRTcU(BmCpFGILMNSgSoTbY *om*. E).   39 Si *add*. non AdCcCiTu-
(L *add*. autem I).   non *om*. PTuZ(KSo) nisi *insert*. Ad.   42 sufficit AcJRTcU(Bm-
CpEFGLMNSgSoTbY).   conductu AcJRTcU(BmCpEFGIMNSoTbVY) conducto Ck
conditu H (condutu L) *auctor videtur scripsisse* condictu *eodem sensu ac* condicto.   43 tantum]
tuum JTu *om*. P.   oculos CcCiP *add*. tuum U.   45 est¹] sit AcCkHJRTcUZ(Bm-
EFGMNTbVY).   46 non *om*. PRTuU.   47 ibi idem] ibidem AdCcCiCkZ.
48 fortasse] forte CkP.   52 alicui Ci quidam H *rasura* Ad.

---

[56] The word *firma* signifies property rented for a fixed price. To possess *ad firmam* is to possess by a contract of rent. Cf. 1 *Compil*. 3.26.6 (JL 14023; X 3.30.8); Thomassin-André, *Ancienne et nouvelle discipline* I 494-499; VII 25, 28; Du Cange s.v. 3 *Firma* III; Po. 3447 (Reg. 11. 128 PL 215.1443-45; issued July 7, 1208).

[57] In this case it is the revenues of the church, not the spiritual offices, which are rented. Since temporal goods are received on both sides, Robert is willing to allow it, provided that both the intention and the terms of the contract are just and not usurious; cf, below sect. 215. Regarding such contracts see Moorman, *Church Life in England* pp. 33-34.

[58] Robert maintains above in sect. 130 (cf. sect. 129 with n. 41) that, while the vicar who administers and serves the church spiritually may not receive a definite amount of money for his services, the parson may receive a stated sum in view of his title. That is what is done in this case.

[59] See St. Ambrose, *De officiis* 1.30.147 (PL 16.71). Cf. Huguccio: "Sed contra videtur quod intentio baptizantis exigatur. Ait enim Ambrosius: 'Affectus tuus operi tuo nomen imponit'. Et idem: 'Intentio dirigit opus'," Hug. ad *De consec.* D.4 c.31 (quoted by Gillmann, *Katholik*⁴ 18 [1916]² 50 n. 4); also Peter of Poitiers, *Sententiae* 2.16 (ed. Philip S. Moore, Joseph N. Garvin and Marthe Dulong, *Sententiae Petri Pictavensis* II [Notre Dame 1950] 112-120; PL 211.1000-05); Müller, *Ethik und Recht* p. 136 with n. 61. Several theologians and canonists of this time allow certain kinds of transactions if one's intention is upright; cf. above sect. 115 and below sect. 136 with notes.

ecclesiam tuam, ut tu haberes aliam; et licet tantum spirituale dedisti,
quia tamen dedisti, simoniam commisisti.[60] Si diceret episcopo clericus
"Date mihi ecclesiam istam et dabo vobis praebendam illam," licet sic 55
daretur spirituale pro spirituali, nonne simonia esset? Item, si diceret
clericus abbati et conventui sancti Victoris "Recipite me in fratrem et
canonicum et dabo vobis ecclesiam istam," nonne simonia esset si ita fieret?

POENITENS. Quomodo ergo debet fieri commutatio spiritualium?

SACERDOS. Tantum ut consideretur honor Dei et salus animarum. 60
Dicat ergo Robertus Petro: "Frater, videtur mihi quod in ecclesia tua
magis essem ad honorem Dei et salutem animarum quam sim in mea,
et tu similiter, ut mihi videtur, magis esses ad honorem Dei et salutem
animarum in mea quam sis in tua. Eamus igitur ad episcopum et ista
ei indicemus." Si igitur episcopus tantum ad honorem Dei et salutem 65
animarum oculum dirigens personas transmutaverit singulas a suis ecclesiis ad alias, credo quod bene facit; nec commutant personae beneficia,
sed episcopus personas.[61] Si autem Robertus et Petrus aliam conditionem
vel alium contractum fecerint inter se, simonia erit, vel ad minus illicitum propter suspicionem quaestus et lucri.   70

137 Unde personae non possunt de commutatione aliter tractare quam
diximus. Monasteria et ecclesiae possunt, quia ibi cessat suspicio quaestus; et bene potest una ecclesia dicere alii: "Renuntia ecclesiam tuam
et concede mihi eam, et ego renuntiabo meae et concedam eam tibi, quia
hoc erit tibi utile et mihi"; et postea poterit istud fieri et confirmari aucto- 75

---

54 tamen *insert.* Ad *corr. ad* tantum Cc.   quia tamen dedisti *om.* Ck.   55 ecclesiam]
praebendam Ck.   praebendam] ecclesiam CkTu.   licet] hoc J si P.   60 SACERDOS
om. CcRTu *insert.* Ad.   61 Petro *om.* CcCiTuZ.   62 sim] sua *corr. ad* sum Ck *om.* J.
quam sim in mea *om. forte insert.* Ad.   64 sis *om.* JR.   igitur] ergo AdCkRTu *om.* U.
ista] ita Tu *om.* Ck.   65 igitur] ergo J *om.* P.   68 aliam] aliquam Ad.   69 fecerunt
HTu.   erit] est HPR.   69-70 illicitum *add.* aliter Cc.   73 ecclesiam tuam] ecclesiae
tuae HTu.   74 et¹ *om.* Ad.

---

[60] This is maintained by Peter Cantor; see his *Verbum abbreviatum* c. 40 (PL 205.132); *Summa
de sacr.* fols. 88va, 92rb. Others deny that this is simony, requiring only the consent of proper
ecclesiastical authority; see Hug. ad C.16 q.7 c.40 *cum alio monasterio* (fol. 243va); *Apparatus*;
Ecce vicit Leo ad C.16 q.7 c.40 *vel commutare* (fol. 76rb). Exchanges of benefices became increas-
ingly common during the later Middle Ages; cf. THOMPSON, *The English Clergy* pp. 107-109;
Franz GILLMANN, "Die Resignation der Benefizien", *ArchivKKRecht* 81 (1901) 222-242.

[61] Cf. JL 15754 (X 3.19.5); CANTOR, *Verbum abbreviatum* c.40 (PL 205.133). ROBERT COUR-
SON, *Summa* 8.25 (fols. 40vb-41ra) says that exchanges of benefices are licit only if motivated by
the utility of the Church and not by temporal gain.

ritate episcopi.[62] Alii dicunt quod non alio modo possunt commutare ecclesiae quam personae.[63]

Quod diximus de simplicibus beneficiis dicunt aliqui etiam de dignitatibus, exceptis episcopatibus et majoribus. Alii dicunt quod solius papae est commutare dignitates quascumque.[64]

80

138 Puto tutius est, quantum ad salutem animarum, sic sentire de simoniacis sicut diximus, ut scilicet ad papam transmittantur ad dispensationem obtinendam et in ordinibus et in beneficiis. Sunt tamen plures et juris peritiores qui dicunt quod episcopi possunt cum quibusdam simoniacis dispensare et in aliis criminibus, ut in homicidiis.[65] Immo dicunt 85 quod nec opus est dispensatione in homicidio occulto; quia peracta poenitentia sine omni dispensatione potest homicida promoveri et in quolibet ordine ministrare; quia, ut dicunt, in confessione et poenitentia non solum dimittitur peccatum, sed et omnis peccati sequela, ut est ordinis impedimentum.[66] Et habent generaliter pro regula quod in omni crimine potest 90

---

76 commutari CcCiJ(BmCpEILMSoVY) *add.* tam R.   78 aliqui] alii CcCiCkPTuZ quidam R.   79 et *om.* CiPZ *insert.* Ad.   81 Puto *ss.* reincipit Pet.   82 diximus] dictum est JU.   83 in[2] *om.* JPTcTuU(BmEGKMSgSoTb).   tamen *add.* et Cc. 83-84 plures et *invers.* H *om.* R.   84 et] de Ck *om.* AcJTcU(BmCpEFMNSgSoTbY). periti H perviores Ci.   85 et] vel HTu.   in[1] *om.* AcRTc.   homicidia Cc *om.* P. 88 et in poenitentia TcU Pet.   88-89 solis dimittatur Cc.   89 et] etiam JU *om.* H.

---

[62] This might have some connection with BERNARD OF PAVIA, *Summa decretalium* 3.16.4 (p. 83). Bernard, however, is speaking about the alienation of ecclesiastical goods rather than about the problem of exchanging spiritual things.

[63] Source not found.

[64] Regarding these "dignities" in the Middle Ages, see P. TORQUEBIAU, "Chapitres de chanoines", *DictDroitCan* 3.547-548. Alexander III at the Council of Tours in 1163 forbade "divisions of prebends or exchanges of dignities" (c.1; see HEFELE-LECLERCQ 5².971; 1 *Compil.* 3. 5.10; X 3.5.8). This decree is variously interpreted. BERNARD OF PAVIA, *Summa decretalium* 3. 16.3 (p. 83) considers exchanges of dignities illicit because these must be acquired by canonical election. In the *Apparatus: Ecce vicit Leo* ad C.16 q.7 c.40 (fol. 76rb) mention is made of an opinion, based on the same decree, that exchanges of prebends are illicit without the authority of the Pope; this opinion is rejected by the author of the *Apparatus.* Cf. also Po. 1806 (X 3.19.7).

[65] The opinions mentioned in this paragraph are supported by several canonists of this time; see following nn. 66-67. They are summarized and defended by the anonymous author of Appendix A below.

[66] See below Appendix A sects. 361-362 with n. 14. Huguccio likewise is opposed to this position: "Quidam tamen ex sua aequitate dicunt quod, si crimen est occultum, et purgatum tamen per poenitentiam, non peccat ille patiendo se promoveri, et sic promotus licite administrat, licet sit tale crimen quod inducat depositionem; quod non credo." HUG. ad D.25 c.6 (text establ. from Paris BN lat. 3891, fol. 30ra and BN lat. 3892, fol. 31ra). However he seems less

episcopus dispensare nisi expresse sit prohibitum, dummodo de illo crimine sit in canone dispensatum alicubi.[67] Unde cum notoriis homicidis non dispensat episcopus,[68] nec cum sortilegis,[69] nec cum ordinatis in excommunicatione, nec cum illis qui ministraverunt in excommunicatione,[70] nec in simonia ordinis quando simonia est in ordinante, id est quando 95 ordinem vendidit, vel in ordinato, id est quando ordinatur sciens et pru-

---

92 alicubi] alicui JTu.   homicidiis CcTu homicidii *corr. ad* homicidis Ck.   94 nec — excommunicatione *om.* Cc Pet (*homoeotel.*).   95 ordinis] ordinatis JPRTuU(BmCp-GKLMTbV).   in simonia ordinis] cum in simonia ordinatis vel in simonia ordinis H (cum simoniace ordinatis I).   96 vendit PR Pet.

---

rigid than Flamborough: "Si enorme est et occultum, ut incestus et homicidium sponte commissum, monendus est ut ab officio abstineat, non cogendus; acta poenitentia, si voluerit, uti poterit officio pristino." Hug. ad D.50 pr. (text establ. from Paris BN lat. 3891, fol. 54[ra] and BN lat. 3892, fol. 56[vb]). See fuller quotations from these texts in Firth, *Thesis* II 471* n. 85 (III 749*-751*); cf. *op. cit.* II 461*-465* with notes.

[67] See below Appendix A sects. 358-360; cf. *Apparatus: Ecce vicit Leo* ad D.17 c.3 (fol. 6[vb]); ad C.1 q.4 dictum p. c.5 (fol. 38[va]); *Glossa ordinaria in Decr.* ad D.50 pr.; ad C.1 q.7 dictum p.c.5 *ut plerisque*; ad C.27 q.1 c.12 *auctoritatem*. This opinion, at least in regard to ordinary and less important cases, seems to be in conformity with canon law as it was until somewhat past the middle of the twelfth century, but current trends were beginning to make it untenable in Robert's time. See Brys, *De dispensatione in iure canonico* pp. 142-146, 243-246; Jean Dauvillier, *Le mariage dans le droit classique de l'Église* (Paris 1933) pp. 201-208. Huguccio in one place says that the bishop can dispense where he is not forbidden to do so (see Hug. ad D.50 c.22 *multotiens*, fol. 59rb); in another place he states that the bishop can dispense where he is so authorized by the law (see Hug. ad C.1 q.7 dictum p. c.5, fol. 125[vb]). In any case he denies that the bishop can on his own authority dispense simoniacs: "*ex concessione episcopi sui* Arg. quod episcopus potest dispensare cum simoniacis; quod non credo; nec hinc habetur, cum hoc specialiter fuerit ei indultum. Quilibet sic posset dispensare, scilicet ubi specialiter a domino papa indulgetur." Hug. ad C.1 q.5 c.3. Cf. *ibid.* ad q.5 pr. (fol. 124[rb-vb]); Heitmeyer, *Sakramentenspendung* pp. 158-166; above sects. 111-113 with notes; below n. 76; Firth, *Thesis* II 443*-458* with n. 22, also II 471*, 482*-486*. cf. also Gabriel Le Bras, Ch. Lefebvre and J. Rambaud, *L'âge classique* (Hist. du droit et des instit. de l'Église en Occident 7) pp. 519-523; in this work it is shown that the older opinion was still defended by some canonists long after our author's lifetime.

[68] See Gratian D.50 cc.4-6; cf. below Appendix A sect. 360.

[69] Probably a prohibition of dispensation for those notoriously guilty of witchcraft was understood from 1 *Compil.* 5.8.3 (JL 13940; X 5.9.2); cf. below sect. 159 with notes.

[70] Regarding ministration in excommunication see Gratian C.11 q.3 cc.6-7. It might easily be inferred from the same canons that one who has received ordination while under sentence of excommunication may never be dispensed; cf. also JL 16597 (X 5.30.3); Po. 1326 (X 5.39.32; issued probably Feb.-April 1201). It is evident from these decrees and also from below Appendix A sect. 363 that a violation of excommunication is regarded as an especially heinous crime; cf. below sect. 154.

dens ad illum ordinem,[71] et in similibus in quibus invenitur prohibita dispensatio episcopo vel non invenitur alicubi in canone de illo crimine dispensatum. 99

139 Sed haec opinio nusquam expressa invenitur, sed argumentis validis roboratur. Praeterea, ut audivi, dominus papa huic opinioni non consentit.[72] Praeterea contra conscientiam meam est. Praeterea expresse invenitur quod cum adulteris et minoribus potest episcopus dispensare, quasi majora crimina excludantur.[73] Praeterea tutius mihi videtur 5 agere cum papa et ejus petere dispensationem quam istam sequi opinionem.[74] Unde etiam ab illis qui in hac sunt opinione mihi consultum est quod potius meam propriam sequar conscientiam quam eorum sententiam vel arbitrium.[75] Et ideo quod dixi dixi; *quod scripsi scripsi*.[76]

Unde et simoniaco poenitenti, quando transmitto eum ad papam, dico: 10 "Frater, non gravet te quod dico, non gravet te quod facio; aliud propter conscientiam meam non audeo tibi dicere; conscientiam meam sequor, animam meam libero. Tu, si placet, episcopum tuum consulas vel alios quos volueris; tu videris quid feceris."

140 Dominus Innocentius dicit quod quando commutatur spirituale 15 purum pro spirituali puro non est simonia, sed tamen propter suspicionem quaestus illicitum est.[77]

97-98 prohibita — invenitur *om.* Tc(*homoeotel.*). 98 vel si non HU. alicui TcTu (ELMSgTb) *abbrev. ambigua* Ac(F). 1 numquam CcZ umquam Ci. 2 Praeterea *usque ad lineam 95 in sect. 145 desinit* Tb *folio perdito.* 6 istam] eorum CkJ. 6-7 opinionem *add.* Tamen secundum aliquos episcopus potest dispensare ubicumque non est ei expresse prohibitum *insert.* Ac (*idem vel simile add. in textu* EMNY *idem add. supra post* est *in linea 3* F). 7 illis] his Ad. 8 propriam *om.* P *post* conscientiam Ck. sequatur Ck sequerer Tu. 9 dixi quod dixi scripsi quod scripsi JU. quod scripsi scripsi *om.* R. 10 et] etiam Tc et si R. 12 tibi *om.* CkTu. 13 places CcTc. 15 non commutatur Ck committatur J immutatur Pet.

---

[71] See below Appendix A sect. 360 with notes.
[72] Perhaps a reference to Po. 5021 (X 5.3.37), a decretal of INNOCENT III (1198-1215) of uncertain date.
[73] See 1 *Compil.* 2.1.6 (JL 14091; X 2.1.4). Cf. above sect. 101 with notes; sect. 138 n. 67.
[74] Regarding *tutius* see FIRTH, *Thesis* II 494*-497*.
[75] See below Appendix A sect. 363.
[76] See *Joan* 19.22. A position similar to that which Flamborough here defends is maintained by BERNARD OF PAVIA, *Summa decretalium* 5.2.6 (pp. 205-206).
[77] Perhaps the decretal which prompted this statement is Po. 1806 (PL 214.1154A; issued Jan. 13, 1203) or Po. 534 (X 3.19.8; issued probably in 1198); see FIRTH, *Thesis* II 396*-397*. Cf. above sects. 136-137 with notes 60, 64.

POENITENS. Praebendam quandam dimisit avunculus meus ut eam mihi daret episcopus; quod et factum est.

SACERDOS. Ut videtur, non gratis habuisti; quia aliquid datum est vel 20 dimissum ut eandem praebendam haberes, eadem scilicet praebenda; ideo dicunt quidam quod hic est simonia.[78] Ut audivi, Dominus Innocentius ita distinguit: Si ille qui renuntiat ecclesiae vel praebendae habet jus eam conferendi et eam liberaliter confert viro bono et honesto, non est simonia; ut si parisiensis episcopus praebendam habet in parisiensi 25 ecclesia, et eidem praebendae renuntians liberaliter eam viro honesto confert, non est simonia; ubi autem renuntians ecclesiae non habet jus conferendi eam, simonia est.[79] Alii dicunt quod, sive renuntians habet jus conferendi sive non, simonia committitur.[80]

POENITENS. Quomodo ergo subveniet aliquis dives plura beneficia habens 30 alicui pauperi honesto?

SACERDOS. Prius renuntiet beneficio, et postea roget episcopum ut illud conferat pauperi.[81] Alii dicunt quod sic potest rogare episcopum: "Domine, rogo ut hoc beneficium meum huic pauperi conferatis."[82]

De excommunicatione 35

141 Excommunicatio etiam impedit promotionem; quia, si ordinatus es ab excommunicato, vel si in quocumque ordine ministrasti excommunicatus, vel si in excommunicatione ordinatus es, de cetero non ministrabis in aliquo ordine sine papae dispensatione nec promoveberis ulterius.[83]

---

18 POENITENS *ss. usque ad finem sectionis 140 om.* Pet.   quandam] unam AdTu.
19 quod *om.* JTu.   et] etiam TcU *om.* CkTu.   20 Ut mihi videtur JTc.   aliquid]
aliud Ck ei J.   27 ubi] ut J vir TcTu.   29 jus *om.* CcJ.   30 habens *om.* CcCiTu.
32 renuntiat AcCcCiCkTcTuZ(LN) *corr. ab* renuntiat Ad remittit J.   36 Excommunicatio *reincipiunt* AbOTa(X) *reincipit* Q¹* *fol. 335ᵛ* (*incipiunt fragmenta* Q²**).   37 si *om.* Ta-
Tu.   ministrari J ministraverit U.   37-38 vel si — excommunicatus *om.* Ta (*forte homoeoarchia*)   38 ordinatus es *om.* Ta.   es] est U.   non] nec CcZ.

---

[78] Cf. HUG. ad C.8 q.1 c.7 *hereditario* (fol. 173ᵃ); CANTOR, *Verbum abbreviatum* c.40 (PL 205. 132-133).

[79] Perhaps this is a reference to Po. 377 (X 3.12.un.; PL 214.346-351); cf. FIRTH, *Thesis* II 393*.

[80] Source not found.

[81] Cf. HUG. *loc. cit.* (above in n. 78).

[82] Source not found.

[83] Cf. GRATIAN C.11 q.3 cc.5-7; 1 *Compil.* 5.23.2-4 (X 5.27.2-4); Po. 1002 (X 5.27.5; issued April 9, 1200); Po. 1906 (X 5.27.6; issued May 21, 1203).

Dicunt tamen aliqui quod hoc verum est si a papa lata est excommuni- 40
cationis sententia in qua ministrasti vel ordinem suscepisti; sed si a canone
a papa constituto excommunicatus hoc fecisti vel illud, exceptis excommunicationibus quarum absolutionem sibi reservavit papa, episcopus
tuus potest dispensare tecum et ad omnia restituere.[84] Sed prior sententia
mihi plus placet quia tutior est. In suspensione autem vera est haec sen- 45
tentia et in minori excommunicatione.[85]

142 Excommunicatio est a qualibet licita et honesta fidelium communione separatio. Unde quot sunt communiones, tot sunt excommunicationes; quia tum separatur quis ab uno sacramento et non ab alio, tum a
communione fratrum et non a sacramentis, tum ab ingressu ecclesiae.[86] 50
Excommunicationis duae sunt species: anathema et simplex excommunicatio. *Anathema* est sollemnis excommunicatio quae fit candelis accensis
cum stola, et haec dicitur major excommunicatio.[87] *Simplex excommunicatio*

---

40 alicui Ci quidam CcRTaTu.   40-41 excommunicationis sententia] excommunicatio JU.
41 ministrari J ministravit U.   suscepit U.   42 fecit U.   illud] id Tu *add.* sine
alia excommunicatione hoc fecisti vel illud *delet, una cum praecedenti* vel illud O.   vel illud
exceptis] vel in Pet.   42-43 exceptis — papa *om.* Ab *insert.* O *infra post* tecum *in linea 44*
Q¹*Q²** *cum signis ad restituendum huc* Q¹* *infra post* restituere *in linea 44* TaTu; *cf. infra in Append.*
C no. 6.   43 reservaverit Cc reservabit J servavit Tu non reservavit Pet.   44 tuus]
suus U. tecum] secum U.   46 excommunicatione] sententia et excommunicatione CkH.
47 Excommunicatio *usque ad finem sect. 158 invenitur fols. 120ᵛ-122ᵛ* Pet.   48 quotquot TaTu.
48-49 excommunicationes] separationes J separationes sive excommunicationes U.   49
tum¹] tamen OQ¹*R cum J cum *insert.* Ck.   quis *add.* tum J.   50 et non a sacramentis
om. RTa.   51 anathema] anathematizatio AcJTcU(BmCpEFGLMNSgSoY anathema vel
anathematizatio Hugᵇ); *hic et infra plures Mss habent abbrev. ambiguam;* Hugᵇ *habet deinceps* anthema.
52 anathematizatio TcU(BmCpLMSo).   excommunicatio *add.* simplex excommunicatio O.

---

[84] Source not found. Quite probably this opinion has some connection with C.11 q.3 dictum
p. c.24, where Gratian maintains that, while those excommunicated by a general canon must
abstain from the sacraments, they are not anathematized in the full sense and the faithful need
not avoid communication with them. Gratian's opinion was soon generally rejected by canonists and by popes in decretals (see FIRTH, *Thesis* II 450* n. 22 [724*-727*]; cf. below n. 96).
The extra words inserted into Form 3 at this place (see variants) may have some connection
with Po. 1326 (X 5.39.32: issued probably Feb.-April, 1201).

[85] Source not found. No doubt this position is based on the fact that these are not anathematized or excommunicated in the fullest sense of the word. The decrees cited above in n. 83
refer to complete excommunication.

[86] See Hug. ad C.11 q.3 dictum p. c.15 *Quia* (fol. 189ᵛᵇ); this dictum is not found in vulgate
editions of Gratian. It is quite probable that sects. 142-143 depend on this text of Huguccio.

[87] According to a mediaeval rubric, twelve priests holding lighted candles are to surround the
bishop; when the excommunication has been pronounced, these are to throw their candles
down and trample on them. See GRATIAN C.11 q.3 c.106.

non fit hoc modo, et haec dicitur minor excommunicatio. Quandoque
tamen pro eodem accipiuntur anathema et simplex excommunicatio.⁸⁸   55
Simplici excommunicatione quandoque seipsum excommunicat quis,
quando scilicet pro reverentia abstinet a sacramentis.⁸⁹

143 Et anathema et simplex excommunicatio tum datur a canone sive
decreto, tum a persona: *a canone* quando canon vel decretum praecipit
aliquem excommunicari; ut per decretum sunt excommunicati qui manus 60
violentas injiciunt in clericos, et incurrunt majorem excommunicationem
sive anathema.⁹⁰ Item simplex excommunicatio datur a canone; ut
quando aliquis communicat excommunicato majori excommunicatione,
nisi in casibus exceptis.⁹¹ Et non oportet eum ulterius excommunicari,
quia in ipsa communione quando communicavit excommunicato excom- 65
municatus fuit; quia qui communicat excommunicato, supple "majori
excommunicatione," excommunicatus est, supple "excommunicatione
minori," sed non transit in personam tertiam.⁹²

A persona datur major excommunicatio quando papa vel episcopus
sollemniter excommunicat aliquem, scilicet cum stola et candelis accensis.⁹³ 70
Simplex etiam sacerdos quandoque sollemniter excommunicat et majorem
dat excommunicationem, sed de speciali praecepto episcopi, et etiam de

---

55 accipimur Ta *om.* R.   anathematizatio Tc(CpMSo).   56 quandoque] quoniam
Ck *om.* O.   57 quando] quandoque quando O quandoque AcCk.   scilicet *om.* Ta Pet.
58 anathematizatio Tc(CpMSo).   58-59 sive decreto] a decreto Tu *om.* TaQ¹* sive a
decreto Pet.   61 clericum CkH.   incurrent O.   62 anathematizationem Tc-
(BmCpGMSo).   63 aliquis] quis JP.   communicat *add.* cum CcTc Pet.   excommunicato *add.* supple RTa.   64 eum *om.* O.   65 communicat Q¹*Tc aliquis communicavit P *add.* cum RTc.   66 quia *om.* AdR.   qui *om.* Ci.   communicat *add.*
cum Cc.   quia — excommunicato *om.* J.   66-67 quia — excommunicatus est *om.*
PTa.   67-68 supple majori excommunicatione *om.* Cc.   70 scilicet *om.* CkTa.
et cum candelis O.   72 speciali *corr. ab* spirituali AcCk.   etiam *om.* Ac.   de *om.*
TaTu Pet.

---

⁸⁸ Cf. Hᴜɢ. *loc. cit.*; also Iᴅᴇᴍ ad C.3 q.4 dictum p. c.11 (fol. 148ᵛᵇ); Rᴜꜰɪɴᴜs, *Summa* ad
C.11 q.3 c.2 (pp. 314-315); Sᴛᴇᴘʜᴇɴ ᴏꜰ Tᴏᴜʀɴᴀɪ, *Summa* ad C.3 q.4 dictum p. c.11 (p. 195);
Apparatus: Ecce vicit Leo ad C.11 q.3 pr. (fol. 58ʳᵇ⁻ᵛᵃ); also texts cited by Artur Lᴀɴᴅɢʀᴀꜰ,
"Sünde und Trennung von der Kirche in der Frühscholastik," *Scholastik* 5 (1930) 240-241.
⁸⁹ Cf. Hᴜɢ. *loc. cit.* (above in n. 86); Rᴜꜰɪɴᴜs *ibid.* (above in n. 88; p. 314).
⁹⁰ See Gʀᴀᴛɪᴀɴ C.17 q.4 c.29; Hᴜɢ. *loc. cit.*; cf. below sects. 144, 148 and 157.
⁹¹ Cf. Hᴜɢ. *loc. cit.*; below sects. 144 and 156.
⁹² See Hᴜɢ. *ibid.* (fols. 189ᵛᵇ-190ʳᵃ); cf. Gʀᴀᴛɪᴀɴ C.11 q.3 c.18; below sects. 150-151.
⁹³ Cf. Hᴜɢ. *ibid.* (fol. 189ᵛᵇ); cf. Sᴛᴇᴘʜᴇɴ ᴏꜰ Tᴏᴜʀɴᴀɪ, *Summa* ad C.3 q.4 dictum p. c.11
(p. 195).

generali, ut quando pro furtis vel aliis forefactis excommunicat.[94] Simplicem excommunicationem dat persona, ut quando sacerdos vel major a communione aliqua aliquem excludit.[95]   75

144 Tam major excommunicatio quam minor tum est datae sententiae tum dandae. *Datae sententiae* est canon vel excommunicatio quando ex ipso facto excommunicatur aliquis, nec oportet eum ulterius excommunicari; ut, quando aliquis animo malignandi percutit clericum, in ipsa percussione est percutiens excommunicatus nec oportet eum ulterius 80 excommunicari. Denuntiatur autem "excommunicatus" et non "excocommunicandus," quia jam excommunicatus est. Vitandus est autem etiam ante denuntiationem ab illis qui sciunt excommunicationem; licet aliqui in contrarium dicant, et male, quia denuntiatio non est nisi excommunicationis notificatio.[96] Simplex quoque excommunicatio quandoque 85 datae est sententiae; ut quando aliquis scienter communicat anathematizato, in ipsa communione est ipse excommunicatus, sed minori excommunicatione, nec oportet eum ulterius excommunicari.[97]

---

73 forefactis] fori factis O.   75 aliqua] alia Tu *om.* JO.   76 major] minor HJU
corr. ab minor Ac.   minor] major HJU *corr. ab* major Ac.   77 ex *om.* AcCkHJU-
(BmCpEMNSgSoVXY *hoc textu caret* Q²**) *corr. ab* in Tc.   78 nec] non JRTc.   79
quando aliquis] quis Q¹* *add.* eum J *add.* cum U.   80 percutiens] percussor Ck ipse percutiens Tc Pet.   81-82 excommunicatur JU.   82 autem *om.* HJRTuU.   83
etiam *om.* Ta *add.* et Ac.   excommunicatum PTa *add.* esse Ta.   84 aliqui] alii CkP
aliquid Tc.   84-85 excommunicati Ta excommunicatis Cc.   85 quoque] autem J *om.*
Ta.   quandoque] quando Ac *ante* J.   86 quando *om.* R.   aliquis] quis JR.
86-87 anathematizato] excommunicato R excommunicato id est anathematizato Tu.
87 minore CkTa.   88 eum] tamen Tc *om.* R.

[94] The power of excommunication possessed by priests inferior to the bishop varied with time and place in the Middle Ages. See BERNARD OF PAVIA, *Summa decretalium* 5.34.3 (p. 272); HINSCHIUS, *System des katholischen Kirchenrechts* V 291-294; cf. N. HÄRING, "Peter Cantor's View on Ecclesiastical Excommunication and its Practical Consequences," *MedStud* 11 (1949) 108-109.

[95] Cf. HUG. *loc. cit.* (in n. 86).

[96] The opinion which Robert rejects here is that of GRATIAN C.11 q.3 dictum p. c.24 (cf. above n. 84). Rufinus teaches a modified version of it, namely that it is a sin to associate with such a one before promulgation of the sentence, but that the minor excommunication for it (see following sentence of text with n. 97) is incurred only if the person has been proclaimed excommunicated; see RUFINUS, *Summa* ad C.11 q.3 c.2 (p. 315). Huguccio attributes this latter opinion to John (of Faenza); Huguccio himself maintains that even before sentence is passed on such an individual he is excommunicated in the full sense; see HUG. ad C.11 q.3 dictum p. c.24 §3 *anathemati* (fol. 191ra); cf. IDEM ad C.17 q.4 c.29 *mandatum* (fol. 247va); ad D.93 c.1 *absque commotione* (fol. 98vb). Robert follows Huguccio in regard to this matter; cf. below sect. 150 with n. 19.

[97] Cf. HUG. ad C.11 q.3 c.16 *communione* (fol. 190ra).

Dandae sententiae est canon vel sententia aliqua quando non ipso facto est aliquis excommunicatus, sed si non acquieverit vel emendaverit, ex- 90 communicari potest, ut aliquis qui praelato suo rebellis est.

145 Quando aliquis majori excommunicatione excommunicatus est, sollemniter absolevendus est, id est ante fores ecclesiae et extra jurabit quod stabit mandato ecclesiae, vel pignus praestabit vel fidejussorem si causa pecuniaria fuerit vel alia ratio exegerit.[98] Hoc facto, nudus et pro- 95 stratus verberabitur in conspectu populi cum *Miserere mei Deus*, tandem subjuncta absolutione.[99] Quando aliquis minori excommunicatione excommunicatus est, non est necessaria ista sollemnitas, sed privatim et absque omni sacramento absolvi potest.[100] Mulieres in absolutione non 99 exuunt, sed in manibus verberantur vel aliter puniuntur.

146 Quando aliquis excommunicatus est a canone, credo quod a quolibet absolvi potest si occultum est, nisi reservata fuerit alicui absolutio; alioquin a suo episcopo, ut videtur velle Alexander in extra. *Eminenti*.[1]
[ut]   5

93 est id est] id est *corr. ad* est Ac.   et extra] e contra Tu.   extra jurabit *invers*. JU.
97 adjuncta P subjecta Pet.   absolutione *add. formulam liturgicam* Pet (*post* absolutione
cessat Q²**).   98 et *om.* PTa.   99 omni *om.* P Pet.   1 exuuntur CkOQ¹*RTcZ
exeunt Tu ejiciunt J.   3 observata Ta revelata J.   fuit U sit Ck.   alicui excommunicationis absolutio CkJ.   4 extra.] ecclesia JTu.   In eminenti JPU.   5 ut
AbOQ¹*TaZ(VX) *om. cett.*(*cett.*) *Vocabulum* ut *videtur conjungere decretalem sequentibus, quod tamen est contra sensum decretalis*; *cf.* FIRTH, *Thesis III* 581*-582* n. 33.

[98] Cf. GRATIAN C.11 q.3 c.108; HUG. ad C.11 q.3 c.4 *ante cognitionem* (fol. 188ᵛᵇ); BERNARD OF PAVIA, *Summa decretalium* 5.34.8 (p. 275); E. VERNAY, *Le "Liber de excommunicatione" du cardinal Bérenger Frédol* (Paris 1912) pp. lxiv-lxxi.

[99] See *Ps* 50.1; the whole psalm would be recited. The verberation was not universal in the Middle Ages. Several texts simply say that the repentant sinner must lie prostrate and ask for pardon; see *Ordo excommunicationis* (PL 138.1125-26); MARTÈNE, *De antiquis Ecclesiae ritibus* Liber 3 cap. 4 formula 5 (II 912-913). Flogging is mentioned by BERNARD OF PAVIA *loc. cit.* and towards the middle of the thirteenth century by Hostiensis (quoted by E. VERNAY, *op. cit.* p. lxvi n. 2). Hostiensis insists that this is not necessary, in fact is often omitted (quoted *ibid.* n. 3). In the latter part of this century William Durand of Mende produced a *Pontificalis ordinis liber* in which he distinguishes between major excommunication and anathema. For absolution from major excommunication he prescribes a ceremony with verberation (Liber 3 cap. 8 no. 6; ed. ANDRIEU III 610), but oddly enough in the ceremony for absolution from anathema, the most severe excommunication, prescribes only prostration with expression of repentance (Liber 3 cap. 8 no. 18; III 615).

[100] Cf. BERNARD OF PAVIA, *Summa decretalium* 5.34.7 (pp. 274-275); Po. 700 (X 5.39.29; issued May 16, 1199). *Sacramentum* in this text apparently signifies "oath."

[1] Cf. HUG. ad C.11 q.3 dictum p. c.15 *Quia* (fol. 189ᵛᵇ; cf. above sect. 146 n.86); ad C.11

Communicans excommunicato a quolibet simplici sacerdote suo potest absolvi. Quando tamen papa vel alius excommunicans reservat sibi absolutionem, ab alio absolvi non potest nisi in mortis articulo, et tunc sollemniter, ut diximus.[2]

147 Quando aliquis excommunicatus est a persona, dicunt aliqui quod 10 non nisi ab excommunicatore vel ejus successore vel superiori absolvi potest; ut, si ego excommunico aliquem pro furto, non nisi a me vel successore meo vel majori absolvi potest.[3] Sed ecce parisiensis aliquis Romae excommunicatus est pro tribus solidis quos ibi furatus est; numquid Romam mittam eum pro absolutione ad suum excommunicatorem? Di- 15 cunt aliqui et periti quod sic; sed crudele est valde. Ideo mihi videtur sic distinguendum esse: excommunicatus quandoque tenetur simpliciter ecclesiae satisfacere, ut fur, et tunc a quolibet potest absolvi; quandoque alicui certae personae satisfacere tenetur, ut contumax qui in judicio comparere non vult judici; tunc ab illo solo potest absolvi. Tutius tamen est ut, si 20 commode fieri potest, quilibet a suo excommunicatore absolvatur.[4]

---

8 articulo] periculo OTc.   11 successori J.   superiore AcCkHP(BmCpEIKMN)
ejus superiore Pet(Tb) majori Tc majori sive superiori U.   12-13 ut — potest om.
TaTc insert. Ad (homoeotel.).   12 ego om. CkHP.   excommunicarem PTu.
13 a majori AcCkHJ(CpEFMNSgSoVY) a superiori U meliore Tc (majore X).   16 sed
— valde] hoc credi brutale est valde cum aliqua rasura in brutale O.   sic[2] om. CkHJU.
17 esse om. CkHJU.   excommunicatus add. simplex Pet.   simpliciter om. CkHTa Pet.
19 satisfacere tenetur om. Q[1]*Ta.   apparere JR.   20 tunc] tamen corr. ad et ille O.
solo om. Tu insert. Ci.

---

q.3 c.29 regulare judicium sui episcopi (fol. 191[va]); ad C.17 q.4 c.29 absolvere (fol. 247[rb]); ad C.11 q.3 c.16 communione (fol. 190[ra]). In each of these places Huguccio refers to a decretal In eminenti; this is apparently JL 12411, which includes 1 Compil. 2.1.3, 1 Compil. 2.20.36 and 1 Compil. 5.33.3 (X 5.38.4); probably he had in mind the last mentioned part of it.

[2] See Po. 700 (X 5.39.29; issued May 16, 1199); cf. Hug. ad C.17 q.4 c.29 absolvere (fol. 247[rb]). Robert's exposition follows the decretal rather than Huguccio, who requires such absolution, at least if the offence is public, to be received from the bishop. — If the absolution of those who should communicate with the excommunicated person were reserved, then the decree of excommunication would explicitly excommunicate not only the person, but also those who should communicate with him. These latter would then, according to the canon law of the time, be excommunicated by a major excommunication or anathema, and would require solemn absolution. See Summa parisiensis ad C.11 q.3 c.25 et dictum p. c.26 (p. 151); Po. 390 (X 5.39.30; issued Oct. 11, 1189). Cf. below sect. 150 with n. 19, sect. 153 with n. 27.

[3] Cf. Hug. ad C.11 q.3 c.40 successori (fol. 192rb); Häring, "Peter Cantor's View," MedStud 11 (1949) 108-109; below sect. 152 with n. 26.

[4] Robert's lenient opinion is somewhat in harmony with Po. 700 (X 5.39.29) ad finem.

148 Tria tantum genera excommunicatorum reservavit sibi papa: sacrilegos qui manum miserunt in clericum vel personam religiosam, falsarios
litterarum domini papae (de aliis enim litteris non loquor) et incendiarios
excommunicatos. De aliis non memini quod ad papam pro absolutione 25
mittendi sint.[5]

Si ergo manum misisti in clericum vel personam religiosam,[6] vel ad
hoc auctoritatem vel consilium vel auxilium vel aliquod adminiculum
(nisi in casibus exceptis, de quibus in sequentibus dicetur) praestitisti,[7]
a solo papa vel ad praeceptum ejus absolveris, nisi religionem intraveris; 30
quia tunc te absolvere poterit abbas tuus, nisi enormis fuerit excessus
tuus.[8] In articulo mortis te poterit quivis sacerdos absolvere.[9] Personas
religiosas voco non solum monachos et canonicos, sed etiam templarios,[10]
hospitalarios,[11] leprosos qui sunt de congregationibus (de vagis enim non

---

22 tantum] tamen TaTu Pet.   reservat P servat Ta retinuit O.   dominus papa
CkP.   23 manum add. violentam P manus violentas Z.   mittunt U injecerunt Ck
om. Pet.   clericos JZ corr. ab clericos H.   vel add. in JTa.   24 enim] autem J
etiam P.   26 sunt AcCcCiCk JOQ¹*Tc(BmCpMSgSoTbVY) sicut Tu.   27 vel¹ add.
in U Pet.   28 aliquod] aliud Tu Pet om. TaU.   31 quia tunc] tunc enim AcCkHJU-
(BmCpEMNSoTbY) tunc Tu.   potest TaTu.   tuus om. CcTc.   fuit Ac.
32 tuus] ejus Pet om. Q¹*TaTuU.   quivis] quilibet RTa.   33 et] vel Cc.

---

[5] See following text to the end of sect. 149 with notes.
[6] See GRATIAN C.17 q.4 c.29; 1 Compil. 5.34.6 (JL 13893; X 5.39.5); 1 Compil. 5.34.9 (JL
14025; X 5.39.7). Cf. FIRTH, Thesis II 451* n. 22 (III 724*-727*) 456*-457*, 481*-483*.
[7] Cf. 1 Compil. 5.34.7 (JL 13768; X 5.39.6); 1 Compil. 5.10.7 (JL 12180; X 5.12.6); HÄRING,
MedStud 11.107; below sect. 157.
[8] See Po. 1326 (X 5.39.32; issued probably Feb. 22-April 1201).
[9] Cf. GRATIAN C.26 q.6 dictum p. c.11; 1 Compil. 5.34.6 (JL 13893; X 5.39.5); JL 16623
(X 5.39.13; Collectio seguntina no. 52 RevHistEccl 50.433-434 CELESTINE III).
[10] These are the Knights Templars, a religious order founded at Jerusalem very early in the
twelfth century, cf. Max HEIMBUCHER, Die Orden und Kongregationen der katholischen Kirche I 339;
Louis BRÉHIER, L'Église et l'Orient au Moyen âge: Les Croisades 2nd ed. pp. 96-97; Records of the
Templars in England in the Twelfth Century ed. Beatrice A. LEES (London 1935).
[11] See 1 Compil. 5.34.15 (JL 13967; X 5.39.10). These were religious, both men and women,
who cared for the sick in hospitals. Most famous were the Hospitallers of St. John of Jerusalem, founded there about the same time as the Knights Templars; before long the latter Hospitallers took on a military character like the Templars. See HEIMBUCHER, Orden und Kongregationen I 614; Léon LE GRAND, Statuts d'Hôtels-Dieu et de léproseries esp. pp. ix-xxiv, 1-21;
Louis BRÉHIER, loc. cit.: Jean IMBERT, Les hôpitaux en droit canonique (Paris 1947) esp. pp. 261-
263; LE BRAS, Institutions ecclésiastiques pp. 472-475.

loquor)[12] et illos qui se domibus Dei dederunt et similes.[13] Qui in aliquem 35 talem manus violentas injecerit, et etiam in clericum degradatum,[14] ipso facto est excommunicatus et a solo papa absolvendus.

149 Si litteras papae (de aliis non loquor) quocumque modo falsasti, vel ad hoc auctoritatem vel consilium vel auxilium vel aliquod adminiculum praestitisti, vel falsatas ultra quindecim dies penes te reservasti, ipso facto 40 excommunicatus es et a solo papa absolvendus.[15]

Si domunculam trium solidorum incendisti, non es ipso facto excommunicatus; sed si postea quivis simplex sacerdos te excommunicaverit, a solo papa absolveris.[16] Incendiarii ecclesiarum et coemeteriorum non sunt

---

35 illis JTa.   consimiles Ta Pet *add.* supple qui habitum habent religionis Tc *add.* supple qui habent habitum religionis *insert.* O.   36 injecerunt OTc injiciunt J.   37 absolvendus *corr. ad* absolvendi O *add.* est J.   38 falsatis Ac falsati Cc falsificasti P.   39 aliquod] aliud Ck *om.* Pet.   vel aliquod adminiculum] aliquod Q¹* vel aliud Tc aliquod vel adminiculum Ta.   40 falsitas *corr. ad* falsas OR.   quindecim] quadraginta Cc viginti Tu.   servaveris JU observasti Tc.   42 es] ex Ac *add.* ex O.   43 quivis] quamvis AcR.   44 sint JORTcTu Pet.

---

[12] There were also various religious communities who cared for lepers; then the lepers themselves usually took vows and lived the religious life. Quite famous were the Order of St. Lazarus of Jerusalem and the leprosary of Saint-Lazare at Paris. See HEIMBUCHER, *Orden und Kongregationen* I 612-613; LE GRAND, *Statuts d'Hôtels-Dieu* pp. xxv-xxix, 181-252. The Third Lateran Council in 1179 provided that lepers living in congregation must be allowed to have priests, churches and cemeteries, and to be exempt from the tithe; see c.23 (HEFELE-LECLERCQ 5².1104; 1 *Compil.* 3.35.1; X 3.48.2).

[13] This refers to *conversi, donati* or *oblati.* Many of these took vows like modern lay-brothers; others were lay men who devoted themselves to the service of a religious house; see DU CANGE s.vv. *conversi, oblati.* Huguccio says of them: "Si sunt obligati ecclesiae perpetuo singulari obligatione, scilicet ratione conversionis, non possunt verberari sine sacrilegio; si non sunt obligati ecclesiae nisi generali obligatione, scilicet qua servi omnes et coloni sunt obligati dominis suis etiam laicis, credo eos posse verberari sine sacrilegio." HUG. ad C.17 q.4 c.21 *ecclesiasticis* (text establ. from Paris, BN lat. 3891, fol. 212ᵛᵃ, and BN lat. 3892, fol. 246ᵛᵇ); cf. *ibid.* s.v. *devotis.* See also 1 *Compil.* 5.34.6 (JL 13893; X 5.39.5); 1 *Compil.* 5.34.15 (JL 13967; X 5.39.10); Gilles G. MEERSSEMAN and E. ADDA, "Pénitents ruraux communautaires en Italie au xiiᵉ siècle", *RevHistEccl* 49 (1954) 343-390; Gilles G. MEERSSEMAN, *Dossier de l'ordre de la pénitence au xiiiᵉ siècle.* Cf. also texts cited below in sect. 239 n. 29.

[14] See HUG. ad D.81 c.8 *saeculariter* (fol. 89ʳᵃ⁻ᵇ).

[15] See Po. 202 (X 5.20.4; issued May 19, 1198); cf. Po. 1276 (X 5.20.7; issued apparently not later than Feb. 21, 1201). The first of these decretals mentions a period of twenty days, beyond which one cannot retain false papal letters without incurring the penalty, but some MSS of this decretal read *quindecim dies* according to Friedberg's edition of the *Corpus Iuris Canonici* II 818 cap. 4 n. 8. See also Peter HERDE, "Römisches und kanonisches Recht bei der Verfolgung des Fälschungsdelikts im Mittelalter", *Traditio* 21 (1965) 334-362.

[16] See JL 16607 (X 5.39.19; *Collectio seguntina* no. 69 *RevHistEccl* 50.438; CELESTINE III); cf. Po. 220 (Reg. 1.237 PL 214.204).

ipso facto excommunicati nisi consuetudo loci habeat; vel si sunt excom- 45
municati, ab episcopo loci absolvi possunt nisi consuetudo loci contradicat.[17]

150   Par parem, minor majorem excommunicare non potest. Quid igitur ?
Episcopus aliquem excommunicat; illi excommunicato communicat archiepiscopus vel metropolitanus. Nonne excommunicatus est quia com- 50
municat excommunicato ? Utique, et quilibet praeter papam; sed non
ab episcopo suo suffraganeo, sed a canone excommunicatus est, isto scilicet: Qui communicat excommunicato excommunicatus est.[18]

    Cameracensis sic excommunicavit: "Excommunico omnes cives came-
racenses et omnes communicantes eis." Sic sunt excommunicati majori 55
excommunicatione et cives et eis communicantes.[19] Numquid omnes communicantes ? Numquid parisienses ? Credo quod nullum sic excommunicare potuit nisi diocesianum suum.[20]

151   Sacerdos excommunicat pro furto quod ipsemet fecit. Numquid est
excommunicatus ? Non, quia nemo seipsum potest excommunicare; sed 60

    45 ex ipso facto OTc Pet.   48 igitur] ergo JOTc *add.* si Cc.   50 vel metropolita-
nus *om.* Q¹*R.   quia] qui JTa Pet.   51 cum excommunicato JOTc.   51-53 Utique — est *om.* J.   52 suo *om.* CkTc Pet.   est] et Ck *om.* Tc.   excommunicatus
est *om.* Q¹*.   iste CcORZ(CpLMSgTb) et isto H primae Tu.   52-53 isto — est
om. Ta Pet (*homoeotel.* ?).   53 cum excommunicato OTc.   55 cum eis AcJH Pet-
(CpELMNSo).   56 et¹ *om.* R.   et² *om.* Cc *add.* omnes Tc.   eis *corr. ab* ei Tc *om.*
J.   57 Numquid *add.* omnes AcTaTc(EFGLNSo).   Numquid parisienses *om.* Ck.
58 potest Ta poterit Cc *add.* auctoritate propria nisi forte dominus papa sic dedisset sententiam Tc.   suum *add.* auctoritate propria nisi forte dominus papa dedisset sententiam
insert. O.   59 ipsemet] ipse HTa.   Numquid] nonne JR *add.* ipse JU.

    [17] See Hug. ad C.17 q.4 c.5 *anathematizamus* (fol. 245va; Franz Gillmann, "Die Abfassungs-
zeit", *ArchivKKRecht* 94 [1914] 249-250). Huguccio maintains that the excommunication proclaimed in this canon is not *latae sententiae*. He cites as a possible counter-indication a "*capitulum* of Alexander *Conquesti*". He says that perhaps this was a particular sentence against certain
individuals, or perhaps they had done violence to ecclesiastical persons, or else Alexander was
alluding to the contemporary custom of many places according to which those who commit
sacrilege against churches or cemeteries are *ipso jure* excommunicated. Possibly the decretal
to which he refers is the one which we know as JL 17642 (X 5.39.22); if so, this cannot be a decretal of Celestine III. Cf. Bernard of Pavia, *Summa decretalium* 5.34.6 (p. 273).
    [18] See Hug. ad C.11 q.3 c.17 *quicumque* (fol. 190ra); ad C.11 q.3 c.29 *regulare judicium sui epis-
copi* (fol. 191va).
    [19] See above sect. 146 with n. 2; below sect. 153 with n. 27; cf. *Apparatus: Ecce vicit Leo* ad
C.11 q.3 c.25 (fol. 59va); Bernard of Pavia, *Summa decretalium* 5.34.7 (p. 274).
    [20] Cf. JL 17053 (X 5.39.21); Bernard of Pavia, *Summa decretalium* 5.34.4 (p. 272).

graviter peccat excommunicando. Tutius tamen petet absolutionem a superiori suo.[21]

Episcopus excommunicat aliquem; postea sciens et prudens communicat eidem excommunicato. Numquid et ipse idem excommunicatus est quia communicat excommunicato? Dicunt quidam quod, eo ipso quod com- 65 municat excommunicato quem ipse excommunicavit, absolvit eum.[22] Mihi videtur hoc verum esse de papa et de episcopo qui sua auctoritate excommunicat.[23] Qui autem aliena auctoritate excommunicat aliquem, et illi postea communicat, excommunicatus est, vel ab eo cujus auctoritate ipse excommunicavit, vel a canone, isto scilicet: Qui communicat 70 excommunicato excommunicatus est.[24]

152 Excommunicato non debet esse lucrosa sua nequitia; unde quae tibi debet extorqueas ab eo, ut decimas, debitas pensiones, etc. In aliis non communices ei, nisi in his quae ad correptionem ejus pertinent.[25]

In duobus episcopatibus duas habuisti praebendas; unus episcopus 75 tuus excommunicavit te; reliquus non potest te absolvere.[26]

153 Nominatim excommunicatur quis dupliciter: tum proprio nomine, ut "Excommunico Petrum," tum aequipollenter, ut "Excommunico illum

---

63 excommunicavit JO.   64 eidem] ei O.   excommunicato *add.* quem ipse excommunicavit Ad.   idem *om.* PRTa.   excommunicatus est] excommunicatur JU excommunicatus Ac.   65 cum excommunicato JTc.   quod[2] *insert.* Ab qui Ac.   65-66 Dicunt — excommunicato *om.* JU (*homoeotel.*).   67 de[2] *om.* CkU.   68 autem] enim R *om.* U.   70 ipse] ipsum AdJU *om.* CkQ[1]*Z.   isto] ipso J illo Ta.   scilicet *om.* Q[1]*Ta.   71 excommunicato *om.* Tc cum excommunicato R.   72 nequitia] malitia J malitia sive nequitia U.   quae] qui Cc.   73 debes J debent Ck.   eo] illo J ipso Q[1]* eos *corr. attentat.* Ab.   debita AbOQ[1]*RTa Pet(CpGSgV *om.* I).   aliis] his Ab. 74 correctionem AcAdCkRTaU Pet(BmCpEGNSgSoY).   75 duabus JOTc.   76 tuus *om.* CkP.   te *om.* CkHJ.

---

[21] Cf. Hug. ad C.11 q.3 c.101 *anathema sit* (fol. 195[vb]); Robert Courson, *Summa* 3.13 (fol. 26[ra]), maintains that a priest is excommunicated by a general sentence previously passed by himself.

[22] Source not found.

[23] Cf. *Glossa ordinaria in Decr.* ad D.93 c.1 *exspectare*; Po. 2421 (X 5.39.41; issued Feb. 21, 1205).

[24] In *Apparatus: Ecce vicit Leo* ad C.11 q.3 c.17 *simili* (fol. 59[ra]) it is maintained that this holds true for every excommunicator except the Pope.

[25] Cf. below sect. 156 with n. 38.

[26] Cf. Hug. ad C.11 q.3 c.2 *ab aliis* (fol. 188[rb]); above sect. 147 with n. 3.

qui equum istum furatus est," si Petrus eum furatus est. Et cum dico "Excommunico Petrum et omnes fautores ejus," omnes fautores Petri 80 sunt nominatim excommunicati.[27]

154 Etsi injusta est excommunicatio, non contemnas eam; alioquin mortaliter peccabis. Dicat episcopus "Excommunico te si hodie Deum adoraveris"; propter hoc non dimittam Deum adorare, sed statim cum adoravero, pro excommunicato me habebo. In tantum timenda est 85 omnis excommunicatio.[28]

Qui clericum verberaverit in gravi infirmitate desperatus, sicut debet, absolvitur, sed sub sacramento quod si convaluerit ad papam recurret. Ad quid? Nonne jam absolutus est? Utique, et de cetero quilibet ei licite communicabit; sed poenitentiam petet a papa.[29]   90

155 Simplex sacerdos sic excommunicat: "Excommunico omnes qui in ecclesia ista furtum fecerint." Postea in eadem ecclesia furatur sacerdos par excommunicanti vel episcopus. Nonne ambo excommunicati

---

79 equum istum] idem Tu.   si — est] sed — est *delet.* Tc *om.* R.   eum] illum HU id Tu.   est[2] *om.* Ac.   80 omnes futores ejus *om.* Ta.   ejus] suos JU *add. et* J. Petri] ejus Q[1]*Tc Pet.   omnes fautores Petri *om.* Ck.   81 nominatim *om.* Ck.   82 eum O.   83 Si dicat HPTaTu Pet.   83-86 Dicat — excommunicatio *delet.* O *insert.* Tc.   85 habeo Pet habet *corr. ad* habeo Ck.   87 desperatus *om.* O.   87-88 sic debet absolvi TuZ.   88 absolvatur J.   recurrat P adibit Ta.   90 sed *ss. usque ad lineam 70 in sect. 170 desinit* Tb *duabus foliis perditis.*   92 ista *om.* Cc.   ecclesia ista] hac ecclesia Ck Pet.   fecerunt PTu *corr. ab* fecerunt Ac.   ecclesia[2] *om.* RTu. eadem ecclesia] ecclesia illa Q[1]*.   93 excommunicanti] excommunicati CcORTuZ *corr. ab* excommunicati Ad *om.* Ck.   par excommunicanti *om.* Pet.   episcopo Ta.

---

[27] Cf. Hug. ad C.5 q.1 c.2 *percutiatur* (fol. 159[ra]); ad C.9 q.1 c.5 *excommunicatis nominatim* (fols. 176[vb]-177[ra]); ad C.11 q.3 dictum p. c.24 *in causa "quidam presbyter"* (fol. 191ra). John of Faenza had maintained that one was excommunicated for communicating with a person who was under a major excommunication only if that person was excommunicated *nominatim*; no doubt this was based on 1 *Cor* 5.11, which was much quoted in this connection (see Häring *MedStud* 11.104). To explain why those excommunicated by a general sentence were subject to the same ban in regard to communication with others, Huguccio and others had to find a way to maintain that they were *nominatim excommunicati*. Cf. above sect. 144 with n. 96; sect. 150 with n. 19.

[28] See Hug. ad C.11 q.3 dictum p. c.101 *Gelasii* (fols. 195[vb]-196[ra]; quoted in Firth, *Thesis* II 473*-474*); ad C.11 q.3 c.27 *licet injuste liget* (fol. 191rb). Robert Courson maintains the opposite in regard to such extreme cases; see his *Summa* 6.1 (fol. 32ra). Cf. also J. Zeliauskas, *De excommunicatione vitiata apud glossatores (1140-1350)* (Studia et textus historiae juris canonici 4; Zürich 1967); the present editor has not been able to examine this work.

[29] Cf. JL 16623 (X 5.39.13). This is also the explanation of Peter Cantor, *Summa de sacr.* fol. 129va.

sunt, et ita par parem et minor majorem excommunicat? Secundum
quosdam verum est, et est specialis iste casus;[30] alioquin non sunt isti ex- 95
communicati propter hanc regulam quia par parem et minor majorem
ligare non potest.[31]

Tu solus scis aliquem excommunicatum; privatim vita eum. Coram
aliis teneris ei communicare; numquam enim prodas aliquem alicui qui 99
nescit eum esse excommunicatum.[32]

156 Communicans excommunicato cuicumque sex modis excusatur ne
sit excommunicatus: justa ignorantia, domestica necessitate, adventitia
necessitate, numero, humanitate, correptione. *Justa ignorantia*, quia
ignorans aliquem excommunicatum, communicans ei non es excommuni- 5
catus, nisi bruta et grossa sit ignorantia tua.[33] *Domestica necessitate*, quia
per exceptionem Gregorii licite communicat pater filio et e converso, et
vir uxori et e converso, et servus domino et e converso.[34] *Adventitia necessi-*
tate, quia, si peregrinus non potest vitare castrum excommunicatum, com-

---

94 et²] vel Tc *om.* U.   95 est² *om.* Cc.   specialis] spiritualis AcCk *corr. ab* spiritualis Ab
spirituales Tu.   96 quia *om.* Cc.   98 vita eum *add.* in communi non Ad *add. et* Z.
99 enim *om.* CkJQ¹*.   1 esse *om.* OR.   esse excommunicatum] excommunicatum est
U.   2-14 *Sect. 156 invenitur in fol. 120*rb *Pet.*   2 excusatur] excommunicatur CcTa.
3-4 domestica — ignorantia *om.* Pet (*homoeotel.*).   4 correptione] correctione AdJZ *et* correctione U correptione *ut vox reclamans* Q¹* *et statim cessat* Q¹*.   5 ignoras OTu ignorantia
J.   communicas P si communicas U.   es] est AcTaTcZ Pet *corr. ab* est H.   6
tua] ejus Ta *om.* CkJ Pet.   7 filio *add.* suo Ta.   converso] contrario OTaTcTu (*abbrev.*
ambigua in quamplurimis codd. hic et infra).   et² *om.* TcTu.   7-8 et vir uxori et e converso *om.* J *post et* servus domino et e converso *ad lineam 8* Ac.   8 vir uxori] uxor marito
U.   converso¹] contrario TcTu.   et² *om.* OTc.   converso²] contrario Tc.

---

[30] Cf. Huc. ad C.3 q.6 c.1 *agatur* (fol. 150rb); *Glossa ordinaria in Decr.* C.3 q.6 c.1; 1 *Compil.*
5.14.1 (X 5.17.1).

[31] Cf. above sect. 150.

[32] Cf. Huc. ad D.93 c.1 *commonitione* (fol. 98vb); ad C.5 q.1 c.2 *percutiatur* (fol. 159ra); JL
17639 (X 5.39.14).

[33] Huguccio speaks in this connection of *ignorantia supina* or *crassa* as distinguished from *ig-*
norantia vera: see ad C.11 q.3 c.103 *partim ignorantia* (fol. 196va *secunda expositio post mediam partem*
columni); *ibid.* verbo *subtrahimus* (fol. 196vb). Regarding distinctions of various kinds of ıgno-
rance made at this time see below sect. 356; KUTTNER, *Kanonistische Schuldlehre* pp. 135-179;
FIRTH, *Thesis* II 474*-475* with n. 92, 478*-479* with n. 7.

[34] See GRATIAN C.11 q.3 c.103. Most of this paragraph is based fundamentally on this canon, which is a decree of St. Gregory VII (Hildebrand). Huguccio interpreting it (*ad eundem*
locum verbo *uxores*, fol. 196vb) considers the excuse reciprocal only in the case of husband and
wife, not in the case of father and son or of master and servant.

municans hominibus illius castri non est excommunicatus.[35] *Numero*, 10
quia excommunicatio non transit in tertiam personam.[36] *Humanitate*, quia,
deficientibus vitae necessariis excommunicato, subvenire ei teneris.[37]
Correptione, quia in his quae ad correptionem pertinent communicabis excommunicato.[38]

157 Item quod dicitur, quod qui manus misit violentas in clericum ex- 15
communicatus est, octo habet casus exceptos, in quibus si quis mittit
manum in clericum, vel non est excommunicatus, vel si est ab episcopo
suo absolvitur vel ab abbate suo.[39]

Primus casus est si, quando mittebas manum in clericum, nondum
quatuordecim annos compleveras.[40]   20

Secundus, si ignorabas eum esse clericum, vel propter tonsuram irregularem vel habitum. Si autem sciens eum esse clericum manus violentas in eum mittis, quantumcumque se irregulariter habeat, excommunicatus es.[41]

---

12 excommunicato *add.* ei RTa *add.* ei *delet.* Ac.   ei] eum Tc *om.* Ac RTa.   13 Cor-
reptione] correctione AcAdCkJU Pet(BmCpMNSoY corruptione Sg).   correptionem] correctionem CkJRTaU Pet(BmCpEMNSoY corruptionem Sg) *add.* ejus AdZ.   communicabit
TaTu communicandum O *add.* cum R.   15-50 *Sects. 157-158 fol. 122*[r-v] Pet.
15 Item] Idem Cc.   quod] quia J *om.* Tu.   miserit O mittit RTa injicit U.
16 casus *om.* Tu.   casus exceptos] exceptiones Ta.   immittit Cc mittat R misit P.
16-17 in quibus — clericum *om.* Ta.   17 manus PR.   si est *om.* CcRTu *add.* excommunicatus U.   18 absolvitur] absolvi potest ORTaTc absolvi *add.* potest *suprascr.* Ab
potest absolvi Tu.   absolvitur — suo] vel abbate absolvi potest Pet.   ab *om.* CkTa
insert. Tu.   20 inpleveras JU compleverit Ck completos Tu.   21 eum] istum Ac ipsum
R.   22 eum] ipsum AdR *om.* Pet.   23 habebat OTc habuerit *vel* habuit Ck haberet
Pet.

---

[35] See GRATIAN *loc. cit.*
[36] See GRATIAN *loc. cit.*; cf. HUG. ad C.11 q.3 dictum p. c.15 (fol. 190[ra]); BERNARD OF PAVIA,
Summa decretalium 5.34.7 (p. 274).
[37] Cf. GRATIAN *loc. cit.*; HUG. ad C.11 q.3 c.103 *in sustentatione* (fol. 196[vb]).
[38] Cf. HUG. ad C.11 q.3 c.18 *ad eandem excommunicationem* (fol. 190[ra]); ad C.11 q.3 dictum
p. c.15 (fol. 190[ra]).
[39] A similar list of eight cases is found in HUG. ad C.17 q.4 c.29 *mandatum* (fol. 247[va]); Robert seems to depend on this place. These exceptions are based originally on a decretal of Alexander
III cited by Huguccio: *Sicut dignum* JL 12180 (X 5.39.1-3); cf. below n. 41; also FIRTH, *Thesis* II 403*
with nn. 55-56; 474*-475* with n. 92.
[40] See 1 *Compil.* 5.34.2 (JL 12180; X 5.39.1); HUG. *loc. cit.*
[41] See HUG. *loc. cit.*; cf. IDEM ad C.17 q.4 c.21 *clericis arma non ferentibus* (fol. 246[vb]). Huguccio cites for this a decretal: *De illis* JL 13771 (1 *Compil.* 5.34.5; X 5.39.4; perhaps originally
part of JL 13767; see LOHMANN, *ZSavignvStRG* kan. Abt. 22.67). This decretal then is apparently not part of JL 12180; cf. PL 200.894-896.

Tertius est si ex jocosa levitate manum mittis in clericum.[42] 25

Quartus, si propter disciplinam.[43]

Quintus, si te defendendo; quia vim vi repellere omnia jura permittunt;[44] tribus observatis: scilicet ut in continenti fiat, cum moderamine inculpatae tutelae, non animo vindicandi, sed animo defendendi. *In continenti*: quia statim quando clericus invadit te, repellas eum; alioquin 30 timendum est tibi de excommunicatione. *Cum moderamine inculpatae tutelae*: quia si invadit te pugnis, non defendas te armis. *Non animo vindicandi, sed defendendi*: alioquin timendum est tibi de excommunicatione.[45]

Sextus casus est de religiosis qui se ad invicem verberant; eorum abbas potest eos absolvere, vel abbates eorum si sint de diversis domibus.[46] 35

Septimus casus est si arcendo turbam, id est cohibendo vel repellendo, manum mittis in clericum; non es excommunicatus, vel si es, episcopus tuus potest te absolvere, nisi dolose elegeris in turba aliquem cui tu velles nocere.[47]

Octavus casus est si inveneris clericum turpiter agentem cum matre 40 tua vel filia vel sorore vel uxore; si mittis manum in eum, non es excommunicatus.[48]

Servum, domino invito ordinatum vel ignorante, solus dominus ejus potest verberare ita quod non incurrit excommunicationem.[49]

158 Post mortem etiam excommunicatur quis et absolvitur. Verbi 45 gratia, aliquis in parochia sepultus est in coemeterio; post mortem pro-

---

25 Tertius *add.* casus TaTc Pet. 27 omnia *om.* P omnes leges et *praem.* JU. 32 vindicandi sed *om.* Ta. 33 sed defendendi *om.* Tu. 37 mittit Cc mittas Pet. manum mittis in clericum *add.* sine personae delectu *insert.* O in clericum manum mittis sine delectu personae Tc. vel] et J ideo Pet. 38 elegeris] egeris TaTu Pet. circa aliquem Ta cum aliquo Tu videns aliquem Pet. tu *om.* Ck. tu velles] te vellet Tu. velis J nolles Ac. 41 tua] sua CcTu. 43 ordinato Ck ordinationi Tu. 44 potest *add.* eum OPTu Pet. incurret Tc incurreret Tu incurrat H. *add.* ejus Z. in communicationem *corr. ad* in excommunicationem O. 45 Post mortem etiam] Item post mortem O. excommunicatus est quis Tu. excommunicatur — absolvitur] quis excommunicatus absolvitur Tc. 46 parochia *add.* ista O. est *om.* RTu. 46-47 pro-

---

[42] See 1 *Compil.* 5.34.2 (JL 12180; X 5.39.1); Hug. ad C.17 q.4 c.29 *mandatum* (fol. 247va).
[43] See *locc. citt.*
[44] See 1 *Compil.* 5.34.4 (JL 12180; X 5.39.3); Paulus in *Digesta* 9.2.45.4; Ulpianus in *Digesta* 43.16.1.27.
[45] Cf. Kuttner, *Kanonistische Schuldlehre* p. 340.
[46] See 1 *Compil.* 5.34.3 (JL 12180; X 5.39.2); Hug. ad C.17 q.4 c.29 *mandatum* (fol. 247va); Po. 1326 (X 5.39.32; issued probably Feb.-April, 1201).
[47] See 1 *Compil.* 5.34.4 (JL 12180; X 5.39.3); Hug. *loc. cit.*
[48] See *locc. citt.*
[49] Cf. Hug. ad D.54 c.2 *ejus conditionis* (fol. 65vb).

batur fuisse haereticus vel excommunicatus; ejiciendus est a coemeterio et excommunicandus.⁵⁰ Item aliquis mortuus est in excommunicatione et probatur non contempsisse absolutionem et laborasse quantum potuit ad absolutionem; absolvendus est et transportandus in coemeterium.⁵¹ 50

De sortilegio

159 Sortilegium impedit promovendum et dejicit promotum; sed hoc intelligo de illis sortilegis qui daemonibus immolant, vel imagines vel alia baptizant, vel de corpore Christi sortilegia faciunt. Quicumque aliquid tale fecerit, vel consilium vel auctoritatem vel auxilium vel consen- 55 sum ad hoc praestiterit, etsi occultum fuerit, nec promovebitur nec post promotionem ordinis habebit exsecutionem. De aliis sortilegis hoc non credo, nisi infamia notati fuerint. Idem mihi videtur de illis qui sortilegos consulunt et divinos.⁵²

De sollemniter poenitente   60

160 Sollemniter poenitens non promovetur; quia sollemnis poenitentia non datur nisi pro maximo crimine, quod et per sollemnem poenitentiam

---

batus Tu probatus est J. 47 esse R Pet *om.* Tu. 50 in] ad Ta Pet. coemeterio O coemeteriis J. 51 *tit. om.* CcO *insert.* Ac. 52 Sortilegium *usque ad lineam 47 prope finem sect.* 177 *aliquibus omissis et mutatis invenitur fols. 139ᵛ-141ʳ* Pet. promovendum] promotionem J *corr. ab* promotionem Tc. dejecit O *corr. ab* dejecit Pet. 53 intelligendo O intelligendum est Tc. sortilegiis TuZ *corr. ad* sortilegiis O *om.* Ta. de illis sortilegis *om.* Pet. 53-54 vel alia baptizant] baptizant aqua Tu. 54 alia] aliqua U. vel *add.* qui Ta. 54-55 aliquod JU. 56 etsi] etiam si J Pet si Tu. fuerit] sit CkH. nec¹] non AcCcCkHJPRTcTuU Pet(CpEIKLMNSgSoXY). 57 sortilegiis TaZ Pet *corr. ad* sortilegiis O *corr. ab* sortilega Ci. 58 nisi — fuerint *om.* Ad. 60 *tit. om.* AbOJ. 61 poenitens] poenitentes Pet *corr. ab* poenitentes Tc. promovebitur AcCkHJTuU promoventur Pet. 62 pro magno H proximo *corr. ad* pro eximio O.

⁵⁰ Cf. GRATIAN C.24 q.2 c.6; Po. 627 (Reg. 2.14 PL 214.546-547; issued March 17, 1199); Po. 1128 (X 3.28.12; issued approximately Aug.-Sept. 1200). This was done at Paris in 1210 in the case of Amaury of Bène; see *Chartularium Universitatis parisiensis* ed. DENIFLE and CHATELAIN I 70 no. 11.

⁵¹ Cf. RUFINUS, *Summa ad* C.24 q.2 pr. (p. 419); HUG. (?) *ad eundem locum* (fol. 277ᵛᵇ; quoted in FIRTH, *Thesis* II 362* n.37 [III 646*-648*]). Regarding the authorship of this part of Huguccio's *Summa* see Luigi PROSDOCIMI, "La 'Summa decretorum' de Uguccione da Pisa", *Studia Gratiana* 3.361-374; Corrado LEONARDI, "La vita e l'opera di Uguccione da Pisa Decretista", *Studia Gratiana* 4.83-85.

⁵² Cf. GRATIAN C.26 q.5 cc.5, 13; the first of these is the canon *Si quis episcopus* quoted below in sect. 329. Cf. also 1 *Compil.* 5.8.3 (JL 13940; X 5.9.2); 1 *Compil.* 5.17.3 (JL 13943; X 5.21.2).

publicatur.[53] Dictum est autem quod maximum crimen et publicum promotionem impedit.[54]

De infamia   65

161 Infamia enim promotionem impedit. Infamia cujusque notorii et
maximi criminis irremissibilis est. Notorium est crimen tuum quando
ita notum est quod tuill ud negare non potes. Remissibilis est infamia
quae nec est de notorio nec de crimine maximo.[55] Huic sententiae consonat
Caelestinus papa dicens: Qui in sacro ordine perdidit bonum conscien- 70
tiae per crimen homicidii vel adulterii vel perjurii vel falsi testimonii, si
notorium est ejus crimen, nec utatur ordine suscepto nec ulterius promoveatur; si occultum est, admonendus est in periculo animae suae ut nec
hoc nec illud faciat;[56] supple: "sine dispensatione papae in homicidio et
majoribus adulterio, vel episcopi sui in adulterio et aequalibus et minori- 75
bus."[57] Cum plures sint infamiae, credo quod ista sola impediat promotionem. Si laboras infamia irremissibili, si vis famam reparare, consule
papam; pro remissibili consule episcopum tuum, et ante nec promovearis
nec ministres.

De rebaptizatis et aliis   80

162 Alia etiam crimina impediunt promotionem, ut rebaptizatus[58] et
eundem ordinem suscipiens bis,[59] qui adhaesit haeretico ad fidei subver-

---

63 publicabitur O duplicatur Ck *add.* Clericus — *poenitentia ex lineis 50-52 infra in sect. 237*
Pet.   autem *om.* Ta Pet.   64 impedit *add.* Ista — dispensationem *ex lineis 53-55 infra in*
sect. 237 Pet.   65 *tit. om.* JOPTc *insert.* AbAc.   66 infamia enim] id est infamia O.   enim
promotionem impedit] impedit etiam promotionem Pet.   Infamia[1] — impedit *om.* JTa.
notarii J *corr. ab* notarii O notorium U.   68 tu *om.* JU.   69 quae] quando Tu.
nec[1]] non JPTc.   nec[2] neque JU.   consonat] consentit TaTu.   70 perdiderit JTc.
71 per] propter JU.   vel adulterii *om.* JTa.   vel[2] *om.* Ci.   vel perjurii *om.* Ck
post falsi Tu.   vel[3] *om.* AbO.   75 adulterio *om.* P Pet *delet.* AcO.   vel *add.* sine
dispensatione O.   76 istae solae AbOTaR(F) illae solae Tu ita sola Cc.   impediant
AbOTaTcTu(BmEFMSo) impediunt R impedit Pet(CpIV).   78 promoveris Ac.

---

53 Cf. GRATIAN D.50 cc.55-68; D.51 pr., c.5; below sects. 236-237 with nn. 19-22.
54 See above sect. 101 with n. 79. Regarding this reasoning cf. HUG. ad D.33 c.2 *publica*
(fol. 41[ra]).
55 Cf. RUFINUS, *Summa* ad C.2 q.3 dictum p. c.7 (pp. 245-246).
56 See JL 16617 (2 *Compil.* 1.8.3; *Collectio seguntina* no. 45; *RevHistEccl* 50.432; CELESTINE
III); cf. FIRTH, *Thesis* II 387*-393*.
57 Cf. above sects. 101-102 108.
58 See GRATIAN D.50 c.65; D.51 c.5; *De consec.* D.4 cc.117-118; cf. above sect. 82 with nn.
35-36; sect. 83 with n. 37.
59 See GRATIAN C.1 q.7 c.21; cf. above sect. 82 with nn. 33, 36; sect. 83 with n. 37.

tionem, qui elegit ab haeretico ordinari,[60] qui differt baptizari usque ad
mortem vel infirmitatem;[61] tales omnes nec dispensationem recipient ut
ordinentur.   85

163   Ecce jam diximus de criminibus quae hodie promotionem impediunt et ordinis exsecutionem. Sunt et alia crimina quae apud antiquos,
apud quos viguit religionis vigor, promotionem impediebant et ordinis
exsecutionem; ut ista: sacerdos revelans confessionem deponatur et pro-
fugus et vagus sit super terram;[62] clericus, a quocumque deponatur, eo ipso 90
infamis sit et a solo papa restituatur;[63] clericus clericum invitum ad judicem
trahens saecularem suspendendus est.[64] Et generaliter quodcumque crimen in veteri testamento morte mulctabatur, in novo promotionem antiquitus impediebat.[65] Quod si hodie servaretur, qui semel ad menstruatam
accessit non promoveretur; qui semel patri vel matri maledixit non pro- 95
moveretur; qui semel est excommunicatus non promoveretur; quia contumacia et alia quae dicta sunt in veteri testamento morte mulctabantur,[66]
et pro sola contumacia excommunicatur quis.[67] Sunt et alia plura crimina
quae antiquitus promotionem impediebant, sed hodie non reputantur.   99

84 nec] non OP *om.* J *insert.* H.   86 Ecce *ss. usque ad* dicamus *ad linea 4 in sect. 164 om.*
Pet.   promotiones AcZ.   88 viguit] erat O.   religio Ta religionis et *corr. ad*
religio et Ab *om.* Tu.   vigor *om.* Ta.   91 sit] fit AdCcCiU est Ta(BmEGLMNSgSoY)
om. RTu.   92-93 quocumque crimine RTu.   crimen *om.* Ta.   93 testamento
om. O.   in veteri testamento] invenitur Tu.   94-95 qui semel ad menstruatam —
promoveretur *om.* CkTaTu *infra post* promoveretur *ad lineas 95-96* AcH(BmELMNSoY) *infra
post* promoveretur *ad finem lineae 96* JU(CpX).   95 accesserit HJ accedit R.   vel] et JP.
maledixerit HJORU.   96 est] esset JTcU *om.* H.   (qui semel est — promoveretur
om. LSoV *supra post* promoveretur *ad lineam 95* X).   98 excommunicatus CiTu excommuni-
cabatur Z.   alia *om.* CkTa.   plura plurima Cc *om.* R.

[60] See above sect. 82 with n. 36.
[61] See GRATIAN D.57; HUG. ad D.57 pr. (fols. 70[vb]-71[ra]).
[62] See GRATIAN *De poen.* D.6 c.2 (reproduced below sect. 350).
[63] See GRATIAN D.50 c.10; HUG. ad D.50 pr. (fol. 56[vb]).
[64] See GRATIAN C.11 q.1 c.42; C.11 q.2.
[65] See GRATIAN D.54 c.23 *ad finem*; D.61 c.18.
[66] Regarding cursing of father see *Ex* 21.17; *Lev* 20.9. Regarding intercourse with a menstruous woman see *Lev* 18.19, 29; *Ezech* 18.6, 9. Regarding obstinate disobedience see *Deut*
17.12.
[67] Cf. HUG. ad C.11 q.3 c.14 *lapidabatur. . . aut gladio* (fol. 189[va]); KUTTNER, *Kanonistische
Schuldlehre* p. 35 n. 2.

164 Recollige ergo praemissa. Diximus quod sunt quaedam quae non sunt de ordinis substantia et promotionem impediunt, ut crimen, conditio et casus.[68] Prout potuimus de crimine diximus, consequenter de conditione dicamus.

De conditione   5

In conditione quatuor intelligo: servitutem, nativitatem, conjugium et officium.

De servitute

165 De servitute cum multa multipliciter dici possint, hoc puto ad propositum sufficere: quod de licentia domini sui ordinetur servus, vel reli- 10 gionem intret, vel alio modo alienetur ab eo vel ad tempus vel in perpetuum. Alioquin domino tenetur satisfacere tam servus quam ejus alienationis cooperator, ut ejus ordinator, ejus praesentator et monasterium quod eum recepit.[69]

De nativitate   15

166 Nativitas impedit promotionem; quia, etsi liber sit aliquis, non tamen de matrimonio natus, de jure communi promoveri non potest.[70] Dispensative tamen etiam saecularis sacerdos fieri potest, immo episcopus, immo archiepiscopus, immo patriarcha, immo papa; secundum Huguccionem etiam presbyteri filius, licet Gratianus contradicat.[71]   20

---

1 *praem. tit.* Quae impediunt exsecutionem ordinis tantum AcAdCcCiHRZ(NY) *idem tit. delet.* Tc *idem insert.* R *similes titt.* P(FKM) *similis insert.* O; *vide* Firth, *Thesis II* 344*.   praemissa] praedicta R *add.* quae O *add.* quae impediunt ordinis exsecutionem *delet* Tc   quod sunt *om.* P.   quod sunt quaedam] quorum quaedam sunt O.   3 et *om.* CkRTu.   6 In *reincipi.* Pet.   9-10 De — quod *om.* Pet.   9 possunt CkRTcTuZ possent J. 10 quod] et O et quod J *add.* si Tu *add.* non nisi P.   vel] et Ac.   16 etsi] etiam si Ck si PRTu.   sit *om.* TaTu.   18 dispensantem O dispensationem Pet dispensatione Tc-TuU *om.* J.   etiam] et Cc *om.* AcJRU.   19-20 Hugonem CkPTaTcUZ.   20 etiam] et JRTaTuU *om.* O.

---

[68] See above sect. 100.

[69] Cf. Hug. ad D.54 dictum post c.8 (fol. 66ra); ad D.54 c.19 *permanente, duplice* (fol. 67vb); ad D.54 c.20 *triennium* (fol. 68ra); ad C.17 q.2 c.3 *aut servus* (fol. 244vb); 1 *Compil.* 1.10.2 (D.54 c.6; X 1.18.2; cf. Hefele-Leclercq 4¹.28).

[70] Cf. Hug. ad D.56 pr. (fol. 69vb-70ra; cf. Paris BN lat. 3891, fol. 66rb).

[71] See Hug. ad D.56 dictum p. c.13 (fol. 70vb; partly quoted in Firth, *Thesis* II 363* n. 40 [III 649*-651*]). Robert has misunderstood the precise point of Huguccio's disagreement with the text of Gratian on which he is commenting; see Firth, *Thesis, loc. cit.*

Religio etiam cotidie filium presbyteri legitimat; ut, si in religione honestae fuerit religionis et non paternae imitator incontinentiae, sacerdotii dignitatem suscipere possit legitime; praelationem autem non praesumat suscipere, nec saecularis ubi pater ejus praelatus fuit,[72] nec alicubi in religione sine episcopi sui vel majoris dispensatione. Alicubi tamen in- 25 venitur quod qui non sunt nati de matrimonio religionem intrent ut facilius cum illis dispensetur;[73] quod fortasse de illis dicitur qui de graviori nati sunt incestu. Ego enim aliquem sacerdotis filium et religiosae sive conversae pro dispensatione Romam misi, quam obtinere non potuit.

167 Hoc etiam memoriter teneas: quod natus in fornicatione per sequens 30 matrimonium etiam post quantumlibet tempus legitimatur. Verbi gratia, natus es in fornicatione; non potes sine dispensatione promoveri; post triginta annos contrahent pater tuus et mater, et tunc legitimaberis ad ordinandum; nec oportebit te dispensationem petere.[74]

De conjugio   35

168 Conjugium impedit promotionem, quia maritus viduae vel corruptae et bigamus non promoventur; quia, si contraxisti cum aliqua ab alio cognita

21 etiam *om.* JTa.   cotidie] hodie CcJ.   religionem Ck.   in religione] religionis O.   22 religionis] et religione *corr. ad* et religiose O conversationis Ta conversatus CkP.   23 recipere AcCk.   autem *om.* JRTu.   24 ejus] suus Ad est J *om.* R. fuerit O.   alicui CcJTaTu a¹ Ac alibi Tc aliquam U.   24-25 alicubi in religione] in aliqua religione Pet.   in religione *om.* R.   25 religione] regione P.   sui vel] vel sine H sui auctoritate vel Tc.   auctoritate et dispensatione AcCkHJU.   alicui JTaTc.   26 qui] si CkP *om.* Cc.   de] in R *om.* J.   intrant CcTa *corr. ad* intrant O.   27 illis] eis AcHJRTu.   quod] quia Cc.   graviore Tc majori Ta. 28 aliquem] quandoque JU.   28-29 religiosae sive conversae] religiose conversatum P religiose conversatum sive converse Z religiose sive converse viventem Pet religiosae conversationis Ta religiosae vitae sive conversatione H.   31 etiam *om.* AcTcTu *add.* hoc Tc. quantumlibet] quantulum O quantum hoc Tu.   32 es *delet.* Ac est Cc.   potest Ac. 33 contrahunt JTcU Pet contrahet AbPRTa contrahat Tu.   mater *add.* tua CcOU Pet. 34 oportet AcHRTu.   te] de Ad de *delet.* Tc.   dispensationes AbZ Pet dispensatione Ad.   petere *add. sect. 172* Pet.   36 vel] et Pet.   viduae vel *om.* R. 37 et] vel AcCkHJRTaTuU(BmCpELMNSgSoXY).   promovetur AcRTu promoveretur U.   aliqua] alia Tu *insert.* Cc.   alio] aliquo J Pet.

[72] Cf. Hug. ad D.56 c.1 *nisi aut* etc. (fol. 70ra; cf. Paris BN lat. 3891, fol. 66rb); 1 *Compil.* 1.9.1-4 (X 1.17.1-4).

[73] Cf. Hug. ad D.56 pr. (fols. 69vb-70ra; cf. Paris BN lat. 3891, fol. 66rb); *Glossa ordinaria in Decr.* ad D.56 c.1 *coenobiis.*

[74] Cf. 1 *Compil.* 4.18.1 (JL 14167; X 4.17.1) 1 *Compil.* 4.18.6 (JL 13917; X 4.17.6); Robert Génestal, *Histoire de la légitimation des enfants naturels en droit canonique* pp. 38-42, 71-76, 80-90.

et postea eam cognovisti, non promoveberis.[75] Ideo dico "si eam cognovisti," quia, si non, credo quod hoc non obstante poteris promoveri, quia carnem tuam in duo non divisisti, quod impedit promotionem, non ma- 40 trimonium.[76] Item ideo dico "ab alio cognita," quia, si aliquam corrupisti et postea cum ea contraxisti, credo quod hoc non obstante poteris promoveri, quia carnem tuam in duo non divisisti.[77] Item oportet, ut credo, quod a te solo fuerit cognita; alioquin non promoveberis, quia uxor tua carnem suam in duo divisit. *Oportet* enim, ut dicit apostolus, 45 *episcopum esse unius uxoris virum*,[78] et similiter sacerdotem, immo quemlibet ad sacrum ordinem promovendum. Quod ergo dicitur *unius uxoris virum* etc. sic intellige: id est unius unius, id est uxoris quae non fuerit nisi unius.[79]

Item si contraxisti cum vidua ab alio cognita, idem dico quod dixi de illa quae ab alio est cognita. Item ideo dico "cum vidua ab alio cognita;" 50 quia aliqua cum pluribus contraxit, sed a nullo est cognita, quod morte

---

38 postea] post O.   38-39 non. — cognovisti *om.* TuZ (*homoeotel.*).   40-43 quod — divisisti *insert. hic* H *infra in textu post* in duo divisit *ad lineam 16* U (*homoeotel. corr.*). 40-48 quod — etc. *om.* Ta (*forte idem homoeotel. et alia omissio cum* Ab *infra ad lineas 43-48; cf. supra in Proleg. ad p. 48 cum nn. 46-47 et infra in Append. C ab initio*).   43-48 Item — etc. *om.* Ab *cf. loc. cit.*   45 enim] etenim AcO etiam Cc autem U.   46 quamlibet Ci quilibet Tu quantumlibet J.   48 etc. *om.* AcHJORTuZ.   id est[1] *om.* CcCiCkHJPRTuUZ(EGKLVX *rasura* Bm).   id est unius unius *om.* Tu(G).   (unius[1]] virum X). unius[2]] uxoris U *om.* CcCiCkHJPTcZ(EKLMSoVY uni Cp).   unius, id est] id est unius O (*om.* INSg).   fuit JPU Pet est Ck.   49 dico] dixero O.   49-50 idem — cognita[2] *om.* CkTa (*homoeotel.*).   50 quae ab] de Cc quae Tu.   alio] illo R aliquo H Pet. est] sunt Cc.   Item] Idem J Iterum U *om.* Pet.   ideo dico *invers.* JU.   51 quia] quae R *add.* si Tc *add.* si *insert.* Ab.   aliqua] aut Ta aliquando R.

---

[75] Cf. Hug. ad D.26 c.2 *episcopus significat* (fol. 31rb; partly quoted below in n. 79); 1 *Compil.* 1.13.2 (X 1.21.1; cf. Hefele-Leclercq 2².1062.

[76] See Hug. ad D.34 c.20 *ad hunc articulum* (fol. 43ra).

[77] Huguccio mentions this opinion *loc. cit.* without accepting it.

[78] See 1 *Tim* 3.2.

[79] Robert's analysis of *unius uxoris virum* seems to be based on the following passage in Huguccio: "*episcopus significat* Ergo episcopus est sacramentum? Non est dubium; nec est inconveniens si episcopus sit sacramentum; res enim corporales sunt sacramenta, scilicet oleum et aqua. Et nota quod in hoc sacramento non tantum exigitur ut sit unus unius uxoris, sed etiam exigitur ut sit una [*corr. ad* unus] unius [*add. in marg.* uxoris quae sit una unius]. Nam si uxor fuit vidua vel ab alio corrupta, vir tamquam non habens in se integrum sacramentum repellitur a promotione. Mariti enim viduarum vel corruptarum non debent promoveri, ut Dist. xxxiv. *Si quis viduam* (c.13) et Dist. li. *Qui in aliquo* (c.5). Exigitur ergo virginitas ex parte uxoris et non ex parte viri; etsi enim mille habuit concubinas vel uxorem et concubinam vel concubinas, non ideo deest ei sacramentum, et ideo ratione defectus sacramenti non repellitur." Hug. ad D.26 c.2 *episcopus significat* (fol. 31rb; cf. Paris BN lat. 3891 fol. 30rb). Cf. Idem ad D.34 c.11 *admitti potest* (fol. 42rb); ad D.34 *eodem vitio* (fol. 42va).

interveniente possibile est; credo quod hoc non obstante promoveri poteris si cum ea contraxeris, quia carnem tuam in duo non divisisti.[80]

169   Si postquam uxor tua cum alio fornicata est eam cognovisti, non promoveberis, quia postquam uxor tua facta est non unius, immo plu- 55 rium, cognovisti eam.[81]

Eadem ratione si post matrimonium cum aliqua fornicatus es, non promoveberis, quia carnem tuam in duo divisisti.[82] Eadem ratione videtur quod qui cum pluribus fornicatus est vel adulteratus est non possit promoveri; sed non est verum; quia non intelligitur carnis divisio in fornica- 60 tione, sed in matrimonio, quia in matrimonio intelligitur unio Christi et ecclesiae, non in fornicatione.[83] Ergo quando tu in matrimonio cum aliqua adulteraris, quantum in te est, rumpis illam unionem; et ideo quia injuriam facis sacramento quod est in matrimonio, id est unioni Christi et ecclesiae, non promoveberis; quod non est in fornicatione.   65

170   Si habuisti duas legitimas, unam post aliam, quas ambas cognovisti, si contraxisti cum duabus, legitime cum una, cum alia de facto, vel cum duabus de facto, et ambas maritali tractasti affectu, non promoveberis. Ideo dico "maritali affectu," quia per hoc, quantum in te fuit, bigamus fuisti; et ideo non promoveberis. Huic attestatur Innocentius in decretali 70

---

52 superveniente JU praeveniente H.   53 contraxisti HJTcU.   54 alio] aliqua P.   cum alio *om.* J.   55 immo] sed TaTc Pet.   57 aliqua] alia Tc qua O. es, non promoveberis] est aliquis non promovebitur U.   58 tuam] suam OU.   dividisti Tc Pet divisit U.   59 est[2] *om.* AcCkHJU.   60 sed] quod AcCkHJU.   62-63 cum aliqua] cum alia Tc cum adultera Pet tuo *add.* cum *delet.* Ck *om.* R.   66-74 Si — promovebitur *om.* Pet.   68-69 non — affectu *om.* Ta (*homoeotel.*).   69 dico *add.* de O. 70 Huic] hoc Cc hinc P.   (Innocentius *reincipit* Tb).   decretis Cc.

---

[80] Cf. GRATIAN D.34 c.20; HUG. ad C.27 q.2 dictum p. c.29 *Item sponsa* (fol. 291ra; ed. ROMAN p. 784); Po. 2875 (X 1.21.5; issued Aug. 28, 1206).

[81] Cf. GRATIAN D.34 cc.11-12; HUG. ad D.34 c.11 *admitti non potest* (fol. 42rb).

[82] Cf. GRATIAN D.34 c.8; 1 *Compil.* 1.13.1 (see HEFELE-LECLERCQ 2².1159). Canonists generally interpret this prohibition, not as an instance of the canonical impediment of bigamy, but as declaring unsuitability because of crime, a mediocre crime, which can be removed by sincere contrition and proper penance, after which one could be promoted by dispensation of one's bishop. See e.g. HUG. ad D.34 cc.7-8 (fol. 42ra); cf. above sect. 101. In contrast to what he says here, Flamborough normally follows the canonists in this. Hence in the marriage case in which the penitent is found to be involved at the end of Book 3 below (sects. 188-195) the confessor judges that the penitent has not incurred the impediment of bigamy, even though he has been involved in several invalid marriages after entering into one valid one; cf. above n. 79 and below n. 84; also FIRTH, *Thesis* II 469*-471* with nn. 81-83.

[83] See the quotation from Huguccio above in n. 79.

sub hoc sensu: Si aliquis in sacro ordine contraxit cum duabus, licet de facto tantum, et ita nec hic nec ibi fuerit matrimonium, quia tamen maritalem habuit affectum, et per eum non stetit quin ibi esset matrimonium, bigamus judicatur et non promovebitur.[84]

Eadem ratione, si quis cum corrupta contraxit in sacro ordine cum 75 maritali affectu, non promovebitur.

171 Memoriter tene: si alicui fidem dedisti vel jurasti quod eam duceres et non dolose, si eam maritali affectu postea cognovisti, consummatum est matrimonium.[85] Si igitur vel duabus vel uni corruptae hoc fecisti, non promoveberis; immo per omnia in isto facto judica sicut et judicares si 80 aliter contractum esset matrimonium.

De officio

172 Consequenter de officio dicamus. Officia quaedam impediunt promotionem, ut curialium. Curiales dicuntur tum advocati vel causidici, tum judices, tum officiales, tum histriones, scilicet qui ludibria sui corporis 85 exercent vel ursos ducunt vel simias. Quandoque curiales strictius dicuntur a cruciatu, qui scilicet reos sanguinis faciebant apparere in judicio, vel damnatos morti tradebant vel mutilabant. Nam et curiales a cruore vel a cura dicti sunt. Igitur histriones, qui ipso jure sunt infames, et qui

---

71 aliquis] quid O.   72 ita] illud Tu *om*. Tc.   et ita *delet*. O.   fuit PTaTc. 71-72 maritale Cc matrimonialem Ta.   tamen maritalem habuit] tantum maritale fuerit Tu.   quia — matrimonium *om*. J (*homoeotel*.).   73 in affectum *corr*. *ad* affectum Cc *corr*. *ab* effectum O.   75 contraxerit CcHTaTu traxit Ck.   77-81 *sect. 171 om*. Pet.   77 tene *add*. quod O.   eam *om*. AbOTu.   79 vel[1]] illis Ck *om*. AcHJ-TaTcU(BmCpEFGMNSoTbXY).   hoc *om*. AbOTaTu.   80 et *om*. AcCkHJPRTcU-(BmCpEGIKMNSoTbVXY).   (et judicares] praejudicares Sg).   83-96 *Sect. 172 interpolatur supra intra sects. 167 et 168* Pet.   84 vel] tum AcHJTcU(BmCpEGMNSgSoTbVY) et Ta *obscur*. Pet.   86 simias] ursicuas Ck similia Pet.   87 curiatu TaTu crucia Ck. qui] quia AcHTc.   88 vel[2]] et CkJU.   et *om*. CkPTu.   cruore] cruce Ta cruciatu P.   89 a *om*. JTu.   cura] curia HPRTaTcTuU Pet(BmKSgX) *corr*. *ad* curia O (curio *add*. dicuntur vel Cp cruciatu M crure So cura Hug.).   Igitur *om*. R.   Igitur histriones] Hi ergo Ta.   qui[2] *add*. ipsa O.

---

[84] See Po. 700 (X 1.21.4; issued May 16, 1199). Pope Innocent in this decretal speaks of a priest, and Robert understands it as applying to one who has acted thus *in sacro ordine*. Probably this is why he does not judge his penitent as bigamous below in sects. 188-195, even though he has consummated one valid marriage and several invalid ones before his ordination to the subdiaconate (see below sect. 191).

[85] See above sect. 56 with n. 32; cf. below sect. 192. Cf. also J. A. CORIDEN, *The Indissolubility Added to Christian Marriage by Consummation* esp. pp. 16-18.

saeva praecepta exercuerunt circa sanguinem non promoventur, nec judex, 90
nec advocatus, nec assessor, nec testis in causa sanguinis, ut mihi videtur.
Alii curiales ordinari possunt, sed si prius absolvantur a curia, aliter non;
et hoc ideo quia irregulares sunt, vel quia molestantur ecclesiae cum
iterum repetit eos curia, vel quia praesumitur contra eos quod transeunt
ad clericatum non voto religionis, sed ut fugiant consilia dominorum 95
suorum.[86]

173   Diximus superius, si bene memini, quod tria impediunt promotionem: crimen, conditio, casus.[87] Duo prima prosecuti sumus; restat tertium,
scilicet casus.   99

De casu

Casum hic voco eventum aliquem in corpore humano ex quo quis
promoveri impeditur, ut est aliquis morbus vel corporis vitium ex incisione vel laesione proveniens. Dico ergo generaliter quod omnis morbus
vel tale vitium promotionem impedit quod in celebratione scandalum 5
introducit, vel ex mentis alienatione, vel ex inordinata corporis disposi-
tione. *Morbus*, ut lepra, impetigo enormis in facie, id est sicca scabies,
epilepsia, apoplexia.

174   Tamen de epileptico dicunt quod epilepticus omnino curatus celebrare potest. Item, si frequenter accidit ei morbus, vel raro et cum spu- 10
mae jactatione vel vocis confusae emissione, omnino debet cessare a
celebratione missae. Si sine istis duobus raro ei accidit, celebrare potest,
ita tamen quod secum habeat alium sacerdotem qui incepta officia possit

90 exercent TuU.   94 repetet O poterit Tu.   97-99 Diximus — casus *om.* Pet.
98 persecuti CcOTcTu exsecuti P consecuti Z.   sumus *add.* sed AcHJU *add.* modo Tc.
2 hic] hoc JOR.   aliquem *om.* PTu.   3 vel *om.* Ta.   vel corporis *invers.* P.
4 generaliter *om.* J.   generaliter quod *invers.* TaTu.   4-5 omnis — vitium] omne vitium tale vel omnis morbus RTaTu Pet.   6 introduxit J Pet includit Tu.   ex² *om.*
Ta Pet.   ex inordinata] in exordinata J.   7 ut] vel Ab.   8 epilemsia *vel* epilsensia
in perplurimis MSS add. morbus caducus Ad *add.* id est morbus caducus J.   apoplexia *add.*
morbus celebris et cogit hominem mori subito *insert. margin.* Ad.   10 si *insert.* AbO.
et *insert. post* cum Ab.   11 debent JU.   12 Si] sed Ck Sed si JU Sed *add.* si *insert.*
O *om.* Cc.   sine] in J.   duabus Tu *om.* P.   13 alium] aliquem J *om.* Pet.

[86] See Hug. ad D.51 pr. (fol. 64[rb]; quoted in Firth, *Thesis* II 356*-358*); cf. Hug. ad D.
51 c.1; R. Cheney, *From Becket to Langton* pp. 16-18, 21-24; above sect. 105; below sects. 247,
249-250.
[87] See above sect. 100.

complere si ille deficiat; sed tutius consulerem ut ipse penitus cessaret.[88]
Idem credo de furioso vel alio morbo unde quis fit amens vel ad terram 15
colliditur. Si a daemonio quandoque tangitur, ex toto cesset quousque
ex toto sanetur.[89]

175 Vitium quoque corporis promotionem impedit sacerdotii. Si in
brachio vel humero vulneratus est quis vel laesus quod in missae celebratione non potest brachia ordinate levare, non promovebitur ad sacer- 20
dotium. Si in virilibus pateris ita quod necesse sit ut abscindantur, per
medicum peritum hoc fiat, vel per te vel per alium, et promovearis.[90]
Si ex indignatione hoc fecisti, non promoveberis. Nec erroneam illam
sequaris opinionem quod non potest quis celebrare nisi secum virilia
habeat sicca vel pulverizata vel alio modo, quia non exiguntur ad cele- 25
brationem.[91]

176 Sponte debilitatur qui ferrum sibi apposuit vel apponi fecit vel
concessit absque necessitate violenta; talis non promovetur tamquam sui

---

14 implere PTu.   ipse] ille AdH *om.* J.   15 quis] si quis UZ qui Ta quisquis Pet.
fit] sit CiCkJPRTcTuU Pet(CpLSgV).   16 Si] vel Ta Vel si Pet.   16-17 Si — sanetur *insert. margin.* Ad.   ex toto] omnino AcHRTc(BmEGMNSoTbY).   quousque]
donec AdJRTaTuU Pet(CpSg).   17 ex toto] omnino Ad(Tb) *om.* U.   19 vel in humero AcHPTuU.   vel laesus] ita O.   21 ut] quod PRTc.   abscidantur HJPTa-
TuUZ Pet(CpEFKSoX abscidatur LM) accidantur Tc(G).   22 (hoc — alium] vel per te
vel per alium hoc L *hic cessat L*).   vel[1] *om.* AcHTuU.   vel per te *om.* R.   et *om.*
JTc.   promoveberis Tc Pet.   24 quod] quia Tc quasi Ac *om.* Tu.   25 pulverulenta
TaTu Pet *corr. ab* pulverulenta Tc.   28 concessit] consensit RTaTu (consensit Hug. Rufinus).

---

[88] Cf. Hug. ad D.49 c.1 *Jugem, Impetiginem* (fol. 56[rb]); also texts cited in the following note.
[89] Cf. Hug. ad D.33 c.3 (fol. 41[ra-b]); ad C.7 q.1 c.15 *singulariter* (fol. 168[ra]); Rufinus ad
C.7 q.2 (p. 295).
[90] Cf. Gratian D.33 c.2; D.55 c.9; JL 16604 (X 1.20.3; *Collectio seguntina* no. 87 *RevHist-
Eccl* 50.443 Celestine III); *Apparatus: Ecce vicit Leo* ad D.33 c.2 *indignatione* (fol. 15[ra]).
[91] Source not found. According to the general tenor of the canon law (see texts cited in nn.
90, 92-95), grossly evident mutilation is an impediment to orders whether voluntary or not,
but hidden mutilation, including sexual mutilation even if grave, is not an impediment unless
it has been voluntarily, and hence criminally, produced with at least the consent of the person himself. It seems from our text that some canonist added to all of this the stipulation that
in no case could one be promoted if his sexual organs had been completely removed. For, his
argument probably claimed, if the organs have not just been withered or shredded, but have
been totally removed, then one would not be properly of the male sex, which is required for
valid reception and exercise of orders (see above sect. 76 with n. 10). Robert repudiates this
added stipulation and follows the general canonical teaching that sexual mutilation is not an
impediment unless voluntary.

homicida et promotus dejicitur, nisi modici membri pars abscisa fuerit.[92]

Casu debilitatur qui a medico secatur propter aegritudinem vel alio 30 casu. Talis, si in secretioribus partibus laeditur, promovetur; si autem in magno membro et evidenti, non promovetur aliquo modo. Magnum autem membrum dicitur quantitate vel decore, ut oculus, nasus, manus, pes, tres digiti manus dextrae, pollex, index, medius et verpus, id est medicus.[93] Si autem post susceptum ordinem aliquo modo mutilatur ut sine 35 deformitate ministrare non possit, cessabit a celebratione. Si oculum amisit post promotionem, non cesset; sed si nasum radicitus cum labio superiori, cesset.[94] Si medicorum incisione claudus efficitur, non prohibetur ordinari.[95]

<Cap. iv.>   <QUAE IMPEDIUNT EXSECUTIONEM   40
ORDINIS TANTUM>

177   Sunt et alia quae, etsi promotionem non impediant, ordinis tamen principaliter exsecutionem impediunt: ut si ordinatus es a non tuo episcopo, si aetatem ordinandi praevenisti, si extra tempus ordinandi ordinatus es, si saltum in ordinibus fecisti, si plures ordines simul suscepisti, si 45 furtive ordinatus es, si in suspensione vel a suspenso, si in excommunica-

---

29 abscissa TaTc *corr. ab* abscissa R.   30 qui a] quia Cc quia *corr. ad* qui Ab.
32 promovebitur Tu promoveatur Pet.   33 autem *om.* RTu.   34 et verpus] et ut
post *corr. ad* verpus O (*om.* Tb).   verpus] ut post AbTa(IV Hug^b) verpos P(K) impus H
(ympus So umpus Bm impus et verpus M) simpus J limpus U(G erumpus Y erupus E infipus
N) duo post Pet (non post X ubi prius Hug^a) vermis Ck.   verpus id est] secunda prima
Tu *om.* R.   (medius — est *om.* Sg).   id est] sive Tc (idem I) *om.* Ta Pet(X).
37 cum labio] est *cum lacuna in qua script.* cum labro Cc.   labio] labro HP Pet lapra J.
38 superiori *add.* amisit Ck *add.* amiserit U.   Si] Sed si R se Cc.   inficitur Ac.
39 ordinari] promoveri PR.   40-41 *tit* DE HIS QUAE NON IMPEDIUNT ORDINEM
SED ORDINIS EXSECUTIONEM Pet (DE HIS QUAE IMPEDIUNT ORDINIS EXSE-
CUTIONEM M) *om. cett.(cett.) Vide* FIRTH, *Thesis II 344**.   42 et] etiam J *lacuna* Cc.
impediunt JTu.   43 a non *invers.* HRTc.   45 recepisti U accepisti Pet.   46 si^l
— es *om* J (*homoeotel.*).

---

[92] Cf. RUFINUS, *Summa* ad D.55 pr. (pp. 145-146); GRATIAN ad D.55 cc.5-6; 1 *Compil.* 1.12.1 (JL 14091; X 1.20.1); also the text from Huguccio cited in the following note.

[93] The vulgar word *verpus* normally signifies the middle finger, as in Huguccio: "tres digiti manus praesertim dextrae, scilicet pollex, index, <verpus>, qui et medius et impudicus dicitur." HUG. ad D.55 pr. (text established from Paris BN lat. 3891 fol. 65ra-b and BN lat. 3892 fol. 68va). Robert has understood this word to designate the fourth finger; thus he mentions four fiingers in all.

[94] Cf. RUFINUS *loc. cit.* (in n. 92); HUG. *loc. cit.*; FIRTH, *Thesis* II 374*-377*.

[95] Cf. GRATIAN D.55 c.10; RUFINUS *loc. cit.*

tione vel ab excommunicato ordinatus es. Haec omnia in inquisitionibus
nostris prosequemur.[96]

178 His intellectis, propone si quid te gravat vel in matrimonio vel in
his quae ad clericos pertinent. Deberem quidem secundum ordinem 50
naturalem a superbia confessionem tuam inchoare et per cetera vitia
producere. Sed quia, sicut superius memini,[97] in primis de difficilioribus
me expedire consuevi, de matrimonio scilicet cum laicis, de ordine et
simonia et aliis cum clericis, circa ordinem hoc inquiro.

Cujus ordinis es ? 55

POENITENS. Sacerdos sum.

SACERDOS. In primis habuisti coronam ?

POENITENS. Habui, sed a simplici sacerdote; sic enim mos est in partibus meis.

SACERDOS. Nisi esset consuetudo terrae, oporteret te ab episcopo coro- 60
nam suscipere. Quid de illis agendum sit qui corona praetermissa alios
ordines suscipiunt in tractatu de ordine determinatum est.[98]

179 De matrimonio natus es ?

POENITENS. Non.

SACERDOS. Scivit hoc ordinator tuus ? 65

POENITENS. Non.

SACERDOS. Si districte tecum ageretur, judicari posses furtive ordinatus.
Quid de talibus furtive ordinatis dicendum sit in sequentibus dicetur.[99]

Diximus etiam quod illi qui non sunt nati de matrimonio per religionem, si illam intraverint, legitimantur; id est si honeste in religione conver- 70
sati fuerint, ad sacerdotii dignitatem promoveri possunt.[100]

---

47 ab *om.* Pet *insert.* RTa.   Haec *ss. usque ad finem sect. 180 om.* Pet.   in *om.* CcPR.
48 nostris *om.* CkTu.   prosequimur PTaU prosequetur J.   49 si *om.* RTa.   propone si] propositione Tu.   50 quidem] quid JTa.   51 tuam *om.* O.   52 quia
om. CkTa.   54 hoc] haec HRTaTcTu enim Ck.   56 Sacerdos] acolythus JU.
58 mos] mox OZ.   60 oportet Tu *corr. ab* oportet Ci.   (ab *ss. usque ad lineam 66 in
sect. 189 desinit* Tb *folio perdito*).   episcopo *add.* tuo U *add.* tuo *insert.* J.   61 accipere
JORTcU.   62 tractu JO.   63 De *praem.* SACERDOS PU.   65 hoc] haec O *om.*
R.   67 districte *ss. cessat* Tu.   70 id est *om.* Ta *insert.* Ci.   71 possint Ab.

---

[96] See below sects. 178-187.
[97] See above Book 1 sects. 9-10.
[98] See above sect. 78; cf. sect. 74.
[99] See sect. 182.
[100] See sect. 166.

Poenitens. Numquid possunt tales in religione ministrare in ordine ante conversionem suscepto?

Sacerdos. Credo quod possunt, ex quo potuissent in religione illum ordinem suscepisse; tamen consule discretiores.   75

Poenitens. Licet negaverim me de matrimonio natum, tamen non intelligo plane an sim de matrimonio natus; quia diu postquam natus sum, contraxerunt parentes mei.

Sacerdos. Si legitimi fuerunt ad contrahendum, per sequens matrimonium legitimatus es (sic enim superius dictum est), et bene et legitime 80 ordinatus es si ante ordines tuos contraxerunt.[1]

Poenitens. Aliquem ordinem antequam contraherent parentes mei suscepi, aliquem post. De illo quem ante suscepi quid erit? Ministrabone in illo?

Sacerdos. Credo quod bene ministrabis; consule tamen peritiores.   85

180   Cujus conditionis fuisti?

Poenitens. Servilis.

Sacerdos. Si sine licentia domini tui et ordinatore tuo conditionem tuam ignorante ordinatus es, et te domino tuo furatus es, et ordinatori tuo ordinem quem suscepisti; et ideo domino tuo pro te satisfacias, et 90 episcopo tuo pro ordine hoc modo: ut sine ejus licentia in ordine tuo non ministres, nec antequam domino tuo satisfeceris.[2]

De aetate ordinandorum

181   In qua aetate ordinem suscepisti?

Poenitens. Quinquennis eram.   95

Sacerdos. Aetatem ordinandi male praevenisti; quia corona conferri debet in septimo anno et supra, acolythatus in duodecimo et supra, sub-

---

74 potuissent *corr. ab* possent Ad.   religionem JO.   in religione *om.* Tc.   77
an] aut O.   78 sum] fui CkP.   79 fuerint CiJORTcU.   80 sic] sicut RTaTc.
enim *om.* HO.   et[2] *om.* JTc.   82 ordinem *om.* O.   Poenitens — mei *om.* Cc.
contraxerunt CkH *corr. ab* contraxerunt Tc contraxerent Ci.   83 ministrabo RTa ministrare
ne Cc *add.* ego H.   88 Si *om.* Ac.   89 tuam *om.* Tc.   te] de AbCkTc.   94
In qua *reincipit* Pet *sects.* 181, 185-186 *abbrev. et mutat. fol.* 135r-v.   96 conferri] fieri O prae-
ferri Ck.   97 acolythus JR Pet acolatus CkO.   duodecimo *add.* anno CcJPTa.

---

[1] See above sect. 167.

[2] See Hug. ad D.54 c.2 *ejus conditionis* (fol. 65vb); cf. ad D.54 c.19 *permanente* (fol. 67vb). Huguccio says of a slave who has received ordination without being released by his master *Furtum sui corporis fecit* and *Facit furtum sui ipsius.* Cf. also Gratian D.54 cc.2, 6; Hug. ad D.54 c. 19 *eum esse servum nescierit* (fol. 67vb); above sect. 165. Regarding restitution of the order to the bishop cf. below sect. 182 and Appendix A sect. 363; also Hug. ad D.50 pr. (fol. 56vb).

diaconatus in vicesimo et supra, diaconatus in vicesimo quinto et supra, presbyteratus in tricesimo et supra; rationabili tamen causa potest epis- 99 copus contra istud dispensare.[3]

De furtive ordinatis

182 Ab episcopo tuo omnes ordines tuos suscepisti, vel de licentia ejus?

POENITENS. Subdiaconatum ab alio suscepi et ordinatore meo ignorante.

SACERDOS. Furtive ordinatus es; et si nec in excommunicatione nec ab 5 excommunicato ordinatus es, episcopus tuus tecum dispensare potest ut in subdiaconatu ministres et ulterius promovearis.[4]

183 Saltum fecisti in ordinibus?

POENITENS. Feci; quia sacerdos sum et numquam diaconatum suscepi.

SACERDOS. Ad episcopum tuum recurre, quia ipse tibi hic sufficiet, et 10 pete ab eo diaconatum; et tamdiu cessa ab omni administratione quamdiu diaconatu caruisti; et tandem, post dignam poenitentiam vel perfectam vel saltem bene inchoatam, de licentia tui episcopi in quovis ordine ministra.[5]

De eo qui plures ordines simul suscepit 15

184 Aliquos ordines simul suscepisti?

POENITENS. Suscepi acolythatum et subdiaconatum.

SACERDOS. Numquam ulterius promovearis nec in aliquo ministres ordine sine papae dispensatione, quia ille solus tecum potest dispensare.[6]

---

98 vicesimo[1] *add.* primo R *add.* anno CcJ *add.* anno *delet.* Tc.   diaconus Ci.   diaconatus— sumra *om.* R (*homoeotel.*).   quinto] octavo H *add.* anno CcJ.   99 tricesimo *add.* anno J Pet.   1 contra *om.* P Pet.   istud] illud PTa hujusmodi Z.   3 Ab] de Tc *corr.* ab *de* Ab.   Ab *ss. usque ad finem sect. 184 desinit* Pet.   tuos *om.* JTc.   vel] et Ta. ejus] episcopi Ta episcopi tui R.   4 et *om.* JU. 5 in *om.* CkO.   6 ordinatus es *om.* JU.   10 hic] in hoc Ta *om.* Tc.   sufficit Ta *corr.* ab sufficit R.   10-11 et — diaconatum] pete ab eo diaconatum *insert.* Ad.   11 ministratione HTc.   12 caruisti] carens in sacerdotio ministrasti Tc *corr.* ad carens in sacerdotio administrasti O.   condignam OP.   12-13 ministres Cc.   17 acolythum RTcU acolatum O.   18 ultro Cc vel Tc *om.* P.   19-26 quia — dispensatione *om.* Cc (*homoeotel.*).

---

[3] Cf. HUG. ad D.77 pr. (fol. 86rb); *Glossa ordinaria in Decr.* ad D.77 pr.

[4] Cf. 1 *Compil.* 5.25.un. (JL 13988; X 5.30.1); *Hug.* ad C.9 q.2 c.10 *poterit* (fol. 177va); FIRTH, *Thesis* I 162*, 178*. Cf. also above n. 2 *ad finem.*

[5] Cf. GRATIAN D.52; Po. 2381 (X 5.29.un.; issued Jan. 21, 1205); FIRTH, *Thesis* I 162*.

[6] Cf. Po. 1327 (X 1.11.13; issued probably March-April 1201); JL 16603 (X 5.30.2; *Collectio seguntina* no. 80 *RevHistEccl* 50.442 CELESTINE III).

185　In temporibus ordinandi ordinatus es?

POENITENS. Quae sunt tempora ordinandi?

SACERDOS. Sex in anno: sabbata quatuor temporum, sabbatum *Isti sunt dies*, sabbatum sanctum paschae.[7] Si extra ista tempora ordinatus es, numquam promovearis nec in aliquo ordine ministres sine papae dispensa- 25 tione, quia ipse solus hic tecum dispensare potest.[8]

In quolibet die dominico dictorum sabbatorum potest ordinari subdiaconus, sed privatim et continuato jejunio tam ab ordinatore quam ab ordinando;[9] si tamen omittatur jejunium, credo quod non propter hoc impeditur ordo vel ordinis exsecutio. Quidam dicunt quod personale 30 est istud et alicui a papa concedendum, aliter minus canonice fiet.[10] Nec extenditur ultra subdiaconatum, id est major ordo quam subdiaconatus in tali dominica conferri non potest.[11]

Similiter acolythatus extra omnia dicta tempora conferri potest, sed privatim et cum paucis et in aliqua magna sollemnitate.[12] Si aliquod 35

21-47 *sects. 185-186 textu abbrev. et mutat.* Pet *fol. 135ᵛ.*　　　24 sanctum] sacrum Ck *om.* Ta. 28 ordinatore] ordinato P ordinante Tc.　　　29 ordinato Cc ordinante OP.　　　29-31 si — fiet *om.* Pet.　　　31 fieret JPU.　　　34 acolythus RTa acolatus O.

[7] See GRATIAN D.75 c.7; cf. STEPHEN OF TOURNAI, *Summa* ad D.75 dictum p. c.2 (p. 99); *Glossa ordinaria in Decr.* ad D.75 c.7; 1 *Compil.* 1.6.3 (JL 13948 X 1.11.3). The words *Isti sunt dies* (*Esth* 9.28) are the incipit of the first responsory at matins on Passion Sunday, two Sundays before Easter. This Sunday was often called "dominica *Isti sunt dies*" or "dominica in qua cantatur *Isti sunt aies*" (see DU CANGE s.v. *dominica*). Flamborough apparently means by "sabbatum *Isti sunt dies*" the Saturday before Passion Sunday. This is one of the traditional and canonical *tempora ordinandi* (see texts cited at beginning of this note).

[8] Cf. 1 *Compil.* 2.17.11 (JL 15742; X 1.11.8); 1 *Compil.* 1.6.2 (JL 13948; X 1.11.2); FIRTH, *Thesis* I 162*-163*, 179*.

[9] Cf. HUG. ad D.75 c.4 *continuato* (fol. 85ʳᵇ); RUFINUS ad D.75 pr. (p. 164); *Glossa ordinaria in Decr.* ad D.75 c.4 *sabbati*; Po. 1327 (X 1.11.13; issued probably March-April, 1201).

[10] Source not found; cf. 1 *Compil.* 1.6.1 (JL 13769; X 1.11.1); 1 *Compil.* 1.6.3 (JL 13948; X 1.11.3).

[11] None of the sources mentioned above in n. 9 restricts this to the subdiaconate; yet in Form 1 we find as here: "nec extenditur ultra subdiaconatum". (below Appendix B sect. 378). Possibly this supposed restriction has been surmised from the fact that in Po. 1327 (X 1.11.13) Innocent III condemns the ordination of someone to the diaconate and to the priesthood on two successive days, a Saturday and a Sunday *continuato jejunio*. However the pope's condemnation is not based on the fact that these are orders beyond the subdiaconate, but on the fact that two such successive days are considered liturgically one; hence this an instance of simultaneous ordination to two orders (cf. above sect. 184).

[12] Cf. 1 *Compil.* 1.6.3 (JL 13948; X 1.11.3); HUG. ad D.75 c.7 *presbyterorum et diaconorum* (fol. 85ᵛᵃ).

istorum trium tibi defuerit, id est non cum paucis et sollemniter et in die profesto[13] acolythatum suscepisti, de consilio meo sine papae dispensatione non ministrabis.

186   Umquam in excommunicatione ministrasti vel ordinem suscepisti, vel ab excommunicato ? Si hoc fecisti in majori excommunicatione, num- 40 quam ordineris nec in aliquo ordine ministres sine papae dispensatione; de isto plenius superius dictum est in tractatu de excommunicatione.[14]

Umquam in officio diaconatus ministrasti non habens diaconatum ? Si fecisti, non promovearis nec in aliquo ordine ministres sine dispensatione ad minus tui episcopi; tutius ages cum papa.[15]   Quid dicendum sit de 45 ministrante vel ordinato in suspensione vel a suspenso superius dictum est.[16]

187   Alia etiam inquiri possunt circa clericos, de quibus nos expedivimus cum de simonia tractaremus.[17]

Est aliud quod te gravat in his quae circa clericos inquiri possunt ?   50 POENITENS. Non memini.

188   SACERDOS. Et de matrimonio quid dicis ?

POENITENS. Et hic quaeso diligenter attende, quia de aliquot cum quibus contraxi nescio an aliqua mea fuit uxor; quia puellae cuidam juravi et fidem dedi quod eam in uxorem ducerem si permitteret me rem 55 habere cum ea.

---

36 tibi] cui Cc.   defuit PU.   non *om.* OP.   non cum *invers.* CkJU.
37 profesto] festo OP *corr. ab* festo Ad   profecto J *add. et* P.   acolytham R acolatum O.
40 vel *om.* CcCkOPTaTc(BmKNSgSoV).   42 isto] hoc Ad.   superius] supra PTa.
44 sine *add.* papae O.   45 episcopi] praelati JU.   ageres Ad.   46 vel[1]] sive Ck sine ordine vel H (*Nota marginalis in* H *indicat lectionem* Ck *tamquam* Alia litera).   48 alia *ss. usque ad finem sect. 236 desinit* Pet.   50 aliud] aliquid JPU(CpKV) aliquid aliud AcTc(Bm-EFGMNSgSoXY *etiam* Aliquid I).   gravet HRP.   circa] contra JU.   52 Et *om.* OPR.   53 aliquot] illis O.   cum *om.* J *insert.* Ci.   54 fuerit H sit Ck *corr. ab* sit U (sit Q[1]W).   55 me *om.* Ck.   ea] illa CkHP.   cum ea] secum Ta.

---

[13] A ferial (i.e. non-festal) day.

[14] See above sects. 141-142. Robert uses the term *major excommunicatio* as equivalent to *sollemnis excommunicatio*, i.e. *anathema*, and *minor excommunicatio* as equivalent to *simplex excommunicatio*.

[15] See 1 *Compil.* 5.24 (X 5.28); cf. FIRTH, *Thesis* II 495*-497* with n. 54 (III 769*-770*).

[16] See sect. 141.

[17] See above sects. 110-140; cf. sects. 74-109.

SACERDOS. Serio hoc fecisti an fraudulenter ?[18]

POENITENS. Serio.

SACERDOS. Exstitit umquam conditio, id est rem cum ea habuisti ?

POENITENS. Aetatis impossibilitas hoc impedivit; novennis enim erat, 60
ego vero duodennis.

SACERDOS. Attentasti quod tamen facere non potuisti ?

POENITENS. Sic est.

189   Processu vero temporis, quia ista absolvit me, aliam amavi, apud
quam ab amicis ejus deprehensus, compulsus sum eam ducere.   65

SACERDOS. Violenta fuit coactio quae debuit movere virum discretum,
an in eam consensisti ?[19]

POENITENS. Et violenta fuit et grata mihi, quia in eam consensi.

SACERDOS. Virginem eam invenisti ?

POENITENS. Inveni ante contractum matrimonium.   70

190 Post aliquantum tempus, hac relicta et vivente et nesciente, contraxi
cum tertia, cum qua aliquamdiu vixi post mortem secundae.

SACERDOS. Istam tertiam virginem invenisti ?

POENITENS. Inveni.

SACERDOS. Scivitne aliquid de aliis ?   75

POENITENS. Nihil.

191   Item, tertia relicta, vivente et nesciente, contraxi cum quarta.

SACERDOS. Scivitne aliquid de aliis ?

POENITENS. Nihil, nisi post mortem earum.

SACERDOS. Tunc consensit tibi ?   80

---

59 Exstitit umquam] exstititne HU.   60-63 POENITENS — est *om.* Ck.   62 SACER-
DOS *add.* attamen O.   tamen *om.* RTaTc.   64 quia *delet.* O.   absolvit *corr. ad*
absolvi O.   me *corr. ab* te O.   65 amicis *corr. ab* inimicis O.   sum *om.* J.
sum eam ducere] ut eam ducerem R.   66 (quae *reincipit* Tb).   debet O deberet Ad.
71 aliquantulum U quantum Z.   76 Nihil *add.* nisi post mortem earum PR.   76-78
POENITENS — aliis *insert.* AcTc (*homoeotel.*).   77 relicta *add.* et Tc *add.* et *delet.* R.
79 Nihil *add.* de aliis Cc.   80 Tunc *om.* Cc.

---

[18] Cf. HUG. ad C.27 q.2 c.51 *vel etiam pro consensu* (fol. 293ra; ed. ROMAN p. 804); FIRTH, *Thesis*
II 469*, 476*-477*. Philippe ARIÈS, *L'enfant et la vie familiale sous l'ancien régime*, points out that
in mediaeval art down to the twelfth century the child is depicted as a small adult. He con-
cludes that mediaeval children from about the age of seven years were considered in many ways
as adults and entered into the stream of adult life. See Eng. tr. *Centuries of Childhood* (New York
1962) pp. 33-43, 411-412. Cf. above sects. 12, 33, 51-54.
[19] Cf. above sect. 62; FIRTH, *Thesis* II 489*-492*.

POENITENS. Utique.

SACERDOS. Virgo fuit?

POENITENS. Immo corrupta et vidua, sed numquam eam cognovi.

SACERDOS. Sollemniter in facie ecclesiae cum ea contraxisti?

POENITENS. Ita est.   85

SACERDOS. Alicujus ordinis tunc eras?

POENITENS. Acolythus eram; parentes enim mei in tertio decimo anno per verba de praesenti me monasterio dederunt.

SACERDOS. Tonsuram et habitum suscepisti?

POENITENS. Neutrum; immo etiam post annum reclamavi.[20] Tandem 90 compunctus, istam quartam intactam relinquens, in claustrum reversus sum.

SACERDOS. Illa reclamante vel non?

POENITENS. Reclamante.

SACERDOS. Fuit hoc infra duos menses post contractum matrimonium? 95

POENITENS. Immo post sex.

SACERDOS. Postea continue ordini adhaesisti?

POENITENS. Continue.

192 SACERDOS. Superstites sunt aliquae illarum mulierum?   99

POENITENS. Tantum prima et ultima.

SACERDOS. Attende tibi, quia res intricatissima est. Ego hic mallem audire quam audiri; tamen ita sentio. Utique si serio alicui fidem dedisti de matrimonio contrahendo et postea eam cognovisti, ratum et consummatum est matrimonium;[21] si non est secuta carnis copula, non est matri- 5 monium, sed ad contrahendum teneris, et neuter reliquum potest absolvere nisi auctoritate majoris, ut episcopi.[22] Unde quando tu et puella absolvistis vos ad invicem, nihil actum est.

Immo plus dico: licet non sit secuta carnalis copula, impediente aetatis impossibilitate, quia tamen attentasti quod facere non potuisti [et] 10

---

83 POENITENS *om.* O.   88 monasterio] in monasterio J ecclesiae CkH.   90 etiam] et O.   reclamavit Ta *corr. ab* reclamavit Tc.   98 Continue *praem.* Adhaesi CkH.
5 carnalis RTa.   7 ut *insert.* O id est Ck.   8 absolvisti AbAcCcCiJTc(CpNSg) *corr. ab* absolvisti O(*et forte* Bm absolvistis Q¹W),   ad] ab CcP *om.* H.   9 licet *add.* quod Ab.   carnis R *corr. ab* carnis H.   10 et AbCkORTaTc(BmCpFGINVX *et* Q¹W) *insert.* Ac *om. cett.*(*cett.*).

[20] Cf. above sect. 33.
[21] Cf. above sect. 56 with n. 32; sect. 171; FIRTH, *Thesis* II 477*; below Appendix B sect. 392.
[22] See above sect. 53 with n. 23; cf. sect. 21.

(quidam praeveniunt aetatem coeundi, dicente beato Gregorio quod puer quidam novennis nutricem suam impregnavit),[23] bene posset judicari matrimonium fuisse inter te et primam. Ita enim judicat Alexander in eodem vel simili casu.[24] Quia inter te et eam tantum sponsalia contracta sunt, id est per verba de futuro, et hoc clandestine, in secundam autem 15 per verba de praesenti consensisti et sollemniter, et grata tibi fuit ejus coactio, verius videtur fuisse matrimonium inter te et secundam.[25]

193   Cum tertia autem non fuit matrimonium, nec etiam post mortem secundae. Alexander enim in illa decretali *Propositum* dicit in eodem casu: Si vivente uxore tua contraxisti cum alia nesciente te esse uxoratum, et 20 post mortem prioris reclamas et vis recedere a secunda quia vivente tua legitima contraxisti cum secunda, in arbitrio illius erit ut maneat vel recedat a te.[26] Hac ratione potuit tertia a te recedere, quando scivit post mortem secundae te tunc uxoratum esse quando cum ea contrahebas; ergo inter te et eam non fuit matrimonium. Ad hoc enim ut inter vos fuisset 25 matrimonium, oportuisset quod, praeter primum consensum qui inter

11 quidam — coeundi] aetatem coeundi praevenisti quam quidam praeveniunt Ta. beato] bono Cc.   Gregorio *add.* vel Augustino R.   12 possit O.   13 fuisse *om.* CkPR *insert.* Ad.   14 Quia] quod O *delet.* Ac.   16 fuit *om.* Ab.   17 coactio *add.* ideo *insert.* Ac.   18 autem] ante O *om.* Ta.   fuit *corr. ab* fuerit O.   etiam *om.* R *insert.* Ci.   20 te *insert.* O.   21 reclamans AbCcCk.   secunda] ea Cc. 23 tertia *om.* O.   25 non *insert.* AbO.   fuisset] esset OTc.   25-26 ad — matrimonium *insert.* CkH (*homoeotel.* ut *om.* H).   26 oporteret Tc oportuit JU.

[23] Cf. *Glossa ordinaria in Decr.* ad C.20 q.1 pr. The attribution of this story to St. Gregory is perhaps the result of a misinterpretation of Hug. ad C.20 q.1 c.1 *quae solet apta nuptiis* (fol. 253rb). Huguccio there cites a decretal attributed, probably erroneously, to St. Gregory VII (Hildebrand), namely JL 5291 (1 *Compil.* 4.2.3), and then relates this story, attributing it to St. Jerome. Cf. also 1 *Compil.* 4.1.18 (JL 9655; X 4.1.3). Several of these texts quote the dictum of Roman law *Malitia supplet aetatem*, usually inserting the word *quandoque* (see *Codex* 2.42.3; cf. KUTTNER, *Kanonistische Schuldlehre* p. 128). Cf. also above n. 18 and texts cited in the following note.

[24] Reference probably to JL 13969 (1 *Compil.* 4.2.12; X 4.2.9); this has likely become known to Flamborough through the use made of it by Hug. ad C.31 q.3 c.1 *servetur* (fols. 307vb-308ra); Huguccio cites the decretal as *De illis*. Cf. Willy ONCLIN, "L'âge requis pour le mariage dans la doctrine canonique médiévale", *Proceedings of the Second International Congress of Medieval Canon Law* pp. 237-247.

[25] This solution seems to be out of harmony with the principles implied above in sect. 28 and rather in conformity with those applied in Form 1 in the text corresponding to sect. 28; see Appendix B below pp. 285, 291; cf. above Proleg. pp. 41, 44; also FIRTH, *Thesis* I 182*-186*, 477*.

[26] See 1 *Compil.* 4.7.1 (JL 12636; X 4.7.1).

vos fuit, novus supervenisset et post mortem prioris et postquam ista tertia scivit te uxoratum esse.[27] Hac ratione nec matrimonium fuit inter te et tertiam, nec tu bigamus judicandus es.[28]

194 Ex his patet quod inter te et quartam fuit matrimonium; sed quia 30 post contractum matrimonium eam non cognovisti, nec judico te viduae maritum nec corruptae; quia carnis divisio, non matrimonium, irregularitatem facit.[29]

195 Tandem cum ista quarta reclamante claustrum intrasti infra duos menses post contractum matrimonium et ante carnalem copulam, licite 35 te claustro dedisti, et ideo maxime si ea sciente et non contradicente sacros ordines suscepisti; quia usque ad duos menses post contractum matrimonium ante carnis copulam potest uterque reliquo invito monachari.[30] Postquam autem semel convenerunt, neuter potest intrare religionem reliquo manente in saeculo, nisi remanens ita provectae aetatis fuerit quod 40 incontinentiae suspicio de eo non habeatur.[31] Oportet etiam quod in praesentia episcopi vel ejus vicarii idem remanens in saeculo voveat con-

---

27 et¹ *om.* HTa. 34 claustram O. 38 reliquo] relicto CkR. 39 autem] ante O *om.* P. convenerint PRTa. 41 quod] ut O. 42 idem *om.* CkTa. 42-43 continentiam] castitatem JU.

---

[27] The need for new consent is at least implied in Po. 3669 (X 4.7.7; issued probably in February 1209). This decretal is quite probably of later origin than the composition of this text of our penitential, since the latter is found also with little difference in Form 1; see below Appendix B sect. 369.

[28] Our author apparently does not consider a series of invalid marriages or concubinages occurring before ordination as constituting a very serious impediment to orders, as he would a series of concubinages after ordination; cf. above sects. 168-170 with nn. 79-84.

[29] Cf. above sects. 168-169.

[30] See above sect. 56 with notes.

[31] Whether their consent has been a solemn promise for the future (i.e. an engagement) or present matrimonial consent, after they have had intercourse *maritali affectu* they are considered to be married; see above sect. 56 with n. 32, sects. 171 and 192; below Appendix B sect. 392. Moreover consummation adds a new kind of permanence to marriage; see above sect. 56 with n. 30. Thereafter either of them to enter a monastery must follow the procedure *De conversione conjugatorum*, which is described here, and more fully above in sects. 21-23. Cf. also HUG. ad C.27 q.2 c.19 *in pollutione* (fol. 289ʳᵇ; ed. ROMAN pp. 767-768); *Glossa ordinaria in Decretum* ad C.27 q.2 c.21 *dimittere*; 1 *Compil.* 3.28.4-6, 8 (X 3.32.4-6, 8).

tinentiam, ad minus usque ad mortem alterius, et ita post ejus mortem nubere poterit.[32]

196   Hic inquirere consuevi de omnibus impedimentis matrimonii, ut de 45 consanguinitate tam carnali quam spirituali, de omni genere affinitatis, de justitia publicae honestatis et aliis quae supra enumeravimus.[33]

46 sanguinitate JO.   spirituali *add.* et TaTc.   47 supra] super CkZ.

[32] Cf. above sect. 23 with n. 39.
[33] See Book 2 esp. sects. 38-58.

INCIPIT LIBER QUARTUS

197 Ecce de difficilioribus nos expedivimus, scilicet matrimonio et ordine et simonia et aliis, sicuti promisimus.[1] Ut igitur diligentius omnia
peccatorum genera perquiramus et prosequamur, commissa scilicet et
omissa sive delicta, virtutum species distinguamus ut omissa et delicta tua 5
intelligas, id est quae debuisti et non fecisti. Iterum vitia distinguamus
et eorum species ut commissa tua intelligas, id est quae facere non debuisti
et fecisti. Vitiorum originem et radicem ponamus superbiam, virtutum
humilitatem.[2]

<Cap. i.> <DE SUPERBIA> 10

198 Incipiamus ergo a superbia et dicamus: Superbia laborasti?

Poenitens. Quid est superbia?

Sacerdos. Superbire est super alios ire: quando ergo super alios te ex-
tollis, tunc superbis.[3]

Poenitens. Frequenter hoc feci et ex consuetudine. 15

Sacerdos. Pete veniam et cessa de cetero.

Poenitens. Peto, domine, et per gratiam Dei cessabo de cetero.

<Cap. ii.> DE VANA GLORIA

199 Sacerdos. Vana gloria laborasti? Ad vanam gloriam pertinent ista:
hypocrisis, jactantia, inobedientia, insolentia (quando aliquid faciendo 20

---

1 INCIPIT *ss. reincipit* Aa.   2 scilicet] id est AbORTa.   de matrimonio PRZ.   et
om. PU.   3 et¹ *om.* Ci.   sicut HJ.   diligentius *om.* RTa.   4 proquiramus
Cc.   persequamur CcO.   scilicet *om.* Ta.   5 sive] et Ci.   delicta *add.* et
O.   6 Iterum] Item HPTa.   6-8 Iterum — fecisti *om.* Tc (*homoeotel.*).   10 *tit.*
om. hic omnes MSS.   11 dicamus *add.* DE SUPERBIA AaCc *add.* Sacerdos OTa *add.* DE
SUPERBIA Sacerdos P.   17 Peto *add.* veniam P.   domine *add.* veniam Tc.
18 *tit. om.* CiJR; *tit. invenitur post* Sacerdos *in perplurimus MSS hic et in sequentibus capitulis hujus*
libri.   19 Sacerdos *om.* JOPTaZ.   Vana *praem.* Si Ad.   Ad vanam gloriam P.

[1] See above in Book 1 sect. 10.
[2] Regarding the questions in the order of the seven capital vices in these sects. 198-230 see
above sect. 9 and Proleg. p. 13 with notes 70-71. Regarding the sources of these sects. see Proleg. p. 15 with notes. Regarding this paragraph cf. Alan of Lille, *De virtutibus et vitiis et de*
donis Spiritus sancti 2.1 (*Psychologie et morale* VI 71).
[3] Cf. Alan, *De virtutibus* 2.1 (*Psych. et morale* VI 69 lines 32-33).

modus exceditur), irreverentia, inverecundia, contentio, contemptus, contumacia, praesumptio, arrogantia (ut quando homo sibi omnia ascribit), loquacitas, vaniloquium, curiositas, adulatio tum acceptando tum exhibendo (quod fit quatuor modis: primus modus est quando aliquid in eo commendatur quo in eo vituperandum est; secundus modus est quando 25 alicui attribuitur bonum quod in eo non est; tertius modus est quando bonum quod in aliquo est ei ex meritis suis attribuitur; quartus modus est quando bonum quod est in aliquo plus quam in eo sit extollitur), scandalum (quando homo contemnit alios scandalizare).[4] In aliquo istorum offendisti, et tu de omnibus petis veniam et de cetero cavebis? 30

POENITENS. Peto, domine, et de cetero per gratiam Dei cavebo.

<Cap. iii.> DE INVIDIA

200 SACERDOS. Invidia laborasti? Ad indiviam pertinent ista: ingratitudo (accepti scilicet beneficii), malitia, inventio mali (scilicet quando scit homo invenire malitias, seditiones, nequitias), susurratio (scilicet 35 quando scit homo spargere voces ambiguas et seminare inter fratres discordias), conjuratio, conspiratio, dissensio, schisma, suspicio, seditio, odium, exsultatio (scilicet de alienis malis), afflictio (de alienis scilicet bonis), detractio (tum loquendo tum, quod deterius est, audiendo), depravatio (cum dico "Iste multum orat, multum jejunat, multas facit eleemo- 40 synas," et tu respondes "Frater, hoc non facit pro Deo, sed quia ad illam

---

21 contentio *om.* CkTc.   contemptus] contentus O.   32 tum[2]] cum OR tunc H.
24-28 (quod — extollitur) *om.* O *insert.* Ab; *cf. infra in Append.* C no. 7.   24 est *om.* JTa.
24-25 aliquid — quando *om.* Ci (*homocotel.*).   25 in eo *om.* TaTc *add.* aliquo R.   est[2]
om. JTa.   quando *add.* aliquid Ta.   26 alicui *add.* aliquid Ck.   bonum *om.*
RTa.   modus est *om.* Ta.   est[2] *om.* AdRTc.   28 aliquo] alio AaJTc.   30
offendisti *add.* POENITENS. Immo saepissime et fere indesinenter. SACERDOS H.   omnibus
add. istis AaU *add.* peccatis istis J.   cavebis *om.* Cc.   31 Dei *om.* JU *add.* mihi P.
32 *tit.* DE VANA GLORIA Ci *om.* JR.   33 SACERDOS] De JO *om.* HPZ.   34 scilicet[1]
om. CkPR.   malitia *corr. ab* malefitia O.   35 malitiam JTa.   nequitia OTa
corr. ad nequitia H.   susurrationes AaCkJUZ.   35-37 (scilicet — discordias) *insert.*
hic et iterum infra in textu post schisma *ad lineam 37* (scilicet *om. in textu et ordo vocabulorum* homo scit
quando) O *post* schisma conspiratio *ad lineam 37* RTa (*post* schisma *ad lineam 37* Tb); *ordo vocabulorum hic variatur in pluribus MSS; cf. infra in Append.* C no. 13.   37 conspiratio dissensio
insert. O.   dissensio *om.* Ta.   suspicio seditio *om.* OTa.   38 odium *add.* conspiratio
O.   scilicet[2] *om.* CkPZ *ante* de alienis[2] AaORTa.   39 est *om.* AdRTc.   40 cum]
enim Ck *add.* scilicet U.   multum[2]] iste Ck *om.* CiP.   40-41 multas eleemosynas facit
add. pro Deo O.   41 tu *om.* P.   et tu *om.* R.   Frater] super CkJ semper Tc *om.* P.

---

[4] Cf. *De fructibus carnis et spiritus* c.4 (PL 176.999-1000); ALAN, *De virtutibus* c.1 (*Psych. et morale* VI 69-70).

vel illam aspirat dignitatem," depravatio est); compressio est: cum dico
"Iste bonus est," et tu respondes "Verum est, sed non ita bonus ut tu
credis," compressio est; amaritudo (quando scilicet alii sunt in prosperitate, in felicitate, et amaricatur animus tuus; frequens est hoc in hominibus 45
invenire).[5] In aliquo istorum offendisti et tu de omnibus petis veniam et
de cetero cavebis?

POENITENS. Peto, domine, et de cetero per gratiam Dei cavebo.

<Cap. iv.> DE IRA

201 SACERDOS. Ira laborasti? Ad iram pertinent ista: impatientia, 50
indignatio, injuria, rixa, contumelia, blasphemia (quando scilicet homo
obloquitur Deo vel sanctis ejus), discordia (quando homo est dyscolus,
nec potest cum aliquo pacem habere), luctus (quando scilicet homo
semper est in anxietate quadam), temeritas, furor (quando homo se habet
furiose in domo sua vel ubi ipse praeest; istum percutit, illum verberat), 55
clamor (quando homo clamosus est in domo sua vel ubi ipse praeest, modo
contra istum, modo contra illum).[6] In aliquo istorum offendisti, ut supra?

SACERDOS. Vide quod de cetero sis pacificus, id est pacem habens tecum
et cum aliis, et ad pacem labores inter discordes. Vide quod tu sis modes-
tus (id est modum et mensuram servans in omnibus), socialis. Vide 60
quod tu sis longanimis, id est bonae sustinentiae, ut rerum eventum pa-
tienter exspectes, et sic tibi et tuis melius dispones. Vide quod sis patiens adversitatum; immo cum gratiarum actione suscipe adversa. Maxima enim est Dei misericordia quod hic vult secare et urere ut in futuro

---

42 vel] et Z *add.* ad CcPRTaTc(BmCpKMSgSoTbVX).   vel illam *om.* Ck(I).
illam[2]] istam Tc.   42 est[2]] ut HR(E *add.* ut V) *om.* TaTcZ(CpGMXY).   compressio
est] et compressio Ck *om.* P(KSg).   (est compressio est] compressio *ex parte eras.* est So).
44 compressio est *insert.* J.   44-45 prosperitate et in felicitate P felicitate et prosperitate Aa-
U.   in felicitate *om.* Ta.   45 et *om.* JU.   hominibus] omnibus AbCkR.   48
Dei *om.* JU.   49 *tit. om.* JU DE INVIDIA Ci.   50 SACERDOS *om.* JOTaTc.   52
vel] et U *corr. ab* et Ad.   dyscolus] discors Ta discors vel dyscolus Tc dyscolis Ac.   53
nec] non JR.   aliquo] alio AaJ.   scilicet *om.* AaPTa.   54 semper *om.* HTa.
55 praeest] potest Ck est dominus U *corr. ab* est Aa.   istum] illum JTc.   illum] istum
R.   55-56 istum — praeest *om.* Cc (*homoeotel.*).   56 praeest] est J *corr. ab* est Aa.
modo *insert.* Ac.   56-57 modo contra istum *om.* Tc.   57 istum] ipsum AaJ.   58-
59 tecum et *om.* HORTa *insert.* AbAc.   59 quod] ut H.   tu *om.* AaCkHJOTaTcU-
(CpEGMSgTbY).   60 modus AdCc.   socialis *om.* AbOTa.   61 tu *om.* Ta.
62 et[1]] ut CkJ.   sic] sit Ck.   quod *add.* tu JP.   64 vult *add.* te JU.

---

[5] Cf. *De fructibus* c.5 (PL 176.1000); ALAN, *De virtutibus* 2.1 (*Psych. et morale* VI 70-71).
[6] Cf. *De fructibus* c.6 (PL 176.1000); ALAN, *De virtutibus* 2.1 (*Psych. et morale* VI 70).

parcat. Audi David: *In die*, inquit, *mandavit Dominus misericordiam suam* 65
et nocte canticum ejus, ʰ ʰˢ ʰⁿ ᵃⁿᵛᵉʳˢ̣ʰᵗᵃᵗ̣ᵉ ᵍʳᵃᵗ̣ᵃʳ ᵘⁿᵘ ᵃᶜᵗ̣ᵒⁿ̣ᵉⁿ̣."

Ecce hic in tractatu de ira mentionem feci de modestia et longanimi-
tate, quae virtutes sunt; et hoc ideo feci quia contrariae sunt irae. Idem
in sequentibus facio ut per unum contrariorum memoriam habeas alterius.

<Cap. v.>   DE TRISTITIA ET ACCIDIA   70

202 Tristitia vel accidia laborasti? Ad tristitiam pertinent ista: ignavia,
desidia, negligentia.[8]

Numquid ex negligentia tua aliqua offensa accidit vel in officio divino
vel in sacramentis, ut in baptismo vel in sacramentis altaris, ut scilicet
omitteres chrisma vel oleum vel panem vel vinum vel aquam vel ignem 75
vel stolam vel aliquid de canone; vel canonem reiterasti; vel aliquid de
sacramento tibi decidit? Quia vero periculosum est canonem reiterare,
diligenter caveas ne umquam in hora consecrationis remaneat in altari
panis vel vinum.[9]

Ad tristitiam etiam pertinent: improvidentia, incircumspectio, rancor 80
(qui est quando homo hilarem vultum nequit exhibere), pusillanimitas,
querela, desperatio, remissio (quando homo remisse agit et corrigit), suspicio, taciturnitas (de qua dicitur *Vae mihi quia tacui*, quod scilicet dicendum erat).[10] In aliquo istorum offendisti, etc.?

SACERDOS. Vide quod de cetero agas cum consilio, cum discretione, 85
cum deliberatione, et perspicaciter consideres praeterita, praesentia et
futura.

66 actione AcTc.   70 ET] VEL AcCi.   71 ista *add.* inertia P.   ignavia *add.* taciktur-
nitas, de qua dicitur: Vae mihi quia tacui, quod scilicet (*om.* U SACERDOS *add.* De accidia *delet.*
Sg) dicendum erat AaJU(CpSg) *cf. infra ad lineas 83-84 cum var.*   72 desidia] taciturnitas
P.   73 tua *om.* AaCi.   74 ut¹ — sacramentis *om.* O (*homoeotel.*).   in² *om.* CkP.
vel²] et AcTc.   75 omittens R *corr. ad* omittens Aa.   77 cecidit AdHTa.   80
etiam *om.* TaTc *add.* ista Cc.   pertinent *add.* ista AaAcCkTc(CpEFGMNSoTbVY).
etiam pertinent *invers.* H.   81 qui] quae Ta.   qui est *om.* Tc.   83-84 taciturnitas —
erat *om.* AaCkHJTaU(CpSg) *insert.* AbO *cf. supra var. ad lineam 71 et infra in Append. C no. 14.*
83 quia] quod Cc.   85 SACERDOS *om.* OPR *insert.* Tc.

[7] *Ps* 41.9; cf. PETER LOMBARD, *Commentarium in Psalmos* 41.11 (PL 191.420).
[8] Cf. ALAN, *De virtutibus* 2.1 (*Psych. et morale* VI 71); Siegfried WENZEL, "Acedia, 700-1200",
Traditio 22 (1966) 73-102.
[9] Cf. RUFINUS, *Summa* ad *De consec.* D.2 c.1 (p. 552); above sect. 83 with nn. 37-38.
[10] *Is* 6.5; cf. ALAN, *loc. cit.*; *De fructibus* c.7 (PL 176.1001).

\<Cap. vi.\> DE AVARITIA

203 Avaritia laborasti? Ad avaritiam pertinent ista: ambitus, philargyria (quando homo delectatur in munusculis),[11] simonia, inquietatio, 90
violentia, rapina, fraus, fallacia, calumnia, perjurium.[12]

Numquid fecisti perjurium? Dic quot et quae. Attende quia in sacramento quandoque obligat se quis Deo tantum, ut cum juro me intraturum
religionem, quandoque homini tantum, ut cum juro me tibi marcam
daturum, quandoque Deo et homini, ut cum juro tibi quod tecum religio- 95
nem intrabo.[13] Item sacramentum quandoque est simplex, ut praedicta;
quandoque duplex, ut cum juro quod infra pascha.

Item ad avaritiam pertinent ista: furtum, homicidium et omnis modus
aliquem damnificandi.
99

204 Furtum fecisti?

POENITENS. Alicui servivi qui mihi mercedem meam abstulit, in cujus
recompensationem aliqua ei furatus sum.

SACERDOS. Si aequaliter eum damnificasti ut et ipse te, sustinebo; si
plus, redde ei; si minus, juste quaere quod tuum est. Si alia fecisti furta, 5
vel simplicia vel sacrilegia, dic.

POENITENS. Aliquis alicui equum furatus est; eundem equum eidem
furi furatus sum. Cui equum illum restituam?

SACERDOS. Mihi videtur quod vero domino, ita quod furi nota fiat
solutio, ne forte, si poenituerit fur, per confessionem cogatur iterum vero 10
domino equum vel pretium restituere. In ipsa etiam solutione equi admonendus est dominus equi ne umquam de cetero aliquid in recompensationem equi recipiat.

---

89 Avaritia *praem.* SACERDOS PTc.   ista *om.* AaJ *add.* POENITENS Tc.   89-90 phi-
largia O.   92 Numquid fecisti perjurium *om.* Ck (*forte homoeotel.*).   Numquid] Quae
quid J.   fecisti perjurium *om.* J *insert.* Aa.   96 praedictio Ck praedictum est Ta.
97 cum juro] conjuro O *add.* tibi P.   quod *om.* Cc.   pascha *add.* intrabo Ta *add.* religionem intrabo H *add.* reddam tibi decem solidos Z *add.* etc. R.   98 ista *om.* Ab.
1 Aliquod furtum Z SACERDOS Furtum H.   2 mercedem meam] servitium meum CkH.
meam *om.* OP.   cujus] ejus R *om.* Ck.   4 ut *om.* Ta *insert.* AbO.   et *om.* CkHJP.
7 eundem equum *insert.* Ad.   8 furi *om.* O.   9 fiat] sit JR.   12-13 recompen-
satione CcRTaTc.

---

11 The word *philargyria* is used by some writers as equivalent to *avaritia*; see *De fructibus* c.8
(PL 176.1001); JOHN CASSIAN, *De coenobiorum institutis* 5.1 (PL 49.203; CorpusScrEccLat 17.81).

12 Cf. *De fructibus, loc. cit.*; ALAN, *De virtutibus* 2.1 (*Psych. et morale* VI 72).

13 Peter Cantor makes similar distinctions in his *Summa de sacr.* fols. 112[rb-va], 115[vb], 148[va];
cf. FIRTH, *Thesis* II 407* n. 69 (III 678*-679*).

205   Ita de consilio meo facies si dominum rei invenire poteris; alioquin
ipsi furi redderem equum. Similiter eidem furi redderem equum si 15
constaret mihi quod fur equum vero domino reddere vellet. Forte aliquis
non incompetenter dicet quod, quidquid sit de voluntate furis, non in-
vento vero domino equi equus pauperibus distribuendus sit. Et dico: si
hoc fiat, admonendus est fur et de peccato poeniteat, sed ad solutionem
non tenetur. Dominus etiam rei admonendus est, si inventus fuerit, ut 20
ratam habeat equi distributionem.

   Quod hic dixi de furto aliquando dixi de usuris. Ecce aliquis a judaeo
per usuram habuit decem libras; quaesivit in confessione cui redderet
illas decem libras. Dixi quod praesente judaeo distribueret eas pauperibus,
quia judaeus eas per usuram rapuerat. Hoc ideo dixi ut constaret judaeo 25
quod reddendae essent usurae et quod ei non essent reddendae quia eas
rapuerat. Si autem scivissem aliquam personam quam judaeus per usuram damnificasset, ei fecissem restitui.[14]

De rapina

206   Rapinam fecisti vel fraudem, vel in ludo vel male computando vel 30
falsis deciis vel vendendo vel emendo ? Quia si vendidisti aliquam rem,
omne vitium latens propalare debuisti; alioquin de dolo satisfacias.

De incendiis

   Incendium fecisti ? Segetes vel vineas vel virgulta exstirpasti vel suc-
cidisti ?
                                                                                    35

207   Umquam fuisti judex corruptus vel testis, advocatus vel assessor vel
arbiter ? Umquam accusasti aliquem unde malum ei proveniret, vel consilium dedisti ? Umquam sustinuisti quod aliquis damnificaretur ? Umquam habuisti aliquid a judaeo vel fure vel praedone vel raptore vel
foeneratore vel simoniaco ? Umquam aliquid invenisti vel mutuasti quod 40
non solveres ? Mercedem alicujus retinuisti ? Numquid per calumniam

---

15 Similiter — equum *om.* CcJTc *insert.* Aa (*homoeotel.*).   16 equum *om.* RTc iterum
equum J.   vero] ut Cc non Tc *lacuna vel rasura* J.   18 sit] est AcOTc(BmCpEFGMN-
SoTbY).   20 fuerit] sit Tc.   inventus fuerit] inveniatur R.   26 quod[1] *om.* Cc.
et *om.* Ci.   quia] qui Cc.   36 testis *add.* vel CkHJPRTaU.   vel[2] *om.* AcTc.
vel assessor *om.* H.   assessor] accessor O.   40 aliquid *om.* AaO.   invenisti]
habuisti P *corr. ab* advenisti Aa.   mutuasti *add.* vel invenisti P.   41 restituisti Ac *cor-*
rupt. Ta.

---

[14] Cf. Courson, *Summa* 10.18 (fol. 51[ra-b]); cf. Firth, *Thesis* II 410* n. 74 (III 680*-681*).

vel extractionem aliquem damnificasti? Numquid ad aliquod istorum
consilium vel auxilium vel aliquod adminiculum praestitisti?

Si fuisti judex corruptus vel testis vel advocatus vel assessor vel arbiter,
et per te damnificatus est aliquis, satisfacere ei teneris de damno et de 45
expensis et de vexatione. Si aliquid habuisti a judaeo vel fure vel praedone vel raptore vel foeneratore vel simoniaco, redde. Immo plus dico:
si aliquid habuisti ex empto vel dono a judaeo vel alio foeneratore vel
aliis similibus quos superius enumeravi, non potes illud retinere; de illi-
cite acquisitis dico.[15]   50

208 Numquid ab amasiis tuis aliquid habuisti?
POENITENS. Multa.
SACERDOS. Si aliquid habuisti ab aliqua persona quae proprium non
habuit, ut a moniali vel conjugata quae nihil habuit nisi de illis quae com-
munia erant sibi et viro suo, reddendum est. Si aliquid habuisti ab aliqua 55
persona quae habuit proprium, illud tuum est; et secundum quosdam
purgato vitio, id est inchoata poenitentia vel peracta, potes illud retinere.[16]
Mihi non placet quod aliquid retineas pro carnali commercio; nec aliquid reddes mulieri a qua habuisti, sed ut ipsa puniatur dabis pauperibus.[17]   60

209 Numquid aliquid acquisivisti in expeditionibus?
POENITENS. Multa.
SACERDOS. Si bellum fuit justum ex parte tua, de auctoritate illius
qui erat auctor belli potes illud retinere, nisi aliquid habuisti a miserabili

---

42 vel *om.* Ta *add.* per JU.   exactionem PTaTc subtractionem CkH *corr. ad* subtractionem Aa exsecrationem Ci.   43 fecisti vel praestitisti Ck praebuisti Ta.   44 fueris
O.   45 de[2] *om.* Aa J.   46 de *om.* HR.   48 dono] dato Ck a dono J *add.* vel AdJ.
vel alio *om.* H.   alio] a Cc *om.* Tc.   49 non *om.* Ab.   illud] id Ta *om.* P.
49-50 illicitis Cc.   54 conjugatis H a conjugatis AaJ.   habuit[2]] habent Aa habuerunt
H *om.* J.   55 erant] sunt JTc.   est] erit AaJ *add.* ei Cc.   ab] de AaHJU.
ab aliqua] a Ta.   58 quod] ut CkR.   59 reddas AaCkHJOUZ(BmCpEFGIMSgSo-
TbXY) reddat *corr. ad* reddas R.   habuisti] recepisti PTa.   dabit Ta.   61 ac-
quisisti CkPTaU.   63 bellum *add.* tuum O.   64 retinere] recipere Cc.

---

15 Cf. COURSON *loc. cit.*; IDEM, *Summa* 11.7 (fol. 53[rb]).
16 Cf. HUG. ad C.14 q.5 pr. (fol. 219[ra]); *Glossa ordinaria in Decr.* ad C.14 q.5 pr.
17 Cf. CANTOR, *Verbum abbreviatum* c. 46 (PL 205.144). Cantor uses language similar to that
of Flamborough and decides that the money should be given to pious causes. Cf. also COUR-
SON, *Summa* 1.43 (ed. KENNEDY pp. 323-324).

vel religiosa persona; illis credo quod reddendum sit.[18]   65

Si aliquid habuisti per extorsionem, ut per talliam injustam, redde.[19]

210 POENITENS. Ita convenit inter me et extraneum aliquem, quando
terram meam intravit, ut quandocumque et quantamcumque vellem ab
eo talliam extorquerem.

SACERDOS. Iniqua est conditio, nec est observanda.   70

POENITENS. Quomodo ergo faciendae sunt talliae?

SACERDOS. Non video nisi hoc modo: scilicet ut taxentur et in quantitate et in tempore, ut dicas illi: "Frater, tu vis terram a me accipere vel
hospes meus esse;[20] quocumque anno" (vel "biennio"; ita determina
tempus ad libitum tuum) "habueris valens centum libras; dabis mihi in 75
illo anno" (vel "biennio," vel secundum quod aliter determinatum est)
"quadraginta solidos" (vel plus vel minus secundum quod determinatum
fuerit). Aliter, ut credo, tallia tua rapina erit et ad restitutionem teneberis. Hoc dico de liberis.[21]

---

65 vel *add.* a AaTc.   sit] est Ci.   67 extraneum aliquem] aliquem alium extraneum
R.   aliquem] quendam CkU quendam vel aliquem Ad.   68 in terram J.   meam
om. JR.   quandoque Ta *corrupt.* R.   et] vel OP.   quantumcumque PR.
et quantamcumque *om.* Ta.   70 est[1] *om.* AbOTaTc.   nec] non OTaTc.   73 tu
om. O.   tu vis *corr. ab* tuus Ab.   terram *add.* illam AaJU *add.* meam Ta.   recipere
ORTc excipere CkJ.   vel *om.* J.   73-77 vel hospes — solidos] anno vel biennio. In
illo tempore dabit mihi triginta solidos Ta.   75 vel cum habueris R habuisti J.   valentes
Aa *om.* CcU.   habueris valens] valet H.   76 est] fuerit AbAdCkO.   78 fuerit]
est CkH.   79-82 Hoc — sustentare *om.* Ta *insert.* AbO; *vide infra in Append. C no. 8.*

---

[18] Cf. HUG. ad C.23 q.1 c.5 *sed propter praedam* (fol. 267rb).

[19] The word *tallia* has been used for various kinds of mediaeval tax. See W. M. NEWMAN,
Le domaine royal sous les premiers Capétiens (Paris 1937) pp. 22-24; C. STEPHENSON, "The Origin
and Nature of the Taille", *Revue Belge de philologie et d'histoire* 5 (1926) 801-870; IDEM, *Mediaeval
History* (New York 1935) pp. 270-271; Marc BLOCH, *La société féodale: La formation des liens de
dépendance* pp. 386, 427.

[20] The word *hospes* properly signifies a type of mediaeval tenant who held his land on better
terms than a serf, but did not enjoy all the privileges of a free man. Originally he came from
outside the estate and often obtained his land on favourable terms upon payment of a fixed
rent because he undertook to clear hitherto uncultivated soil. In the latter part of the Middle
Ages the word was sometimes used more loosely for any tenant who cultivated land. See A.
LUCHAIRE, *Les premiers Capétiens* (E. LAVISSE, Histoire de France 2[2]) pp. 23-24; J. W. THOMPSON,
An Economic and Social History of the Middle Ages pp. 758-759.

[21] Several theologians condemn the exaction from feudal or manorial subjects of anything
beyond the just dues established by ancient contract or custom. This applied only to free subjects; for serfs had no property of their own. Cf. CANTOR, *Summa de sacr.* fols. 102[vb]-104[va]; COUR-
SON, *Summa* 1.37 (ed. KENNEDY pp. 314-315); 15.4-6 (fols. 64[rb]-65[rb]). In *Apparatus: Ecce vicit
Leo* ad C.1 q.1 c.124 *ex usu* (fol. 36[vb]) there is mention of an opinion much like that here expressed by Flamborough.

De servis autem nec consulo quod facias tallias, nec dico quod mortaliter 80
pecces si feceris; sed si per te ad extremam redacti fuerint necessitatem,
teneberis eos sustentare.²²

211 Sunt fortasse et alii modi aliquem damnificandi; quis enim omnes
dinumerare poterit ? Igitur quocumque modo aliquem damnificasti, vel
facto vel consilio vel auxilio, redde damnificato, vel heredibus ejus si eum 85
non inveneris; vel si nec illum nec illos, da pauperibus, vel ecclesiae suae
si fuerit persona ecclesiastica.²³ Si non audes per teipsum restituere, per
fidelem aliquam personam restitue, ita quod nihil sciatur de te, ne forte
aliquid mali tibi contingat.²⁴ Si non potes in integrum restituere, saltem
aliquid restitue, ut pro illo totum tibi remittatur; sed hic debes omnem 90
fraudem et dolum vitare, sicuti velles tibi fieri. Si plus non potes, veniam
pete vel per te vel per fidelem aliquam mediam personam, ita quod nihil
de te sciatur. Si nullum istorum potes, a Domino Deo veniam pete, et de
cetero cave tibi ab omni tali peccato, et firmum habeas propositum omnia
reddendi quando poteris.   95

212 POENITENS. Scivi quod sex homines equum unum furati sunt, quod
ego impedire potui et non feci. Cum aliis sex equum unum furatus sum.
Quid faciam ?
    SACERDOS. Inducas tam istos sex quam illos sex ut quilibet portionem 99

---

80 nec¹] non CcHTcU.   81 fuerint] sunt CcJ.   85 ejus] suis CcU.   86 non
inveneris] invenire non poteris AaCkHJU.   87 (si¹ *om.* Sg).   fuit AcCcCiO(CpNV)
forte fuit Ck sit AaP(KSg) *om.* J.   88 aliquem Ci aliam Cc.   aliquam personam]
aliquem AaJU.   ita *om.* Cc.   89 mali] inde JU.   continguat O.   in *om.*
CcCkHPRTc.   90 tibi *om.* OR.   dimittatur AaJU.   91 et omnem dolum O.
92 vel¹ *om.* AdR.   mediam] mediantem Cc.   92-93 vel per te — pete *om.* PTa
(*homoeotel.*).   93 Deo] tuo O.   96 POENITENS *om.* Ta *corr. ab* SACERDOS Ad.   96-
97 quod — sum *om.* R (*homoeotel.*).   97 equum *om.* Cc.   99 istos] illos AaJPU.
sex¹ *om.* O.   illos] istos P alios Ck.   sex² *om.* P.   quilibet] quicumque R *corr. ab*
quibus J.   portionem] partem JU.

---

²² Cf. COURSON, *Summa* 15.4-6 (fols. 64ʳᵇ-65ᵛᵇ); Marc BLOCH, "The Rise of Dependent Cultivation and Seignorial Institutions", *The Cambridge Economic History of Europe* I 240-243; Hans
NABHOLZ, "Medieval Agrarian Society in Transition", *The Cambridge Economic History* I 496-
497.
²³ Cf. GRATIAN C.14 q.5 c.4; HUG. ad C.14 q.5 c.6 (fol. 219ʳᵇ-ᵛᵃ); ALAN OF LILLE, *Liber
poenitentialis* 2.10 (ed. LONGÈRE II 52-53; cf. *Archives HDLMA* 32.201-202; PL 210.292); COUR-
SON, *Summa* 11.14 (fol. 55ʳᵃ-ᵇ; ed. LEFÈVRE, *Le traité "De Usura" de Robert de Courson* [Lille 1902]
pp. 45-47).
²⁴ Cf. COURSON, *Summa* 1.42 (ed. KENNEDY pp. 320-321).

suam restituat; et tu pro portione tua, id est pro septima parte pretii utriusque equi, absolutus eris. Alioquin utrimque ad integram teneberis restitutionem.[25]

<De decimis>

213 Decimas bene solvisti ?   5
   POENITENS. De quibus debeo decimas ?
   SACERDOS. De omnibus quae terra gignit: de terris, vineis, hortis, pra-
tis, furnis, molendinis, de omni venatione (id est feris, avibus, piscibus),
de omni peculio (gallinis, anseribus, caseis, butyro, melle), et si quis
alius excogitari potest fructus, ut etiam pluma anserum. Dicunt etiam 10
viri periti et boni quod foenerator et meretrix lucra sua decimare debent.[26]
Omnia igitur decimare debes, id est de omnibus decimam partem dare.[27]
Unde graviter offendunt qui decimam garbam dant messoribus, undeci-
mam decimae, et nonam ad campi partem.[28] Similiter offendunt qui de

---

1 suam *om.* AaJU.   tua *om.* CcR.   septima] sexta JR.   pretii *corr. ab* pretium O *om.* R.
2 utrimque] utriusque J de utroque Ta.   integram *add.* equi Ad.   4 *tit. sic* Z *insert.*
AcP *om.* AdCcCi *et al.*   7 terris *add.* frugibus Tc *add.* de J.   8 id est] scilicet de Ck *om.*
Ta.   10 aliud R *om.* P.   etiam] in H *om.* Ta.   11 viri] juris AaAbJTcU.
et boni *om.* O.   viri — boni] juris periti et viri boni H.   debet Ac.   12 igitur]
etiam O.   decimare] determinare Cc.   13 garbarum Cc gerbam HTcZ *corr. ab* partem
Ad.   messoribus *add.* suis AaJU.

---

[25] Regarding the necessity of one participant in the theft making restitution for the whole
see COURSON, *Summa* 1.31 (ed. KENNEDY p. 311); cf. GRATIAN C.23 q.8 c.32 (quoted below in
sect. 315). Peter Cantor considers that one would be obliged to restitution if one had been neg-
ligent in preventing loss to another as well as for positive acts of thefts or damage. However
he is not so certain of this as to insist upon it in practice; see his *Summa de sacr.* 2.3.128-129 (ed.
DUGAUQUIER II 261-278).
   [26] Cf. HUG. ad C.16 q.1 c.66 (fols. 232vb-233ra); ad C.16 q.7 c.4 (fol. 240ra); *Glossa ordinaria
in Decr.* ad C.16 q.1 c.66 *negotio*; COURSON, *Summa* quoted by K. WEINZIERL, *Die Restitutionslehre
der Frühscholastik* pp. 149-150.
   [27] Cf. *locc. citt.*; GRATIAN C.16 q.7 cc.4-6 (c.5, based on *Lev* 27.30-33, is quoted below in Book
5 sect. 317); 1 *Compil.* 3.26.2 (JL 13821; X 3.30.5); 1 *Compil.* 3.26.3 (JL 14157; X 3.30.6);
LE BRAS, *Institutions ecclésiastiques* pp. 255-258; VIARD, *Histoire de la dîme ecclésiastique dans le royaume de France aux XIIe et XIIIe siècles* pp. 5-21.
   [28] See COURSON, *Summa* 14.14 (fol. 62vb; partly quoted in FIRTH, *Thesis* II 409*-410*). Canonists and theologians of the time condemn two practices, first the practice of paying the eleventh
part rather than the tenth, and secondly the practice of paying the reapers before deducting
the tithe. Flamborough here combines these two practices under one condemnation, when
he says: « Hence they offend gravely who give the tenth sheaf to the reapers, the eleventh for
the tithe and the ninth for rent.» Cf. HUG. ad C.16 q.1 c.66 *et novem* (fol. 233ra); *Apparatus:*

vino non dant decimam partem.²⁹   15

POENITENS. Ex quo talis est loci consuetudo et sacerdotes tacent, videntur tacendo consentire et remittere illa quae non bene decimantur.

SACERDOS. Credo quod consuetudo illa, immo potius abusio, non excusat; et sacerdos non potest decimas remittere quin solvantur, sed solutas potest cui voluerit dare; sic enim habetur in decretali quadam.³⁰   20

POENITENS. Rusticus debet mihi decimas et decem libras; ego possum ei remittere decem libras, quare non decimas?

SACERDOS. Quia Deus dicit: Decimas dabis omnium quae possides; ergo quod istud non fiat nemo potest facere.³¹ Item dico quod laici tenentes decimas debent decimas decimare.³²   25

---

16 est *om.* Cc.   loci *insert.* Ad.   17 decimantur] determinantur Cc.   19 sacerdotes non possunt P.   20 potest cui voluerit] poterunt si voluerint P potest culibet RTc. voluerit] vult OTa.   dare] donare O.   23 omnia *corr. ad* omnibus O.   24 Item] Idem JPZ.   24-25 retinentes O.   25 decimare] dare J dare vel decimare Aa.   debent decimas decimare] decimas de decimis debent dare U.

Ecce vicit Leo ad C.16 q.1 c.66 *de novem partibus* (fol. 72ᵛᵃ); ad C.16 q.7 c.4 *nec minus* (fol. 75ʳᵇ); 1 *Compil.* 3.26.4 (JL 13928; X 3.30.7); VIARD, *Histoire de la dîme ecclés. dans le r. de France aux XIIᵉ et XIIIᵉ siècles* pp. 28-30. *Campi pars*, in French *champart*, is a kind of mediaeval rent paid as a certain portion of the crop; see DU CANGE s.v. *campipars*; Augustin FLICHE, *L'Europe occidental de* 888 *à* 1125 (G. GLOTZ, Histoire du Moyen-âge 2; Paris 1941) p. 171.

²⁹ Most of the texts quoted in the two preceding notes insist on the all-inclusive nature of the tithe; regarding their practical application (including tithing of wine) see VIARD, *op. cit.* pp. 29-30.

³⁰ Possibly this has some connection with Po. 3812 (Reg. 12.112 PL 216.146; issued Nov. 2, 1209); cf. FIRTH, *Thesis* II 399*-400*. Cf. also HUG. ad C.10 q.1 cc.13-14 (fol. 180ʳᵇ⁻ᵛᵃ); below sect. 215.

³¹ See *Lev* 27.30-33 (quoted below sect. 317); *Deut* 14.22-23; cf. *Luc* 18.12. It is taught by some theologians of this time that tithes are due by divine law, and hence cannot be dispensed, as was said above concerning vows (see sect. 25) and close consanguinity (see sect. 38). Robert Courson writes of tithes: *nec angelus de caelo posset hoc immutare* (*Summa* 14.13 [fol. 62ᵛᵇ]); cf. *Gal* 1.8; cf. fuller quotation in FIRTH, *Thesis* II 409*-410*. Cf. STEPHEN LANGTON, quoted by HÖDL, *Die Geschichte der Schlüsselgewalt* (Beiträge 38.4) pp. 344-345. Some decretals of this period seem to imply that God has commanded all Christians to pay tithes, e.g. Po. 898 (X 3.30.26; issued Dec. 11, 1199); Po. 3459 (Reg. 11.116 PL 215.1434; issued July 14, 1208). Other decretals might be taken to imply that this is a matter of church law, e.g. Po. 889 (X 3.30.24; issued Dec. 2, 1199); Po. 2708 (X 3.30.27; issued March 10, 1206).

³² Regarding possession of tithes by laymen in the Middle Ages see P. THOMAS, *Le droit de propriété* pp. 25-27, 82-88; Paul VIARD, *Histoire de la dîme ecclésiastique principalement en France jusqu'au décret de Gratien* pp. 129-139, 205-222; above sect. 127 with note.

214 POENITENS. Si ita examinatim dandae sunt decimae, quis salvabitur, quia de tot milibus quis bene decimat ? Et laici tenentes decimas, numquid omnes damnabuntur ?

SACERDOS. De consilio meo numquam laicus tenens decimas, quamdiu tenet eas, accedet ad corpus Christi, nec aliquis nisi dicto modo deci- 30 maverit.[33]

POENITENS. Numquid faber, sutor et alii officiales opera sua decimabunt ?

SACERDOS. Credo quod debent.[34]

POENITENS. Videtur quod ecclesia erret; quia multi laici decimas tenent ab ecclesiis et hominium[35] pro illis faciunt ecclesiis et contra alios ab ec- 35 clesiis defenduntur; et ita videtur quod ecclesiae vel laicos in errore suo foveant vel eis auctoritatem dent decimas retinendi. Quid ergo eis imputatur ?

SACERDOS. Ecclesiae accipiunt de decimis quod possunt. Ex quo non possunt ipsas decimas retinere, habent dominium[36] ut facilius possint de- 40 cimas recuperare; et laicos defendunt, non ut eos in errore foveant, sed ne decimae ad alios dispergantur et non possint ab ecclesiis recuperari.

215 POENITENS. Potest laicus vendere decimas quas tenet ? Videtur enim quod simonia sit ex quo decimae spirituales sunt.

SACERDOS. Duplex est jus possidendi decimas: unum temporale, quod 45 habent laici et possunt vendere sine simonia, aliud spirituale, quod habent clerici et non possunt vendere sine simonia, nec potest a laicis haberi. Verbi gratia, sacerdos potest dare decimas suas laico ad duos annos vel

---

26 examinate Ck *corr. ab* examinate Aa *corrupt* CcTc.   30 accedat CkJTcU accederet Ta.
32 faber *add. et* HOTc.   34 errat CcJ.   35 et hominium — ecclesiis *om.* Ck (*homoeotel.*).
hominum CcCiJTcU(K) *corr. ab* hominum AcO(G homagium MNSoTbX humagium V).
hominium... faciunt] homines... sunt Z.   alios] illos Cc.   35-36 ecclesiis — ecclesiis]
et ab ecclesia Ta.   36 ecclesia CcCkTa.   37 foveat CkTa *corr. ab* fovent Ac.   det
Ta dant OR.   40 ipsas *om.* CiTc.   dominum AaAbCcTc(GM) *corr. ab* dominum J
corr. ab dominum *forte manu originali* O hominium P (hominum K *corr. ab* hominium *forte manu
originali* X).   possunt Ck *corr. ab* possunt AbAc.   42 possunt CkJO *corr. ab* possunt
Ab.   ecclesia Ta aliis R.   43 tenetur Ci possidet Ta.   47 laico Tc laici Ac.
48 vel *add.* ad U *add.* a J.   48-49 vel tres *om.* Ta.

---

[33] Cf. HUG. ad C.14 q.6 c.1 *Si res* (fol. 220rb-va).

[34] Cf. HUG. ad C.16 q.1 c.66 (fol. 232vb).

[35] Feudal homage; see DU CANGE s.v. *hominium*; François L. GANSHOF, *Qu'est-ce que la féodalité* (Brussels-Neuchâtel 1947) pp. 91-94. Regarding tithes held in fief see VIARD, *Histoire de la dîme ecclésiastique dans le Royaume de France aux XIIe et XIIIe siècles* pp. 144-165; THOMASSIN-ANDRÉ, *Ancienne et nouvelle discipline* VI 54-70.

[36] Feudal overlordship, signified by feudal homage.

tres; ecce laicus jam habet jus in decimas illas, sed temporale, et potest
illud vendere; hoc modo habent laici decimas.[37]   50

POENITENS. Nonne hoc licitum est ? Quare ergo damnas tu laicos pro
decimis ?

SACERDOS. Quia ipsi eas sibi usurpant; et cum eis non fuerint datae
nisi ad tempus et in necessitate, scilicet ut in periculo ecclesiae ingruente
ecclesias defenderent (cum tamen gratis debent eas defendere), ipsi non 55
instante necessitate et in perpetuum eas retinere volunt; ex quo patet quod
violenter eas tenent et mortaliter peccant.

De usura

216   Usuras exercuisti vel ad exspectationem vendidisti et emisti ?[38]

POENITENS. Quod scio dicam. Modium tritici valentem marcam cui- 60
dam praestiti; quando recepi, valuit duas.

SACERDOS. Non est usura. Nonne licuit tibi ad libitum tuum repetere ?
Quando ergo repetisti, licuit tibi eandem rem in genere quam praestitisti recipere, vel aliam quae eam tunc valuit.[39]

POENITENS. Domum quandam exposuit mihi quidam pro decem libris 65
hac conditione ut, si infra certum terminum non redimeretur, mea esset.

SACERDOS. Usura est, quia conditio illa lucrosa tibi fuit.[40]

---

51 ergo *om.* O.   54 scilicet ut] vel O.   in *om.* AaTaTc.   55 (cum — defendere) *om.* U.   debeant JTaTc(BmEGISoTb) deberent AbHP(FKVX debebant Cp).
debent eas] eas debent tot O.   non *om.* Ta. autem non Tc.   57 violenter eas tenent
et] quia volunt eas violenter tenere O.   59 et] vel AaCkHJRTcU.   et emisti *om.* P.
60 Quod] Quid AaJ.   63 recepisti CkHO(E) repitisti AdCc(K) repetiisti U (petisti
BmSo recepisti W *corr. ab* recepisti Q¹).   rem *om.* OTa.   64 aliam quae eam] aliud
tantum valens quantum R.   quae] quod O *corr. ab* quod Ab.   quae eam] quantum
Ta.   66 si infra *om.* J scilicet *add.* infra *insert.* Aa.   non redimeretur *om.* AaJ.
67 lucrosum J *corr. ab* lucrosum Aa.   tibi] tantum O *om.* Ck.

---

[37] Cf. JL 14193 (1 *Compil.* 3.11.1). This is an application of the distinction made by many
writers between the right of receiving the tithe, the *jus decimarum*, which belongs to the clergy
by divine right and cannot be alienated, and the fruits of the tithe, the grain or wine, etc., which
may be given to laymen. See HUG. ad C.16 q.7 pr. (fol. 239ᵛᵇ); *Glossa ordinaria in Decr.* ad C.1
q.3 c.13 *laicalibus; Summa parisiensi* ad C.1 q.1 pr. (p. 79); COURSON, *Summa* 2.14 (ed. KENNEDY
p. 335).

[38] Cf. CANTOR, *Verbum abbreviatum* c.50 (PL 205.157); COURSON, Summa 12.2. (fol. 56ʳᵃ; ed.
LEFÈVRE pp. 57-61); 1 *Compil.* 5.15.8 (JL 13965; X 5.19.6); 1 *Compil.* 5.15.12 (JL 15726; X
5.19.10); Terence P. MCLAUGHLIN, "The Teaching of the Canonists on Usury", *MedStud* 1
(1939) 117-120.

[39] Cf. HUG. ad C.14 q.4 cc.5-6 (fol. 218ʳᵇ⁻ᵛᵃ).

[40] To contract for the exaction of a penalty, should a loan not be paid at the proper time,

217 Poenitens. In nundinis mercatorum consuetudo est ut sibi ad invicem credant debita sua usque ad generalem solutionem, quae est in fine nundinarum et gallice dicitur *paement*.[41] Pro viginti libris parisiensium 70 non potui habere de manu ad manum nisi viginti tres libras andegavensium; accepi ergo viginti sex ad generalem solutionem.

Sacerdos. Ut mihi videtur, non est usura, quia non emitur exspectatio temporis; si enim creditor tuus accessisset, statim ei satisfecisset debitor tuus. Sed emitur contractus cum aliis personis, ac si diceret debitor tuus: 75 "Non potes habere pro viginti libris parisiensium de manu ad manum nisi viginti tres libras andegavensium; dabo tibi viginti sex si permiseris me satisfacere pro te aliis creditoribus tuis." Ecce hic non exspectatur aliquis certus dies, sed quandocumque aliquis creditor tuus repetet aliquid a te, satisfaciet ei ille qui argentum tuum emit; et ideo non est hic exspectatio 80 nec usura. Alioquin esset ibi exspectatio et usura.

218 Cum essem Parisius, pro marca argenti non potui habere de manu ad manum nisi quadraginta solidos parisiensium, sed dedi pro quadraginta quinque solidis ut unaquaque septimana tantum quinque solidos reciperem ad expensam meam.[42]   85

Sacerdos. Usura fuit.

---

68 ad] ab Ad.   69 ad *om.* Ac.   70 et *om.* O.   (et — paement *om.* ISg).   paiement JOTaU(CpGTbV) paiment Cc(BmEX) *corr. ab* pement AdTc pagiement P(K peagiment M paiement W paiment Q¹). *Auctor scripsit* paiement *in Formis 1 et 2, quod tamen videtur mutasse in* paement *in Forma 3.*   Pro] et pro OTa.   71 tres] duo AaJ *om.* Ck sex *corr. ad* quatuor O.   71-72 andegaviensium AbP.   non potui — andegavensium *om.* Tc (*homoeotel.*). 72 solutionem *add.* quae est in fine nundinarum AaJU.   74 statim *om.* Aa.   ei *om.* U.   debitor *corr. ab* creditor J.   76 potes *insert.* O potest AbZ.   77 tres] quatuor AaJ.   libris Tc *om.* J.   andegaviensium P *add.* de manu ad manum Aa.   78 pro te *om.* RTa.   te *om.* Aa.   79 quandoque Tc quantumcumque J *corr. ab* quantumcumque O.   80 satisfaceret OTa *corr. ab* satisfaceret Ab.   ille *om.* AbORTa. emit] habet J *corr. ab* habet Aa.   hic *om.* O.   82 Cum *praem.* Poenitens HPTcZ. 84 solidis *om.* AbJTa *add.* parisiensium P.   unaquaque] quaeque Ab quaque RTa quaqua O.   tantum *om.* AaJ.

---

is usually held to be licit by mediaeval canonists unless it is a fraudulent cloak for usury; see McLaughlin, *MedStud* 1.140-143. Robert Courson maintains that such a penalty must enrich not the lender but the poor; see Courson, *Summa* 12.5 (fol. 56ᵛᵇ; ed. Lefèvre pp. 65-67).

[41] Cf. O. Verlinden, "Markets and Fairs", *The Cambridge Economic History of Europe* III 119-153, esp. 136-137 ; F. Bourquelot, *Études sur les foires de Champagne* 2ᵉ partie, p. 103. It is probably not the fairs of Champagne which Flamborough has principally in mind. He mentions pounds of Antwerp in his example. Bourquelot treats of the money in use at the fairs of Champagne, but without mention of Antwerp currency.

[42] Another example of usurious contract under cover of currency exchange is presented by Courson, *Summa* 12.5 (fol. 56ᵛᵃ⁻ᵇ; ed. Lefèvre p. 65).

219 Patrimonium habuisti?

POENITENS. Habui et decimas et vadia, quae reliquit mihi pater meus jure hereditario.

SACERDOS. Omnia quae ultra sortem et expensas percepta sunt a te vel 90 a patre tuo de vadiis, solvere teneris.[43] Quid tibi agendum sit de decimis quas praeter consensum episcopi tenuisti superius dictum est in tractatu de simonia.[44]

POENITENS. Agros etiam et possessiones alias reliquit mihi pater, quas omnes usura emerat; et adhuc eas detinet frater meus. Quid ei agendum 95 est?

SACERDOS. Si vult eas retinere, solvat earum pretium illis a quibus receptae [sunt] usurae [si] sciuntur; si non, [dentur] pauperibus; vel dentur possessiones illae alicui domui religiosae ut ipsa annuatim aliquid 99 solvat quousque persolutae sint usurae quae illas possessiones contingunt.

Tu etiam ad illorum forte solutionem teneris de quibus vixisti in domo patris tui, maxime postquam adultus fuisti. Hoc dico si nil habuit nisi de usurus. Si quaedam bene habuit, quaedam male, tutius tibi fuisset recessisse ab eo; vel si tu non habuisti aliunde vivere, accepisses ab eo se- 5 cundum proportionem bene habitorum, et de bene habitis portionem

88 Habui] licet una Aa *om.* J. et vadia *corr. ab* et vadimonia H vadiavi et Tc.
90 recepta O accepta Ck. 90-91 percepta — tuo] recepisti vel pater tuus U. 91 vadis R vadio O. tibi] ergo Ck *add.* igitur JU. 94 etiam *om.* CcO *add.* ipsos Tc.
etiam et *invers.* R. alias *om.* J *insert.* Aa. pater *add.* meus CcCkPTa. 95 omnes *add.* de R *add.* de *insert.* O. meus *add.* et O. 97 earum *insert.* Ad eorum Tc.
98 sunt AaAbOPRTa(BmEGIKMSgVX *et* Q^{1}W) *om. cett.(cett.).* si^1 OPRTa(BmIKMVX *et* Q^{1}W) *om. cett.(cett.).* si sciuntur *insert.* Aa (*om.* GSg). sciuntur] fuerint J inveniuntur Ta (sciantur V sequuntur So). (sciuntur si non] si non inveniuntur E).
dentur O(W *post* pauperibus BmIKMSoTb dantur *corr. ad* dentur *post* pauperibus V) detur *post* pauperibus P a Ck *om. cett.(cett.).* 98-99 vel dentur possessiones illae *om.* O.
99 illae *om.* Aa *add.* scilicet H *add.* vel Tc. 1 sint] sunt O. 2 illarum R aliorum Cc.
3 nihil AdJRTa. habuisti O. 4 usuris] vadiis Cc. 5 tu *om.* AdR. habuisses AaU. 6 proportionem] portionem HRTcU. secundum proportionem] pro portione Aa.

[43] Cf. MCLAUGHLIN, *MedStud* 1.113-115; HUG. ad C.14 q.3 c.3 *accedit* (fols. 217vb-218ra); COURSON, *Summa* 12.4 (fol. 56va; ed. LEFÈVRE p. 63); 12.12 (fol. 58rb; p. 83); 1 *Compil.* 5. 15.6 (JL 14155); 1 *Compil.* 5.15.7 (JL 13998); 1 *Compil.* 5.15.1 (Council of Tours c.2 HEFELE-LECLERCQ 5^2.971; X 5.19.1); 1 *Compil.* 5.15.4 (JL 13819; X 5.19.2); 1 *Compil.* 5.15.10 (JL 13979; X 5.19.8). Regarding the obligation of one's heirs to restitution see texts cited below in n. 45.

[44] See sect. 127; cf. sects. 214-215.

[45] Cf. 1 *Compil.* 5.15.5 (JL 14093; X 5.19.5); 1 *Compil.* 5.15.11 (JL 14065; X 5.19.9); BERNARD OF PAVIA, *Summa decretalium* 5.15.10 (p. 238).

tibi assignasset; vel ad minus quanto parcius potuisses ab eo accepisses, et
hoc etiam de licentia episcopi tui, in cujus dispensatione debent illa esse
quae foenerator pauperibus distribuenda relinquit.[46]

220 Hic potest quaeri de bobus et ovibus et aliis jumentis, quae vulgus 10
dicit "ferrea" vel "immortalia," quae dantur vel ad censum vel ad medietatem, et de aliis medietariis.[47]

    Scis tu plus de usura vel de avaritia?

    Poenitens. Non memini.

    Sacerdos. De omnibus dictis et similibus petis veniam et cavebis de 15
cetero?

    Poenitens. Peto, domine, et per gratiam Dei cavebo de cetero.

    Sacerdos. Vide ergo quod de cetero sis benignus, liberalis, misericors,
pius, compatiens, aliis indulgens, aliis mansuetus et affectuosus erga alios.

---

9 distribuendo Cc.   reliquit AaAbCkRZ.   11 ferrea] ferea Cc(Bm) fera Ci ferae
Ac(EIMSo) corr. ab ferae Tc ferrea corr. ad ferritis [?] corr. ad ferrea Aa firma Ck firmam
R.   vel[1]] et JU.   mortalia Cc in mortalia R(BmFSo) in mortalia corr. ad in mortaria
corr. ad immortalia Aa.   dantur add. ad illis delet. Aa.   vel[2] om. CkPTaTc.   12 et]
vel AaHPU.   13 tu] in Cc om. OU.   de[2] om. AcCkTc.   16 ceteris AaJ.
19 patiens HU.   20 tit. om. Ci.   GULOSITATE PTaZ.   22 de om. AaCk-
JOPTaTcU(BmCpEGIKSgSoTbXY).   23 suos AaCkJPRTaU(BmCpEFGIKMNSgSo sex
hos X).   14 delicate JRTa.   16 et[1] om. CkHJPR.   16-17 et visum om. Ta insert.
AbO.   17 De] et de OZ.   istis] his OR.   etc. om. CcJTa add. ut supra Ck add.
ut prius Aa.

---

[46] Cf. Courson, Summa 1.39-41 (ed. Kennedy pp. 316-320). Courson insists on the authority of one's own bishop in such matters; see his Summa 11.9 (ed. Lefèvre p. 31) 11.14 (ed. Lefèvre p. 45).

[47] The word medietas, with its derivatives medietaria, mediatarius, and the French métairie, mé-
tayer and métayage, was used in connection with farming on a crop-sharing basis. So a payment
made ad medietatem is one made as a certain fraction of a profit or revenue; see Du Cange
s.vv. 1 medietas, medietaria and medietarius. On the other hand a payment made ad censum is one
computed in value as a fixed amount; see E. Lavisse and A. Rambaud, Histoire générale du IVe
siècle à nos jours II 12-13; Ch.-E. Perrin, Recherches sur la seigneurie rurale en Lorraine pp. 746-747;
Marc Bloch, La société féodale: La formation p. 382. The sentence could then be rendered: "Here
we could ask about the oxen, sheep and other domestic animals which the common people call
ferrea or immortalia, which are rented out either for fixed payments or for fractional payments,
and we could ask about other fractional payments." The adjective immortalis in this context
probably means "fructifying perpetually for its owner", on the analogy of such expressions as
vadium vivum (see Du Cange s.v. vadium). Cf. also Germain Sicard, "L'usure en milieu rural:
notes sur le bail à cheptel dans la doctrine de la fin du Moyen âge", Études d'histoire du droit canonique dédiées à Gabriel Le Bras II 1395-1405, esp. 1398 where bestes de fer are mentioned.

<Cap. vii.> DE GULA   20

221 Es tu gulosus, crapulosus, ut ita dicam, ebriosus, delicatus, id est
de deliciis sollicitus?

Gula habet suas comites: nimis mane comedere, nimis saepe, nimia
quantitate, nimis delicata, nimio apparatu, nimia aviditate; et introducit
multa mala: torporem, somnolentiam, nauseam, vomitum; aufert usum 25
pedum, usum linguae et usum memoriae, et obtundit ingenium et visum.[48] De omnibus istis petis veniam, etc.?

<Cap. viii.> DE LUXURIA

222 Luxuria laborasti? Ad luxuriam pertinent ista: prodigalitas, im-
pudicitia, lascivia, petulantia, titubatio, blanditiae, deliciae, voluptas, 30
dissolutio, imbecillitas, scurrilitas et coitus.[49] Prodigalitas patet; impu-
dicitia similiter. Titubatio est quando homo quod agit non agit confidenter. Blanditiae, quando homo blanditur aliis et ab aliis acceptat
blanditias. Deliciae patent. Voluptas, quando homo sequitur concupis-
centias suas, desideria sua. Dissolutio est in gestu, in dictis, in factis, in 35
habitu. Imbecillitas patet. Scurrilitas est quando homo se habet ut
scurra. De istis omnibus petis veniam, etc.?

SACERDOS. Illa quae de cetero ages, age confidenter (ita disponas tibi
et tuis quod ea quae ages bona confidentia agas) et toleranter (quod scias
et possis tolerare) et stabiliter (quod non sis inconstans) et perseveranter 40
(quod ad debitum finem omne bonum perducas) et mente quieta (quod
non sis turbulentus).

223 Restat coitus, qui stricto vocabulo dicitur luxuria. Umquam luxuria pollutus es?

POENITENS. Nimis.   45

SACERDOS. Umquam contra naturam?

POENITENS. Nimis.

SACERDOS. Umquam cum masculo?

32 similiter *om.* AaJ.   33 Blanditiae *om.* Ci.   34 patet JTaU *corr. ab* quia Aa.   35
suas *om.* O.   36 est *om.* AcTc.   38 dispone AaHJ.   39 ages] agis CcTa agas
Aa.   conscientia U fiducia Tc confidenter Ck.   46-47 SACERDOS — Nimis *om.* PTa
insert. Aa (*forte homoeotel.*).

[48] Cf. St. GREGORY, *Moralia* 31.45.87 (PL 76.621); WARNER, *Gregorianum* 4.10 (PL 193.153).
This paragraph is perhaps related to one or both of these sources through some intermediary.
[49] Cf. *De fructibus* c.10 (PL 176.1002). Here too the author probably depends on some unknown source as well.

Poenitens. Nimis. ⸗

Sacerdos. Cum clericis an cum laicis?   50

Poenitens. Et cum clericis et cum laicis.

Sacerdos. Cum laicis conjugatis an solutis?

Poenitens. Et cum istis et cum illis.

Sacerdos. Cum quot conjugatis?

Poenitens. Nescio.   55

Sacerdos. Ergo nec vices scis?

Poenitens. Ita est.

Sacerdos. Accipiamus ergo quod possumus: Quanto tempore fuisti cum eis?

Poenitens. Per septennium.   60

Sacerdos. In quo ordine?

Poenitens. In sacerdotio per biennium, in diaconatu per biennium, in subdiaconatu per biennium, in acolythatu per annum. Cum aliis solutis peccavi, quorum nescio numerum nec vices.

Sacerdos. Cum clericis peccasti?   65

Poenitens. Peccavi et cum saecularibus et cum religiosis.

Sacerdos. Dic cum quot saecularibus et cum quot religiosis, et cujus ordinis eratis tu et illi quando simul peccastis, et an in dignitate erant, an archidiaconi, an decani, an abbates, an episcopi.

Umquam innocentem aliquem introduxisti in istud peccatum? Dic 70 quot, et cujus ordinis eratis.

224   Postea potest quaeri si umquam plus contra naturam peccavit, si extraordinarie habuit aliquem. Si quaerat quomodo extraordinarie, non respondebo ei; ipse viderit. Numquam ei mentionem de aliquo faciam de quo peccandi occasionem accipere possit, sed tantum de gene- 75 ralibus quae omnes sciunt esse peccata.[50] Mollitiem autem dolose ab eo

---

50 an] aut JTcU.   51 Et[1] om. AdCkRTa.   52 an] aut Tc add. cum CkR.
53-54 Poenitens — conjugatis om. Cc.   56 Ergo om. CkO.   Ergo nec] Numquam J.
nec] non AaP.   nec vices scis] vices nescis Ck.   58 ergo insert. Ac.   63 in subdiaconatu per biennium om. Ta ante in diaconatu ad lineam 62 O.   66 et[1] om. O insert.
Aa.   saecularibus] scholaribus P laicis AaHJU clericis Z.   et cum[2] om. AaHJ.
67 saecularibus] scholaribus P.   Sacerdos — religiosis om. CcCk insert. Ad (homoeotel.).
saecularibus et cum quot om. Ta (homoeotel.).   68 eratis] eras CkTa.   peccasti RTc
peccavisti J.   et[2] om. CiCk.   70 istud] illud AaJPU.   73 aliquam R.   habuit
aliquem om. P.   74 non respondebo ei] ego non respondebo Ta non dicam ei nec respondebo
U.   75-76 de omnibus generalibus JU.   76 ab eo om. Ck.

---

50 Cf. Bart. c.38 (p. 205); Alan of Lille, Liber poenitentialis 1.4 (ed. Longère II 27; cf. ArchivesHDLMA 32.191-192, PL 210.286); Theodulf of Orleans, Capitulare PL 105.219.

extorqueo, et de muliere similiter, sed modus extorquendi scribendus
non est.[51]

Sicuti etiam quaesivi de masculo si contra naturam aliquid egerit, ita
quaero de muliere, immo de omni genere fornicandi. Secundo quaero 80
de adulterio et deinceps de omni genere fornicandi; postea de incestu
hoc modo.

225 Ad consanguineam tuam accessisti? Dic ad quot, et quam propinquae erant tibi. Postea quaero ut supra. Ad duas sibi consanguineas accessisti? Dic ad quot paria, et quam propinquae sibi erant, et postea ut 85
supra.[52] Aliquas habuisti post consanguineos tuos? Dic quam propinqui
tibi erant; et post ut supra.[53]

Ad monialem accessisti vel aliam conversam.[54] Dic cujus religionis
erant; et post ut supra.

Virginem deflorasti? Ad commatrem tuam accessisti? Ad matrinam 90
tuam? Ad filiolam tuam? Ad filiolam patris tui? Ad filiolam patrini
tui? Ad menstruatam? Ad infidelem, scilicet judaeam, gentilem, haere-
ticam? Dic ad quot et quotiens ad quamlibet. In puerperio? Ad non
purificatam? In omnibus istis quaere ut supra.

226 Ad praegnantem accessisti? Hoc quaero, quia multi parvuli tunc 95
debilitantur et claudi efficiuntur et opprimuntur. Si ex concubitu tuo

---

77 extorquebo CkTa.   79 Non sicuti Tc Sicut Ta si Cc.   etiam] et CcR *om.* AaTa.
80-81 Secundo — fornicandi *om.* CcR *insert.* Aa (*homoeotel.*).   81 deinceps *add.* et OUZ.
et deinceps — fornicandi *om.* Ta.   83 Ad¹] Et ad CcCi.   83-85 Dic — accessisti *om.*
O (*homoeotel.*).   84 Postea quaero ut supra *om.* U *insert.* Aa.   sibi] tibi CcCk igitur RZ
om. TaTc.   sibi consanguineas] consanguineas si P.   85 propinqui J propinqua CcZ.
sibi] tibi CcTaTc *om.* Ck *add.* ad invicem P.   86 Aliquos JP.   86-87 Aliquas —
supra *om.* Ck (*homoetel.*).   87 postea CcTcU.   88 vel *add.* ad TcU.   89 postea
CkTc.   90 commatrem *lacuna* com *insert.* O.   tuam *corr. ab* ejus O.   90-91 Ad
matrinam tuam *delet. et postea insert.* Aa.   91 Ad filiolam tuam *om.* CcTa *ante* Ad matrinam
tuam Aa.   patrini] patrui CcJP.   91-92 Ad filiolam patrini tui *om.* R.   92 scili-
cet] sive Cc.   92-93 Ad infidelem — quamlibet *om.* HTa *insert.* AbO *post* purificatam *ad
lineam 94* R; *cf. infra in Append. C no. 15.*

---

[51] Cf. below *De mollitie* sect. 294.

[52] See sect. 223. The mediaeval Church, influenced apparently by 1 *Cor* 6.16, regarded affinity as established by intercourse rather than by marriage; cf. above sects. 39-41, 45, 65-66;
below sects. 276-277; 386-387.

[53] Cf. *locc. citt.*; also *Amos* 2.7.

[54] Cf. below sects. 278-279. The adjective *conversus* designates one who has dedicated himself by vow to a religious life, such as that of a monk or a nun; cf. above sect. 148 with n. 13.

aliquis oppressus est, de consilio meo numquam ministrabis in aliquo
ordine vel promoveberis sine papae dispensatione.[55] In menstruo et puerperio multi generantur leprosi, epileptici et aliter male se habentes.[56]   99

227 In loco sacro vel die fornicatus es?[57] Quaere quo et quotiens, in
quo ordine, cum qua persona, quo genere fornicandi.

Si in loco sacro fornicatus es, ut in ecclesia dedicata vel coemeterio,
reconciliandus est locus, vel a simplici sacerdote privatim vel ab episcopo
sollemniter; a simplici sacerdote privatim si occultum est crimen, sol- 5
lemniter ab episcopo si notum est crimen. Unde ad hoc proprium habetur officium et propria missa. Sacerdos simplex debet circuire locum et
aspergere aqua benedicta quae fit in dedicatione ecclesiae, decantando
septem psalmos et litaniam. Reconciliatur autem pro homicidio, pro
quacumque fornicatione, si in rixa ibi fuerit effusus sanguis, pro furto 10
secundum quosdam.[58]

228 Ad meretrices accessisti? Timendum est tibi ne sint consanguineae
vel conjugatae vel de religione, vel aliquis consanguineus tuus eam habuit,
vel aliam aliquam circumstantiam.

Aliquam procatus es non tibi? Dic quot et quibus et quas. Ex prae- 15
dictis inquisitionibus satis intelliges quae hic sint inquirenda. Per interpositam personam umquam aliquam sollicitasti? Quaere ut supra.

---

98 vel] nec OPZ.   99 se] sese P om. Ta.   1-3 Quaere — fornicatus es om. Ta (homoeotel.).   2 ordine add. et JU.   3 ut om. U.   in ecclesia — coemeterio] in
coemeterio vel in (om. J) monasterio JU corr. ab eodem Aa in ecclesiam Tc.   vel add. in
HPR.   4-5 vel[2] ab — privatim om. AaCiTa (forte homoeotel.).   5-6 sollemniter[2] ab —
crimen om. Z (homoeotel.).   6 notum] notorium J corr. ab verum Tc.   8 quae fit] quasi
P om. Tc.   9 autem] etiam Ta om. AcTc.   10 si in] sive AaJU.   rixa add. in JU.
fusus Aa om. R.   12 tibi — consanguineae] ne sint tibi consanguineae Aa add. sibi P add.
tuae JRTa.   13 eam] eas PTa.   habuerit HUZ.   15 et[1] om. CcCiP.   16 satis intelliges] patet AaJ.   intelligens Cc patet H intelligi potest U.   sunt O.   17
umquam om. HJTaU.

---

[55] See above sect. 104 with n. 84; cf. below sect. 296 De coitu in puerperio.
[56] See below sect. 288.
[57] Cf. GRATIAN, De poen. D.5 c.1; ALAN, Liber poenit. 1.5-8 (ed. LONGÈRE II 28; cf. Archives-
HDLMA 32.192; PL 210.286-287).
[58] Reference to furtum not found. Regarding this reconciliation cf. HUG. ad De consec. D.1
cc.18-20 (fol. 360[ra-b]); STEPHEN OF TOURNAI, Summa ad De consec. D.1 c.20 (p. 266); 1 Compil.
5.13.6 (JL 12183; X 5.16.5); Po. 3123 (X 3.40.4; issued Jan. 20, 1207); Pontificale Romanum
of the twelfth century c.18 (ed. Michel ANDRIEU, Le pontifical romain au Moyen-âge I 195-197);
SICARD OF CREMONA, Mitrale 1.6 (PL 213.37).

Infamis fuisti pro fornicatione? Superius dictum est de infamia.[59]
Umquam inconfessus vel non contritus ad altare accessisti post fornicationem vel in odio vel in voluntate peccandi? Quaere quotiens et volun- 20
tatem et genus fornicandi et alia similia.

229 Multas personas, et masculos et feminas, male aspexisti, concupi-
visti, sollicitasti, tractasti, osculatus es. Multa alia exciderunt tibi a memoria; multa sunt occulta tua; multae sunt omissiones tuae. Bona etiam
quae fecisti minus pure fecisti. Multotiens es ingratus Deo; multotiens 25
repellis gratiam Dei. Non ita detestaris malum ut deberes; in bono non
es ita progressivus ut deberes. Sed tu de omnibus petis veniam et paratus es confiteri et satisfacere si Deus reduxerit tibi aliquid ad memoriam,
quidquid illud fuerit?

POENITENS. Ita est, domine. 30

SACERDOS. Bene notes quod ultimo dixi; quia si alicujus peccati voluntatem retines, vel si aliquod latet te de quo tu nolles poenitere si rediret
tibi ad memoriam, si sic decederes, damnareris.[60] Idcirco dixi: "quidquid illud fuerit."

POENITENS. Per omnia per gratiam Dei tibi obediam. Restat, ut mihi 35
videtur, ut poenitentiam mihi injungas.[61]

230 SACERDOS. Non es ad praesens de foro meo; Deus enim ad libitum

---

19 vel *om.* Ci.   non contritus] incontritus JPR inconstrictus Tc contritus Cc.
20 in[2] *om.* R *insert.* Ac.   22-23 concupisti CkJ *om.* U.   23 tibi *om.* JU *insert.* Aa.
23-24 tibi a memoria] a memoria tua H.   24 commissiones JP.   etiam] est J *om.*
Ta.   26-27 in bono — deberes *om.* J *insert.* Aa (*homoeotel.*).   27 ita *om.* OPR.
ut] sicut Ta ita ut U.   28 aliquid *om.* JTaU *insert.* Aa.   29 fuerit] sit PTc.
30 est *om.* Ck.   Ita est domine. SACERDOS *om.* *forte insert.* U.   32 te] in te Ck *om.*
AaJTa.   te de] de te O.   tu *om.* JORU.   tu nolles] nolles te Aa.   nolles]
non velles R.   33 si] et JU.   sic] sibi J.   discederes CcHPTc dicederes Ci.
Idrirco *add.* illud O.   37-42 Non — revertaris Pen (*hoc siglo indicantur lectiones ex libro poenitentiali de quo supra in Proleg. ad pp. 6-7 et 27*).   37 enim *add.* tibi AbAcCkHOTaTcZ(NTbVX).

---

[59] See sect. 161.
[60] Cf. GODFREY OF POITIERS, *Summa* quoted by ANCIAUX p. 477. This author wrote at a slightly
later date than Flamborough; see ANCIAUX p. 99.
[61] Flamborough, in harmony with contemporary theology, considers that the official act of
the priest in confession is to authoritatively assign a penance: *injungere poenitentiam*. By doing
so he signifies that the penitent has been released from sin by God and he exercises his authority as confessor in regard to temporal punishment. Cf. above sect. 4; below sects. 236, 241,
356; LOMBARD, *Sent.* 4.18.6.187 (ed. Quaracchi II 863); FIRTH, *Thesis* II 435*-440*.

suum tibi poenitentiam imponit, quia infirmaris. Et ideo innuenda est tibi poenitentia et nulla injungenda, nisi haec tantum: ut studeas ad dolendum de universis peccatis tuis et singulis et ad Deum diligendum, 40 et firmiter proponas quod de cetero ab omni cavebis peccato, et quando convalueris ad me vel ad alium pro poenitentia revertaris.[62]

POENITENS. Fiat ut libet.

Ita, optime decane, in confessionibus inquirere consuevi; et non solum mala quae gessit, sed etiam bona, ut secundum hoc plus vel minus 45 aliquem puniam. Postea considero circumstantias confitentis: aetatem, conversationem, divitias et paupertates, vires corporis et similia; et secundum quod eum video, punio.[63] Si canonicam non vult recipere poenitentiam, id est a canonibus institutam, diligenter eum admoneo ut naturam suam nullo modo laedat, et promptissimum me offero ad quantam- 50 libet poenitentiae alleviationem.[64]

<Cap. ix.> DE POENITENTIA

231 In tribus consistit poenitentia: jejuniis, orationibus et eleemosynis. Quandoque commuto unum pro alio, secundum quod video expedire

38 tibi AdCcCiP(GIK) suam J *om. cett.(cett.).* poenitentiam *add.* tibi RU(FSoX). imponet Ad imponat R(BmM ponat So *add.* tibi BmM) *add.* tibi *insert.* Pen. quia infirmaris *om.* Ta *insert.* AbO *Cf. supra in Proleg. ad p. 47 cum n. 41.* Et *om.* AaU. innuenda] munienda *vel* minuenda Ck(imminenda F minuenda V nuntianda E) innotescenda PTa(K) invenienda Tc injungenda Cc *corr. ab* injungenda Z *corr. ab* imponenda Aa. innuenda est] non est injungenda R(So). 38-39 (innuenda — injungenda] nulla injungenda est tibi Tb). 39 et *om.* AaJPU. et nulla] nulla et Ck. nulla] non J *corr. ab* non Aa. injungenda] imponenda Ta. haec] hoc AcCkORZ(BmEGIMNSgTbX). 42 ad[2] *om.* AbAcAdR. reverteris AaJRU. 43 Fiat *insert.* Ac. 44 decane *add.* salesbur. Ac *add.* salaber. Tc *Cf. supra in Proleg. ad pp. 7-8 et 44.* 46 aliquem] aliquando Ta. aliquem puniam] aliquam poenitentiam Z *corr. ab* aliquam poenitentiam Tc. confitentis] poenitentis AaCkHJRU. aetatem *add.* et HJU. 47 et[1] *om.* CkPTaTc. paupertates *add.* et Ab. 48 eum] ego TaTc. non *add.* eum Ta. 49 eum *insert. alia manu* O. 50 promptissima Cc promptissimam Ci. 51 poenae Aa *corr. ab* poenitentia Tc *corr. ab* poenitentiam O. 52 *tit. om.* AbCiORTa. 53 in jejuniis CkHJP et jejuniis et Aa jejunio R *add.* et J *add.* in Ck. et *om.* CcOR. 54 committo CkRTcU *corr. ab* committo O percommuto J. quod *insert. alia manu* O. videro Ta. expedire *add.* quod *delet.* O *add.* sed Ta.

[62] Cf. GRATIAN C.26 q.7 c.1; BART. c.39 (pp. 206-209); above Proleg. pp. 6-7, 16, 47, 50.

[63] Cf. GRATIAN *De poen.* D.1 c.19; BART. c.25 (p. 194); ALAN, *Liber poenitentialis* 1.5-37, 2. 5-7 (ed. LONGÈRE II 28-37, 47-51; cf. *Archives HDLMA* 32.192-197, 199-201; PL 210.286-289, 291-292); also ANCIAUX p. 43 n. 1 *ad finem*, p. 124 n. 1; below sect. 234 nn. 2 and 3. Regarding the connection between *punio* and *poenitentia* cf. LOMBARD, *Sent.* 4.14.2.

[64] Cf. below sects. 234-235, 241, 356; COURSON, *Summa* 1.45 (ed. KENNEDY pp. 325-326); FIRTH, *Thesis* II 439*-441*.

propter varios rerum eventus, ut quando unum non potest facere, aliud 55
faciat.

Aliquando patitur recidivum peccandi, sed raro; tunc aggravo antiquam
ejus poenitentiam, vel extendendo eam, vel exasperando, vel utroque
modo si expedit.

Quandoque patitur aliquis recidivum peccandi, sed frequenter; tunc, 60
si timeo quod desperet vel succumbat si ei semper aggravetur poenitentia,
non solum cum antiqua remitto eum poenitentia, sed quandoque eam
allevio, immo quandoque eam relaxo, quandoque et ex toto relaxo, semper monens ut a peccato cesset.[65]

232   Quandoque quaerit aliquis: "Domine, si cavero mihi a peccato et 65
istam quam dedisti mihi prosecutus fuero poenitentiam, umquam plus
confitebor?" Et dico: "Frater, in fine vitae tuae omnia debes evomere;
vel si frontem habes teneram et de facili rubes, vel si virum inveneris de
quo bene speras ut ejus utaris consilio, secundum conscientiam tuam quando
volueris confitearis; multum enim valet quod quis pluribus confiteatur.[66] Sed 70
quamdiu tibi portabilis est, numquam quam dedi tibi poenitentiam minuas."

Quatuor sunt quadragesimae in anno quas oportet, quandoque ex toto,
quandoque ex parte, alicui injungere, praeter dominicas quadraginta
continentes dies. Prima incipit ante natale in festo quatuor coronatorum;
secunda, quarta feria post octavas pentecostes; tertia, quarta feria post 75
octavas assumptionis beatae Mariae. Quarta, quae pascha praecedit,
omnibus nota est.[67]

---

57 recidium J recidinum R rescidimum O.   58 eam om. AaCkJO.   vel[2] om. O.
60 aliquid JU quis RTa.   recidium J recidium Ck rescidimum corr. ad recidimum O.
Quandoque — frequenter] Si frequenter patitur aliquis recidivum Ta.   61 ei] enim O.
63 eam] eum HTc.   relaxo[1] add. ex parte R.   relaxo[1] quandoque[2] et om. PU.
quandoque[2] et ex toto relaxo[2] om. Z insert. Aa om. forte aliquid insert. J ex toto Ta.   et] etiam
O eam R corr. ab eam Ck om. CcCiTcU.   et ex toto] ex toto et Ab add. eam H add. eum Tc.
relaxo[2]] remitto Ck.   65 caveo AaJORTa cavebo Ta.   peccatis CkTc.   66
numquam AaJU numqua Tc.   68 vel[1]] ut P corr. ab et O.   70 quis corr. ab quisque
[?] O.   71 tibi[1] om. AaJ.   tibi portabilis] importabilis Tc.   tibi[2] om. Ta insert.
O quando Tc.   mutas vel minuas Cc corr. ad mutas vel minuas Ci.   74 natale add.
Domini RTaZ.   76 beatae add. virginis AaU.   Mariae] virginis RTa add. virginis J.

---

[65] Cf. Courson, loc. cit.
[66] Cf. Gratian De poen. D.1 c.88; De vera et falsa poenitentia c.10.25 (PL 40.1122); Amédée
Teetaert, La confession aux laïques dans l'Église latine depuis le VIIIe jusqu'au XIVe siècle pp. 38-
42; Firth, Thesis II 427*-428*.
[67] Cf. below sect. 352 (pp. 277-278); Ivo 10.133 (PL 161.731); Benedict the Levite, Capitularia 2.187 (MonGerHist Leges [folio] II[2].82; PL 97.770). Three of the lents, i.e. fasts of

233 Quandoque ad cautelam sine omni recidivo confitetur aliquis; cui
sic dico: "Tu peccasti in cibo et potu, in verbis vanis, otiosis, joculatoriis,
adulatoriis, detractoriis, audiendo, loquendo, mentiendo et jurando, 80
contendendo cum aliis. Multa exciderunt tibi a memoria; multa sunt
occulta tua; multae sunt omissiones tuae. Bona quae fecisti minus pure
fecisti. Multotiens es ingratus Deo; multotiens repellis gratiam Dei. Non
ita detestaris malum sicut deberes; in bono non ita es progressivus ut deberes. Sed tu de omnibus petis veniam et paratus es confiteri et satis- 85
facere si Deus reduxerit tibi ad memoriam, quidquid illud fuerit?" Ego
autem aliquantulam ei injugnam poenitentiam unam vel aliam.[68]

---

78 resciduo O reciduo Ck *corr. ab* recidivio Ci.   79 et *om.* Ta.   in[2]] et R et in
Aa *om.* Ta.   vanis] variis AaJ paucis R *add.* et OP.   80 adulatoriis *om.* RTa.
et *om.* CkR.   et jurando *invers.* H.   82 tua *om.* Ta.   sunt *om.* CiTa.   tuae
om. Ta.   84 sicut] ut HOP.   progressus CkP.   ut] sicut AaP.   85 tu *om.*
AaHJ.   87 autem *om.* AaJ.   ei] tibi Tc *om.* O.   unam vel aliam *om.* JTa.

---

forty days mentioned by our author, are found in these sources. I have not found a source for
the fast which he indicates should begin after the octave of the Assumption.
    [68] Cf. ALAN, *Liber poenitentialis* 4.1 (ed. LONGÈRE II 161-162; cf. *Archives HDLMA* 32.226;
PL 210.299-300). Concerning the ending of Book 4 at this place see above Proleg. p. 16 n. 87.

\<INCIPIT LIBER QUINTUS\>

234   Postquam per poenitentis propalationem et poenitentiarii indagatio-
nem vitia et vitiorum membra et virtutum omissiones modo superius enu-
merato[1] inventa sunt et deprehensa, consequens est ea digna animadver-
sione prosequi et percutere, hoc est dignos facere fructus poenitentiae.   5
    Ad hoc autem necessarium est scire quae cui respondeat peccato poeni-
tentia. Poenitentiae autem arbitrariae sunt, et ad arbitrium sacerdotis
ex causis inspectis mitigandae sunt et exasperandae.[2] Nos tamen, potius
quam a nobis et per nos aliquid fingamus, canonicas a sanctis patribus
praetaxatas proponemus poenitentias.[3] Quae licet graves sint admodum 10
et asperae ut vix sit aliquis qui vel eas suscipere velit vel imponere praesumat,[4] praeterea licet in libris poenitentialibus non singulas singulorum
invenias expressas (licet peccatorum invenias poenitentias), tutius tamen
et honestius prae oculis habita antiquorum auctoritate, modo et conside-
ratione (nam et ipsi mitigant)[5] mitigabimus eas et forte exasperabimus. 15

1 *tit.* Quartus liber O Necessaria huic operi *obscur.* Ab De fructu poenitentiae Ta De poenitentia
pars prima Cc De poenitentiae indagatione J(Cp) De imponenda satisfactione P(K) De discretione habenda in dandis poenitentiis H (De poenitentia V Incipit quartus liber Tb Incipit liber
quintus de poenitentiae indagatione X De injunctione poenitentiae So De in propalatione poenitentiae caret [*lege* quaerit ?] cujusmodi poenitentia et quomodo debet inju\<ngi\> M) *om. cett.-*
(*cett.*) *Cf.* FIRTH, *Thesis II 345*-350*.*   2 per] pro O *om.* U.   3-4 annotato vel enume-
rato Ad.   4 ea] ut ea J *om.* H.   4-5 ea... prosequi et percutere... facere] ut ea... prosequamur... faciamus Ta.   5 persequi AaCkH.   8 asperandae AaP.   11 vel[1] *om.*
CcTaTc.   excipere Aa recipere J *corr. ab* sustinere Tc.   vel[2]] aut O ut Ck.   12
licet *om.* U.   13 invenias[1] *om.* Ad *delet.* Ab.   expressas *add.* poenitentias R.
licet *om.* AbAdCkHOPTaUZ(KTbVX *delet.* Bm) *lacuna vel rasura* CcCi.   invenias[2] *om.*
CkHOPTaU(KTbVX *delet.* Bm; *lectiones hic inventae in Forma 2 et in KPTb praebent clariorem sensum*).
(peccatorum invenias *invers.* F).   15 nam et *rasura* Cc.   nam — mitigant *om.* Ta.
eas *om.* H.   forte eas et JU eas forte et Aa.   asperabimus AaJ exasperamus *add.* eas
R *corr. ab* exasperavimus Tc.

    1 Reference to Books 1-4, sects. 3-230; cf. above sects. 2, 3, 9-10, 197.
    2 Cf. GRATIAN C.26 q.7 c.5; *De poen.* D.1 c.84, c.86; Ivo, *Decretum* 15.46-49 (PL 161.868-
869); ANCIAUX p. 31 n. 1, pp. 43-46 with notes; Pierre MICHAUD-QUANTIN, "A propos des premières *Summae confessorum*", *Rech ThAncMéd* 26 (1959) 268-269 with n. 16; Philippe DELHAYE,
"Deux textes de Senatus de Worcester", *Rech ThAncMéd* 19 (1952) 203-224.
    3 Cf. GRATIAN *De poen.* D.5 c.6; Ivo, *Decretum* 15.47 (PL 161.868); GODFREY OF POITIERS
quoted by ANCIAUX p. 533 (end of first quotation); texts cited in preceding note.
    4 Cf. ALAN, *Liber poenitentialis* 2.13-14 (ed. LONGÈRE II 54-56; cf. *ArchivesHDLMA* 32.202-
203; PL 210.293-294).
    5 Cf. texts cited above in n. 2; below sects. 241, 246, 253, 256-257, 351, 353-354, 356. Re-
garding Flamborough's appeal to what is *tutius* see FIRTH, *Thesis* II 494*-497*.

Et cum peccato conformem non invenimus poenitentiam canonicam, per majus et minus eam inveniemus et per simile.[6]

235 Ego autem in confessionibus jus illaesum semper servare volo vehementer, poenitentias autem non ita. Quando enim poenitens canonicam suscipere non vult pocnitcntiam, moneo eum et rogo: "Amice, incipe et 20 proba si sustinere potes poenitentiam istam. Dabit tibi Deus gratiam et fortitudinem; alioquin mitigabo tibi." Et subjungo: "Si aliud fieri non potest, cessa a peccato, et ad libitum tuum quod volueris tibi mitigabo."[7]

Elegi enim semper magis misericors esse quam rigidus.[8] Quando enim gravem aliquam suscipit quis poenitentiam, dico ei: "Frater, rationabile 25 sit obsequium tuum;[9] ego me expedio,[10] rogo, praecipio, praemoneo et praemunio[11] ut naturam tuam semper serves illaesam." Nolo ut sub pondere poenitentiae in tantum gemat quis ut a studio cogatur cessare, scholaris a scholis, vel ab officio suo faber vel agricola vel alius laboriosus, ut domui suae praevidere non possit, vel ut dominum suum sequi non pos- 30 sit cursor, vel conventum claustralis.

Ordinem autem superius praenotatum hic non observabimus,[12] sed de illis quae frequentiora sunt et nota magis tractabimus.

---

18 jus] vix Ck *om.* R.   19 enim] autem Tc *om.* Ta.   20 recipere AaHO.   21 possis AaJU.   23 tibi *om.* CkTaTc.   24 semper *om.* O.   25 aliquem TcU *om.* Aa. aliquam suscipit quis] aliquis suscipit P.   quis] aliquis AaO.   26 praecipio *add.* et U et praecipio et Aa.   praemoneo] moneo O *corr. alia manu ad* praemunio H. 26-27 praemoneo et praemunio] praemunio moneo P.   et praemunio *om.* J.   28 in *om.* Cc *insert. alia manu* H.   in tantum *corr. ab* interea O.   29 a scholis *om.* Tc *insert.* O.   30 providere AaCkJPRTaTcU(BmCpFGIKNSgSoTbVX) provideat *corr. ad* providere Tc (*Auctor videtur intellexisse* praevidere *eodem sensu ac* providere).   32 hic *corr. ab* hoc O.   33 magis *add.* hic O.   tractabimus *add. aliam materiam ex qua pars invenitur infra in sect. 351* O *Vide infra in Append. C ad nos. 20, 27.*

---

[6] Cf. BART. c.37 (p. 203 lines 20-25).

[7] Cf. HUG. ad *De poen.* D.3 c.34 natura (fol. 336ra); ALAN, *Liber poenitentialis* PL 210.293-294; above sect. 230; below sects. 241, 356; FIRTH, *Thesis* II 439*-441*.

[8] Cf. GRATIAN C.26 q.7 c.12; below sect. 351.

[9] Cf. *Rom* 12.1.

[10] From its original meaning "to prepare oneself for light and speedy travel", and hence "to hasten with urgency", this word seems to have come to mean in this context "to urge, to insist".

[11] This verb was sometimes used in the Middle Ages with the same meaning as *praemoneo*; see DU CANGE s.v. *praemunio*.

[12] See above sects. 9-10.

<Cap. i.>   <DE POENITENTIA>

236 Poenitentia alia sollemnis, alia publica, alia privata. *Sollemnis* est 35 quae fit in capite jejunii, quando cum sollemnitate in cinere et cilicio ejiciuntur ab ecclesia poenitentes.[13] Haec etiam est publica, quia publice fit. *Publica* et non sollemnis est quae fit in facie ecclesiae sine supra dicta sollemnitate, ut peregrinatio.[14] *Privata* est illa quae cotidie fit privatim coram sacerdote.[15]

40

Sollemnem poenitentiam non injunget aliquis nisi episcopus vel aliquis ejus auctoritate, nisi in necessitate;[16] tunc etiam poterit laicus eum reconciliare, ut *De consec.* Dist. iv. *Sanctum est.*[17] Publicam poenitentiam, sicut et privatam, simplex injungit sacerdos et quolibet tempore.[18]

237 In sollemni poenitentia sex attenduntur: quia clericus non poenitet 45 sollemniter, et sollemniter poenitens non promovetur; item sollemnis poenitentia non iteratur pro aliquo crimine; item sollemniter poenitens non contrahit matrimonium; item non militabit; item non revertetur ad saecularia negotia.

Clericus non poenitet sollemniter, ne scandalizentur laici et insultent 50 clericis.[19] Sollemniter poenitens non promovetur, quia pro enormi crimine,

---

34 De poenitentia Z De tribus generibus poenitentiae Ad *om. tit.* Ci *et plures alii; diversi tituli in aliis.*   35 alia[1]] autem AaJ.   37 etiam *om.* Tc *insert.* O.   quia] quae Cc *corr. ab quae* Aa.   39 illa *om.* Cc.   42 etiam] enim Aa et R vero Ta.   eum *om.* Cc.   48 militabit] immutabitur O.   50-52 Clericus — poenitentia *interpolat. supra post* publicatur *in sect.* 160 *ad lineam* 63 Pet *fol. 139*[v].   51 clerici R laici U.   poenitens] confitens U poenitentes Pet pe. R.   promovebitur Tc promoventur R Pet contrahit nec promovebitur H.

---

13 Cf. GRATIAN D.50 c.64; BURCHARD, *Decretum* 19.26 (PL 140.984). This is a mediaeval survival of the public penance of the early Church; see e.g. Bernhard POSCHMANN, *Busse und letzte Ölung* (Handbuch der Dogmengeschichte LV 3; Freiburg im Br. 1951) esp. p. 82; Eng. tr. *Penance and Anointing of the Sick* (Freiburg im Br. 1964) esp. pp. 153-154.

14 Regarding this public, non-solemn penance see ALAN, *Liber poenitentialis* 3.9, 20 (ed. LONGÈRE II 131, 138; cf. *ibid.* I 185-186; *Archives HDLMA* 32.218, 221-222; PL 210.295-297); PETER MANDUCATOR (Comestor) *De sacramentis* sects. 24-25 (ed. Raymond M. MARTIN in the appendix to Henri WEISWEILER, *Maître Simon et son group, De sacramentis* [Louvain 1937] pp. 73*-75*); ANCIAUX pp. 370-373.

15 Cf. *locc. citt.*; also FIRTH, *Thesis* II 426*-441* with notes.

16 Cf. HUG. ad D.50 c.63 *a sacerdote* (fol. 63rb); ad *De poen.* D.6 c.1 (fol. 340va).

17 Cap. 36; cf. *De poen.* D.6 c.1. Regarding the part of the layman in the administration of penance according to various mediaeval opinions see A. TEETAERT, *La confession aux laïques dans l' Église latine.*

18 Cf. HUG. ad D.50 c.64 *in capite, ibidem adesse* (fol. 63va).

19 Cf. HUG. ad D.50 dictum p. c. 64 (fol. 63vb).

quod jam per sollemnitatem publicatur, datur sollemnis poenitentia.[20]
Talia autem, sicut superius dictum est, impediunt promotionem.[21] Ista duo,
scilicet quod clericus non poeniteat sollemniter et quod sollemniter poenitens non promoveatur, non recipiunt dispensationem.[22]   55

Tertium, scilicet quod sollemnis poenitentia non iteratur, forte secundum diversas diversarum ecclesiarum consuetudines in una observatur,
in alia non, *De poen.* Dist. iii. in fine.[23]

238 Quartum, scilicet quod sollemniter poenitens non contrahit, res-
tringunt aliqui ad tria: ad raptum, ad incestum, ad uxoricidium;[24] quia 60
qui propter raptum sollemniter poenituit de cetero non contrahet; item,
si sollemniter poenituisti quia post contractum matrimonium cognovisti
consanguineam uxoris tuae in tertio gradu vel infra, non contrahes postea;
idem est in uxoricida. Nec mirum; quia, si occulta essent ista, non possent
tales contrahere nisi cum dispensatione;[25] digne igitur propter sollemni- 65
tatem poenitentiae debet talibus dispensatio negari. De illa rapta loquor
quae numquam post raptum ante sollemnem poenitentiam libere consensit in raptorem.[26] In istis tribus casibus interdicitur sollemniter poenitentibus contrahere; si tamen contraxerint, stabit matrimonium.[27] Cum
talibus etiam ut contrahant potest papa dispensare.[28]   70

---

52 jam *om.* Ck *corr. ab* laici Aa.   publicatus Cc publicatum est Pet.   53 sicut] ut
AaO.   53-55 Ista — dispensationem *interpolat. supra post* impedit *in sect. 160 ad lineam 64*
Pet.   54 quod¹] ut JU.   non *insert.* AbO.   poeniteat *add.* non *delet.* O.
55 promovetur J *corr. ab* promovetur O.   58 non *add.* ut CkPRTaTcZ.   in fine *om.*
PTc.   60 aliqui *om.* AdH.   61 qui *reincipit* Pet *textu abbrev. fol. 158*va.   poe-
nitet R poenitens est JU.   64 quia si] si enim AaHJU.   65 digne *ss. cessat* Pet.
66 denegari UZ.   67 post] ante J ante *delet.* Aa.   69 contraxerint] contraxerunt
CcCiCkHTc.

---

[20] Cf. Hug. ad D.33 c.2 *publica* (fol. 41ra); ad D.50 dictum p. c.54 (fol. 62va); above sect.
160.
[21] See above sect. 101.
[22] See Gratian D.50 c.68. Hug. *locc. citt.* (in n. 20) says there may be a dispensation, but
not beyond the subdiaconate.
[23] Dictum p. c.49; cf. D.50 dictum p. c.61, c.62; Anciaux pp. 365-366 with notes.
[24] Cf. Hug. ad C.33 q.2 dictum p. c.11 §1 *De poenitentibus* (fol. 321vb).
[25] See above sects. 59-67. Flamborough probably understands "third degree" according to
the computation of Roman law; see above sect. 38 n. 73.
[26] See above sect. 63.
[27] Cf. Hug. *loc. cit.* (in n. 24); ad C.36 q.2 c.10 *tolerabilius* (fol. 356vb).
[28] Huguccio is still more liberal. He leaves it to the discretion of the bishop imposing penance to permit marriage or forbid it.

239 Item quod sollemniter poenitentes non militent, non revertantur ad
saecularia negotia, vel antiquus est rigor, vel de honestate fieri debet; quia
honestum est ut qui illicitorum veniam petit a multis etiam licitis abstineat. Antiquorum etiam opinio fuit quod de enormibus poenitens non
debet redire ad negotia saecularia, maxime quae sine peccato transigi 75
non possunt, ut *De poen.* Dist. v. c. *Fratres.*[29] Quare ergo non idem dicunt
moderni, cum qui sollemnem poenitentiam sponte suscipit vovisse videtur,
ut Causa xxxiii. quaest. ii. c. *De his*?[30]

Publica poenitentia imponitur clericis, ut in Causa xxx. quaest. i. *Si
quis sacerdos,*[31] et post poenitentiam ad officia sua redire possunt, ut Dist. 80
lxxxii. *Presbyter.*[32]

240 Si propter raptum, ut decet, sollemniter poenituisti, et ex dispensatione postea contraxisti (quia aliter non debuisti), nec secundo sine nova
dispensatione contrahes, nec tertio sine nova, et sic ulterius; sicut si ex
dispensatione suscepisti aliquem ordinem, ex eadem dispensatione ulte- 85
riorem ordinem non suscipies, sed novam petes.[33] Quod dixi de raptore,
de secundis nuptiis et ulterioribus ei inhibendis, idem fortasse et eadem
ratione de incestuosis superius memoratis[34] et uxoricidis dici potest. Istis

---

71 poenitens... militet... revertatur RZ.   militant U.   non[2]] nec RTaU nec scilicet Ck.
revertentur Ck reiterantur J.   72 quia] quod Cc.   73 petis J petivit Aa.   etiam
om. Cc.   74 etiam] et J enim H.   enormitatibus Tc *add.* etiam O.   poenitentes
AbTa.   75 deberent Ta.   maxime *om.* J *insert. alia manu* Aa.   quae] quia J.
transigi] exerceri R *corr. ab* transire O.   76 Dist. *om.* H.   v. *add.* et O *add.* i. H.
c. *om.* Tc.   ergo *om.* AaJU.   77 cum] ut Cc.   cum qui] qui cum AaJ.
suscepit CcJPU *corr. ab* suscepit Ab.   novisse CkJR *corr. ab* novisse O.   77 xxiii.
AaJ.   ii.] v. CcCiHP.   quaest. — his] quidem O.   79 non imponitur U.
in *om.* H.   in Causa] causa Deo Ck *om.* OPRTa.   i.] v. P vi. J *add.* c. R.   80-
81 Dist. lxxxii.] ff. ii. H ff. lxxiii. U.   81 lxxxii.] lxxx. AaJTc.   82 raptum *corr. ab*
raptam O.   82-83 ex dispensatione postea] post ex dispensatione R praeterea ex dispensatione Ta.   83 nova *om.* OR.   84 sicut] sunt Ck *corr. ab* quia U.   si *om.* AaJ.
85 accepisti Aa *om.* Ta.   eadem] ea Cc.   85-86 ex eadem — ordinem *om.* Ta (*homoeotel.*).   86 recipies JU.

---

[29] Cap. 8; cf. *ibid.* cc.2-7. Cf. also B. Poschmann, *Busse und letzte Ölung* pp. 55-57, Eng. tr.
Penance and Anointing pp. 105-109; Cyrille Vogel, *La discipline pénitentiel en Gaul des origines à la
fin du VII*e *siècle* (Paris 1952) esp. pp. 128-138.

[30] Cap. 12; cf. below sects. 346-347; also *locc. citt.*

[31] Cap. 9; copied below sect. 280.

[32] Cap. 5; copied below sect. 290.

[33] See Hug. ad C.36 q.2 c.10 *iterare conjugium* (fol. 356vb).

[34] See sect. 238; sect. 59.

autem tribus interdicitur matrimonium quia in matrimonium peccaverunt;
sed et his tribus quare potius secunda est dispensatio vel ulterior neces- 90
saria quam prima ? Quia propter maturiorem aetatem melius continere
possunt.[35]

241 Attende tibi, sacerdos, quia quam plures subscriptae poenitentiae
publicae sunt vel sollemnes; tu autem numquam pro occulto peccato publicam vel sollemnem dabis poenitentiam; alioquin per poenitentiae sol- 95
lemnitatem prodes vel publicabis poenitentis peccatum, quod est pessimum.[36] Quando ergo pro peccato quod est occultum publica vel sollemnis danda esset poenitentia si publicum esset peccatum, detrahe poenitentiae sollemnitatem et ipsam puram injunge poenitentiam.   99
   De alio etiam te moneo, quod vix aliquem invenies qui subscriptas (quia
graves sunt et austerae) suscipiat poenitentias; tu igitur paulatim et paulatim eas mitigabis, ut aliquam habeat poenitens poenitentiam.[37] Numquam enim, dum modo a peccatis cessare velit, omnino sine poenitentia a
te recedet aliquis; alioquin, quod absit, in desperationem eum detrudes 5
et damnationem.[38]

---

90 et] in PRTa *om.* AaCkJU.   90-91 necessarior R *insert. alia* manu O.   93 *tit. praem.*
De homicidio Ci *cf. infra var. ad lineam 7.*   poenitentiae *corr. ab* poenae O.   94 sunt
insert. O.   numquam *om.* R *corr. ab* namque [?] O.   95 dabis *insert. alia manu* O *non* dabis
R dabitur Ta.   96 poenitentis *corr. ab* poenitentiae AbO.   97 publica] publicata O.
98 esset[1]] est AaAbCkTaTc(FGTbY *om.* M).   danda esset] non est danda R datur *insert.*
O.   publicum] occultum R.   si — peccatum *om.* AaHOU(CpSgV) *insert.* Ab (*cf.
infra var. ad lineam 99*).   publicaum esset peccatum *insert.* AcJ *Cf. infra in Append. C no. 16.*
esset[2]] est RTaTc(FG).   99 sollemnitatem *add.* si publicum esset peccatum AaHJU(Cp-
Sg).   puram] paucam O *om.* JTa *insert.* Aa.   2 suscipiet AbAcCiZ suscipient Ck.
3 habeat *insert.* Cc habeas H.   5 recedat CkHPRTaTc recedit *corr. ad* recedat O.

---

[35] See Hug. *loc. cit.* (in n. 33).
[36] Cf. Gratian C.2 q.2 c.19.
[37] Cf. above sects. 230, 234-235; below sects. 351, 356.
[38] Cf. above sect. 229 with n. 61; sect. 233; Alan, *Liber poenit.* 2.13 (ed. Longère II 54-55;
cf. *Archives HDLMA* 32.202-203; PL 210.293-294).

\<Cap. ii.\> \<DE HOMICIDIO\>

242   i. De eo qui semetipsum occidit.

    ii. De interfectoribus clericorum, ex concilio warmacensi.[39]

    iii. De parricidio.

    iv. De eo qui infantem opprimit.

    v. De illo qui inhonoravit patrem aut matrem.

    vi. De mulieribus quae fornicantur et partus suos necant.

    vii. De impedientibus conceptum.

    viii. De homicidiis simplicibus.[40]

    ix. De viro qui interficit uxorem vel de muliere quae interficit virum.

    x. De eo qui publice poenitentem occidit, ex concilio Silvestri papae.[41]

    xi. De homicidio pro vindicta facto.

7 DE HOMICIDIO AbAc DE HOMICIDIO Pars Prima De eo qui se ipsum occidit Cc CA-PITULA LIBRI QUINTI HP Incipiunt capitula libri quinti *insert.* Aa *om.* AdCiZ (*cf. supra var. ad lineam 93*) *alii tituli rubricales hic in aliis MSS, om. in multis. Tituli rubricales quos posui in capite hujus et subsequentium indicum titulorum sumuntur ex Ab; AcCcCi habent tantum hunc primum. Tituli rubricales in capite subsequentium indicum titulorum forte decisi sunt in Ac una cum marginibus paginarum; N habet eosdem titulos ac Ab in capite trium priorum indicum; in aliis MSS plerumque desunt tituli rubricales in capite cujusque indicis titulorum hujus libri. Cf. supra in Proleg. ad p. 16 cum nota 88.*   8-29 *Ordo titulorum variatur in pluribus MSS (loco horum G habet alios titulos)* H(G) *carent omni indicio conciliorum et auctorum.*   8 seipsum CkTa.   9 ex concilio warmacensi *om.* HJ.   warmatensi Cc warmatien. Ad warmascensi Z wormacen. Ta uarinanem Tc.   10 patricidio CkHPTa.   11 eo] illo Cc.   de eo *om.* Z.   De eo — opprimit *infra post* occiderit *ad lineam 29* OU *corr. ab eodem ordine* Ab *in utroque loco (posteriore eraso* Ac) AaAcJ *Vide infra var. ad lineam 29 et in Append.* C *no. 21.*   12 illo] eo AaJPR.   De illo *om.* Z.   honoravit Cc inhonorat AaHJPU.   13 partum suum JU.   14 De impedientibus conceptum *om.* O *insert.* Ab.   15 simplicibus] sponte commissis ex decreto meldensi papae et tiburiensis concilii capitulo iv. O *corr. ab eodem* Ab.   16 interficit[1]] interfecit Ta *corr. ad* interfecit Tc occidit AaJPU occiderit H.   vel] et H *om.* JRTaTc.   vel de] aut Ck.   muliere] uxore AaAcCkJU.   interficit[2]] interfecit PTaTc interfecerit H occidit AaJU.   17 ex — papae *om.* H.   concilio] decretis AaJ.   18 De — facto *om.* U *add.* ex poenitentiali Theodori O.

[39] This title, apparently intended for sect. 244 below, is found at the beginning of that text in BART. c.46 (p. 212), perhaps because the second part of that passage is ascribed to a Council of Worms; see below n. 53.

[40] This is evidently the reading of Form 3. The reading of Form 2 (see variants) is taken from BART. c.41 (p. 210), where the name of the pope is written *Melchiadis papae,* a form often used in mediaeval times to designate Pope Miltiades (A.D. 310-314). Cf. Ivo 10.130 (PL 161. 730); BURCH. 6.1 (PL 140.763). The second reference in this reading is probably to cc.55-58 of a council held at Tribur A.D. 895 according to HEFELE-LECLERCQ 4².697-708; see MANSI 18¹.156-157. Those canons have some rather remote similarity to sects. 260-263 below, for which this title is intended.

[41] Title derived from Bartholomew for the first canon of sect. 265. Burchard and Ivo designate the source *ex decretis Silvestri papae.* Original source not found.

xii. De homicidio non sponte commisso, ex concilio mannecensi, lviii.[42]

xiii. De illo qui domino suo praecipiente homicidium fecerit, ex eodem, capi-   20
      pitulo xxv.[43]

xiv. De illis qui veneficio homicidia committunt, ex concilio heliberitano, ca-
      tulo v.[44]

xv. De illo per cujus delationem aliquis interfectus fuerit, ex eodem concilio,
      capitulo i.[45]   25

xvi. De homicidiis in bello factis, ex concilio mangontiensi.[46]

xvii. De eo qui christianum mancipium seduxerit et sic vendiderit, ex concilio
      apud confluentia.[47]

xviii. Si domina ancillam per iram occiderit.

19 commisso] facto PTc.   Nanneten. Ad (Nannetensi N) manacensi R (mannensi I ma-
nacen. So) mannacensium Ck (mammon⁸ Tb) maten. Ta (matensensi MY meranensi F) ūra-
nēsi Tc warmacensi JU (yarmacensi Y om. Sg) Lectio Nanneten. videtur provenisse correctione.
lviii. om. TaZ.   20 fecit CkRTaTc.   20-21 capitulo] concilio AaRTc.   ex-xxv. om.
H.   22 heleberritano O heliberitino Ck helibertino R liberitura Tc.   22-23 capitulo v.
om. CcJ insert. Aa.   23 v.] vi. P.   De illo om. Z.   24 fuerit] est JPTc om. AaCc.
24-26 De illo — mangontiensi om. O.   26 (De — mangontiensi om. X).   ex concilio
mangontiensi om. H.   mangonciensi Ab(IK) mangoncien. U mangoncensi Ci mag̃censi
P magociensi Tc(BmSoVY) magontiensi CcZ magoncienci Ck manguncien. AdRTa(FN magun-
ciensi M magñtmāsi Tb) magorieni J (magoren. Cp magar. Sg) add. xvi. RTa (add. xvii. So)
Forte numerus derivatur ex numero proximi tituli.   27-28 et sic — confluentia] etc. H.   (ex—
confluentia om. X).   28 confluentiam PTaZ(BmCpFMV Burch. Ivo confluentam K)
circumfluentiam J circumfluentiam corr. ad circumfluentia Aa (confluentia corr. ad circumfluentia
N flu cum lacuna Y circumsententiam Sg) confec. R.   29 ancilla J ancilla ante domina Aa.
iram] iracundiam Ta vim Tc.   occiderit add. De eo qui infantem opprimit. De eo qui semetipsum occidit AaJ Hic ultimus titulus videtur susceptus ex rubrica proximi capituli. Quoad alios titulos
hic inventos in AbAcOU(Sg) vide infra in Append. C no. 21.

[42] Title for the first canon of sect. 266. Bartholomew, Burchard and Ivo ascribe this, as Flamborough does, to a Council of Nantes, but in Morey's edition of Bartholomew no number is
mentioned, and in Burch. 6.16 (PL 140.769) and Ivo 10.145 (PL 161.735) it is designated as
cap. 2 of that council. Actually it is c.18 of a council held at Nantes probably in A.D. 658; see
Hefele-Leclercq 3¹.296-298; Mansi 18.171. Robert's reading lviii. is probably a corruption
of xviii., and so is closer to the original number of the canon than the currently available editions of Burchard, Ivo or Bartholomew.

[43] This title for the first canon of sect. 267 is from Burch. 6.17 (PL 140.769) or from Ivo 10.
146 (PL 161.735). Bartholomew before this canon in c.53 (p. 221 lines 15-17) has the indication Ex concilio namnetensi without any designation of a number.

[44] This is the title for the last canon of sect. 267 below. Actually this canon is based on c.6
of the Council of Elvira (circa A.D. 306); see Hefele-Leclercq 1¹.225; Mansi 2.6. Regarding
this title see Firth, Thesis II 421* n. 16 (III 691*-693*).

[45] This title is for sect. 268. This canon is not found among the decrees of the Council of
Elvira; c.37 of that council does condemn and provide penance for the delator (see Hefele-Leclercq 1¹.260; Gratian C.5 q.6 c.6; Burch. 6.27, PL 140.771; Mansi 2.17), but it is very different from sect. 268. Regarding the origin of this title see Firth, Thesis loc. cit.

[46] Title for sect. 269; original source for this section not found.

[47] Title for the first canon of sect. 270. This is c.7 of the council held at Coblenz A.D. 922;
see Hefele-Leclercq 4².751; Mansi 18.345.

i. *De eo qui semetipsum occidit* 30

243   De eo qui semetipsum occidit aut laqueo se suspendit consideratum est ut, si quis patiens velit eleemosynam dare, tribuat, et orationes in psalmodiis faciat; oblationibus tamen et missis careat.[48]

Quicumque se propria voluntate aut in aqua jactaverit, aut collum ligaverit, aut de arbore praecipitaverit, aut furiose percusserit, aut qualibet occasione sponte 35 sua se morti tradiderit, istorum oblata non recipiantur.[49]

Tu dixisti: "Laqueo traditor periit; laqueum talibus dereliquit." Hoc ad nos omnino non pertinet; neque enim veneramur nomine martyrum eos qui sibi collum ligaverunt.[50]

Placuit ut his qui sibi ipsis voluntarie per ferrum aut per venenum aut per prae- 40 cipitium aut per suspendium vel quolibet alio modo inferunt mortem nulla prorsus in oratione commemoratio fiat; neque cum psalmis ad sepulturam eorum cadavera deducantur. Multi enim sibi hoc per ignorantiam usurparunt. Similiter et de his placuit fieri qui pro suis sceleribus moriuntur; "impoenitentes" subaudiatur.[51]

31 occiderit CkP.   De — suspendit *om.* Tc.   32 quis] aliquis CiP.   compatiens AdCcCiCkZ(CpFTbV Ivo) *corr. ad* compatiens O(Y est patiens est *insert. in rasuram* Bm) parens J(NSgX) *corr. ab* parens Aa mortuo compatiens H mortuo compatiens parens U *om.* P(K) *Cf.* FIRTH, *Thesis II 318*-319*.*   eleemosynas AaHJ.   et *om.* AaJ.   in] et J vel Cc in *insert. in rasuram* Aa.   34 aquam CkPRU(FIKMNVX BURCH. Ivo *orig* (aqua *Capitula* THEODORI *c. 26 PL 99.945*).   in aqua] iniqua So).   35 octõne O actione Tc.   36 recipiatur Cc recipientur Tc.   37 Tu] Qui R.   Tu dixisti] audisti Ta.   derelinquit OTc relinquit J *corr. ab* relinquit Aa.   nos] vos AcCk. 38 enim] nos R *add.* nos Ta.   venerantur AaJ.   martyrium CkTc.   39 ligaverint J ligaverit Tc.   40 ut] et Ck ex R in J *add.* in Cc *corr. ab* in Aa *corr. ab* non O. his *corr. ab* hi O (hi BART. BURCH. Ivo²) pro his P.   ipsi Ck.   ipsis voluntarie *invers.* J(Ivo¹) *add.* aut Aa(BART. BURCH. Ivo²).   40-41 per praecipitium *om.* AaJ.   41 per *insert.* Ab (per Ivo¹ *om.* Ivo² BART. BURCH. GRATIAN).   (aut per *om.* Cp).   vel] aut AaCkP.   42 in *insert. alia manu* O.   sepultura Ta sepulchrum H.   43 hoc *om.* PZ *insert. alia manu* Aa.   usurpant AaCkOTa(BmSgSoVX Ivo¹ GRATIAN usurpaverunt MTb) talia usurparunt Z (*add.* ista Tb usurparunt Ivo² BART. BURCH. *orig*).   et] etiam R *om.* Aa.   44 subaudiantur OTc subaudiuntur Z subauditur U subaudi J *om.* Ck.

[48] See Ivo 10.5 (PL 161.693); BENEDICT THE LEVITE, *Capitularia* 2.70 (MonGerHist Leges [folio] 2².77). Regarding the sources for these penitential canons see above Proleg. pp. 16-17.

[49] See Ivo 10.6 (PL 161.693); cf. IDEM 15.141 (PL 161.890); BURCH. 19.131 (PL 140.1009); *Capitula Theodori* c.26 (last sentence; PL 99.945); regarding these *Capitula* see below sect. 294 n. 65. Cf. also PL 99.1143 c.10; MANSI 9.913 c.17.

[50] See Ivo 10.7 (PL 161.693); GRATIAN C.23 q.5 c.10; cf. AUGUSTINE, *Contra litteras Petiliani* 49.114 (PL 43.299; CorpusScrEcclLat 52.87 lines 14-16).

[51] See BART. c.51 (p. 220); cf. Ivo 10.188 (PL 161.746); 15.140 (PL 161.890); BURCH. 19. 130 (PL 140.1009); GRATIAN C.23 q.5 c.12; *Capitula Theodori* c.26 (PL 99.945). The concluding words *"impoenitentes" subaudiatur* are found in Bartholomew and in Gratian, but not in the other sources.

ii. *De interfectoribus clericorum ex concilio warmacensi*   45

244 Si quis clericum vel quemlibet ex ecclesiasticis occiderit, per singulos ordines
et gradus singulos singulariter poenitere debet. Quapropter omnis qui interfecerit
presbyterum ita debet poenitere sicut sponte commiserit septem homicidia, et
numquam debet esse sine poenitentia.[52]

Haec est ejus poenitentia qui presbyterum occiderit secundum warmacense 50
concilium.[53] Carnem non manducet nec vinum bibat cunctis diebus vitae suae.
Jejunet cotidie usque ad vesperam, exceptis festis diebus atque dominicis. Arma
non ferat; equum non ascendat; ecclesiam per quinquennium non ingrediatur,
sed ante fores stet. Post quinquennium ecclesiam intret; nondum vero communicet,
sed in angulo ecclesiae stet vel sedeat. Cum autem fuerit duodeni anni circulus 55
finitus, communicandi ei licentia concedatur et equitandi tribuatur remissio. Maneat tamen in reliquis observationibus tres dies per hebdomadam ut perfectius purificari mereatur.[54]

245 Poenitens praesentium portitor ad nos veniens rettulit se instinctu diaboli quendam presbyterum armatum super se irruentem ictumque ferentem occidisse. Unde, 60
quia in canonibus pro interfectione armati presbyteri simplicem poenitentiam
esse dandam legimus,[55] injunximus poenitentiam decem annorum, ita ut hinc usque ad pascha jejunet tribus diebus per septimanam in pane et aque et non utatur
calceamentis neque lino. Ab octava pentecotes usque ad festivitatem sancti Martini jejunet duobus diebus per septimanam; et a festivitate sancti Martini usque 65
ad natale Domini faciat carcerem vel carinam, id est tugurium juxta eccle-

45 ex concilio warmacensi *om.* AdCc.   46 ecclesiasticis] clericis Ta.   ex ecclesiasticis]
ecclesiasticum AaJ *add.* viris H(Bart.) *add.* personis Ck.   47 interficit CcCkU interfecit Ci
interficit *corr. ad* interfecit Tc interfecerint J.   48 commisit Tc commisisset R commiserint
J.   50 Haec — poenitentia *om.* O.   warmacien. Ad.   51 nec] neque AaCkRTa
et neque J non Tc.   cunctis] omnibus AdR.   52 festivis RTa.   54 vero *om.* J.
nondum vero] dummodo non Ta non tamen Aa.   55 sed *om.* J.   duodenni Ac *corr.*
ad duocecimi Ad.   56 concedatur] exhibeatur AaJ.   59 se *insert. alia manu* O *corr. ab*
scilicet Tc.   62 legimus *insert. alia manu* O (*om.* Bart. Ivo).   63 per septimanam] in
septimana AaJ.   in pane et aqua] ad panem et aquam J ad panem et aquam *corr. attentat.*
Aa.   64 lineo AaCiU.   festum AaJPU.   sancti] beati AaJRTc.   65 septi-
manam] hebdomadam Ck.   per septimanam] in septimana Ta.   a] in Ta *om.* Cc.
66 Domini *om.* AaR.   faciat *om.* H.   vel *om.* H.   carenam JP carnam Aa.
66-70 vel — minui *insert.* AbO *distinct. signis diacriticis* Ad (*om.* Bart. Ivo *orig*) Cf. *infra in Append.*
C no. 9.

[52] Sects. 244-247 have been taken from Bart. cc.46-47 (pp. 212-214) omitting lines 14-29
of p. 213. No other literal source found for this paragraph; cf. below sects. 246, 248.

[53] There have been many councils of Worms. This canon corresponds in part to c.26 of a
council held there A.D. 868; see Hefele-Leclercq 4¹.458-465; Mansi 15.874; cf. above sect.
242 title ii with n. 39; also sources cited in the following note.

[54] See Bart. c.46 (p. 212); cf. Ivo 10.137 (PL 161.733-734); Burch. 6.8 (PL 140.768); below sect. 250.

[55] Cf. Burch. 6.10 (PL 140.768); below sects. 248-249.

siam ad hoc aedificatum; non exeat (quod dicitur carina a quadraginta, quia tot diebus ibi includendus est, vel a carendo, quia tot diebus hominum communione carere debet; de hac carina dicitur alibi quod non debet dividi, id est minui)[56] jejunans in pane et aqua, aut exeat tribus 70 diebus exsul jejunans in pane et aqua. Ab octava epiphaniae usque ad quadragesimam jejunet diebus duobus; a quadragesima vero usque in pascha jejunet tribus diebus in pane et aqua. Et haec faciat usque ad annos quinque; ab ingressu vero ecclesiae et communione septem annos poeniteat.[57]

246 Presbytero huic, quem perpetrati homicidii reatu ad judicium canonicae 75 poenitentiae suscipiendum ad apostolicam sedem misisti, noveris nos hujus ordinis poenitentiam injunxisse respectu misericordiae. Nam, quia presbyter presbyterum occidit, quadrupliciter, viginti octo videlicet annis, eum poenitere oportet.[58] Quatuordecim annos sibi injunximus, irrecuperabiliter eum dejicientes a presbyteratu et omni administratione altaris. Quos quidem quatuordecim annos hoc ordine 80 servabit. Tribus prioribus annis extra ecclesiam nisi ad extrema mortis absque communione et mensae participatione et pace sit, sed a caena Domini solum modo reconcilietur usque ad octavas pentecostes. Hac praesenti quadragesima cotidie jejunet, in pane et aqua tribus diebus hebdomadae, usque ad pascha. Ab octavis pentecostes usque in festum sancti Michaelis duobus diebus, deinde tribus. Post 85 tres annos, reddita sibi communione ecclesiae et mensae participatione, inter idiotas sit usque ad expletos septem annos, eodem modo totum tempus poenitentiae servans. Et quia convenit eum esse sub regimine abbatis, mandamus tibi ut mittas

---

67 aedificatum *add.* ut Ta *add.* unde P *add.* et idem Ck.   carena JP carentena Ta a carina Aa.   68 ibi *om.* AaPR.   69 hominum communione carere] ibi includi O.   carena P carentena Ta.   70-71 aut exeat — aqua *om.* JP *insert.* Aa (*homoeotel.*). 72 vero *om.* Tc(BART. Ivo).   in AbAcAdCcZ(Bm BART. Ivo) ad *cett.*(*cett.*).   73 haec] hoc AaCcCiJOPRZ(CpFGIKMNSgSoX haec BART. Ivo).   74 et *add.* a HP.   communicatione JR.   annis AaRTaU.   poeniteat] abstineat P *corr. ad* abstineat O. 75 Presbytero *add.* vero AaR *add.* tertio J.   perpetrato PTa perpetrasti Cc propter ecclesiastici Ck *corr. ab* per peccata Tc.   judicium] remedium O.   76 ad apostolicam sedem *om.* O.   78 occidit *add.* debet poenitentiam agere O.   videlicet] scilicet HU.   78-79 Quatuordecim *add.* autem Cc.   79 annis OTa.   sibi] ei H *om.* PU.   80 omni administratione] administratione omnis R.   ordine] modo JR. 81 servabis AaORTa duabus J.   83 pentecostes OZ(IMY BART. Ivo) pentecosten AbAcCiTa(BmCpN) pent. *cett.*(*cett.*).   cotidie *om.* HJR *insert.* Aa *rasura attent.* Ci.   85 in] ad CkJOPRTaU(CpFGKMNSgSoTbVXY in BART. Ivo).   86 idiotas] fideles audientes O *add.* vel audientes *insert.* Ab.   87 completos PTc.   tempus *om.* Ab.

---

[56] Cf. Ivo 15.183, 185 (PL 161.896-897). The word *carina* (*carena, carentena*) is used to designate a penance of forty days or a solemn penance; see BURCH. 19.5 (PL 140.951-958); ALAN, *Liber poenitentialis* e.g. 2.14, 3.8 (ed. LONGÈRE II 56, 131); ANCIAUX p. 366 n. 2, p. 371 lines 1-4. The hut is mentioned by PETER MANDUCATOR, *De sacramentis* 24 (p. 73*; cf. above sect. 236 n. 14) as belonging to the practice of solemn penance customary in Italy.

[57] See BART. c.46 (pp. 212-213); cf. Ivo 10.16 (PL 161.695).

[58] Cf. below sects. 248-249.

eum in aliquo monasterio, ut poenitens condigne salvetur; et si tibi vel abbati videtur sibi remittere, si hunc condigne observasse poenitentiam videris, post tres annos 90
liceat.[59]

247 Homicidium quam sit detestabile crimen clericis etiam ex hoc satis apparet,
quod nec judicium sanguinis eis habere licet nec praecipere quemquam crudeliter
caedi.[60]

His a quibus sacramenta Domini tractantur judicium sanguinis agitare non 95
licet, et ideo magnopere talis excessus prohibendus est, ne indiscretae praesumptionis
motibus agitati aut quod morte plectendum est sententia propria judicare praesumant aut truncationes membrorum quibuslibet personis per se inferant aut in-
ferendas praecipiant. Quod si quisquam horum immemor praeceptorum aut in 99
ecclesiae suae familiis aut in quibuslibet tale quid perpetraverit, et concessi ordinis honore privetur et loco; sub perpetuae quoque damnationis ergastulo reli-
getur. Cui tamen communio de hac vita exeunti non est neganda propter Domini
misericordiam.[61]

248 Si quis subdiaconum calumniatus fuerit,[62] vulneraverit vel debilitaverit, et 5
convaluerit, quinque quadragesimas sine subditis annis poeniteat, et trecentos
solidos cum sua compositione et episcopalibus bannis episcopo componat.[63] Si autem

---

89 aliquo] alio AaJR.   89-90 videtur *add.* quod debeas aliquid O.   90 hunc] hanc
O habeat J.   92 quam] quod J quantum H.   clericis etiam] cunctis etiam clericis
TaTc cunctis etiam *add.* clericis *insert.* Ab.   93 eis] ei Ck *corr. ab* ei Ad eos P *om.* JR.
habere] agitare OTa(Bart.) agere P *corr. ab* habitare Ab.   quamquam Tc *om.* Ta.
95 exagitare AaJR.   96 magno opere AaAbAcCiJRTcUZ(CpMNSgSoVY *corr. ab* magno
opere Bm magnopere Bart. Burch. Ivo).   97 agitata O agitari J(Ivo agitati Bart.
Burch.).   plectendus Cc.   98 truncationem AaJR.   personis] modis O.
99 memor JR.   1 famulis Tc *corr. ab* famulis Ci.   quibus JR.   2 perpetrarunt
JR.   3 deneganda AaHJR.   Domini] Dei AaJU *om.* P.   5 fuerit *add.* aliquem
insert. corr. attentat. ad quem Ab.   vel *om.* AaHJR.   6 sine subditis *corr. ab* de subsequentibus Aa *add.* aliis Ta.   annis *add.* subsequentibus JR.

---

[59] See Bart. c.47 (pp. 213-214); cf. Ivo 10.14 (PL 161.694-695).

[60] See Bart. c.47 (p. 214 lines 17-20). Cf. above sects. 103-106, 172; below sect. 250.

[61] See Bart. c.47 (p. 214 lines 21-32); cf. Ivo 5.315 (PL 161.421); Burch. 1.201 (PL 140.
609-610); Gratian C.23 q.8 c.30; also texts cited in preceding note.

[62] The verb *calumniari* is often used in the Latin Vulgate where the Septuagint has the Greek
verbs *sykophanteo* or *adikeo*; these in turn have been used to translate the Hebrew *ashaq*, which
means "to oppress", "to wrong", "to defraud". See e.g. *Prov* 22.16; *Job* 10.3; *Mal* 3.5. So also
the word *calumnia* has been used to translate corresponding nouns; see e.g. *Lev* 6.2. In these
texts this Latin verb has evidently come to have the meaning "to wrong", "to do someone an
injustice". Normally this has to do with possessions. In this section of our penitential and in
its sources *calumniari* evidently means "to injure", "to mistreat", "to do violence to someone".
Here it quite definitely refers to physical violence.

[63] See Burch. 6.5 (PL 140.766-767); Ivo 10.134 (PL 161.731-732); cf. Burch. 6.6 (PL 140.
767); Ivo 10.135 (PL 161.732-733); Gratian C.17 q.4 c.27; original edited by Alfred Bore-
tius, MonGerHist Leges (quarto) sectio 2, I 359-362. Albert Werminghoff, MonGerHist

mortuus fuerit, singulas supra dictas quadragesimas cum sequentibus annis poeniteat, et quadringentos solidos cum tripla sua compositione et episcopalibus bannis triplicibus episcopo componat.[64]   10

Si diaconum calumniatus fuerit, et convaluerit, sex quadragesimas sine subditis annis poeniteat, et quadringentos solidos cum compositione sua et episcopalibus bannis episcopo componat. Si autem mortuus fuerit, singulas supra dictas sex quadragesimas cum sequentibus annis poeniteat, et sexcentos solidos cum tripla sua compositione et episcopalibus bannis triplicibus episcopo componat.[65]   15

Si presbyterum calumniatus fuerit et passaverit, sex quadragesimas sine subditis annis poeniteat, et sexcentos solidos cum triplici sua compositione et episcopalibus bannis triplicibus episcopo componat. Si autem mortuus fuerit, duodecim annorum poenitentia secundum canones ei imponatur, et nongentos solidos cum triplici compositione sua et episcopalibus bannis triplicibus episcopo componat.[66]   20

Si quis episcopo insidias posuerit, comprehenderit vel in aliquo dehonestaverit, decem quadragesimas cum subditis annis poeniteat, et presbyteri occisi triplicem compositionem componat. Si autem casu et non sponte occiditur, cum comprovincialium episcoporum consilio homicida poeniteat.[67] Si quis autem sponte eum occiderit, carnem non comedat, vinum non bibat, omnibus diebus vitae suae; cin- 25 gulum militare deponat; absque spe conjugii in perpetuum maneat.[68]

---

8 fuerit *om.* O *insert.* Ab.   quadragesimas *corr. ab* quadragesimis O *om.* Z.   subsequentibus Aa *add.* consequentibus Z.   9 quadringentos] trecentos AaCkR *corr. ad* trecentos H. triplicata Ta *om.* P.   9-10 tripliciter J *om.* PR.   componat] constituat J consonat vel componat R.   11 sine *corr. ab* cum Ab.   12 quadringentos] trecentos HU. 13 sex *om.* AaR.   14 annis] bannis H *om.* O.   sexcentos] ducentos Cc dictos Ci do. Ta.   14-15 et — componat *om.* Tc.   15 bannis triplicibus *om.* Aa.   triplicibus *om.* CkJR.   16-18 Si — componat *insert.* Ab (*om.* So).   16 passaverit] pulsaverit AdHJOPZ(BmCpKTbY pacaveret Sg) convaluerit AbRTa(FGV Ivo[1]) pulsaverit *corr. attentat. ad* convaluerit Ck (spassaverit Ivo[2] Burch.[1-2] *orig*) *Vide adnotationem 66.*   (et passaverit *om.* X).   subditis] subsequentibus J subditis *cum* supradictis *suprascr.* Ck.   17 tripla HP.   18 triplicibus *om.* AaJR.   19 ei *om.* AaJ.   20 et *om.* AcJ.   21 posuerit *add.* et JRTcU *add.* vel Ck.   in *om.* HJRU.   aliquo] alio J *add.* modo HJR.   22 quadragesimis Cc.   23 casu et *om.* casu *insert. alia manu* Aa.   et *om.* JRU.   occidatur Tc occiderit P occisus fuerit HJR.   23-24 provincialium CcCkJR provinciarum H. 26 in perpetuo AbHTa(Ivo).

Leges (quarto) sectio 3, II[2] 834-835 gives an account of the MSS in which the original is found and a discussion of its origin; he maintains it is not from a genuine council, but is a fabrication from about the tenth century. The words *compositio* and *bannum* or *bannus* (the latter alternatives often used in the plural) in this context signify each some kind of fine or financial payment. See Du Cange s.vv.

[64] See *locc. citt.* (at the beginning of n. 63).

[65] See *ibid.*

[66] See *ibid.* The word *spassaverit* which occurs in the original means "he gets well"; see Du Cange s.v., noting the observations of later editors. Both Forms 2 and 3 seem to have had the reading *passaverit*; this reading best explains the origin of other readings found in MSS of Flamborough. Here it means "he gets away", "he makes his escape".

[67] See *locc. citt.* (at the beginning of n. 63). Cf. below sect. 251.

[68] See *locc. citt.* (at the beginning of n. 63). Cf. below sect. 250, 316.

249 Ex istis collige quanto aliquis alio plus debeat puniri quando aliqui eodem genere peccati peccant, unus in episcopum, alius in presbyterum, alius in diaconum, alius in subdiaconum. Item ex istis collige quanto plus puniri debeat episcopus quam presbyter, et presbyter 30 quam diaconus, et diaconus quam subdiaconus, quando eodem genere peccati peccant.[69]

250 Qui sacerdotem voluntarie occiderit carnem non comedat nec vinum bibat cunctis diebus vitae suae; jejunet usque ad vesperam, exceptis diebus festis atque dominicis. Arma non sumat; equum non ascendat. Ecclesiam per quinque an- 35 nos non ingrediatur, sed ante fores ecclesiae stet. Post quinque annos ecclesiam ingrediatur; nondum vero communicet, sed inter audientes stet. Cum autem fuerit duodecimi anni cursus finitus, communicandi ei licentia concedatur et equitandi tribuatur remissio. Maneat tamen in reliquis observationibus, id est duos dies per hebdomadam, ut perfectius purificari mereatur.[70]   40
     Saepe princeps contra quoslibet majestatis obnoxios sacerdotibus negotia sua committit. Et quia sacerdotes a Christo ad ministerium salutis electi sunt, ibi consentiant regibus fieri judices ubi jurejurando supplicii indulgentia promittitur, non ut discriminis sententia praeparetur. Si quis sacerdotum contra hoc commune consultum discussor in alienis periculis exstiterit, sit reus effusi sanguinis apud 45 Christum, et apud ecclesiam proprium perdat gradum.[71]

---

27 quanto] quando O quantum P.   alio *om.* O.   alio plus *invers.* CcHU.
debet HJRU *add.* puniat Ck.   quando] tanto AaJ.   in eodem Ta.   27-30
quando — debeat *om.* Tc (*homoeotel.*).   28 alius] alter O.   30 debet J *om.* R.
et *om.* AaHTcU.   et presbyter *om.* J.   31 et *om.* AaJRU.   (33-40 Qui —
mereatur *om.* G).   33 nec vinum] vinum non PZ (et vinum non Burch. Ivo).   bibat
ss. usque ad lineam 61 desinit Ck *folio perdito.*   (34-40 jejunet — mereatur *om.* VX).
35 assuamat Ta ferat O.   37 non ingrediatur J *praem.* non *delet.* Aa.   38 concedatur]
tribuatur exhibeatur Aa.   39 tribuatur] concedatur P *om.* Ta.   id est] scilicet
U *om.* AaOTa(Burch. Ivo).   per duos H tres O(Burch. Ivo).   40 hebdo-
madam] septimanam AaJ.   per hebdomadam] in septimana H.   41 principes
HTcZ(BmCpFGMNSoTbVX Bart. Burch. Gratian *orig*) *corr. ad* principes Ab (principe
corr. ad principes *forte manu originali* I).   42 committunt AaAbAcCcCiHTcZ(Bm-
CpFGIMNSgSoTbVX Bart. Burch. Gratian *orig*) committit *forte corr. ab* committunt Ad
(committent Y) *Auctor videtur scripsisse* princeps... committit *in Forma 2 et forte* princeps...
committunt *in Forma 3, sed haec lectio est valde incerta.*   a Christo *om.* R *insert* Aa.
electi *corr. ab* dediti O.   si ibi U.   43 consentiunt JR.   ubi] nisi AaAcCc-
CiZ(IMNSgSoXY) *corr. ad* nisi *forte manu originali* U (ubi Bart. Burch. Gratian *orig*).
promittuntur Cc permittitur P.   44 ut] ubi P(Bart. Burch. Ivo Gratian *orig*).
praeparatur PTc(BmGIKTb Bart. Burch. Ivo Gratian) properetur Cc (perpetretur Cp).
45 consultum] consilium CcTa.   discursor AcHPTaTcU(BmCpIKSgSoTbXY) *lacuna* Cc
obscur. O (discussor Bart. Burch. Ivo).

---

[69] Cf. above sects. 244, 246, 248.
[70] See Burch. 6.8 (PL 140.768); Ivo 10.137 (PL 161.733-734); cf. above sect. 244.
[71] See Bart. c.47 (pp. 214-215); cf. Gratian C.23 q.8 c.29; Hefele-Leclercq 3[1].271.
Cf. above sects. 103-106, 172, 247.

251 Studeat sanctitas tua persuadere episcopo tuo sibi canonicum sociare numerum collegarum, id est ex vicinis provinciis fratres et coepiscopos tuos, quibus tecum
junctis et decernentibus diligenter investigare et omni annisu scrutari procurate
quatenus invenire valeatis utrum percussione jam nominati presbyteri, an cervicis 50
fractione, idem diaconus, ut fertur, exstinctus est. Et si quidem a saepe fato presbytero non ad mortem percussus est, sed ex equo cadens cervice fracta interiit,
secundum arbitrium vestrum pro percussione incaute agenti presbytero poenitentiam competentem indicite, et aliquanto tempore a missarum sollemniis suspendatur, denuo ad sacerdotale post haec rediturus officium. Quod si veraciter qua- 55
licumque percussione istius presbyteri ille mortuus est diaconus, nulla hunc ratione
ministrare sacerdotis more decrevimus; quoniam, etsi voluntatem occidendi non
habuit, furor tamen et indignatio ex quibus motio illa mortifera prodiit in omnibus,
sed praecipue in Dei ministris, multipliciter inhibenter atque ubique damnantur.
Verum si presbyter adeo vestro studio noxius forte claruerit, praecipimus ut tale 60
beneficium sibi ecclesiae suae concedatur, quo et ipse et sui sufficienter possint
habere suae sustentationis solatium.[72]

iii. *De parricidio*

252 Parricidium dicitur non solummodo patris vel matris interfectio, sed et fratris
et sororis et filii et filiae, avi, patrui, avunculi, materterae et amitae et reliquorum 65
qui valde affines parentes sunt; et secundum hoc dicitur parricidium quasi parenticidium. Omnium autem poenitentia ex paucis potest perpendi, habita ratione
personarum, locorum et temporum, maxime autem causarum et utrum casu vel
sponte perpetrata sint.[73]
De Wimaro, qui tres filios suos occidit, ita statutum est: ut triennio ante fores 70
ecclesiae pro peccatis suis oraturus assistat, et deinde inter auditores permaneat
quadriennio; ut septem annorum curricula absque communione dominici corporis
atque sanguinis transeat, ita quidem ut in omnibus diebus vitae suae carnem non
manducet et isto septennio vinum non sumat nisi diebus dominicis et festivitatibus;

47-62 *alius paragraphus* O; *vide infra in Append. C no.* 22.   48 id est] idem Ci idem est
Cc.   49 annisu] animositate Tc animi nisu H animi jussu R studeo Ta.   procurare
AaCc.   51 fato] facto CiJ dicto P.   saepo fato] praefato U.   52 equo] quo
AaRTc *corr. ab* quo Ab.   53 vestrum] nostrum CcCiJZ *corr. ab* tuum Tc.   54 sollemnitate AaJ.   56 hunc] hinc Cc habet J humana *corrupt.* Ac.   57 decernimus AdHPZ-
(Ivo Gratian) permittimus vel decrevimus Ta.   occidenti J occidi Ta.   59 in
om. Aa.   in Dei] si R.   61 sibi *add. et* AaRZ.   sufficienter *reincipit* Ck.
62 suae *om.* CkTa.   63 *tit. om.* Cc.   65 avi] aut O *add. et* Ta.   affines *add. vel* AcTc
add. et Cc.   66 patricidium HJR.   66-67 quasi parenticidium *om.* Ta *insert.* CcH.
67 Omnis OZ.   68 et¹ *om.* AcTc.   autem] aut Cc *om.* Ta.   69 sunt CkOTc.
perpetrata sint] perpetrentur U.   70 Wimario O Guimario Tc Wimauro Z Vicunato J
Weramaro Cc.   71 orans O.   exsistat AaTc.   deinde] demum AaCcHTa.
73 in *om.* AaHOP(GKTbV Ivo).   74 sumat] bibat RTa.   festivis JORTaZ festivibus
Cc sollemnitatibus H (festivitatibus Ivo).

---

[72] See Ivo 10.24 (PL 161.698); cf. Gratian D.50 c.39.
[73] See Bart. c.48 (p. 215); no other source found.

abinde quinquennio tribus diebus per septimanam a vino abstineat, ut duodecim 75
annis quantitas poenitentiae extendatur. Liceat itaque illi uxorem propriam non
deserere, ne forte incidat in adulterium, et pro occasione unius delicti praecipitetur
fragilitate carnis in pejus. Concessimus etenim ei calceatum ad nos pervenire, ac
deinde triennio discalceatum ire debere, et vestimentis secundum quantitatem temporis et aeris temperiem indui, ac lacte perfrui. Ceterum vero ita actus ipsius dis- 80
cernentes per omnia considerate atque disponite quatenus et evangelica misericordia
in illo agnoscatur et canonica auctoritas conservetur. Attamen permittimus ca-
seum sumere atque possessionem suam habere; et post septimum annum usque ad
diem mortis perseveret in jam dicta poenitentia, atque arma nisi contra paganos
non ferat.[74]
85

253   Thiotar matricida sub jugo poenitentiae permaneat, ita ut unum per annum
ecclesiam non ingrediatur, sed ante fores basilicae orans ac deprecans Deum perseveret quatenus tanto eripiatur piaculo. Completo vero anni circulo, introeundi
in ecclesiam habeat licentiam; tamen inter audientes stet et nondum communicet.
Completis autem trium annorum circulis, sacrae communionis illi gratia concedatur; 90
oblationes vero non offerat nisi postquam aliorum trium annorum curricula expleantur. In his autem omnibus annis atque temporibus carnem non manducet nec vinum bibere praesumat exceptis festis diebus atque dominicis et a pascha usque ad
pentecosten; et quocumque ire voluerit nullo vehiculo deducatur, sed pedibus
proficiscatur; arma non sumat nisi contra paganos. Jejunet autem tres dies per 95
hebdomadam usque ad vesperam. A propria quidem ac legitima sua non sepa-
retur conjuge, ne in fornicationis voraginem corruat; quod ne fiat optamus. Si
autem ante trium annorum cursum finis vitae illius appropinquaverit, corporis et
sanguinis Domini nostri Jesu Christi particeps fiat; sin autem, ut supra statuimus 99
efficiatur. Tamen, si illius conversationem et lacrimarum fontem in omnibus vi-

76 propriam *om.* JR.   77 decidat JR.   delicti *om.* R *insert.* Aa.   78 etenim]
enim AaCkHU etiam P.   venire AaCkJORU(CpFSoVX) *corr. ab* venire Tc (pervenire
Ivo).   79 qualitatem Tc(*orig*) caritatem J *om.* P (quantitatem Ivo).   80 aeris] aetatis R annus *corr. ad* anni O.   ita *om.* Aa.   ita actus ipsius] actus ipsius ita P actus ipsius itaque R.   81 considerare atque disponere JOR.   cognoscatur JRTc.   82 observetur AaCk in illo conservetur P.   permittamus OTc *add.* ei AbH (*add.* eum Ivo).
83 atque] et O at Ta.   et] atque AaCkU.   septennem annum Tc septennium Ad
lacuna Cc.   86 Abiotar Ad Chiotar H Phiotar CcCiZ *om.* JPRU *obscur. corr. alia manu ad*
omnis O.   maneat RTc.   87 orans] stans Ta stet orans Cc (orans Ivo stans orans
BART. GRATIAN).   88 a tanto O.   piaculo] periculo JRTc.   vero] autem O.
circulo] curriculo CkJR.   89 in *om.* HOPTaTc.   90 curriculis JR.   communicationis CcR orationis Ck.   illi *om.* O.   91 trium *om.* OTc *insert.* Aa.   92 atque]
ac Aa vel Tc.   nec] neque JR.   92-93 nec vinum bibere] vinum sumere non P.
93 bibere praesumat] bibat O.   atque] ac Ad et AaCk.   94 pentecostes AbAcCiO.
96 ac] et PTa.   sua *om.* AaCkPTc(FIKMSgTbVY BART. GRATIAN sua Ivo).
98 ante *om.* Aa *corrupt. delet.* Tc.   cursus HP.   99 nostri *om.* Aa.   Jesu Christi
om. AaO.   1 conversationis AaCkH conversationis fructum U.

[74] Cf. Ivo 10.33 (PL 161.700-701).

deritis floridis actionibus et optimis operibus pullulare, humanius circa eum vestra sollicitudo pervigil appareat mitisque omnibus demonstretur.[75]

De patricidis et fratricidis

254 De patricidis et fratricidis praecipimus ut per unius anni circulum ante fores 5 basilicae orantes Domini clementiam perseverent. Completo vero anni circulo, introducantur in ecclesiam; tamen inter audientes, usque dum unius anni spatium finiatur, stent, cum ad missarum sollemnia vel alia sacra audire officia venerint. His itaque peractis, si poenitentiae fructus in eis conspicitis, corporis et sanguinis Domini nostri Jesu Christi participes fiant ne desperationis indurentur caligine. 10 Carnem non manducent omnibus diebus vitae eorum; jejunent autem usque ad nonam diei horam cotidie, exceptis festis diebus atque dominicis; vinum atque pulmentum sumere non praesumant nisi tres dies per hebdomadam; arma gerere non audeant vel sumere nisi contra paganos; et ubicumque ire voluerint nullo vehiculo deducantur, sed pedestri more proficisci studeant. Tempus hujus poenitentiae in 15 vestrae beatitudinis arbitrio ponimus, ut secundum conversationem illorum aut extendere vel minuere valeatis. Ab uxoribus, si habuerint, non separentur. Si autem non habuerint et se continere non valuerint, legitimas in conjugio accipiant feminas, ne in fornicationis voraginem incidere videantur. Si autem, antequam duorum praedictorum finiantur curricula annorum, finis vitae illorum pervenerit, 20 viaticum illis non negetur.[76]

255 Statuimus ut patricidae et fratricidae per unius anni circulum ante fores basilicae orantes Domini clementiam perseverent. Completo anni circulo, introducantur in ecclesiam; tamen inter audientes, usque dum unius anni spatium finiatur, stent, cum ad missarum sollemnia vel alia sacra audire officia venerint. His 25 ita peractis, si poenitentiae fructus conspicitur, corporis et sanguinis Domini participes fiant ut non obdurentur desperatione. Carnem non manducent omnibus diebus vitae suae. Jejunent autem usque ad nonam cotidie exceptis festis diebus

---

4 *tit.* De parricidis et fratricidis *insert.* Ad *om.* AbORTa.   5 parricidis Aa(Ivo).
6 Domini] Dei HU.   vero] autem O unius Ck.   curriculo R curriculo *corr. attent.*
Ad.   7 introducentur Aa introducuntur Ck.   8 finiatur *corr. ab* finiantur O complea-
tur J.   cum *add.* aliis Cc.   alia] aliqua O.   9 itaque] ita AdCc.   10 Domini
nostri Jesu *om.* R.   nostri Jesu Christi *om.* O.   11 eorum] suae HTaU.   12 atque[1]]
et Ck.   festis — dominicis] diebus dominicis et festis U.   13-14 gerere — sumere] ge-
rant O.   15 studeant] debent JR.   16 vestro J nostrae CiTc nostra Z.   17 vel] aut
AaAdCkHPU(BmCpFGKSgTbVX) *obscur.* O (vel Ivo).   (vel minuere *om.* I).   18 valeant
CkR.   19 in *insert. alia manu* O (*om.* Ivo).   20 fines O.   illorum] eorum CcP.
22-34 *sect.* 225 *om.* P(GKX).   23-29 introducantur—dominicis] ut supra usque dominicis Ad.
24 in *om.* O.   25 cum — His *insert.* O *Cf. infra in Append. C no. 23 cum nota 23.*   26
ita] itaque AcTc *corr. ab* itaque H autem ita Ck.   fructus *add.* in eis Ta(BART. BURCH. Ivo)
add. in eis *insert* O.   27 ut non] ne Aa ut *corr. ad* ne O.   28 autem *om.* JR.

---

[75] Cf. Ivo 10.173 (PL 161.741); BART. c.49 (pp. 215-216); GRATIAN C.33 q.2 c.15.
[76] See Ivo 10.180 (PL 161.743-744); cf. following sect.

atque dominicis. Abstineant se a vino, a medone atque cervisia mellita tribus diebus per hebdomadam. Arma portare non debeant vel audeant nisi contra paganos, 30
et ubicumque ire voluerint, nullo vehiculo deducantur, sed propriis pedibus per-
gant. Ab uxoribus, si habuerint, non separentur. Tempus autem poenitentiae in
episcoporum ponimus arbitrio, ut secundum conversationem illorum aut extendere
aut minuere valeant.[77]

256   Praesentium portitor litterarum, ad nos perveniens, lacrimabiliter confessus 35
est se fratricidii crimen incurrisse. Qui, licet tanti facinoris efficiens causa fuerit,
tamen minime voluntate sua peractum intimavit. Cum enim fratrem inimican-
tem paratis insidiis cepisset, et ipsum ut secum iret percussione capuli ensis coegisset,
consobrinus quidam suus secum perveniens, sine consilio et praemeditatione, sine
etiam voluntate ipsius, ut astruit, interfecit. Cui licet condignam religio vestra 40
conjunxerit et laudabilem poenitentiam, tamen circa eum viscera misericordiae
exhibentes, praecipimus ut cum domum redierit, medietatem totius patrimonii sui
pro fratris sui et animae remedio pauperibus tribuat, alterius quoque hereditatis
suae portionem nihilo minus pro eadem causa distribuens, usufructum necessitati
suae reservet; et sic omnibus ordinatis suis liber in monasterium ingrediatur, et 45
ibi per unum annum hujusmodi poenitentia maceretur: scilicet ut a pentecostes usque ad sancti Michaelis festivitatem bis in unaquaque hebdomada in pane et aqua
jejunet, dehinc autem usque ad quadragesimam tribus diebus jejunet similiter
in pane et aqua, et ut a corpore Domini et sanguine usque ad tres annos expletos

29 atque[1]] et AaCk.   a[2]] et Ad atque Ck.   atque[2]] a R et a Ck.   mellita om. O
insert. alia manu Tc.   (atque cervisia mellita} mellita cervisia BART. BURCH. Ivo).
30 debeant vel om. AdTa(CpMTb BART. BURCH. Ivo).   debeant vel audeant] audeant neque
debeant CkHU(V audeant vel debeant So) debent vel audent JR (praesumant Sg).   vel]
neque Aa nec Z(F).   (paganos add. nec debeant Cp).   36 Qui licet tanti] Quibus
tamen O.   efficiens causa] causa non J add. non Aa.   38 scapuli Z corr. ab capituli
vel capitali Ci corr. ab capsi alia manu O.   40 etiam] et delet. Cc om. Ta.   asseruit Tc
asserit P ascivit Ck.   41 injunxerit PRTaTcU(BmCpGFKNX BART. Ivo corr. ad injunxerit
Bm junxerit So) injunxit J (conjunxit SgTbV commenserit M).   tamen] tunc O.   circa
eum invers. O.   43 et om. CkHJRZ add. suae P.   fratris sui et om. U.   et animae]
animaeque O(BART. Ivo) add. suae Ta(BART. Ivo).   44 usum fructum AaAdTc(CpFSgTbY)
usum fructuum H usum fructum corr. ad usuum fructuum O usufructui J (usu fructu So usufructum BART. usum fructumque Ivo).   necessitatis J.   44-45 usufructum necessitati
suae] usum necessitati suae tantum U.   45 reservans O reservavit corr. ad reservat Aa observet
Tc.   in om. TcU.   monasterio O.   46 unum om. O.   pentecostes AbAcCiZ
pentecoste corr. ad pentecostes Ad pentecostem corr. ad pentecoste O pentecosten Ta(BART.)
pentecoste HJTc(Ivo) abbrev. ambig. cett.   47 ad om. AbAcJZ.   festum OTa.
48 ad om. CcCk.   quadragesimam tribus diebus] quadraginta tres dies Z.   tribus om.
Ta.   diebus om. Tc.   similiter om. Ta.   48-49 similiter — aqua] eodem modo
O.   49 et[2] om. AaO.   completos TaTc.

[77] See BART. c.49 (p. 216 lines 9-24); cf. Ivo 10.163 (PL 161.738-739); BURCH. 6.34 (PL
140.772-773); also preceding sect.

abstineat nisi periculum mortis imminuerit. Quadragesimae totos [dies] praeter 50
[dies] dominicos jejunet; arma nullo modo in vita sua ferat; conjugio usque ad
peractam septem annorum poenitentiam non utatur; sexta feria donec vixerit jejunet. Haec omnia ita illi injunximus ut, si infirmitatem ejus haec minime ferre
posse providentia vestra praesenserit, licentiam habeat miserendi prout placuerit.[78]

257 Diligentia vestra noscat huic Theoderico pro parricidio, morte videlicet filii, 55
sponte non commisso auctoritate beatissimorum apostolorum et canonum poenitentiam nos septennio imposuisse, in eodem poenitentiae peractae tempus connu-
merantes, ita ut amodo usque ad festum sancti Martini duobus diebus in hebdomada jejunet, quarta videlicet feria et sexta, in pane et aqua. A sancti Martini
festivitate usque ad Domini nativitatem continuum agat jejunium in pane et aqua, 60
exceptis dominicis et quinta feria, in quibus quadragesimali cibo vescatur. Ab octavis epiphaniae usque ad quadragesimam duobus in hebdomada jejunet diebus,
quarta et sexta feria, in pane et aqua exceptis festis principalibus, in quibus eleemo-
syna se redimat. In quadragesimali vero tempore est agendum jejunium in pane
et aqua exceptis dominicis; in quinta feria tamen tantum ei vinum bibere et qua- 65
dragesimali cibo uti concedimus. Post annum vero completum, in toto anno duobus in unaquaque hebdomada diebus in pane et aqua jejunet; in quadragesima
tamen continuum agat jejunium in pane et aqua; et in unoquoque anno usque ad
expletum poenitentiae tempus hujusmodi jejunium agendum est, et a carne se
abstineat. Per unum annum ei ecclesiam denegamus; post ingressum ecclesiae 70
tribus annis a communione separamus nisi mortis fuerit timore praeventus. Si
quis autem episcopus vel religiosus presbyter causa pietatis aliquid sibi relaxare
voluerit, hoc ei ex apostolica auctoritate concedimus.[79]

50 imminerit HJ *corr. ad* imminerit O (*add.* dies X) *add.* dies *insert.* O.   quadragesimas Ta(CpNSoTbVX) quadrgenas U xl. AaCcCiJR(Sg *corr. ab* xl. Bm) *om.* Ck (quadragesimam BART. Ivo) *add.* dies Ad.   totas JRTaU(CpNSoTbV) totae O (totot M) *om.*
AaCk(Sg totam BART. Ivo).   dies AaHTcZ(GF BART. Ivo) *om. cett.(cett.).*   prae-
ter] nisi Aa(BmCpSgSo nisi praeter IY).   51 dies AaCk(NSgSoTb BART. Ivo) *om.*
cett.(cett.).   dominicas JRTaU(INV dominicos BART. Ivo).   ad *om.* O *insert.* Ck.
53 Haec *add.* autem R *add. ante* J.   ita *om.* JR *insert.* Aa.   ejus] illius JR *add.* vel
J.   55 cognoscat JR.   Theoderico AcCiHPRTc(IKMNSoTbVY) Theodrico Ab
Theodorido Aa Tedorico J.   patricidio JR.   56 beatorum TaTc.   57 tempore
P tempore post JR *corr. ad* tempore Tc.   57-58 communicantes CcCiO *corr. ab* commutan-
tes Tc *corrupt.* Ad connumerandi licentiam dedisse P.   58 sancti] beati Ta *om.* Tc.
59 aqua *add.* et PU.   60 festo O.   Domini nativitatem] natale Z natale Domini CkO.
61 dominicis *add.* diebus CkTa *add.* et festis P.   dominicis — feria] festis diebus et O.
vescamur O uti concedimus *add.* vescatur *delet.* R.   62 in hebdomada *om.* Ta.
hebdomada jejunet diebus] hebdomadis Cc.   63-64 eleemosynis AaRU.   66 in *om.*
JR.   68 agat *insert.* Cc.   jejunium *om.* Cc.   69 et *om.* AaCkU.   72 quis]
quisquam Ta.   quis autem] autem aliquis Cc.   73 ei *om.* O.

[78] See BART. c.49 (pp. 216-217); cf. Ivo 10.177 (PL 161.742-743).
[79] See BART. c.49 (pp. 217-218); cf. Ivo 10.178 (PL 161.743).

iv. *De eo qui infantem opprimit*

258   Si mater filium suum sponte oppresserit vel occiderit, quindecim annis poe- 75
niteat, et numquam mutet nisi die dominico.   Mulier autem paupercula, si pro
difficultate nutriendi fecerit, septem annos poeniteat.[80]

Hi qui infantem oppresserunt tres annos poeniteant, unum ex his in pane et aqua;
si clericus fuerit, quatuor annos, unum ex his in pane et aqua.[81]

Mater si juxta focum infantem poseruit, et alius homo aquam in caldariam mi- 80
serit, et ebullita aqua superfusus mortuus fuerit, pro negligentia mater poeniteat et
ille homo securus sit.[82]

v. *De illo qui inhonoravit patrem aut matrem*

259   Si quis autem inhonoraverit patrem aut matrem, tres annos poeniteat; quod
si manum levaverit vel percussionem intulerit, septem annos poeniteat.[83]   85

vi. *De mulieribus quae fornicantur et partus suos necant*

De mulieribus quae fornicantur et partus suos necant, vel agunt secum ut utero
quae concepta sunt excutiant, antiqua quidem definitio usque ad exitum vitae ab
ecclesia removet; humanius autem nunc definimus ut eis undecim annorum secundum praefixos gradus poenitentia largiatur.[84]   90

---

74 *tit. om.* Cc.   De eo *om.* AcOZ(Y) De illis Aa (*Plerumque in talibus titulis De eo, De*
illo, De eis vel De illis om. Ac[Y]).   75-82 *sect. 258 una cum alia materia infra post sect.*
270 in O; *varr.* O *hic positae sumuntur ex illo loco. Vide infra in Append. C nos. 24-25.*   76
numquam mutet] jejunet Ck.   mutet *insert.* Tc commutet Aa bis manducet P.
nisi in die Ck(Ivo).   die dominica AaCc diebus dominicis J.   77 hoc fecerit CcTc
om. Ck.   septem] quatuor O.   annis CkHJPRU.   78 oppresserint AaPU(Bart.
Ivo).   poeniteat AcCc.   ex his] erit Cc.   79 si — aqua *insert.* AaCkH (*om.* K
homoeotel.).   80 Pater AbCkZ(K) *corr. ab* Pater O.   caldarium JRTa calderam Tc
caldaria Z.   82 homo *om.* O.   83 *tit. om.* Cc.   84 autem *om.* PU(Bart. Ivo).
aut] et J vel H.   tribus annis HU.   85 intulerit] intellexit Z fecerit J.   percussionem intulerit] percusserit Aa.   86 *tit. om.* Cc.   quae] qui *vel* quae Ab *corr. ab* qui
Ac.   87 quae] qui Ab.   88 quae concepta sunt] conceptos O(Bart. Ivo[1,2]).
excutient O excutiantur PTa.   quidem] quid J *om.* R.   vitae *add.* eas R(Bart. Ivo[1,2]).
89 nunc] non Cc *om.* Tc.   undecim] xl. Cc.

---

[80] See Bart. c.49 (pp. 218 lines 2-5); cf. Ivo 15.164 (PL 161.894).
[81] See Bart. c.59 (p. 224 lines 5-9); cf. Ivo 9.104 (PL 161.685).
[82] See Bart. *ibid.* (p. 224 lines 9-12); cf. Ivo 15.159 (PL 161.893).
[83] See Bart. c.49 (p. 218 lines 5-8); cf. Ivo 15.106 (PL 161.884).
[84] See Bart. c.56 (p. 222); cf. Ivo 10.181 (PL 161.744).

vii. *De impedientibus conceptum*

Si aliquis causa explendae libidinis vel odii meditatione, ut non ex eo soboles nascatur, homini aut mulieri aliquid fecerit vel ad potandum dederit ut non possit generare vel concipere, puniatur ut homicida.[85]

viii. *De simplicibus homicidiis* 95

260 Si quis sponte per cupiditatem suam homicidium perpetraverit, talem poenitentiam agat. In primis, ut licentiam habeat intrandi in ecclesiam, illos proximos quadraginta dies nudis pedibus ambulet et nullo vehiculo deducatur; in laneis vestibus sit absque femoralibus; arma non ferat, et nihil in his quadraginta diebus 99 sumat nisi tantum panem et salem, et puram aquam bibat; et nullam communionem cum ceteris christianis neque cum alio poenitente habeat aut in cibo aut in potu antequam quadraginta dies adimpleantur. Ex cibo quem sumit nullus alius manducet. Considerata vero qualitate personae vel infirmitate, de pomis vel de oleribus sive leguminibus, prout visum fuerit, aliquid per omnia indulgeatur; et ei omni- 5 modis ex canonica auctoritate interdicatur ut in his diebus cum nulla femina misceatur, nec ad propriam uxorem accedat, nec cum aliquo homine dormiat. Intra ecclesiam sit, ante cujus januas peccata sua defleat; et non de loco ad locum pergat, sed in uno loco his quadraginta diebus sit. Et si forte habuerit insidiatores viae suae, interim deferatur ei poenitentia donec ab episcopo pax ab inimicis concedatur. 10 Et si infirmitate detentus sit ita ut non possit poenitere, differatur poenitentia donec sanitati restituatur. Si autem longa aegritudine detentus fuerit, ad sententiam episcopi pertinebit quomodo reum et infirmum tractare debeat. Completis quadraginta diebus, aqua lotus vestimenta et calceamenta accipiat et capillum incidat.[86] 15

91 *tit. om.* Cc.   92 aliquis] quis HORTaTc (aliquis Bart. Burch.).   vel *om.* O.
93 potandum *add.* aliquid O.   95 *tit. om.* Cc.   97 ut] non Ta (*om.* FV) *add.* non R(X *add.* non *insert.* Bm).   licentiam *add.* non P(K Bart. Burch. Ivo) *add.* non *insert.* Ad. in *om.* CkHJORTa(BmCpFGSgTbVXY Bart. Burch. Ivo).   1 puram *om.* JR. bibat *om.* P.   aquam bibat] tantum aquam U.   2 alio] aliquo AaJPRTaTc(BmCpFIKMNSgSoY alio Bart. Burch. Ivo).   3 impleantur RTaU.   4 qualitate] caritate O.   de[2] *om.* CkRTc(Bart. Burch. Ivo).   5 sive] vel J *add.* de AaAdJPTa. per omnia] de misericordia Ad pro misericordia U.   5-6 omnimodis] omnibus modis CkU.   6 interdicantur Cc.   in *om.* Cc.   7 Intra] Extra PTcU(GFKXY) *corr.* ad Extra AdO (Juxta Bart. Burch. Ivo).   8 januam CkTaZ.   9 viae] vitae PTcU(BmFGIKMNSgSoTbV Bart. Burch. Ivo) *corr.* ad vitae AaOTa (vitae *corr.* ad viae *postea corr.* ad vitae N).   10 differatur HPU(Bart. Burch. Ivo) *corr.* ad differatur Aa. ei *om.* AaTc.   pax ab] pax *insert. in rasuram forte corr.* ab et O.   11 si *add.* in AaAbAcRTcUZ(CpGNTb Burch. *add.* in [?] *eras.* Bm *sine addit.* Bart. Ivo).   sit *om.* O. differatur *corr.* ab deferatur *add.* ei *corr.* ad ejus Ad.   donec *add.* ei Cc *add.* ejus H. 13 reum et] jejunet *add.* qui *insert. alia manu* O.   et] vel Cc *om.* U.   14 recipiat AaCkH *corr. alia manu* ad recipiat O.

[85] See Bart. *loc. cit.*; cf. Burch. 17.57 (PL 140.933).
[86] See Bart. c.41 (p. 210). Sects. 260-262 along with the first paragraph of sect. 263 are based on Bart. cc.41-45 (pp. 210-212). Regarding sects. 260-261 cf. Burch. 6.14 (PL 140.763-765); Idem, 19.5 (PL 140.951-952); Ivo 10.130-133 (PL 161.730-731); above sect. 242 title viii with n. 40.

261 In primo anno post quadraginta dies totum illum annum a vino, a medone et mellita cervisia, a carne et caseo et pinguibus piscibus abstineat, nisi festis diebus qui in illo episcopatu a cuncto populo celebrantur, nisi forte in magno itinere vel in regio exercitu vel in infirmitate detentus sit; tunc liceat uno denario vel pretio unius denarii aut tres pauperes pascendo tertiam feriam, quintam feriam et sab- 20 batum redimere, ita dumtaxat ut una re de tribus utatur, scilicet vino vel medone vel cervisia; postquam domum venerit aut sanitati restitutus fuerit, nullam licentiam habeat redimendi. Completo anni circulo, in ecclesiam introducatur et pacis osculum ei concedatur.[87]

In secundo anno et tertio similiter jejunet, nisi quod tertiam feriam, quintam 25 et sabbatum potestatem habeat redimendi praetaxato pretio ubicumque est. Cetera vero omnia diligenter observet ut in primo anno.[88]

Per singulos quatuor annos qui remanent tres quadragesimas et legitimas ferias debet jejunare; et in his quatuor annis accipiat quidquid voluerit tertia feria, quinta et sabbato; secundam autem feriam et quartam pretio supra dicto redimere potest; 30 sextam feriam semper observet in pane et aqua. Et his expletis sacram communionem [accipiat] ea ratione ut non sit sine poenitentia quamdiu vivat, sed in omni vita sua omnes sextas ferias poeniteat. Si tamen redimere voluerit, potestatem habeat modo supra dicto redimendi, et hoc secundum misericordiam, non secundum canonum mensuram, quia canones sic praecipiunt: Si quis per industriam et 35 cupiditatem hoc fecerit, saeculum relinquat et ingrediatur monasterium et ibi jugiter Deo serviat.[89]

262 Sicut septem anni publicae poenitentiae hic sunt distincti, sic etiam distinguantur ubi in publica poenitentia distincti non inveniuntur, sed simpliciter dicitur de poenitente: "Quadraginta dies in pane et aqua poeniteat et septem sequentes 40 annos," non utique in pane et aqua sicut primos quadraginta dies, sed sicut hic vel ibi aut in aliqua scriptura authentica eorum distinctio facta reperitur.[90]

16 et a medone Cc.   17 et[1]] a AcCkHJPRTcZ(BmGIKMNSoTbVY et Bart. Burch. Ivo).   a *om.* Ta.   et a caseo CkU.   et[2]] a Ta.   nisi *add.* in AaCkPTaU. 18 cunctis populis AaCkHU.   19 in[2] *om.* CcCkHJPRTaU(BmFKMSoTbVX Bart. Burch. Ivo).   vel[2]] aut AaCkU.   20 quintam feriam *om.* Cc insert. Aa.   feriam[2] *om.* CkHPRTc.   22 domi AaCk.   venerit *add* et laudabiliter AaJU.   aut] cum O et laudabiliter Ck.   23 circulo *add.* et laudabiliter H.   in *om.* O.   25 tertiam] quarta *vel* quartam Cc.   feriam *add.* et CkR.   feriam quintam] et quintam feriam U. 26 est] sit Ad *insert.* O.   28 et] vel *delet.* O.   31 completis AaAdCcCkHOPU(BmF-KMNSgSo exceptis V expletis Bart. Burch. Ivo).   32 accipiat HPTaZ(KMNX Bart. Burch. Ivo) accipiat *insert.* R sumat U sumat *insert.* O recipiat Ad(TbY non sumat G) percipiat Ck (percipiat *insert.* Bm) *om.* AaAbAcCcCiJTc(CpFISgSoV).   34 modo *add.* ut Ac. misericordiam *add.* et Cc.   37 Deo serviat] serviat omnipotenti Deo O.   38 distincti] destricti Cc.   etiam] et O et *insert.* Ad.   38-39 distinguuntur CkJTa.   39 in *om.* O.   distincti *om.* O.   inveniantur Ta *corr.* ad invenitur O.   40 sequentes *ss.* *cessat* Ck.   41 utique] itaque J umquam O.   42 aliqua] alia JR *add.* alia U.

---

[87] See Bart. c.42 (pp. 210-211); cf. *locc. citt.*

[88] See Bart. c.43 (p. 211); cf. *locc. citt.*

[89] See Bart. c.44 (p. 211 lines 19-31); cf. *locc. citt.*

[90] See Bart. c.44 (pp. 211-212); this paragraph seems to be a dictum of Bartholomew. Cf. below sects. 351-356.

263 Si quis voluntarie et per insidias hominem interfecerit, jugi poenitentiae sub-
mittatur. Et si hoc publice actum constat, si laicus est, a communione orationum
quinquennio removeatur; post quinquennium tamen orationum communionem re- 45
cipiat, non autem offerat, non corpus Domini contingat; in quo perdurans quatuordecim annis, tunc ad plenam communionem cum oblationibus recipiatur.[91]

Si quis voluntarie homicidium fecerit, ad januam ecclesiae semper subjaceat, et
communionem in exitu vitae suae recipiat. Si autem non ex voluntate, sed ex
casu aliquo, homicidium fecerit, prior canon septem annis agere poenitentiam 50
jussit, quinque secundus mandavit.[92]

Si quis homicidium sponte commiserit, et non violento resistens, sed vim faciens,
innocentem et simpliciter gradientem interfecerit, usque ad finem vitae suae graviter poeniteat ; sic tamen ut, si poenitentiam bene peregerit, in exitu ei communionis
viaticum non negetur.[93] 55

ix. *De viro qui interficit uxorem vel de muliere quae interficit virum*

264 Occidisti uxorem tuam sine causa mortis. Ingredere monasterium; observa
cuncta simplici animo quae tibi fuerint imperata. Hoc levius et etiam melius tibi
esse certissime scias. Si autem publicam poenitentiam permanens in domo tua
vel in hoc mundo vis agere (quod tibi pejus et durius et gravius esse non dubites), 60
ita tamen agere debes. Exhortamur omnibus diebus quibus poenitere debes vinum
et omnem siceram non bibes, carnem ullo modo non comedas praeter quam in
pascha et in die natalis Domini et pentecostes. In pane et aqua et in sale poenitentiam age; in vigiliis, in jejuniis, in orationibus, in eleemosynis omni tempore
persevera. Armis numquam te cingas, nec in quolibet loco litigare praesumas. 65
Numquam uxorem ducere, concubinam non habere, nec adulterium comittere

43 interfecit JTc.   44 Et] sed et Cc.   hoc *om.* JP(BART. Ivo).   46 non[2]] nec
O.   47 cum oblationibus *om.* J *insert.* Aa.   48 jaceat TaU jacebit JR.   49 exitu]
fine AaU.   ex[2] *om.* AaTa(GRATIAN).   50 aliquod Ci.   aliquo homicidium]
hominis aliquod *corr. ad* hominum aliquod *manu originali* O.   annis *om.* O.   53 simplex
Cc simplicem JR.   54 egerit Cc.   ei] tamen ei Aa ea Cc ejus R.   ei communionis]
tunc ei U.   54-55 communionis viaticum] communio O.   56 *tit. om.* Cc.
uxorem] mulierem Z.   57 Si occidisti JR Accidisti Z *corr. ab* Accidisti O.   58 tibi[1]]
tunc O.   imperata *add. et* JR.   60 vis agere *insert.* Aa *post* dubites H.   pejus]
potius JR.   durius] diutius RTa.   et durius *om.* J.   61 omnibus] singulis
AaU.   62 omnem *om.* JR.   sinceram HO ejiceram Tc.   bibas HP(BART. Ivo
BURCH. GRATIAN).   ullo modo non] nullo modo OPTa nullo modo non Cc.
comedes J comedatur Ta.   63 in[1] *om.* AcTa(Ivo BURCH. in BART. GRATIAN).   et[2]
add. in AaJP.   pentecosten J.   et pentecostes *om.* O.   et in sale *om.* JOR.
in[3] *om.* HP(BART. Ivo GRATIAN).   64 in[2]] et JR *om.* Tc.   in vigiliis in jejuniis *om.*
Z.   in[3]] et JR *om.* Tc(Ivo GRATIAN in BART.).   in[4]] et in J(BURCH.) *om.* Tc(BART.
et Ivo GRATIAN).

[91] See BART. c.45 (p. 212); cf. Ivo 10.141 (PL 161.734).
[92] See Ivo 10.39 (PL 161.702); cf. GRATIAN D.50 c.44; Ivo 10.142 (PL 161.734).
[93] See Ivo 10.143 (PL 161.734).

audeas, In balneo numquam laveris; in convivio laetantium numquam te misceas.
In ecclesia segregatus a christianis post ostium et postes humiliter te repone; in-
gredientium et egredientium orationibus suppliciter te commenda. Communione
corporis et sanguinis Domini cunctis diebus vitae tuae indignum te existimes; in 70
ultimo tamen vitae tuae, si merueris, pro viatico, si sit qui tibi tribuat, tantum
modo ut venialiter accipias tibi concedimus.[94]

x.   De eo qui publice poenitentem occidit

265 Si quis hominem publice poenitentem interfecerit, ut homicidium sponte
commissum dupliciter poeniteat, et nisi in fine non communicet.[95]   75

xi.   De homicidio pro vindicta facto

Qui pro vindicta fratris aut aliorum parentum occiderit hominem, ita poeniteat
ut de homicidio sponte commisso, cum ipsa Veritas dicat: *Mihi vindictam [et] ego re-
tribuam.*[96]

xii.   De homicidio non sponte commisso   80

266 Si quis casu non volens homicidium perpetraverit, quadraginta dies in pane
et aqua poeniteat. Quibus peractis, biennio ab oratione fidelium segregetur, nec
communicet nec offerat. Post biennium in communionem orationis suscipiatur;
offerat autem, tamen non communicet. Post quinquennium ad plenam communionem recipiatur. Abstinentia ciborum in arbitrio sacerdotis maneat.[97]   85
Haec poenitentia de illo intelligenda est qui non omnem quam pro homicidio
vitando debuit diligentiam adhibuit, ut mater quae dormiens filium oppressit, vel

---

68 post] praeter *corr. ad* prope O.   repones AaHU.   69 simpliciter RU simplex J.   A communione JR.   70 existimes] aestimes HO.   71 tamen] autem
U *add.* exitu O.   tibi *om.* CcZ.   72 ut *om.* O.   74 interfecerit] occiderit
AaPRTa.   ut] propter H ut (*delet.*) propter U *corr. alia manu ad* et O *om.* P.   75 com-
misit O.   77 fratrum O patris P.   occiderit aliquem hominem O.   78 ipsa *om.*
O.   vindictam *omnes MSS* (vindicta Bm vindictam *cett.*) *secundum antiquam sacrae Scripturae
versionem vulgatam.*   et HJOPRTaTc(CpFGIKMNSoVXY BART. BURCH. Ivo *et insert.* Bm)
om. cett.(*cett.*).   81 diebus O.   82 ab] absque JR.   oratione] ordine O communione
J.   83 communione JRU.   orationum OR.   85 Ab abstinentia R *add.* autem
AaU.   remaneat Tc sit AaU.   87 filium] alium Z *add.* suum O.

---

[94] Cf. BART. c.50 (pp. 218-219); BURCH. 6.40 (PL 140.774-775); Ivo 8.126 (PL 161.610-
612); GRATIAN C.33 q.2 c.8. Bartholomew has abbreviated this text and Flamborough has
abbreviated it still more.
[95] BART. c.52 (p. 221); BURCH. 6.20 (PL 140.769); Ivo 10.149 (PL 161.735).
[96] See BART. c.57 (p. 223); BURCH. 6.32 (PL 140.772); Ivo 10.161 (PL 161.738); *Rom* 12.
19; *Heb* 10.30.
[97] See BART. 58 (p. 223 lines 7-14); cf. BURCH. 6.16 (PL 140.769); Ivo 10.145 (PL 161.735);
HEFELE-LECLERCQ 3¹.298, C.18; MANSI 18¹.171.

qui nolens occidere, sed percutere, percussum tamen iratus occidit. Qui enim omnem quam debuit diligentiam adhibuit non est homicidii reus.[98]

xiii. De illo qui domino suo praecipiente homicidium fecerit 90

267 Si quis liber jubente domino suo servum ejus occiderit, ut homicidium sponte commissum poeniteat.[99]

Si quis servum proprium sine conscientia vel judicio judicis occiderit, ut homicidium sponte commissum lugeat.[100]

xiv. De illis qui veneficio homicidia committunt 95

Si quis vero veneficio interfecerit alterum, eo quod sine idolatria perficere scelus non potuit, nisi in fine impertiendam non esse illi communionem.[1]

xv. De illo per cujus delationem aliquis interfectus fuerit

268 Periculose decipiunt qui existimant eos tantum homicidas esse qui manibus 99 hominem occidunt, et non potius per consilium quorum et fraudem et exhortationem homines exstinguuntur. Nam judaei nequaquam Dominum propriis manibus interfecerunt, sed ipsi eum lingua crucifixerunt dicentes: *Crucifige eum.*[2] Unde unus evangelista dicit Dominum crucifixum esse hora tertia, alius sexta; quia judaei crucifixerunt eum hora tertia lingua, milites hora sexta manibus.[3] 5

---

88 percussus Tc *om.* Z *insert.* Ad.   peroccidit O occiderit R.   90 praecipiente] jubente Z.   fecerunt Ci facit AdJR.   91 ut] si *corr. ad* sicut O.   95 committunt] faciunt Z.   (95-97 De — communionem *om.* SoTb).   96 alterum] alium HJ aliquem AdOP. 97 impertienda U in percipiendam Cc *corr. ab* percipienda Aa.   impertiendam — communionem] impertienda ei non est communio U impertiendam ei communionem non esse H. non *lacuna* Aa.   illi *om.* Ta *insert. in lacunam* Aa *add.* censemus Tc.   98 dilationem Cc. 99 Periculo se Ci(MY periculossissime V) *corr. ab* pediculose Tc *add.* se Ad(Bart. Ivo Burch. Gratian).   decipiuntur AaAbCcHJOPRU(BmFGIKV existimant M dicipiunt Bart. Burch. Ivo *add.* eos So).   (periculose — esse] Periculosum est tantum eos aestimare homicidas X).   1 et²] in JR *om.* AaU.   1-2 fraude et exhortatione AaPTaUZ. 2 nequaquam Dominum] quoque Dominum nequaquam JR.   3 eum¹] cum AaR. 5 linguis TaTc.

---

[98] See Bart. c.58 (p. 223 lines 14-19; cf. following lines to p. 224); cf. Rufinus ad D.50 c. 37 (p. 126); Kuttner and Rathbone, *Traditio* 7.295 n. 23. Cf. above sect. 107; Firth, *Thesis* II 418*-420* with nn. 5, 14; also 483*-486*.

[99] See Bart. c.53 (p. 221 lines 16-17); Burch. 6.17 (PL 140.769); Ivo 10.146 (PL 161.735).

[100] See Bart. c.54 (p. 222 lines 11-13); Burch. 6.18 (PL 140.769); cf. Ivo 16.80 (PL 161. 921); Mansi 8.335; Firth, *Thesis* II 421* with n. 15 (III 691*).

[1] Ivo 10.155 (PL 161.737); Burch. 6.26 (PL 140.771); cf. Hefele-Leclercq 1¹.225; Mansi 2.6.

[2] *Marc* 15.14; cf. *Luc* 23.21; *Joan* 19.6.

[3] See Bart. c.53 (p. 221 lines 7-15); cf. Burch. 6.31 (PL 140.772); Ivo 10.160 (PL 161.738). Cf. *Marc* 15.25; *Luc* 23.44.

xvi. De homicidiis in bello factis

269 Oportet autem eos diligentius admonere qui homicidia in bello perpetrata
pro nihilo ducunt, excusantes se non ideo necesse habere de singulis facere poenitentiam eo quod jussu principum peractum sit et Dei judicio ita definitum. Sci-
mus enim quod Dei judicium semper justum est et nulla reprehensione dignum, 10
sed tamen oportet eos considerare qui ad hanc necem nefariam currunt, utrum se
coram oculis Dei innoxios excusare potuerunt, qui propter avaritiam, quae *om-*
nium malorum est radix et idolorum servituti comparatur, atque propter favorem
dominorum suorum temporalium Dominum aeternum contempserunt, et mandata illius spernentes non casu, sed per industriam, homicidium fecerunt.[4]   15

xvii. De eo qui christianum mancipium seduxerit

270 Item interrogatum est quid de eo faciendum sit qui christianum hominem
seduxerit et sic venderit; responsumque est ab omnibus homicidii reatum ipsum
hominem sibi contrahere.[5]

xviii. Si domina ancillam per iram occiderit   20

Si qua furore zeli accensa flagellis verberaverit ancillam suam ut infra tertium
diem cum cruciatu animam effundat; eo quod incertum sit si voluntate an casu
occiderit, si voluntate post septem annos, si casu post quinque annorum tempora,
acta poenitentia legitima, ad communionem placuit admitti. Quod si infra tertium diem fuerit infirmata, accipiat communionem.[6]   25

\<Cap. iii.\>   \<DE FORNICATIONE\>

271 i. De fornicantibus sodomitice vel cum brutis.
    ii. De incestu.

8 dicunt CcJOR habent U habent *delet.* Aa.   9 principium Cc principis Ad.
10 semper *om.* O.   justum] dignum AaU.   12 Dei *add.* quasi O(Bart. Burch. Ivo).
se excusare R *add.* non *insert.* Ab.   poterunt AaAdHPTaZ(CpKSgSo) *corr. ad* poterunt
Ab potuerint RU(IX potuerint *corr. ad* poterunt Bm) poterint J(M) (possint Bart. Burch.
Ivo).   16 seduxerunt Cc subduxit O.   17 Item *om.* JR.   18 responsum OR.
est *om.* AbJTa *add.* ei Cc.   19 sibi] si Cc ibi Ta *om.* U.   21 verberavit CcOR.
suam] ita Aa *add.* ita H.   22 an] aut CiJRTa.   23 tempora] spatium Ta *om.* Cc.
annorum tempora] annos U.   24 si *om.* Ac.   25 communionem *add. aliam materiam* O
Vide infra in Append. C no. 25.   26-42 *sect.* 271 *om.* J.   27 fornicationi Cc *corr. ab* for-
nicationibus R.   sodomestice AbCi sodomite *vel* sodomitae O sodomistice H *corr. ab* so-
domeitice Ac sodomisticae pravitatis Z.

[4] See Bart. c.54 (pp. 221-222); cf. Ivo 10.152 (PL 161.736); Burch. 6.23 (PL 140.770);
1 *Tim* 6.10; *Col* 3.5.
[5] Ivo 10.176 (PL 161.742); Burch. 6.49 (PL 140.778).
[6] See Bart. c.55 (p. 222); cf. Burch. 6.19 (PL 140.769); Ivo 10.22, 148 (PL 161.697, 735);
Gratian D.50 c.43.

i. De fornicantibus sodomitice

272   Mulier quocumque molimine aut in se ipsa aut cum altera fornicans duos annos poeniteat.[7]   45

Si sanctimonialis cum alia sanctimoniali per aliquod machinamentum fornicatae sint, septem annos poeniteant.[8]

Mulier, si cum muliere fornicata fuerit, septem annos poeniteat. Sic et illa quae semen viri sui cibo miscet ut inde plus ejus accipiat amorem poeniteat.[9]

Qui cum pecude peccat, quidam judicant annos decem, quidam septem, qui- 50 dam tres, quidam centum dies; juxta qualitatem personae poeniteat.[10]

Qui fornicatus fuerit sicut sodomitae, si servus est, scopis castigabitur, duos annos; si liber est et conjugatus, decem annos; si privatus, septem annos poeniteat;

---

31 adulteris AcOR.   33 vii. Quod *om.* PTc.   nec[1]] non Cc.   38 procatoribus AaHOTc *corr. ad* procatoribus *postea ad* jocatoribus Ad.   39-42 Quod — lavant *om.* AaOU *Cf. infra in Append. C no. 17.*   43 sodomestice AbAcCi *corr. ab* sodomestice Cc sodomistice Z sodomite O *add.* vel cum brutis CcCiZ.   44 cum] in HO.   (46-47 Si — poeniteant *om.* Y).   46 alia] altera Ta *insert.* Ad.   46-47 fornicatae sunt AdO fornicatae fuerint HP fornicata sit TaTc fornicata fuerit JR.   47 poeniteat PR.   48 cum *add.* aliqua O.   Mulier — poeniteat *insert.* AaH.   poeniteant HZ *corr. ab* poeniteant Tc. et] etiam Aa *om.* AcCc (et Ivo).   49 sui *om.* UZ *add.* cum Cc.   cibo *om.* O.   ut *corr. ab* si O.   50 Qui] Quicumque Tc.   Qui cum] Quicumque Ac.   peccat *insert.* Aa peccant O *corr. ab* peccant J.   quidam *add.* autem JR.   50-51 Qui — poeniteat *om.* U *infra post* debet *ad lineam 58* P(K).   52 sicut *insert.* Aa.   sicut sodomitae] sodomitice CcTa ut sodomita Tc.   est] fuerit O *om.* P.   castigetur AaTa.   52-53 duobus annis OU.   53 est *om.* JTc.   decem annis U *add.* poeniteat JRTa.

---

[7] Ivo 9.85 (PL 161.681).
[8] See Ivo 9.86 (PL 161.681).
[9] See Ivo 9.87 (PL 161.681).
[10] See Ivo 9.90 (PL 161.682).

pueri centum dies. Si in consuetudine est: laicus conjugatus, si in consuetudine habet, quindecim annos poeniteat; si ex ordinibus est et in consuetudine habet, de 55 gradatus poeniteat ut laicus. Qui autem cum fratre naturali fornicatus fuerit, propter tam sordidam commixtionem ab omni carne se abstineat vel quindecim annos poeniteat; si clericus est, amplius pelli debet.[11]

Stupratoribus puerorum nec in fine dandam esse communionem censuimus.[12]

273   De his qui irrationabiliter versati sunt sive versantur, id est qui cum pe- 60 coribus vel masculis se coinquinaverunt, quotquot ante viginti annos tale crimen commiserunt, quindecim annis in poenitentia peractis, communionem orationum mereantur; deinde, quinquennio in hac communione durantes, tunc demum oblationis sacramenta contingant. Discutiatur autem vita eorum, qualis tempore poenitudinis exstiterit, et ita misericordiam consequantur. Quod si inexple- 65 biliter his haesere criminibus, ad agendam poenitentiam prolixius tempus insumant. Quotquot autem post viginti annos aetatis uxores habentes in hoc peccato prolapsi sunt quindecim annis poenitentiam agentes ad orationis communionem recipiantur; in qua quinquennio perdurantes tunc oblationis sacramenta percipiant. Quod si et uxores habentes et transcendentes quinquagesimum annum aetatis ita delique- 70 rint, ad extremum vitae communionis gratiam consequantur.[13]

274   Clericus vel monachus parvulorum insectator, vel qui osculo vel qualibet occasione turpi deprehensus fuerit, publice verberetur et coronam amittat; decalvatus, turpiter sputamentis oblinitus in facie, vinculisque artatus ferreis, carcerali sex mensibus angustia maceretur et triduo per hebdomadas singulas ex pane hor- 75 deaceo ad vesperam reficiatur. Post haec aliis sex mensibus sub senioris spiritualis custodia segregatus, in curticula degens, operi manuum et orationi intentus, vigiliis

---

54-55 si in consuetudine habet *delet.* O(*om.* X).   55 annis O.   quindecim — habet *om.* Ta (*homoeotel.*).   57 se *om.* Cc.   58 pelli] poenitere P *corr. ad* puniri Aa *om.* U. 59 esse] omnem O.   censemus JR *add.* nisi digne poenituerint intellige Tc.   60 De] Ex CcH *om.* Z.   versati sunt sive *om.* Ta.   sive] vel JR.   60-61 peccatoribus O. 61 vel *add.* cum HU.   coinquinaverint CiPTa(BmCpINSoV Ivo communiquinaverint Sg) coinquinaverit AaAc(Y) inquinaverint R(K) coinquinant Tc(X coinquinaverunt Вакт.). ante] autem JR anni Tc *insert.* Aa.   62 commiserint O(Вакт. Ivo).   quindecim] viginti quinque JU.   63 deinde] demum O.   64 oblationes RTa oblationum Cc *add.* et Ta.   contingunt O.   65 plenitudinis CcR.   66 insinuant AcCcCiJOTcZ(GSo-TbV) *ambig.* insumant *vel* insinuant AaAb(Bm) insinuamus Ta (insinuerit Y insinuatur FM *corr. ab* insinuant N) sumant U(Cp insumant Вакт. Ivo).   69 durantes JRTa.   70 et [1]] etiam JR.   70-71 deliquerunt J delinquerunt R.   (72-79 Clericus — conjungendus *om.* X).   72 qui] cum Aa.   vel[3] *add.* cum Aa *add.* Qui Cc.   73-74 decalvatur O discalciatus Aa.   74 in *om.* Z.   in facie *om.* Tc *corr. ab* infame R.   vinculis O. 77 curricula CcORZ craticula P carticula Ta *add.* vel curtilla H (curticula Вакт. Ivo). orationi *corr. alia manu ab* oratio O orationum U.   intentus *add.* et O.

---

[11] See Ivo 9.92 (PL 161.682).
[12] Ivo 9.109 (PL 161.686).
[13] See Вакт. c.69 (pp. 235-236); cf. Ivo 9.88 (PL 161.681).

et fletibus subjectus et sub custodia semper duorum fratrum spiritualium ambulet, nulla privata locutione vel consilio deinceps juvenibus conjungendus.[14]

Si quis cujuslibet animalis commixtione peccaverit, quindecim annis in humi- 80 litate subjaceat ad januam ecclesiae, et post hos aliis quinque annis in orationis communione receptus poenitentiam agat, et sic sacramenti gratiam percipiat. Interrogentur autem alii de eo qualem in poenitentia egerit vitam, et sic misericordiam communionis consequatur. Si quis autem post viginti annos habens uxorem huic peccato irruerit, viginti quinque annis humilitati subjaceat, et quinque 85 annis orationi communicans postea recipiat sacramentum. Quod si et hanc mensuram aliquis transgressus fuerit, sacramentum in exitu consequatur.[15]

275 Episcopus faciens fornicationem contra naturam degradetur et duodecim annis poeniteat. Presbyter aut diaconus contra naturam fornicationem faciens praelato ante monachi voto degradentur et quinque annos poeniteant, et veniam 90 omni hora rogent, et superpositionem patiantur in unaquaque hebdomada exceptis quadragesimis diebus.[16]

Sunt multi qui considerantes magnitudinem praedictorum criminum, id est adulterii, incestus, fornicationis contra naturam, omnem reliquam fornicationem, quam et simplicem vocant, nullum vel modicum putant esse peccatum. Sed quan- 95 tum sit ex subscriptis auctoritatibus intelligi potest.[17]

---

79 vel] aut O.   81 ad januas O ante fores Z.   quinque] quindecim JR.   hos — annis] annos quinque O.   orationibus Ci.   81-82 orationis communione *corr. ab* oratione Tc.   82 communionem AaCcPU commixtione JO *corr. ab* commixtione R.   83 interrogantur O interrogent J.   autem *om.* AaR.   qualem in] qualiter O.   84 communionis] communicationis R orationis O.   85 huic] hoc JRTa.   irruit Ta uxtus erit J. viginti quinque] xx. RTaTc *corr. ab* xx. Ab *corr. ab* xv. Aa xxii. Cc xxx. O.   humiliter U humiliatus Z.   quinque²] x. Ta.   et quinque] xx. annis et xxv. J.   86 orationum AbAcJTcU(BmGNSoTbY) orationem Z(K) orationis R(FSg) orationibus Aa (in orationibus Cp orationi tantum Bart. Ivo orationibus *in contextu differenti* Burch.).   et] in J etiam R.   si et *invers.* AaO.   86-87 hac mensura O.   89 aut] autem aut AaHU vel Ta.   90 praelati Tc(FGIMNSgSoTbVY) praelati *vel corr. ad* praelati O praelatus Z praestito H (praelato Bart. Burch.).   praelato ante] praelatione U.   ante] aut JTc(IMSgSoTbVY) *ambig.* aut *vel* autem CcRTa(CpFG) autem Z au *corr. ad* aut O (sive N ante Bart. Burch.).   praelato — voto] degradetur; a praelato autem suo monachi P(K *corr. ab* praelati monachi autem voto Bm) *Cf.* Firth, *Thesis II 296*-297*.*   votum R (voce Tb sint N).   degradetur H *corr. ab* degradeantur O.   annis AaHJU.   90-91 poeniteat... roget... patiatur H. 92 quadragesimalibus AaU quadragesimae H quinquagesimae P (quinquagesimis Bart. Burch.). 93 praedictorum] peccatorum JR.   94 adulteri Tc.   adulterium incestum fornicationem O.   fornicationes AbAc.   96 auctoritate J actibus Cc.

---

[14] See Bart. c.69 (p. 236 lines 6-17); cf. Ivo 9.93 (PL 161.682); Burch. 17.35 (PL 140.925). *Curticula* means "a small yard".

[15] See Bart. c.69 (p. 236 lines 17-28); cf. Ivo 9.107 (PL 161.686); Burch. 17.38 (PL 140. 926).

[16] See Bart. c.69 (p. 236 lines 29-35); cf. Burch. 17.56 (PL 140.932).

[17] See Bart. c.69 (pp. 236-237).

ii. *De incestu*

276   Si quis fornicatus fuerit cum duabus sororibus, vel cum noverca sua, vel
cum sorore sua, vel cum amita sua, vel cum matertera sua, vel cum filia patrui sui 99
et avunculi sui, vel cum filia amitae suae sive materterae suae, vel cum nepte sua,
vel cum commatre sua, aut filiola sua, sive quam de fonte suscepit vel ante episcopum tenuit, et si qua mulier simili modo fornicata fuerit, abstineat ab ingressu
domus Dei unum annum, et eodem anno nisi dominicis et festis diebus solummodo
pane et aqua et sale utatur; arma non ferat; osculum nulli praebeat; sacrificium 5
nisi pro viatico minime accipiat. Sed deinde autem ingrediatur quidem domum
Dei, sed carnibus et vino ac sicera nisi festis diebus non utatur; de armis et osculis
sive de sacrificio sicut supra dictum est. Postea vero duobus annis, quando carne
vescitur, a potu omni quo inebriari potest se contineat; et si potum biberit, carne
minime vescatur absque praecipue festis diebus; de armis vero et osculo sive sacri- 10
ficio modum teneat jam dictum. Inde usque ad obitum suum nisi praedictis festis
a carne abstineat, tres ferias legitimas in omni hebdomada et tres quadragesimas
in anno legitime custodiat; de armis vero ut supra dictum est, et numquam aliquando conjugio copuletur. Haec eadem poenitentia est imponenda parricidis
et fratricidis vel consanguinicidis, nec non et qui sponte per fraudem et avaritiam 15
hominem innoxium occidunt.[18]

---

99 sua[1] *om.* JR.   vel cum amita sua *om.* Ta vel amita sua *insert. alia manu post* sua[3] Ad.
amita] avita Z *corr. ab* avita Tc.   sua[2] *om.* JR.   cum[3] *om.* R.   sua[3] *om.* AaR.
sui *om.* HJ.   99-1 vel cum matertera — avunculi sui *om.* O.   (patrui — sive *om.* Sg).
1 et] vel AaAdJRTaTcUZ(CpFIMNSoTbVXY) aut H (et Bart. Ivo).   vel[2]] et AaP aut
H.   amitae]avitae Z *corr. ab* avitae Tc.   sive] vel JORTaU et AaH (sive Bart. Ivo).
suae[2] *om.* AaJRU.   vel cum nepte sua *om.* P.   nepta AbAcCi *corr. ab* nepote O *corr. ab*
nepta R necte H.   2 commatre] matre AaHJOU.   3 tenuerit O.   abstineat
add. se CcO(Bart. Ivo).   4 Dei] Domini J *add. per* HJRTa.   festivis AdJ.   dominicis et festis] in solis dominicis Aa solummodo dominicis U.   5 panem et aquam R.
et aqua et sale] sale et aqua Cc.   6 recipiat AaHJU *corr. ab* recipiat Ad.   Sed *om.*
HJRTaU(FX sex Cp Bart. Ivo et V).   deinde] demum AaAbAdTa(MNSo deinde Bart.).
autem] annis O(Bart. Ivo) *om.* AdP(CpGFKNV *delet.* Bm).   quidem *om.* AaJORTaTcU-
(GSgSoTbVX) *corr. ab* autem quidem H (quidem Bart. Ivo).   7 et[1]] ac O a H *om.* Aa.
carnibus et *invers.* Z.   ac] et JPTaZ.   sicera] cervisia JPRTa.   nisi *insert.* Aa
add. in AaP.   et[2]] de PRTc *add.* de Ta.   osculo PU.   8 de *om.* JOTaU.
sacrificiis O.   sicut] ut OP.   sicut supra dictum est] modum teneat jam dictum Aa
cf. infra ad lineam 11.   9 possit JR.   se *om.* Cc.   abstineat OTaTc.   10 et
osculo *om.* J.   10-11 osculo — teneat] osculis sive de sacrificio teneat modo O.   11
Inde *om.* JR.   praedictis] jam dictis O jam praedictis U *add.* jam Aa.   13 in anno
legitime] legitimas in anno JR.   13-14 aliquando] alio O *om.* PTaZ *insert.* Aa.   14
patricidis AdCcJPRU(FKSoTbVX patricidiis M parricidis Bart. Ivo).   15 et[1]] vel Aa-
AbCiHORTcUZ(CpSgV Bart. Ivo *om.* G).   vel] et AdHTaU.   consanguineicidis
Aa consanguineis O(Bart. Ivo).   et[2]] etiam JR *om.* O *add.* his H *add.* illis U.
sponte *add.* et O.   16 occiderunt Ta occiderit PR.

---

[18] See Bart. c.66 (pp. 231-232); cf. Ivo 9.70 (PL 161.678); Burch. 19.5 (PL 140.966).

277 Iste poenitens venit ad nos confessusque est se filiam patrui sui corrupisse. Cui quatuordecim annorum poenitentiam injunximus, ut jejunet quidem tribus quadragesimis. In quadragesima post pentecosten duobus diebus in septimana in pane et aqua, et in adventu tribus, et in majori quadragesima tribus, et abstineat 20 se ab ingressu ecclesiae et a communione duobus annis. [19]

Interrogatum est si pater et filius, vel si duo fratres, vel si avunculus et nepos cum una muliere fornicati sunt, quid inde faciendum sit. Theodorus judicavit eum qui incestum fecerit annos duodecim poenitere debere, alii quindecim, alii decem, alii septem ; sed nos, priscorum patrum vestigia sequentes, his solum spatium poe- 25 nitentiae temperemus qui devote et cum lacrimis poenitentiam egerint ; ceteri definitum tempus observent. [20]

iii. De lapsu personarum religiosarum

278 Monachi filios procreantes in carcerem recludantur, et tantum facinus continua lamentatione deflentes, ut eis vel ad mortem sola misericordia in communionis 30 gratia possit indulgeri. [21]

Fili serpentis, minister diaboli, violator virginis, id est templi Dei, qui in uno scelere duo crimina perpetrasti : adulterium utique et sacrilegium, sacrilegium plane ubi vas oblatum Deo et Christo dedicatum dementi temeritate polluisti. [22]

Ex his perpenditur masculos et feminas praedicti criminis reos sacrilegii et adul- 35 terii poena esse plectendos. Est etiam incestus sive adulterium omnis spiritualis cognationis carnalis violatio. [23]

279 Si qui scientes sanctimonialibus feminis in matrimonio sunt ad injuriam Christi copulati, ita ad censuram zeli separentur ut numquam eis concedatur conjugali vinculo religari, sed in poenitentiae se lamentis vehementer, dum vivunt, afficiant. [24] 40

Virginibus sacris temere se quosdam sociare cognovimus et post dicatum Deo propositum incesta foedera sacrilegaque miscere ; quos protinus aequum est a sacra

17 confessusque] et confessus OR confessus J.   corrupuisse Tc corr. ab corrupuisse O.
19 quadragisimis] diebus xl. (lege : diebus quadragesimae ?) Cc.   pentecostem CiO.
in septimana om. AaJPU insert. Tc..   21 se om. CcP.   ecclesiae] monasterii Ta.
22 vel¹] et AbJRTa.   si² om. PZ   vel²] et JR.   23 sunt] sint AaZ(Ivo) fuerint
Ad (sunt Bart.).   eum om. O.   24 annis AaJU.   25-26 poenitentiae] poenae O.
29 carcere Ta.   concludantur Ta retrudantur P.   30 defleant HP.   sola miseri-
cordia] solamina Ci.   in] vel P om. U.   32 virginum O.   33 utique] quippe JTa.
34 et om. O.   35 et¹] vel CiHPZ.   et feminas — reos] praedicti criminis reos et feminas
AaU.   36 sive adulterium om. Ta insert. Tc.   37 cognationisve Ta conjunctionis JR
insert Tc.   39 ut] et O (Bart. Ivo Gratian).   41 dicatum] dicant J corr. ab dicant Aa.

[19] See Bart. c.66 (p. 232 lines 22-29) ; cf. Ivo 9.10 (PL 161.659).
[20] See Bart. c.66 (p. 233 lines 31-38) ; cf. Ivo 9.79 (PL 161.679-680) ; above p. 197, nn. 52-53.
[21] See Bart. c.67 (p. 234 lines 15-18) ; cf. Ivo 7.86 (PL 161.565).
[22] See Bart. c.67 (p. 234 lines 19-22) ; cf. Ivo 7.134 (PL 161.576).
[23] See Bart. c.67 (p. 234 lines 23-26) ; no other source found.
[24] See Bart. c.67 (p. 234 lines 10-14) ; cf. Ivo 7.50 (PL 161.556) ; Gratian C.27 q.1 c.13.

communione detrudi et nisi per probatam publicamque poenitentiam omnino non recipi; sed tamen his viaticum de saeculo transeuntibus, si digne poenituerint, non negetur.[25]   45

Si qua monacharum, vel per anteriorem licentiam vel per impunitatis pravam consuetudinem, ad lapsum adulterii deducta fuerit aut in futurum fuerit perducta voraginem, hanc post competentis severitatem vindictae in aliud districtius virginum monasterium in poenitentiam volumus redigi, ut illic orationibus atque jejuniis vacet, et sic poenitendo proficiat et metuendum ceteris artioris disciplinae 50 praestet exemplum. Is autem, qui cum hujusmodi feminis in aliqua fuerit iniquitate repertus, communione privetur si laicus; si vero clericus est, a suo quoque remotus officio pro suis continue lugendis excessibus in monasterium detrudatur.[26]

iv. *De spirituali incestu*

280 Si quis sacerdos cum filia spirituali fornicatus fuerit, sciat se grave adul- 55 terium commisisse. Idcirco femina, si laica est, omnia derelinquat et res suas pauperibus tribuat, et conversa in monasterio Deo usque ad mortem serviat. Sacerdos autem qui malum exemplum dederit hominibus ab omni officio deponatur, et peregrinando quindecim annis poeniteat; postea vero ad monasterium vadat, ibique cunctis diebus vitae suae Deo serviat.[27]   60

Omnes quos in poenitentia suscipimus nostri ita spirituales sunt filii ut et ipsi quos, vel nobis suscipientibus vel sub trinae mersionis vocabulo mergentibus, unda baptismatis regeneravit.[28]

Non debet episcopus aut presbyter commisceri cum mulieribus quae eis peccata sua confessae fuerint. Si forte, quod absit, hoc contigerit, sic poeniteat quomodo 65 de filia spirituali: episcopus quindecim annis, et presbyter duodecim annis poeniteat, et deponatur tamen si in conscientiam populi devenerit.[29]

43 detrudi] excludi JR arceri Ta.   probatam publicamque] publicam probatamque O. publicamque] et publicam CcJR.   44 recepi Ac *corr. ab* recepi Cc.   47 perducta] deducta Cc deducenda Ta.   49 redigi ut] redigii Ac.   50 et[1]] vel O.   perficiat JR.   artioris] altioris J amoris Cc *insert.* O.   51 Is] His OR *corr. ab* His Tc. fuit AcTc.   52 laicus *add.* est O *add.* fuerit Z.   est *om.* CcR.   quoque *om.* AaTa. 53 retrudatur Cc.   56 femina si *invers.* AaCcHO.   omnia *add.* sua O.   relinquat AaPU.   57 Deo *delet.* Ad.   Deo — mortem] usque ad mortem Deo Z *add.* suam O. 58 dedit AaHPTcU(BmCpFIKMNSgSoTbXY Bart. Gratian *orig*).   59 quindecim] xx. Cc. vero *om.* P *forte om.* O.   61 et] etiam JR *om.* AaP.   63 regeneraverit AbAcCi.   64 eis *om.* O.   65 fuerunt O.   Si] quod si O.   forte] autem fortasse Ta eis AaU. hoc] sic Ta *om.* O.   contingerit HR.   quomodo] sicut AaU.   66 et] poeniteat Tc *om.* AcHPTaU(Gratian *orig et* Bart.).   annis[2] *om.* AcTcU.   66-67 poeniteat *om.* Tc(Gratian *orig* poeniteat Bart.).   presbyteri... poeniteant et deponantur U.   67 deponatur *add.* et O.   conscientia AcJ(Bart.) continuam Cc.   tamen — devenerit] si tamen populus sciverit U.

[25] See Ivo 7.51 (PL 161.556); Gratian C.27 q.1 c.14.

[26] See Gratian C.27 q.1 c.28; Ivo 7.123 (PL 161.572).

[27] See Bart. c.67 (p. 234 lines 26-34); Gratian C.30 q.1 c.9; cf. JK 382; Mansi 4.472; PL 50.565; above sects. 43-49.

[28] See Bart. c.68 (p. 235 lines 2-5); cf. Gratian C.30 q.1 c.8; JK 768; Mansi 8.230; PL 62.80; Lombard, *Sent.* 4.42.2.379; above sect. 48 with notes.

[29] See Bart. c.68 (p. 235 lines 5-10); cf. Gratian C.30 q.1 c.10.

281 Quia peculiare flagitium commisit qui duabus commatribus velut duabus sororibus nupsit, magna juxta modum culpae poenitentia sibi debet injungi.[30]

Si quis cum matre spirituali fuerit fornicatus, anathematis, ut scitis, percutitur 70 ictibus. Similiter autem et illum percutere promulgamus qui cum ea quam de sacro fonte baptismatis susceperit, aut cum illa quam ante episcopum tenuerit cum sacro chrismate fuerit uncta, fornicationis perpetraverit scelus; legitimam tamen, si habuerit, non dimittere cogatur uxorem.[31]

v. De adulteris

75

282 Si quis habens uxorem semel fuerit lapsus, placuit eum quinquennio agere debere poenitentiam.[32]

Si cujus uxor adulterata fuerit, vel si ipse adulterium fecerit, septem annorum poenitentia oportet eum perfectionem consequi secundum pristinos gradus.[33]

Si cui etiam non contingat facultas concumbendi cum conjuge aliena, planum 80 tamen sit eum aliquo modo id cupere, et si potestas ei detur, esse facturum, non minus reus est quam si in ipso facto deprehenderetur.[34]

Si conscio marito et ipsa consciens uxor fuerit moechata, placuit nec in fine dandam eis communionem. Si vero eam reliquerit et separati fuerint et digne poenituerint, post decem annos accipiant communionem.[35] 85

283 Si quis uxorem suam invenerit adulteram et postea deinceps placuerit habere eam in matrimonium, duobus annis poeniteat, ideo quod adulterae mixtus sit quae adhuc crimine suo non purgata est; aut abstineat se a matrimonio ejus

---

68 velut] vel JR.   70 matre] commatre Ad.   71 Simul Cc.   illis O. permulgamus AbAc praeintelligamus O *corr. ab* provulgamus Tc.   72 suscepit PU susceperat O.   illa] aliqua O.   tenuit PZ.   73 fuit OP.   perpetravit JOPRZ. 75 *tit. om.* Ci.   adulteriis Z.   76 eum] eo Cc.   77 debere *om.* PTa. 78 cujus] ejus OTc.   fuit O.   si[2] *om.* JRTa(Ivo si BART.).   79 poenitentiam AaJ.   eum] eam J eos H *om.* O.   81 tamen *lacuna vel rasura* Cc.   id *om.* Cc. esse *om.* Cc id esse U.   82 in *om.* AaRTa.   83 ipsa *corr. ad* ipso O.   consciens] conscia Aa(CpFGM) sciens P(K) consentiens Ad(BmSoX) conscienti *corr. ad* consentienti O (consentiente BART. Ivo).   consciens uxor *invers.* H uxor conscia U.   uxor *om.* AaTc. moechata] machinata Ta *corr. ab* enchoata O.   placuit *add.* vero J *add.* mihi *insert.* O. 84 eis *om.* Cc *add.* esse TcU.   85 poenituerunt Ac.   recipiant AaHU.   86 suam *om.* AaP.   placuit JR *om.* placuit *insert.* Aa.   87 matrimonio Ta(BART. GRATIAN). ideo] eo AdJ.

---

[30] See BART. c.68 (p. 235 lines 11-14); cf. GRATIAN C.30 q.4 c.6; LOMBARD, *Sent.* 4.42.6.386. Regarding a possible meaning of the word *nupsit* here see below sect. 287 with n. 47. Cf. also above sects. 43-49 and sect. 225 with n. 52.

[31] See Ivo 9.36 (PL 161.664); IDEM 1.138 (PL 161.92); GRATIAN C.33 q.2 c.17.

[32] BART. c.61 (p. 227 lines 2-4); Ivo 8.281 (PL 161.645); cf. Council of Elvira c.69 (HEFELE-LECLERCQ 1[1].259).

[33] BART. c.61 (p. 227 lines 4-7); cf. Ivo 8.284 (PL 161.646).

[34] See BART. c.61 (p. 227 lines 8-11); cf. Ivo 8.104 (PL 161.605); GRATIAN *De poen.* D.1 c.30.

[35] See BART. c.61 (p. 227 lines 12-15); Ivo 8.206 (PL 161.626).

donec expleatur satisfactio criminis poenitentiae suae, ideo quia post satisfactionem
poenitentiae non meretur vocari adultera. Similiter, si uxor maritum invenerit 90
adulterum, non ad imparia judicatur.[36]

Quod si vir non habens uxorem cum alterius uxore adulterium perpetraverit,
aut si qua mulier non habens virum cum alterius viro, ille qui foedus conjugii vio-
lavit septem annos poeniteat. Neque enim aequalis poenitentia danda est his
quibus sufficere poterat ad explendam libidinem suam conjugum ardore amplexus, 95
et illis qui conjuge carentes ardore libidinis impellente in fornicationem decide-
runt.[37]

284 Quicumque, propria uxore derelicta vel sine culpa interfecta, aliam duxerit
armis depositis publicam agat poenitentiam; et si contumax fuerit, comprehendatur 99
a comite et ferro vinciatur et in custodiam mittatur.[38]

Si quis fidelis habens uxorem cum judaea vel gentili fuerit moechatus, a communione arceatur. Quod si alius eum detexerit, post quinquennium acta legitima
poenitentia dominicae communioni sociari potest.[39]

vi. *Quando abstinendum sit ab amplexibus*   5

285 Si causa creandorum filiorum ducitur uxor, non multum temporis videtur concessum ad ipsum usum; quia et dies festi et dies processionis et ipsa ratio conceptus
et partus juxta legem cessare temporibus his debere demonstrant.[40]

Oportet legitimam carnis copulam ut causa prolis sit, non voluptatis, et carnis
commixtio creandorum liberorum sit gratia, non satisfactio vitiorum. Si quis vero 10
sua conjuge, non voluptatis cupiditate raptus, sed solum modo creandorum liberorum gratia, utitur, iste profecto, sive de ingressu ecclesiae sive de sumendo dominici
corporis et sanguinis mysterio, suo est relinquendus judicio; quia a nobis prohiberi

---

89 impleatur AaRU.   90 poenitentiae *add.* suae Cc.   91 adulterium AcU *corr. ab*
adulterium AbCi adulteratum O adulterantem Tc.   judicatur *corr. ab* judicantur O.
92 altera O.   93 altero O.   95 conjugium Cc conjugii P.   ardore *om.* AbJOR-
Ta(X Bart. Ivo) *brevissima rasura* Tc in ardore H.   96 in *corr. ab* cum O.   fornicatione
H.   96-97 ceciderunt O(Bart. Ivo) inciderunt TaTc inciderint Aa.   98 relicta P
delicta U.   interfecta] derelicta AaU.   99 publicam *om.* JR.   comprehendan-
tur Ta deprehendatur JR.   1 custodia CiOPTaTc(BmFIKSgXY carcerem G custodiam
Ivo).   et in custodiam] in custodiamque JR.   2 vel] et R *add.* cum HTc.   fuit
Ci.   3 eum] eam Tc *om.* Ta.   4 poterit AaOUZ(Ivo).   7 et[1] *om.* CcTa.
8 demonstrat Z demonstravit Tc monstrant R.   11 voluntatis AcCc.   sed] sit
AcAd.   12 profecto] pro facto O.   de[1]] pro J *om.* Z.   13 quia *corr. ab*
quod O.

---

[36] See Bart. c.61 (p. 227 lines 16-24); Gratian C.32 q.1 c.4.
[37] See Bart. c.61 (p. 227 lines 24-32); cf. Ivo 8.207 (PL 161.626-627).
[38] Ivo 8.241 (PL 161.636); cf. Idem 10.166 (PL 161.739); Gratian C.33 q.2 c.7.
[39] See Ivo 8.282 (PL 161.645-646).
[40] See Ivo 8.84 (PL 161.601); Bart. c.64 (p. 230 lines 1-5); Gratian C.33 q.4 c.4; cf. above
sects. 71-72, 226-227; below sect. 296.

non potest qui in igne positus nescit ardere. Cum vero amor procreandae sobolis, si voluptas, dominatur in opere commixtionis, habent etiam conjuges quod de sua 15 commixtione defleant.[41]

Item, tunc vir qui post commixtionem conjugis lotus aqua fuerit etiam sacrae communionis mysterium valet accipere, cum ei juxta praefinitam sententiam etiam ecclesiam licuerit intrare.[42]

286 Caveat uxor ne forte victa desiderio celet virum, et maritus ne vim faciat uxori, 20 putans omni tempore conjugii voluntatem licere.[43]

Quicumque uxori debitum reddit vacare non potest orationi, nec de carnibus Agni comedere.[44]

Item, si panes propositionis ab his qui uxores suas tetigerant comedi non poterant, quanto magis panis ille *qui de caelo descendit* non potest ab his qui conjugalibus paulo 25 ante haesere complexibus violari atque contingi. Non quod nuptias condemnemus,

---

14 non potest] non debet *insert.* O (non debet Ivo GRATIAN).   nescit *add.* non Ta
add. lacunam vel rasuram Cc.   (Cum vero] quia So cum nec V).   vero *add.* non PTa-
Tc(FGKMNSgTbXY Ivo).   amor *corr. ab* amore Ab.   sobolis *add.* adsit *insert.* O.
15 si] sed PTaTc(BmFGKNTbVXY Ivo GRATIAN).   etiam] et AaJ tunc Ta *om.* Z.
17 vir] ubi CcUZ ibi H nisi Ta *om.* JR.   admixtionem AbAcAdCiRTcZ(GIY Ivo GRA-
TIAN commixtionem *orig*).   etiam] et AaJR.   18 valet *corrupt. corr. ad* licet O.
etiam] et JO.   19 licuit AaJR.   20 Sed caveat O Saveat (*magna littera mutata*) Ci.
celet] zelet Ta(BmTbXY) *corr, ad* zelet Tc (*corr. ab* scelet F celat Cp debet Sg celet Ivo illi-
ciat *orig*) *Vide adnotationem.*   21 voluptatem AbAdPTaU(KTbVX *om.* F voluntatem
Ivo).   licere *om.* O.   24 Item] quod JTa.   propositionis *om.* J *insert.* Tc.
26 violari] immolari O.   Non quod] Numquid AaCcCiHOU(ISgSoVY) Numquam J
Non R.

---

[41] See Ivo 8.88 (latter part; PL 161.602); cf. GRATIAN C.33 q.4 c.7 §2-3. This is taken from a well-known letter purporting to contain the answers of Pope St. Gregory the Great to some questions posed by St. Augustine of Canterbury, JE 1843, preserved by the Venerable Bede in his *Historia ecclesiastica Gentis Anglorum* 1.27 (the portion quoted here by Flamborough, which is from the answer to question 8, is found in the edition of Bede's *Historia* by Charles PLUMMER I 58). The authenticity of the letter, or at least of considerable portions of it, has long been questioned (see e.g. Michael MÜLLER, *Ethik und Recht* pp. 57-58 n. 128). Reasons which would indicate that long portions of the letter, including this part, cannot have been composed literally by St. Gregory have recently been presented by Margaret DEANESLY and Paul GROSJEAN, "The Canterbury Edition of the Answers of Pope Gregory I to St. Augustine", *Journal of Ecclesiastical History* 10 (1959) 1-49; on the other hand Paul MEYVAERT, "Les 'Responsiones' de S. Grégoire le Grand à S. Augustin de Cantorbéry", *RevHistEccl* 54 (1959) 879-894, maintains that this is still an open question.

[42] See *locc. citt.*; cf. *Lev* 15.16-18.

[43] See Ivo 8.86 (PL 161.601); cf. IDEM 9.121 *ad finem* (PL 161.689); ST. JEROME, *Super Ezechielem* 6.18.5 (PL 25.173C). COURSON, *Summa* 31.7 (fol. 108ra) understands *ne . . . celet* in the sense that the wife is not to conceal her menstruous state from her husband; see FIRTH, *Thesis* II 276*-278*.

[44] Ivo 8.87 (PL 161.601); cf. GRATIAN C.33 q.4 c.1; 1 *Cor* 7.5; *Lev* 7.20; 15.16-18.

sed quod eo tempore quo carnes Agni manducaturi sumus vacare a carnibus debeamus.[45]

287 Sponsus et sponsa, cum benedicendi sunt a sacerdote, a parentibus vel a paranymphis in ecclesia sacerdoti offerantur; et cum benedictionem acceperint, 30 eadem nocte pro reverentia ipsius benedictionis in virginitate permaneant.[46]
   Et sponsus et sponsa cum precibus et oblationibus sponsetur ac donetur, et a paranymphis custodiatur, et publice sollemniterque accipiatur. Biduo etiam ac triduo abstineant se et doceantur ut castitatem inter se custodiant, certisque temporibus nubant ut filios non spurios, sed hereditarios, Deo et saeculo generent.[47]   35

288 Per singulos menses gravia atque torpentia mulierum corpora immundi sanguinis effusione relevantur. Quo tempore si vir coierit cum muliere, dicuntur concepti secum vitium seminis trahere, ita ut leprosi et elephantici ex hac conceptione nascantur, et foeda in utroque corpora pravitate vel enormitate membrorum sanitas corrupta degeneret. Praecipitur ergo ut non solum in alienis mulieribus, sed in 40 suis quoque, quibus videntur conjungi, certa concubitus norint tempora, quando coeundum, quando ab uxoribus sit abstinendum.[48]

   vii. *Quod nec vir nec mulier potest continere sine alterius consensu*

289 Si tu abstines sine uxoris voluntate, tribuis illi fornicandi licentiam, et peccatum illius abstinentiae tuae imputabitur.[49]   45
   Consulitis praeterea si liceat viro, dominico nocturno vel diurno tempore, cum

27 carnibus *corr. ad* carnalibus Aa carnalibus U carnalibus ampleximus P (carnalibus amplexibus K).   27-28 debeamus *add.* ostendimus U.   29-30 vel a paranymphis *om.* O.   30 receperint AaJ receperunt R.   31 reverentia *add.* virginitatis AaU. virginitate] bendictione Ta ipsa virginitate U.   32 Et¹] Ut AdPU(Ivo) *corr. ad* Ut Aa Si O.   cum] in U *om.* JTa.   ac] et JTc.   et⁴] ac O.   a *om.* AbTa. 33 etiam] autem Aa *om.* RTa.   34 ut] et OR.   (36 Per *ss. incipit* Bt).   37 relaventur JRZ *corr. ab* relaventur U revelantur Cc.   si *add.* tunc Ab.   dicitur CcP. 37-38 concepti *insert.* O conceptus P.   38 secum] foetus AdTa (foetus secum Ivo). elephantia O epileptici H *add.* fiant et AaU.   39 corpore AbH.   40 ergo *om.* PU *insert.* Aa.   solum *om.* AaU.   41 quibus *insert.* O.   videntur *add.* lege O(Ivo). conjungi] junguntur P *add.* posse Ta.   certa] cuncta J *om.* P.   42 coeundum *add.* sit AcP *add.* es Tc.   43 abstinere Z.   44 illi] ei OPR(GRATIAN illi BART. Ivo). 46 praeterea *om.* Ac.   in dominco P *om.* R *add.* vel Tc.

[45] See Ivo *loc. cit.*; cf. GRATIAN *loc. cit.*; BART. c.62 (pp. 228-229); 1 *Sam* 21.4; *Joan* 6.33; above sects. 71-72; below sect. 296. Regarding a possible meaning of *nuptias* here cf. below n. 47.
[46] See Ivo 8.143 (PL 161.616); cf. IDEM 8.6 *ad finem* (PL 161.585); GRATIAN D.23 c.33; C. 30 q.5 c.5.
[47] See Ivo 8.145 (PL 161.616). Regarding the meaning of *nubere* here see DU CANGE *s.v.*; cf. GRATIAN D.34 c.20; C.27 q.2 c.29; C.33 q.1 c.1.
[48] See Ivo 9.121 (PL 161.688-689).
[49] BART. c.65 (p. 230 lines 22-24); cf. Ivo 8.130 (PL 161.612); GRATIAN C.27 q.2 c.24.

uxore sua conjungi aut dormire. Quibus respondemus quoniam, si dominico ab opere mundano cessandum est, sicut supra docuimus, quanto magis a voluptate carnali et omnimoda corporis pollutione cavendum ?[50]

Apostolus nec ad tempus ut vacetur orationi, nisi ex consensu, voluit conjuges 50 carnali invicem defraudari debito.[51]

viii. *De fornicatione clericorum*

290 Presbyter, si fornicationem fecerit, quamquam secundum *Canones apostolorum* debeat deponi,[52] tamen juxta auctoritatem sancti Silvestri papae,[53] si non in vitio perduraverit, sed sua sponte confessus adjecit ut resurgeret, viginti annis poe- 55 niteat in hunc modum.[54] Tribus quidem mensibus a ceteris remotus pane et aqua a vespera in vesperam utatur. Diebus autem dominicis et praecipuis modico vino et pisciculis atque leguminibus recreetur sine carne et sagimine, ovis et caseo. Sacco indutus humi adhaereat, die ac nocte jugiter misericordiam imploret. Finitis tribus mensibus continuis exeat; non tamen in publicum prodeat ne grex fidelis in 60 eo scandalum patiatur; nec enim debet sacerdos publice poenitere sicut laicus. Postea aliquantis resumptis viribus unum annum et dimidium in pane et aqua expleat exceptis dominicis diebus et praecipuis festivitatibus, in quibus vino et sagimine, ovis et caseo juxta canonicam mensuram uti poterit. Finito autem primo anno et di-

---

47 aut] vel O.   dominica Aa *add.* tempore H *add.* die *insert alia manu* O.   48 est *om.* TaZ.   docuimus] diximus O.   voluntate CiO.   48-49 voluptate carnali] opere voluptatis carnalis Tc.   49 corporis] carnis JR *om.* U.   cavendum] abstinendum est et cavendum Ta *om.* J cessandum est P *add. aliam materiam* O *Vide infra in Append. C no. 26.*   50 Apostolus nec] Apostolus non *corr. alia manu ad* Unde Paulus ait O.   ad — orationi] vacetur orationi nisi ad tempus O.   nisi] nisi ad *delet.* O.   noluit AbAc-AdCcJORZ(NTb) voluit *vel* noluit Tc(CpV volunt *vel* nolunt G velint F) voluerint Ta.   50-51 Apostolus — debito *insert.* Cc.   51 fraudari Ta destinari *corrupt.* J.   53 canonem O.   54 sancti *om.* JORTc (beati BART. GRATIAN).   55 adjiciat R *corr. ab* adjicit Tc.   viginti] decem JPRTaU(BtG GRATIAN per decem V *corr. ad* decem M viginti BART.) *Cf. infra ad lineam 74.*   annis *insert.* Tc annos HRU.   56 a] cum JTa.   57 praecipuis *add.* sollemnitatibus AaHJPRTaU(BmCpKMNSgSoVXY) *add.* festibus Tc(G *add.* festivitatibus F) *add.* festis *insert.* O (*add.* festis BART. GRATIAN).   et[2]] atque AaJRTa.   58 atque] et RTaTc.   sagimine] sanguine AaCcCiJRTaTcUZ(BtGMSgSoV) *corr. ab* sanguine O *corr. ab corrupt.* Ad(I *corrupt. corr. attentat. ad* sagimine Y sagimine BART. GRATIAN).   59 indutus] induitur O.   60 ne] nec Ac.   62 aliquantum JR aliquantulum Ta.   63 sanguine CcCiTc sanguinibus AaJTa sagiminibus H leguminibus R.

---

[50] See Ivo 8.83 (PL 161.601); cf. JE 2812 c.63 (MonGerHist *Epistolae* 6.590).

[51] See BART. c.65 (p. 230 lines 25-27); cf. Ivo 8.133 (PL 161.613); GRATIAN C.33 q.4 c.12; 1 *Cor* 7.5.

[52] See *Canones apostolorum* c.35 (tr. of DENIS THE SHORT in *Ecclesiae occidentalis monumenta iuris antiquissima* ed. C. H. TURNER I [Oxford 1899] 18). This sect. is from Bartholomew; see below n. 57.

[53] See ST. ANSELM OF LUCCA, *Collectio canonum* 8.10 (*Anselmi episcopi Lucensis collectio canonum una cum collectione minore* ed. Fr. THANER I [Innsbruck 1906] 442).

[54] Cf. *Ps* 40.9; Ivo 6.85 (PL 161.464B).

midio, corporis et sanguinis Domini, ne indurescat, particeps fiat, et ad pacem veniat. 65
Psalmos cum fratribus in choro ultimus canat; ad cornu altaris non accedat; juxta
beati Clementis vocem minora gerat officia.[55] Deinde usque ad expletionem septimi anni, omni quidem tempore exceptis paschalibus, tres legitimas ferias in unaquaque hebdomada in pane et aqua jejunet. Expleto septimo circulo, si fratres
apud quos poenituit ejus condignam poenitentiam laudaverint, episcopus in pris- 70
tinum ordinem juxta beati Calixti papae auctoritatem cum revocare poterit.[56] Sane
sciendum est quia in secunda feria unum psalterium psallendo aut unum denarium
dando pauperibus, si opus est, redimere poterit. Septem annis finitis, deinde usque
ad finem decimi anni sextam feriam nulla interveniente redemptione observet in
pane et aqua. Eadem quoque poenitentia erit sacerdoti de omnibus aliis peccatis 75
et criminibus quae eum in depositionem adducunt. Neque hoc cuilibet videatur
onerosum si sacerdos post lapsum, ut supra dictum est, digne poenitens ad pristinum redeat honorem.[57]

291 Si quis clericus adulterasse aut convictus aut confessus fuerit, depositus ab officio suo communione concessa in monasterio toto vitae suae detrudatur tempore.[58]   80
    Si quis presbyter a plebe sibi commissa mala opinione infamatus fuerit, et ipsi
legitimis testibus approbare non potuerit, suspendatur presbyter usque ad satisfactionem dignam ne populus fidelium in eo scandalum patiatur. Digna enim est
satisfactio si eis a quibus reus creditur post rectam securitatem de imposito crimine
innocens esse manifestetur. Quod ita a nobis et a majoribus constitutum esse dinos- 85
citur ut, sive secundum canones sive ad arbitrium episcopi, sibi collegas septem
conjugat et juret in sacro coram positus evangelio quod eum sancta Trinitas et
Christus Filius Dei, qui illud fecit et docuit, et quod evangelium continet et sancti
quatuor evangelistae, qui illud scripserunt, sic adjuvent quod praenominatam actio-

---

67 gerat] agat HRTa age J.   minora gerat] minor agat Aa.   Deinde] Demum HJTa.
67-68 septimi anni] septem annorum Cc semianni Z.   69 expleto add. itaque TcU.
septimo] septem annorum AaJRTaTcU(BmCpFGIMNSgSoTbVXY) septimo annorum H corr.
ab septem Ab (septimo BART. GRAT[r] septimi anni GRAT[f]).   septimo circulo] septem circulo
annorum P(K).   circulo] curriculo RTc(ITbVXY anno Bt).   71 ordinum O.
poterit corr. ab potuerit O potest Tc.   72 quia] quod CcJRTa.   73 pauperibus add.
vel O.   deinde] demum HJTa.   76 quae eum] quaecumque RTa.   depositione RZ.
in depositionem adducunt] deponi inducunt Ta.   cuilibet corrupt. AbAc lacuna vel rasura
Cc.   haec... videantur Cc.   77 ut supra] ut insert. O.   79 quis om. OP.
81 ipse JRTcU(GISg) ipsis Ta episcopus O(BART. Ivo GRATIAN).   (81-82 et ipsi — potuerit
om. V).   82 probare HP.   potuerint AbCc poterint AaZ poterunt P (potuerit BART.
Ivo GRATIAN).   83 dignam] condignam AaZ.   84 credatur Cc esse dicitur Tc add.
reus H.   interposito O.   85 a[2] om. HTc.   constituitur Cc.   85-86 constitutum
esse dinoscitur] institutum est U.   87-88 et Christus] et Spiritus J et Filius et Spiritus sanctus
corr. forte manu originali ad et Spiritus R.   88 illud] id JR eum O.   89 praemonitam Ab.

---

[55] See St. ANSELM OF LUCCA, Collectio canonum 8.2 (I 438).
[56] See Decretales pseudo-isidorianae ed. Paul HINSCHIUS pp. 142-143; GRATIAN D.50 c.14.
[57] Regarding this whole section see BART. c.71 (pp. 237-238); cf. GRATIAN D.82 c.5.
[58] See BART. c.61 (pp. 226-227); cf. Ivo 8.285 (PL 161.646); GRATIAN D.81 c.10.

nem ita non perpetrarit sicut ei de illo oblatum est; et in hac satisfactione purgatus, 90
deinceps secure suum exerceat ministerium. Quam satisfactionem non nulli prae-
cedentium patrum sanctum papam Leonem in basilica sancti Petri apostoli coram
reverendissimo caesare Karolo ac clero et plebe ita fecisse commemorant, atque
ita mox venerandum principem contra ejusdem sancti papae adversarios dignae
ultionis vindictam exercuisse.[59] 95

292 Presbyter, si uxorem acceperit, deponatur ab ordine; si vero fornicatus fuerit
aut adulterium perpetraverit, amplius pelli debet et ad poenitentiam redigi.[60]

Si qui sunt presbyteri aut diaconi aut subdiaconi qui in crimine fornicationis
jaceant, interdicimus eis ex parte Dei omnipotentis et sancti Petri auctoritate in- 99
troitum ecclesiae usque dum poeniteant et emendent. Si qui vero in peccato suo
perseverare maluerint, nullus vestrum audire eorum praesumat officium; quia bene-
dictio eorum vertitur in maledictionem et oratio in peccatum, testante Domino per
prophetam Malachiam: *Maledicam*, inquit, *benedictionibus vestris*. Qui vero huic
saluberrimo praecepto obedire noluerint, idolatriae peccatum incurrent, testante 5
Samuele: *Peccatum hariolandi est* non obedire *et scelus idolatriae* non *acquiescere*; peccatum
igitur paganitatis incurrit dum christianum se esse asserit et sedi apostolicae obedire
contemnit.[61]

Interdixit per omnia magna synodus non episcopo, non presbytero, non diacono vel alicui omnino qui in clero est, licere subintroductam habere mulierem, 10

90 ita *om.* U *insert.* AaO.   perpetraverit OTaU(BmCpFSoVY Bart.) *corr. ad* perpetraverit Aa perpetravit JPR(BtGKMX perpetrarat Tb perpetrarunt Sg perpetrarit Ivo).
91 deinceps] deinde OZ.   ministerium] officium JP *corr. manu originali ab* officium Tc.
92 patrum] presbyterum Tc *om.* O.   sancti] beati HJRTa.   apostolis Tc *om.* PTa.
93 ac] et Ad.   et] ac PTaTc.   ac plebe et clero HU.   94 mox] morum Cc.
(96-97 Presbyter — redigi *supra inter sects.* 290 *et* 291 So).   97 depelli JU.   *et insert.*
O.   98 sint AaRU.   diaconi aut subdiaconi] subdiaconi R diaconi *corr. ad* subdiaconi J.   fornicationis *add.* aut adulterii H.   99 interdiximus O.   Dei] Domini
O.   1 suo *om.* AaTa.   2 nulli Ac.   officia AaR.   3 peccatum *add.* quia
O.   5 voluerint Cc contempserint Aa.   idolatriae peccatum incurrent *om.* Ta (*ho-*
moeotel. ?).   incurrunt AaJP incurrant Z.   7 esse *om.* HJRTa.   8 contempsit O.
9 Item dixit Tc interdicit JPRTa interdit Z.   magna] romana Tc moguntina Ta viana
Z.   non²] nec O.   non³] nec O.   10 omnino *corr. ab* homini O.

[59] See Bart. c.71 (pp. 238-239); Ivo 6.229 (PL 161.494-495); cf. Gratian C.2 q.5 c.13;
Ivo 6.419 (PL 161.535-536); Idem 5.313 (PL 161.421); Howard Adelson and Robert Baker,
"The Oath of Purgation of Pope Leo III in 800", *Traditio* 8 (1952) 35-80; Liutpold Wallach,
"The Genuine and Forged Oath of Pope Leo III", *Traditio* 11 (1955) 37-63; Idem, "The Roman Synod of December 800 and the Alleged Trial of Leo III: A theory and the historical facts",
Harvard Theological Review 49 (1956) 123-142. The last mentioned author contends with considerable reason that only the form of the oath recorded in the *Liber pontificalis* can be genuine.
[60] Bart. c.71 (p. 239 lines 11-14); cf. Ivo 6.185 (PL 161.487); Gratian D.28 c.9.
[61] See Bart. c.71 (p. 239 lines 14-27); cf. Ivo *Pan* 3.134 (PL 161.1161); Gratian D.81
c.15; *Malac* 2.2; 1 *Sam* 15.23.

nisi forte matrem aut sororem aut amitam vel eas tantum personas quas suspiciones effugiunt.[62]

293　Hi qui altario Dei deserviunt, si subito in flendam carnis fragilitatem corrue-
rint, et Domino respiciente digne poenituerint ita ut mortificato corpore cordis
contriti sacrificium Deo offerant, maneat in potestate pontificis vel veraciter afflic- 15
tos non diu suspendere vel desidiosos prolixius ab ecclesiae corpore segregare, ita
tamen ut sic officiorum suorum loca recipiant ne possint ad altiora officia ulterius
promoveri. Quod si iterato velut canis ad vomitum reversi fuerint, non solum offlicii
dignitate careant, sed etiam sanctam communionem nisi in exitu non percipiant.[63]

ix. *De defloratione virginum*　　　　　　　　　　　　　　　　　　20

294　Virgines quae virginitatem suam non custodierint, si eosdem qui eas violaverint
maritos acceperint, eo quod solas nuptias violaverint, post poenitentiam unius anni
reconcilientur; si alios cognoverint viros, eo quod moechatae sunt, quinquennio
poeniteant et sic ad communionem accedant.[64]

x. *De mollitie*　　　　　　　　　　　　　　　　　　　　25

Si quis peccaverit in mollitie, quocumque modo per delectationem
semen emittendo, triginta dies in pane et aqua poeniteat; hoc dico de
laicis pueris, quia alii gravius sunt puniendi.[65]

---

11 quas] quae Ta(Bart. Burch. Ivo Gratian).　　　11-12 suspiciones *add.* quaeque P.
13 qui *add.* in O *add.* ad *insert.* R.　　　altari JOZ(FSoTbX Bart.) altare R (altario Ivo Gratian).　　　flendam] fremdam Ac foedam JPR.　　　14 digne *om.* O.　　　ut in mortificato Ci.　　　15 sacrificium] sacerdotium O.　　　maneant AcTc moneant Cc.　　　18 non
solum] ne soli O.　　　20-24 De — accedant *om.* J *infra post* feminarum *ad lineam 51 in sect.*
297 R.　　　21 suam *om.* AcO.　　　custodiunt AaP.　　　23 reconcilietur R reconcilian-
tur Cc.　　　sunt] sint AaTc(Ivo).　　　28 puris JRTa(GXY) poenitentiis PZ(K) *ambig.*
pueris *vel* poenitentiis AbAcAdCcCiO(Cp poenitentibus BmSo *add.* poenitentibus FM personis
N) *om.* AaHU(BtSgV).

---

[62] See Bart. c.71 (p. 239 lines 28-32); Ivo 6.186 (PL 161.487); Burch. 2.109 (PL 140.645);
cf. Gratian D.32 c.16.
[63] See Bart. c.72 (p. 241 lines 14-24); cf. Ivo 15.87 (PL 161.882); Gratian D.50 c.52; C.15
q.8 c.2; *Prov* 26.11; 2 *Pet* 2.22; *Ps.* 50.19.
[64] See Ivo 8.152 (PL 161.617); cf. Council of Elvira c.14 (Hefele-Leclercq 1[1].230).
[65] Source not found. Cf. PL 94.570; *Capitula Theodori* cc.248, 252 (PL 99.971-972; these
latter *Capitula* are Frankish in origin, some of them as late as the tenth century; see *Councils and
Ecclesiastical Documents relating to Great Britain and Ireland* ed. Arthur West Haddan and William
Stubbs III [Oxford 1881] 175 n. 9; cf. Thomas Pollock Oakley, *English Penitential Discipline
and Anglo-Saxon Law in their Joint Influence* p. 109 with n. 2). Cf. also F. W. A. Wasserschleben,
Die Bussordnungen der abendländischer Kirche p. 223 no. 34, p. 261 c.3; and above sects. 224, 272.

xi. *De fornicatione laicorum*

295 Si laicus cum laica femina, id est uterque absolutus a lege conjugii, concu- 30
buerit, tres annos poeniteat; et quanto saepius et neglegentius cum ea peccatum
commiserit, tanto magis et tempus et modus poenitentiae addatur.[66]

xii. *De procuratoribus*

Si quis ex juvenibus vel aliqua suspiciosa persona cum parvulis jocatus fuerit,
diuturna poenitentia maceretur.[67]   35
Si deprehensus fuerit aliquis frater ludere cum pueris et habere amicitias aetatis infirmae, tertio commoneatur ut memor sit honestatis atque timoris Dei; si non
cessaverit, severissime corripiatur.[68]

xiii. *Quod conjugati in quadragesima abstinere debent*

296 Qui in quadragesima cognoverit uxorem suam et noluerit abstinere ab ea 40
unum annum poeniteat, aut pretium, videlicet viginti quinque solidorum, ad
ecclesiam tribuat aut pauperibus dividat. Si per ebrietatem et sine consuetudine
acciderit, quadraginta dies poeniteat.[69]

xiv. *De coitu in puerperio*

Si quis coierit cum muliere in puerperio, decem dies poeniteat in 45
pane et aqua.[70]

30-31 concubuerint Ab.   31 cum ea *om.* AaHU.   peccata Cc peccator CiZ.
32 commisit CcTa.   33 procatoribus AbAc procatoribus *corr. ad* jocatoribus *add.* vel procu-
ratoribus *insert.* Ad procreatoribus Z.   34 jocatus] procatus Cc locutus U.   35 diurna
O diutina P.   36 deprehensus — frater] quis deprehensus fuerit U.   frater] semper Tc
juvenis JPRTa *om.* AaH.   37 honestatis] aetatis et honestatis HJRTaU.   atque] et
HJRTa.   38 saevissime Cc.   40 suam *om.* AaHJRU.   41 videlicet *om.* AdPRTa-
(BmBtCpFGKMNSoTbV) *insert.* Aa *obscur.* O (videlicet BART. Ivo).   viginti quinque]
triginta Ta quindecim J.   42 tribuat *om.* JPR.   dividat] tribuat JR *om.* Aa.
sine] et J.   et sine consuetudine *om.* R.   (45-46 Si — aqua *infra post* feminarum *ad
lineam 51* So).

---

[66] See Ivo 8.205 (PL 161.626); BART. c.70 (p. 237 lines 12-16).
[67] Ivo 9.94 (PL 161.682).
[68] Ivo 9.95 (PL 161.682).
[69] See Ivo 15.88 (PL 161.882); BART. c.110 (p. 275 lines 5-10). Cf. above sects. 71-72, 285-
286: also PETER OF POITIERS, Canon of Saint-Victor, *Liber poenitentialis* quoted by A. TEETAERT,
"Le 'Liber Poenitentialis' de Pierre de Poitiers", *Aus der Geisteswelt des Mittelalters* (Beiträge
Suppl. 3) 1.325; cf. *Traditio* 16.552.
[70] Source not found. Cf. WASSERSCHLEBEN, *Bussordnungen* p. 238 (c.7); above sect. 226; below Appendix B sect. 385.

xv. *De illis qui libidinose obtrectant pudenda*

297 Si quis obtrectaverit puellae vel mulieris pectus vel turpitudinem, si clericus
est, quinque dies, si laicus, tres dies poeniteat; monachus vel sacerdos, a ministerio
divino suspensi, si aliquid tale fecerint, viginti dies poeniteant. Scriptum est enim: 50
Neque tetigeritis neque obtrectaveritis turpitudinem feminarum.[71]

xvi. *De illis qui in balneo cum mulieribus se lavant*

Si quis in balneo cum mulieribus se lavare praesumpserit, tres dies poeniteat
et ulterius non praesumat.[72]

<Cap. iv.>   <DE PERJURIO>   55

298 i. De usuali perjurio.
    ii. De indiscreto perjurio.
   iii. De illicito perjurio.
   iv. De sophisticis perjuriis.
    v. De eo qui vi vel metu perjuravit.   60
   vi. De eo qui trahit vel provocat aliquem in perjurium.
  vii. Quod juramentum revocetur.
 viii. De illis qui perjurant se in manu episcopi aut in cruce sacrata.
   ix. De illis qui lingua lascivi fuerint.
   x. De transgressione voti.   65

Episcopis, presbyteris, diaconibus canes ad venandum aut accipitres habere non
liceat. Quod si quis talium personarum in hac voluntate detectus fuerit, si episcopus, tribus mensibus se a communione suspendat, presbyter duobus mensibus
se abstineat, diaconus ab omni officio vel communione cesset.[73]

---

48 vel[2] *om.* AcTc *insert.* Ab.
Cc.   laicus *add.* est CcHTc.
51 tetigeris... obtrectaveris JP.
suali TaTc spirituali CiP.   58 De illicito perjurio *om.* Ta.
add. se AcTc.   perjuraverit AaHJRU perjurat Tc.
Quando P.   revocatur O.   62-65 Quod — voti *om.* AaHJRU *Cf. infra in Append. C*
no. 18.   63-65 De — voti *om.* O *Cf. loc. cit.*   64 in lingua TaTc.   65 De —
voti *insert.* Ad.   66-69 Episcopis — cesset *om.* P(K) *supra ad lineam* 55 *ante titulos hujus sect.*
Tc(V).   66 ancipitres HJRTcU aucipitres O ancipitres *vel* aucipitres Cc.   67 voluptate
AdTa.   detentus AdCcTaTcUZ(BmBtCpFGIMSgTbVY Gratian) deceptus R (detectus
Bart. Ivo).   69 vel communione *om.* TcZ.

49 est *om.* JR.   dies[1] *add.* poeniteat TaTc *add. lacunam*
poeniteat *om.* Tc *add.* si JR.   50 si *om.* J *insert.* Aa.
53 muliere AaJOR (mulieribus Ivo Burch.).   56 ca-
perjuris O.   60 metu
61 procat J.   62 Quod]

---

[71] See Ivo 15.147 (PL 161.891); Burch. 19.137 (PL 140.1010); *Capitula Theodori* c.29 (PL
99.946); cf. *Lev* 18.6-19.
[72] Ivo 15.148 (PL 161.891); Burch. 19.138 (PL 140.1010); cf. *Capitula Theodori* c.30 (PL
99.946).
[73] See Bart. c.105 (p. 274); Ivo 13.30 (PL 161.808); cf. Ivo 6.288 (PL 161.505); Gratian
D.34 c.2.

299 Juramentum tres habet comites: justitiam, judicium et veritatem. 70
Justitia est ut justum et licitum juretur et nihil quod sit contra Deum
et veritatem. *Veritas* est ut verum juretur et nihil quod sit contra conscientiam jurantis. *Judicium* est ut discrete juretur. Indiscretio potest referri tum ad jurantem, tum ad id super quod juratur, tum ad
tempus quo juratur, et si placet ad locum in quo juratur, tum ad mo- 75
dum jurandi. *Ad jurantem* refertur indiscretio jurandi: quia impubes
et filius familias et filia sine licentia parentum non debent jurare, nec
uxor sine viri licentia, nec monachus sine licentia abbatis, nec aliquis
non jejunus. *Ad id super quod juratur* refertur indiscretio jurandi: quia
tantum super sancta jurandum est. *Ad tempus* refertur indiscretio: quia 80
a septuagesima usque ad octavas paschae, ab adventu usque ad octavas epiphaniae, in quatuor temporibus, in litaniis majoribus, in dominicis diebus et in diebus rogationum nullus super sancta evangelia jurare
debet nisi pro concordia et pace, nec *in loco* inhonesto. *Ad modum jurandi* refertur indiscretio: quia nullus praepropere vel sophistice jurare 85
debet. Si igitur aliquod trium dictorum defuerit, videlicet justitia,
judicium vel veritas, statim committitur perjurium.[74]

i. *De usuali perjurio*

300 Talis de perjurio poenitentia imponi debet qualis et de adulterio, de fornic-
catione et homicidio sponte commisso et de ceteris criminalibus vitiis. Si quis per- 90
petrato vero perjurio aut quolibet criminali peccato timens poenitentiam longam
ad confessionem venire noluerit, ab ecclesia repellendus est sive a communione fidelium et consortio, ut nullus cum eo comedat, neque bibat, neque canet, neque in domo
sua eum recipiat.[75]

70 justitiam *add. et* O.   72 est] enim R *om.* Aa.   quod sit *om.* AaJR.
74 jurantem] juramentum AaR.   super quo PTaU de quo JR.   74-75 tum ad tempus quo juratur *om.* Ta (*homoeotel.*).   75 tempus in quo AaHJPRU tempus et (*insert.*) quo
Tc.   76 jurandi] juramentum J veritatem Tc.   77 debet Ac.   78-79 nec aliquis
non jejunus *insert. alia manu* O.   79 non] nisi PTaTc(BtCpFGIKMNSoTbVXY nec Sg
nisi *corr. ad* nec Bm).   quod] quo PTaU.   juratur — jurandi] jurandi refertur in
discretio Cc.   refertur indiscretio] indiscretio *insert.* O.   80 indiscretio *add.* jurandi
HP.   82 temporalibus Ci.   83 et *om.* AaHJ.   et in diebus rogationum *om.* R.
diebus rogationum] rogationibus AaHJPTaU.   84 concordia et pace] pace vel concordia HP.   honesto OR.   85 quia] quod AbAcZ.   propere J propere *insert. in
lacunam* R impropere Ci perperam Ta *om.* P.   vel] et Aa *om.* P.   86 igitur] ergo J *om.*
Ta.   aliquid PTa.   scilicet AaHJORTaU.   87 vel] et AaTaTcU *om.* HJR.
89 et *om.* PR.   de[3]] et de R.   90 et[1]] de H de et Cc.   sponte] saepe AaJ.
90-91 perpetrato vero *invers.* AdJOP.   92 a *om.* OTa.   93 et consortio *om.* AaHJRU
add. et Ta.   eo *add.* neque Ad.   neque[1]] nec AaJPRTc.   neque[2]] nec PTc(Cp-
KN).   neque canet *om.* AaJRZ(BmBtSoTb Grat[f]).   cantet Tc(FGIMSgY eat AdH-
PTaU(KVX) oret *add.* neque canet *insert.* O (oret Bart. Ivo Grat[r]).   neque[3]] nec AaJRU.

[74] Literal source not found. Cf. Bart. c.82 (p. 246 lines 17-20); Ivo *Decr.* 12.22 (PL 161.
785); Ivo *Pan* 8.123 (PL 161.1334); Gratian C.22 q.2 c.2; Ivo *Decr.* 4.16 (PL 161.267); X 2.
9.1; *Jer* 4.2.
[75] See Bart. c.73 (p. 242 lines 6-13); Ivo 12.71 (PL 161.798); cf. Gratian C.22 q.1 c.17;
Theodulf of Orleans 1.26 (PL 105.99).

Quicumque sciens se perjuraverit quadraginta dies poeniteat in pane et aqua et 95
septem sequentes annos, et numquam sit sine poenitentia, et numquam in testimonium recipiatur, et post haec communionem recipiat.[76]

Si quis per cupiditatem suam perjuraverit, omnes res suas vendat et pauperibus
distribuat, et monasterium ingressus jugi poenitentiae se subdat.[77]   99

Si quis suspicatur quod ad perjurium inducatur, et tamen ex consensu jurat,
quadraginta dies poeniteat et septem sequentes annos, et numquam sit sine poenitentia.[78]

Si quis per capillum Dei vel caput juraverit, vel alio modo blasphemia contra
Deum usus fuerit, si in ecclesiastico ordine est, deponatur, si laicus, anathematiza- 5
tur. Et si quis per creaturas juraverit, acerrime castigetur et juxta quod dijudicaverit synodus poeniteat. Si quis autem talem hominem non manifestaverit, non est
dubium quin divina coerceatur damnatione.[79]

ii. *De indiscreto perjurio*

301 Ecce dico caritati vestrae: Et qui super lapidem falsum jurat perjurus est. 10
Unde hoc dico ? Quia multi in hoc falluntur et putant quod nihil est per quod jurant nec se crimine teneri perjurii. Prorsus perjurus es, quia per id, quod falsum
non putas, falsum juras. Si tu illud falsum non putas, falsum putat cui juras. Non

---

96-97 testium *corr. ad* testem O.   97 haec] hoc O.   98 suam *om.* H(BART. BURCH. IVO).
99 tribuat AaCcPTc(BtKMSgV) restituat AcAdCiJRUZ(Cp) *corr. ad* restituat O restituit *corr. ad*
restituat Ab (distribuat BART. BURCH. IVO).   ingressus *add.* jure JU.   subdat] subeat O.
2 et[2] *om.* JR.   4 Dei *om.* AaHRTa.   vel[1] *add.* per AaCcPTc.   alio] aliquo OP.
6 Et[1] *om.* AaCcHJRTaU.   6-7 judicaverit AaAdJORU(BmISgSoV BART.) diu duraverit
H (indicaverit Tb dijudicaverit IVO GRATIAN).   7 autem *om.* JR.   talem *om.* Ab malum
O.   hominem *om.* Cc.   8 coerceatur AaO coercentur Ac *corr. ab* coercentur [?] Ab
coercebitur P.   11 Quia] quod JRU.   quod[1]] quia HOTa(BART. IVO GRATIAN) *add.*
perjurio Ad.   est] sit HR.   12 Prorsus *add.* et Cc.   es] est AaJPRTaU(CpFKM-
NSgSoY IvoPan) *corr. ab* est Ac *corr. manu originali ab* est Tc *obscur.* O (es BART. IvoDecr GRATIAN).
falsum] sanctum Ta(BART. IVO GRATIAN) *Cf.* FIRTH, *Thesis II 278*-281*.*   (12-13 per id —
falsum juras] per quod per id falsum juras quod sanctum non putas Cp).   (falsum non
putas *om.* N).   13 non[1] *insert.* Tc (*om.* G).   non putas[1]] juras JR(V).   juras[1]]
non putas JR(V) non juras Cc dicitur jurasse Z (*om.* Y).   (falsum juras — putas *om.* Tb
BART. *homoeotel.*).   Si] sed Ac(BmMSgSoY) sed si Tc(G quia quamvis X).   illud]
id Cc istum R inde Ta.   falsum[2]] sanctum Ta(BART. IVO GRATIAN falsum sanctum Cp)
obscur. O.   non putas, falsum[2]] putas, falsum non Tc.   falsum[3]] sanctum Ta(Cp
BART. IVO GRATIAN).   (falsum putat *om.* SoV).   putat] putas O(BmMSg *corr. ab* putas
G) *add.* ille J.   cui *add.* tu Ta.   juras[2]] perjuras Z.   13-14 Non enim] Nonne
enim Aa.

---

[76] See BART. c.73 (p. 242 lines 14-18); cf. IVO 12.65 (PL 161.796); GRATIAN C.6 q.1 c.18.
[77] See BART. c.83 (p. 247 lines 14-16); BURCH. 12.3 (PL 140.876); IVO 12.60 (PL 161.796).
[78] See BART. c.83 (p. 247 lines 16-19); BURCH. 12.11 (PL 140.878); IVO 12.68 (PL 161.797).
[79] See BART. c.74 (p. 243 lines 27-33); IVO 12.72 (PL 161.798); cf. IDEM 12.32 (PL 161.788);
GRATIAN C.22 q.1 c.10.

enim qui juras tibi aut lapidi, sed proximo, juras. Homini juras ante lapidem; sed numquid non ante Deum? Non te audit lapis loquentem, sed punit Deus te 15 fallentem.[80]

Sciendum etiam quod non majus est per evangelium vel per quodlibet aliud jurare quam per Deum.[81]

iii. *De illicito perjurio*

302 Qui sacramento se obligaverit ut litiget cum aliquo, nec ad pacem ullo modo 20 redeat, pro perjurio uno anno a corpore Domini segregetur et reatum suum jejuniis et eleemosynis absolvat; ad caritatem vero, quae *operit multitudinem peccatorum*, celeriter redeat.[82]

iv. *De sophisticis perjuriis*

Quacumque arte verborum quis juret, Deus tamen, qui conscientiae testis est, 25 ita hoc accipit sicut ille cui juratur intelligit. Dupliciter autem reus fit, quia et nomen Dei in vanum assumit et proximum dolo capit.[83]

v. *De eo qui vi vel metu perjurat*

303 Qui compulsus a domino perjurat, sciatis utrique perjuri sunt, et dominus et miles: dominus, quia praecepit; miles, quia plus dilexit dominum quam ani- 30 mam. Si liber est, quadraginta dies poeniteat in pane et aqua et septem sequentes annos; si servus est, tres quadragesimas et legitimas ferias poeniteat.[84]

(14 qui] tu qui Cp *om.* FNTbV).   lapidi *add.* juras U.   proximo] pro Christo AbCcCiHZ.   sed proximo, juras] juras sed proximo Ta.   juras. Homini *invers.* U. Homini — lapidem *om.* Ta.   ante] autem per J.   ante lapidem] aut lapidi Z. 15 non[1] *om.* JTa.   Non te] Nonne Cc.   lapis *insert.* H.   punit] unus *cum voca-bulo obscuro* O.   te[2]] autem Tc.   17 Sciendum *add.* est AaHJRU(Bart.) *forte olim add. est folio nunc lacerato* O.   etiam] autem J tamen Tc *add.* est Ta.   non *om.* Cc. majus] magis Cc.   per[1] *om.* HPR.   quodlibet] quod JU (quidlibet Bart.) *add.* tale Tc.   20 aliquo] alio AaJRU (quolibet Bart. Ivo Gratian).   ullo] aliquo AaHRTaU nullo Cc.   ullo modo *om.* J.   24 perjuriis *om.* Cc.   25 Quicumque Ci Quicum-que *corr. ad* Quocumque Ab.   26 hoc] haec Tc *corr. ab* hac[?] O *om.* Aa.   et *om.* AcP. 27 assumens AaJR sumit H.   29 sciatis] sciens O (se sciens Bart. Ivo) *add.* quod HPTc. uterque HJ utique Tc.   perjurii AcTc.   30 miles[1]] servus U servus et miles Z *add.* et Ci.   praecipit CcH.   miles[2]] servus U.   32 si servus est] sit servus J.   est *om.* AaAdRTa.

---

[80] See Bart. c.74 (p. 243 lines 13-20); cf. Ivo *Decr* 12.34 *ad finem* (PL 161.788-789); Ivo *Pan* 8.116 (PL 161.1332-1333); Gratian C.22 q.5 c.10; St. Aug. *Sermo* 180.12.3 (PL 38.378-379).

[81] See Bart. c.74 (p. 243 lines 21-22); cf. Gratian C.22 q.1 C.10.

[82] See Bart. c.75 (p. 244); cf. Ivo 12.74 (PL 161.798); Gratian C.22 q.4 c.11; 1 *Pet* 4.8.

[83] See Bart. c.73 (p. 243 lines 7-11); cf. Ivo 12.36 (PL 161.789); Gratian C.22 q.5 c.9.

[84] See Bart. c.73 (p. 242 lines 24-30); Ivo 12.61 (PL 161.796); cf. Gratian C.22 q.5 c.1.

Si quis coactus pro vita redimenda vel pro qualibet causa vel pro necessitate se
perjurat, quia plus corpus quam animam dilexerat, tres quadragesimas poeniteat.
Alii judicant tres annos in pane et aqua; unum ex his poeniteat.[85]   35

vi. *De eo qui trahit vel provocat aliquem in perjurium*

304 Si quis se perjuraverit et alios sciens in perjurium duxerit, quadraginta dies
poeniteat in pane et aqua et septem sequentes annos, et numquam sit sine poenitentia; et alii, si socii fuerint, similiter poeniteant.[86]

Ille qui hominem provocat ad jurationem et scit esse falsum juramentum vincit 40
homicidam; quia homicida corpus occisurus est, ille animam, immo duas animas,
et ejus quem provocaverit jurare et suam.[87]

Si quis convictus fuerit alios ad falsa testimonia vel perjuria attraxisse vel quacumque corruptione sollicitasse, ipse quidem usque ad exitum vitae non communicet; hi vero qui ei consensisse in perjurio comprobantur postea ab omni testimonio 45
sunt removendi et secundum legem infamia notabuntur.[88]

vii. *Quod juramentum revocetur*

305 Juratos comiti milites ne ipsi, quamdiu excommunicatus est, serviant pro-
hibemus. Qui sacramentum praetenderint moneantur oportere Deo magis servire
quam hominibus; fidelitatem enim christiano principi Deo ejusque sanctis adversanti 50
et eorum praecepta calcanti nulla coguntur auctoritate persolvere.[89]

Tribus modis juramenta contracta solvenda sunt: primo, cum quis male jurat;
secundo, cum quis incaute jurat, non putans hoc esse peccatum; tertio, si pueri vel

---

33-34 Si — poeniteat *infra post* poeniteat *ad lineam 39* P(K).   33 quis] civis J *om.*
Tc.   se *om.* AaHJRU(GRATIAN).   35 Alii — poeniteant *om.* P(K).   37 se *om.*
Cc.   39 si socii *invers.* HRU.   fuerint] sint AaTaU.   si socii fuerint] sint si
socii J.   41 corpus] chorus *corr. ad* corpus tantum O.   42 et¹ *om.* JR.   quem]
quae Ac.   suam] animam *add.* propriam *insert.* O.   43 falsa testimonia vel purjuria]
perjuria vel falsa testimonia J perjuria vel ad falsa testimonis AaHRTaU.   43-44 quali-
cumque Aa quocumque modo Ta.   44 vitae] suum J *add.* suae RTaTcU (vitae *sine addit.*
BART.).   45 probantur U(BART. Ivo) probentur Aa.   48 est] fuerit Tc.   excommunicatus est] excommunicati sint J.   49 praetendunt Ta protenderint Aa.   50 enim
add. quam OZ(BART. GRATIAN).   ejusque sanctis] et sanctis ejus J sanctisque ejus U.
52 persolvenda AaJORTaTc retractanda U (solvenda BART.).

---

[85] See BART. c.83 (p. 247 lines 20-23); Ivo 12.63 (PL 161.796); cf. GRATIAN C.22 q.5 c.3.
[86] See BART. c.73 (p. 242 lines 18-21); cf. Ivo 12.66 (PL 161.796-797); GRATIAN C.22 q.5
c.4.
[87] See BART. c.73 (pp. 242-243); cf. Ivo 12.28 (PL 161.787); GRATIAN C.22 q.5 c.5.
[88] See BART. c. 73 (p. 243 lines 1-6); Ivo 12.26 (PL 161.786); cf. GRATIAN C.22 q.5 c.7.
[89] See BART. c.77 (p. 244); cf. GRATIAN C.15 q.6 c.5; *Act* 4.19.

puellae in domo parentum se juramento constrinxerint, patribus post quam audie-
rint contradicentibus.[90]   55

Quod David juramentum per effusionem sanguinis non implevit major pietas fuit.
Video David, pium hominem et sanctum, in jurationem temerariam incidisse et
maluisse non facere quod juraverat quam jurationem suam fuso hominis sanguine
adimplere.[91]

306 Non solum in jurando, sed in omni quod agimus, haec est moderatio sollici- 60
tius observanda, ut si in talem forte lapsum versuti hominis inciderimus insidiis ex
quo sine aliquo peccati contagio surgere non possumus, illum potius evadendi aditum petamus in quo minus periculi nos perpessuros esse cognoscimus vel cernimus.[92]

Si aliquid nos incaute jurare forte contigerit quod observatum pejorem vergat in
exitum, illud salubriori consilio mutandum novimus, ac magis instante necessitate 65
perjurandum nobis quam perfecto juramento in aliud crimen majus esse diverten-
dum.[93]

viii. De illis qui perjurant se in manu episcopi aut in cruce sacrata

307 Qui perjurat se in manu episcopi aut in cruce consecrata, tres annos poeniteat; si vero in cruce non consecrata, annum unum poeniteat. Qui seductus fuerit 70
et ignorans se perjuraverit et postea cognoscit tres quadragesimas poeniteat.[94]

ix. De illis qui lingua lascivi fuerint

Si quis lascivus in lingua fuerit, triduana poenitentia expietur.[95]

---

54 constrinxerunt PU constringunt JR *obscur.* O.   57 Video] judicio AaJRU in domo Z
Ideo dicunt P Quidem O.   pium] pueri JTcU *corr. ab* pueri Z.   60 sed *add.* etiam
Ad.   60-61 sollicius JO *corr. ab* sollicius R sollicitudinis Ta.   61 homines R(MSo)
hostis PTc(BmGKTbX Bart. Gratian) *add.* vel hostis *insert.* O.   incidimus O.   63
cognoscimus vel *om.* Ad(Bart. Gratian).   64 aliquod AaJ *corr. ab* aliquod O.   nos]
vos Aa *om.* Ta.   forte *om.* R *post* observatum U.   vergat] ungat AbCi.   65 noveri-
mus P(Bart. Burch. Ivo Gratian) cognoscimus Ta.   66 profecto Ta pro facto J.
majus] magis AaCcJ *om.* P.   68 sacra Z secreta Cc.   69 perjurant AaAcJRTcU(CpF-
GIMNTbVY perjuravit SgSo) perjuraverit H perjurant *corr. ad* perjuravit O (perjurat Ivo Gratian) *Forma pluralis videtur derivasse ex titulo.*   69-70 poeniteant JRU.   72 fiunt CcCi.
73 in *om.* AaH.

---

[90] Bart. c.83 (p. 246 lines 21-26); cf. Gratian C.22 q.4 c.19; C.32 q.2 c.14; *Num* 30.4-6.

[91] See Bart. c.83 (pp. 246-247); Gratian C.22 q.4 c.3; Ivo *Decr* 12.11 (PL 161.783); cf.
Ivo *Pan* 8.92 (PL 161.1328); 1 *Sam* 25.22-33.

[92] See Bart. c.83 (p. 247 lines 3-8); Gratian C.22 q.4 c.7.

[93] See Bart. c.83 (p. 247 lines 9-13); cf. Ivo 12.75 (PL 161.798-799); Burch. 12.18 (PL 140.
879); Gratian C.22 q.4 c.6.

[94] See Ivo 12.62 (PL 161.796); cf. Gratian C.22 q.5 c.2; Wasserschleben, *Bussordnungen*
pp. 343, 515.

[95] Ivo 13.57 (PL 161.814); Burch. 10.56 (PL 140.852).

x. *De transgressione voti*

Transgressionem voti et perjurium, quantum ad poenitentiam in- 75
jungendam, satis ad paria possumus judicare, eo quod votum tum privatum est tum sollemne, ita et juramentum.

<Cap. v.>   <DE DAMNIS ILLATIS>

308   i. De sacrilegio.
   ii. De incendio ecclesiae.   80
   iii. De decimis.
   iv. De simplici furto.
   v. De inventis.
   vi. De rapinis.
   vii. De usuris.   85
   viii. De injustis mensuris et ponderibus.

i. *De sacrilegio*

Si quis de ministerio ecclesiae quolibet alio aliquid furatus fuerit, septem annos
poeniteat.[96]

Si quis clericus vel monachus furtum fecerit, quod potius sacrilegium dici potest, 90
id censuimus ordinandum ut junior virgis caesus tanti criminis numquam ecclesiasticum officium excipiat; si vero jam ordinatus in hoc facinore fuerit deprehensus,
nominis ipsius dignitate privetur; cui sufficere potest pro actus sui levitate, impleta
poenitentiae satisfactione, sola communio.[97]

---

75 Transgressionum O Trangressorem Tc.   76 tum] tunc H *om.* Aa.   76-77 tum
privatum *om.* Ac.   tum privatum — sollemne] tum sollemne est tum privatum CcTa.
77 tum] tunc H cum Ci.   80 ecclesiae *add.* De hospitalitate *delet.* Tc.   82 De] et
JRU.   (furto *add.* De hospitalitate BmSoTb).   83 inventis *corrupt.* R (juramentis Bt
hospitalitate Y *add.* De hospitalitate M).   85 De] et JRU.   86 ponderibus *add.* De
hospitalibus AdCcCi *add.* De hospitalibus *insert.* Ac *add.* De hospitalitate *cum signis ad inserendum
supra ad lineam 83 post* inventis Tc (*add.* De hospitalitate FNV *add.* inhospitalitate G) *Cf. supra in
Proleg. ad p. 52 cum n. 64.*   (88-89 Si quis — poeniteat *om.* V *supra post* sacrilegio *ad lineam
79* Cp).   88 ecclesiae *add.* vel AaHJRTaZ(BmBtCpINSg *add.* aliquid G *nihil add.* BART.
Ivo).   (quolibet alio] quodlibet ac So aliquo modo Tb).   alio] modo P(FGKX
BART. Ivo) *add.* modo *insert.* Ad (alicubi M) *om.* Tc.   90 furtum *om.* Ac.   poterit HJR-
TaU.   91 id] idem AcTc hunc O.   censuimus *add.* non *insert.* O.   ut] nec ut
AaAbAcCcCiHJRUZ(BmBtINSgSoTbY ut nec M ut si V) nec O *om.* P(K).   (junior vir-
gis] si probatus fuerit X).   junior] minor CcJU *add.* quidem H.   caesus (census
So reus NX) *add.* reus Ad.   (tanti criminis *om.* G).   criminis *add.* reus HPU(CpK
BART. Ivo BURCH.).   92 suscipiat AaPRTaU.   jam *om.* JR.   facinore *insert.* Aa
crimine R.   94 poenitentiae *add.* suae HU.

---

[96] See BART. c.86 (p. 253 lines 6-8); cf. below sect. 313 with n. 9.

[97] See BART. c.87 (p. 253 lines 10-16); Ivo 13.50 (PL 161.813-814); BURCH. 11.64 (PL 140.
871).

309 De viro nefando purgando nomine qui rabie insana commotus, collectis ma- 95
litiae suae sequacibus iniquitatisque complicibus, nefarias invasiones et depraeda-
tiones violentas inferre daemoniaco ausu praesumpsit et, ut epistolae vestrae textus eloquitur, sacrum altare sacrataque dominici corporis et sanguinis vasa insuper et sanctum chrisma pollutis arripere manibus, quasi vilia et ad usum com- 99
munem apta, praesumpsit, dilectio vestra nos consulit. Si ipse, vel qui cum eo in
tam impio et iniquo scelere fuerunt, ad poenitentiam quandoque gratia tracti divina
venire voluerint, quo eos poenitentiae vinculo astringatis nostrae institutionis censuram curastis exposcere. Ex quibus, si tamen ita est, jubemus qui ad poenitentiam reverti acceleraverint uno anno extra ecclesiam Dei consistere, cujus sacra- 5
tissima vasa extra ritum fidei christianae diripiendo auferre non dubitaverunt.
Secundo autem anno ante fores ecclesiae sine communione maneant. Tertio autem
anno ecclesiam Dei intrent et inter audientes astent sine oblatione, non manducantes
carnem neque bibentes vinum praeter natalis et resurrectionis dominicae diebus.
Quarto praeterea anno, si in his prioribus tribus eorum fructuosus fuerit poenitentiae 10
labor, communioni fidelium restituantur, tota mentis intentione spondentes talia
se ulterius numquam facturos, et corpus et sanguinem Domini recipere mereantur,
et usque ad septimum annum tribus in hebdomada diebus sine esu carnium et vini
potatione maneant poenitentes.[98]

310 Omnes ecclesiae raptores atque suarum facultatum alienatores a liminibus 15
ejusdem sanctae matris ecclesiae anathematizamus et apostolica auctoritate pelli-
mus atque damnamus atque sacrilegos esse judicamus, et non solum eos, sed omnes
consentientes; quia non solum qui faciunt rei judicantur, sed etiam qui facientibus
consentiunt; par enim poena et agentes et consentientes comprehendit.[99]

95 Burgando Ta(Ivo GRATIAN) Bulgardo P (purgando BART.).   insignia *corr. ad* insania
O.   collectis *corr. ab* collectus O caelestis JR.   96 iniquitatisque *corr. ab* iniquitatis O
iniquitatis suae Ta.   97 et *om.* CcCiJRTa.   vestrae] nostrae AaAbAcCiRTcZ(Bm
FGNSgTb) *lacuna* Cc.   98 deloquitur O.   sacraque AaAdR(ISgSoTb BART. GRA-
TIAN) sacrumque Ac(NY sacramentumque Cp).   99 accipere AaJPRU.   et[2] *om.*
AaJTaU.   1 qui *insert.* O.   qui cum] quicumque AaHJU.   in] vel AaHJRU
om. Ta.   2 fuerint AaJRTaU.   3 noluerint Tc voluerunt OZ.   quo] quos P
corr. ab quos O.   perstringatis AaHJTaU constringatis R (BART. GRATIAN).   nos-
trae] vestrae OTc.   5 reversi JR veram O *om.* H.   acceleraverit AbAcCiTc celera-
verit Aa acceleravit Z acceleraverunt *add.* reverti *insert.* O *om.* Cc.   6 decipiendo Cc.
dubitaverint CcRTa(N BART.).   8 stent AaHJRTcU.   manducantes] comedentes
JR.   9 carnes AcTaTc(BmGISoTbXY Ivo*secundumFriedb.* carnem BART. GRATIAN).
neque] nec Tc non P.   praeter] nisi O praeterquam Ta *add.* in TaU *add.* diem P.
dies HTc.   10 tribus *praem.* annis R *add.* annis HTa.   15 *tit.* De raptoribus ecclesiarum *praem.* Z.   16 matricis AaAbAcCiZ.   16-17 compellimus JR.   17 sed *add.*
etiam JR.   18 rei *om.* O.   rei judicantur *om.* Ta.   19 enim — comprehendit] poena
constringit Ta.   comprehendit] constringit J.

[98] See BART. c.87 (p. 254 lines 7-32); cf. GRATIAN C.12 q.2 c.17; JE 2840 (PL 119.1124).
[99] See BART. c.87 (pp. 254-255); cf. Ivo 3.140 *ad finem* (PL 161.230); IDEM 14.89 (PL 161.
850); GRATIAN C.17 q.4 c.5; *Rom* 1.32.

Sicut antiquitus a sanctis patribus statutum est, major ecclesia per circuitum 20
sexaginta passus habeat; capellae vero vel minores ecclesiae triginta.[100] Qui autem
confinium eorum confringere temptaverit, aut personam hominis aut bona ejus
inde subtraxerit, natura publicus latro erit quousque emendet, et quod rapuerit
reddat aut excommunicetur.[1]

Si quis contumax vel superbus timorem Dei vel sanctarum ecclesiarum non ha- 25
buerit, et fugientem servum, vel quem ipse persecutus fuerit, de altario ecclesiae
et de porticibus ejus quemlibet ecclesiae adhaerentibus per vim abstraxerit, pro
temeritate nongentos solidos componat et publica poenitentia juxta judicium judicum plectetur.[2]

311   Si quis inventus fuerit reus sacrilegii, episcopis vel abbatibus, sive personis ad 30
quas sacrilegii querimonia juste pertinuerit, triginta libras argenti examinati puris-
simi componat.[3]

Sacrilegium committitur si quis infregerit ecclesiam, vel triginta ecclesiasticos
passus qui sunt in circuitu ecclesiae, vel domos, vel quae infra praedictos passus
fuerint, aliquid inde diripiendo vel auferendo, seu qui injuriam vel ablationem 35
rerum intulerint clericis arma non ferentibus vel monachis sive Deo devotis omnibus
ecclesiasticis personis. Capellae quae sunt infra ambitum murorum castellorum
non ponuntur in hac triginta passuum observatione.[4]

Si qui monasteria et loca Deo dicata et ecclesias confringunt, et deposita vel quae-

---

21 sexaginta] quadraginta AaCcHJRTaTcUZ(BtCpGIMNSgSoTbVXY) ix. (*error pro* lx.) Ci
(sexaginta Bart.).   22 eorum] earum PU(KMTbX Bart. eorum Ivo).   constringere
AcCcCiJOTaTc(CpIMNSoTbY contringere V contingere BmBtX configere G confringere Bart.
Ivo Gratian).   temptaverint O.   23 subtraxerit *corr. ad* subtraxerint O distraxerit J.
natura] nisi R(Bart. Ivo Gratian) ut JP(K) velut Tc(Tb nec So) natura *vel* hujus O (illud G)
om. Ta(VX).   quousque] donec AaHJRTa *obscur.* O.   24 reddit *corr. ad* reddiderit
O.   aut] vel H(G) *om.* AaAbJOTaU(VX Bart. Ivo).   26 quem] quod O.   27 et]
vel Ta *forte om.* O.   de *om.* Aa.   quemlibet] quomodolibet O(Bart. Gratian quolibet
modo Ivo) cuilibet Cc (quamlibet V quodlibet Sg de *delet.* G).   quemlibet ecclesiae ad-
haerentibus] adhaerentibus quemlibet P(K) ecclesiae adhaerentibus quemlibet Ad quemlibet
adhaerentem Ta (*om.* X).   subtraxerit O.   28-29 judicum *om.* AaCcJPRTa(BtCp-
FGIKMNSoTbVY Bart. Gratian canonum X episcopi Ivo).   29 plectatur AdP.
31-32 purissime JR.   33 triginta *add.* quinque Cc.   34 vel[2] *om.* AdHPR(BtFKSg Bart.
Ivo) *eras.* Aa(Bm).   35 oblationem JR.   36 rerum *om.* Cc.   intulerit JPTcU(Bt-
FGIKSgXY Bart. Gratian) intellexerint Z.   39 dedicata PTc(IKMTbVY Bart.) devota
O(GSo) sacrata Aa(Cp sacrata vel dicata X).   Deo dicata] sancta Deo JR sacrata Deo
U.   constringunt JR.   vel *om.* O.   39-40 vel quaelibet *corrupt.* J *om.* Cc.

---

[100] See Council of Toledo c.10 (A.D. 681; Hefele-Leclercq 3[1].546; Gratian C.17 q.4
c.35); cf. below second paragraph of sect. 311.

[1] See Bart. c.87 (p. 255 lines 4-10); cf. Ivo 3.104 (PL 161.221); Gratian C.17 q.4 c.6;
JL 4404.

[2] See Bart. c.87 (p. 255 lines 11-16); cf. Ivo 3.114 (PL 161.223); Gratian C.17 q.4 c.20.

[3] See Bart. c.87 (p. 255 lines 17-20); cf. Gratian C.17 q.4 c.21 *ab initio.*

[4] See Bart. c.87 (p. 255 lines 21-28); cf. Gratian C.17 q.4 c.21 §1; above at n. 100.

libet alia exinde abstrahunt, damnum novies componant et immunitatem tripliciter, 40 et velut sacrilegi canonicae sententiae subjugentur.[5]

De rebus ecclesiasticis quo modo restituantur

312 Si quis ecclesiasticas oblationes et quod Deo consecratum fuerit rapuerit, vel consenserit facientibus, ut sacrilegus dijudicetur et damnum in quadruplum restituat et canonice poeniteat.[6]

45

De eadem re

Fures et latrones, si in furando et praedando occiduntur, visum est pro eis non orandum; sed si comprehensi aut vulnerati presbytero aut diacono fuerint confessi, communionem eis non negamus.[7]

De clericis si in demoliendis sepulchris inventi fuerint

50

Si quis clericus in demoliendis sepulchris fuerit deprehensus, quia facinus hoc pro sacrilegio legibus publicis sanguine vindicatur, oportet in tali scelere proditum a clericatus ordine submoveri et poenitentiae triennio deputari.[8]

De illis qui de ministerio ecclesiae aliquid furati fuerint

313 Si aliquis de ministerio ecclesiae quolibet modo aliquid furatus fuerit, sep- 55 tem annis poeniteat.[9]

De his qui Christi pecunias rapiunt vel auferunt

Qui abstulit, inquit, aliquid patri vel matri homicidae particeps est.[10] Pater noster sine dubio est Deus, qui nos creavit; mater vero nostra ecclesia, quae nos in

---

40 alia] aliqua O.   abstrahent Ta extrahunt H.   component JR componat AaTa. 41 sacrilegii AcTc.   subjungentur AaOTc subjungantur Cc subjiciantur JRTaU subigantur H(GRATIAN subjugentur BART.).   42-89 *sects. 312-315 inveniuntur infra post* gratiam pervenire *ad lineas 92-93 in sect. 327 Aa fol. 37ᵛ.*   42 quo modo] quando Z.   46 *tit. om.* Z.   47 si *om.* Ac.   et²] vel HPR.   visus AbAcCcCi usus P jussum O. 48 sed *om.* OR *obscur.* J.   aut¹] et AaHJRTaU.   51 in *insert.* O non R.   demoliendum Ac.   deprehensus] inventus AaHJRTaU.   hoc *om.* RZ.   52 vindicantur CcP judicatur Ta.   54 *tit. om.* Z.   55 aliquis] quis HRTc(BART. aliquis Ivo). 55-56 Si — poeniteat *infra post* judicandus est *ad lineam 62* P (*om.* BtK).   56 annos HO-(BART. Ivo).   58 abstulerit AdHOPTa(BtCpFKMSoVX abstulit Ivo).   inquit] vi Tc *om.* AaOPTa.   aliquid *om.* CcJ.   59 vero *om.* Ad.   nostra *om.* JR.

---

[5] See BART. c.87 (p. 255 lines 28-32); cf. Ivo 14.92 (PL 161.850-851); GRATIAN C.17 q.4 c.21 §4; below sect. 313 with n. 12.

[6] See Ivo 13.37 *ad finem* (PL 161.811); cf. GRATIAN C.12 q.2 c.10 *ad finem*.

[7] See Ivo 13.45 (PL 161.812); BURCH. 11.59 (PL 140.870); GRATIAN C.13 q.2 c.31.

[8] Ivo 13.49 (PL 161.813); BURCH. 11.63 (PL 140.871).

[9] See Ivo 13.51 (PL 161.814); BURCH. 11.65 (PL 140.871); cf. above sect. 308 with n. 96.

[10] See *Prov* 28.24.

baptismo spiritualiter regeneravit. Ergo qui Christi pecunias et ecclesiae aufert, 60
rapit aut defraudat, homicida est atque ante Deum homicida deputatur. Qui
enim res ecclesiae abstulerit sacrilegium facit et ut sacrilegus judicandus est.[11]

De eadem re

Et hi qui monasteria et loca Deo sacrata et ecclesias infringunt, et deposita vel
alia quaelibet exinde abstrahunt, damnum novies componant et emunitatem tripli- 65
citer, et velut sacrilegi canonicae sententiae subigantur.[12]

Quod sacrilegi sunt ecclesiarum praedones

314 Sacrilegi sunt ecclesiarum praedones. Unde et in concilio agathensi sub
quatuor capitulis decretum habetur ita: Amico quippiam rapere furtum, ecclesiae
vero fraudari vel abstrahi surripique sacrilegium.[13] Omnes enim contra legem 70
facientes resque ecclesiae diripientes vel ecclesias sacerdotesque contra divinas
sanctiones vexantes sacrilegi vocantur atque indubitanter infames sacrilegique
habendi sunt.[14]

---

60 spirituali AcTc *obscur.* O.   aufert *add.* et AaJU.   61 aut] et HJR.   63 *tit. om.*
Z.   re *om.* Cc.   64 Et *om.* OTcU.   hi] hujusmodi JU.   sacrata] devota O.
vel *om.* Tc.   64-65 vel alia quaelibet *om.* J.   64-66 Et hi — subigantur *om.* RTa(BtGX
infra post praedones *ad lineam 68* Bm).   65 alia] aliqua O.   immunitatem HP muni-
tatem O *corr. ab* emunitem Tc.   66 subjungantur CiJOU subjungentur Aa (subigantur
Ivo).   68 Sacrilegii Ac.   et *om.* RTaTc.   69 quarto Cc(M) iv. AaAbJRTc(Bm-
BtFISgSoTbY Ivo).   caput AcCc cap. AbAdCiOTc(FI capitulo M capituli V causa Bm
om. So).   (capitulis decretum habetur] discretum habetur caput Y).   decretum *corr.*
ab decertum Ci discretum Tc de rerum Cc (decretorum Tb).   habetur *corr. ab* habe-
retur O.   quispiam AaJRTc.   furtum *add.* est AdHP(Ivo).   70 vero] nec Cc
om. J.   defraudari Cc.   sacrilegium *add.* est HTc *add.* est *insert.* O.

---

[11] See Ivo 14.88 (PL 161.850); cf. GRATIAN C.12 q.2 c.6; cf. also c.1 in the same question of
GRATIAN.

[12] See Ivo 14.92 (PL 161.850-851); cf. above sect. 311 with n. 5.

[13] Cap. 4 of the Council of Agde (Languedoc, 506 A.D.) dealt with alienation of ecclesiastical goods; this canon has been reproduced in GRATIAN C.13 q.2 c.11; cf. MANSI 8.324. However what is attributed to it here is closer to C.13 q.2 c.10 *ad finem*, which is practically the same
as C.12 q.2 c.71 §2; this is from St. Jerome, *Epistolae* 52.16 (PL 22.539; CorpusScrEccLat 54.
439 lines 15-16). These words perhaps came to be attributed to chapter 4 of the Council of
Agde because they may have been found immediately preceding it in some earlier collection,
as afterwards they preceded it in Gratian. Flamborough seems to have written *sub quatuor capitulis* in error for *sub quarto capitulo* as found in his sources; see texts cited in the following note.

[14] See BURCH. 11.28 (PL 140.865); Ivo 13.38 (PL 161.811). The readings here are a little
closer to Burchard than to Ivo.

De pauperes defraudantibus

Si quis pauperibus destinata male distraxerit, tres annos poeniteat.[15]   75

ii. *De incendio ecclesiae*

315 Si quis ecclesiam igne comburit, quindecim annos poeniteat et eam sedule restituat et pretium suum distribuat pauperibus.[16]

Pessimam quidem et depopulatricem et urendam incendiorum malitiam auctoritate Dei et beatorum apostolorum Petri et Pauli omnino detestamur et interdicimus. 80
Si quis igitur post hujus nostrae prohibitionis promulgationem malo studio, sive
pro odio sive pro vindicta, ignem apposuerit vel apponi fecerit, aut appositoribus
consilium vel auxilium scienter tribuerit, excommunicetur; et si mortuus fuerit
incendiarius, christianorum careat sepultura; nec absolvatur nisi prius damno cui
intulit resarcito et juret se ulterius ignem non appositurum; poenitentia autem ei 85
detur ut Hierosolymis aut Hispaniam per integrum annum in servitio Dei permaneat. Si quis autem episcopus aut archiepiscopus hoc relaxaverit, damnum
restituat et per annum ab officio episcopali abstineat. Sane regibus et principibus
faciendae justitiae facultatem consultis archiepiscopis et episcopis non negamus.[17]

316 Quisquis per dolum mittit manum suam in christum Domini, episcopum 90
videlicet patrem et pastorem suum, et qui ecclesiam Dei devastat et incendit, placuit sanctae synodo ut in uno loco idem in monasterio poeniteat omnibus diebus
vitae suae.[18]

De illis qui aream vel domum proximi sui incendunt

Si quis domum vel aream cujuscumque voluntarie igne cremaverit, sublata 95
vel incensa omnia restituat et tribus annis poenitentiam agat.[19]

---

75 male distraxerit] maledixerit U.   detraxerit AaHJRTaTc(CpFISgSoVXY destruxit
Tb ditraxerit G) *add.* per AaR.   (Si — poeniteat *infra post* suae *ad lineam 93* G).
77 comburat Ta combusserit HP(GRATIAN).   78 pauperibus *om.* AaJU.   79 populatricem JTa *corr. ab* populatricem O de populantem R.   horrendam P(GRATIAN *orig*) *corr.*
ab verendam O *corr. ab* urandum Tc *om.* Ta (urendam BART.).   incendiarum Ta incendo-
rum Cc.   83 excommunicatur JRU.   85 intulerit O.   86 in Hispania AdPTa-
(K GRATIAN *orig* in Hispaniam G Hispania V BART.) Hispaniae AaRU(Cp) Hispane *corr. ad*
Hispaniae J.   86-87 maneat O poeniteat Aa.   87 autem *om.* AaHJRTaTcU(BmBtCp-
GIMSgSoTbVXY autem BART. GRATIAN).   aut] vel CcH(GRATIAN).   90 Quisquis]
Si quis AaCcHJRTaU *obscur.* O.   suam *om.* TcZ.   92 ut] non O *om.* Aa.
idem] id est P(BURCH. IVO GRATIAN).   95 cujusque Ad.   96 restituet AaHJTa.
poenitentiam agat] poeniteat RU.

---

[15] Source not found.
[16] See BART. c.87 (p. 254 lines 3-6); Ivo 3.127 (PL 161.226); GRATIAN C.17 q.4 c.14.
[17] See BART. c.125 (pp. 285-286); cf. GRATIAN C.23 q.8 c.32; HEFELE-LECLERCQ 5[1].730-731.
[18] See Ivo 12.86 (PL 161.802); IDEM 13.65 (PL 161.815); BURCH. 10.65 (PL 140.853-854);
cf. GRATIAN C.24 q.3 c.22; *Sam* 24.7; 26.9-23; 2 *Sam* 1.14; *Ps* 104.15.
[19] BURCH. 19.136 (PL 161.1010); cf. 1 *Compil.* 5.31.7 (X 5.36.6).

iii. *De decimis*

317 *Omnes decimae terrae* suae *de* fructibus *sive de pomis arborum Domini sunt et illi sanctificantur,* boves *et* oves *et caprae quae sub pastoris virga transeunt; quidquid decimum* 99 *venerit sanctificabitur Domino.* [*Non eligetur nec bonum nec malum, nec altero commutabitur; si quis mutaverit, et quod* mutat et quod *mutatum est sanctificabitur Domino*] *et non redimetur.*[20] Sed quia multi modo inveniuntur decimas dare nolentes, statuimus ut secundum praeceptum Domini nostri admoneantur semel, secundo et tertio; si non emendaverint, anathematis vinculis constringantur usque ad satisfactionem et 5 emendationem congruam.[21]

iv. *De simplici furto*

318 Si quis per necessitatem furatus fuerit cibaria vel vestem vel pecus per famem vel per nuditatem, poeniteat hebdomadas tres; si reddiderit, non cogatur jejunare.[22]
  Si quis capitale furtum commiserit, id est quadrupedia tulerit vel casas fregerit, 10 septem annos poeniteat et quod furatum est reddat. Si quis vero de minoribus semel aut bis furtum fecerit, reddat quod tulit et unum annum poeniteat. Vel si quis sepulchrum violaverit, septem annos poeniteat, tres ex his in pane et aqua.[23]

v. *De inventis*

319 Multi sine peccato putant esse si alienum quod invenerint tenent, et dicunt: 15 "Deus mihi dedit. Cui debeo respondere?" Discant hoc peccatum simile esse rapinae, si quis inventa non reddat.[24]

---

98 suae] sive AaHJOPRTaUZ(BmBtCpFGKMNSgVXY Bart. Burch. Ivo) *corr. ad* sive Ad- (BmF *om.* G).   fructibus — arborum] fructibus arborum sive de pomis AaJRTa fructibus arborum sive de aliis U.   1 sacrificabitur AbAcCcCi.   Non] nec H et non Ta.
1-2 Non — Domino *om.* AbAcAdCcCiTcZ(BmBtFGIMSoTbY *homoeotel.*) *Hic textus videtur pertinere ad Formam 2, sed non ad Formam 3.*   2 quis] quid AaHU.   mutatum est] mutatur OPU.   sacrificabitur O.   3 ut *om.* AaHJRU.   4 nostri *om.* PZ. ut admoneantur H admoneatur Ta.   et *om.* AaP.   5 emendaverit O.   astringantur AaJORTaU(CpSoXY astringatis M confringuntur Sg).   ad *om.* AaH.   8 cibaria *praem.* necessaria AaHJRTaU(CpMNSgX).   vel pecus] per pecus *corr. ad* coactus O. 11 furatus AaHJRTaU.   vero] autem OTa nec Cc.   12 Vel] Et JRU *om.* H.
12-13 Vel — aqua *om.* Ta (*homoeotel.*).   15 se esse Cc.   esse si] se esse Ci.   16 respondere] reddere AdR(BtSg Bart.) ferre Cc.   17 reddit AaTa reddidit JU reddiderit R.

---

[20] See *Lev* 27.30-33.
[21] See Bart. c.91 (p. 257 lines 1-12); Ivo *Decr* 3.196 (PL 161.245); Ivo *Pan* 2.58 (PL 161. 1093); Burch. 3.130 (PL 140.698-699); Gratian C.16 q.7 c.5; cf. *Matt* 18.15-18.
[22] See Bart. c.86 (p. 252 lines 34-37); Ivo 13.42 (PL 161.812); cf. Wasserschleben, *Bussordnungen* p. 275; PL 99.961.
[23] See Bart. c.86 (pp. 252-253); cf. Ivo 13.44 (PL 161.812); Wasserschleben, *Bussordnungen* p. 272; Gratian C.17 q.4 c.17.
[24] See Bart. c.86 (p. 251 lines 18-21); Gratian C.14 q.5 c.8.

Si quod invenisti non reddidisti, rapuisti; quantum potuisti fecisti, quia plus non invenisti. Qui alienum negat, si posset, et tolleret; Deus cor interrogat, non manum.[25] 20

vi. *De rapinis*

320 Forte aliquis cogitat et dicit: "Multi sunt christiani divites, avari, cupidi; non pecco si illis abstulero et pauperibus dedero. Unde enim illi non bene agunt, mercedem habere potero." Sed hujusmodi cogitatio ex diaboli calliditate suggeritur; nam, si totum tribuat quod abstulerat, auget potius peccatum quam minuat.[26] 25

vii. *De usuris*

321 Si quis clericus detectus fuerit usuras accipere, placuit degradari et abstinere.[27]
Clerici ab indignis quaestibus noverint abstinendum et ab omni cujuslibet negotiationis ingenio vel cupiditate; aut in quocumque gradu sint, mox a clericalibus officiis abstinere cogantur.[28] 30
Si quis clericus pecuniam dederit ad usuram, aut conductor alienae rei voluerit esse, aut genus aliquod aliud turpis negotiationis exercuit, depositus a clero et communione alienus fiat.[29]

viii. *De injustis mensuris et ponderibus*

322 Si quis justas mensuras vel justa pondera mutare praesumpserit, in pane et 35 aqua viginti diebus poeniteat.[30]

18 quod] quid JPTa quis Cc.   et non HTa nec P.   reddisti AbCcCiHO.
rapuisti — fecisti] quantum potuisti rapuisti *add.* fecisti *insert.* H rapuisti quantum fecisti potuisti Aa.   19 et *om.* HJO.   interrogat *add.* et JR.   22 aliquis] si quis Cc.
divites *om.* Cc et cupidi AdP *om.* O.   non] nec AdJORTc.   23 dedero] do AaHJRTaU.
24 Sed *add.* ejus AaH.   calliditate] suggestione AaHJRTa.   27 detectus] deductus
AaJ devictus U detestatus R convictus Ta.   28 quaestionibus AaAbAcJOPRTaU(BmBt-
CpKMNSgSoTbVY) quaestubus H quaestubus *corr. ad* quaestionibus Tc (quaestibus BART. Ivo
GRATIAN).   31 quis *om.* Cc.   dedit RU.   alienae] alicujus JR.   32 aliud]
ad Cc *om.* AaHJORTaU(FVX BART. Ivo) *add.* aut Ac(GI) *add.* aut *delet.* Ab.   et] a Ta-
(BART. Ivo GRATIAN) *om.* H *add.* a JOPTc(BmFGKMNSoX).   33 communionem Cc.
35 justas] injustas CcCTa.   36 poenitebit H poenitebis *corr. ad* poenitebit O *hic add.* De hospitalibus (inhospitalibus Ad non hospitalibus Ac) Quicumque hospites non recipit (recepit Tc
receperit Ta) in domo sua, sicut Dominus (Deus Ci) praecipit (praecepit TaTc[IMSgTbVXY]
Ivo) et propter hoc regna caelorum promisit, quanto tempore hospitibus humanitatem denegaverit et mandata evangelica juxta possibilitatem suam non adimpleverit (servaverit vel adimpleverit Ta), nec pedes laverit, nec eleemosynam fecerit, tanto tempore in pane et qua, si non emendet,
poeniteat AdCcCiTaTc(BmFIMNSoTbVXY) *idem hic insert.* Ac; *idem supra in principio hujus
sect.* Z (*idem supra inter sects.* 320 *et* 321 Sg) *cf. supra in Proleg. ad p.* 52.

[25] BART. c.86 (p. 251 lines 12-15); cf. GRATIAN C.14 q.5 c.6.
[26] See BART. c.86 (p. 251 lines 6-11); cf. GRATIAN C.14 q.5 c.3.
[27] See BART. c.92 (p. 257 lines 28-31); Ivo 13.12 (PL 161.805); GRATIAN D.47 c.5.
[28] See BART. c.92 (p. 258 lines 5-8); Ivo 13.28 (PL 161.808); cf. GRATIAN C.14 q.4 c.1.
[29] See BART. c.92 (p. 258 lines 9-12); Ivo 13.11 (PL 161.805).
[30] See BART. c.92 (p. 258 lines 17-19); cf. Ivo 15.158 *ad finem* (PL 161.893); BURCH. 19.148
(PL 140.1012); X 3.17.2; *Capitula Theodori* c.58 (PL 99.952).

\<Cap. vi.\>   \<DE DIVINATORIBUS\>

i. De haereticis et schismaticis et excommunicatis

324 Si quis dederit aut acceperit communionem de manu haeretici et nescit quod 55
ecclesia catholica contradicit, postea intelligens annum integrum poeniteat. Si
autem scit et neglexerit et postea poenitentiam egerit, decem annos poeniteat; alii
judicant septem; quidam judicant humanius ut quinque annos poeniteat. Si quis
permiserit haereticum missam suam celebrare in catholica ecclesia et nescit, quadraginta dies poeniteat; si vero pro reverentia ejus, annum unum poeniteat; si 60
pro damnatione ecclesiae catholicae et consuetudinis romanorum, projiciatur ab
ecclesia sicut haereticus nisi poenitentiam habuerit; si habuerit, decem annos
poeniteat. Si recesserit ab ecclesia catholica in congregatione haereticorum et
alios persuaserit, si postea poenitentiam egerit, duodecim annis poeniteat, tribus

---

38-53 *alii tituli* P(K *item alii* X) *cf.* Firth, *Thesis II 255*, 294*-296**; Idem, *Traditio 16.547-548.*   38 et²] De Tc *om.* Z.   et excommunicatis *insert.* Ab.   42 vel] et Tc *om.* J.
44 De *om.* Z.   De — dare *om.* AaHJTaU *infra post* poenitentias *ad lineam 49* R.   46 De] et
AaU *om.* H.   47 post] in HJ in *insert. forte manu originali* Aa *om.* O.   49 non *insert.* O *insert.*
forte manu originali Aa.   debet TaTc.   50 retinent AaCcHJRTaU(BtIMSoV retinent
vel reticent Cp recitent *add.* sua Sg) retinens O.   53 remissionibus *add.* xvii. De hospitalibus AcTa (*add.* De inhospitalibus V) *Cf. supra in Proleg. ad p.* 52.   54 et¹ *om.* AdJ.
et excommunicatis *om.* OTa.   57 et² *om.* AaTa.   58 quidam] alii HJRTaU.   ju-
dicant² *om.* JRTa.   ut] quod AaHJRTaU.   quinque] sex CcCi.   poeniteant
Cc promiserit O.   61 consuetudine AaJRU suetudinis Ac.   63 recessit RZ.
64 aliis Ta(Ivo alios Bart. Gratf).

extra ecclesiam et septem inter audientes et duobus adhuc extra communionem.[31] 65
Idem potest dici de excommunicatis et schismaticis.

De presbyteris ecclesiae ministrantibus in excommunicatione

325 Presbyteri qui excommunicati praesumpserint contingere sacrum ministerium
studeant tribus annis continuis per hebdomadam omni secunda et sexta feria a vino
[aut] aceto penitus jejunare et ultra lugenda nequaquam committere.[32]   70

De eo qui communicaverit vel oraverit cum excommunicato

Qui communicaverit vel oraverit cum excommunicato, si laicus est, excommunicetur, si clericus, deponatur.[33]

ii. *De apostatis*

326 De his qui sacrificare coacti sunt insuper et coenaverint in idolio: quicumque 75
eorum cum ducerentur laetiore habitu fuerunt et vestimentis pretiosis usi sunt et
praeparatae coenae indifferenter participes exstiterunt, placuit eos inter audientes
uno anno constitui, subjacere vero poenitentiae tribus annis, in oratione autem
communicare biennio, et ita ad perfectionis gratiam pervenire. Quot autem ascen-
derunt templa veste lugubri et recumbentes per omne tempus deflevere discubitus, 80
si compleverint poenitentiam triennii, sine oblatione suscipiantur; si autem non
manducaverint, biennio subjecti poenitentiae, tertio anno communicent sine
oblatione, ut perfectionem quadriennio consequantur. Penes episcopos autem erit
potestas conversationis eorum, probantes vel humanius circa eos facere, vel tempus
adjicere amplius. Ante omnia vero praecedens eorum vita et posterior inquiratur, 85
et ita eis impertiatur humanitas.[34]

65 audientes] poenitentes Ta poenitentes audientes AaH poenitentes et audientes JR.
duos Ta(BART. Ivo) duo O.   adhuc] annis H *om.* AaJRTa.   68 praesumpserunt
JTa.   mysterium JPTaZ.   69 hebdomadas Cc.   et] aut AaJ.   et sexta
feria *infra post* aceto *ad lineam 70* H.   a] aut AaCiJO(IvoPan *orig*) *corr. ab* aut Ab *inser.*
Cc *om.* AdRUZ(V a IvoDecr GRATIAN).   70 aut AaCcJOTa(Ivo) ac Ad et HRU(BtFGKt-
MNSgX GRATIAN) *om.* AbAcCiTcZ(BmCpINTbV).   (aut aceto] ac ceto So).   ace-
to] cervisia PTa *corr. ad* a carnibus O.   75 insuper *om.* AaJRTaU.   coenaverunt
AdHPU(BmBtFGIKN BART. *orig* coenaverit V) celaverint AaJ *corr. ab* celaverint O.
76 laetitiore Cc *corr. ad* laetitiore Tc.   fuerint AaJORTaU.   77 scenae JR.   exsti-
terint AaJRTaU.   78 autem] vero H *add.* non Ta.   79 ita] tunc AaAdOP item U rei
R *om.* J.   Quod AaCcJR Qui PTa.   80 flevere HJRPU.   81 triennii — suscipian-
tur] triennium si non (*vel forte* triennium sine) ablatione agant Ta.   suscipiantur] restituantur AaHJR.   84 conversationem PTa.   85 inquiritur Cc.   86 humanius
Ta *corr. ab* humanitatis J.

[31] See BART. c.96 (pp. 260-261); GRATIAN C.24 q.1 c.41; cf. Ivo 15.117 (PL 161.886); BURCH.
19.105 (PL 140.1004-1005) WASSERSCHLEBEN, *Bussordnungen* p. 166.

[32] Cf. Ivo *Decr* 14.35 (PL 161.834); Ivo *Pan* 5.104 (PL 161.1234) GRATIAN C.11 q.3 c.109.

[33] Ivo 14.108 (PL 161.853); cf. GRATIAN C.11 q.3 c.19.

[34] This and the following sect. seem to be taken from BART. c.129 (pp. 287-288); cf. *Decretales pseudo-isidorianae* ed. Paul HINSCHIUS pp. 261-262.

327   De his qui minis cessere tantum poenarum, aut privatione facultatum territi
aut demigratione, sacrificaverunt, et hactenus poenitudinis negligentes neque conversi,
nunc idem concilii hujus tempore semet obtulerunt conversionis suae consilia ca-
pientes, placuit usque ad magnum diem eos inter audientes suscipi, et post magnum 90
diem eos triennio poenitentiam agere, et postmodum duobus annis sine oblatione
communicare, et tunc demum septem annis completis ad perfectionis gratiam
pervenire.   Si vero quidam ante hanc synodum suscepti sunt ad poenitentiam,
ex illo tempore initium eis sexennii computetur.   Si quod autem periculum vel
mortis exspectatio aut ex infirmitate aut ex alia occasione contigerit, his sub de- 95
finitione statuta communio non negetur.

      Si qui secundo et tertio sacrificaverunt coacti, quatuor annis poenitentiae sub-
jiciantur, duobus autem aliis oblatione communicent, et septimo anno perfecte
recipiantur.   99

      Si qui vero dolore victi et pondere persecutionis negare vel sacrificare compulsi
fuerint, duobus annis inter catechumenos, triennio inter poenitentes, a communione
habeantur suspensi.[35]

328   Si in alicujus praedio infideles aut fideles ascenderint, aut arbores fontesve aut
saxa venerantur, si hoc eruere neglexerint, sacrilegii reum se esse cognoscant; do- 5
minus aut ordinator rei ipsius, si admonitus ordinare noluerit, communione privetur.[36]

      Quod dictum est de apostatis dici potest de his qui ab haeresi rever-
tuntur.

---

      88 dimigratione Ab denigratione AaJTa.   sacrificaverint AaJTa.   88-89 conversi
— obtulerunt *om.* Ci.   89 obtulerint Ta.   suae] hujus AaJTaU.   93 pervenire *insert.* Aa *postea sequuntur in* Aa *sects. 312-315; vide supra var. in capite sect. 312.*   quidem
CcCiP.   antehac O hanc ante AaJ hanc autem R.   recepti HRTa.   94 eis] ei
AaJOTa ejus Cc.   sexennii *corrupt.* J *insert.* Aa.   95 ex[1] *insert. forte manu originali* O.
ex[2] *om.* AaJ.   97 sacrificaverint AaJPRTaU(BtCpFGKTbVX sacrificaverit So sacrificaverunt BART. *orig*).   98 aliis] annis P annis aliis U.   sine oblatione PTaU(BART.).
2 fuerint *om.* AaJ(BART.).   4 aut[1] fideles *om.* Cc (aut faculas BART. *orig*).   accenderint
AbCc(BART. *orig* accenderit M) ignem ad sacrificandum accenderint H acciderint Z ascendant
Ta (conscenderint So).   aut[2]] ut H ac J.   fontesve] aut fontes JRTaU fontes P.
4-5 aut saxa] saxave JRU vel saxa P(BART.).   5 neglexerit AaHJRTaU(BtX BART.).
sacrilegii *corr. ad* sacrilegi O.   reos AdCcTc(BmFGIMTbVY) *corr. manu originali ad* reos
Z (rei Cp).   reum se esse *corr. ab* rei sint O reatum se habere PTa(K reum esse M).
Lectio reum *habet sensum in canone originali, ubi legitur* si hoc eruere neglexerit, sacrilegii reum se
esse cognoscat dominus aut ordinator rei ipsius, *id est dominus vel villicus praedii in qua infideles
sinuntur faculas accendere aut arbores aliave venerari; lectio* reum *videtur perseverasse usque in Formam 3,
quamvis verba* neglexerit *et* cognoscat *probabiliter ibi mutata sunt in numerum pluralem.*   cognoscat AaHJORU(BART.) agnoscant Ta.   6 aut] autem AdHPRTaZ(BtCpFGKMNSoTbY)
corr. ad autem O *abbrev. ambig.* CcTa(BmGSg aut BART.).   ordinator] dominator AbTc.
voluerit Cc noluerint Ta.   8 de apostaticis *insert.* H de apostaticis Tc.

---

[35] See BART. c.129 (p. 288 lines 3-24); cf. *Decretales pseudo-isidorianae, loc. cit.*
[36] See BART. c.129 (p. 288 lines 25-29); cf. *Decretales pseudo-isidorianae, loc. cit.*; BURCH. 10.
21 (PL 140.836).

iii. *De divinatoribus* 10

329 Qui divinationes expetunt et morem gentilium sequuntur, vel in domos suas hujusmodi homines introducunt exquirendi quid arte magica aut experiendi causa, sub regula quinquennii jaceant secundum gradus poenitentiae definitos.[37]

Si quis episcopus aut presbyter sive diaconus vel quilibet ex ordine clericorum magos aut haruspices aut hariolos aut certe augures vel sortilegos aut eos qui pro- 15 fitentur artem magicam aut aliquos eorum similia exercentes consuluisse fuerit deprehensus, ab honore dignitatis suae depositus, monasterium ingressus, ibique perpetuae poenitentiae deditus, scelus admissum sacrilegii luat.[38]

330 Commoneant sacerdotes fideles populos ut noverint magicas artes incantationesque quibuslibet infirmitatibus hominum remedii nil posse conferre, non anima- 20 libus languentibus claudicantibusque vel etiam moribundis quidquam mederi, sed haec esse laqueos et insidias antiqui hostis quibus ille perfidus genus humanum nititur allicere; et si quis haec exercuerit, clericus degradetur, laicus anathematizetur.[39]

Qui auguriis vel divinationibus inserviunt, vel qui credit ut aliqui hominum sint 25 immissores tempestatum, vel si qua mulier divinationes vel incantationes diabolicas fecerit, septem annos poeniteat.[40]

De illis qui ritum paganorum observant

331 Si quis paganorum consuetudinem sequens divinos et sortilegos in domum suam introduxerit, quasi ut malum foras mittat aut maleficia inveniat, quinque 30 annos poeniteat.[41]

---

11 Qui *om.* AaJ.   expectunt AcCcO.   et] cum O.   mores AaHJRTaU. 12 exquirendi *add.* causa Ta.   quid] aliquid HTaU.   13 subjaceant AaJRTa poeniteant P.   15 auruspices PTa airupices *corr. ad* arupices R.   auriolos R.   hariolos — augures] auguros aut hariolos aut certe augures Ta.   auguros J.   vel] aut JRTa.   16 aliquid P alios Tc *om.* Ta.   eorum] horum Ta illorum JU.   18 poenitentiae] poenae JR.   sacrilegi Cc.   luant AaR solvat Ta.   19-20 incantationesque] quae Tc incantationes quia R.   21 moribundus CcTa.   quis quam Cc. 22 haec] hoc RTa(Bart. Gratian haec Ivo Burch.) hic Cc.   23 haec] hoc RTc(Gratian *aliquiMSS* haec Bart. Ivo).   25 vel¹] et Cc.   credunt AaHJRTaUZ.   ut] quod P vel Cc.   sint] sicut AaJO *om.* Cc.   31 annis TaU.

---

[37] See Bart. c.104 (pp. 271-272); Ivo *Decr* 11.2 (PL 161.746-747); Ivo *Pan* 8.62 (PL 161. 1317); Burch. 10.5 (PL 140.834); Gratian C.26 q.5 c.2.

[38] See Bart. c.104 (p. 272 lines 5-11); Burch. 10.48 (PL 140.851); cf. Ivo *Decr* 11.5 (PL 161.747): Ivo *Decr* 11.73 (PL 161.772); Ivo *Pan* 3.169 (PL 161.1169-70); Ivo *Pan* 8.64 (PL 161. 1317); Gratian C.26 q.5 c.5.

[39] See Bart. c.104 (p. 272 lines 12-18); Ivo 11.65 (PL 161.759-760); Burch. 10.40 (PL 140. 839); Gratian C.26 q.7 c.15.

[40] Bart. c.104 (p. 273 lines 30-34); Ivo 11.36 (PL 161.755).

[41] Ivo 11.34 (PL 161.754); Burch. 10.6 (PL 140.834); cf. Gratian C.26 q.5 c.3 §2.

De illis qui sortem observant

Auguria vel sortes quae dicuntur false sanctorum vel divinationes, qui eas observaverint, vel quarumcumque scripturarum, vel votum voverint vel persolverint ad arborem vel ad lapidem vel ad quamlibet rem excepto ad ecclesiam, omnes ex- 35 communicentur. Si ad poenitentiam venerint, clerici annos tres, laici unum et dimidium poeniteant.[42]

De illis qui lapides vel arbores colunt

332   Si quis veneratur lapides vel arbores vel ligna, quasi Deum suum negat et abrenuntiat christianitati, et talem poenitentiam inde suscipiat quasi idola adoras- 40 set.[43]

De illis qui daemonibus immolant

Nam de his qui daemonibus immolant Theodori episcopi constitutiones habemus, in quibus scriptum est: Qui immolant daemoniis in minimis anno uno poeniteant; qui vero in magnis decem annos poeniteant.[44]
                                                      45

De mulieribus illis quae infantes suos in fornacem aut super tectum ponunt

Mulier si qua filium suum ponit supra tectum aut in fornacem pro sanitate febrium, unum annum poeniteat.[45]

De illis qui manducant aut bibunt aut portant super se aliquid ad Dei judicium subvertendum

333   Si quis manducat aut bibit aut portat super se unde existimat Dei judicium 50

---

32 sortes Ad.   33 Auguria] Jurgia JRU.   vel²] et J *om.* RTa.   33-34 observarint Ci observant AaHJRTaU.   34 quarumcumque] illarumcumque R quandocumque J.   voverunt Tc fecerint Ta.   34-35 vel persolverint ad arborem] ad arborem et persolverint Ac.   35 ad² *om.* CcTa.   ad³ *om.* TaU.   36 annos *om.* Ta.   unum *add.* annum TaTc.   36-37 dimidium *add.* annum U.   38 *tit. om.* CcZ.   39 vel¹] aut Tc.   vel arbores *om.* R.   quasi] contra JR *om.* P.   43 Nam] Jam H *om.* AaJRU.   44 immolat HR.   qui immolant daemoniis *om.* Ta.   daemonibus AaHJRUZ.   minimis] minoribus U muneribus J muneribus *corr. ad* minoribus Aa.   poeniteat HO.   45 annis AaCcHJRTa(BtCpMVX) *om.* P(K annos Ivo).   poeniteat H *om.* O.   47 super AaHJRTaU(BmBtCpSgSoVX Ivo).   49 super se *om.* Z.   pervertendum Z.   50 aut aliquid portat Tc.   se *add.* aliquid AaJPR.   aestimat Cc putat Ta.

---

[42] See Ivo 11.37 (PL 161.755); Burch. 10.9 (PL 140.834); cf. Idem 10.27 (PL 140.837); Wasserschleben, *Bussordnungen* p. 597 §12; p. 394 c.26.

[43] Cf. Ivo 11.38 *in medio* (PL 161.755); Burch. 10.10 (PL 140.834).

[44] Ivo 11.39 (PL 161.755); Burch. 10.12 (PL 140.835).

[45] Burch. 10.14 (PL 140.835); see Ivo 11.41 (PL 161.756).

pervertere posse, et exinde comprobatus fuerit, eadem sententia feriatur qua magi et harioli et incantatores feriuntur.[46]

De illis qui in tabulis vel codicibus futura requirunt

In tabulis vel codicibus sorte futura non sunt inquirenda, et nullus in psalterio vel evangelio vel in aliis rebus sortiri praesumat nec divinationes aliquas in ali- 55 quibus rebus observare; quod si fecerit, quadraginta dies poeniteat.[47]

De illis maleficis qui sperant se mentes hominum posse pervertere

Malefici vel incantatores vel immissores tempestatum vel qui invocatione daemonum mentes hominum perturbant anathematizati abjiciantur; et si emendare voluerint, clerici tribus annis, laici unum annum poeniteant.[48] 60

De illis qui ad suas vanitates perficiendas daemones invocant

334 Quicumque pro curiositate futurorum vel invocator est daemonum, vel divinos quos hariolos appellant vel haruspices qui auguria colligunt consuluerit, clerici ab omni officio remoti tribus annis, laici duobus annis poeniteant.[49]

De illis qui nocturna sacrificia daemonibus celebraverint 65

Quicumque nocturna sacrificia daemonum celebraverint, vel incantationibus daemones quacumque arte ad vota sua invitaverint, tres annos poeniteant.[50]

---

51 evertere R pervertendum Z.   probatus JR.   qua *add. et* AaJU.   52 incantores CiO.   53 exquirunt Ci.   54 vel] et Ac *add. in* OPTa.   sorte] forte CcJTc.   requirenda Z(Ivo).   et *add. ut* AaHJORTa(Ivo *om.* G).   55 vel[1]] et Ac *add. in* CiPTa(Ivo).   54-55 psalterio vel evangelio] evangelio vel in psalterio Tc. 57 sperant] putant Ad.   se *om.* Ci.   58 incantores Ci.   59 subjiciantur AaJRTaU.   60 noluerint AcAdCcTaTcUZ *obscur. forte corr. ab* noluerint Aa (voluerint Ivo).   uno anno U.   annum *om.* JR.   62 furtorum JR.   vel[1] *om.* CcTa. 62-66 vel divinos — daemonum *om.* Cc (*homoeotel.*).   63 hariolos — haruspices] haruspices appellant vel hariolos HRTa haruspices appellant et hariolos vel hariolos AaJU.   consuluerint JTaZ consulerint AaH consulunt P *corr. attentat. ab* consulunt Ad *corrupt.* Ci.   64 omni *om.* JR.   tres annos P(Ivo).   laici — poeniteant] poeniteant, laici (lici Ci) duobus annis CiP.   66 daemonibus AaHJRTaUZ *om.* O.   67 invitaverit Tc invocaverint H mutaverint CcCiO.

---

[46] Ivo 11.51 (PL 161.757); Burch. 10.25 (PL 140.836).

[47] See Ivo 11.52 (PL 161.757); Burch. 10.26 (PL 140.836-837); cf. 1 *Compil.* 5.17.1 (X 5. 21.1).

[48] See Ivo 11.53 (PL 161.757); Burch. 10.28 (PL 140.837).

[49] See Ivo 11.55 (PL 161.757-758); Burch. 10.30 (PL 140.837).

[50] Ivo 11.56 (PL 161.758); Burch. 10.31 (PL 140.837).

De illis qui balationes fecerint et se aliena forma mutaverint

Si quis balationes ante ecclesias sanctorum fecerit, seu qui faciem suam transfor- maverit in habitu muliebri et mulier in habitu viri, emendatione pollicita tres annos 70 poeniteat.[51]

De illis qui ad fascinum incantationes fecerint

Si quis praecantaverit ad fascinum vel qualescumque praecantationes excepto symbolo et oratione dominica, qui cantat et cui cantatur tres quadragesimas in pane et aqua poeniteat.[52]   75

De illis qui scabiem aut vermiculos qui pedulae dicuntur aut urinam bibunt et de illis qui talia aliis porrigunt

335   Qui comederit scabiem aut vermiculos qui pedulae dicuntur, aut urinam biberit sive stercora comederit: si infantes sunt vel pueri, vapulent; si virili aetate, septem dies poeniteant.[53]   Idem potest dici de illis qui talia aliis porri- 80 gunt.

Qui sanguinem aut semen biberint

Qui sanguinem aut semen biberint pro aliqua re tres annos poeniteant.[54]

iv. De ebrietate et gula

336   Magnum malum ebrietatis, unde omnia mala pululant, christianis omnibus 85

---

68 immutaverint Z.   69 balationes] oblationes O bachinationes Ta.   69-70 trans- formaverint Ta transmutaverit J(BART. Ivo transformaverit Ivo *alia lectio*).   70 mulier *add.* etiam Ta.   71 poeniteant CcTaTc *corr. ab* poeniteant J.   72 fascinum] fallacia Ci. 73 praecantaverit] peccaverit AaHTa *corr. ab* peccaverit O.   (qualescumque] quacumque Cp *postea cessat* Cp).   frequentationes vel praecantationes JTa frequentationes vel preca- tiones R precationes U *corr. ab* praemeditationes Aa.   73-74 excepto — dominica] praeter symbolum et orationem dominicam AaHJRTaU.   74 incantat... incantatur O.   75 poeniteant Tc *corr. alia manu ad* poeniteant O jejunet AaHJRTa jejunent U.   76 dicuntur] vocantur Z.   de illis[2] *om.* Z.   (78-81 Qui — porrigunt *om.* X).   78 pedulae] pediculi JP(Ivo).   79 biberint Tc bibit AaJU(Ivo) *corr. ab* bibit [?] O bibunt Z.   sive] aut HU.   comedit AaJU *corr. ab* comedit [?] O comedunt Z.   infans sit Tc infans fuerit J.   vel pueri *om.* AaP.   vapuletur JTc.   si in virili AdPTa.   80 poeni- teat J.   aliis *om.* Ta.   82 Qui *praem.* De illis AaAdP.   bibunt Z.   83 (Qui — poeniteant *insert.* X).   biberit Z(Ivo) bibunt JP *corrupt.* O.   poeniteat Z(Ivo). 85 ebrietas U *corr. ab* ebrietas R.

---

[51] BURCH. 10.39 (PL 140.839); see Ivo 11.64 (PL 161.759); BART. c.90 (p. 256).
[52] Ivo 11.74 (PL 161.772-773); BURCH. 10.49 (PL 140.851); BART. c.104 (p. 273 lines 3-6).
[53] See Ivo 15.96 (PL 161.883).
[54] See Ivo 15.103 (PL 161.884).

modis cavere praecipimus; qui autem hoc evitare noluerit excommunicandum esse decrevimus.[55]

(i.) De ecclesiastica persona ebriosa.

(ii.) De eo qui per ebrietatem vomitum facit.

(iii.) De eo qui se vel alium quocumque modo inebriat.   90

(iv.) De eo qui per ebrietatem vel voracitatem eucharistiam evomit.

(v.) De ebrietate laici.

(vi.) De eo qui carnes comedit in quadragesima.[56]

(i.) De ecclesiastica persona ebriosa

Si ecclesiastica quis praeditus ordinatione fuerit ebriosus inventus, aut mona- 95 chus, in pane et aqua tribus mensibus poeniteat.[57]

Ante omnia clericis vetetur ebrietas, quae omnium vitiorum fomes ac nutrix est, ita ut quem ebrium esse constiterit, ut ordo patitur, aut per triginta dierum spatium a communione submoveatur.[58]   99

(ii.) De eo qui per ebrietatem vomitum facit

337   Qui per ebrietatem vomitum fecerit, si presbyter aut diaconus est, quadraginta dies poeniteat; si monachus, triginta; si clericus, viginti; si laicus, quindecim dies.[59]

(iii.) De eo qui se vel alium quocumque modo inebriat   5

Sacerdos quilibet, si inebriatur per ignorantiam, septem dies poeniteat in pane et aqua; si per negligentiam, quindecim dies; si per contemptum, quadraginta dies.

---

86 noluerint AcCcTc.   excommunicandos Tc.   esse] eum AaHU.   decernimus UZ.   88 *praem.* Sextus liber Ab *praem.* Istud quod sequitur debet interponi, sed tamen est de alio O.   88-93 De — quadragesima *om.* AdZ(X) *supra post* poeniteant *ad lineam* 83 U *add.* *alios titulos* P(K); *cf. adnotationem 56.*   89 fecit O.   95 ordinatione] ordine Ta dignitate J. 97 est *om.* O.   98 ut²] aut AaHJR *om.* P.   patiatur JR.   ordo patitur] ordine privetur P.   98-99 *Auctor suppressit conclusionem canonis relinquens cetera syntaxi imperfecta.* 1 fecerit CcZ *obscur.* Ad.   4 dies *add.* poeniteat CiJRU.   5 se vel *om.* Z.   6 si] qui AdPTa (si Bart.).   inebrietur Tc inebriabitur Z *corr.* (*forte manu originali*) ab inebrietate R.   septem] sex AaTa.   7 per²] propter JR.   dies² *om.* AaTaTc.

---

[55] See Bart. c.102 (pp. 269-270); Ivo 13.70 (PL 161.816).

[56] This list of titles does not begin a new chapter of Book 5, but a subdivision of chap. 6. Chapter 6 includes sects. 323-357; this subdivison includes sects. 336-339. Regarding another arrangement in MS X see Firth, *Thesis* II 255* with nn. 15-16; regarding a different one again in KP see *ibid.* pp. 294*-296* with n. 59; cf. *Traditio* 16.547 n. 37.

[57] See Bart. c.102 (p. 270 lines 3-5); Ivo 13.77 (PL 161.817).

[58] See Bart. c.102 (p. 270 lines 6-10); cf. Gratian D.35 c.9; Ivo 13.79 (PL 161.817); Burch. 14.11 (PL 140.892). The final words of the canon have been omitted.

[59] See Bart. c.102 (p. 270 lines 16-18); Ivo 13.81 (PL 161.818).

Diaconus vel monachus secundum ordinem, ut scriptum est, seu et ceteri clerici et ministri juxta ordinem judicio sacerdotis poeniteant. Laici, velut vota non ha- bentes, si inebriantur, arguantur a sacerdote quod ebriosi regnum Dei non habebunt, 10 et compellat eos poenitere.[60]

Qui cogit hominem ut inebrietur humanitatis gratia acerrime corripiatur et sep- tem dies poeniteat; si per contemptum, triginta dies poeniteat.[61]

(iv.) *De eo qui per ebrietatem vel voracitatem eucharistiam evomit*

338   Si quis per ebrietatem vel voracitatem eucharistiam evomit, quadraginta dies 15 poeniteat; clerici vel monachi seu diaconi quinquaginta dies poeniteant; presbyter septuaginta dies poeniteat; episcopi nonaginta. Si pro infirmitate evomerint, sep- tem dies poeniteant.[62]

Si vero per negligentiam de calice Domini aliquid stillaverit in terram, linguabi- tur; tabula radetur; si non fuerit tabula, ut non conculcetur, locus corradetur et 20 igne consumetur et cinis intra altare recondetur et sacerdos quadraginta dies poeni- teat.[63]

Si super altare stillaverit calix, sorbeat minister stillam et tres dies poeniteat; si super linteum altaris et ad aliud stilla pervenerit, quatuor dies poeniteat; si usque tertium, novem dies poeniteat; et linteamina quae tetigerit stilla minister abluat 25 tribus vicibus calice subtus posito, et aqua ablutionis sumatur et juxta altare recon- datur.[64]

---

8 seu *om.* H *delet.* Ab.   et] etiam AaJPRU.   10 inebrientur U ebriantur Ta.   ha- bebunt] possidebunt CcHTa(Bart. Ivo).   11 compellunt Cc compellant P *corrupt.* AbO. 12 hominem] aliquem J *om.* RTa.   inebrietur R *add.* quis Ta.   ut inebrietur] inebriari H.   corripiatur] puniatur AaHJRU.   13 dies[2] *om.* O.   poeniteat *om.* JO(Bart. Ivo).   14 per *om.* Cc.   per — voracitatem] vel ebrie vel voraci Ci.   15 vel] et O.   voracitatem *add.* vomitum facit et AaHJRTaU.   16 seu] vel AaOTaU et H. seu diaconi *om.* J.   dies *om.* U.   poeniteant *om.* RU.   presbyteri HOTaU(Bart. Ivo Burch. Gratian).   17 dies *om.* UZ.   poeniteant OTa(Bart.) *om.* HU(Ivo Burch. Gratian).   episcopus CcP.   nonaginta] viginti Ta *corr. ab* viginti O centum J *add.* dies poeniteant JR.   evomuerint AdHPUZ(Bart. Ivo evomuerit BtFNTb Burch. Gratian) evomerit AaCcO(M) *corr. ab* evomerit Tc (vomerit V) evomatur J evometur R *om.* Ta(SoX). 18 poeniteat Ta(BtFGMNSoTbX Burch.) poenit. AaAdJR(Sg) *add.* si non, nonaginta poeni- teat Z.   19 terra U.   in terram *om.* Ta.   19-20 linguabitur] lignea Ta lignabitur Cc lingua lambetur P(Ivo Grat[r] linguabitur Grat[f] Burch).   20 radetur] corrodetur U reddetur J.   corradetur] corrodetur Ta corodatur Aa cum-radetur O radetur JP. 21 intra] infra Ta in terra sub Tc.   recondatur AaHTc.   24 usque *add.* ad AaHP(Ivo[l] Gratian *sine additione* Ivo[2] Burch.).   25 contigerit JRU tetigerat H.

---

[60] Cf. 1 *Cor* 6.10; see the following note.

[61] See Bart. c.102 (p. 270 lines 19-29); Ivo 13.76 (PL 161.817).

[62] See Bart. c.102 (p. 270 lines 29-34); Burch. 5.46 (PL 140.761); cf. Ivo *Decr* 2.55 (PL 161.172); Ivo *Pan* 1.154 (PL 161.1081); Gratian *De consec.* D.2 c.28; *Capitula Theodori* c.50 (PL 99.950).

[63] See Burch. 5.47 (PL 140.761); Ivo *Decr* 2.56 (PL 161.172-173); cf. Ivo *Pan* 1.155 (PL 161.1081); Gratian *De consec.* D.2 c.27; *Capitula Theodori* c.51 (PL 99.950).

[64] See Burch., Ivo *Decr locc. citt.*; cf. *locc. citt.*

Qui evomerit sacrificium et a canibus consumitur, annum unum poeniteat; sin autem, quadraginta dies poeniteat. Si in die quando communicaverit sacrificium evomerit, si ante mediam noctem, tres superpositiones faciat; si post mediam noc-30 tem, duas; si post matutinum, unam.[65]

Si vero sacrificium evomerit, quadraginta dies poeniteat; si in ignem projicit, et centum psalmos cantet. Si vero canes lambuerint talem vomitum, centum dies qui evomit poeniteat.[66]

Omne sacrificium sordida vetustate perditum igne comburendum est et cinis juxta 35 altare sepeliendus.[67]

(v.) *De ebrietate laici*

339 Laicus, si per ebrietatem vomitum facit, tres dies a carne et vino et cervisia abstineat.[68]

Si quis per nequitiam alium inebriat, quadraginta dies poeniteat. Quod si in 40 consuetudine habuerit, communione privetur donec digne poeniteat et emendationem promittat.[69]

(vi.) *De eo qui carnes comedit in quadragesima*

Quicumque in quadragesimae diebus esum carnium attentare praesumpserit non solum reus erit resurrectionis dominicae, verum etiam alienus ab ejusdem diei sancta 45 communione; et hoc illi cumuletur ad poenam ut in ipsius anni circulo ab omni esu carnium abstineat, quia sacris diebus abstinentiae oblitus est disciplinam.[70]

---

28 evomuerit AdPTaU(BtKNTbX Ivo Burch.) *corr. ad* evomuerit R (evomit F) vomerit Cc. sumitur P consumptum fuerit Ad.   29 poeniteat *om.* HJRTaU.   quando] qua HJRTaU. 30 evomuerit AaAdPTaU(BmBtFKNTbX Ivo Burch.) *corr. ad* evomuerit R *add.* xxl. dies poeniteat J (*add.* et a canibus non consumetur Tb).   interpositiones J *corr. ad* prostrationes O. 31 matutinas Ta *add.* vel nas *suprascr.* Ad.   32 evomuerit AaAdPTaU(BmBtKNTbX Burch. Ivo).   igne CcJ.   projecit AaJR projecerit HU projiciat Ta.   et *om.* AdHJPR-TaTcU(BmBtFGIKMNSgSoTbVXY Burch. Ivo) *delet.* Ab.   33 tabuerint AcCcCiZ. 35 cinis *om.* JRU.   36 sepeliendum CcJR recondendum U reponendus H *add.* est HTa. 38 Laicus *add.* hic Ab.   et[1] *om.* Cc.   40 in] ex Tc *om.* Aa.   42 permittat Ac promiserit Z.   43 quadragesimis J quadragesimalibus AaU xl. CcCiO *forte corr. ab* xl. R. diebus *insert.* R.   44 attentare] acceptare O.   45 etiam *add.* et JR.   46 poenam] poenitentiam O.   in *om.* AaHJPRU.

---

[65] See Burch. 5.48 (PL 140.762); Ivo 2.57 (PL 161.173); cf. *Capitula Theodori* c.52 (PL 99. 950).

[66] See Burch. 5.49 (PL 140.762); Ivo 2.58 (PL 161.173); cf. *Capitula Theodori* c.53 (PL 99. 950-951).

[67] Burch. 5.50 (PL 140.762); Ivo 2.59 (PL 161.173); cf. *Capitula Theodori* c.54 (PL 99.951).

[68] Bart. c.102 (pp. 270-271); Ivo 13.82 (PL 161.818).

[69] Bart. c.102 (p. 271 lines 2-5); Ivo 13.83 (PL 161.818).

[70] Bart. c.110 (p. 275 lines 10-16); cf. Ivo 15.89 (PL 161.882).

v. *De sacerdote negligenter tractante eucharistiam*

340 Si cediderit sacrificium de manu offerentis terra tenus, uti non conculcetur, omne quodcumque inventum fuerit in quo ceciderit comburatur, et cui accidit 50 medium annum poeniteat; si vero sacrificium inventum fuerit, locus scopis mundetur et stramine igniatur et cinis recondatur, et sacerdos viginti dies poeniteat.[71]

Qui non bene custodierit sacramentum, et mus vel aliquod aliud animal comederit illud, quadraginta dies poeniteat; qui autem perdiderit illud in ecclesia, aut pars ejus ceciderit et non inventa fuerit, triginta dies poeniteat. Perfundens aliquid 55 super altare de calice quando offertur sex dies poeniteat; aut si abundantius, septem dies poeniteat; qui autem perfuderit dum sollemnitas missae celebratur quadraginta dies poeniteat. Si vero celebrata missa presbyter neglexerit accipere acrificium, quadraginta dies poeniteat; et qui accipit sacrificium pollutus nocturno tempore septem dies poeniteat.[72]   60

Et post pauca: Qui negligentiam erga sacrificium fecerit, ut in eo vermis consumptus sit et ad nihilum devenerit, tres quadragesimas in pane et aqua jejunet; et si integer in eo vermis inventus fuerit, comburatur, et cinis sub altari recondatur, et qui neglexerit quaternis diebus propter negligentiam suam solvat. Si cum amissione saporis decoloratur sacrificium, viginti dies expleantur; conglutinatum vero, 65 septem qui merserit poeniteat.[73]

vi. *Quibus danda sit eucharistia et quando*

341 Nulli nisi poenitenti detur eucharistia, nec etiam in fine vitae, nec etiam omnibus talibus, tum propter corporis vitium tum propter rationis defectum: *propter corporis vitium*, ut continuam nauseam patien- 70 tibus; *propter rationis defectum*, ut parvulis; licet quidam sub specie vini talibus sacram communionem porrigant, quod non est tutum ne forte

---

49 uti *corr. ad* ut Ad ut CcJOR(MX Bart. Ivo) *om.* Aa(V prout uti Tb ubi *corr. ad* ut Bm). non] si Aa.   50 fuerit *om.* AaJU.   inventum fuerit] inventem O.   50-51 in quo — fuerit *om.* Cc (*homoeotel.*).   50 acciderit PTa.   52 viginti] xxii. JR.   53 aliquod *om.* CiPTaTc(Ivo² aliquod Bart. Ivo¹ GRATIAN BURCH.).   aliud *om.* Cc.   55 Et perfundens AaJRU.   56 dies poeniteat] diebus U.   57 dies *om.* O diebus U.   poeniteat *om.* OTc.   58-59 sacrificium] ministerii sacrificium Z sacramenta H.   62 devenerit] redigerit JRU.   in] cum AbJORUZ.   63 cinis] ignis AaU.   64 propter] per AaJ.   pro negligentia sua Ta.   Si cum] et si cum JR sicut CcCiZ *corr. ab* sicut Aa *corr. ad* si anima tamen Tc.   65 decoloratur *add.* et Cc.   conglutinant Ci et glutinatum Tc.   65-66 conglutinatum — poeniteat *om.* Ta.   66 septem *om.* JR *add.* dies P. 68 petenti J *corr. ab* poenitent O.   nec] nisi CiZ ut Tc.   69 etiam *add.* in PU. tum¹] tunc H qui O.   tum²] tunc H.   71 ut] aut Ci *om.* Z.   quidem Cc. 72 ne] nisi Aa nisi ubi H.

---

[71] See BART. c.100 (p. 267 lines 14-20); cf. Ivo 2.61 (PL 161.173); BURCH. 5.52 (PL 140.762).

[72] See BART. c.100 (p. 267 lines 20-31); cf. Ivo 2.60 (PL 161.173); BURCH. 5.51 (PL 140. 762); GRATIAN *De consec.* D.2 c.94.

[73] See BART. c.100 (pp. 267-268); cf. BURCH. and Ivo *locc. citt.*

evomatur.[74] Fatuis naturaliter et furiosis non est danda nisi in inter-
polatione furoris. Illis etiam qui pro peccatis suis extremam poenam
persolvunt, ut suspendendis, decollandis, vivis sepeliendis et similiter 75
puniendis, apud quosdam, sicut ecclesiastica sepultura, sic et sacra
communio negetur, licet confitentibus vel confiteri desiderantibus.[75]
Sed credo quod male hoc fit, licet ad aliorum fiat terrorem. Quibusdam etiam, licet confitentibus et poenitentibus, nec in fine vitae datur
eucharistia propter criminis enormitatem, ut in supra dictis, et hoc ad 80
terrorem.[76]

342 Saeculares qui in natale Domini, pascha, pentecosten non communicaverint
catholici non credantur, nec inter catholicos habeantur.[77]
  In coena Domini a quibusdam perceptio eucharistiae negligitur; quae quoniam
in eadem die ab omnibus fidelibus, exceptis his quibus pro gravibus criminibus in- 85
hibitum est, percipienda sit ecclesiasticus usus demonstrat, cum etiam poenitentes

---

73 evometur Cc.   danda add. eucharistia Ta add. communio H.   nisi] licet AaHJ-
ORTa.   in om. AaCcCiHJORTaTc(BmFGMSoTbVX).   (73-74 nisi in interpola-
tione] sed ubi inter pollationes Sg).   74 Illis etiam] nihil et Cc vel eis H.   qui om.
Cc.   75 persolverint CcCiRU persolverunt P corr. ad persolverunt Tc.   ut add. in
HJORTa.   suspendiis Ta suspensis Cc.   76 sic] ita J si Cc.   et om. AaHJRTaU.
77 negatur PU corr. ad negatur Ab.   confidentibus Cc.   confitentibus vel confiteri]
confitentibus corr. manu originali ad confiteri Tc.   78 fit] sit Tc fiat H.   79 vitae om.
JP.   80-81 ad aliorum terrorem AaHJPRU add. aliorum Ta.   82 natali AaAdHJ-
TaU(Ivo Burch. Grat^r natale Bart. Grat^f Burch^f nativitate BtG).   in pascha U vel
pascha vel Cc add. et HJU.   pentecoste HTa(GX Ivo Grat^r Burch. pentecosten Bart.
Grat^f Burch^f) pentecost. AdCcJR(BmBtIKTbV petent Sg) add. poenitent J.   84 quoniam]
quem Cc quia U.   85 eodem AaJRTcU.   86 etiam] in ecclesia R add. ecclesia AaHJU.
poenitentes add. in ecclesia P.

---

[74] Source not found. In the early Church Holy Communion was given to children, even
infants, especially after baptism; most often this was under the form of wine alone. This practice was continued into the Middle Ages, then gradually discontinued toward the end of the
twelfth century. See P. Browe, "Die Kinderkommunion im Mittelalter", Scholastik 5 (1930)
1-22, esp. 4-9; Josef Andreas Jungmann, "Kinderkommunion", Lexikon ThKirche² 6.154-155;
Gilbert of Poitiers, Epistola ad Matthaeum Abbatem Sancti Florentii Salmuriensis PL 188.1256.
  [75] See Gilbert of Poitiers, op. cit. PL 188.1258; Robert Pulleyn, Sententiae 6.53 (PL 186.
903-905); Thomassin-André, Ancienne et nouvelle discipline IV 57-62; cf. above sect. 243 ad finem;
the last two words of sect. 243 are found in Bartholomew, but not in the ancient sources. Cf.
also Bart. c.115 (pp. 277-278); Burch. 11.76 (PL 140.874); Ivo 14.124 (PL 161.857-858);
Alan, Liber poenitentialis 3.17, 24, 37 (ed. Longère II 136-137, 141, 148; cf. ArchivesHDLMA
32.221; PL 210.296-297).
  [76] The use of the first person in the preceding sentence might suggest that this passage is Robert of Flamborough's own composition, so also the words in supra dictis. These words apparently refer to the end of sect. 272; cf. the last paragraph of sect. 282.
  [77] Bart. c.103 (p. 271 lines 7-9); Gratian De consec. D.2 c.19; cf. Ivo 2.33 (PL 161.168);
Burch. 5.23 (PL 140.757); Peter of Poitiers as cited above at sect. 296 in n. 69.

eadem die ad percipienda corporis et sanguinis Domini sacramenta reconcilientur.[78]

343 Cyprianus Eucharistio confratri salutem. Pro dilectione tua et reverentia consulendum me aestimasti, frater carissime, quid mihi videatur de histrione et mago illo qui apud nos constitutus adhuc in artis suae dedecore perseverat, et 90 magister et doctor non erudiendorum, sed perdendorum, puerorum, id est quod male didicit ceteris quoque insinuat, an talibus sacra communio cum ceteris christianis debeatur. Hanc vobiscum communicare puto: nec majestati divinae nec evangelicae disciplinae congruere ut pudor et honor ecclesiae tam turpi et infami contagione foedetur.[79]   95

Qui acceperit sacrificium post cibum aut post aliquam parvissimam refectionem, nisi pro viatico, pueri tres dies, majores septimanam, clerici viginti dies poeniteant.[80]

vii. De sacerdotibus subter fugientibus baptismum et poenitentiam dare

344 Quicumque presbyter in propria provincia aut in alia, ubicumque inventus 99 fuerit, commendatum sibi infirmum baptizare noluerit, vel in profectione itineris vel de aliqua excusatione, et sic sine baptismo moritur, deponatur.[81] Idem dici potest de eo qui in extremo alicui negat poenitentiam.

viii. De detractoribus

345 Si quis detraxerit ei qui praeest, septem dies a conventu ecclesiae separatus, 5 ut Maria soror Aaron quae detraxit Moysi, poeniteat.[82]

---

87 reconciliet U.   88 Eubaristio J Eubaristo R Euchario Ta Eucherio AaU (Eucratio Ivo BURCH. *orig*).   tua] vestra Cc.   89 existimasti JPTaTc(BtGIKMNSgTbVXY Ivo[1-2] BURCH. GRATIAN *orig*) aestimavi H (aestimasti Ivo[3]).   videtur AaH.   90 nos] vos AdCcHPTaU(KSoX Ivo GRATIAN BURCH. *corr. alia manu ad* vos N) nos *vel* vos Ab(Sg). constitutus] est et J *om.* AaHRU *add.* est O.   decore Ta (So) indedecore AbAcCcCiTcZ (in dedecore IvoDecr IvoDecr GRATIAN BURCH. indecore F de decore GSg errore V) decorare R.   91 id est] idem P et J (id Ivo GRATIAN BURCH.).   quod] quid J qui R. 92 cum] et J *om.* Ci.   93 Hanc] Haud O(IvoPan) aut AaHJTaU(TbVX BURCH. GRATIAN) an P(KSg hunc BmBtSo) *Circa sensum* Hanc *in Forma 3 cf. Ps 26.4.*   nobiscum AaJRTaU(FTb IvoDecr GRAT[r] BURCH. *orig* nobiscum *vel* vobiscum IX vobiscum IvoPan nobis V nobis *vel* vobis Sg vobis non BmSo) *add.* non O.   94 ecclesia Z *om.* J.   tam] tamen O.   et infami *om.* J *insert.* Ad.   94-95 et infami contagione] contagione et infami R.   96 parvam R perituram J.   98 et poenitentiam dare *om.* Ci.   99 alia] aliqua O aliena J.   1 in] de Cc *om.* AaHJ *delet.* R.   2 vel de *corr. ad* sine O.   3 moriatur H moriuntur Ta. in *om.* Ci.   5 quis *add.* discors Cc.   conventu] communione H.   ecclesiae *om.* JU *insert.* Aa.   6 Moysi *om.* J *insert.* Aa.

---

[78] BART. c.103 (p. 271 lines 11-17); BURCH. 5.20 (PL 140.756); Ivo 2.30 (PL 161.167); GRATIAN De consec. D.2 c.17; cf. PETER OF POITIERS *loc. cit.*

[79] See Ivo *Pan* 1.152 (PL 161.1080); cf. BURCH. 5.21 (PL 140.756-757); Ivo *Decr.* 2.31 (PL 161.167-168); Ivo *Decr.* 11.83 (PL 161.774); GRATIAN *De consec.* D.2 c.95; St. CYPRIAN, *Epistulae* 2 (CorpusScrEccLat 3².467-468; *Epistola* 61 PL 4.373).

[80] See BURCH. 5.35 (PL 140.759); Ivo 2.45 (PL 161.170).

[81] BART. c.98 (pp. 264-265); cf. Ivo 1.241 (PL 161.117); BURCH. 4.47 (PL 140.736); GRATIAN De consec. D.4 c.22.

[82] See BART. c.106 (p. 274); Ivo 13.67 (PL 161.815); BURCH. 10.67 (PL 140.854); cf. *Num* 12.1-15.

ix. *De conjuratoribus et conspiratoribus*

Si quis discors et litigans et per odium dissidens exstiterit, quousque ad concordiam redeat a conventu et societate ecclesiae, ut canones jubent, alienus exsistat.[83]

Si qui clerici vel monachi reperti fuerint conjurantes vel conspirantes aut insidias ponentes episcopis aut clericis, gradu proprio penitus abjiciantur.[84] 10

Igitur si clerici aut monachi inventi fuerint conjurati aut per conjurationem calumniam machinantes episcopis vel clericis, proprium amittant gradum, similiter et eis consentientes; ceteri vero, scilicet laici, communione priventur et ab ecclesia extorres fiant et omnes infames censeantur.[85] 15

x. *De his qui post publicam poenientiam relabuntur*

346 De his vero non incongrue dilectio tua apostolicam sedem credidit consulendam qui acta poenitentia tamquam canes et sues ad vomitus pristinos et ad volutabra redeuntes, et militiae cingulum et ludicras voluptates et nova conjugia et inhibitos denuo appetiere concubitus, quorum professam incontinentiam generati post absolutionem filii prodiderunt. De quibus, quia jam subterfugium non habent poenitendi, id duximus decernendum ut sola intra ecclesiam fidelibus oratione jungantur; celebrationi, quamvis non mereantur, intersint; a dominicae mensae convivio segregentur, ut in hac districtione correpti et ipsi sua errata castigent et aliis exemplum tribuant quatenus ab obscenis cupiditatibus retrahantur. Quicumque tamen carnali fragilitate ceciderunt, viatici munere, cum ad Dominum coeperint proficisci, per communionis gratiam volumus subveniri. Quam formam et circa mulieres quae post poenitentiam se talibus pollutionibus devinxerunt servandam esse censemus.[86] 20 / 25

8-9 Si — cxsistat *supra post* poenitentiam *ad lineam* 3 RU(Sg) *infra post* censeantur *ad lineam* 15 Aa.   10 reperti] inventi AaJ.   11 penitus *om.* JR *insert.* Aa.   abjiciantur] deponantur JR *corr. ab* deponantur Aa.   12 aut¹] atque Cc.   13-14 similiter] sic Cc.   14 scilicet] videlicet J si Ta.   15 sentiantur Cc.   17 sedem] se Cc *corr. ab* se J.   crediderit O *om.* J *insert.* Aa.   17-18 esse consulendum AaHJRTaU.   18 volutrabrum Aa voluptatem R voluptaria J.   20 aperiere R appetere OZ appetere praesumumt P petiere Ta.   21 prodierint JTa perdiderunt OPTc.   quia] qui TaU.   22 diximus Ci.   duximus decernendum] decrevimus J.   23 meruerint HJRTaU.   intersint] interesse Ta interfuit Tc.   convivio] communione JTa. communio R conjugio Tc.   26 ceciderint AaAbRTaU occiderunt J.   27 et per O.   28 devinxerint CcJ devinxerint *vel* dejunxerint *corrupt.* R convinxerint *vel* conjunxerint Ta.

[83] Bart. c.107 (p. 274 lines 13-16); Ivo 13.58 (PL 161.814); see Burch. 10.57 (PL 140.852).

[84] See Bart. c.82 (p. 245 lines 28-30); Burch. 10.68 (PL 140.854); Ivo 12.87 (PL 161.802); Gratian C.11 q.1 c.23.

[85] See Bart. c.82 (p. 246 lines 1-3); Burch. 10.69 (PL 140.854); Ivo 12.88 (PL 161.802); cf. Gratian C.11 q.1 c.21. The last part of this paragraph, *similiter* ff., seems to have been composed by Flamborough abbreviating the basic concepts found in Bart. c.82 (p. 246 lines 4-17); cf. Gratian C.11 q.1 c.22; Ivo 6.346 (PL 161.516); above sect. 310 with n. 99. Regarding a possible meaning of *calumnia* here see above sect. 248 n. 62.

[86] See Bart. c.117 (p. 279 lines 7-24); Ivo 15.71 (PL 161.879); Burch. 19.57 (PL 140.997); Gratian C.33 q.2 c.12; JK 255; 2 *Pet* 2.22.

347 Nemo ex praemissa et similibus auctoritatibus, saepe criminaliter lapsus, 30
existimet veniam omnem et poenitentiam esse negandam; sed pro sollemni poenitentia id dictum intelligat, quae secundum specialem morem quarundam ecclesiarum
non est iteranda pro reverentia sacramenti et ne vilescat et contemptibilis fiat hominibus.[87]

    Caute et salubriter provisum est ut locus illius humillimae poenitentiae semel 35
in ecclesia concedatur, ne medicina vilis et minus utilis esset aegrotis; quae tanto
magis utilis est quanto minus contemptibilis fuerit. Quis tamen audeat Deo dicere: "Quare huic homini, qui post poenitentiam primam rursus se laqueis iniquitatis obstrinxit, adhuc iterum parcis?"[88]

348 Quicumque vocati per gratiam primum quidem impetum monstraverint 40
deponentes militiae cingulum, postmodum vero ad proprium vomitum sunt re-
lapsi, ita ut quidam et pecunias tribuerent et beneficiis malitiam repeterent, hi
decem annis post triennii tempus quo inter audientes erunt in afflictione permaneant.
Sed in omnibus propositum et speciem poenitentiae convenit explorari. Quotquot
enim metu et lacrimis atque poenitentia vel bonis operibus rebus ipsis conversa- 45
tionem suam non simulatione monstrant, hi definitum tempus auditionis implentes
tum demum fidelibus in oratione communicent; postmodum vero licebit episcopis
his aliquid humanius cogitare. Quicumque ergo indifferenter tulerunt et aditum
introeundi ecclesiam sibi arbitrati sunt ad conversionem posse sufficere, hi definitum modis omnibus tempus impleant.[89]   50

---

30 Nemo *add.* enim JRU.   lapsis AdHP(BtK Bart.).   32 id] idem AdTc.   spe-
cialem] spiritualem AaCcHJTc.   35 est *add.* hominibus HJRTaU *add.* homini O.
37 fuerit] est J *om.* HRU.   39 obstrinxerit HTcZ astrinxit U astringit Ta(Ivo) obstruit
Cc (obstringit Bart.).   iterum] tantum J crimen tam *corr.* ad crimen tamen U.
40 monstraverunt AaCcHJPRTcUZ(BtFKMNVY demonstraverit G numeraverint Tb monstrarunt Bart.) *Aliqua exemplaria versionis Dionysianae hujus canonis habent* monstrarunt, *aliqua*
monstraverunt, *sed Forma 3* Roberti *videtur habuisse* monstraverint.   41 malitiae JR.
41-42 lapsi Ta reversi P.   42 ut *om.* Cc quidem ut Aa.   quidam] quidem CcTa.
tribueret Cc tribuent Tc *om.* R.   militiam P(Bart. *orig*) maleficium Tc maleficia U.
43 anni Cc.   post] poeniteant Ta poeniteant post P.   44 speciem] spem HJTc(FNSo-
TbVY) spē AaRTa(GMX) *obscur.* O.   poenitentiae] continentiae AaR.   convenit]
oportet AaHRTaU.   45 rebus *om.* Cc et rebus H.   vel — ipsis] rebus ipsis vel bonis
operibus R.   46 non] ne O.   non simulatione] insimulatione Ac.   monstrent Z *corr.*
ab monstrent Tc numerant Ta.   47 tum] tunc PTa(Bart.) tamen R.   vero] ne J nec
Aa.   48 his *praem.* de P *praem.* de *insert.* Ab.   ergo] autem Ta igitur J.   tulerint
RTa(Bart.).   49 in ecclesiam AaHU.   conversationem OTc.   50 modum AbZ
ambig. AaAcORTa.

---

[87] See Bart. c.117 (p. 279 lines 25-31); cf. Rufinus ad C.33 q.2 c.12 (p. 500); Kuttner
and Rathbone, *Traditio* 7.295 n. 23; above sects. 236-241. This paragraph is a dictum of Bartholomew commenting on the preceding paassge; the following three paragraphs, also from
Bartholomew, are quotations in support of the position taken here.

[88] See Bart. c.117 (pp. 279-280); cf. Ivo 15.24 *in medio* (PL 161.862); Gratian D.50 c.62;
Lombard, *Sent.* 4.14.3.

[89] See Bart. c.117 (p. 280 lines 4-19). This is c.12 of the Council of Nicea (see Hefele-

349 Si qui per Dei gratiam vocati primo quidem ostenderunt fidem suam deposito militiae cingulo, post haec autem ad proprium vomitum reversi sunt ut pecunias darent et abirent rursus ad militiam, isti sunt decem annis inter poenitentes post primum triennium quo fuerint inter audientes; ab hominibus vero praecipue observetur ut animus eorum ad fructus poenitentiae accendatur. Quicumque 55 enim cum Dei timore et lacrimis perseverantibus et operibus bonis conversationem suam non verbis solis, sed opere et virtute, demonstrant, cum tempus statutum ab his fuerit impletum et orationibus jam coeperint communicare, licebit episcopo et humanius aliquid circa eos cogitare. Qui vero indifferenter habuerint lapsum et sufficere sibi quod ecclesiam introierint arbitrantur, isti omnino tempora statuta 60 implebunt.⁹⁰

xi. *De poena sacerdotis publicantis peccata poenitentis*

350 Sacerdos ante omnia caveat ne eorum qui ei confitentur peccata alicui recitet, non propinquis, non extraneis, nec quod absit pro aliquo scandalo; nam si hoc fecerit, deponatur et omnibus diebus vitae suae ignominiosus peregrinando poeniteat.⁹¹ 65

xii. *Quod non ad libitum suum arbitrari debeat sacerdos poenitentias*

351 Nemo sic intelligat ut semper secundum rigorem et districtionem canonibus constitutam absque omni misericordia poenitentia imponi debeat, sed quod cano-

---

51 Si] Hi Ad.   vocati *om.* JR *insert.* Aa.   ostendunt CcOPTaZ ostenderint J.
52 malitiae JR.   sunt *om.* O.   53 malitiam AaJRU *corr. ad* malitiam H.   sint AaAdHJPU(GIKMNSoX Bart. Gratian).   54 fuerunt AaAcCcHPTcZ(FIKNTbY *corrupt.* Sg fuerint Bart. Gratian).   (quo fuerint] sint Bt).   hominibus] omnibus HJTaTc-(BmGIKMNSgTbVXY Bart. Gratian).   55 observentur JR.   ut *om.* J *insert.* Ad. attendatur AaAcPZ(KMSgSoTbV Bart. Gratian) accendatur *vel* attendatur Tc attendat H (accedatur Y) incendatur Ta (*corr. alia manu ab* observatur G).   58 coeperit CcCi. episcopo et *invers.* AaJRU.   et *om.* HPTa.   60 arbitrentur JZ.   isti] illi O ipsi Y.   tempora] ipsa Cc.   62 poenitentis] confitentis Ad.   63 aliquibus Ta aliqui Ci.   recitent Ta reticet JR.   67-74 Nemo — tenere *una cum alia materia supra intra sects.* 235 et 236 O; varr. O *hic positae sumuntur ex illo loco; cf. infra in* Append. *C ad nos.* 20 *et* 27. 67 sic] si praedictas O (sic praedictas Bart.).   intelligat *add.* auctoritates O(Bart.). strictionem Cc *add.* in JRU *add. a* PTa.   68 institutam AaTc.   quod] quia JR.

Leclercq 1¹.591) according to a translation found in *Collectio Dionysiana*; concerning this collection see J. Rambaud-Buhot, "Denys le Petit", *DictDroitCan* 4.1138-1153; Fournier-Le Bras, *Histoire des collections canoniques* pp. 23-24, 94-98. Flamborough's text here is closest to that published by Adolf Strewe, *Die Canonessammlung des Dionysius Exiguus in der ersten Redaktion* p. 28; cf. *Codex canonum ecclesiae* PL 67.39. Cf. 2 *Pet* 2.22.

⁹⁰ See Bart. c.130 (p. 289 lines 21-35); cf. Gratian *De poen.* D.5 c.4. This is another translation of the same c.12 of Nicea, derived from the *Collectio Hispana*; regarding this collection see R. Naz, "Hispana ou Isidoriana (collectio)," *DictDroitCan* 5.1159-62; Fournier-Le Bras, *Histoire* pp. 65-71, 100-103. Cf. 1 *Cor* 2.1-5; 2 *Pet* 2.22.

⁹¹ Bart. c.29 (p. 198 lines 6-10); cf. Gratian *De poen.* D.6 c.2; Lombard, *Sent.* 4.21.9.

num rigor non pro sacerdotum libito, sed per canonum dispensationem, sit tempe- 70
randus, ita ut in poenitentiis dandis semper memor sit sacerdos et districtae satisfac-
tionis, ad quam peccatores tenentur ex culpa, et indulgentiae, per quam canones
vere poenitentibus subveniunt ex misericordia. Et si in altero necesse sit excedere,
minus malum credimus misericordiae lenitatem absque dissolutione servare quam
rigorem justitiae semper ubique tenere.[92]

xiii. De illis qui diu retinent peccata   75

    Sciendum vero est, quanto quis tempore moratur in peccatis, tanto ei augenda est
poenitentia.[93]

xiv. Qualis debeat esse poenitentia anni illius qui in pane et aqua jejunandus est

352 Poenitentia illius anni qui in pane et aqua jejunandus est talis esse debet:
ut duos dies, scilicet secundam et quartam feriam, in unaquaque hebdomada je- 80
junet usque ad vesperam, et tunc reficiatur de sicco cibo, id est pane et leguminibus
siccis sed coctis aut pomis aut oleribus crudis (unum eligat ex his tribus) utatur, et
cervisiam bibat et sobrie, et tertium diem, id est sextam feriam, in pane et aqua
observet. Et tres quadragesimas jejunet, unam ante natale Domini, secundam
ante pascha, tertiam ante missam sancti Joannis; et si totam quadragesimam ante 85
festum sancti Joannis implere non possit, post missam impleat. Et in his tribus quadragesimis jejunet duos dies in hebdomada ad nonam, et sic de cibo sicco comedat
ut supra notatum est; et sextam feriam jejunet in pane et aqua. Et in diebus do-

<hr/>

69 non *insert.* H quasi Ta.   per] pro P.   dispensatione PU.   sit] sic Ci *om.* Tc.
69-70 temperandum J imperandus O crepandus Cc.   71 et *corr. ab* ex Tc *om.* AaH.
74 semper (*om.* X) *add.* et Tc(BmFIMNSoTbY Bart. *add.* etiam Sg).   tenere] reservare
Ta observare U.   76 vero *om.* Z.   vero est] quoque quod U.   quis tempore]
aliquis plus Tc *add.* magis U.   ei] eis CiZ plus ei Ta magis ei U.   78 in *om.* Ci.
81 de *om.* AaHJRTaU.   82 aut[1]] vel PU.   sed coctis aut] scilicet AaJ.   unum]
unde AbCi inter [?] O.   quo utatur PTa et utatur H(Bart. Burch.) his utatur U.
et] sed AaJ *om.* H.   83 et[1]] sed AaHJORTaU(NVX Bart. Burch. *om.* P(K).
(et sobrie] *om.* M).   tertium diem id est *om.* O.   id est] scilicet Tc aut Ta *om.*
Cc.   84 quadragenas U scilicet xl. Ci.   85 missam] festum AaJPRTaTcUZ(Bm-
FGMSgTbY) *corr. ad* festum AbO (missam Bart. Burch.).   sancti] beati AaR sanctis
H.   sancti Joannis] Joannis Si J *add.* baptistae AcHPRTc(BmGIKMNSgSoTbVXY)
obscur. O (*sine addit.* Bart. Burch.).   85-86 et si — Joannis *om.* AaJ (*homoeotel.*).
ante festum *om.* Ta.   86 festum] missam H(TbV) *corr. ab* missam AbO (*om.* X).   poterit
AaHJRTaU.   missam] festum AaJRU(FGMSgY *corr. ad* festum Ab *corr. ab* mis festum
Tc *obscur.* O.   his *om.* JR.   tribus] tria J *om.* Ta.   86-87 quadragenis U.
87 usque ad nonam PTcUZ *obscur.* O *om.* Ta.   de *add.* aliquo O.   88 sexta feria TaZ.

<hr/>

[92] See Bart. c.33 (pp. 200-201); cf. Idem c.29 (p. 198 lines 10-16); Ivo 15.46-49 (PL 161.
868-869). This is a dictum of Bartholomew; cf. below Appendix C no. 20 with n. 18 and no. 27.
[93] Burch. 19.118 (PL 140.1006).

minicis, et in natale Domini quatuor dies, et in epiphania Domini unum diem, et in pascha usque ad octavum diem, et in ascensione Domini et pentecosten qua- 90 tuor dies, et in missa sancti Joannis baptistae et sanctae Mariae et duodecim apostolorum et sancti Michaelis et sancti Remigii et omnium sanctorum et sancti Martini et illius sancti festivitate qui in illo episcopatu celebris habetur, in istis supra dictis diebus faciat caritatem cum ceteris christianis, id est utatur eo cibo et potu quo illi; sed tamen ebrietatem in ventris distensionem semper in omnibus caveat.[94] 95

xv. *De commutatione poenitentiae*

353 Pro uno die quem in pane et aqua jejunare debet, quinquaginta psalmos genibus flexis in ecclesia, si fieri potest, decantet; sin autem, in convenienti loco eadem faciat et unum pauperem pascat; et eodem die, excepto vino et carne et sagimine, 99 sumat quidquid velit.[95]

Si autem talis est quod tamdiu in genibus jacere non possit, faciat sic: infra ecclesiam si fieri potest, sin autem in uno loco stando intente, septuaginta psalmos per ordinem cantet et pauperem pascat; et eo die, excepto vino et carne et sagimine, sumat quidquid velit.[96]   5

Qui in ecclesia centies genua flexerit, id est si centies veniam petierit (si fieri potest ut in ecclesia fiat, hoc bonum est; si autem fieri non potest, secrete in loco con-

---

89 in[1] *om.* Ab *insert.* Cc.   natali RTaUZ(Burch.) natalis Aa (natale Bart.). Domini[1] *add.* et in epiphania Aa *add.* et in epiphania illos JRU *add.* illos HO(Bart. Burch). et in epiphania Domini *om.* R.   et in epiphania Domini unum diem *om.* U.   Domini[2] *om.* PTa.   90 et[1] *om.* Ci.   octo dies JRU.   Domini *om.* Cc *add.* unum diem *insert.* O.   et[3] *add.* in CcOP.   pentecoste U(Burch.).   91 missa] festo U *corr. ad* festo AbO.   baptistae *om.* JR.   93 et *add.* in HOP(Bart. Ivo).   illo *om.* O.   95 in[1]] et AdHU(FNX Bart. Burch.).   in ventris distensionem *om.* Ta(G).   distensione P defensione J defensionem AaO difensionem Ac ingluviem et distensionem H.   97 quem] quam R quando Ta.   98 convenienti] continenti AaJ conventu U.   loco *om.* AaJOU. 99 et eodem die *om.* AaJ.   sanguine AaCcCiJTaU.   (2-5 Si — velit *om.* Bt *infra post* velit *in linea 13* X).   2 Si *ss. incipit* O[2] *cf. supra in Proleg. ad p.* 26.   talis — tamdiu *om.* P.   tamdiu *corr. ab* diu O.   sic *om.* O[2].   intra AaHJORTaU(NSgVX *infra* Bart.).   4 eo] eodem RTaTcUZ(Bart.).   eo die] cotidie Cc.   sanguine AaCcCiJTaU.   5 voluerit JR.   (6-9 Qui — velit *om.* So).   7 ut *om.* HPTa. ecclesia *add.* hoc Cc.   autem *add.* hoc HRTaU.   si — potest] sin autem P. secreto HTa.   7-8 secrete in loco convenienti] in secreto conveniente loco O[2].

---

[94] See Bart. c.135 (p. 297 lines 4-28); Burch. 19.10 (PL 140.981); Ivo 15.189 (PL 161. 897-898). The use of the expression *faciat caritatem* in this context is probably derived from the *agape* of the early Christians; see Du Cange s.v. *caritas*.

[95] See Bart. c.135 (pp. 297-298) Burch. 19.12 (PL 140.981; Ivo 15.192 (PL 161.899). Regarding this section cf. Thomas P. Oakley, « Alleviations of Penance in the Continental Penitentials, » *Speculum* 12 (1937) 488-502; Idem, « Commutations and Redemptions, » *Catholic Historical Review* 18 (1932) 344-351.

[96] See Bart. c.135 (p. 298 lines 3-8); Burch. 19.13 (PL 140.981); Ivo 15.193 (PL 161.899).

venienti eadem faciat), sed si fecerit, eodem die, excepto vino et carne et sagimine, sumat quod velit.[97]

354 Pro una hebdomada quam in pane et aqua jejunare debet, trecentos psal- 10 mos genibus flexis in ecclesia decantet; si autem hoc facere non potest, tria psalteria in ecclesia vel in loco convenienti intente decantet; et postquam psallerit, excepto vino et carne et sagimine, sumat quidquid velit.[98]

Pro uno mense quem in pane et aqua jejunare debet, psalmos mille ducentos flexis genibus decantet; si autem hoc facere non potest, sine genuflexione sedendo aut 15 stando faciat, si fieri potest; sin autem, mille sexcentos octoginta psalmos decantet; et omni die, si velit et se abstinere non vult, reficiat se ad sextam, nisi quod quartam feriam et sextam jejunet usque ad nonam, et a carne et sagimine et a vino per totum mensem abstineat. Alium autem cibum, postquam psalmos supra dictos decantaverit, sumat.   20

Isto ordine totus ille annus redimendus est.[99]

xvi. *De remissionibus*

355 De remissionibus quae fiunt in ecclesiarum aedificatione vel pontium vel alibi diversi diversa sentiunt, scilicet quantum vel quibus valeant. Nos autem, quidquid dicatur, omnibus consulimus tales remissiones, 25 maxime illis qui peccatis et poenitentiis onerati sunt et gravati.[100]

---

8 eadem] hoc AaHJRTaU.   faciat] fiat Cc.   fecerit] fieret *corrupt.* Cc.   sanguine AaCcCiJO²TaU.   9 quod] quidquid AaHJRTaTcU(BmFGMSoVX Bart. Ivo quod Burch.).   voluerit AaJR.   10 Pro *ss. cessat* O.   11 cantet PR.   hoc *om.* PU.   12 in² *add.* uno AaHRU.   psallet Ta psalmos decantaverit P cantaverit vel psallerit O².   13 et¹ *om.* O².   sanguine AaCcCiJO²U.   quidquid] quod Ad. voluerit AbAcCcO²Z (velit Bart. Ivo Burch.).   14 ducentos *om.* O² et ducentos J. 15 hoc *om.* AbO².   17 velit] vult AaHJRU.   se¹] si JPR.   sextam¹] sexta feria JR.   quod *om.* AaHJRTa.   17-18 quarta feria et sexta U iv. fer. et vi. R quarta et sexta feria J.   18 a¹] in R *om.* AaJTa(X).   et³ *add.* a AbCcHPU (*add.* a *insert.* F). sanguine CcCiO²(Bt).   a² *om.* O²PRUZ(Bt).   carne — vino] vino et carne et sagimine AcTc(BmMTb vino et carne et sanguine SoV vino et a carne et sagimine Y vino et a carne et a sagimine K vino carne et sanguine G).   sagimine — vino] vino et sagimine Ta(X) vino et sanguine AaJ.   19-20 cantaverit AaHTaU.   21 totus ille annus *om.* O².   25 ab omnibus JR.

---

[97] See Bart. c.135 (p. 298 lines 9-13); Burch. 19.14 (PL 140.982); Ivo 15.194 (PL 161. 899).

[98] See Bart. c.135 (p. 298 lines 23-28); Burch. 19.18 (PL 140.982); Ivo 15.198 (PL 161.899).

[99] See Bart. c.135 (p. 298 lines 29-38); Burch. 19.19 (PL 140.982); Ivo 15.199 (PL 161. 899).

[100] Regarding the matter discussed in this section cf. Huguccio: « Item aliquis episcopus facit remissionem parochiano alterius episcopi de poenitentia ei injuncta, et sic absolvit eum quamvis non possit eum ligare. Sed dico quod eum sic non absolvit nec talis remissio valet ei nisi suus episcopus vel ejus patrinus [*lege* parochus ?] ei sic imposuit poenitentiam ut talis remissio valeat ei, et tunc non intelligitur absolvi ab isto episcopo, sed ab illo qui imposuit ei poeni-

356 Postremo monere te volo, sacerdos, quia, si per ignorantiam grossam vel negligentiam vel propter gratiam aliquam vel favorem vel personae acceptionem ad arbitrium tuum et libitum et non canonum inspecta dispensatione citra merita punis poenitentem et minus quam 30 canonicae et authenticae exigant poenitentiae [dummodo ipse petat et paratus sit suscipere quantamlibet et canonicam poenitentiam], ipse quidem, ut puto, salvabitur et etiam a purgatorio liberabitur, peracta dico poenitentia a te sibi injuncta, tu autem in periculo eris. Quid enim ei imputabitur si tibi per omnia obedit et quantamlibet paratus est suscipere 35 poenitentiam ? Sanum igitur mihi videtur consilium ut, quantumcumque potes, poenitentem inducas ut canonicam et authenticam suscipiat poenitentiam; et sic tibi et ei bene erit. Quod si obtinere non poteris, dicas ei: "Frater, oportet te vel in hac vita puniri vel in purgatorio. Incomparabiliter autem gravior est poena purgatorii quam aliqua in hac vita. 40 Ecce anima tua in manibus tuis; elige ergo tibi vel in hac vita sufficienter secundum poenitentias canonicas vel authenticas puniri vel purgatorium exspectare." Quod si elegerit poenitens, ad petitionem ejus et libitum et arbitrium tuum poteris canonicas mitigare poenitentias et authenticas; sed paulatim et paulatim hoc facias, ut postea potius alleviationem petat 45 poenitens quam aggraviationem; et sic, ut puto, tu securus eris.[1]

27 sacerdos *corr. ad* sacerdotes Z *om.* Ta. 29 acceptionem *add.* vel CiTc. 31 exigant *om.* O² exigunt Tc. 31-32 dummodo — poenitentiam O²(FGMNXY) *insert.* Ac si tamen paratus sit (est K) suscipere quantamlibet poenitentiam P(K) dummodo paratus sit et petat suscipere *lacuna add.* vel quantamlibet poenitentiam *delet.* Tc *om. cett.(cett.) Haec parenthesis videtur non pertinuisse ad poenitentialem* ROBERTI, *sed apte exprimit mentem auctoris alibi in hac sectione explicatum.* 32 suscipere] ad Ac(MNY *om.* Sg). 33 etiam *om.* JP *add.* forte *insert.* Ab. 34 sibi] ei Tc sic CcCi cui *delet.* J *om.* O². 34-36 a te — poenitentiam *insert. alia manu* Ci. 35 est] sit PTaTc. 36 consilium *om.* Cc. quandocumque Cc. 38 et¹ *om.* JPR. poteris] possis AaHJRU. 39-40 incomparabilior JR. 41 Ecce *ss. cessat* O². tibi *om.* Ab. 42 puniri *ss. cessat* Z. 43 et] ad AaHTcU(G) *add.* ad PRTa(KMSoX). 44 et¹ *add.* ad JR. tuum *om.* Cc. poenitentias] sententias Cc. 45 et paulatim *om.* CcTc. facies J. 46 sic ut] sicut AaAdJRTaU(FX). tu *om.* CcPTc.

tentiam, ut in extra. *In eminenti.* » HUG. ad D.21 c.4 *adjicere* (text established from Paris BN lat. 3892, fol. 21ᵛᵃ, and BN lat. 3891, fol. 21ʳᵇ⁻ᵛᵃ) citing JL 12411 (X 5.38.4). Cf. also ALAN, *Liber poenitentialis* 4.21-23 (ed. LONGÈRE II 174-177) ; COURSON, *Summa* 1.46-2.8 (ed. KENNEDY pp. 326-331); HINSCHIUS, *System des katholischen Kirchenrechts* V 153 ff.; a gloss quoted by Artur LANDGRAF, « Cod. Bamberg... Magister Alanus, » *Philosophisches Jahrbuch* 54 (1941) 489; LANGTON quoted by HÖDL, *Geschichte... Schlüsselgewalt* (Beiträge 38.4) pp. 347-348; a quotation in ANCIAUX p. 129 n. 2 ; Franz GILLMANN, « Zur Ablasslehre der Frühscholastik, » *Katholik*⁴ 11 (1913)¹ 365-376; Bernhard POSCHMANN, *Der Ablass im Licht der Bussgeschichte* (Bonn 1948); IDEM, *Busse und letzte Ölung* pp. 112-120; Eng. tr. *Penance and Anointing of the Sick* pp. 210-226; Nikolaus PAULUS, *Geschichte des Ablasses im Mittelalter* esp. I 1-267.

¹ Cf. *Synodicae constitutiones* 6.9 (PL 212.61); COURSON, *Summa* 1.45 (ed. KENNEDY pp. 325-326); FIRTH, *Thesis* II 439*-441* with nn. 61-68; above sects. 6-8, 230, 234-235, 241.

De hospitalibus

357   Quicumque hospites non recipit in domo sua, sicut Dominus praecipit et
propter hoc regna caelorum promisit, quanto tempore hospitibus humanitatem
denegaverit, et mandata evangelica juxta possibilitatem suam non adimpleverit, 50
nec pedes laverit, nec eleemosynam fecerit, tanto tempore in pane et aqua, si non
emendet, poeniteat.[2]

47-52 *Sect. 357 om. hic* AdCcCiTaTc(BmFSoTbVX); *in his et etiam in* AcZ(IMNY) *idem canon
invenitur supra in sect. 322 (et in* Sg *post sect. 320) Cf. supra in Proleg. ad p. 52 cum n. 64.*   47 De
inhospitalibus AaAbP.   48 receperit P.   praecepit PRTc(GIKMSg Ivo).   *et om.*
R.   50 impleverit H obediverit U.   51 eleemosynas J.   fecerunt Ab.   52 *add.*
Poeniteat Fiat Amen J.

---

  [2] See Ivo 15.127 (PL 161.888); cf. *Matt* 25.35, 43; above Proleg. p. 52.

APPENDICES

APPENDIX A

An appendix¹ found at the end of the penitential in AcKPSg

[358]   Canones dispensabiles propositi sunt tantum episcopis. Non enim potest papa praejudicium suis successoribus generare quin dispensent prout sibi videbitur, ut dicit Innocentius in decretali sua *Innotuit* quae loquitur de Wigorniensi.²
Sic ergo ubicumque canon permittit dispensari simpliciter, illa permissio fit
5 episcopo, ut xxxiv. Dist. *Lector,*³ ubi dicitur quod cum bigamo usque ad subdiaconum potest dispensari et nihil supra; nec negatur quin papa possit ulterius dispensare si velit, sed episcopus non potest. Hodie tamen secundum nova jura non potest episcopus dispensare cum bigamo in sacris ordinibus, ut extra. *De bigamis, Super eo.*⁴

10 [359]   Ex jam dictis patet quod ubicumque invenitur dispensatum in canone potest episcopus dispensare nisi specialiter fuerit inhibitum sibi; sicut dicitur in lege quod quilibet est restituendus nisi specialiter fuerit prohibitus per legem, ut ff. *Quibus ex causis majores in integrum restituuntur,* l. *Necnon* § i.⁵ Cur enim negaretur quod nulla ratione prohibetur, ut extra. *De desponsatione impuberum,* c. i. in fine ?⁶
15 Respice canonem illum qui habetur lxxxii. Dist. c. *Presbyter si fornicationem fecerit,*⁷ ubi notatur qualiter episcopus potest dispensare circa adulterum injungendo ei poenitentiam et postea admittendo eum ad exsecutionem officii, et postea adjungitur

---

1 praepositi Ac.   episcopis *om.* P(KSg).   2 successoribus *add.* episcopis P(K).   (generare *add.* episcopis Sg).   3 iste Innocentius Ac(Sg *lege* iii. Innoc. ?).   quae loquitur *om.* P.   Wigorniensi] Widone P.   4 permissio *om.* P.   5 dicitur quod] dicit P(Sg).   6 nec *add.* tamen P.   8 ut in extra. *et sic per totam hanc appendicem* P.   11 episcopus *om.* P(KSg).   13 1.] lege P.   § i.] lege prima P.   Cur] cui P(KSg).   (enim *om.* Sg).   14 c. *om.* P.   17 et¹ *om.* P.   ad] in P.

---

¹ The author is unknown; see Firth, *Traditio* 16.547, 554-556; Idem, *Thesis* II 257*-258*.

² See Po. 953 (X 1.6.20; issued probably in Febr. 1200).

³ Cap. 18. Regarding this dispute about the power of the bishop to dispense from ecclesiastical laws see above sects. 111-113, 138-139 with notes. The author of this appendix apparently regards the impediment of bigamy to holy orders as a matter of church law, whereas Huguccio and Flamborough seem to regard it as a matter of Divine law; see above sects. 168-170 with notes. No doubt these latter so regard it because of its basis in Scripture (1 *Tim.* 3.2), from which, they constantly assert, no one can dispense; see above sects. 25 and 38 with notes. It seems to be implied in the decretal cited in the following note that this impediment comes from Divine inspiration and so cannot be changed.

⁴ See 1 *Compil.* 1.13.3 (X 1.21.2; forte JL 11690).

⁵ See *Digesta* 4.6.28.1-2.

⁶ See 1 *Compil.* 4.2.1 (Gratian C.27 q.2 c.18).

⁷ Cap. 5; copied above in sect. 290.

in fine: "Eadem quoque poenitentia erit sacerdoti de omnibus aliis criminibus
quae eum in depositionem inducunt." Unde, cum ex hoc habeatur quod, sicut
20 episcopus disponit circa adulterum, eodem modo et circa alia quae inducunt in
depositionem, dico quod episcopus potest in omnibus dispensare in quibus specialiter non inhibetur.

[360]   Sunt enim plures casus speciales in quibus episcopus inhibetur dispensare,
ut in homicidio notorio spontanee commisso, prout legitur l. Dist. *Miror*.[8] "Spon-
25 tanee" dico; quia, si ex necessitate vel casu fiat, secus est, ut l. Dist. *De his clericis
qui in obsidionis*.[9] Item nec potest dispensare cum eo qui excommunicatus exsequitur
officium suum, ut xi. quaest. iii. *Si quis episcopus damnatur a synodo*,[10] nec cum
simoniaco qui ratione praelaturae habendae contraxit simoniam. Non enim
potest episcopus dispensare cum aliquo ut habeat praelaturam emptam, ut extra.
30 Caelestini tertii, *Nobis*, tit. *De simonia*,[11] et i. quaest. v. c. i. in fine. Sed tamen
cum eo qui beneficium emit in aliqua ecclesia potest episcopus dispensare ut habeat
illud, prout legitur in praeallegato capitulo: i. quaest. v. c. i. Item cum eo qui
emit ordinem non potest episcopus dispensare, ut extra. *De simonia, Tanta*.[12]
Si tamen ordinandus non dat pecuniam nec ordinator accipit, sed mediatores
35 quidam accipiunt ab amicis ordinandi ut episcopum inducant ad ordinationem
faciendam citra conscientiam tam ordinatoris quam ordinandi, licet talis ordinatio
sit simoniaca, tamen episcopus potest cum tali dispensare, ut i. quaest. v. *Praesentium*.[13]

[361]   Quae autem dixi vera sunt in manifestis. In occultis autem non est opus
40 dispensatione; quia per poenitentiam deletur tam peccatum quam infamia peccati,
ut habetur evidenter de clerico fure qui post poenitentiam admittitur ipso jure
ad exsecutionem officii, ut extra. *De furtis*, c. ult.,[14] et hoc quia furtum fuit oc-

---

18 aliis *om.* P.   20 disponit] dispensat P.   20-21 in depositionem] dispensationem P.
24 legitur l.] dicitur P.   26 nec] non P.   35 quidam accipiunt] accipiunt quiddam P.
36 tam ordinatoris quam] tamen P.   37 simonia P.   40 tam] tum Ac.   peccati] peccatum P.

---

[8] Cap. 4; cf. above sects. 100-106 with notes.
[9] Cap. 36; cf. above sects. 107-109 with notes.
[10] Cap. 6; cf above sect. 138 n. 70.
[11] See JL 16466 (2 *Compil.* 5.2.9; X 5.3.27).
[12] See 1 *Compil.* 5.2.16 (X 5.3.7); cf. below n. 22.
[13] Cap. 3.
[14] See 1 *Compil.* 5.26.7 (JL 13860; X 5.18.5). This opinion is in harmony with the position
of Simon of Bisignano: "... si ante poenitentiam divina celebraret, in judicium suum hoc faceret,
quod tamen licuit acta poenitentia. Unde ex hoc non probatur quod de occultis criminibus
non possit quis retento ordine poenitere." *Summa in decreta* ad D.33 c.7 *ad ministerium nullo modo
...accedere*; see *op. cit.* ad C.15 q.5 c.2 *non potest per aliquam poenitentiam*; also ad D.5 c.6. Cf. *Summa
parisiensis* ad D.50 pr. (ed. McLaughlin pp. 43-44); *Apparatus: Ecce vicit Leo* ad D.50 pr. (fols.
19vb-20ra); *Glossa ordinaria in Decr.* ad D.50 pr.; Stephan Kuttner, "Ecclesia de occultis non
judicat," *Jus pontificium* 17 (1937) 13-28 with notes; above sects. 138-139 with n. 66.

cultum. De occulto autem peccatore dicitur quod gradu servato agat poenitentiam,
ut l. Dist. *De his vero visum.*[15] Qui enim in occulto peccato est unicum solum
45 habet judicem, scilicet Deum, ut xxxii. Dist. *Erubescant.*[16] Sed Dominus, dum
poenitentiam nostram suscipit, hoc quod erravimus abscondit, prout legitur xxxii.
quaest. i. *Apud misericordem.*[17] Deus enim neminem sanat quem omnino non sanat,
ut *De poen.* Dist. iii. *Sunt plures,*[18] et ita sanat tam a reatu peccati quam ab infamia.
Unde occultus peccator per poenitentiam restituitur in integrum. Unde dico
50 illum legitimatum ad omnes actus, argum. ii. quaest. iii. § *Notandum,* in fine.[19]

[362] Secus est de manifesto peccatore; ille enim duos habet judices, scilicet
ecclesiasticum et Deum. Unde, licet per poenitentiam restituatur quantum ad
Deum, non tamen restituitur quantum ad ecclesiam. Licet enim poenitentia
acquirat gratiam, non tamen restituit in potestatem primam, prout legitur *De*
55 *poen.* Dist. vi. c. i. versus finem. Unde tale peccatum quod est notum dicitur
crimen a criminando, quia licet sit purgatum per poenitentiam, tamen homo
potest inde accusari; et de tali dicitur in apostolo *Oportet episcopum esse sine crimine,*
ut xxv. Dist. § *Criminis appellatio.*[20]

[363] Quod autem dico in occultis non esse opus dispensatione, hoc intelligas
60 "nisi poenitentia exigat carentiam exsecutionis officii," ut patet in ordine empto.
Cum enim talis ordo sit furtivus, licet occultum sit peccatum, tamen quia non
remittitur peccatum nisi restituatur ablatum, ut xiv. quaest. vi. *Si res,*[21] oportet
quod in injunctione poenitentiae suspendatur talis ab exsecutione officii in perpetuum. Unde dicitur quod omnis peccator praeter simoniacum potest cantare
65 missam, videlicet praeter talem simoniacum qui ordinem emit, ut extra. *De*
simonia, Tanta.[22]
Licet itaque dicam in occultis non esse opus dispensatione et ita doceam secundum jura, tamen ut securus procedam in enormibus peccatis, videlicet in homicidiis
et cum excommunicatus recipit ordinem, licet sint occulta, consulo venientibus
70 ad me quod adeant dominum papam, licet de juris rigore hoc non exigeretur.

---

44 unicum *om.* P.   47 misericordiam P.   quem—sanat] nisi omnino sanet P(KSg).
48 tam] tum Ac.   50 Notandum *add.* est P(KSg).   53 tamen *om.* P.   poenitentia] per
poenitentiam P.   54 restituitur P.   55 quod *om.* P(KSg).   68 securius P(K).

15 Cap. 34.
16 Cap. 11.
17 Cap. 10.
18 Cap. 42.
19 Dictum post c.8 §8. Cf. above n. 14.
20 Dictum post c.3 §4; cf. *Tit* 1.7.
21 Cap. 1. See Simon of Bisignano, *Summa* ad C.1 q.1 c.11. Huguccio says the same in regard
to purchase of a benefice, in fact of any ecclesiastical office: "Habet enim beneficium furtivum;
unde oportet restituere tamquam rem furtivam si salvari vult." Hug. ad D.50 pr. (fol. 56vb)
quoted more fully in Firth, *Thesis* II 471* n. 85 (III 750*-751*); cf. Hug. ad C.1 q.5 c.1 *pro*
magna misericordia (fol. 124va); cf. also above sect. 180; below Appendix B sect. 374.
22 See 1 *Compil.* 5.2.16 (X 5.3.7); cf. above n. 12.

APPENDIX D

Form 1 (formerly called Form W)[1] *the form of the penitential found in* W, *less completely in* Q[1], *with fragments also in* Q[2]

Form 1 has no rubrics or lists of titles; it is not divided into books or chapters. It begins in W on fol. 19[rb] with the incipit *Res grandis* and continues as in sections 1-6 of Form 3 with the following variations:

Sect. 1: 6 satisfecit W.   7 tantus] tacitus W.   totum *om.* W.   9 facultatem] facilitatem W.   10 igitur *add.* et W.   11 decane salesburiensis *om.* W.   quod] quia W.   quidlibet] quilibet W.   15 enim *om.* W.   16 re perfectionem] perfectione W.   17 penitus *om.* W.   18 viam W.   19 ergo] igitur W.   dilectissimi W.   20 affectum] ad effectum W.   commensurare] mancipare consumere W.   20-21 alterum] reliquum W.

Sect. 2: 22-35 Quia — competentes *om.* W.   36 Verumtamen] Verum W.

Sect. 3: 41-48 INCIPIT—Poenitens *om.* W.   50 illa] illius W.   53 spero W.   54 debeamus *add.* omne W.   58 sint *add.* Resp. W.   quae] qui W.

Sect. 4: 72 te *om.* W.   73 in *om.* W.   ut] ubi W.   76 enim *om.* W.

Sect. 5: 79-80 A poenitente—operatio] Fili, *Deum qui te genuit dereliquisti* et recessisti a Domino Creatore tuo;[2] domum Domini et familiam peccando exivisti. Vis ergo reverti in domum tuam unde exivisti?[3]

Poenitens. Volo, domine.

Sacerdos. Ad poenitentem duo exiguntur: ut christianus sit et poenitens. Domus haec, scilicet poenitentia, quatuor continetur partibus: fide, spe, caritate et operatione. W.   83 semperque tenebo *om.* W.   84 de *om.* W.   86 et times *om.* W.   87 et timeo *om.* W.   88 de operatione W.   92 igitur *om.* W.   93 licet *add.* nemini W.   93-95 Fac—reducaris] Prius ergo per opera poenitentiae ad innocentiam reducaris W.   95 et postea W.

Sect. 6: 97-1 Dixi—obedientia] Et quia poenitentiam petis, quatuor a te exiguntur: dolor de praeteritis omnibus peccatis (quia uno retento omnia retinentur), cautela de futuris (ut scilicet velis abstinere ab omni mortali peccato),[4] integra et nuda confessio (ac si numquam locutus fuisses sacerdoti);[5] quartum est poena vel obedientia. W.   3 Poenitens — observare *om.* W (*homoeotel.*).   8 possum *add.* ab omni cavere peccato W.   10 non *om.* W.   15 tibi *om.* W.   16 scilicet — sis] ut habilior sit ad gratiam habendam W.   17 tibi *om.* W.   id est *om.* W.   22 relinquere W.   25 igitur] ego W.   abstinere] cavere W.   27 peccato *om.* W.   32 a te exigo] tibi impono W.   33 tibi *om.* W.   sollemne *add.* Si importabile est tibi, cum episcopo agas vel papa. W (*cf.* sect. 26).

---

[1] Regarding Form 1 see above Proleg. pp. 34-45.
[2] Cf. *Deut* 32.15, 18.
[3] Cf. *Luc* 15.17-20; *Matt* 12.44.
[4] Cf. above sect. 6 with n. 12.
[5] Cf. above sect. 7 with n. 17.

Then Form 1 in W continues as follows (cf. above sect. 17):

[364] Poenitens. Quid est votum?

Sacerdos. Licet digressionem facere videamur, quia tamen ad propositum pertinet, scias quod votum est conceptio melioris boni animi deliberatione firmata;[6] quod tribus modis sollemnizatur:...

Then Form 1 in W continues as in sects. 23-29 with the following variations:

Sect. 23: 36 Votum] quod W (*vide proxime supra*).   et *om.* W.
Sect. 24: 44 Similiter *add.* si W.   dat] det *vel* debet W.   45 mutat W.
48 aliquis *om.* W.   49 recipit W.   54-55 Ubi — simplex *om.* W.
Sect. 25: 60-61 Alioquin — fecisse *om.* W.   64 autem vel evangelium *lacuna* W.   66 lex — praesumet *om.* W.
Sect. 26: *nulla variatio.*
Sect. 27: 72 quid *add.* est quod W.   73-74 contrahendum — dirimit] sed non impedit W.   74-75 post — contraxi] post simplex votum continentiae contraxerim cum aliqua privatim solus cum ea W.   75 an] vel W.   77 tum] tamen W.   78 tum quadam subtilitate] propter quadam subtilitatem W.   81 ideo] ergo W.
Sect. 28: 82 quia] quod W.   89 vocat W.   91 vel[1] *om.* W.   93 secundam] alteram W.   nec] vel W.   95 consentio] non consentio, quia majus peccatum est scandalum facere excommunicationem sustinendo quam debitum reddere uxori putativae; sic enim quilibet propria ab ecclesia posset recedere excommunicationem sustinendo W.[7]   ut] quod W.   96 pie deluderes] praedivideres W.   97 eam] ipsam W.
Sect. 29: 98 subdiacono] subdit W.   99 contrahatur W.   1 illa *om.* W.   6 est *om.* W.   8 quod] quidquid W.   hoc — destruere] potest destruere papa W.   9-10 scilicet hoc *om.* W.   11 subdiacono] subdito W.   12 tutius mihi videtur W.

Then Form 1 in W continues as follows (see notes below for indications of parallel places in Form 3):

5 [365]   Tu post aliquantam digressionem perge propositum prosequi. Vis ergo quatuor illa quae a te exiguntur observare?

Poenitens. Volo, domine.

Sacerdos. Pone ergo cor tuum super vias tuas, immo super devia tua; quae super bivium dispersa sunt, quia dupliciter deviasti a Deo, committendo scilicet,
10 ut ita loqui liceat, vel omittendo, id est vel quod non licet faciendo vel quod faciendum erat omittendo.[8] Hoc fit quando quod tibi vis fieri tibi vel aliis subtrahis. Illud fit quando vitium aliquod sequeris.

---

6 Cf. Rufinus, *Summa* ad C.27 q.1 pr. (p. 435); above sects. 17 and 23; also above Proleg. pp. 35-36 with n. 86.

7 Cf. above Proleg. p. 41 with notes; sect. 28 with n. 48.

8 Cf. above sect. 197.

Sunt autem septem vitia criminalia vel capitalia cum suis speciebus.[9] Sed
ante quam illa prosequamur, ut more solito procedatur, dic mihi. Clericus es an
15 laicus? In primis enim de difficilioribus me expedire consuevi, de simonia cum
clerico, de matrimonio cum laico.[10]

POENITENS. De utroque mecum disputandum est.

SACERDOS. Vis ergo ut amodo incipiamus.

POENITENS. Ut libet.

20 SACERDOS. De ovili nostro es?

Sed de licentia abbatis mei ad vos venio. Monachus enim sum et prior.
Alioquin adultera esset confessio, immo nec confessio.[11]

Dic ergo: Uxoratus fuisti?

POENITENS. De aliquot quas habui nescio an aliqua mea fuerit.[12]

25 SACERDOS. Quare? An nescis quid sit matrimonium?

POENITENS. Quid enim est?

SACERDOS. Matrimonium est...

At this point the text of Form 1 begins to occur in Q^1Q^2 and continues
in Q^1Q^2W as in sects. 11-16 lines 8ff. (excluding titles) with the following
variations:[13]

Sect. 11: 8 SACERDOS. Matrimonium W (SACERDOS *om.* Q^1Q^2; *vide proxime supra*).
9-14 Legitima — suae *om.* Q^1Q^2W.

Sect. 12: 16 animorum *add.* et Q^1.   17 consensus *om.* Q^2.   19 enim *om.*
Q^2 *insert. alia manu* Q^1.   vovit] novit W.   21 nec[1]] non Q^1Q^2W.   consentiunt *om.* Q^1Q^2.   nec[2]] non Q^1Q^2.   22 nec etiam sponsalia *om.* Q^2 *add.*
nisi de facto tantum Q^1 *add.* de facto tantum W.   Cum — contraxisti] Unde
(*add.* si W) contraxisti sponsalia cum aliqua infra septennium Q^1Q^2W.   23
ea dimissa *om.* Q^2.   25 actum] factum Q^2W.   quam] nisi Q^1Q^2W.   26-
27 furiosi non contrahent W.   27 contrahet Q^1Q^2.   in *om.* W.   si — furor
om. Q^2.

Sect. 13: 29 contrahit Q^1W.   30-31 Si — matrimonium *om.* W (*homoeotel.?*).
31 dicuntur *add.* esse Q^1Q^2.   32 ut — erigi] et non possunt erigi W *om.* Q^2.
accesseris] ieris W.   33 et cognoveris *om.* W.   34 Si *add.* vero Q^1Q^2.
frigiditatem] fragilitatem W.   37 vel *om.* W.

Sect. 14: 41 etiam] autem W.   etiam perpetuum *insert. manu forte originali*
Q^2.   42 neque hoc neque illud Q^1Q^2.   erecta — virilia] passus est tetiginem
W^{14} passus es tentiginem erecta sunt virilia Q^1 passus es tetiginem vel aucta sunt
virilia tua Q^2.

---

[9] Cf. above sects. 9-10; below sects. 382-383.

[10] Cf. above Proleg. pp. 13-14; sects. 2 and 10.

[11] These lines 20-22 are an abbreviation of a portion which has already occurred in unab-
breviated form in Form 1; see above Proleg. pp. 35-36; cf. sect. 4 and p. 284.

[12] Cf. above sect. 188.

[13] Cf. above Proleg. pp. 27-28.

[14] Cf. above Proleg. pp. 37-38.

Sect. 15: 52 Aliquis — obtinuit] de virga ingrossata per morbum Q^1Q^2 *om.* W.[15]   53 tutius dicit] dicitur Q^1.   quod *om.* Q^1.   54 non] nec Q^2. suam *om.* Q^2.   56-57 vel si — dictum est *om.* Q^2.   57 et] vel Q^1.   59 et — matrimonium^2 *om.* Q^2.

Sect. 16: 61 impedit W.   etiam] et Q^1.   ordo *om.* Q^2.   62 cognitio, agnitio W.   63 raptus *om.* W.   tempus (*add.* personarum W) feriarum interdictum ecclesiae Q^1Q^2W.

Then Form 1 in Q^1Q^2W continues as in sects. 31-37 with the following variations:

Sect. 31: 23-24 Ita — habitu *om.* Q^1Q^2W.   25 Ordo — dirimunt] Votum et ordo et habitus patet W (*Vide sect. 16 et proxime supra*) impediunt ordo et habitus matrimonium et dirimunt Q^1Q^2.   25-26 quia — religionis] si enim aliquod istorum Q^1Q^2W.   27 tibi *om.* Q^2.   et *om.* Q^2.   27-28 et — matrimonium *om.* W.   matrimonium *om.* Q^2.   28 alioquin *add.* assidue Q^1Q^2.   ecclesia *add.* assidue W.

Sect. 32: 29 si — religionis] si tantum non praemisso voto religionis ad probandum intrasti religionem Q^1 tamen si non praemisso voto religionis tantum ad probandum intrasti religionem Q^2 *lacuna* probandum intrasti religionem W.   30 remanendi W.   31-34 quia — exibis] praemisso quidem voto exire non poteris Q^1Q^2 *om.* W.

Sect. 33: 35 monasterium] religionem Q^1Q^2.   38 in^1 *om.* W.   39 *invert.* monasterio a parentibus W.   39-43 et consensisti — parentibus monasterio *om.* W (*homoeotel.?*) *Scriba* Q^1 *coepit habere tale homoeoteleuton scribens hic*: capax doli vel non; *tunc deletis his verbis scripsit textum fere integrum cum varr. ut infra.*   40 ut maneas vel non *insert.* Q^1.   non] recedas Q^2.   41 Hoc est verum] Et hoc intelligitur Q^2.   42 vel^1] aut Q^1Q^2.   vel^2] aut Q^2.   42-43 *invert.* Secundum alios et secundum Caelestinum Q^1Q^2.   14 capax doli vel non *om.* hic Q^1 (*vide supra var. ad lineas* 39-43).   44 sed] si Q^1Q^2W.   accepisti] suscepisti W *om.* Q^2.

Sect. 34: *hanc sect. om.* Q^2 48 non] nec W.

Sect. 35: 51 et dirimit *om.* Q^1Q^2W.   52 ut dicunt *om.* Q^2.   separabat W.   53 contraxerunt W.

Sect. 36: 55 autem *om.* Q^2.   56 tu *om.* Q^1Q^2.   tantum] tecum W tamen Q^1.   57 ea *om.* Q^2.   60 alter *add.* eorum Q^2.   62 vivente] manente Q^2. vivente prima *om.* W.   64-66 Solutum — continere *om.* Q^2.   65 quidam *om.* W.   66 retinere Q^1.

Sect. 37: 69 Berta] Deberga W.   tibi *om.* Q^1.   Teberga] Berta W.   70 consensis W.   Tebergam] Bertam W.   72 et *om.* Q^1.   73 eam] illam Q^2. 74-75 matrimonium Q^1Q^2 *om.* W.

---

[15] Cf. above Proleg. pp. 38-40.

Then Form 1 in Q¹Q²W continues as follows:

[366] Interdictum ecclesiae et tempus feriarum non dirimunt matrimonium, licet impediant; quia quandocumque contractum fuerit stabit nisi aliud impediat.[16]
30   Delicti enormitas impedit matrimonium, ut uxoricida, non tamen in matricida, licet majus sit peccatum; quia in quo deliquit quis in eo puniendus est.[17]

Item cognovisti consaguineam uxoris tuae in primo vel in secundo gradu; sine spe conjugii manebis.[18]

Item si adulter adulterae fidem dederit de contrahendo matrimonio post mortem
35 viri sui, vel si machinatus est in mortem viri sui et ideo eum interfecit ut adulteram duceret, et impeditur et dirimitur matrimonium. Aliae enormitates non dirimunt, licet impediant, matrimonium.[19]

Item si adulter adulteram publice tenuerit, post mortem viri ejus si duxerit eam, <dirimitur> matrimonium secundum quosdam; secundum alios tamen
40 impeditur.[20]

Item uxoricida et incestuosus qui cognovit consanguineam uxoris suae cum nulla potest contrahere, et alii forte si nupserit, stabit matrimonium.[21]

Adulter et adultera qui sibi invicem fidem dederunt, vel in mortem viri machinati sunt, sibi invicem non possunt conjungi sed aliis.[22]
45   Item secundum quosdam, si sollemniter poenitens contraxerit, non tenet matrimonium.[23]

Coactio non modica sed absoluta quae cadit in virum perfectum dirimit matrimonium contractum, ut minae mortis, verbera, captio corporalis. Si tamen postea benigne consensisti, vel quando potuisti non recessisti, praejudicabitur
50 tibi.[24]

---

29 impediant *add.* quia in adventu et in quadragesima et in interdicto ecclesiae non contrahuntur matrimonia, id est non debent contrahi Q¹ *Pluralis numerus in his verbis monstrat ea pertinere non ad Formam 1 sed ad Formam 2 vel ad Formam 3.*   quotiescumque Q¹Q².   impediat] impedit Q².
30 ut in uxoricida Q¹.   in *om.* Q².   31 delinquit Q².   32 in¹ *om.* Q².   in² *om.* Q¹Q².
secundo *add.* vel tertio Q¹ *Cf. supra in Proleg. ad p. 40 cum n. 5, pp. 42-43 cum n. 25.*   33 manebit W.
34 dedit Q².   35 eum *om.* Q².   36 ducet Q².   38-40 Item — impeditur *om.* Q¹Q².   39
dirimitur] dimittitur W.   41-46 Item — matrimonium *om.* Q².   41 consanguineam] sororem Q¹.   42 si nupserit] aliqui si tamen forte contraxerint Q¹.   43 invicem *om.* Q¹.   47
absoluta *add.* et violenta Q¹Q².   48 verbera *add.* et Q¹Q².

---

[16] Cf. above sect. 72.
[17] Cf. above sect. 59.
[18] Cf. above Proleg. pp. 42-43; sect. 59.
[19] Cf. above sects. 60-61.
[20] Cf. above sect. 60.
[21] Cf. above sects. 59 and 61.
[22] Cf. above sect. 61.
[23] Cf. above sects. 237-238.
[24] Cf. above sect. 62.

Then Form 1 in Q¹Q²W continues as in sections 38-39 with the following variations:

Sect. 38: 78 in infinitum *om.* Q¹Q². usque hodie Q¹Q². 80 sed a solo] a domino Q². 80-83 et tantum — potest *om.* Q². 82 autem *om.* Q¹. 82-83 papa — potest *om.* W (Q¹ *habet forte hic textum corr. ex Forma 2*).
Sect. 39: 85 Agnatio] cognatio Q¹. 87 in primo *om.* W. 89 quoto] quarto W. consanguinitatis *om.* Q². 90 tibi²] cui W.

Q² does not contain any text corresponding to sects. 40-41,[25] but Form 1 continues in Q¹W as the text of these sections with the following variations:

Sect. 40: 96 affini tuo] affinitivo W. 98 ut *om.* W. genus *add.* exclusive Q¹. 99 quintum] quartum Q¹. judicandum *add.* est W. 99-1 "usque" dico exclusive *om.* Q¹W. 1 quoto] quarto W. 3 illa W. 8 "usque" dico inclusive *om.* Q¹W. 9 dinoscitur Q¹W. tibi *om.* W. 10 tertii] gradu istius W.
Sect. 41: 12 genus *add.* et Q¹W. 14 illa erit Q¹W. 16 parte *add.* enim W. omnem *om.* W. 19 et *om.* W. 20 carnis *add.* copulam vel Q¹. 21-22 affinitatis *add.* hodie Q¹W.

Sect. 42 is not found in Form 1, but this form continues immediately in Q¹Q²W as in sects. 43-44 with the following variations:

Sect. 43: 30 salis] salutis W. 31 ecclesia Q¹W. vel melius in] et W *om.* Q¹Q². 34 consummatio] confirmatio Q¹Q². 35 et impediunt *om.* Q¹Q²W. matrimonium *add.* et impediunt Q¹.
Sect. 44: 38 accepisti W. 39 quilibet *add.* alius Q¹Q². 40-41 Dicunt — errant *om.* Q¹Q²W. 44 Si] sed W. 46-47 Sed — est *om.* Q²W (Q¹ *habet hic textum forte corr. ex Forma 2*). 48-50 Aliqui — ducere *om.* Q¹Q²W.

Then Form 1 in Q¹Q²W continues as in the first paragraph of sect. 51 with the following variations:

Sect. 51: 14 vel *add.* cum Q¹. 15 progressum Q². 16-23 Igitur — intelligunt *om.* Q¹Q²W.

Then it continues as in the first paragraph of sect. 58 with the following variations:

Sect. 58: 96-97 "usque" dico inclusive *om.* Q¹Q²W. 97-99 alii — est *om.* Q². 98 sed — ecclesia *om.* Q¹W. Quidam] quia W. 1-9 Poenitens — mei *om.* Q¹Q²W.

---

[25] These sections have been omitted in Q² most probably because they had been rendered obsolete by the Fourth Lateran Council in 1215; cf. above Proleg. pp. 8-9 with n. 44.

Then Form 1 continues as follows (see *apparatus criticus* for variations of MSS):

[367]   Sequitur raptus. Si rapuisti innubilem, vel aliquam aliam ad stuprum, reddenda est. Si nubilem rapuisti ad matrimonium et illa consensit, stabit matrimonium.[26]

    Religio etiam, ut videtur, dirimit matrimonium, quia ante carnalem copulam, 55 maxime infra duos menses, potest uterque reliquo invito intrare religionem, et imponunt Alexandro quod manens in saeculo potest statim cum alia contrahere, sed non auderem hoc consulere.[27]

Then Form 1 in Q^1Q^2W continues as in sects. 110-113 with the following variations:

    Sect. 110: 48 Consequenter — dicamus *om*. Q^2.   49 aliquod *om*. W.   vel[2] *add*. aliquid W.   adnexum spirituali] ei adnexum Q^1Q^2.   52 si *om*. Q^2.   56 si *om*. Q^1Q^2.   quia] quod Q^1Q^2.   istorum[2]] illorum Q^1 illarum W.   57 autem] enim Q^1Q^2W.

    Sect. 111: 59 in promovendo et non *insert*. Q^2.   61 nec] et non W.   61-62 est — ordinaris] quando aliquis te nesciente laborat pro te ut ordinetur et non ordinatur; secundum est quando aliquis etiam laborat pro te te nesciente ut tu ordineris W.   62 laboret Q^1.   et tu ordinaris] ut tu ordineris Q^1Q^2W.

    63 itaque] ita W.   Quandoque] quando W.   66 stricta *lacuna* Q^1.   69 sine *add*. speciali Q^1Q^2W.   quidam] alii Q^2.   70 enim *om*. Q^1Q^2W.   70-71 vel praebendae *om*. Q^2.   73 praebendam *om*. Q^2.

    Sect. 112: 76 ordine *add*. scilicet de —rigore Q^1 (*cf. infra var. ad lineam* 80).   te *om*. Q^2.   77-79 Et — titulum *om*. Q^1Q^2W.[28]   80-81 ab — deponi *om*. Q^2. 80 de rigore *om*. Q^1 (*vide supra var. ad lineam* 76).   81-84 Immo — dispensatione *om*. Q^1Q^2W.[29]

    Sect. 113: 86 averteris Q^2.   87-90 Dicunt — credo *om*. Q^1Q^2W.   93 semel *om*. W.   simoniace suscepit] sermocinare recepit W.   numquam] non Q^2. 94 papae *om*. W.

This is the end of the text of Form 1 in Q^2; what follows in this MS is derived from Form 2.[30] But in Q^1W the text of Form 1 continues as follows:

51 innubilem *add*. aliquam Q^2.   52 reddenda est] redde Q^2.   consensit] concessit W.   52-53 matrimnium *om*. Q^2.   54-57 Religio — consulere *om*. Q^2.

---

[26] Cf. above sect. 63.
[27] Cf. above sect. 56 with nn. 30 and 31.
[28] Cf. below Appendix C no. 2.
[29] Cf. *ibid*. no. 3.
[30] Cf. above Proleg. p. 28.

[368]   His intellectis, propone si quid gravat te in simonia vel in matrimonio.[31]
Dixisti enim: "De aliquot quas habui nescio an aliqua mea sit."[32]
60   POENITENS. Ita est; quia puellae cuidam juravi et fidem dedi quod eam in
uxorem ducerem si me permitteret rem habere cum ea.

Then Form 1 in Q¹W continues as in sects. 188-192 with variations
as follows:

Sect. 188: 52-56 SACERDOS — cum ea *aliter* Q¹W *vide proxime supra sect.* 368
cum apparatu critico.   62 Attentasti quod tamen] Attamen attentasti quod Q¹W.
    Sect. 189: 68 POENITENS — consensi *om.* W.   69 SACERDOS *om.* Q¹W.
    Sect. 190: 71 tempore W.   hac relicta] haec W.   et¹ *insert.* Q¹ *om.* W.
    Sect. 191: 82 SACERDOS *add.* Si W.   84 Cum ea contraxisti] eam duxisti
Q¹W.   91 intactam *om.* W.   95 infra] post W.
    Sect. 192: 99 illarum] aliarum W.   2 tibi *om.* W.   3 ita] ista W.   5
carnalis Q¹W.   6 et] sed W.   9 carnis Q¹.   12-13 bene — primam]
securius est judicare quod matrimonium fuit inter te et puellam quam non Q¹-
W.   13 enim *add.* si bene memini Q¹W.   14 vel simili *om.* Q¹W.   14-17
Quia — secundam] Sed quia iste iste contractus fuit clandestinus et secundus
sollemnis, ut mihi videtur, praejudicabit secundus contractus et fuit verum matrimonium, nec fuit impeditum per coactionem quia grata tibi fuit et consensisti
in secundam Q¹W.[33]

Then Form 1 in Q¹W continues as follows:

[369]   Sed cum tertia non fuit matrimonium quantum ad te, nec etiam post
mortem secundae. Alexander enim in illa decretali *Propositum* dicit in eodem
casu quia, si vivente legitima uxore tua contraxisti cum alia quae nescivit te esse
65 uxoratum, si post mortem prioris reclamas et vis recedere quia vivente tua legitima
contraxisti cum secunda, in arbitrio illius erit ut remaneat vel recedat a te.[34]
Ex quo sic infero: ista potest recedere a te et contrahere cum alio; ergo inter te
et eam non est matrimonium. Ad hoc enim ut inter vos sit matrimonium, oportet
ut novus consensus interveniat inter vos post mortem prioris et postquam ipsa

58 qua gravant Q¹.   in² *om.* Q¹.
63-64 eodem casu] eadem W.   64 quia] quod Q¹.   legitima *om.* Q¹.   65 recedere *add.*
a secunda Q¹.   69 consensus] sensus W.

[31] Cf. above sects. 114, 178, 187-188.
[32] See above sect. 365. Sect. 365 of Form 1 is not found in Q¹Q²; cf. above Proleg. p. 28
with n. 48.
[33] Cf. above in Book 2 sect. 62. Cf. also 1 *Compil.* 4.17.3 (JL 14311; X 4.16.2; *AppConcLat*
6.28 ed. MANSI 22.295-296); FIRTH, *Thesis* I 182*-186*, 477*.
[34] See 1 *Compil.* 4.7.1 (JL 12636; X 4.7.1); cf. above Book 3 sect. 193; also FIRTH, *Thesis* I
178*-179*.

70 scivit te ∞∞∞ unoratum quando primo contraxisti cum ea. Ideo nec matrimonium
fuit inter te et tertiam, ut mihi videtur, nec tu bigamus es.[35]

[370] Ex his patet quod inter te et quartam matrimonium fuit, sed quia post
contractum matrimonium non cognovisti eam, forte non es dicendus viduae
maritus vel corruptae. Ita mihi videtur, quia divisio carnis, non matrimonium,
75 facit irregularitatem.[36]

[371] Tandem quando ista quarta reclamante claustrum intrasti, injuriam ei
fecisti; et quia post duos menses post contractum matrimonium, licet ante carnis
copulam, claustrum intrasti, credo quod posset te revocare nisi ea sciente et non
contradicente sacros ordines suscepisti, quia sic videtur tibi licentiam dedisse.
80 Usque ad duos menses autem ante carnis copulam potest uterque reliquo invito
monachari. Postquam autem semel carnaliter convenerunt, neuter potest intrare
religionem reliquo manente in saeculo nisi ita provectae aetatis fuerit quod suspicio incontinentiae non habeatur de eo. Oportet etiam quod in praesentia
episcopi voveat continentiam usque ad mortem alterius ad minus.[37]

85 [372] Est aliud quod gravat te in matrimonio ?
    Poenitens. Non memini.[38]
    Sacerdos. Expediamus ergo nos de simonia. Cujus ordinis es ?
    Poenitens. Sacerdos sum.
    Sacerdos. In primis habuisti coronam ?
90 Poenitens. Habui, sed a simplici sacerdote; sic enim mos est in partibus meis,
scilicet in Alemannia.
    Sacerdos. Nisi esset consuetudo terrae, oporteret te coronam ab episcopo
recipere et bene consulo quod accipias.[39]

[373] In qua aetate factus es acolythus ?
95 Poenitens. Decennis eram.
    Sacerdos. Ordo acolythi debet dari in duodecimo anno vel ultra, in vicesimo
subdiaconatus, in vicesimo quinto diaconatus, in tricesimo sacerdotium. Episcopus tamen in talibus potest dispensare.[40]

76 quia] quod Q[1].   77 quia *om.* W.   78 quod *add.* non W.   79 contradicente] credente
W.   81 autem *om.* Q[1].   conveniunt W.   83 eo] eis Q[1].   84 episcopi *add.* remanens Q[1].
85 Est *praem.* Item Q[1].   90 sed] Sacerdos W.   93 accipere Q[1].   suscipias Q[1].
95 decennius Q[1].

[35] Cf. above Book 3 sect. 193 with n. 28.
[36] Cf. above sect. 194; also sects. 168-169.
[37] Cf. above sect. 195 with notes.
[38] Cf. above sects. 187 and 196.
[39] Cf. above sects. 178 and 78.
[40] Cf. above sect. 181.

99 [374] SACERDOS. Ab episcopo tuo vel de licentia ejus ordinatus es in subdiaconatum ?
    POENITENS. Suscepi ab alio quam ab episcopo meo, et eo nesciente qui me
ordinavit.
    SACERDOS. Ordinem furatus es, et ideo degradationem meruisti.
5   POENITENS. Dispensavit mecum papa.
    SACERDOS. Ipse solus potest.[41]

[375] Aliquos ordines simul sucepisti ?
    POENITENS. <Acolythatum> et subdiaconatum.
    <SACERDOS.> Et hic degradationem meruisti.
10 POENITENS. Papa mecum dispensavit etiam hic.
    SACERDOS. Ipse solus potest.[42]

[376] Praepostere aliquos suscepisti ?
    POENITENS. Prius factus sum sacerdos quam diaconus.
    SACERDOS. Et hic pessime fecisti. Cesses ergo a sacerdotio quousque ordinem
15 praetermissum suceperis, et tunc demum ministres, et hoc totum fiet ex dispensatione tui episcopi ad minus.
    POENITENS. Ita factum est.[43]

[377] SACERDOS. In temporibus statutis ordinatus es ?
    POENITENS. Quae sunt statuta tempora ?
20 SACERDOS. Sex in anno, scilicet sabbata quatuor temporum, sabbatum *Isti
sunt dies*, sabbatum sanctum paschae. Si extra ista tempora ordinatus es, nisi
consuetudo regionis id moris habeat, deponeris. Tutius quaeres dispensationem
domini papae quam alterius.
    In qualibet etiam die dominica istorum sabbatorum potest ordinari subdiaconus
25 continuato jejunio tam ab ordinante quam ordinando. Quidam dicunt quod
personale est illud et alicui a papa concessum; nec extenditur ultra subdiaconatum;
et privatim debet fieri, sicut acolythatus potest privatim conferri extra sex dicta
tempora in aliqua magna sollemnitate.[44]

[378] De matrimonio natus es ?
30 POENITENS. Non.

99 SACERDOS *om.* Q¹.   99-1 in subdiaconatum *om.* Q¹.   2 POENITENS *add.* Subdiaconatum Q¹
6 Ipse] Ille Q¹.   8 Acolythum Q¹W.   subdiaconum W.   9 SACERDOS *om.* Q¹W.   11
Ipse solus potest *om.* Q¹.   14 pessime fecisti] peccasti Q¹.   quousque] usque dum Q¹.   15
fiat Q¹.   20-21 Isti sunt dies] pentecostes W.   21 sanctae Q¹.   22 regionis *corr ab* religionis
W.   23 domini *om.* Q¹.   24 quolibet die dominico Q¹.   25 ordinante] ordinatione W.
26 concedendum Q¹.   29 Item de Q¹.

[41] Cf. above sect. 182; also sect. 180 and Appendix A sect. 363 with n. 21.
[42] Cf. above sect. 184.
[43] Cf. above sect. 183.
[44] Cf. above sect. 185; JL 13948 (1 *Compil.* 1.6.2; X 1.11.2); FIRTH, *Thesis* I 179*.

Sacerdos. Scivit hoc ordinator tuus ?

Poenitens. Non.

Sacerdos. Si districte ageretur tecum, deberes judicari furtive ordinatus et
ita degradandus si dum scholaris eras ordinem sacrum suscepisti. Religio enim,
35 statim cum intras eam, istam purgat irregularitatem; sed numquam potest quis
in religione uti ordine ante religionem suscepto, maxime si sis genitus in sacerdotio.

Poenitens. Non satis intelligo plane an sim natus de matrimonio, quia diu
postquam natus sum contraxerunt parentes mei.

Sacerdos. Si legitimi fuerunt ad contrahendum, per sequens matrimonium
40 legitimatus es et regularis factus, maxime si ante tuos ordines contraxerunt. Sed
quid si post ?[45]

[379]   Item cujus conditionis fuisti ?

Poenitens. Servilis.

Sacerdos. Si sine licentia domini tui et ordinatore tuo ignorante te esse talem
45 ordinatus es, furatus es te domino tuo, et ideo debes ei satisfacere et de jure stricto
degradari, quia ordinem furatus es.[46]

Item redditus ecclesiasticos habuisti ?

Poenitens. Habui diversos; quia patronus...

Then Form 1 in Q¹W continues as in Book 3 sects. 114-117 with the
following variations:

Sect. 114: 95-2 *aliter* Q¹W *vide supra in sect.* 368 *et proxime supra in sect.* 379.
Sect. 115: 9 fuit] erat W.   14 porrexerit W.   14-16 Idem — Sed *om.*
Q¹W.   17 liberalitate] libertate W.   18-19 voluptas W.   19 vel — spiri-
tuale] etc. W.   22 Poenitens] Peccator W.   23 te *om.* W.   23-24 remur-
murat] remordeat te W.
Sect. 116: 26 fuit W.   29 quia *add.* et Q¹W.   31 et *om.* W.   33 uter]
utrum Q¹W.   34 uni] jus Q¹W.   36 admittant W.
Sect. 117: 39 etiam] et W.   autem *om.* W.   42-43 Alexander *add.* tertius
W.   43-49 Ita — conferendo *om.* Q¹W.[47]

Then Form 1 in Q¹W continues as follows:

[380]   Postremo diversas ecclesias singulas sufficientes tibi sine licentia domini
50 papae habuisti; male fecisti.[48]

Sacerdos. Decimas umquam non tuas habuisti ?

Poenitens. Quasdam emi a laico, quasdam in vadimonium recepi.

31-32 Sacerdos — Non *om.* (*probabiliter homoeotel.*) Q¹.   35 cum *om.* Q¹.   numquid Q¹.
36 sis genitus] genitus fuit Q¹.   37 natus] generatus Q¹.   diu *om.* Q¹.   49 singulas *om.*
Q¹.   sine *add.* speciali Q¹.

[45] Cf. above sect. 179.
[46] Cf. above sect. 180 with n. 2; also sect. 374.
[47] Cf. below Appendix C no. 12.
[48] Cf. above sect. 128; **Proleg.** pp. 35 and 47.

SACERDOS. Si tuae erant de jure et ad tuam attinebant ecclesiam, vel ad licentiam ecclesiae cujus erant de jure et consensu episcopi hoc fecisti, licitum est. Sin
55 autem, primum simonia est, secundum usura, et quidquid praeter sortem habuisti
debes restituere.[49]

[381] Monachus gratis factus es ?
  POENITENS. Immo simoniace, et etiam prior, et ut idem aliis fieret saepius
cooperator fui.
60   SACERDOS. Renuntia prioratui et numquam sine speciali dispensatione domini
papae praelatus sis, et postea religionem quam intrasti simoniace exi, et artiorem
intra; vel si gravior importabilis est tibi, quasi novitius intra eandem religionem
de speciali licentia domini papae.[50]
  De redditibus ecclesiasticis scis tu aliquid quod gravat te ?
65   POENITENS. Non memini.

  Then Form 1 in Q^1W continues as in Book 4 sect. 219 with the following variations:

  Sect. 219: 88 vadia] vadimonia W.   reliquerat W.   91 tuo *om.* W.
vadiis] vadimoniis W.   91-93 Quid — simonia] De decimis quas praeter consensum episcopi (*add.* tui Q^1) tenuisti, redde quidquid percepisti ecclesiae cujus
erant de jure Q^1W.[51]   94 pater *add.* meus Q^1.   95 eas *om.* W.   97 eas]
ea W.   98 perceptae W.   sunt Q^1W.   si[1] Q^1W.   dentur W *om.* Q^1.   1
quousque] usque dum Q^1W.   sint] fuerint W.   3 Haec W.   nihil Q^1W.
      habuit *add.* pater W.   4 Si *add.* vero Q^1.   bene *om.* W.   quaedam[2]
om. W.   5 tu *om.* Q^1W.   aliunde vivere] aliud unde viveres W.   5-7 secundum proportionem — accipisses] quanto parcius potuisses, vel ad minus secundum
proportionem (portionem Q^1) bene habitorum vel de bene (*om.* W) habitis portionem
(proportionem W) tibi (sibi Q^1) assignasset Q^1W.   7-9 et hoc — relinquit *om*
Q^1W.

  Then follow in Q^1 (fol. 330[v]) the following two paragraphs; these
paragraphs are not found in W:

[382] Ecce jam ea quae in confessionibus magis sunt periculosa et difficilia et
disputabilia tetigimus, simoniam scilicet et matrimonium.[52] Nemo enim (cum
infiniti sunt) omnes qui circa contingunt casus proponere posset; si tamen ea quae
proposita sunt diligenter advertantur, frequenter nos expedient.

53 SACERDOS *om.* W.   ecclesiam] parrochiam Q^1.   55 praeter] ultra Q^1.   63 domini
om. Q^1.   64 gravet Q^1.   68 sunt *lege* sint ?

[49] Cf. above sect. 127.
[50] Cf. above sect. 126.
[51] Cf. above sects. 127, 380.
[52] Cf. above sects. 10, 197, 365.

70   Nunc de aliis criminibus expedias te. Sed ut melius et commissa tua intelligas
et omissa sive delicta, congruum duxi virtutes et vitia cum suis speciebus tibi breviter proponere, ut in virtutibus tuum dinoscas defectum et in vitiis errorem.
Et proponimus illarum humilitatem, istorum superbiam originem et radicem.
Superbia igitur est singularis excellentis animi super omnes coetus quidam appe-
75 titus; cujus comitatus sunt principales isti: vana gloria, invidia, ira, tristitia, avaritia, ventris ingluvies et luxuria.[53]

Then Form 1 in Q^1W continues as follows:

[383] Inter vitia supra enumerata frequentiora sunt et asperiora avaritia et
luxuria; de aliis vix aut raro confitetur quis, nisi discretus et litteratus, nisi ad
inquisitionem sacerdotis discreti et diligentis. Caveat autem sacerdos in inqui-
80 rendo ne aliquid ignotum confitenti inquirat, ne ex mentione illius peccati occasionem peccandi poenitens accipiat, quod frequenter fit.[54] Alia autem peccata
a luxuria et avaritia, licet sint mortalissima, vel raro puniuntur vel venialiter.
Vis ergo ut illa inquiram quae experimento didici usitatiora in confessionibus,
sive in avaritia, sive luxuria, sive in aliis ?
85 POENITENS. Immo rogo, domine.
SACERDOS. Vis ergo incipiamus a luxuria ?
POENITENS. Ut libet; tamen vellem secundum ordinem vitae meae procedere
et omnia, sicut dixistis, confiteri.
SACERDOS. Ut melius tibi putas expedire; propone tamen, si mihi credis, ut
90 me melius instruas (quoniam oportet tandem, postquam omnia dixeris, omnia
prae oculis habere, ut sciam aequa lance contra peccata poenitentiam librare),
omnia quae sunt ejusdem articuli simul dicas.[55]
POENITENS. Ita fiat.

[384] SACERDOS. Ad quot mulieres accessisti ?
95 POENITENS. Nescio.
SACERDOS. Ergo vices nescis ?
POENITENS. Ita est.
SACERDOS. Umquam ad conjugatam accessisti ?
99 POENITENS. Ad septem.

---

73 illarum *add.* virtutem et Q^1 *Haec vocabula forte originem ducere potuissent ex vocabulo* virtutum *antea
forte inserto ad explicandum* illarum.   74 coetus *lege* ceteros ?   77 vitia supra enumerata] haec
vitia Q^1.   asperiora] apertiora Q^1.   78 aut] et W.   quis] aliquis Q^1.   nisi[2] *add.* forte
Q^1.   79 discreti et *om.* Q^1.   80 illius] alicujus Q^1.   82 vel fere venialiter Q^1.   83 usitato-
ria W.   84 sive[2] *add.* in Q^1.   86 ergo *add.* ut Q^1.   87 libet] licet W.   91 aequa lancea]
aequalem Q^1.

---

[53] Cf. above sects. 9, 197-198. This definition of pride, which is not found in Forms 2 and 3,
seems to be derived from *De fructibus carnis et spiritus* c.3 (PL 176.999).
[54] Cf. above sect. 224 with n. 50.
[55] Cf. above sect. 9; also sect. 229 n. 61, sect. 230 with n. 63.

Sacerdos. Quotiens ad quamlibet?

Poenitens. Nescio.

Sacerdos. Accipiamus ergo quod possumus. Quamdiu in adulterio mansisti cum una, tum cum alia?

5 Poenitens. Per septennium.

Sacerdos. In quo ordine?

Poenitens. Tres in sacerdotio et monachus per triennium, duas diaconus et monachus per biennium, duas per triennium subdiaconus et monachus.[56]

[385] Sacerdos. Ad menstruatam accessisti, vel praegnantem vel nondum puri-
10 ficatam?

Poenitens. Saepe.

Sacerdos. Si ad tuam talem requisitus accessisti, ei est imputandum; si non requisitus, tibi est imputandum; quia in menstruo et ante purificationem leprosi et caduci et alii male se habentes nasci solent.

15 Quando cum gravida coitur, multi opprimuntur vel claudi nascuntur. Um-quam ex concubitu tuo aliquis oppressus est?

Poenitens. Non memini.

Sacerdos. Si fuisset, irregularis esses ad promovendum.[57]

[386] Aliquam consanguineam tuam cognovisti?
20 Poenitens. Ita est.

Sacerdos. Dic quot et quotiens quamlibet et quam propinquae tibi erant et ordinem tuum.

Poenitens. Neptem meam per dimidium annum tenui subdiaconus, diaconus consobrinam meam per annum.

25 Sacerdos. Duas sibi consanguineas cognovisti?

Poenitens. Cognovi.

Sacerdos. Dic quot paria et quotiens quamlibet et quam propinquae sibi erant et ordinem tuum.

Poenitens. Duas sorores per annum subdiaconus, duas consobrinas per annum
30 diaconus.

Sacerdos. Aliquam habuisti quam ante habuerat consanguineus tuus?

Poenitens. Habui.

Sacerdos. Dic quot et quotiens quamlibet et ordinem tuum et quam propin-quus erat tibi ille.

35 Poenitens. Post fratrem meum per duos menses duas in subdiaconatu.[58]

Sacerdos. Ad religiosam accessisti?

Poenitens. Ad monialem unam et conversam unam semel diaconus.

---

8 per² — monachus] subdiaconus et monachus per biennium Q¹.   9-10 nondum purificatam] purificandam Q¹.   11 Persaepe Q¹.   14 nasci] generari Q¹.   25 sibi] enim W.   27 Dic] Sed W.   27-28 et quam — erant *om.* W.   31 habuerat *add.* aliquis Q¹.   34 ille *om.* Q¹.

[56] Cf. above sect. 223.
[57] Cf. above sects. 225-226, also sect. 104.
[58] Cf. above sects. 223, 225.

Sacerdos. Virginem deflorasti?

Poenitens. Tius subdiaconus.

40 Sacerdos. Ad commatrem tuam accessisti vel ad fillolam tuam vel patris tui vel filiam patrini tui?

Poenitens. Non.[59]

[387] Sacerdos. Aliquam consanguineam uxoris tuae cognovisti?

Poenitens. Sororem ejus.

45 Sacerdos. Si post contractum matrimonium cognovisti aliquam consanguineam uxoris tuae in primo vel secundo gradu et occultum fuit crimen, et uxor tua conscia fuit facti, nec exigere debuisti, nec reddere, quia ipsa non debuit exigere. Si ipsa non fuit conscia facti et occultum fuit factum, reddere debuisti, sed non exigere, quia jus tuum perdidisti. Si manifestum fuit crimen, separari debuistis

50 tu et uxor tua, ut dicit Alexander, et ita uxor tua sine culpa sui puniri debuit; quod frequenter fit. Secundum alios in voluntate uxoris tuae esset retinere te.[60]

Consanguineas sibi quas dicis te cognovisse cognovisti carnaliter? Et illas quas habuisti post consanguineos tuos cognovisti carnaliter? Et illi consanguinei tui fuerunt illius aetatis quod potuerunt rem habere cum muliere?[61] Alioquin

55 non fuit contracta affinitas, quia affinitas non contrahitur nisi per carnalem copulam.[62]

[388] Sacerdos. Cum masculo peccasti?

Poenitens. Cum multis.

Sacerdos. Umquam aliquem innocentem introduxisti ad hoc?

60 Poenitens. Tres scholares et subdiaconum.

Sacerdos. Dic quot tu es abusus et quotiens et ordinem tuum et ordines illorum si clerici, si laici, an uxorati fuerint.

Poenitens. Tribus subdiaconis et ego subdiaconus per dimidium annum, uno uxorato semel. Tunc temporis iste et ego ad invicem polluti sumus, isti tantum.[63]

65 Sacerdos. Nocturnam pollutionem passus es?

Poenitens. Frequenter.

Sacerdos. Si ex crapula consuetudinaria vel ex concupiscentia, mortale est; sin autem, veniale.[64]

---

40 accessisti *om.* Q^1.   41 filiam *om.* Q^1.   48 factum *om.* Q^1.   sed] et Q^1.   50 sui] sua Q^1.
57 Item Sacerdos Q^1.   60 scholaris Q^1.   subdiac. Q^{1}W.   62 clerici *add.* fuerunt Q^1.
fuerint *om.* Q^1.   64 iste] isti Q^1.

---

[59] Cf. above sect. 225.

[60] Cf. above sects. 65-66 with n. 53; Firth, *Thesis* II 479*-481*. Cf. also Bernard of Pavia, *Summa decretalium* 4.13.1 (p. 163).

[61] Cf. above sects. 188, 192; texts cited in the following note.

[62] Cf. Hug. ad C.35 qq.2-3 pr. (fol. 346vb); Idem ad C.35 qq.2-3 c.11 (fol. 348^{ra-b}); Rufinus ad C.35 qq.2-3 c.11 (pp. 518-519).

[63] Cf. above sect. 223.

[64] Cf. Ivo 2.51-52 (PL 161.170-172). This is the answer to question 9 in the letter believed to have been sent by St Gregory the Great to St Augustine of England, the letter mentioned above sect. 285 n. 41; see Bede, *Historia ecclesiastica* ed. Plummer I 59-62; cf. Gratian D.6 cc.1-2; Bart. c.101 (p. 269).

Umquam in loco sacro peccasti ?
70 POENITENS. Non.
SACERDOS. Umquam in die sacro ?[65]
POENITENS. In vigilia paschae et pentecostes accessi ad mulierem.
SACERDOS. In sequenti die paschae communicasti ?
POENITENS. Ita est.
75 SACERDOS. Consilio meo exspectasses usque ad pentecosten.[66]
Ad meretrices accessisti ?
POENITENS. Frequenter.
SACERDOS. Fortasse conjugatae sunt vel consanguinae, vel aliquis consanguineus
tuus aliquam habuit illarum.[67]
80 Post istas enormitates umquam accessisti ad altare ad celebrandum inconfessus ?
POENITENS. Numquam.[68]

[389] SACERDOS. Umquam procuratus es aliquam nisi tibi ?
POENITENS. Multis.
SACERDOS. Dic quot et quibus, an sacerdoti vel conjugato, et quas personas,
85 utrum virgines an conjugatas an moniales, et utrum convenerint per te.
Et tu ipse umquam per interpositam personam sollicitasti aliquas ?
POENITENS. Multas.
SACERDOS. Dic quot et quas personae, utrum conjugatas an virgines vel moniales,
et personae interpositae, utrum fuerint clerici an laici et cujus ordinis, et utrum
90 consecutus fueris effectum an non.[69]

[390] Item multas male aspexisti et sollicitasti. Dic quot et quas et qualiter.
Multas amplexatus es et deosculatus et tractasti.[70]
Unum scias quod contra te est: quod scripsit Caelestinus dicens: Si quis in sacro
ordine perdidit bonum conscientiae per crimen homicidii vel adulterii vel perju-
95 rium falsi testimonii, si notorium est crimen, non utatur suscepto ordine nec ulterius
promoveatur; si occultum fuit crimen, admonendus est in periculo animae suae
ne utatur suscepto ordine.[71] Sed talis es tu; tu ergo videris. Ego ad nihil arto te.[72]

71 in *om.* Q¹.   72 pentecoste W.   78 Fortasse *om.* Q¹.   79 earum Q¹.   82 nisi]
non Q¹.   84 an *om.* Q¹.   vel] an Q¹.   86 numquam Q¹.   sociasti Q¹.   89 an] vel
Q¹.   92 et¹ *om.* Q¹.   93 te *om.* W.   quod scripsit *om.* W.   94-95 vel per perjurium Q¹.
95 non] nec Q¹.   96 fuit crimen] est Q¹.   97 tu² *om.* W.   Ego] Ergo W.

⁶⁵ Cf. above sect. 227.
⁶⁶ Cf. above sect. 71.
⁶⁷ Cf. above sect. 228.
⁶⁸ Cf. above sect. 71; also FIRTH, *Thesis* II 425*-439*.
⁶⁹ Cf. above sect. 228.
⁷⁰ Cf. above sect. 229.
⁷¹ See JL 16617 (2 *Compil.* 1.8.3); cf. above sect. 161 with n. 56; FIRTH, *Thesis* I 169*-170*.
⁷² Cf. above sects. 100-101, 108, 138 with n. 66, 161. If we suppose Robert to be the author
of Form 1, we may conjecture that when he wrote it he had perhaps not yet obtained from the
bishop of Paris the authority mentioned in sect. 108, and that he was then accustomed to leave
those guilty of mediocre crimes to apply to their bishops for dispensations if their own consciences
so directed them.

Umquam aliquem damnificasti furto vel rapina, fraude in ludo vel extra, usura
99 emendo vel vendendo ad exspectationem, Incendio, segetes vel vineas succidendo ?
Judex fuisti corruptus, testis, advocatus, assessor vel consiliarius ?[73]

Then Form 1 in Q^1W continues as in sects. 216-217 with the following variations:

Sect. 216: 59 *aliter* Q^1W *vide proxime supra ad finem sect. 390.*   60 valentis Q^1.
      62 Nonne] Solutione Q^1.   63 repetisti] recepisti W *corr. ab* recepisti Q^1.
64 aliam quae] aliud quod Q^1W.   66 infra] juxta W.   67 fuerit W.
      Sect. 217: 70 paiment Q^1 paiement W.   74 statim accessisset, statim Q^1.
75 debitor] creditor W.   78 pro te *om.* W.   creditoribus] debitoribus Q^1W.
78-81 Ecce — usura *om.* Q^1W.

Then Form 1 in Q^1W continues as follows:

[391]   Aliud scis de usura ?
    POENITENS. Non memini.
    SACERDOS. Caveas tibi, quia infiniti sunt casus et subtiles.[74]
5   Incendiarius fuisti ?
    POENITENS. Fui.
    SACERDOS. Si coemeterium vel ecclesiam incendisti, ipso facto fuisti excommuni-
catus et episcopus loci potest te absolvere nisi consuetudo loci habeat ut tales excommunicati a solo papa absolvantur. Si domorum communium incendiarius
10 fuisti, non es ipso facto excommunicatus, sed si te excommunicaverit quis sacerdos,
solus papa potest te absolvere etsi domus vilis incensa fuerit.[75]
    Ubicumque aut quocumque modo aliquem damnificasti, satisfacias ei per te,
vel per interpositam personam si damnum times vel scandalum; si damnificatum
non invenis, heredibus ejus. Si nec istum nec illum invenis, pauperibus des. Si
15 ecclesiam vel ecclesiasticam personam damnificasti, ecclesiae ejus satisfacias, quia
ecclesia est heres personae.[76] Si dominus tuus mercedem tuam retinuit et tu eum
aequipollenter furte damnificasti, dummodo nihil ab eo plus recipias et ipse se
non sciat teneri tibi, sustinebo.[77]

[392]   Perjurium fecisti vel fidem violasti ?
20   POENITENS. Saepius.[78]

98 Item umquam Q^1.   10 quis] quivis Q^1.   11 etsi] etiamsi Q^1.   12 aut] autem Q^1.
14 non *om.* Q^1.   istum ... illum] illum... istos Q^1.   invenis[2]] inveneris Q^1.   15 satisfacias
corr. ab satisfacies Q^1.   16 ecclesia — personae] ecclesiastica erat persona W.   18 sustinebo
om. W.   19 Item perjurium Q^1.

[73] Cf. above sects. 206-207.
[74] Cf. above sect. 220.
[75] Cf. above sect. 206; sect. 149 with nn. 16, 17.
[76] Cf. above sect. 211.
[77] Cf. above sect. 204.
[78] Cf. above sect. 203.

SACERDOS. Mulieri jurasti vel fidem dedisti quod eam duceres in uxorem?
Si serio hoc fecisti et postea eam cognovisti, uxor tua est.[79]

Si in sacro ordine cum diversis contraxisti, licet de facto tantum, bigamus es,
nec potes in suscepto ordine ministrare aut ulterius promoveri.[80]

25   Incantationes fecisti, vel sortilegos consuluisti, vel ipse sortilegus fuisti, vel de
re sacra vel per invocationem daemonum, vel eis sacrificasti?[81]

[393] Excommunicatus fuisti? Manum misisti in clericum vel in personam ecclesiasticam vel religiosam, ut est conversus vel apud leprosos vel domum Dei vel
alibi? Consilium vel auxilium dedisti ad aliquid tale? Si fecisti, solus papa absol-
30 vet te nisi in exceptis casibus.[82] Consentiens enim et faciens eadem poena ligantur;
quod dicitur de illo consentiente vel communicante qui consilium vel auxilium dat.[83]

In tribus casibus mittitur excommunicatus ad papam: pro incendio (de quo
jam dixi), si clericum verberaverit, si convictus fuerit falsarius.[84]

Umquam causa fuisti homicidii vel mutilationis? Umquam stetisti in causa
35 sanguinis judex vel advocatus vel assessor? Umquam litteras legisti vel scripsisti
ad hoc faciendum, vel principis litteras ad villam comburendam? Si quid tale
fecisti, timendum est tibi de ordine, nec consilio meo promoveberis sine dispensatione
papae.[85]

Umquam officium scribatus gessisti? Secundum quosdam, si semel suscepisti,
40 licet non gessisti, irregularis es, id est si saeva praecepta regis exercuisti et forisfacta
sanguinis et similia crimina ei detulisti.[86]

Umquam notarius foeneratoris fuisti?[87]

Cave tibi quia de causa sanguinis infiniti sunt casus et subtiles.[88]

[394] Aliquem odis? Omnibus dimitte odium et rancorem.[89] Jus tuum prose-
45 quaris, si aliquod habes erga aliquem? Si aliquis de te conqueritur, vis laborare
ad gratiam ejus habendam?

POENITENS. Volo et haec et alia quae dixisti facere.

SACERDOS. Multa fecisti quae non advertis, licet forte in januis sint. Multa

---

21 fidem add. ei Q¹.   23 tantum om. W. transp. huc ex loco originali post bigamus es Q¹.
24 aut] nec Q¹.   25 Incantatores W.   26 vel¹ om. W.   29 vel] et Q¹.   29-30 absolvat Q¹.
30 poena] sententia Q¹.   35 scripsisti] fecisti Q¹.   36 principi Q¹.   quid] aliquod Q¹.
37 tibi om. Q¹.   40 forisfacta] forsitan W.

---

[79] Cf. above sect. 56 with n. 32; sects. 171, 192.

[80] Cf. above sects. 168-170 with nn. 79-84.

[81] Cf. above sect. 159.

[82] Cf. above sects. 148, 157.

[83] Cf. above ibid.; sect. 310 with n. 99; sect. 103.

[84] Cf. above sects. 148-149, 391.

[85] Cf. above sects. 103-109; FIRTH, Thesis II 483*-486*.

[86] Cf. above sects. 105, 172.

[87] Cf. above sects. 110, 207.

[88] Cf. above sects. 103-109.

[89] Cf. above sect. 200.

per fragilitatem tuam et negligentiam a memoria tibi exciderunt. Omissiones
50 multas fecisti. Quae fecisti bona minus pure fecisti. De quibus omnibus veniam
petis?

POENITENS. Peto, domine.[90]

SACERDOS. Quantum est quod cessasti ab omni mortali?

POENITENS. Septem anni sunt elapsi.

55 SACERDOS. Quot annorum es tu?

POENITENS. Quinquaginta.

SACERDOS. In qua aetate peccare incepisti?

POENITENS. In anno quinto decimo.

SACERDOS. Ab illo tempore usque ad istud septennium continue fuisti in peccatis
60 supra dictis?

POENITENS. Quandoque interpolavi unum annum, quandoque dimidium,
quandoque minus.

SACERDOS. Ad minus per viginti annos?

POENITENS. Ita est.

65 SACERDOS. In isto septennio quid boni fecisti? Quia secundum quod plus
vel minus fecisti, plus vel minus puniam te.[91]

[395] Ita, optime decane, consuevi inquirere in confessionibus. Postea considero
circumstantias confitentis, aetatem, conversationem, divitias et vires corporis et
similia; et ita tempero poenitentiam quod semper potius petet alleviationem quam
70 gravamen. In fine tamen quantum artius possum prohibeo ne naturam suam
laedat, et promptissimum me offero ad quantamlibet alleviationem.[92]

This is the end of Form 1 in Q¹, but in W it continues as follows:

<Huic> quem introduxi confitentem injungerem tota vita sua afflictionem
in pane et aqua in sextis feriis, et a carnibus feriis secundis, et a carnibus et <sagi-
mine> feriis quartis et sabbato, et in anno quatuor quadragesimas cibo quadrage-
75 simali: unam ante natale quae incipit in festo quatuor coronatorum; alia incipit
quarta feria post octavas paschae; tertia incipit post octavas assumptionis.[93]

Si redditus haberet decem marcharum, redemptionem diei injungerem ei sex
peris*, nisi esset debitis vel familia impeditus. Ista enim tria considero in redemptione. Si vacare posset, <injungerem> qualibet septimana psalterium; si redditus
80 haberet, decimam partem reddituum suarum in eleemosynis.[94]

53 SACERDOS] Sed W.   est insert. W.   61 unum annum] annum integrum Q¹.   67 optime
decane] lector optime Q¹.   69 semper] sperem Q¹.   72 Hunc W.   73-74 sanguine fer.
iv. W.   78 peris W Emendationem congruam non inveni.   79 injungeret W.

[90] Cf. above sects. 229-230.
[91] Cf. above sect. 230.
[92] Cf. loc. cit.; also sect. 235.
[93] Cf. above sect. 232.
[94] Cf. above sects. 230-231, 353-354.

Ad minus ista offerrem ei; si suscipere nollet, extraherem quantum possem. Cilicium etiam ei offerrem ad minus uno die in septimana.[95]

[396]   Quando aliquis <recidivum> peccati patitur: si recenter post confessionem, facio eum reincipere poenitentiam, ut post dimidium annum si grave est peccatum,
85 ut adulterium vel majus. Et dico: "Ab hodie incipias poenitentiam tuam quam tibi injunxi." Si simplex fuerit fornicatio et mensis vel minus transiit a confessione, similiter faciam reincipere poenitentiam. Quandoque aliter, quia aut extendendo poenitentiam, ut pro simplici fornicatione in simplici persona decem dies, pro tribus adulteriis vel circa hoc dimidium annum, vel exaspero quantum possum.
90 Si non frequenter patitur <recidivum>, mollius tracto eum et sine omni poenitentia remitto, ne dum semper aggravatur peccatum ipse succumbat vel desperet.[96]
      Quandoque quaerit aliquis: "Domine, si cavero mihi a peccato de cetero et istam prosecutus fuero poenitentiam, <umquam> plus oportebit me confiteri?" Et dico: "Frater, in fine vitae tuae omnia debes evomere; vel si frontem habes
95 tenerum et de facili rubes, secundum conscientiam tuam confitearis aliquotiens, vel si virum inveneris de quo bene speras ut ejus utaris consilio. Sed quamdiu portabilis est, numquam minuas poenitentiam quam dedi tibi."[97]

[397]   Ita generaliter procedo in confessionibus. Speciales poenitentias nemo
99 determinare posset, cum arbitrariae sint et infiniti sunt casus quibus respondent. Ignoscite ergo; aliquas tamen vobis transcribam.[98]

Explicit poenitentiale magistri Roberti sancti Victoris

83 reciduum W.   90 reciduum W.   93 numquam W.

[95] Cf. above sects. 230-231, 235-236, 241.
[96] Cf. above sect. 231.
[97] Cf. above sect. 232.
[98] Cf. above sect. 234; Proleg. pp. 34-35.

APPENDIX C

The principal differences between From 2 and 3[1]
(formerly called Forms O and A)
Peculiarities in the text of AbOTa *and* $Q^{1*}Q^{2*}Q^{2**}$

Ten portions of text which are found in all the MSS of Form 3 (insofar as these are complete enough to contain the context where they should be found) are lacking in two or more of the above mentioned manuscript texts. One of these omissions, the lack in AbTa of the words *Item oportet — dicitur unius uxoris virum etc.* of sect. 168 (lines 43-48), does not fit into the regular pattern of the others; these words probably belonged originally to the text of the penitential and were afterwards omitted in some MSS.[2] Hence this variation is not included in this appendix as a peculiarity of Form 2. The other nine portions of text are enumerated below as items 1-9. Two of these portions are out of their regular place in the text of Tu.[3] Two of them are missing in X, which contains a special form of the work, called Form 4.[4]

Nine other portions are missing from their regular place in one or more of the aforementioned MSS and in others as well. These portions are listed below under numbers 10-18. The other MSS in which one or more of the portions are missing or out of place are AaAcCkCpHJRSgTbTuUV. Two of these, namely AcTb, do not agree with the others very often. Tb has closer affinities with the generality of MSS of Form 3. This is the case also with Ac; however it has some other special relations with Form 2. The rest of these MSS, namely AaCkCpHJRSgTuUV, are designated as "the intermediate MSS." In some ways they are intermediate between Form 2 and Form 3.[5]

---

[1] See above Proleg. p. 33 and pp. 45-51.

[2] See *ibid.* p. 48 with n. 46.

[3] A portion which is out of place in one or more MSS and missing in others has quite probably found its way into the text of each MS where it is out of place by way of a marginal insertion into an earlier MS. Such a marginal insertion can easily come to be copied into a different place. Tu is quite incomplete; it contains the context for only six of these nine passages, namely nos. 1-6; these are found in Tu, but two of them, namely nos. 1 and 6, are out of place. For these reasons Tu seems to have a closer affinity to Form 2 than any other of the intermediate MSS. Cf. above Proleg. p. 50.

[4] See above Proleg. p. 51.

[5] See above Proleg. pp. 49 and 52. Regarding these special affinities of Ac see below nos. 16 and 21 with n. 19.

One short sentence is found in the MSS of Form 2 and in a number of other MSS as well, but in lacking in the majority of the MSS of Form 3. This is portion 19 below.

Finally there are certain peculiarities of the text of O in Book 5; one of these (21) has left traces in some other MSS as well. These peculiarities are listed below as portions 20-27. At least some of these probably belonged to Form 2 in its original state.[6]

This form of the work, found in AbOTa and $Q^{1*}Q^{2*}Q^{2**}$, is called Form 2. It seems to represent a redaction of the penitential composed by Robert of Flamborough later than Form 1, but before Form 3, within the period 1208-13.[7] The intermediate MSS have composite texts which are probably derived from some early stage or stages in the development of Form 3 from Form 2.[8]

I *Nine portions lacking in the text of*
two or more of $AbOTaQ^{1*}Q^{2*}Q^{2**}$

1. In sect. 83 the second paragraph: *Ecce — Credo.* — marginal insertion in AbO, found in the text in a different place in Tu.[9]

2. In sect. 112 a sentence: *Et ita simoniacus — titulum.* (lines 77-79) — lacking in AbTa (also Q^1Q^2WX),[10] marginal insertion in O.

---

[6] Because O seems to be the most faithful witness to the original text of Form 2 (see above Proleg. p. 48 with n. 48), its peculiarities probably belonged to that text. However there is special difficulty in accepting this in regard to portion no. 23; see below no. 23 with n. 23. On the other hand, the presence in some other MSS of titles pertaining to some of these peculiarities would suggest that the same peculiarities quite probably belong to some early stage in the history of the text; see below nos. 21 and 25.

[7] Form 2 contains the same indications of date mentioned above Proleg. pp. 8-9. However there is evidence in the texts of all MSS of Form 2, even in O, of correction from Form 3 (e.g. AbOTa contain portion 10) and there is also evidence of survival of some features of Form 1 in MSS of later forms (e.g. the opinion expressed in Form 1 that one should live in a marriage contracted after a private vow rather than incur excommunication reappears in X and a possible trace also in Ck; see above Proleg. p. 31 with nn. 13-14, also p. 51). All of this suggests that the original Form 2 may have been more like Form 1 than the present contents of $AbOQ^{1*}Ta$ and may have been composed somewhat before 1208.

[8] See above Proleg. pp. 49-51.

[9] This is the only one of these portions which is in Q; it is found in Q^{1*}. Quite probably this is a result of correction from Form 3 in some MS from which Q^{1*} is derived; cf. above n. 7, also above Proleg. p. 49 with n. 50.

[10] None of the portions 1-18, in fact none of these features of Form 3 by which it differs from Form 2, is found in any text of Form 1, i.e. in Q^1Q^2W. Likewise none of these portions or peculiarities is found in Q^{1*} or Q^{2*} or Q^{2**} except portion no. 1 (see preceding note). So when

3. In sect. 112 the final sentence: *Immo generaliter — dispensatione.* — lacking in AbTa (also Q^1Q^2W), marginal insertion in O.

4. In sect. 124 a few words: *vel licentiam in aliquo ordine ministrandi, vel aliquid spirituale?* (lines 18-19) — lacking in AbTaQ^1*, marginal insertion in a different place in O.

5. Sects. 129-140, a long passage at the end of the discussion on simony: POENITENS. *Patronus — pauperi conferatis.* — lacking in AbOTa (also Q^1-WX), probably lacking in Aa even before the loss of its third gathering.[11]

6. In sect. 141 a few words: *exceptis excommunicationibus quarum absolutionem sibi reservavit papa* (lines 42-43) — lacking in Ab, a marginal insertion in O, found in the text in a different place in Q^1*Q^2**, found in the text in still another place in TaTu.[12]

7. In sect. 199 a long parenthesis: (*quod fit — extollitur*) (lines 24-28) — lacking in O, a marginal insertion in Ab.

8. In sect. 210 a short passage: *Hoc dico de liberis — sustentare.* (lines 79-82) — lacking in Ta, a marginal insertion in AbO.

9. In sect. 245 a short portion of text: *vel carinam — minui*) (lines 66-70) — a marginal insertion in AbO, set off by diacritical marks in Ad, not found in the sources.[13]

---

it is indicated that one of these portions 1-18 is lacking in W or in some text of Q, it is meant that the MS indicated contains the context for this portion, but lacks the portion itself. When these texts are not mentioned, it is understood (except in the case of portion 1 found in Q^1*) that they lack even the context where this portion might be found. — Conversely, the other MSS usually contain these portions; when they are not mentioned, it is to be understood that they do contain them. This is true of AbAcAdBmCcCiCpFGHIJKMNOPRSgSoTaTcUVXYZ. AaCkDELTb-Tu are incomplete because of some accidents in the transmission of their texts and lack the contexts where some of these portions belong, but this fact does not indicate any affinity with Forms 1 or 2. When these MSS are not mentioned, it is understood that they contain the portion in so far as they are complete enough to contain its context. Regarding Tu see above n. 3; regarding Aa see below no. 5. Bt contains the context for only one of these portions, namely 18, which it contains.

[11] Regarding Aa see FIRTH, *Traditio* 16.544 n. 13; cf. above Proleg. pp. 20-21. Regarding this passage see above Proleg. p. 47 with nn. 42-43 and p. 35 with n. 82. Q^1W do not have the precise context in which this passage is found in Form 3, but they do have something akin to that context; see above Appendix B sects. 380-381.

[12] Q^1* has marks indicating that the passage should go into its proper place, but Q^2** has no such marks.

[13] The diacritical marks here in Ad are apparently the work of a corrector who elsewhere in this MS, on fol. 108^r, corrected it from canonical sources.

II *Nine other portions lacking or out of place
in the text of one or more of* AbOTaQ¹*Q²*Q²**
and in other manuscripts as well

10. In sect. 85 the second paragraph: *Item, si mutet — baptizat.* — lacking in Q¹*R, found in the text in a different place in AaJHU.

11. In sect. 95 two lines of poetry with introductory phrase:

[Et iterum secundum magistrum Stephanum de Langetonne:]
Collige, sustena, stimula vaga, morbida, lenta;
Hoc est pastoris; hoc virga figurat honoris.

(lines 4-6) — all three lines lacking in AaAbJSgTaTuUV (also X), marginal insertion in O, found in the text in a different place in Ck and in another different place in R, not found in the source; — introductory attribution lacking also in AdCcCiCkKLPZ (*Item* Ad, *Demum* Z); — introductory attribution (*Item* H) and last line lacking in H.[14]

12. In sect. 117 a long sentence: *Ita, inquam — conferendo.* (lines 43-49) — lacking in AbOTaTu (also Q¹W), found in the text in a different place in H.

13. In sect. 200 a short parenthesis: (*scilicet quando scit homo spargere — discordias*) (lines 35-37) — found in the text out of its proper place in ORTaTb, also a marginal insertion in its proper place in O; this peculiarity is combined in these MSS with a great variation in the order of the words which follow the parenthesis in our text; moreover *suspicio, seditio* are lacking in ORTa.[15]

14. In sect. 202 a few words: *taciturnitas* (*de qua — dicendum erat*) (lines 83-84) — lacking in CkHTa, marginal insertion in AbO, found in the text in a different place in AaCpJSgU.

---

[14] Besides these variations, in L lines 5 and 6 are separated by the line of poetry which in our text is found in line 1; however this seems to be of no special significance for the relations of the different forms of the penitential to one another. Regarding these lines of poetry and their introductory attribution see FIRTH, *Thesis* I 222*-224*, 226*-228*, 236*-239* with nn. 26-27 (III 590*-592*) 315*-316*, 414*-415*; IDEM, *Traditio* 16.543-544, 17.531.

[15] In the text of OTaTb the parenthesis comes after *schisma*, where it can hardly have belonged originally; in R it comes after *conspiratio*. Quite probably it was originally lacking in Form 2 and afterwards was inserted into the wrong place in some early MS of this form. There is great variation in the order of the words in several MSS at this part of the text; see variants.

15. In sect. 225 a short question: *Ad infidelem — quamlibet.* (lines 92-93) — lacking in H1a, marginal insertion in AbO, found in the text in a different place in R.[16]

16. In sect. 241 four words: *si publicum esset peccatum* (line 98) — lacking in OV, inserted in Ab, found in the text in another place in AaCpHSgU. Moreover the last three of these words are an insertion in AcJ, and in J (but not in Ac) the four words occur again in the text in that other place.

17. In sect. 271 the last four titles: *xiii. Quod conjugati — se lavant.* — lacking in AaOU (J lacks the whole list).

18. In sect. 298 the last four titles: *vii. Quod juramenti — voti.* — lacking in AaCpJHRU; — the last three titles: *viii. De illis — voti.* lacking in O; — the last title an insertion in Ad.

III *One sentence found in MSS of Form 2 and in some others*

19. One sentence at the end of sect. 88: *Nos tamen in proximo capitulo breviter ostendemus.* — found only in the text of AbBmLMORSoTaTu and as an insertion in Aa.

IV *Peculiarities of O in Book 5*

20. In sect. 235. At the end of this section MS O adds:

> Quoniam plerique canones tempora poenitentiarum et formas in sacerdotum arbitrio ponunt, quidam sacerdotes, non intelligentes arbitrii modum ex aliorum canonum auctoritate sumendum, existimant indandum [*lege* in dandis] poenitentiis totum sibi licere quod libeat. Sed modus tempusque poenitentiae peccata sua confitentibus aut per antiquorum institutionem aut per sanctam scripturarum auctoritatem aut per ecclesiasticam consuetudinem probatam imponi debet a sacerdotibus.[17]

The text of O continues with the paragraph *Nemo si praedictas intelligat auctoritates ut semper secundum rigorem — semper ubique tenere,* which is the first paragraph of sect. 351 in the present edition, with variations noted

---

[16] Cf. above Proleg. p. 50 with n. 54.

[17] Cf. Burch. 19.28, 31 (PL 140.984-986); Ivo 15.46, 49 (PL 161.868-869); Bart. c.26 (p. 195 lines 24-36); c.33 (p. 200 lines 20-31); Gratian *De poen.* D.1 c.86.

in the *apparatus criticus* of that section.[18] Then it continues with sect. 236: *Poenitentia alia sollemnis...*

21. In sect. 242 the titles are arranged in O and in a few other MSS as follows.

Title iv *De eo qui infantem opprimit* is not found in its place after *De parricidio* in OU. Instead it comes in these MSS after the title which is last in the present edition: *Si domina ancillam per iram occiderit.* This corresponds to the place where the canons designated by title iv are actually found in O; see below nos. 24-25. In Ab likewise title iv originally came at the end of the list, but this has been corrected in Ab; the title has been inserted after *De parricidio* and erased at the end of the list. In AaAcJ the title *De eo qui infantem opprimit* occurs in both places. However it has been erased at the end of the list in Ac.[19]

Title vii *De impedientibus conceptum* is lacking in O and is a marginal insertion in Ab. The next title reads thus in AbO: *De homicidiis sponte commissis ex decretis Meldensi papae et Tiburiensis concilii, capitulo iv. xii.*[20] In Ab this has been corrected to the reading of the text of the present edition.

Title xi *De homicidio pro vindicta facto* has *ex poenitentiali Theodori lviii.*[21] added in O; this title is missing in U.

After the last title of the list in our text AaAbAcJO have *De eo qui infantem opprimit* as noted above; then follows in O:

xvii. De fure interfecto qui capi potuit.
xviii. De eadem re.
xix. De illis qui christiana mancipia captivaverint [*verbum ult. corrupt.*]
xx. De illis qui truncationes membrorum fecerint.
xxi. De illis qui per amorem venefici fiunt.
xxii. De se invicem percutientibus.

These titles indicate canons found in O; see below item 25.

---

[18] The beginning of this canon in O is actually quite close to the reading of BART. c.33 (pp. 200-201), its source: *Nemo praedictas sic intelligat auctoritates ut...* This can be explained if we suppose that the canon was first introduced into Form 2 in the place in which it is now found in O, and that afterwards the reading was changed to the present reading of Form 3 *Nemo sic intelligat ut...* because no penitential canons preceded it there. Finally, according to this conjecture, it would have been moved to its present position in Form 3.

[19] This is definitely a trace of Form 2 in Ac; cf. above no. 16.

[20] See above sect. 242 title viii with variants and n. 40.

[21] Source not found.

22. In sect. 251; instead of this canon, O has the following:

> Parricidium [*corr. ad* Patricidium] autem quam sit detestabile crimen judicio
> facto inter Chaim et Abel fratrem suum Dominus ipse ostendit cum ad Chaim
> fratricidam ait: *Maledictus eris super terram quae aperuit suum os et suscepit san-*
> *guinem fratris tui de manu tua. Cum operatus fueris* terram, *non dabit tibi fructus*
> ejus et *vagus et profugus eris super terram.* In quo posuit signum ut tremens et
> gemens et profugus viveret super terram nec auderet usquam sedes habere
> quietis. Sed quia modernis temporibus parricidae [*vel* patricidae *corr. ad*
> fratricidae] profugae discurrunt.[22]

This is the end of the canon in O, but not in its source. O then continues
with sect. 252: *Parricidium dicitur...*

23. In sect. 255 a few words: *cum ad missarum sollemnia vel alia sacra*
audire officia venerint. His (line 25) — an insertion in O. All of these words
except the last one are missing in the sources.[23]

24. In sect. 258: the three canons of this section, *Si mater — securus sit,*
are not found in this part of the text of O (fol. 43ʳ), but do occur farther
along in this MS; see next item.

25. In sect. 270: after the end of this section O reads thus:

> *Qui ducatum praestant et praedatores super christiano****. conc. xvii.*
>
> Si quis ducatum praebet super christianos ut deprehendentur et non accidit
> strages christianorum, tres annos poeniteat. Si vero electis armis ad usque
> mortem, mundo mortuus fiat.[24]

---

[22] See Ivo 10.164 (PL 161.739). The text of this canon in O breaks off in the midst of a sentence
which is in the middle of the canon in Ivo.

[23] The words *cum ad missarum — venerint* are missing from the sources of this canon, but are
found in the corresponding place in similar canons, both in this penitential and elsewhere;
see e.g. above sect. 254 (line 8). It was no doubt from the influence of those other canons that
these words were introduced into this one in Flamborough's penitential. This might seem to
indicate that O here contains Robert's text in its original state. But the omission of *His* in O
suggests rather the contrary. A very plausible explanation for the omission of *His* in O is the
supposition that it may have been deleted in error by someone who, in correcting the text from
the sources, was deleting the preceding sentence in an archetype of O. Such correction from
canonical sources was common in mediaeval times; cf. above n. 13. Correctors sometimes deleted
more than was necessary; see e.g. above sect. 141, line 42, with its *apparatus criticus.* Hence
this peculiarity in O does not necessarily indicate priority of its text over that of Form 3.

[24] See Ivo 15.115 (PL 161.886); WASSERSCHLEBEN, *Bussordnungen* p. 480 §28; p. 507 c. vi.
The last sentence in Ivo (with which other sources correspond) reads as follows: *Sin vero, ejectis*
armis usque ad mortem mundo mortuus vivat. Possibly the reading of O should be punctuated: *Si*
vero electis armis, ad usque mortem mundo mortuus vivat.

Then follow in O the three canons *Si mater — securus sit* of sect. 258 not found in their regular place above; see last item. Then:

Si fur aut latro captus in praeda absque occisione potest comprehendi et tamen interficitur, quia ad imaginem Dei creati et in nomine ejus baptizati sunt, interfectores eorum quadraginta diebus non intrent ecclesiam, lanea [*corr. ab* linea] veste induti ab escis et potibus qui interdiciti sunt, a thoro et gladio et equitatu se abstineant. In tertia [et *insert.*] quinta feria et sabbato, aliquo genere leguminum vel oleum et pomis, parvulis piscibus cum mediocri cervisia vicissim utantur et temperate. Sin autem comprobatur a veridicis testibus quod sine odii meditatione se suaque liberando diaboli membra interficiunt et capi non poterant, poenitentiam pro homicidio ejus [*lege* eis] non injungimus nisi ipsi voluerint aliquid quod humanius est facere.[25]

<*Si*> [Sunt *delet.* MS] *effringens domum fur sive effodiens fuerit inventus et accepto vulnere fuerit mortuus* [marg. insert.] *percussor non erit reus sanguinis. Quod si orto sole fecerit, homicidium perpetravit et ipse morietur. Si non habeat quod pro furto reddat, venumdabitur. Si inventum fuerit apud eum quod furatus est vivens* [?], *sive bos sive asinus sive ovis, duplum* retinet [*lege:* restituet.][26]

Si quis contristatus reconciliari noluerit satisfaciente eo qui contristavit, acerrimis maceretur inediis usque dum gratanti animo satisfactionem recipiat.[27]

Si quis non vult reconciliari fratri suo quem odio habet, tamdiu in pane et aqua poeniteat usque reconcilietur ei.[28]

De clericis maledictis xxv.

Clericus maledictus maxime a sacerdotibus cogatur ad postulandum veniam; si noluerit, degradetur, nec umquam ad officium absque satisfactione revocetur.[29]

Qui christiana mancipia captivaverit xxvi.

Quicumque hominem quolibet ingenio captivaverit <aut> inde transmiserit, tribus annis poeniteat.[30]

Qui per rixam ictu debilem <vel> deformem hominem fecerit, reddat impensas medici et medium annum poeniteat; si non habuerit unde reddat, unum annum poeniteat. Si laicus per dolum sanguinem effuderit, reddat illi quantum nocuit, et si non habet unde reddat, solvat in opera proximi sui quamdiu ille infirmus est, et praeterea quadraginta dies poeniteat in pane et aqua.[31]

---

[25] See Ivo 13.46 (PL 161.813); GRATIAN C.13 q.2 c.32.

[26] See Ivo 13.47 (PL 161.813); *Exodus* 22.2-4.

[27] See BURCH. 10.59 (PL 140.852); cf. GRATIAN D.90 c.10.

[28] See BURCH. 10.60 (PL 140.852).

[29] See BURCH. 10.66 (PL 140.854); Ivo 11.11 (PL 161.748); IDEM 13.66 (PL 161.815).

[30] See Ivo 15.145 (PL 161.891).

[31] See Ivo 15.113 (PL 161.885); cf. WASSERSCHLEBEN, *Bussordnungen* p. 225 2.9; p. 398 c. lxv.

Qui per amorem venefici fiunt

Si quis per amorem fit veneficus et neminem perdiderit, si clericus est, unum annum poeniteat in pane et aqua, si subdiaconus, duos, si diaconus, tres, unum ex his in pane et aqua; si laicus, dimidium annum poeniteat; maxime si per <hoc> mulieris partum quisque deceperit [deciperit MS], tres annos unusquisque superaugeat in pane et aqua ne homicidii reus sit.[32]

De se invicem percutientibus

Qui ictum proximo dederit et non nocuerit, tres dies poeniteat in pane et aqua; si clericus, annum et dimidium. Si quis alicui quodlibet membrum voluntate sua truncaverit, tres annos poeniteat, unum ex his in pane et aqua. Parvuli se invicem percutientes tres; si vero adolescentes, viginti dies poeniteant.[33]

Then follows in O the list of titles of sect. 271.

26. In sect. 289. This section is arranged thus in O. The first canon is not found at the beginning. Instead O begins with the second canon of our text: *Consulitis — cavendum ?* Then as follows:

Ergo ad enixae mulieris concubitum vir suus non accedere debet quoadusque qui gignitur ablactetur. Prava autem in conjugatorum moribus consuetudo subrepsit ut mulieres filios quos gignunt nutrire contemnant, eosque aliis mulieribus ad nutriendum tradant. Quod videlicet sola causa incontinentiae videtur inventum; quia quod [*corr. ab* de se] continere nolunt, despiciunt lactare quos gignunt. Hae itaque quae filios suos ex prava consuetudine ad nutriendum tradunt, nisi purgationis tempus transierit, viris suis non debent commisceri, quippe etiam si <sine> partus [?] causa cum consuetis menstruis detinentur, viris suis misceri prohibentur.[34]

This is the end of the canon in O, but not in the sources. Then follows in O the title *Quod nec vir nec mulier potest abstinere sine consensu alterius* with the canon *Si tu abstines — tuae imputabitur abstinentiae*, which is missing at the beginning of this section in O, finally the last canon *Apostolus — debito.* [incipit *Populus non* delet.] Differences of reading in these two canons here (see *apparatus criticus* of sect. 289 above) seem to result from scribal errors and attempts to correct them.

27. In sect. 351: the first paragraph, *Nemo sic intelligat — semper ubique tenere*, is not found in this part of the text in O (fol. 60[r]). It was included earlier; see above no. 20.

---

[32] See Ivo 15.116 (PL 161.886).
[33] See Ivo 15.114 (PL 161.886).
[34] See Ivo 8.88 (PL 161.601-602); cf. BEDE, *Historia eccl.* 1.27 (ed. PLUMMER I 55).

APPENDIX D

TABLE OF CONTENTS OF

FIRTH, *THESIS*

One typewritten copy of this thesis is deposited at the Pontifical Institute of Mediaeval Studies, 59 Queen's Park Crescent, Toronto 181, Ontario, Canada; another typewritten copy is deposited at l'*Institut de recherche et d'histoire des textes*, 40 Avenue d'Iéna, Paris 16ᵉ, France.

TABLES AND INDEX

TABLE OF CITATIONS, QUOTATIONS, PARAPHRASES
AND VERBAL PARALLELS
FOUND IN THE TEXT OF OUR AUTHOR

This table contains a considerable number of references not found in the notes to the text.

SACRED SCRIPTURE — Latin Vulgate

(data in parentheses refer to the corresponding Hebrew text)

Chapter.verse	page:line of our text
Genesis	
2.24	. . . . 63: *13-14*
Exodus	
21.17	. . . . 160: *92-97*
22.2-4 (1-3)	. . . . 311 at n. 26
Leviticus	
18.6-18	. . . . 78: *81-82*
18.19, 29	. . . . 160: *92-97*
20.9	. . . . 160: *92-97*
27.30-33	. . . . . 189: *23*, 256: *98-3*
Numbers	
12.1-15	. . . . 270: *5-6*
Deuteronomy	
14.22-23	. . . . 189: *23*
17.12	. . . . 160: *96-98*
32.15, 18	. . 284 var. for sect. 5: *79-80*
1 Kings (1 Samuel)	
15.23	. . . . 241: *6*
25.21-33	. . . . 249: *56-59*
4 Kings (2 Kings)	
5.20-24	. . . . 124: *57-58*
1 Esdras (Ezra)	
10.11	. . . . 77: *52-54*
Esther	
9.28	. . . . 172: *23-24*
Job	
7.1	. . . . 58: *95-96*
13.15	. . . . 58: *85*

	page:line
Psalms	
41.9 (42.7)	. . . . 182: *65-66*
50 (51).1	. . . . 148: *96*
67.5 (68.4)	. . . . 114: *83*
75.12 (76.11)	. . . . 72: *64*
138 (139).16	. . . . 54: *15*
Proverbs	
28.24	. . . . 253: *58*
30.18-19	. . . . 54: *17-18*
Ecclesiastes (Qoheleth)	
9.10	. . . . 58: *92-93*
Isaias	
6.5	. . . . 182: *83*
52.7	. . . . 114: *76-77*
Jeremias	
17.9	. . . . 54: *16-17*
Ezechiel	
3.20, 33.8	. . . . 57: *1*
Malachias	
2.2	. . . . 241: *4*
Matthew	
5.32	. . . . 95: *89-90*
12.44	. . 284 var. for sect. 5: *79-80*
13.52	. . . . 113: *53-54*
15.14	. . . . . . 56-57: *62-63*
18.15-18	. . . . 256: *3-4*
19.5	. . . . 63: *13-14*
25.35,43,46	. . . . 278: *48-50*
Mark	
4.11	. . . . 114: *75*
15.14	. . . . 227: *3*
15.25	. . . . 227: *4*

Non-biblical sources prior to BUCHARD OF WORMS have not been included in these tables because research into these has been quite incomplete.

BURCHARD OF WORMS

IVO OF CHARTRES

.96	264: *76-80*
.103	204: *82-83*
.106	222: *84-85*
.113	311 at n. 31
.114	312 at n. 33
.115	310 no. 25
.116	312 at n. 32
.117 *a princ.*	258-259: *55-65*
.127	278: *48-52*
.130	274: *75-77*
.140	211: *40-44*
.141	211: *34-36*

.145	311 at n. 30
.146	255: *94-96*
.147-148	244: *47-54*
.158 *ad finem*	257: *35-36*
.159	222: *80-82*
.164	222: *75-77*
.183	213: *69-70*
.189	274-275: *79-95*
.190	274-275: *79-95*
.192-194	275-276: *97-9*
.198-199	276: *10-21*
16.80	227: *93-94*

Ivo of Chartres

Panormia (PL 161.1045-1344)

Book.chapter   page: *line*
                                   in our text

1.152	270: *88-95*	.99	259: *72-73*
.154-155	266: *15-27*	.104	259: *68-70*
.156	268: *53-55*	.111	248: *48-51*
2.58	256: *98-6*	6.20	238: *29-31*
.70	255: *77-78*	.21	236: *6-8*
.79	252: *33-38*	.79 *a princ.*	238: *44-45*
.80	252: *30-32*	.79 (col. 1259D) . . .	239: *50-51*
.81	252: *20-24*	7.16	225-226: *57-72*
3.41	110-111: *92-21*	.19	235: *80-82*
.91	241: *96-97*	.64	235: *70-74*
.112	241-242: *9-12*	8.62	261: *11-13*
.134	241: *98-8*	.64	261: *14-18*
.143	240: *79-80*	.92	249: *56-59*
.156	257: *27*	.94	249: *64-67*
.167	244: *66-69*	.95	249: *60-63*
.169	261: *14-18*	.108	248: *40-42*
5.2	240-241: *81-95*	.112	247: *25-27*
		.116	246-247: *10-16*
		.118	249: *64-67*
		.154 (14)	255: *79-85*

Gratian of Bologna

Decretum

First Part   page: *line*
                                   of our text

D.5 c.4 *cum palea*	312 no. 26	D.34 c.2	244: *66-69*
D.23 c.33	238: *29-31*	c.18	281: *5*
D.24 c.7	122: *24-26*	D.35 c.9	265: *97-99*
D.25 c.1	110-111: *92-21*	D.47 c.5	257: *27*
dictum p. c.3 §4 . .	283: *58*	D.50 c.4	142: *91-93*, 282: *24*
D.28 c.9	241: *96-97*	c.34	283: *44*
D.32 c.11	283: *45*	c.36	282: *25-26*
c.16	241-242: *9-12*	c.39	217: *47-62*
		c.43	228: *21-25*
		c.44	225: *48-51*
		c.52 *cum palea* . . .	242: *13-19*
		c.62	272: *35-36*

BARTHOLOMEW OF EXETER, *Liber poenitentialis*

Speculum ecclesiae

Decretal letters of popes

Alexander III

13860	. . . . 282: *42*
13887	. . . . 061 *30 32*
13912 (13917 ?)	. . . 117: *39-40*
13946	. . . . 70: *24-28*
13969	. . . . 176: *11-14*
14091	. 88: *78-81*, 143: *3-5*, 290: *54-56*

CLEMENT III

JL 16466 ad finem	. . . 282: *29-30*
16580	. . . . 128-129: *41-49*

CELESTINE III

JL 16607	. . . . 151: *42-44*, 300: *9-11*
16617	. . 159: *69-74*, 299: *93-97*
16637	. . . . 76: *42-46*
17606	. . . . 126: *6-8*

INNOCENT III

Po.202	. . . . 151. *90-11*
377 (?)	. . . . . . 144: *22-28*
502	. . . . 71: *46-51*
534 (?)	. . . . . . 143: *15-17*
700	. . . 164-165: *70-74*, 149: *6-9*
953	. . . . 281: *3*
1326	. . . . 150: *30-32*
1806 (?)	. . . . . 143: *15-17*
2749	. . . . 102: *48-53*
2836 (?)	. . . . . 65-66: *48-52*
3168	. . . . 87-88: *62-66*
3812 (?)	. . . . . 189: *19-20*
5021 (?)	. . . . . 143: *2-3*

Collections of papal decretals

Compilatio prima

Book.title.chapter	page: *line*
1.13.3	. . . . 281: *8-9*
2.1.6	. . . . 143: *3-5*
3.15.3	. . . . 257: *35-36*
.27.8	. . . . 76: *47-48*
.11 (?)	. . . . . . 76: *42-46*
.28.1	. . . . 70: *24-28*
.2	. . . . . 88: *78-81*, 290: *54-56*
.7	. . . . . . 88: *78-81*, 290: *54-56*
4.2.1 ad finem	. . . . 281: *13-14*
.6	. . . . 86: *30-32*
.12	. . . . 176: *11-14*
.7.1	. . . . .176: *19-23,*293: *63*
.13.2	. . . . 94: *76-85*, 298: *45-50*
.20.6	. . . . 95: *90-95*, 298: *45-50*
5.2.16	. . . . . . 282: *33*, 283: *65-66*

.17.1	. . . . 263: *54-56*
.26.4	. . . . 253: *47-49*
.7	. . . . 282: *42*
.31.7	. . . . 255: *95-96*
.33.3	. . . . 148: *2-4*
.34.2	. . . . 156: *15-20*, 157: *25-26*
.3	. . . . 157: *34-35*
.4	. . . . 157: *27-28*, *36-42*
.5	. . . . 156: *21-24*

Compilatio secunda

1.8.3	. . . . . . 159: *69-74*, 299: *93-97*
3.4.3	. . . . 126: *6-8*
.13.2	. . . . 128-129: *41-49*
.18.3	. . . . 76: *42-46*
5.2.9	. . . . 282: *29-30*
.18.8	. . . . 151: *42-44*

The *Libri sententiarum* of PETER LOMBARD are not included in this table because research into them has been quite incomplete. It is improbable that our author used this work directly. The works of PETER CANTOR and ROBERT COURSON are not included here because no relationship could be found close to enough to come within the scope of this table.

TABLE OF MANUSCRIPTS

References are to pages in the present edition
"6n31" indicates footnote no. 31 on page 6.

GENERAL INDEX

References are to pages; the italicized numbers following a colon refer to lines. Thus:

"2:32-35" refers to lines 32-35 on page 12.

"56n42" refers to footnote 42 on page 56.

See also: Admonition

Exorcist: office of, 110: *99-1*

Experience, pastoral: influence on manuals, 10

Extra (vagantes). See: Decretals

Extreme unction, money not to be exacted for, 131: *97-2*

FABRICIUS, JOHN ALBERT: attributes other works to our author, 6n30

Falsarii. See: Forgers ...

Fairs (*nundinae mercatorum*), 192: *68-81*

Faith: necessity of, 58: *79-83*
    baptism of the spirit, 102: *48-53*
    how symbolized, 112: *45-47*, 114: *79-90*

Falcons (*accipitres*): higher clerics are not to keep, 244: *66-69*

Fascinus, incantation to, 264: *72-75*

Fasting: complete before reception of the eucharist, 270: *96-97*
    required of penitents, 200-201: *52-56*, 201: *72-77*, 212-240 *passim*, 247: *20-22*, 256: *8-9*, 270-276 *passim*, 302: *72-76*
    See also: Bread and water

Fathers: not to promote their own sons, 126: *6-8*n9
    See also: Parents

Favouritism in assigning penance, 277: *27-36*

Feast days: penances relaxed on, 212-225 *passim*, 232: *4-13*, 239: *57-64*, 251: *7-9*, 275: *89-95*
    sexual intercourse forbidden on, 198: *1*, 236: *6-8*

Femoralia (drawers): use of forbidden to penitents, 223: *97-99*

Ferias, three legitimate. See: Legitimate ferias

Ferrea (*bêtes de fer*), 194: *10-12*

Fetus: animated distinguished from non-animated, 120: *89-91*

Fictive consent. See: Consent, simulated

Fighting: leading to death creates irregularity, 119: *80-81*, 121: *11-15*
    penances for, 311 at n31, 312 at n32

Filiola: meaning of, 232: *2-3*

Finding lost articles, 184: *40-41*

Fine (composition): part of penance for homicide, 214-215: *5-24*
    inflicted for sacrilege, 252-253: *25-45*, 254: *63-66*

Fire. See: Incendiarism

Firma: meaning of, 139: *38*n56

First tonsure. See: Tonsure

Fish: forbidden to penitents, 224: *16-17*
    allowed to penitents, 239: *57-58*, 311 *a princ.*

Flamborough, Yorkshire (*Flainesburc*): 1-2, 21, 22, 24, 26, 29, 30, 31, 54: *2*

Flattery, 180: *23-28*

Flogging. See: Beating

Font, sacred: how infant is to be received from, 82: *64-70*

Food: eucharist not to be received after, 270: *96-97*

Force, to repel with, 157: *27-28*

Forgers of papal letters: excommunication for, 150: *22-26*, 151: *38-41*, 301: *32-33*

Forgive, one unwilling to: penance for, 311 at nn27-28

Forgotten sins: admonition to include, 199: *22-35*, 301-302: *48-52*

Form 1 of our penitential: character and origin, 34-44
    doctrinal peculiarities, 40-43, 44
    date, 8, 9, 38-43
    manuscripts of, 27-28, 30-31, 33, 34, 45
    some manuscripts contaminated from Form Two, 40
    relation with Form Four, 41n14, 51
    publication of, 45, 53, 284-303
    limited use of HUGUCCIO, 37, 38-40, 42-43

Form 2 of our penitential: character and origin, 43n28, 45-49
    date, 8-9, 41-42n14, 305n7
    manuscripts of, 21, 26, 28, 29, 33, 48-49
    relation with Form Four, 31, 41-42n14, 51
    publication of, 49, 52-53, 304-312

Form 3 of our penitential: authenticity, 6-7, 32, 43, 46-47
    outline, 12-17
    date, 8-9
    probable development of, 49-50
    manuscripts of, 33, 51-52
    publication of, 52-53

Form 4 of our penitential, 31, 33, 41-42n14, 51

Forma of a sacrament: the whole outward sign, 109: *72-79*
    distinguished from the elements, 101n9
    the *forma ecclesiae* and validity, 100n6, 101n9, 104-105: *95-98*, 105: *5-6*
    power of the Church to determine, 99: *13-14*, 100: *24-26*n6, 117: *30-37*

See also: Spiritual relationship; God-parent

Individuus: possible meanings, 63n3

Indulgences, 276: *22-26*

See also: Relaxations

In facie ecclesiae. See: Marriage, cladestine

Infamy: how incurred, 158: *57-58*, 159: *66-77*, 199: *18*, 240: *79-80*, 248: *13-46*, 254: *68-73*, 299: *93-97*

formerly incurred by any deposition, 160: *87-91*

creates irregularity, 158: *57-58*, 159: *65-79*, 240: *79-80*, 299: *93-97*

how cured in a cleric, 159: *66-79*, 240-241: *79-95*

Infidel (non-Christian): marriage with, 76-77: *50-54*

marriage among, 77: *55-66*

not bound by ecclesiastical constitutions, 83: *78-81*

intercourse with, 197: *92-93*

Infirmitas. See: Sickness

Influence of our penitential: 18-19

Injusta excommunicatio, 154: *82-86*

INNOCENT II, Pope: cited as INNOCENT III, 6-7n34

INNOCENT III (LOTHAR OF SEGNI), Pope: quarrel with King John, 8

letters addressed to our author, 3n12

and case of MAHEU OF LORRAINE, 3-5

and obedience in an invalid marriage, 41

and supervenient affinity, 42

judgment regarding impotency, 39-40, 65-66: *48-52*

decretals cited in our penitential, 8, 14, also above in "Table of Citations..."

decretals cited in Form One, 38

INNOCENT II cited as, 6-7n34

and the unbaptized priest, 102: *48-53*

decretal of 1207, 8, 87-88: *62-66*

references to decretals, 66-198 *passim*, 281: *1-3*

De sacro altaris mysterio, 110n47, 115n67

Insanity: impedes betrothal, 85: *19-23*

impedes marriage, 64: *26-27*, 86: *24-28*

impedes orders and their exercise, 166-167: *9-16*

Insolentia: meaning of, 179-180: *20-21*

Institution of the Church: establishes impediments to marriage, 83: *78-81*, 90: *95-6*, 91: *20-25*

and solemnity of vows, 74: *98-12*

Intention: can make a contract into simony, 127: *9-24*, 139: *38-49*, 140: *59-70*

in the recipient of ordination or sacrament, 116-117: *20-25*

necessary in the minister, 101n9

of doing what the Church intends, 105: *4-6*, 107: *40-43*

Intercourse (sexual): is carnal union, 298:*52-56*

capability of, necessary for marriage. See: Impotence

sometimes possible for children, 174: *59-63*, 175-176: *9-14*

with marital affection between betrothed consummates marriage, 89: *85-89*, 165: *77-79*, 173-174: *52-63*, 175-176: *2-14*, 301: *21-22*

of a cleric in marital affection with several persons establishes bigamy, 165: *77-81*

right of spouse to. See: *Debitum conjugale*

how restricted in marriage, 97: *40-43*, 236-238: *5-42*, 238-239: *46-49*, 243: *39-46*, 312 no. 26

called *Luxuria* in the strict sense, 195: *43*

and Easter communion, 97-98: *40-49*

forbidden to penitents, 221-226 *passim*, 271: *17-21*, 311 *a princ.*

permitted to penitents, 218-221 *passim*, 235: *73-74*

sole basis for affinity, 297: *25-35*, 298: *43-56*, 299: *76-79*

See also: *Debitum conjugale*

Interdictum ecclesiae: impediment to marriage, 98: *51-54*, 288: *28-29*

Intermediate MSS, 20-32 *passim*, 33, 45, 49-51, 304, 305, 307-308

Interrogation of the penitent: necessity of, 56-57: *62-67*, 203: *2-5*

order of, 13-14, 62, 286: *13-16*, 295-296: *66-93*

imprudent questions to be avoided, 196-197: *72-78*, 296: *79-81*

about orders, 15, 169-173: *49-49*, 292-295: *87-65*

about marriage, 15, 173-178: *52-47*, 291-292: *58-86*

based on the seven capital vices, 15, 179-199, 296-302

Interruption by a contrary act, 82: *64-70*, 108: *55-60*

Sollemnitas missae, 268: 57-58

Son of a priest: not to be promoted by his father, 126: 6-8

  not to succeed his father, 126-127n9, 162: 23-24

  See also: Illegitimate birth

Sorbonne: ancient library, 26

  library, 30

Sorcery (*sortilegium*). See: Witchcraft

Sources of our penitential: of Forms Two and Three, 13-17

  of Form One, 38-43, 44

  portions not found in, 47-48, 50, 306 no. 9, 307 no. 11

Spanking of children, 264: 78-81

Spassare, meaning of, 215n66

Speculum [*de mysteriis*] *ecclesiae*: author of, 14n74, 112n51

  teaching about epicopacy, 100-101n8

  used by our author, 14, 112-116nn

  See also: PETER OF ROISSY

Spirit, evil. See: Demon

Spiritual ministry: not to be exercised for a stated sum, 132: 3-15, 135-136: 59-80, 137-138: 1-27, 139: 38-49

  obligation of a benefice-holder to render, 138: 28-37

  See also: Sacrament; Simony; Altar; Judgement; *Census*

Spiritual relationship (*cognatio spiritualis*): how constituted, 80-85: 27-6, 234: 61-63

  impedes marriage, 80-85: 27-6

  violation of, 233: 36-37, 233-234: 54-74

  See also: Compaternity 1, 2; God-parent; Baptism; Confirmation; *Sacramentalia*

Sponsalia. See: Betrothal

Sponsor. See: God-parent; Spiritual relationship

Spouse of the bishop is his church, 114: 86-89

Springs (*fontes*): veneration of, 260: 4-7

Staff (*baculus*, crosier) of bishop, 115: 94-6

Stealing. See: Theft

STEPHEN LANGTON, Archbishop of Canterbury: teacher of RICHARD POORE at Paris, 3

  quarrel over the elevation of, 8

  two lines of poetry attributed to, 50, 115: 4-6, 307 no. 11

STEPHEN OF TOURNAI: our author not a fellow student of, 3n8

—, *Summa*: on episcopacy, 100-101n8

cited, 79-81 *passim*, 117-125 *passim*, 146nn88, 93, 172n7, 198n30

Stercora (dung): consumption of, 264: 76-81

Stole (*orarium*), 112: 30-34

Stones: veneration of, 260: 4-7, 262: 38-41

  oaths upon, 246-247: 9-18, 262: 33-37

STRATTON, WALTER DE, rector of Teversham, 22

Stricta (woman incapable of intercourse), 66: 55-57

Striking another: penance for, 311 at n31

Subdeacon: office of, 111: 4-7

  additional times for ordination to, 172: 27-33, 293: 24-28

  violence to, 214-215: 5-10

  greater penance for, 312 at n32

  See also: Orders, sacred; Pope; Dispensation

Subintroducta (cohabiting woman): forbidden to clerics, 241-242: 9-12

Subprior of Saint-Victor: our author, 5-6

  RALPH, 5

Substantia (essential nature): origin of the term, 100n6, 101n9

  meaning of, 108: 44-64, 110: 83-89, 111: 23-24, 117-118: 35-48

  See also: Betrothal; Marriage; Orders, holy; Sacrament; Vow; Oath; Profession

Sues ad volutabra, 271: 17-21

Suicides: burial rites denied to, 211

Summa: Breves dies hominis, 57n4, 58n5

Summa Bambergensis, 122n90

Summae casuum. See: Manuals for confessors

Summa juniorum: cites our penitential, 7n35

Summa parisiensis, 107n38, 122n90, 149n2, 191n37, 282n14

Sunday: penance relaxed on, 212-222 *passim*, 232-245 *passim*, 274-275: 88-95

Superbia (pride), 179: 8-17

Superpositio (a very strict fast): required of penitents, 231: 89-92

Superstition. See: Witchcraft

Supervenient affinity. See: Affinity, supervenient

Surgical operation: how it impedes orders, 168: 30-39

Suspension of a cleric: orders received or exercised in, 103-107, 145: 40-46, 168-169: 42-48, 173: 45-47

  decreed in ancient canons, 217: 51-55, 239-240: 53-77, 240-241: 81-95, 241: 98-8,

242: *13-19*, 244: *49-50, 66-69*, 255: *87-88*

Susurratio: meaning of, 180: *35-37*

Sweden, CHRISTINA, Queen of: library (*Regin.*), 24-25, 25n32

Swine: symbol of relapse, 271: *17-21*

SYLVESTER, Pope: cited in penitential canon, 239: *53-56*

Symbolism: of liturgical vestments and furnishings, 14, 111-116

of relapse into sin, 242: *18-19*, 271: *17-21*, 272: *40-43*, 273: *51-53*

Symbolum (creed): as incantation, 274: *68-75*

—, "*Quicumque*" *pseudo-Athanasianum*, 114n60

SYMMACHUS, Saint, Pope: decretal attributed to, 234n28

Synodicae constitutiones, 59n12

Synods for reform of the Church, 7n37, 18n98

Tabula: used for divining, 263: *53-56*

Taciturnity, vice of, 182: *83-84*

Tale-bearing. See: *Susurratio*

Talio (penalty paid by the unsuccessful accuser): can impede orders, 120: *98-1*

Tallia (rent or feudal payment), 186-187: *60-82*

Tax. See: *Census, Tallia*

Taxata quantitas. See: *Census*, for spiritual services; Spiritual ministry; Altar; *Persona*; Vicar

Te igitur. See: Canon of the mass

Temperance: chastity pertains to, 111: *26*

Templars, Knights, 150: *33*

Tempora. See: Times

Temporal goods: not to be exchanged for spiritual, 128-129: *38-49*

See also: Simony; Spiritual ministry; Altar; *Census*; Sacrament

Temporal punishment for sin, 60-61: *44-47*, 181-182: *63-65*

TERENCE, 54n7

Testament, New: committed to the deacon to preach, 111: *8-13*

—, Old: Lector commissioned to preach, 110: *97-98*, 111: *12-13*

crimes punished by death in, 160: *92-98*

Testaments, the Two: preaching of, symbolized by deacon's dalmatic, 112: *41-43*

knowledge of, symbolized by bishop's vestments, 113: *51-54, 68-69*

Testis. See: Witness

Teversham: WALTER DE STRATTON rector of, 18n100, 22

Theft: interrogation about, 183-184: *1-21*, 300: *98-99*

impeding orders, 122: *27-34*

by clerics or monks, 250: *90-94*

of church goods, 250: *88-89*, 253: *54-56*

from graves, 253: *50-53*, 256: *12-13*

of necessities, 256: *8-9*

capital theft, 256: *10-12*

from alms for the poor, 255: *74-75*

killing one engaged in, 311 *a princ.*

See also: Dishonesty; Robbery; Usury; Restitution; Thief

THEODORE (of Canterbury): cited in ancient canons, 233: *23-25*, 262: *42-45*

penitential ascribed to (in PL 99), 211n49, 256n22

See also: *Capitula* THEODORI

THEODULF OF ORLEANS, 196n50, 245n75

Theology: influence on manuals, 10

moralizing and Christian life, 11-12

used by our author, 14, 15

less use of in Form One, 34

THOULOUSE, JEAN DE, 2n7, 5-6

Three legitimate ferias. See: Legitimate ferias

Thursday: penances relaxed on, 221: *55-66*, 224: *19-30*, 311 *a princ.*

Thursday, Maundy. See: Maundy Thursday

TIERSONNIER, S.: 26

Time: spent in sin to be considered, 302: *52-66*

Times, canonical: for ordination, 168: *42-45*, 172-173: *20-38*, 293: *18-28*

Tithes (*decimae*): obligation of paying, 256: *97-6*, 188-190: *5-33*

to be exacted from the excommunicated, 153: *72-73*

held by laymen, 189: *24-25*, 190: *27-28*, 190-191: *34-57*

held by clerics or religious by leave of bishop or proper church, 133-134: *40-49*, 193: *91-93*, 294-295: *51-56*

Titubatio, 195: *32-33*

Toledo, Fourth Council of, 216n71

Tongue: murder can be committed by use of, 227: *98-5*

Tonsure, first: one of the orders, 100: *19-22, 27-31*

function to which one is ordained by, 110: *95-96*